SCOTLAND

THE STORY OF A NATION

BY THE SAME AUTHOR

Introducing Archaeology
Viking Expansion Westwards
The Clacken and the Slate (The Edinburgh Academy, 1824–1974)
Viking Hammer of the North
BC: The Archaeology of the Bible Lands
Landlord or Tenant?: A View of Irish History
Iceland
Vikings!
Magnus on the Move
Treasures of Scotland
Lindisfarne: The Cradle Island
Reader's Digest Book of Facts (ed.)
Iceland Saga
Chambers Biographical Dictionary (ed., 5th edition)
The Nature of Scotland (ed.)
I've Started, So I'll Finish
Rum: Nature's Island
Magnus Magnusson's Quiz Book

Saga translations

Njal's Saga
The Vinland Sagas
King Harald's Saga
Laxdaela Saga
The Icelandic Sagas (Vol. I)

SCOTLAND

THE STORY OF A NATION

MAGNUS MAGNUSSON

Grove Press
New York

First published in 2000 by HarperCollins*Publishers*,
Hammersmith, London, England

Published simultaneously in Canada
Printed in the United States of America

FIRST GROVE PRESS EDITION

Library of Congress Cataloging-in-Publication Data

Magnusson, Magnus.
    Scotland : the story of a nation / Magnus Magnusson.
        p. cm.
    Includes bibliographical references (p.) and index.
    ISBN 0-8021-3932-9 (pbk.)
    1. Scotland—History. I. Title.

DA760 .M24 2001
941.1—dc21   2001035859

Grove Press
841 Broadway
New York, NY 10003

03 04 05 06 07   10 9 8 7 6 5 4 3 2 1

Contents

Illustrations

Wooing' of Henry VIII. (Crown copyright, reproduced courtesy of Historic Scotland)

The Palace of Holyroodhouse, the home of Mary during her brief reign in Scotland. (Historic Scotland)

John Knox disputing with Mary Queen of Scots, by Samuel Sidley. (Bridgeman Art Library/Towneley Art Gallery, Burnley)

Mary's second husband, Henry, Lord Darnley. (Scottish National Portrait Gallery)

A rough sketch of the scene following the explosion which killed Darnley. (Public Record Office Image Library)

Death mask of Mary Queen of Scots. (In the collection of Lennoxlove House)

The casket which contained a sheaf of letters allegedly written by Mary to Bothwell at the time of Darnley's illness. (In the collection of Lennoxlove House)

James VI as a child, by Arnold van Bronckorst. (Scottish National Portrait Gallery)

King James's favourite, his cousin Esmé Stuart, Earl of Lennox, by an unknown artist. (Scottish National Portrait Gallery)

The Gowrie Conspiracy, painted by Alexander Douglas in the late nineteenth century. (Reproduced by permission of Perth Museum and Art Gallery, Perth & Kinross Council)

James VI's queen, Anne of Denmark. Portrait attributed to Adrian Vanson. (Scottish National Portrait Gallery)

One of the nearly seventy extant copies of the National Covenant. (© Trustees of the National Museums of Scotland 2000)

James Graham, 1st Marquis of Montrose. Copy of a portrait by Willem von Honthorst. (Scottish National Portrait Gallery)

The Covenanters' Preaching, by George Harvey, a nineteenth-century depiction of a field conventicle. (Glasgow Museums: Art Gallery & Museum, Kelvingrove)

The Martyrs' Memorial in Greyfriars Kirkyard in Edinburgh. (© The Society of Friends of the Kirk of the Greyfriars)

Monument erected at Thankerton in Maybole, Ayrshire, in memory of the Reverend Donald Cargill, executed in 1681. (Postcard reproduced by kind permission of Ann Matheson, Biggar Museum Trust)

John Graham of Claverhouse, 'Bonnie Dundee'. Portrait by David Paton. (Scottish National Portrait Gallery)

The Massacre of Glencoe. A nineteenth-century painting by James Hamilton depicts some of the shivering survivors. (Glasgow Museums: Art Gallery & Museum, Kelvingrove)

A dilapidated former summerhouse in the grounds of the Moray House College of Education in Edinburgh was one of the venues for the signing of the 1707 Act of Union between Scotland and England. (Ian Jacobs/Scottish News Agency)

Queen Anne, the last Stewart monarch of Britain. Portrait by Edmund Lilly. (By kind permission of His Grace the Duke of Marlborough)

The Articles of Union, drawn up on 27 July 1706. (National Archives of Scotland – SP13/209)

Prince James Francis Edward Stuart, the 'Old Pretender'. Portrait by M. Horthemals after Alexis Simon Belle. (Scottish National Portrait Gallery)

General George Wade. Portrait attributed to J. van Diest. (Scottish National Portrait Gallery)

The Scott Monument in Princes Street, Edinburgh. (Scotland in Focus/R. Schofield)

Sir Walter Scott's funeral. Watercolour by J.E. Alexander. (In the collection of Crinan Alexander/courtesy of Scottish National Portrait Gallery)

Demonstration of 'Red Clydesiders' in Glasgow's George Square in January 1919. (Glasgow Museums: The People's Palace)

ILLUSTRATIONS

On 11 April 1951 the young Scottish Nationalists who had abducted the Stone of Destiny from Westminster Abbey deposited it, wrapped in a saltire flag, on the high altar in the ruins of Arbroath Abbey. (*Arbroath Herald*)

Colour

Replica crannog at the Scottish Crannog Centre at Kenmore, on Loch Tay. (Christine Moorcroft)

A male and female Pict, imaginatively drawn by the Elizabethan explorer John White (c.1585). (© British Museum)

According to the medieval origin myths, the original Scots were descended from Scota, daughter of the Pharaoh Ramses II of Egypt, and Gaedel Glas (Gathelos), a prince of Scythia. Illustration from Walter Bower's fifteenth-century *Scotichronicon*. (Masters and Fellows of Corpus Christi College, Cambridge)

Macbeth instructing the murderers employed to kill Banquo, in a painting by George Cattermole (1800–68). (V&A Picture Library)

Malcolm Canmore and his English wife Margaret. Illustration in the sixteenth-century *Seton Armorial* (Sir Francis Ogilvy Bt/Trustees of the National Library of Scotland)

David I and his grandson Malcolm IV. Illustration from the charter of 1159 granted to Kelso Abbey. (By kind permission of His Grace the Duke of Roxburghe/Trustees of the National Library of Scotland)

The inauguration of Alexander III at Scone at the age of seven. Illustration in Walter Bower's *Scotichronicon*. (Masters and Fellows of Corpus Christi College, Cambridge)

John Balliol, later known as 'Toom Tabard', swears homage to Edward I in 1292 after being nominated King of Scots by him. (By permission of British Library, MS.Roy.20.c.vii)

Portrait of Robert Bruce by the seventeenth-century artist George Jamesone. (Private Scottish collection)

The earliest surviving depiction of the Battle of Bannockburn. Illustration in the *Scotichronicon*. (Masters and Fellows of Corpus Christi College, Cambridge)

David II and his first wife, Joan of England, sister of Edward III of England. Illustration in the *Seton Armorial*. (Sir Francis Ogilvy Bt/Trustees of the National Library of Scotland)

Queen Philippa at the Battle of Neville's Cross, by Benjamin West. (The Royal Collection © 2000, Her Majesty Queen Elizabeth II)

Elgin Cathedral, fired by the Wolf of Badenoch in 1390. (Crown copyright, reproduced courtesy of Historic Scotland)

Robert III. Illustration from the *Seton Armorial*. (Sir Francis Ogilvy Bt/Trustees of the National Library of Scotland)

James I. Portrait by an unknown artist. (Scottish National Portrait Gallery)

James's poem *The Kingis Quair*, celebrating his love for Joan Beaufort, cousin of Henry V, was the subject of a series of murals painted in Penkill Castle, Ayrshire, by the Scottish pre-Raphaelite artist William Bell Scott. (Magnus Magnusson, by kind permission of Patrick and June Dromgoole)

James II. Sixteenth-century portrait. (Scottish National Portrait Gallery)

James III and his queen, Margaret of Denmark. (The Royal Collection © 2000, Her Majesty Queen Elizabeth II)

James IV. (Scottish National Portrait Gallery)

The Great Hall of Stirling Castle, built around 1500 by James IV, and now restored by Historic Scotland. (Crown copyright, reproduced courtesy of Historic Scotland)

James V. (From the Blair Castle Collection, Perthshire/courtesy of Scottish National Portrait Gallery)

Mary Queen of Scots' third husband, the Earl of Bothwell. (Scottish National Portrait Gallery)

The execution of Mary Queen of Scots in Fotheringay Castle on 8 February 1587. Sketch by an unknown artist. (Scottish National Portrait Gallery)

A portrait of the 'Bonnie Earl o' Moray', killed in February 1582, commissioned by his grieving mother Lady Doune and showing the wounds inflicted on him. (Robert Harding Picture Library/Earl of Moray)

At the Union of the Crowns in 1603, James VI of Scotland became James I of Scotland, England and Ireland. Portrait by De Critz. (Scottish National Portrait Gallery)

Charles I. Family portrait by van Dyck. (The Royal Collection © 2000, Her Majesty Queen Elizabeth II)

Oliver Cromwell incorporated Scotland into the Commonwealth, abolished its parliament and proclaimed a full union of Scotland and England. Miniature by Samuel Cooper, c.1650. (Bridgeman Art Library/private collection)

Charles II. Portrait by John Michael Wright. (The Royal Collection © 2000, Her Majesty Queen Elizabeth II)

James VII & II, the last Stewart king of Britain. Family portrait painted in 1674 by Sir Peter Lely and Benedetto Gennari. (The Royal Collection © 2000, Her Majesty Queen Elizabeth II)

The Apotheosis of William and Mary, depicted on the ceiling of the Lower Hall of the Royal Naval College at Greenwich. (George Wicks)

The United Parliament of Great Britain was established by the 1707 Act of Union. The House of Commons in session, painted by Peter Tillemans in 1710. (Reproduced by permission of the Palace of Westminster)

Prince Charles Edward Stuart, 'Bonnie Prince Charlie' or the 'Young Pretender'. Portrait by G. Dupré. (King Street Galleries/Bridgeman Art Library)

The Duke of Cumberland; in 1746, at the age of twenty-five, he defeated the Jacobites at Culloden. Portrait by the studio of David Morier. (By courtesy of the National Portrait Gallery, London)

Bonnie Prince Charlie's leave-taking from Flora Macdonald, painted by George William Joy in 1891. (Reproduced by permission of Walker's Shortbread Ltd)

'Bonnie Prince Charlie' became not so bonnie in the years following his escape to France after Culloden. Portrait by Hugh Douglas Hamilton. (Scottish National Portrait Gallery)

Sir Walter Scott's study at Abbotsford. (By kind permission of Dame Jean Maxwell-Scott, Abbotsford House)

The royal visit by George IV in 1822. Cartoon by Thomas Rowlandson. (City Art Centre: City of Edinburgh Museums & Galleries)

In February 1818 Sir Walter Scott masterminded the recovery of the Scottish Regalia from a bricked-up chamber in Edinburgh Castle. (Crown copyright, reproduced courtesy of Historic Scotland)

The Queen's progress up Edinburgh's Royal Mile in an open carriage for the official opening of the new Scottish Parliament on 1 July 1999. (Scotsman Publications Ltd)

Maps

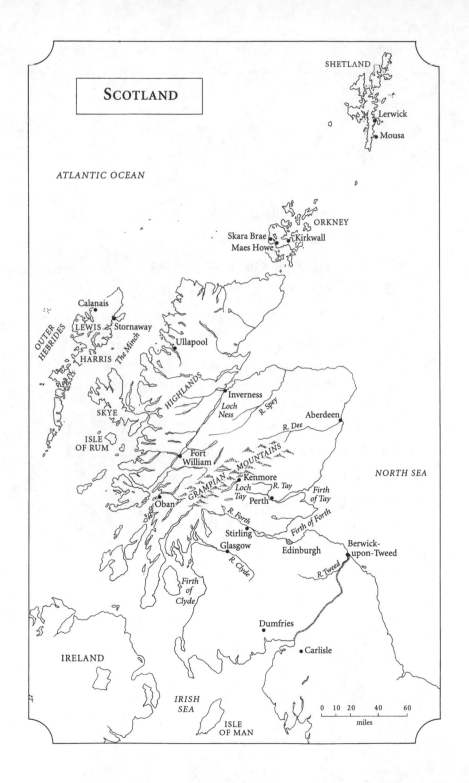

Introduction

These Tales were written in the interval of other avocations, for the use of the young relative to whom they are inscribed [Sir Walter Scott's grandson, John Hugh Lockhart]. They embrace at the same time some attempt at a general view of Scottish History, with a selection of its more picturesque and prominent points ... The compilation, though professing to be only a collection of Tales, or Narratives from the Scottish Chronicles, will nevertheless be found to contain a general view of the History of that country, from the period when it begins to possess general interest.

SIR WALTER SCOTT,
PREFACE TO *TALES OF A GRANDFATHER*

These are stirring times for Scotland. With a parliament of its own – the first for 292 years – Scotland stands on the threshold of a new future. What this future will bring is anyone's guess; all we can be sure of is that it will be informed and influenced by the past, just as our present has been. History gives the present a context.

In this book I have tried to tease out the significant strands in Scotland's history which highlight the key concepts of nationhood and identity. When and how did the many peoples who inhabited Scotland become Scots? When and how did the country of Scotland become the nation of Scotland? How did relationships with England (and other nations) evolve? How did an independent realm develop? How did the role of kingship, the concept of monarchy, develop? When and how did the governance of Scotland evolve into the community of counsels which is now called parliament?

All these threads are woven, often luridly, into the tapestry of Scotland's past. But what was that past? The Scottish history which I absorbed in my childhood was the history of Scotland as expressed and cast in the nineteenth century by the greatest novelist of his day, Sir Walter Scott. Some 175 years ago he wrote *Tales of a Grandfather*

(1827–29), purportedly for the edification of his grandson John Hugh Lockhart, whom he addressed by the neat pseudonym of 'Master Hugh Littlejohn'. In the *Tales*, Scott told history essentially as *story*. He was a brilliant *teller* of history. And he had a wonderful feel for the natural landscape, for the scenes where history happened – history on the hoof, one might call it. This is one of the things which have made his *Tales* such an enduringly popular exposition of history for generations of readers of all ages.

Like every historian, Scott had his own views – there is no such thing as truly objective history: every generation writes its own history to suit its own agenda, for history is part of the process of cultural definition and redefinition. Scott's agenda was very clear. Soon after writing the *Tales*, he expanded his children's book into a 'grown-up' *History of Scotland, 1033–1788* (published in 1831). His purpose, as he put it, was 'to show the slow and interrupted progress by which England and Scotland, ostensibly united by the accession of James the First of England, gradually approximated to each other, until the last shades of national difference may be almost said to have disappeared'.

Implicit in everything Scott wrote was the assumption that this union of England and Scotland was the inevitable outcome of an inevitable historical process – a process which meant progress. He believed passionately that the Union of the Crowns in 1603 and the Union of the Parliaments in 1707 had helped Scotland to mature out of turbulent and rebellious adolescence into adult nationhood, as an equal partner in the corporate nation-state of Britain.

Walter Scott was a meticulous and extremely erudite historian as well as being the first great historical novelist. He was familiar with all the fashionable theories of history of his day. He read extraordinarily widely, had a remarkable memory, and absorbed information from all manner of sources. He searched out medieval manuscripts and founded societies to edit and publish them.[1] He was greatly admired by historians all over Europe for the way in which he breathed fresh life into the musty recesses of the past. He was deeply interested in historical changes and movements and their causes – and even more

---

1 As a historian, Scott 'was familiar with all the historical works of the Scottish Enlightenment as well as that of editors and antiquaries, and he knew also the medieval chroniclers. It is probably true to say that as a political and cultural historian of Western Europe he was better equipped with knowledge of both primary and secondary sources than any of his contemporaries.' (David Daiches, 'Character and History in Scott's Novels', in *The Edinburgh Sir Walter Scott Club Bulletin*, 1993/4).

so in their effects. And in his greatest novels (where his characters are constantly seen as being helplessly trapped in the social and economic forces of history), no less than in his writing of history, he subtly and imaginatively examined the *meaning* of history in terms of the relationship between tradition and progress. Scotland, it has often been said, was *invented* by Walter Scott in his portrayal of its history.

But Scott's version of Scotland's history is now largely out-of-date; and so are the ideas about history which informed it. History is continuously being reassessed and rewritten. That is what Walter Scott was doing – he was harnessing the events of the past to reinforce his agenda for his own time: simultaneously conservative and progressive.

In the last few years there has been a revolution in Scottish historical thinking. Many of our cherished conceptions and ideas about our past are being revised. Where did the 'Scots' come from? What happened to the Picts? And what about Macbeth, whom both Shakespeare and Scott cast as the prototype villain of Scottish monarchy? Did Robert Bruce ever see a spider in a cave? How important was the 'Declaration of Arbroath' (which Scott does not even mention)? What was the Scottish Renaissance? What really happened at the Reformation? What was the significance of the reign of Mary Queen of Scots? Who were the Covenanters? What was the impact of Jacobitism on the Highlands and the Scottish identity? And what were the real, long-term effects of the 1707 Treaty of Union?

All these crucial themes in Scotland's history are being examined, sometimes even turned upside-down, by a generation of brilliant and realistic Scottish academic historians. General books and specialised research papers pour from the presses. Illustrated part-series, like the fifty-two-part *Story of Scotland* published by the *Sunday Mail* in 1988–89 and the current *Scotland's Story* (First Press Publishing), masterminded by Professor Ted Cowan (Professor of Scottish History at Glasgow University), bring Scottish history to a wide and appreciative audience in a highly readable and accessible form.

The study of Scottish history in our universities has been revolutionised since Walter Scott's day. The first chair specifically dedicated to the subject was endowed at Edinburgh University by a bequest as the Chair of Scottish History and Palaeography in 1901. Glasgow followed in 1911, when a joint Chair of Scottish History and Literature was established by public subscription. St Andrews University started a lectureship in 1948 which was elevated to a professorship in 1974. More specialised research institutes have recently been established, like the Institute for Environmental History at St Andrews and Dundee (by the Historiographer Royal in Scotland, Professor Chris Smout) and the Institute of Irish and Scottish Studies at Aberdeen (by Professor Tom Devine, author of the recent *The Scottish Nation 1700–2000*).

The teaching of Scottish history in our schools has also been gradually expanding over the years since I was learning about it (at home) from an edition of *Scott's Tales of a Grandfather* abridged by Elizabeth Grierson (1934). At my school in Edinburgh we were taught only *British* history, about English rather than Scottish monarchs, about the history of the British Empire.[1] In Scotland today there is a formal requirement on schools and teachers to cover, at their discretion, aspects of Scottish history for pupils aged five to fourteen: the Wars of Independence, the vikings, the Jacobites, Victorian Scotland and the impact of the two world wars are the most popular at present. For pupils at Standard grade (the successor to the O-grade) who take History as a subject, Scottish History is compulsory.

Scotland: The Story of a Nation arose from a broadcast series on Scottish history which I presented on BBC Radio Scotland in 1998. It was entitled *Tales of a Grandfather* because it used Scott's *Tales* as its framework. In the series, I interviewed twenty-four contemporary historians who were busy casting new light on Scotland's history; they helped me to show how radically the perceptions of that history have altered in recent years. Extracts from several of these interviews are quoted in this book. The series presented a re-examination and a re-illumination of traditional views about Scotland's past, from its roots in the so-called Dark Ages to the Union of the Parliaments in 1707 and the last throes of Jacobitism in the 1745 Rising – which is where Walter Scott ended *his* history.

I have used almost the same framework in *Scotland: The Story of a Nation*. However, as far as Scott was concerned, Scottish history did not begin until the accession of Macbeth in 1040; all the preceding centuries were wrapped up in a preamble to the story (Chapter 1: 'How Scotland and England came to be separate kingdoms'), for the dreariness of which he apologised to his young grandson: 'This is but a dull chapter, Master Littlejohn.' He gave a brief account of the Roman invasion of Britain, talked about the continual warfare between

---

1 Some pupils of my vintage in Scotland were luckier than I was: other schools showed a greater interest in Scottish history, but everything depended on the enthusiasms of individual teachers.

the Scots and the Picts after the Romans withdrew, and then, with a sigh of relief, moved on to Macbeth – 'The next story shall be more entertaining.' To my mind, the centuries *before* Macbeth are just as fascinating and revealing as those which came afterwards – and just as important for an understanding of the identity of the Scots.

Like Walter Scott, I am a devotee of the *landscape* of history, the monuments, the man-made relics, the places as well as the people of history. *Scotland: The Story of a Nation* takes the reader on a tour of Scotland's history, from the earliest Mesolithic settlers on the Island of Rum nine thousand years ago to the establishment of Scotland's new parliament in 1999. We visit many of the sites and monuments which celebrate significant moments in Scotland's history: the marvellous Neolithic village of Skara Brae on Orkney; the overgrown hill-fort near Inverness where St Columba tried to convert the King of the Picts to Christianity in AD 600; the site of the decisive battle of Nechtansmere (Dunnichen) in Angus where the Picts repelled the Northumbrians in 685, as illustrated by the 'war-correspondent' Pictish stone at nearby Aberlemno; the cliff in Fife where Alexander III fell to his death to create a major succession crisis in 1286; the little-known plaque in Westminster Hall which marks the spot where William Wallace was condemned to a brutal death in 1305; the site of the Battle of Flodden where James IV and the 'Flowers of the Forest' were scythed down in 1513.

We find the site of the house in Perth in which James I was murdered in a sewer in 1437, and of the house in Edinburgh where Mary Queen of Scots' husband, Lord Darnley, was murdered after an explosion in 1567. We visit the superb sarcophagus for Mary in Westminster Abbey which James VI built for his mother. We discover the derelict summerhouse in Edinburgh in which the 1707 Union of the Parliaments of Scotland and England was signed. And we explore not just the battlefield of Culloden but also the magnificent fortress near Inverness which the Hanoverian government built in the worried aftermath of the 1745 Jacobite Rising – Fort George. And all along the way we savour the 'people's history' of Scotland – the living wealth of local legends and traditions about 'Braveheart' William Wallace, for instance, which can have just as much resonance for the general reader as the careful analyses of academics.

History on the hoof, indeed, down the long, helter-skelter trail of Scotland's quest for its identity through nationhood; it is a story of high drama and far-reaching change – change which has never been more striking than in recent years. The words which Sir Walter Scott wrote in the final chapter of his novel *Waverley* (1814), nearly two centuries ago, are even more relevant today:

> *There is no European nation which, within the course of half a century, or little more, has undergone so complex a change as this kingdom of Scotland.*

Magnus Magnusson KBE
April 2000

Chapter 1

IN THE BEGINNING

England is the southern, and Scotland is the northern part of the
celebrated island called Great Britain. England is greatly larger
than Scotland, and the land is much richer, and produces better
crops. There are also a great many more men in England, and
both the gentlemen and the country people are more wealthy,
and have better food and clothing there than in Scotland. The
towns, also, are much more numerous, and more populous.

Scotland, on the contrary, is full of hills, and huge moors and
wildernesses, which bear no corn, and afford but little food for
flocks of sheep or herds of cattle. But the level ground that lies
along the great rivers is more fertile, and produces good crops.
The natives of Scotland are accustomed to live more hardily in
general than those of England.

TALES OF A GRANDFATHER, CHAPTER I

For three billion years Scotland was on a collision course with
England.

I am talking in terms of geology. Scotland's geological past involves
a barely believable story in which whole continents moved around like
croutons floating half-submerged in a bowl of thick soup; a story of
great oceans forming and disappearing like seasonal puddles, of mighty
mountains being thrown up and worn down, of formidable glaciers
and ice-caps advancing and retreating behind mile-thick walls of ice
as they melted and reformed again. Scotland itself has been a desert,

a swamp, a tropical rainforest, and a desert again; it has drifted north over the planet with an ever-changing cargo of lizards, dinosaurs, tropical forests, giant redwoods, sharks, bears, lynx, giant elk, wolves – and also, in the last twinkling of an eye in the geological time-scale, human beings.

And always it was on that inexorable collision course with England.

In their learned writings, geologists tend to toss millions of years around like confetti. About three billion years ago what is now (largely speaking) 'Scotland' was part of a continent known as *Laurentia*, one of the many differently-sized 'plates' which moved slowly around the surface of the globe. Some eight hundred million years ago it was lying in the centre of another super-continent thirty degrees south of the equator. Over aeons of time it wandered the southern hemisphere before drifting north across the equator. By six hundred million years ago Scotland was attached to the North American continent, separated by an ocean called *Iapetus* from the southerly part of what was to become Britain and which was then attached to the European continent.

And then, some sixty million years ago, the *Iapetus* ocean began to close. North Britain and South Britain came together, roughly along the line of Hadrian's Wall. That collision produced the Britain we know today (although it was still connected to Europe). But the weld continued to be subject to stress and strain long after the land masses had locked together: over a three-million-year period a chain of volcanoes erupting off the western seaboard of Scotland created many of the islands of the Hebrides, including Skye, Mull, Arran, Ailsa Craig, St Kilda and Rum.

The foundation of history is geology and its related subject of geomorphology. The underlying rock has shaped the landscape and has influenced, through the soil, the kind of plants, animals, birds and insects in every part of the countryside; it has thereby shaped the lives and livelihoods of the human communities which have lived here.

Agriculture would flourish on the productive farmland on the flatter east coast of Scotland. The more mountainous landscape of the west with its thin, acid soils was suitable only for subsistence husbandry. In the Central Belt of Scotland the abundance of coal and oil-shale entombed in the underlying rocks fuelled the Industrial Revolution and would foster the growth of the iron, steel, heavy engineering and shipbuilding industries.

Edinburgh Castle, at the heart of what became the nation of Scotland, would be built on the eroded roots of a volcano which had erupted some 340 million years ago, when Scotland still lay south of the equator. Castle Rock itself was carved into a classic crag-and-tail shape by the gouging passage of ice during the last glaciation.

When Sir Walter Scott opened his *Tales of a Grandfather* with his summary description of the difference between Scotland and England, the modern science of geology was in its infancy (that science, incidentally, was created by Scotsmen like James Hutton[1] and Sir Charles Lyell[2]. Scott did not know *why* Scotland was so different from England; it took the pioneers of geology to explain it.

The first people in Scotland (c.7000 BC)

One day in the early 1980s a ploughman was working on a potato field near the village of Kinloch, at the head of Loch Scresort on the island of Rum in the Inner Hebrides. As his ploughshare turned over the soil, he caught sight of a beautiful barbed and tanged stone arrowhead. He reported the find at once, and in 1984–85 archaeologist Caroline Wickham-Jones conducted an excavation of the area on behalf of Historic Scotland. What she unearthed was the earliest human settlement site yet discovered in Scotland, dating from the Mesolithic (Middle Stone Age) period, nearly nine thousand years ago.

It was a large camp-site rather than a formal settlement: arcs of stake-holes indicated the locations of several shelters, and there were many traces of fires and broken hearth-stones as well as numerous pits and hollows. These first 'Scots' had built small tent-like shelters out of wood, brushwood and skins; they made hearths on which they could prepare food and even smoke meat and fish to keep for the winter. The climate at that time was moist and relatively warm – perhaps 2°C warmer than today; much of the island was covered by open heathlands with shrubs of juniper and bog myrtle, but there was

---

1   Edinburgh-born James Hutton (1726–97) is now universally recognised as the 'father of modern geology'. He was the first person to grasp the nature of the immense age of geological time and the concept of sequences within that time-scale; until that time, it was widely believed that the earth was precisely 4,004 years old. His book, *Theory of the Earth* (1788), long predated Darwin's *On the Origin of Species by Means of Natural Selection* (1859), and ranks alongside it as one of the greatest scientific contributions of all time.

2   Sir Charles Lyell (1797–1875) was the prophet of the theory of 'continental drift' (plate tectonics) which would later be refined by the German meteorologist Alfred Wegener in 1915. Lyell had been struck by the evidence of massive changes in climate indicated by the rock records. In the year of his death he stated: 'Continents, therefore, although permanent for whole geological epochs, shift their positions entirely in the course of ages.'

also light, low-canopied woodland, while copses of birch and hazel flourished in the more sheltered areas. Remains of carbonised hazelnut shells showed that nuts were an important part of the early inhabitants' diet.

The most significant find at Kinloch was the discovery of an assemblage of more than 140,000 stone tools and discarded flint-like material. The Mesolithic dwellers on Rum had made a variety of tools from stone, including microlithic ('small stone') arrowheads, scrapers, awls, blades and flakes. They used flint which they collected as pebbles from the beaches; but they also had access to a good knapping stone known as bloodstone, which has similar properties to flint. The source of the Rum bloodstone was on the west coast of the island, ten kilometres from the Kinloch settlement: Bloodstone Hill (Creag nan Steàrnan).

Good-quality stone for tools is rare in Scotland, and the presence of bloodstone made Rum very special to the early inhabitants of the western seaboard; we know from archaeological sites elsewhere that people from many of the surrounding islands and the adjoining mainland used bloodstone from Rum for their tools.

Such were the first known inhabitants of prehistoric Scotland. They had moved up from the south (i.e. England) soon after the end of the last Ice Age, ten thousand years ago, during the Mesolithic period. This sounds very ancient indeed, but it is worth remembering that hunter-gatherers had been living in England for at least four thousand years before that; and in the much warmer climate of the Middle East, people were already living in cities and experimenting with woollen textiles, metal-working, pottery and the irrigation of farmlands.

The Mesolithic incomers to Scotland were not 'settlers', as such. They were small family groups or communities of nomadic people who lived by hunting, fishing and gathering plants; they would establish camps where they could spend the winter and then make forays in pursuit of deer herds in the spring and summer. They made tools and weapons of stone, they used fire for cooking and warmth, and they dressed in animal skins. They were mobile on both land and sea, and soon established barter-links with other semi-permanent communities.

It is impossible to say how large the Mesolithic population of Scotland was, but several sites have already been identified at places like Morton on Tentsmuir, north of St Andrews and at various other places from Grampian to Argyll.

The Mesolithic period in Scotland lasted for about four thousand years, and merged into the Neolithic (New Stone Age) period around 3000 BC. By then the last land-link between south-east England and the Continent was submerged, and Britain had become an island. This change had involved an influx of new people from the south, people who started to clear the forests and farm the land. There were now permanent communities, such as the marvellous Neolithic village of Skara Brae, on Orkney.

Skara Brae, Orkney (3100–2600 BC)

In the winter of 1850 a ferocious storm stripped the turf from a high sand-dune known as Skara Brae in the Bay of Skaill, on the west coast of mainland Orkney. An immense midden was exposed, as well as a semi-subterranean warren of ancient stone buildings. What came to light in that storm turned out to be the best-preserved prehistoric village in northern Europe. And not only was it perfectly preserved – it was the earliest in Europe as well: the village of Skara Brae was inhabited around 3100 BC, more than half a millennium before the Great Pyramid of Egypt was built (2500 BC), and long before Stonehenge (2000 BC).

A splendid new £900,000 Visitor Centre was opened in April 1998. It had taken ten years to plan and build, and it provides a graphic introduction to the story of Skara Brae, using interactive computer images and a replica of one of the original stone houses. But nothing can match the extraordinary experience of seeing the place for oneself.

The 'village' comprises half a dozen separate houses and some associated structures, including a very large workshop for manufacturing stone tools. The houses are spacious and cellular, connected by covered passage-lanes. The village was deliberately embedded into the congealed mass of the midden up to roof height, to provide stability and insulation. The walls were made of local Orkney flagstone, which is easily worked and splits naturally into building slabs. All the fittings and furnishings were also fashioned from flagstone – the kitchen dressers, the cupboards, the shelves, the compartments for the beds. Some of the houses had under-floor drains for indoor sanitation.

The houses are roofless now. Visitors walk along the tops of the walls and look down into the interiors of the houses. There is a startling sense of intimacy, peering down into these comfortable, well-furnished homes: it is easy to imagine the families who lived there for some twenty generations, from 3100 to 2600 BC. The village evokes a vivid sense of immediacy, of instant identity with that close-knit, self-sufficient farming and fishing community.

They lived well. The womenfolk owned a lot of jewellery (necklaces, pendants and pins made from bone, as well as ivory and pumice) which they kept in a recess above the bed. They cooked with home-made pottery on a square stone-built hearth in the centre of the room. Farming consisted of keeping cattle and sheep and a few pigs, and growing barley; the sea provided cod and saithe, lobsters and crabs, cockles and mussels. The nearby cliffs were a cornucopia of seabirds' eggs. Wind and weather drove whales, dolphins, porpoises and walrus ashore on their doorstep.

It was a stable, unchanging lifestyle. Then the village was deserted, around 2600 BC – no one knows how or why. There is no archaeological evidence of sudden emergency or destruction.

The merging of the Neolithic Age into the Bronze Age also saw the flowering of an extraordinary architectural phenomenon – the erection of stone circles and standing stones. On Orkney, not far from Skara Brae, the Standing Stones of Stenness and the Ring of Brogar survive. But the most imposing, and probably the oldest, of the megalithic ('big stone') monuments of Scotland is the great complex at Calanais on the Isle of Lewis – Scotland's 'Stonehenge of the North'.

Calanais (Isle of Lewis): 3000–2000 BC

It used to be called 'Callanish' or 'Callernish'. Before that it was 'Classerniss'. But now the original Gaelic form of the name will be enshrined in the next Ordnance Survey maps of the Western Isles of Scotland, so 'Calanais' it is, officially.

Calanais on the Isle of Lewis lies at the head of Loch Roag, some twenty-four kilometres west of Stornoway. It was built in stages from about 3000 BC and was certainly completed by 2000 BC. Briefly, it is a circle of thirteen standing stones huddled round a massive central monolith, 4.75 metres high, and a small chambered cairn. A double line or 'avenue' of stones comes in from the north, and ragged tongues protruding from the circle create a rough cruciform shape.

The importance of Calanais has long been recognised. In the seventeenth century the people of Lewis called the standing stones *Fir Bhrèige* ('False Men'):

IN THE BEGINNING

It is left by traditione that these were a sort of men converted into stone by ane Inchanter. Others affirme that they were sett up in places for devotione.

JOHN MORISONE OF SOUTH BRAGAR, c.1684

By then the complex had been all but drowned in a layer of peat some 1.5 metres deep. In 1857 the owner of Lewis, Sir James Matheson, ordered the peat to be cleared, and the site became a Mecca for visitors. When the first Ancient Monuments Act was passed in 1882, Calanais was in the primary list of sixty-three prehistoric or later monuments to be scheduled for protection.

The landscape setting, and the setting of the stones themselves, have changed considerably since then. The local inhabitants, who had lived in a row of crofting houses built in the 1860s at the southern edge of the site, were 'cleared', like the peat. Various excavations of dubious value were undertaken. Early in the 1980s a 'proper' excavation was mounted, led by Patrick Ashmore of Historic Scotland, to clarify the precise positions of fallen and missing stones and to repair and conserve the site; in 1982, in a BBC documentary to celebrate the centenary of the Ancient Monuments Act (*Echoes in Stone*), I filmed the tricky re-erection of one of the stones at Calanais.[1] There is now a new Calanais Visitor Centre next door to the Edinburgh University Field Centre; here, visitors can find out about the main site before going on to admire the stones *in situ.*

Calanais has a special aura of enchantment, of marvel and majesty and mystery. What was it originally intended to be? That is its continuing enigma. A temple? A huge funerary complex? A megalithic astronomical observatory to mark important events in the movements of the sun and the moon and the stars? Or all three, perhaps? The engineering and surveying skills required to construct such a complex monument are astonishing; they argue a high level of sustained social organisation, and the sophisticated and purposeful use of regional power to express ancient beliefs and rituals which we still cannot fathom.

These beliefs and rituals were given their most impressive and enduring monument in the great prehistoric chambered tomb of Maes Howe, at Tormiston Mill on the Orkney mainland.

---

1 Archaeology is simply architecture after it has collapsed. I cherish Patrick Ashmore's description of how he was planning to re-erect the stone: 'And then we'll lower it down and twiddle it a bit, so that it will fit in precisely.' It sums up neatly the *modus operandi* of dealing with our heritage of crumbling ancient monuments which want nothing better than to fall down.

Maes Howe on Orkney (3000 BC)

In 1861 an assiduous local antiquary named J. Farrer, along with a friend, George Petrie, dug their way into the heart of a great green mound known as Maes Howe. They had no idea what to expect. First they tried to make their way along the entrance passage. When they found it blocked solid, they broke through a hole in the top of the mound. They dropped into a central chamber choked with clay and stones, and had it cleared by their workmen. What they found disappointed them: it was clearly a burial chamber, with three built-in recesses or cells for bodies, but all they found was a fragment of a human skull and some horse bones and teeth.

They also discovered, however, that they were not the first 'moderns' to have broken into Maes Howe. In the middle of the twelfth century AD, a band of Norse crusaders ('Jerusalem-farers') had dug a hole in the roof of what they called 'Orkahaug' and dropped in, and the signs of their incursion were still apparent when Farrer and Petrie made their entry. The Norsemen had had their reasons for breaking into the chamber: they knew that the kings of antiquity had been buried in huge burial mounds accompanied by their choicest treasures and weapons, and ransacking burial mounds was a favoured diversion for viking heroes. But the crusaders had found nothing to satisfy their greed in Maes Howe, and had scrawled their disappointment – and their excuses for failure – in runic graffiti on the walls:

> To the north-west a great treasure is hidden. It was long ago that a great treasure was hidden here. Happy is he who finds the great treasure.
>
> It is surely true what I say, that treasure was taken away. Treasure was carried off in three nights before these Jerusalem-farers broke into this howe.

I make no excuses for returning to Orkney on this lightning tour of prehistoric Scotland, for Orkney is an archaeological paradise, with more outstanding monuments and sites than any other part of Britain of similar size. Maes Howe itself, which is acclaimed as the finest chambered tomb in north-west Europe, is associated with the Orkney farmers who built the Standing Stones of Stenness and the Ring of Brogar, and whose ancestors may have lived at Skara Brae. It was built within a century or two of 3000 BC. The mound stands more than seven metres high, and measures thirty-five metres across. The lofty central chamber is relatively small (some 4.6 metres square) and is approached by a low, stone-flagged entry-passage. The passage points south-west, and in the evenings around the shortest day of the year (21 December) the rays of the setting sun shine directly into the burial chamber.

Maes Howe is a miracle of early engineering. It is built almost entirely of huge flagstone slabs (megaliths), the largest of which weigh more than thirty tonnes. The walls of the central chamber converge in overlapping slabs of stone to form a vaulted ceiling; the final square of space was closed with slabs.

But Maes Howe has even more to offer than this amazing feat of prehistoric architecture, and for that we have the Norsemen to thank. The graffiti carved by the Orkney crusaders are not the only inscriptions in this fascinating place. After the first Norse break-in, the old burial chamber seems to have become a popular venue for courtship. One boastful inscription states boldly, *Thorný bedded: Helgi carved* [it]. Another, more gallantly, says, *Ingigerð is the sweetest woman there is*. Another refers obliquely to the amorous activities of the local merry widow: *Ingibjörg the fair widow: many a woman has lowered herself to come in here; a great show-off. Erlingr.*

They form part of the largest collection of runic inscriptions anywhere in the viking world – and the fact that their subject-matter is so commonplace gives them, for me, a special value. These are not the epics of kings and heroes which you find in the Icelandic sagas, but the authentic voices of the ordinary folk who, throughout history, are usually as anonymous as a flock of birds. Maes Howe was the ancient, brooding, mysterious place which the Norsemen of Orkney made their own.

The Broch of Mousa

Round about 2000 BC the advent of the Bronze Age brought another revolutionary social change to Scotland with the introduction of metallurgy. A new metal, bronze, which was tougher than silver or gold or copper, underpinned the development of sophisticated social hierarchies based on wealth and power. Bronze brought about an increase in trade and an increase in the effectiveness of weaponry; and the new weaponry enabled ambitious leaders to indulge in territorial aggression.

It was now that Scotland made another uniquely Scottish contribution to architecture – the brochs. They were magnificent edifices: tall round towers, with tapering double-skinned dry-stone walls bonded together at intervals by rows of flat slabs. Between the double walls were stairs leading to galleries and small rooms on separate storeys. There was room for livestock at ground level, which had only one small, low and easily defended entrance. There were no windows. The brochs were practically impregnable.

There are some five hundred brochs, or traces of brochs, still surviving in Scotland. They were built in large numbers in the north, especially in the Northern Isles, the Western Isles and Caithness, with occasional examples in the southern part of the country.

When were they built, and why? They seem to have originated in Orkney early in the Iron Age, around 200 BC, and were being built until about AD 200, when they were more or less abandoned; their stones were robbed for newer buildings in the farming communities which had been growing around them. They can only have been built as powerful symbols of local authority and prestige, which could also act as strongholds for the local people in times of danger: part refuge, part status symbol.

And who built them? They used to be called 'Pictish towers', but in fact they were constructed by the ancestors of the Picts – the indigenous inhabitants of northern and western Scotland from whom the historical Picts were descended (see Chapter 3).

My own favourite is a broch which stands on a tiny uninhabited island off the east coast of Shetland – the broch of Mousa. It is the best-preserved of all Scotland's brochs; it is still almost intact, standing to a height of thirteen metres. Many centuries after it ceased to be used by the local population the Icelandic sagas record that it was used on two occasions as a refuge by runaway lovers in viking times.

Egil's Saga relates how, around AD 900, an Icelander in Norway fell in love with the sister of a powerful Norwegian war-chief, Thórir Hróaldsson, named Thóra Hlaðhönd (Lace-Cuff); her suitor was Björn Brynjólfsson. Thórir refused permission for them to marry, whereupon the lovers eloped one night and boarded a ship bound for Iceland, but were shipwrecked on Shetland on the way. They spent a secure and comparatively comfortable honeymoon that winter in the broch of Mousa while their ship was being repaired, and in the spring they completed their journey to Iceland and lived happily ever after. The daughter of that marriage, Ásgerð, who was conceived on Mousa, became the wife of the eponymous hero of the saga, the great viking warrior-poet Egil Skallagrímsson.

Orkneyinga Saga ('The Saga of the Earls of Orkney') tells how, in

1153, a high-born lady named Margaret, the mother of Earl Harald of Orkney, was abducted by an ardent admirer named Sigurður. The couple holed up with a band of supporters in the broch of Mousa. They had brought in plentiful supplies of food and water, and Earl Harald wrathfully but vainly besieged the broch all winter. Eventually he was forced to agree to the marriage.

These stories seem to me to underline the constant need for security in a world which was becoming more and more violent and aggressive. Safety was paramount – and the more prosperous you were, the more important safety precautions became.

Crannogs

Deep in the heart of Perthshire, in the village of Kenmore at the eastern end of Loch Tay along the A827 from Aberfeldy, the historical enthusiast comes upon an extraordinary structure beside an embryo marina. On a solid platform of pile-driven wooden stilts in the water stands a massive wooden, thatched round-house. It is a crannog, reconstructed by the Scottish Trust for Underwater Archaeology.

Crannogs were, essentially, loch-dwellings built on artificial or modified natural islands in inland waters. They were usually linked to the shore by timber walkways or stone causeways, for protection against robbers or invaders. They were built by some of the first farmers in Scotland towards the end of the Neolithic Age (3000 BC), and some of them were still inhabited as late as the seventeenth century AD. Eighteen crannogs have been found in Loch Tay alone; hundreds more have been identified the length and breadth of Scotland north of the Central Belt. Some remain hidden as submerged stony mounds, others have become tree-covered islands. They were mini-castles long before castle-building began in Scotland.

The Kenmore crannog is based on 'Oakbank crannog', on the northern shore of Loch Tay at Fearnan ('Place of the Alder'), which was built around 500 BC, at the start of the Iron Age, and was the first crannog in Scotland to have been thoroughly excavated underwater. The round-house has a floor of stout alder-logs thickly carpeted with bracken. It is furnished with all the kinds of artefacts which the excavation produced: a central flat-stone hearth for cooking and heating, storage areas for provisions, wooden bowls and plates, leather clothes and shoes and bags, jewellery made from jet or polished stone, woven and dyed textiles. It makes an unexpectedly roomy homestead for an extended family of perhaps fifteen to twenty people.

The crannog-dwellers on Loch Tay were farmers, even though they lived on water. They tilled the adjoining land and grew barley and two different types of wheat. They kept cattle, sheep and goats. They cut and coppiced hazel to make hurdles for partitions and wood-panels. Their diet of lamb, beef and boar was supplemented by fish, butter, cheese, hazelnuts, nettles, sorrel and wild carrots, and they enjoyed wild cherries, sloes, blackberries and cloudberries.

And they had water-transport – a 10.5 metre log-boat, hollowed out from a single oak-tree, was found at the site; it was large enough to carry animals and other cargo – the first Loch Tay ferry, perhaps! They presumably had canoes as well.

A visit to the Crannog Centre at Kenmore is a rewarding experience. One comes away more impressed than ever by the evidence of the intelligence and creative skills of these early Scots who pioneered the land-uses and methods of land-management with which we are familiar today. There was nothing 'primitive' about our early and Iron Age ancestors.[1]

Sir Walter Scott made no reference to these early ancestors in his *Tales of a Grandfather*; they were *pre*-history. For him, *history* only began with the coming of the Romans to Scotland.

It was the Roman incursion which caused the first armed collision with the forces from the south, through England.

---

1 I am indebted to American-born Barrie Andrian, director of the Crannog Centre, for an illuminating tour of the Centre, which was opened in 1997. 'The reconstruction crannog', which was started as an archaeological experiment to try out the technique of driving alder-wood piles to a depth of two metres into the soft bed of the loch, using local materials and ancient methods, took two years to build. Crannog research has been conducted by Nicholas Dixon of Edinburgh University for more than twenty years.

Chapter 2

THE ROMANS IN SCOTLAND

A long time since, eighteen hundred years ago and more, there was a brave and warlike people, called the Romans, who undertook to conquer the whole world, and subdue all countries, so as to make their own city of Rome the head of all the nations upon the face of the earth. And after conquering far and near, at last they came to Britain, and made a great war upon the inhabitants, called the British, or Britons, whom they found living there. The Romans, who were a very brave people, and well armed, beat the British, and took possession of almost all the flat part of the island, which is now called England, and also of a part of the south of Scotland.

TALES OF A GRANDFATHER, CHAPTER I

From the road it looks like a genteel suburban garden, discreetly protected by freshly-painted black iron railings, with a small gate inviting access; but for those who take the trouble to stop and enter, it is a magic garden indeed. Inside is one of the most delightful little monuments in the care of Historic Scotland – the excavated remains of the Roman Bath-House at Bearsden, near Glasgow.

A weather-proof interpretive panel mounted on a solid stone pedestal provides a clear and graphic account of what the visitor can see among the manicured lawns: the walls, stone floors and hypocaust of an elaborate and well-appointed sauna for the small cavalry detachment which garrisoned one of the forts on the Antonine Wall.

The Antonine Wall was a solid and continuous barrier which stretched across the narrowest part of Scotland between the estuaries of the Forth and the Clyde – the Forth–Clyde isthmus. It ran for sixty kilometres (forty Roman miles) along the high ground bordering the southern edge of the central valley of Scotland, from Bridgeness at Bo'ness, west of Edinburgh on the south coast of the Firth of Forth, to Old Kilpatrick west of Glasgow on the north bank of the Clyde. It was started around the year AD 140 on the order of the Emperor Antoninus Pius. It took four years to build, and consisted of a massive stone-based rampart of turf, some 3.4 metres high, topped by a timber breastwork to protect the Roman sentries on patrol; the turf came from a wide and deep defensive ditch which was dug on the northern side of the wall. The wall was studded along its length with forts and beacon-platforms, linked by a road running behind the wall known as the Military Way. Because of its turf construction, and the sprawl of modern urban development, little of it has survived; but the remains of some of the forts, and a few short stretches of the wall, are still visible at places like Watling Lodge (ditch), Rough Castle and Seabegs Wood (rampart, ditch and Military Way), between Falkirk and Bonny-bridge.

In a sense the Antonine Wall was as much a customs barrier as a defensive wall; it was a means of controlling trade and traffic moving into and out of the Roman province, as well as a base for military patrols into the native territory to the north. One of those frontier posts was Bearsden.

The fort at Bearsden has long since been engulfed by the tide of neat housing of this douce suburb on the north of Glasgow; the houses now sitting on the site overlook the Bath-House which lay in a large annexe attached to the wall. The legionaries coming off sentry duty were able to choose between a plunge in the Cold Room and Bath (*Frigidarium*), or the Hot Dry Room (*Sudatorium*) with its graded Warm Rooms (*Tepidaria*). To one side lay a stone-built communal latrine housing a wooden bench with round holes cut in it for seating over the sewer channel.

The Bearsden Bath-House with its 'mod cons' presents a vivid picture of the advance of Roman civilisation into the wildlands of Scotland. It brings us from prehistory into history 'proper'. But it also foreshadows the long struggle to settle a border between north and south, between Scotland and England.

Iain MacIvor, former Chief Inspector of Ancient Monuments for Historic Scotland, says:

The first military works to divide north from south Britain were made by the Romans, and for a long time there was a fanciful link between the famous wall from the Tyne to the Solway [Hadrian's Wall] and the border between Scotland and England. The Scots were to find a lasting source of national pride in the notion that, whereas the southern parts of Britannia had been taken over without too much difficulty by the mighty Roman army, their own ancestors had held out against the Roman Empire for centuries, and that this undaunted resistance forced the Romans to build one of the wonders of Europe to protect their province of Britannia – Hadrian's Wall.

The location of the Roman frontier in the north varied considerably over the years. Julius Caesar claimed a 'Conquest' after his two invasions in 55 and 54 BC; but it was not until the massive invasion of AD 43 under the Emperor Claudius that the real conquest of southern Britain began. It took the Romans a full forty years of gradual advance and consolidation to become masters of their new province of Britannia. In the course of these four decades they suffered some severe setbacks, including the ferocious uprising of the Iceni tribe of Norfolk and Suffolk under their redoubtable warrior queen Boudica in AD 60–1. By AD 79, however, all England and Wales had been subdued. Now only the far north remained: the Lowlands and Highlands of Scotland. These were *terrae incognitae* to the Romans: unreconnoitred badlands inhabited by (to them) unknown but ferociously barbarian tribes.

There seem to have been three tribes in the Lowlands at this time: the Votadini in the east with their capital Traprain Law in Lothian; the Novantae in the south-west (Dumfries and Galloway); and in between them the Selgovae, whose territory reached from Eskdale to the Cheviot Hills.

The hill-fort of the Votadini on Traprain Law (152 metres) had earthen ramparts (now almost invisible) enclosing sixteen hectares. It was more than just a stronghold or a refuge: it housed a permanent settlement and the administration of the district – an embryo town or burgh, in effect. The Votadini would later shift their capital from Traprain Law to Edinburgh (Din Eidyn), probably to the Castle Rock, and would be known in heroic legend as the Gododdin (see Chapter 3).

Around the Firth of Clyde were the Damnonii. Above that were the mountainous lands of many Highland tribes, collectively called the Caledonii (Caledonians) by Tacitus.

In AD 78 the newly-appointed Governor of the Province of Britan-nia, Julius Agricola, embarked on a vigorous policy of subduing the native tribes still beyond Roman control in Wales and the north of England. Then he turned his mind to an invasion of Scotland. With him was his son-in-law, the historian Tacitus, who would write (in AD 98) an account of the campaigns in Scotland in his *Life of Agricola*. In AD 80 Agricola launched his blitzkrieg with a pincer movement. He sent his Ninth Legion up through the territory of the Votadini on the east side of Scotland, following the line of today's A68 through Lauderdale and north over the Lammermuirs at Soutra to Lothian and the Firth of Forth. Meanwhile the Twentieth Legion moved up the west side through Annandale, along the line of today's M74 to Clydesdale and the Firth of Clyde. Then the two legions joined forces and marched up to the Firth of Tay. By AD 82 Agricola had subdued the Novantae in the south-west and secured the occupation of Scotland below the Central Belt. He made treaties and alliances with the native peoples where he could, and consolidated his grip by building several garrison forts, the most substantial of which was at Newstead, next to the Eildon peaks near Melrose. He also built a string of small forts (without a continuous barrier) which superintended a line between the Clyde and Forth, with a network of roads to secure the territory to the south.

What was the impact of the Roman incursion into the Lowlands of Scotland? Anna Ritchie, freelance archaeologist and prolific writer on the archaeology and history of early Scotland, says:

> At the time the impact must really have been remarkable, because the tribesmen would never have seen anything like the Roman military machine which marched into Scotland.
>
> And there was also an immense economic effect. Once the Roman army was established in the Lowlands of Scotland, there was an impact on agriculture because the army had to be fed. They needed immense quantities of grain, and that grain had to be obtained locally once the supplies they brought with them were finished. You can see that archaeologically, in fact, in these great souterrains, or earth houses: underground storage chambers, some of which are so large that they cannot just have been for the needs of the little settlements in which they lie; they can only be that size because they were storing the grain for the occupying army.
>
> Another area of impact would have been the transport network they needed for military mobility, for provisioning the army and

for sending messages between battalions. That must have been quite stunning in the eyes of the local peoples, because there had been nothing more than tracks until that time. The roads and the great forts with their ramparts and huge wooden gateways would have been a glimpse of a totally alien world.

Agricola's ambitions did not stop at the Clyde–Forth isthmus. His ultimate aim was the conquest of the whole of northern Britain. In AD 83 he started his march north, with a powerful fleet in support. He had a formidable army under his command: three full legions of crack Roman infantrymen supported by cavalry and squadrons of battle-hardened auxiliaries. He wintered on the Tay, and next spring continued his advance northwards up the coastal plain, taking out any native settlements on the way and building a series of temporary marching camps. Meanwhile the Caledonians, according to Tacitus, 'turned to armed resistance on a large scale'.

Agricola's strategy was to bring the Caledonians, under their leader Calgacus, to pitched battle. In the late summer of AD 84 the strategy succeeded. The locations of Agricola's marching camps suggest that he cut across country from Stonehaven into Morayshire along the line of the modern A96 to Inverurie and Huntly; and there, somewhere in the north-east, at a place which Tacitus called *Mons Graupius* (the 'Graupian Mountain'), the two sides met for the final battle.

More than thirty thousand of the Caledonian tribesmen had gathered in close-packed tiers on the slope of a hill. In the valley between the two armies the Caledonian charioteers careered back and forth, taunting the Romans and displaying their skills, daring them to advance. And advance they did; under the personal command of Agricola, the auxiliary squadrons moved forward in a disciplined frontal attack while the cavalry engaged the charioteers. The Caledonians fought with reckless courage, but gradually they were outflanked and outfought at close quarters. By the end of the day they had been comprehensively routed amid fearful slaughter: ten thousand tribesmen were said by Tacitus to have perished, at a cost of only 360 Roman dead. The survivors scattered and fled 'far into the trackless wilds'.

The location of 'Mons Graupius' has never been positively identified and has been the source of endless debate among archaeologists and historians. Some think the battle took place near Huntly on the slopes of a hill named Bennachie; others opt for somewhere closer to Stonehaven. The apparent similarity between 'Graupius' and 'Grampian' is intriguing, if inconclusive. It is also tempting to think that it may have been somewhere near Inverness – such as Culloden? – where in 1746, more than 1600 years later, another retreating 'Caledonian' army would be brought to battle and shattered by the superior fire-power and discipline of a military machine from the south (see Chapter 28). There, as at Mons Graupius, it was the last strategic point where a native leader could hold an army of Highland tribesmen together before they melted away to their winter straths and glens; there, as at Mons Graupius, defeat would leave what Tacitus called 'a grim silence on every side, the hills deserted, homes smoking to heaven'.

The account by Tacitus of the battle of Mons Graupius makes compelling reading – particularly the noble rhetoric he put into the mouth of Calgacus (his name may be associated with the Gaelic *calgath* and mean 'swordsman') in his pre-battle speech, a ringing denunciation of Rome and its supposed civilisation, and the first recorded despairing cry of 'Freedom!' which would echo through the Highlands and Lowlands for centuries to come:

> *Former battles in which Rome was resisted left behind them hopes of help in us, because we, the noblest souls in all Britain, the dwellers in its inmost shrine, had never seen the shores of slavery and had preserved our very eyes from the desecration and the contamination of tyranny: here at the world's end, on its last inch of liberty, we have lived unmolested to this day, in this sequestered nook of story.*
>
> *But today the farthest bounds of Britain lie open; there are no other peoples beyond us; nothing but seas and cliffs and, more deadly even than these, the Romans, whose arrogance you shun in vain by obedience and self-restraint. Harriers of the world, when the earth has nothing left for their ever-plundering hands, they scour even the sea; if their enemy has wealth, they have greed; if he be poor, they are ambitious; neither East nor West can glut their appetite; alone of people on earth they passionately covet wealth and want alike.*
>
> *To plunder, butcher, steal – these things they misname 'empire': they make a desert, and they call it peace.*

The defeat was a crushing blow to the Caledonians and their northern neighbours, and a significant victory for the Romans; although beaten, however, the tribes were not broken. Agricola sent a reconnaissance fleet round the north coast to confirm that Britain was, indeed, an island. He may have felt the terrain so inhospitable as not to be worth the effort of military conquest; besides, he had already exceeded the normal five-year period as Governor. He contented himself with ordering the completion of a massive legionary fortress at Inchtuthil on the Tay, seven miles east of Dunkeld, with satellite forts blocking the way into the northern mountains. The following year he was recalled to Rome.

There was to be no Roman subjugation of the Highlands. The fortress at Inchtuthil did not last long. The Empire was in a constant state of flux, with troops required in hot-spots which would flare up here and there on the Continent. In AD 87, before it was even completed, the fortress was abandoned and systematically dismantled, its stores removed and its defences slighted. The Romans were in retreat, withdrawing gradually from all their forts and bases in Scotland. The native tribespeople helped them on their way with constant harassment. By 105 the Romans had withdrawn to a line between the Solway and the Tyne.

The tide turned again with the accession of Hadrian as Roman Emperor in 117. He visited Britain more than once, and in 122 he decided to consolidate the northern frontier with that great barrier, Hadrian's Wall, across the isthmus between the Solway and the Tyne. The Lowland tribes of Scotland were left in peace for a time – until 139, when a new Roman Governor (Quintus Lollius Urbicus) marched north from the wall in strength to reoccupy the territory Agricola had seized nearly fifty years earlier. It was then that he decided to consolidate his gains by building the Antonine Wall.

The Antonine Wall did not last very long either – only twenty years or so. After it was abandoned around 161 it was reoccupied, but only for a very short time, and by about 180 the Romans seem to have decided to pull back towards Hadrian's Wall. There were occasional uprisings in the Lowlands, followed by severe punitive campaigns. But by 214 the Romans had finally withdrawn from Scotland, leaving Hadrian's Wall as the ultimate frontier – the most impressive and enduring legacy of Roman rule in Britain. Scotland and its restless tribes were left to their own devices, held in check only by their domestic preoccupations and the Roman soldiery still garrisoning the fortlets of Hadrian's Wall.

By now, however, the graffiti were really on the wall. And in 297, one of the most famous names of the north appears in the documentary record – the Picti, the warlike painted people who are still considered one of the great enigmas of early Scotland, with a kingdom which

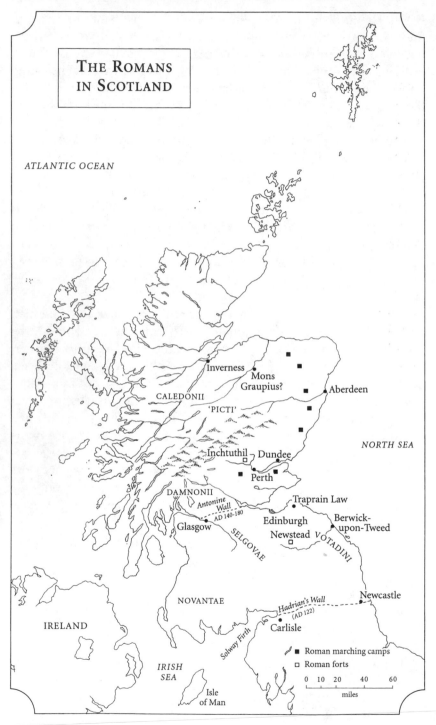

THE ROMANS
IN SCOTLAND

ATLANTIC OCEAN

Inverness
Mons
Graupius?
CALEDONII
'PICTI'
Aberdeen

NORTH SEA

Inchtuthil   Dundee
Perth

DAMNONII
Antonine
Wall
AD 140-180
Glasgow
SELGOVAE

Traprain Law
Edinburgh
Newstead

Berwick-
upon-Tweed
VOTADINI

NOVANTAE
Hadrian's Wall
(AD 122)
Newcastle

IRELAND

Solway Firth
Carlisle

IRISH
SEA

■ Roman marching camps
□ Roman forts

0 10 20   40   60
miles

Isle
of Man

stretched from north of the Firth of Forth to the Moray Firth and beyond (see Chapter 3).

They are mentioned as playing a key part in the great 'Barbarian Conspiracy' which, through accident or design, attacked Roman Britannia simultaneously from all sides in 367; the Angles and Saxons overwhelmed the coastal forts of the south and east, the Gaelic-speaking Scoti from Ireland came sweeping in across the Irish Sea, and the Picti overran Hadrian's Wall from the north. From then on, the Roman hold on Britannia became more and more tenuous. They appointed three generals in quick succession in an attempt to save the province, and the defences were patched up again. But it was to no lasting avail. The Roman Empire was crumbling, and by 410 the last of the Roman army, along with the Roman administrators, had left Britain's shores.

A century before they left, however, the Romans had given this enduring name to their main enemies in the north of Scotland: in the year 297 a Roman poet had referred to them as Picti ('painted ones'). The name stuck, and 'Picts' became a generic term for the many 'Caledonian' tribes who lived north of the Forth–Clyde line and who thwarted the imperial ambitions of the Romans at their ultimate frontier.

Chapter 3

PICTS, SCOTS, BRITONS, ANGLES
AND OTHERS

*These people of the northern parts of Scotland, whom the Romans
had not been able to subdue, were not one nation, but divided
into two, called the Scots and the Picts; they often fought against
each other, but they always joined together against the Romans,
and the Britons who had been subdued by them.*
              TALES OF A GRANDFATHER, CHAPTER I

In the western outskirts of Inverness stands a massive hill crag, now
engulfed in trees – Craig Phadrig. The summit of this crag was
once the site of a great hill-fort, a mighty bastion of the early Pictish
kings.

Not a lot of people know that it is there, or how to find it when
they do know. It stands in the Kinmylies district, near Craig Phadrig
Hospital; you drive up the steep, dead-end Leachkin Brae, which is
not marked as leading to anywhere. Forest Enterprise has provided
two woodland walks which meander through the forest at the lower
levels of the crag; each has its own car park. To reach the summit of
the crag, you use the second (upper) car park and follow the walkway
from it. Then you leave its carefully graded surface, take a very deep
breath, and embark on a fiercely steep scramble up, and up, and up.

Twenty-five years ago, archaeologists cleared the surface vegetation
and revealed two concentric ramparts crowning the summit; these
ramparts had been what is called 'vitrified' – that is to say, the timber

framework inside the walls had been set on fire (deliberately or accidentally) so that the stone and earth of the massive ramparts were fused into a slaggy mass. The ramparts enclosed a flat expanse measuring some eighty metres by forty. When I was chairman of the Ancient Monuments Board for Scotland in the 1980s, we all toiled up to the top to admire the revelation of this great hill-fort, and decided there and then that Something Must Be Done to make this remarkable monument more accessible and comprehensible to the public; it was being used at the time as an obstacle course by trail riders and motorbike scramblers and the old ramparts were being undermined by the roots of invasive trees.

Well, Something Was Not Done – immediately. The whole summit is now overgrown with thistles and other tall plants. The commanding views of both the Beauly Firth to the north-west and the Moray Firth to the north-east are blocked by massive tree-growth. The ramparts are once again smothered by shrubs and undergrowth. Historic Scotland has plans to clear the summit and its ramparts once again, however, and people should soon be able not only to reach the summit with much greater ease but also to understand what is to be seen there.

Craig Phadrig was a major Pictish stronghold in the north of Scotland from the fifth century onwards. Towards the end of the sixth century it was the fastness of one of the most powerful kings named in the Pictish king-lists – King Bridei mac Máelchú, often called by the anglicised name of 'Brude'. In his monumental *A History of the English Church and People* (c.731), the Venerable Bede described King Bridei as *rex potentissimus*, and he seems to have been the over-king of many local kingdoms which comprised the core of the realm of 'Pictland', or 'Pictavia'; this realm extended from around the Firth of Forth and covered the centre and north-east of Scotland as far as Orkney (the name for the sea between Caithness and Orkney is the 'Pentland' Firth, which is a Norse word meaning 'Pictland'). One of his 'capitals' may have been on Castle Hill in Inverness; and it is tempting to see Craig Phadrig as the place where St Columba (see below) may have met King Bridei during an expedition up the Great Glen to convert the northern Picts to Christianity in the latter half of the sixth century.

According to Columba's biographer, Adomnán, King Bridei refused to open the heavy double gates of the ramparts to his missionary visitor. Columba then went up to the gates, made the sign of the cross against them and knocked; the bolts slid back of their own accord and the gates swung open – whereupon King Bridei 'greatly honoured the holy and venerable man, as was fitting, with the highest esteem'.

The 'Picts'

So who were these people, these Picts? The first thing to recognise is that there was nothing 'mysterious' or 'problematic' about them, as scholars used to state. The Picts were not a new element in the population: 'Picts' ('*picti*' – painted ones) was simply the Roman nickname for the tribal descendants of the indigenous Iron Age tribes of northern Scotland.[1] Anna Ritchie, in *Picts* (Historic Scotland, 1989), puts it like this:

> *The Picts were Celts. Their ultimate ancestors were the people who built the great stone circles like Calanais on the Isle of Lewis in the third millennium BC in Neolithic times, and the brochs in the early Iron Age from about 600 BC to AD 200. We have no evidence of any major invasions of Scotland after the initial colonisation by farming peoples soon after 4000 BC – there seems to have been very little fresh blood coming in during the Bronze Age.*

Just outside the town of Brechin, in Angus, by the A90 trunk road from Dundee to Aberdeen, an impressive £1.2 million visitor centre was opened in the summer of 1999 in the country park of the Brechin Castle Centre. It is called *Pictavia*, and can be described as somewhere between a museum and a theme park. The display tells, vividly and graphically, the story of the Picts, and is a splendid introduction to their world for visitors of all ages and abilities; it includes not only many examples of Pictish stones and jewellery but also interactive computer facilities explaining the meanings of Pictish symbols ('Cyber Symbols') and the sounds of Pictish music (the 'Tower of Sound').

Some time after the age of King Bridei, of Craig Phadrig fame, the centre of Pictish power moved southward, to Angus, Perthshire and Fife, but the Picts' distinctive culture did not change. They were not by any means the painted barbarians described by Roman chroniclers;

---

1   The idea that the Picts painted or tattooed their bodies is older than the reference to *Picti* in AD 297 by the the poet Eumenius. Herodian of Syria, who wrote (in Greek) a history of the Roman emperors from AD 180 to 238, said of the Picts: 'They tattoo their bodies not only with likenesses of animals of all kinds, but with all sorts of drawings.'

on the contrary, they were a cultured society ruled by a sophisticated warrior aristocracy which could afford to employ learned men and, more particularly, craftsmen of all kinds – particularly the sculptors who fashioned the magnificent carved stones which are the unique legacy of the Picts.

This period of early Scottish history has long been known as the 'Dark Ages', not because the deeds of the time were so dark but because the documentary sources are too meagre to shed a great deal of light. Modern historians prefer to call the 'Dark Age' of Scotland by a less misleading name – 'Early Medieval'. What *is* clear is that it was a time of considerable and rapid political and ethnic change. By pulling together the sometimes elusive accounts of medieval chroniclers, and calling in all the available archaeological evidence, it is now possible to see various historical patterns developing in Scotland, both north and south of the Forth–Clyde line.

In our attempt to understand the changing shape of early Scotland it would be enormously useful to be able to call upon the aid of television, with its graphic use of 'morphing' – merging collages of images into one another, like long-range weather forecasts. The pattern of conquests and occupations in Scotland in the centuries succeeding the Roman withdrawal presents a confusing kaleidoscope of shifts in power, like an ever-changing jigsaw puzzle. Before we reach a more stable picture of 'Scotland' in the twelfth century, say (the time of David I – see Chapter 6), we have to follow the fortunes of several apparently different groupings: Picts, Gododdin, Angles, Britons/Celts and Scoti/Scots/Gaels, as well as specific kingdoms like Pictland, Fortriu, Strathclyde, Rheged, Alba and ultimately Scotia.

The Gododdin

While the Picts were the power in the north, another martial kingdom had been developing to the south of the Firth of Forth, in the Lothians – the home of the British tribe known to the Romans as Votadini. During the Roman occupation they had been a client kingdom, or at least had lived peaceably under Roman subjugation; archaeologists have found a major hoard of rather battered Roman silverware which was buried at Traprain Law in the fifth century, after the Roman withdrawal.

By 600, however, the Votadini had their stronghold in Edinburgh (Din Eidyn), and emerged in history under their proper British, or Old Welsh, name of 'Gododdin' in an elegiac heroic poem called *Y*

Gododdin, composed by a local bard named Aneirin at about that time. The poem tells the story of a raiding expedition mounted by the king of the Gododdin, Mynyddawg Mwynfawr, who ruled territories stretching from the Forth to the Tees. He gathered a princely war-band of 360 chosen champions from all over his realm and even farther afield. For a year they feasted and caroused in the towering timber hall of his stronghold in Edinburgh, wearing robes of purple and gold, with gold brooches and neck-bands, drinking from goblets of gold or silver. Then they pledged themselves, according to ancient custom, to conquer or die in the service of their lord. Next morning they went clattering down the Castle Rock, riding southward deep into the lands of the Angles. The encounter took place at 'Catraeth', identified as Catterick in what is now Yorkshire:

> *Men went to Catraeth, they were renowned.*
> *Wine and mead from gold cups was their drink.*
> *A year in noble ceremonial,*
> *Three hundred and sixty gold-torqued men.*
> *Of all those who charged, after too much drink,*
> *But three won free through courage in strife,*
> *Aeron's two war-hounds and tough Cynon,*
> *And myself, soaked in blood, for my song's sake.*
>
> *Gododdin's war-band on shaggy mounts,*
> *Steeds the hue of swans, in full harness,*
> *Fighting for Eidyn's treasure and mead.*
> > *On Mynyddawg's orders*
> > *Shields were battered to bits,*
> > *Sword-blades descended*
> > *On pallid cheeks.*
> *They loved combat, broad line of attack:*
> *They bore no disgrace, men who stood firm.*
> FROM *THE GODODDIN* (TRANS. JOSEPH P. CLANCY)

It was the very stuff of heroic legend, that ferocious, unforgiving battle.

Legendary or not, historical fact or poetic fiction, the power of the Gododdin was certainly broken a few years later. In 638 Din Eidyn was besieged and captured by the avenging Angles, and the place seems then to have received the anglicised name Edinburgh, by which it is known today.

The Angles

It may come as a surprise, at first blush, to think of Angles in Scotland – the Angles from northern Germany who had come over to the south-east of England, first in the fourth century as invited auxiliaries to assist the Romans in keeping their hold on Britannia but later, in the fifth century, as invaders bent on conquest. They had created their own kingdom in England, 'Anglia', in the area of today's East Anglia. They were a tough warrior people, the Angles, and in 547, according to the Venerable Bede, the Anglian King Ida thrust his way far northwards over the Humber, across the Tees and the Tyne, and established his royal seat on the formidable fortress crag of Bamburgh on the north-eastern coast of England. By the year 605 all this territory had been consolidated into the Kingdom of Northumbria (literally, 'north of the Humber') under King Æthelfrith, whom Bede described as 'a very powerful and ambitious king'.

We must be careful, when we talk about the ancient name Northumbria, not to be misled by the boundaries of today's Northumberland. Northumbria at its greatest extent in the seventh century extended all the way north (after the capture of Edinburgh in 638) to the Firth of Forth and even beyond, perhaps to the Mounth (the eastern extension of the Grampian massif). In that context, it is possible to see the heroic raid by the Gododdin deep into Yorkshire as an abortive pre-emptive strike against the growing imperial ambitions of the kingdom of Northumbria.

After the collapse of the Gododdin, the aggressive expansionism of the Angles of Northumbria extended their dominance beyond Edinburgh into the southern part of Pictland; the power-centre of Pictland had by then moved from Inverness south to Abernethy, perhaps, and/or Scone, beside today's city of Perth, and a new name was being applied to it – the kingdom of 'Fortriu'. From 653 to 685 much of the southern part of this area seems to have been under Northumbrian control. There was an attempted Pictish uprising in 672, but this was put down with the utmost ferocity and many of the Pictish aristocracy were massacred. The climax came in 685, with a battle between the Picts and the Northumbrians in the Angus glens, north of the estuary of the Tay.

The Battle of Dunnichen (Nechtansmere): 685[1]

In 685 a check was given to the encroachment of the Saxons by the slaughter and defeat of their king Egfrid at the battle of Drumnechtan, probably Dunnichen; and the district south of the Forth was repeatedly the scene of severe battles between the Picts and the Northumbrians, the latter striving to hold, the former to regain, these fertile provinces.

WALTER SCOTT, *HISTORY OF SCOTLAND*, VOL. I (1830)

In front of the parish church in the village of Dunnichen, near Forfar in Angus, a commemorative cairn was erected by Letham and District Community Council in 1985. It was set up to mark the 1300th anniversary of one of the most significant battles of 'Dark Age' Scotland: a battle which, until recently, was referred to as 'Nechtansmere' but is now called the Battle of Dunnichen (as Walter Scott called it in his *History of Scotland*). 'Nechtansmere' is the name by which the battle was known from Northumbrian sources.

In 685 the ruler of Northumbria was a headstrong king named Ecgfrith. Against the advice of all his counsellors and of St Cuthbert, Bishop of Lindisfarne, who had a premonition of disaster, he decided on a massive cavalry attack on Pictland, under its new king, Bridei mac Bili (who also happened to be Ecgfrith's kinsman). Ecgfrith probably marched through the Lowlands to Edinburgh, then may have crossed the Forth at Stirling and the Tay at Perth. As he advanced up Strathmore from Perth, he was diverted from his planned route by the Picts; using classic guerrilla tactics, they fell back towards territory of their own choosing rather than offering pitched battle in open country.

The earliest primary account of the Northumbrian invasion of 685 was written, forty-five years later, by the Venerable Bede:

King Ecgfrith ... rashly led an army to ravage the province of the Picts. The enemy pretended to retreat, and lured the king into narrow mountain passes, where he was killed with the greater part of his forces on the 20th of May and the 15th [year] of his reign.

---

1   I am indebted to Graeme Cruickshank, director of Edinburgh Historical Enterprises, for an enlightening guided tour of the presumed battle-site and its environs; it was due to his dedicated and scholarly researches that the true significance of the Battle of Dunnichen began to be acknowledged.

It was somewhere in these 'narrow mountain passes' that the Picts ambushed the invaders on 20 May 685 with devastating effect. It has not proved possible to identify the location with certainty. The topography in this southern, fertile part of Angus is open and rolling (the terrain is much more mountainous farther to the north-west); but Bede had never been to Scotland, and his description doubtless relied on exaggerated accounts brought back by the survivors to justify the defeat. A plausible scenario can be made for an ambush somewhere in the Dunnichen area, probably between the high ground of Dunnichen Hill ('Dun Nechtan') and the marshy ground known later as Dunnichen Moss ('Nechtan's mire'); the 'mere', or marshland, has now been reconstituted as a large pool by the farmer of Dunnichen Mains farm. The identification of 'Nechtansmere' with Dunnichen Moss is purely circumstantial, and not all scholars agree with it; but it is attractive, nonetheless.

In this scenario, the Pictish cavalry would have lured Ecgfrith into an ambush by feigning fear, until Ecgfrith found himself marching eastward past Dunnichen Hill alongside an extensive stretch of 'mere' at the base of the hill. At that point the trap was sprung: the main Pictish forces came swarming down from behind the top of Dunnichen Hill to attack the Northumbrian cavalry on the flank and cut off its retreat. The Northumbrians were virtually wiped out and Ecgfrith was killed.

In the churchyard of Aberlemno, some ten kilometres to the north of Dunnichen, there is a magnificent Pictish cross-slab (a fawn-coloured sandstone slab with a cross carved on it). The cross, richly decorated in high relief, is on the front of the slab; on the reverse, under two Pictish symbols, is depicted a battle-scene in three tiers. It has been called a 'tapestry in stone', but it is more than that: it is a brilliantly detailed despatch by a war-artist from the front line. It portrays the battle in a series of four vivid cartoon panels. The combatants are carefully distinguished: bare-headed Pictish warriors confronting (and eventually defeating) opponents who are wearing Anglo-Saxon helmets with long nose-guards and distinctive neck-collars. The Pictish cavalrymen are riding long-tailed ponies which they control with their knees and feet, leaving both hands free to wield their weapons, whereas the Northumbrians on their heavier, short-tailed ('bang-tailed') horses need to use one hand for the reins. The Pictish infantrymen are drawn up in ranks with a swordsman in front, defended by a warrior behind him wielding a long thrusting-spear and another armed with a throwing-spear.

The Aberlemno cross-slab seems to have been made early in the eighth century; it is tempting to interpret it as a memorial depiction of the Battle of Dunnichen itself. In the bottom right-hand corner an outsize Northumbrian (the size signifies a person of rank – perhaps Ecgfrith himself) lies dead on his side, his helmeted corpse now carrion for ravens.[1]

The outcome of the battle was decisive, according to the Venerable Bede:

> Henceforward the hopes and strength of the English realm began to waver and slip backwards ever lower. The Picts recovered their own lands which had been occupied by the English . . . Many of the English at this time were killed, enslaved or forced to flee from Pictish territory.

The battle marked the end of the Anglian/Northumbrian ascendancy in Scotland: from then on, the Northumbrians were never to be a power in the lands north of the Forth. Modern historians now claim that it was the Battle of Dunnichen which paved the way for northern Britain eventually to become the independent nation of Scotland and not just a northern extension of England. Some have even compared it to Bannockburn as 'the most decisive battle in Scotland's history'.

As for Bridei mac Bili, the conquering hero of Dunnichen, he died in 693 and was buried in the royal cemetery on Iona.

The Saltire of Scotland

Half a century or more after the Battle of Dunnichen, it is said, there was another battle against the Northumbrians, of symbolic significance at least, which legend associates with the village of Athelstaneford, on the B1347 near Haddington, in East Lothian; this battle is traditionally believed to have provided Scotland with its patron saint, the apostle Andrew, and its banner, the saltire.

According to Walter Bower's massive *Scotichronicon*, a Latin history of Scotland written in the 1440s, around 750 a Pictish warrior-king named Unust (729–61) was having the worst of a battle against the

---

1 For safety's sake, the Aberlemno stone in Aberlemno churchyard is covered in winter by stout wooden crating to protect it from bad-weather erosion. A faithful fibre-resin cast of the stone is now in the Museum of Scotland; it was formerly on display in the Meffan Museum in Forfar.

Northumbrians, when St Andrew appeared to him in a dream and promised him victory; this boost to Pictish morale apparently did the trick, assisted by another supernatural omen – a huge cloud-formation against the blue sky in the shape of a saltire (a diagonal cross, the *crux decussata*, on which Andrew was said to have been crucified at Patras in Achaia). Hence the adoption of St Andrew as Scotland's patron saint, and the blue-and-white saltire banner as the symbol of Scotland's nationhood.

The early Church in Scotland built up the cult of St Andrew by promoting the story that some of the saint's relics had been brought to Scotland at the behest of an angel by St Rule (Regulus) in the fourth century; a shrine was built for the relics at Kilrymont, which later became the site of the great cathedral of St Andrews. Having Andrew as its patron saint was a great coup for Scotland: he had been the first of the apostles whom Jesus had called. St Andrews quickly became a renowned centre for evangelisation and pilgrimage.

The tourist trade today is as important to the Scottish economy as the pilgrim trade was then – and Athelstaneford, as 'the birthplace of Scotland's flag', has seen no reason to miss out. In 1965 a commemorative cairn was erected in the graveyard of the parish church, incorporating a granite panel showing two armed hosts facing one another beneath the St Andrew's Cross in the sky, and the inscription:

> *Tradition says that near this place in times remote*
> *Pictish and Scottish warriors about to defeat an army*
> *of Northumbrians, saw against a blue sky a great*
> *white cross like Saint Andrew's, and in its image*
> *made a banner which became the flag of Scotland.*

Beside the cairn the saltire flies permanently on a tall white flagpole. A Flag Heritage Centre was established there in 1996 in a converted sixteenth-century doocot (dovecote).

The Britons

To the west of the Lowlands there was another realm – or rather, another shifting conglomeration of petty kingdoms and principalities – which took in a huge stretch of land from the Clyde down through today's Dumfries and Galloway, over Hadrian's Wall and across the Solway as far south as the present Lake District. This was the kingdom of the Britons – basically, Cumbria; but, as with Northumbria, we must not confuse its boundaries with those of today's Cumbria. The original Cumbria was the Latinised ancient name for this territory of the Britons, derived from a variant of the same word as modern Welsh *Cymry*, the name of the peoples there. In the sixth century this Brittonic realm may well have been the home ground of Arthur (Arturus), a Romanised British war-leader who was promoted, in legend, into a great European champion of Christianity, the 'once and future king' of the Britons.

Within this British realm of Cumbria two separate kingdoms emerged north of Hadrian's crumbling wall. One was Strathclyde, whose boundaries stretched as far south as Penrith. Its power-centre was at the basalt Rock of Clyde (*Altcluith*, Dumbarton Rock), where Dumbarton Castle now stands. Its 'spiritual' centre seems to have been in the Govan area, somewhere near Govan Old Parish Church; this church now houses an impressive collection of thirty-one pieces of sculpted stonework dating from the ninth to the eleventh centuries, including a magnificently carved giant sarcophagus.

The British of Strathclyde reached the height of their power in the seventh century; Strathclyde survived as a client kingdom of Alba until the Battle of Carham in 1018 (see below), where the last native king of Strathclyde, Owain the Bald, was killed.

The other British kingdom was Rheged, based on Carlisle and covering Galloway in the extreme south-west of Scotland. Rheged is the most shadowy of all the kingdoms of the 'Dark Ages'. One name stands out from ancient Welsh poetry: that of Urien, king of Rheged, whose exploits were hymned by the Welsh bard Taliesin. In 590 he took part in a siege of the Anglian stronghold on the island of Lindisfarne, off the north-east coast of England, but was assassinated by a rival British king who was jealous of his prowess.

The 'Scots'

The people the Romans called *Scoti* originally came from Ireland. The name was just a term of opprobrium applied by the Roman authors to describe raiders from Ireland, and probably meant, simply, 'pirates'; it differentiated the Scoti from the Picti of mainland Scotland. The Scoti had raided in the Hebrides and the western mainland of Scotland, they had taken part in the 'Barbarian Conspiracy' which overran the Roman province of Britannia in 367 (see Chapter 2), and they had probably been coming across the North Channel to settle in the west of Scotland for quite a long time. Around the year 500, however, tradition suggests that there was a positive 'migration' of the Scoti to

Scotland: the seventh-century Irish *Senchus fer nAlban* ('Tradition of the Men of Scotland') records the story that the Scoti, under their king Fergus Mór mac Eirc, an enterprising hero in the legendary mould, moved in strength from Antrim in north-eastern Ireland across the North Channel to the rugged, mountainous, island-haunted terrain of Argyll in the west of Scotland. These people were known as the Dál Riata; they spoke Gaelic, and established a new kingdom in the territory of modern Argyll which came to be known as Dalriada.[1]

The Gaelic-speaking Dál Riata in Argyll and the adjacent Inner Hebrides soon started to colonise farther afield. By the end of the sixth century they were hammering at the boundaries of neighbouring states, led by a series of aggressive warrior kings. One of those whose names are writ large in the *Annal of Scotland* was Áedán mac Gabhráin, overlord of Dalriada from 574 to 603, whose recorded exploits included large-scale raids by land and sea against the territories of the Picts, the Britons of Strathclyde and the Anglians of Northumbria. He was eventually defeated and killed by the Northumbrians in 603.

Dunadd

The massive natural fortress of Dunadd, in mid-Argyll, rears out of the Crinan Moss (Moine Mhor – the 'great moss') at the southern end of the fertile Kilmartin Glen above Lochgilphead. For historical pilgrims intent on getting a 'feel' for ancient Dalriada, there is a new Museum and Visitor Centre (Kilmartin House) in the village of Kilmartin at the head of the valley.[2]

The hill-fort of Dunadd is only one of the many power-bases of the

---

1   The traditional version of an Irish colonisation of Argyll is no longer accepted as uncritically as before: scholars like Ewen Campbell, lecturer in archaeology at Glasgow University, point to the lack of archaeological corroboration of any migration of ideas or artefacts from Ireland to the western mainland of Scotland. Dr Campbell argues that the evidence all points the other way – that there was no change in the population in Argyll and that there was considerable influence in the opposite direction.

2   Kilmartin House won the 1998 Scottish Museum of the Year Award and the 1998 Gulbenkian Prize for Museums and Galleries. Kilmartin Glen contains one of the richest assemblages of prehistoric ritual and ceremonial monuments in Scotland: more than 150 sites within six miles of the village of Kilmartin; an extraordinary collection of cup-and-ring rock carvings; a unique linear cemetery of Neolithic and Bronze Age burial cairns; a fine stone circle at Temple Wood and dozens of other ancient stone monuments, dating back almost to the start of human habitation in Scotland. Kilmartin House, which was opened in 1997, provides a focal point for pilgrims who want to visit the sites, and also houses a research centre for archaeology and landscape interpretation.

old kingdom of Dalriada, but it is perhaps the most striking and evocative. It stands back from the A816 from Lochgilphead to Oban, fifty-four metres high, a grass-grown rock mass made of epidiorite schist and shaped by glacial action – what geologists call a *roche moutonnée*. It is a bit of a scramble in places to reach the top, through natural clefts in the rock, but there is a wonderful panoramic view from the summit which makes the effort well worth while.

The steep zigzag route to the summit leads through two defiles which give access to concentric terraces which girdle it. The terraces are buttressed by the living rock, and any gaps were filled in by walling to complete the defences. The terraces provided space for timber structures, no trace of which now remains. The path leads onwards and upwards to the highest of the terraces, just below the sanctuary of the summit. On this grassy shelf lies the magnet which draws visitors to the top: a carved footprint incised into the bedrock, pointing more or less directly towards the distant Ben Cruachan, the 'holy mountain' of Argyll. There is also a roughly-scratched outline of a boar (a Pictish symbol) and an inscription in the unintelligible alphabet known as ogam. On another rock, just behind the 'heel' of the footprint, is a small hollowed-out basin (possibly for libations).

It is a tantalisingly enigmatic spot, where the imagination can take wing. Most commentators now agree that the carved footprint was used in the ritual inauguration of early Dalriadic kings; the new king would have placed one foot in the carving during the ceremony, in full view of his people gathered on the terrace below, to symbolise a royal 'marriage' with the land. Today's visitors cannot resist trying the fit for themselves.[1]

There is a magic resonance about Dunadd; for the people of Argyll it is the birthplace of the Scottish nation, a royal centre of major importance in the growth of 'Scotland' as a coherent realm. It has an overwhelming sense of place, of belonging to the land, superintending the surrounding countryside: the coiling meanders of the River Add below, Kilmartin Glen to the north, the hills of Knapdale to the south and, to the west, the Crinan Estuary and the Sound of Jura marking the route of the incomers from Antrim.

---

1   The footprint into which visitors place their feet is not quite the original one. In 1979, when erosion and increasing wear and tear were beginning to cause damage to the carvings, an exact mould was made up of reconstituted crushed stone, which matched the texture and colouring of the original in every detail; this replica 'cap', weighing more than fifteen hundred-weight, was helicoptered in by the RAF in 1979 and then manhandled into place to fit snugly and unobtrusively over the stone slab.

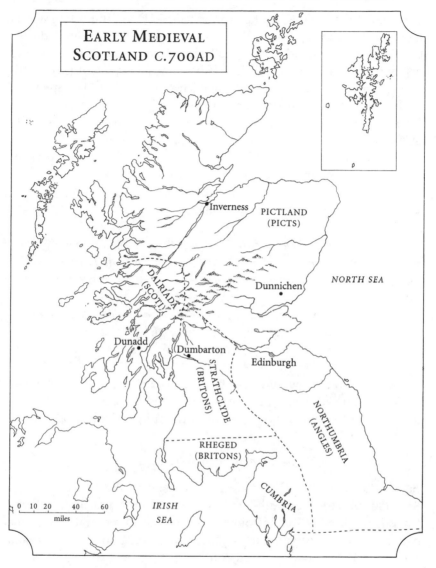

EARLY MEDIEVAL
SCOTLAND *C.*700AD

Inverness

PICTLAND
(PICTS)

DALRIADA
(SCOTS)

Dunnichen

NORTH SEA

Dunadd

Dumbarton

Edinburgh

STRATHCLYDE
(BRITONS)

NORTHUMBRIA
(ANGLES)

RHEGED
(BRITONS)

CUMBRIA

0 10 20   40   60
miles

IRISH
SEA

Recent archaeological excavations have shown that Dunadd was occupied, albeit intermittently, from about AD 500 to 1000; it is usually called 'the capital' – or '*a* capital' – of the kings of Dalriada. It was a place where skilled craftspeople fashioned high-quality jewellery and implements in bronze, silver and gold. It was also a major trading centre in a huge Celtic network which stretched from Ireland, down the west coast of Britain and across to the Mediterranean. Dunadd was clearly an important player in European trade, exporting commodities like hides, leather and metal-work and importing luxury goods from abroad. One of the most intriguing items found during excavations at Dunadd was a small piece of a yellow mineral named orpiment which comes from the Mediterranean; orpiment is the mineral which produced the beautiful golden yellow ink used by medieval scribes for their illuminated manuscripts, and may have been used on Iona to make the Book of Kells. Adomnán, the biographer of St Columba, described a visit paid by Columba to the *caput regionis* (capital of the region) and his talking to sailors from Gaul – perhaps he was there to buy orpiment for his scriptorium on Iona!

Ted Cowan, Professor of Scottish History at Glasgow University, says of the carved footprint on Dunadd:

> *The new king of Dalriada metaphorically (and almost literally) stepped into the shoes of the old king – it's a perfect size nine shoe, by the way. It carried overtones of fitting the role of being king, of being the only person whose foot fitted the footprint; the last echo of that concept is heard in the story of Cinderella and the glass slipper – the Ugly Sisters try it on, but Cinderella, the 'real' princess, is the only person whose foot fits.*

These inaugurations would have been Christian ceremonies, whatever ancient pagan traditions may have been reflected in them. And that brings us to a consideration of the impact of Christianity on early Scotland.

The coming of Christianity

Before the Romans officially declared an end to their occupation of Scotland, in 410, the south-west of Scotland may already have been Christianised; early in the fourth century the Emperor Constantine had declared Christianity to be the official religion of the Roman Empire, and this may have led to the establishment of some kind of 'sub-Roman Church' in Pictland.

The Venerable Bede wrote that, after Constantine made Christianity official, 'faithful Christians who during the time of danger had taken refuge in woods, deserted places and hidden caves, came into the open and rebuilt the ruined churches. Shrines of the martyrs were founded and completed and openly displayed everywhere as tokens of victory. The festivals of the Church were observed, and its rites performed reverently and sincerely.'

The one name which emerges from the scanty sources about south-west Scotland during this period is that of St Ninian. Ninian (Nynia) is the first Christian missionary in Scotland's history who is known to us by name. Bede called him 'a most reverend and holy man of British race', and recorded a tradition that he had been trained in Rome and that his see was at St Martin's Church at Candida Casa (the 'White House'), identified as Whithorn in Galloway. He was, apparently, the son of a converted British chieftain, who began his mission in the south-west late in the fifth century as the bishop of a Romanised community which had been Christian for some time. By the seventh century Ninian had become a cult saint, and many churches were dedicated to him in different parts of Scotland in the ensuing centuries.

In the west of Scotland, St Kentigern, or Mungo,[1] founded a church beside the Molindinar Burn; it was in a 'green hollow' (*glascu*), which gave the city of Glasgow its name. By 600, Kentigern/Mungo was established as the first bishop of the kingdom of Strathclyde centred on Dumbarton; his shrine lies in the crypt of Glasgow Cathedral.

The man most closely associated with the spread of Christianity in the sixth century, however, is Columba (*Colum Cille*, 'Dove of the Church', c.521–97). He was a scion of the Uí Néill, the most powerful royal family in Ireland at the time. Columba was a vigorous and hot-blooded warrior-monk who was banished after a particularly bloody battle and, as a penance, chose to lead a mission to the Scoti of Dalriada. In 563 he set sail in a coracle with twelve companions to do God's work. After some years on an island which Columba called *Hinba* (perhaps Jura), the king of Dalriada gave him the island of Iona, off the west coast of Mull, probably in the early 570s. Here he founded a large monastic community which was to become the spiritual powerhouse of Christianity in northern Britain. It also became a renowned centre of learning and artistic excellence, and owned an extensive library of books: many claim that the magnificently illustrated Book of Kells, now in the library of Trinity College, Dublin, was produced in a scriptorium on Iona. Columba's biographer, Adomnán, wrote that he was engaged in making a new manuscript of a psalter on the day of his death.

The major impact of the Church was the introduction of writing, and the close and mutually beneficial relations between Church and state. The Church was both client and patron of the monarchy. Columba himself ordained one of the kings of Dalriada (Áedán mac

---

1   The name Kentigern means 'hound-lord'. The diminutive Mungo means 'hound'.

Gabhráin) on Iona in 574. Another graphic impact was on Pictish art: following the advent of Christianity the Pictish symbol-stones were shaped into slabs with a dominant cross carved on one face, and Biblical figures like David were introduced to symbolise kingship, alongside the characteristic ornamentation of spirals, snakes, dragons, birds and fish.

Although both the Picti and the Scoti were ethnic Celts, the Picts were not the same *kind* of Celts as those incomers who came from Ireland around 500 to found the kingdom of Dalriada. The language the Picts spoke was 'British' or 'Brittonic' Celtic, akin to Welsh, Cornish and Breton (scholars call it 'P-Celtic'), whereas modern Irish and Scottish Gaelic descend from Goidelic Gaelic (which is classified as 'Q-Celtic'). The eventual assimilation of the Picts into the Gaelic culture of the Scots was made much easier through the influence of Christianity. Having been converted by Columban missionaries, the Picts looked to Iona as the head of their Church. Differences between Picts and Gaels began to be reduced, through intermarriage and the exchange of church personnel. So it is reasonable to assume that it was the rise of the Gaelic Church in Pictland which laid the foundations for the ultimate unification of the Picts and Scots as a new kingdom.

But before that could come about, there was another threat to be faced, in the shape of an enemy who would serve to bring the Picts and the Scots even closer together – the vikings.

The vikings

The vikings have long been considered the bogeymen of history. For centuries they were cast in the role of Anti-Christ – merciless barbarians from Scandinavia who plundered and burned their way across the known world, heedless of their own lives or the lives of others, intent only on destruction and rape and pillage. In fact it was never quite as one-sided as that – history seldom is – but it made a good story at the time. Today there is emerging a much more balanced version of the story which depicts the vikings in a less lurid and more objective light. It is mainly a matter of emphasis: less on the raiding, more on the trading; less on the piracy and pillage, more on the poetry and artistry; less on the terror, more on the technology of the Norsemen and the positive effect they had.

Politically as well as militarily they had a profound effect on the shifting, unstable kingdoms which were developing in what was to become Scotland. The historical record of their incursions into Scottish waters and territory began in 795 with a raid on Iona (the first of three such raids in ten years), and Scotland was then engulfed in the turmoil of what has come to be called the Viking Age (800–1050). While Danish raiders attacked the Continent and southern England, Norwegian invaders established a Norse earldom in Shetland and Orkney which was to last for more than three hundred years, from the middle of the ninth century to the thirteenth.

The Orkney earldom was a semi-autonomous fiefdom of the Norwegian crown, theoretically a Norwegian possession but frequently a recalcitrant one which displayed a large degree of independence. The main source for our knowledge of the Northern Isles during this period is an Icelandic saga, *Orkneyinga Saga* ('The Saga of the Earls of Orkney'), written early in the thirteenth century. It is a sprawling, dynastic chronicle of the lives of the earls of Orkney, a vivid narrative pageant of clashing personalities and dramatic events – not so much a history as a historical novel. It is the only medieval chronicle which has Orkney as the central place of action, but the story has much to say about the Norse impact on the northernmost counties of mainland Scotland, Caithness and Sutherland (which to the Orcadian Norsemen was 'South-land'!).

Today the people of Shetland celebrate their Norse heritage on the last Tuesday of every January with an exhilarating, night-long viking fire-festival called Up-Helly-Aa, which culminates in the ceremonial burning of a viking galley in Lerwick, the capital town of Shetland. It is not an ancient ritual by any means. It was invented by a blind Shetland poet in the 1880s, an aspect of the Victorian 'rediscovery' of the Viking Age by literary figures like Thomas Carlyle and William Morris – and, before them, Sir Walter Scott with his novel *The Pirate* (1821), which was inspired by a fleeting visit to Shetland in 1814 and a glimpse of the ruined medieval baronial building at Sumburgh which he named, romantically, Jarlshof ('Earl's Temple').

From their base in the Northern Isles the Norsemen ruled a miniature empire of the North Sea. It was probably from Orkney that their early raids on Iona were mounted; it was from Orkney that they exercised dominion over the Western Isles, which from then on owed fealty to the Norwegian crown. Viking armies penetrated deep into mainland Scotland in the north and the west, inflicting heavy defeats on the Scoti and the Picts alike. On the west coast, in 870, the vikings stormed the Strathclyde fortress of Dumbarton after a four-month siege; on the east coast in 890 they captured the formidable Pictish fortress of Dunnottar on its apparently impregnable rock projecting from the coast three kilometres south of Stonehaven. Norse power played a potent part in the kaleidoscope of aggression and alliance from which the picture of Scotland was to emerge.

Kenneth mac Alpin (800–58): the union of the Picts and the Scots

One effect of the viking incursions in the west was to force the Scots of Dalriada to look eastwards along Strathearn ('the Strath of the Irish') towards the richer lands of Pictish Fortriu, where the Picts, too, were under fierce pressure from viking attacks from the east. The power of Dalriada was now in decline and, despite occasional hostility between Scots and Picts, there was a certain inevitability about the way in which the two kingdoms began to come together against the common viking enemy.

This process of gradual unification culminated in the middle of the ninth century with the first joint king of the Picts of Fortriu and the Scots of Dalriada – Kenneth mac Alpin (Cináed mac Aílpín), known as Kenneth I. He was born about 800, and is believed to have been of mixed Dalriadan and Pictish stock, with a Gaelic father and a Pictish mother.

Out of the welter of warfare which saw the royal families of both kingdoms crushed, Kenneth mac Alpin emerged as king of Dalriada around 840; a few years later he became king of Pictish Fortriu as well. How exactly that came about is not known; according to a lurid folk-tale he invited the leaders of the Pictish nobility to a feast under a flag of truce and had them all slaughtered, but that yarn is no longer given any credence.

Kenneth mac Alpin soon moved his base out of Dalriada and east-ward to Tayside, the heartland of Pictland itself. The island of Iona, founding centre of the Columban Church, had proved to be too vul-nerable to viking raids; so when another huge viking fleet came prowling down the west coast in 849 on its way to Ireland, Iona and the other 'hallowed' islands were abandoned and the relics of their saints taken to safety on the mainland. The bones and treasures of St Columba were carried from Iona to Dunkeld ('Fort of the Cale-donians'), and installed in a great new church there.

It was the end of Dalriada as a historical identity. Kenneth mac Alpin, or one of his successors, established a new royal seat at Scone, near Perth, which became the capital of a united kingdom. He died in his palace at Forteviot in 858, having in the last ten years of his life invaded the kingdom of Northumbria no fewer than six times. In the course of these incursions he burned the royal fortress of Dunbar and the great early monastery at Melrose.

Kenneth mac Alpin's unification of Dalriada and Pictland as a new political entity was a landmark in the evolution of Scotland as a single kingdom. His authority extended from the Moray Firth in the north to the Firth of Forth in the south. This kingdom soon came to be called Alba, the old Gaelic name for Britain as a whole, which was now applied specifically to the territory ruled by Scottish kings.

Kenneth mac Alpin founded the first recognisably Scottish royal dynasty, and as a result Scotland's kings are formally numbered from him as Kenneth I. However, the perceived significance of Kenneth mac Alpin in the origins of the Scottish nation is now diminished in the eyes of modern historians. Ted Cowan backs another king as the real creator of the kingdom we now call Scotland; his name was Constantin II (Constantín mac Áeda), and he ruled from 900 to 943:

> In my view, Constantín mac Áeda was Scotland's equivalent of England's King Alfred, and he should be on the lips of every schoolchild in this country. Perhaps the only reason that he isn't is because his Gaelic name looks so difficult to pronounce! This Constantín did two things. First, he married members of his family into the viking war-bands and bought peace with them in that way. Second, he manufactured a new origin myth for the 'Scots' to give them a pedigree which showed how the Picts and Scots were related.

The 'original' Scottish origin myth traced the lineage of the Scoti back to Biblical times: they were descended from an Egyptian princess named Scota, the daughter of the Pharaoh of the Oppression (Ramses II, 1304–1237 BC). This enterprising princess left Egypt shortly after the Israelites crossed the Red Sea. She wandered for 1,200 years in the deserts of the eastern Mediterranean, before crossing to Sicily and making her way through the Pillars of Hercules (Straits of Gibraltar), through Spain and then across to Ireland. In her baggage she brought the block of sandstone, weighing 152 kilograms, which was reputed to have been used as a pillow by Jacob when, according to Genesis 28, he had his celebrated dream about Jacob's Ladder ('I am the Lord God of Abraham thy father, and the God of Isaac: the land whereon thou liest, to thee will I give it, and to thy seed'). From the east coast of Ireland, Scota beheld her own Promised Land – Scotland – and crossed over to it with Jacob's sacred Stone.

Constantin II, according to Ted Cowan, made a significant addition to this imaginative account: he instructed his bards to give Scota a husband – Gaedel Glas (Gathelos), a Prince of Scythia and ancestor of the Picts. That gave the Picts and the Scots a common ancestry, as a deliberate part of the nation-building on which Constantin II was engaged. As part of the redefining of the new integrated kingdom, Scota's far-travelled Stone was moved to Scone, where it was put to use as the seat on which the rulers of the united Scottish kingdom were inaugurated – the 'Stone of Scone' or 'Stone of Destiny', as it came to be called.

The origin myth of 'the Scots'

Your identity, both as an individual and as part of a nation, is crucially determined by where you believe you come from – what your origins are, in effect. There comes a time in the growth of any country when it is both politic and imperative to have a respectable pedigree as a nation. And if you don't know it, you invent it.

But how and when, in the case of Scotland, was it done? On what basis was this embryonic origin myth manufactured? Dauvit Brown, a lecturer in Scottish History at the University of Glasgow, has made an exhaustive study of early medieval written sources:

> The earliest surviving text which propounds the idea, in all seriousness, of Scotland being two thousand years old was written during the 1290s, during the ill-fated reign of John Balliol [see Chapter 9]. It is basically a king-list, but it also includes an account of Scottish origins, explaining that the original Scots were descended from Gaedel Glas and Scota, and came from Egypt and eventually ended up in Scotland. The length of reigns in the king-list, we are told, added up to 1,976 years to the coronation of John Balliol in 1292.
>
> The way it was achieved was by an ingenious and simple use of the available material. There was a list of kings from Kenneth mac Alpin. There was also a list of about thirty kings from Fergus Mór mac Eirc, the alleged founder of the 'Scottish' colony of Dalriada around the year 500. There was also a list of sixty-five-plus Pictish kings. All this material was stitched together and presented as if it were a single series of kings, which totalled 113 (once you had included Robert Bruce).
>
> It is noticeable that this text, elaborating in this rudimentary

way the idea that Scotland was an ancient kingdom, was written when Edward I [of England] was knocking on Scotland's door with a vengeance. This Irish identity gave the kingship of Scotland the authenticity of age which medieval institutions required, through a royal genealogy stretching all the way back to Noah via the Irish king-lists.

Any desire to express Scottish identity as a form of ethnicity has an inherent weakness: there is not any one set of 'people' who form the backbone of a group which can be identified as modern Scots. Even in the tenth century this was so, and notions of Scottish ethnicity had to be carefully blended into a constructed notion of Scottish nationality. In the twentieth century, too, the range of peoples and cultures one might mix together when trying to construct a notion of Scottish national identity or national characteristics is as broad as ever. But the one culture still in existence today in Scotland, and the one with the longest track record, is that of the Gaels, who have the strongest claim to being the indigenous people of Scotland.

And that raises a puzzle concerning Walter Scott's *Tales of a Grandfather*: the Celts, these Irish progenitors, were given no mention at all in the opening chapter, and very little mention, indeed, throughout the whole book. Why? Alex Woolf, lecturer in Scottish and Celtic History at Edinburgh University, says:

When I first read Tales of a Grandfather, *what struck me most was that Scott completely passes over the Irish origin of the Scots; he makes it look as if the Scoti were indigenous people alongside the Picts from earliest times. To understand this attitude, we have to look at the period in which Scott is writing – the beginning of the nineteenth century. He grew up in the eighteenth century, when Catholicism was outlawed in the United Kingdom. There was a great anxiety about Catholicism in Britain and Ireland, and the period in which Scott was writing saw a powerful political movement demanding Catholic emancipation, which came in 1829, towards the end of Scott's career as a writer. There was much anxiety, particularly in Ireland, about this upswelling of political fervour of a people who were 'not like us' – people who were not Protestants, people who still spoke Gaelic (which was totally alien to the ruling élites of both Scotland and England and, indeed, of Ireland). I think it was this linkage of Ireland with the threat of Popery which*

probably led Scott to feel somewhat ashamed of his Irish ante-
cedents himself.

Ted Cowan agrees:

> *Walter Scott really fudged this whole issue of the Irish origins of*
> *the Scots: it did not particularly suit a Protestant Scot to make*
> *a big deal of the fact that the Scots came from Ireland, so he*
> *tended to play it down. But it is rather surprising because, in*
> *other contexts, Scott was very interested in Scottish myth and*
> *legend (and did a good deal himself to add to that myth and*
> *legend).*

It is in line with his silence over the Irish connection that Sir Walter
Scott makes no mention at all of Ted Cowan's candidate for the first
real king of the embryo realm of Scotland – Constantin II.

Constantin II

Constantin II was a remarkably long-lived king who was eventually
to outlive his effectiveness. In his prime he fought against the vikings
encroaching from the north and the west; but he was also determined
to extend the boundaries of 'Lesser Scotland' southwards beyond the
Forth–Clyde line. In 914, and again in 918, he made inconclusive
forays as far south as Corbridge; but now the position in Northumbria
was changing dramatically.

The old Anglian kingdom of Northumbria had been overwhelmed
by the Norsemen, and King Alfred of Wessex (Alfred the Great) had
been forced to partition England in 878, yielding to the Norsemen the
huge swatch of east and north England which became known as the
Danelaw. Alfred's son (Edward the Elder of Wessex, r.899–924) and
grandson (Athelstan, r.924–39) succeeded in turning the tide of Norse
domination. By 920, Edward the Elder had won back all the Danelaw
south of the Humber. The next target was York, and in 927 the
vigorous young Athelstan expelled the Norsemen from their power-
base there and assumed the overlordship of Northumbria. Seven years
later, in 934, Athelstan consolidated his position in the north of England with a sweeping invasion of Alba, backed by a fleet which harried
the east coast as far north as Caithness.

The growing power of Wessex posed an obvious and alarming threat
to the fledgling kingdom of Alba, which was also constantly menaced

by the power of the Norse earls of Orkney and Shetland. In 937 Constantin II joined a Great Alliance of the Norsemen in Ireland and the Britons of Strathclyde for a pre-emptive strike against the West Saxons. Together they sailed and marched down to the Humber, a huge host, for a trial of strength with Athelstan. The two sides met at a place called Brunanburh, somewhere on Humberside, perhaps, in a ferocious battle which would be commemorated in contemporary poetry and folk memory as the bloodiest encounter yet fought on English soil:

> *Athelstan the king,*
> *lord of earls*
> *and ring-giver to men,*
> *his brother beside him,*
> *Edmund the Ætheling,*
> *won undying glory*
> *in furious battle*
> *with the blades of their swords*
> *at Brunanburh:*
> *burst through the shield-wall,*
> *hewed at the bucklers*
> *with well-forged swords,*
> *the sons of Edward . . .*
>
> FROM *THE BATTLE OF BRUNANBURH*,
> IN THE *ANGLO-SAXON CHRONICLE* (937)

It was a decisive victory for Athelstan. Among the dead was one of Constantin's sons. The defeat of all his hopes for his kingdom, and the death of his son, seem to have drained the spirit out of Constantin, and in 943 he abdicated and withdrew to monastic life in St Andrews. It was his successors who began to stem the seemingly irresistible Wessex advance. One of his sons, Indulph (r.954–62), managed to capture the formidable stronghold of Edinburgh and gain temporary control of Lothian. But it was not until the next century that the Scots, under the leadership of the forceful and ambitious Malcolm II (Mael Coluim mac Cinaeda, r.1005–34), finally succeeded in wresting control of the Lothians from Northumbria.

The decisive showdown occurred in 1018. Malcolm had already annexed the kingdom of Strathclyde and had shown his mettle with some merciless raids deep into Northumbria, including a siege of Durham on one occasion. The Northumbrians were outraged. They raised a huge army commanded by warrior prelates pledged to recover the Church lands (and revenues) of Lothian. Malcolm met them with his forces at Carham, just south of the Tweed. It was another fierce encounter, but this time the Scots won the day. Many of the English fell, including a score of Northumbrian nobles and eighteen leading churchmen.

One of the casualties on the Scottish side was Owain, who ruled Strathclyde as a vassal of the Scots. He was the last of his family line, and Malcolm now added the kingdom of Strathclyde (the Britons) to the Scottish realm.[1]

The significance of the Battle of Carham in 1018 was only to emerge later. It was the last battle for Scottish control of the Lothians. Carham marked the first firm delineation of a settled frontier between Scots and English along the line of the River Tweed; but it would be a very long time before this line was to emerge as an accepted final boundary. With the hindsight of history, we can see Carham as a real watershed in the evolution of the shape of 'Scotland' as we know it today.

What happened to the Picts?

The Scots and the Picts, after they had been driven back behind the Roman wall, quarrelled and fought between themselves; and at last, after a great many battles, the Scots got completely the better of the Picts. The common people say that the Scots destroyed them entirely; but I think it is not likely that they could kill such great numbers of people.

TALES OF A GRANDFATHER, CHAPTER I

The fate of the Picts has become the great enigma, the great puzzle of Scottish history; and as a result they are probably the most written about of all the Dark Age peoples, simply because they apparently disappeared, and disappeared very suddenly. Scholars used to write darkly of a terrible chapter of genocide.

It is now accepted that there was no wholesale massacre or enslavement of the people known as the Picts; they simply ceased to exist in the historical record as a separate political and ethnic entity. The old Pictish language was swamped by the Gaelic of the Scots, all the Pictish

---

1 In his *Tales of a Grandfather* (Chapter I), Walter Scott referred generally to the inhabitants of Scotland encountered by the Romans as 'British', or 'Britons'. The term 'Britons' properly applies specifically to the people of Strathclyde.

written records perished over time, and the use of the characteristic Pictish symbols on monumental sculptured stones fell into disuse. It was a question of assimilation, of integration, not the kind of 'ethnic cleansing' which is such a horrid aspect of some conflicts of modern times.

Ted Cowan has a typically robust attitude to the so-called 'Problem of the Picts':

> *By Page Three of almost any one-volume History of Scotland, the Picts disappear. And it always used to amaze me that nobody asked what on earth happened to them. After all, we are talking about three-quarters of the population of north Britain.*
>
> *In fact, the Picts did not disappear on Page Three. There must have been intermarriage between the Picts and the Scots, there must have been a process of assimilation through the Church and through the common medium of Latin. And this, to my mind, explains the demise of the Picts, their language and their culture better than anything else. What they did leave behind was the magnificent and unique legacy of their sculptured stones.*

There is no better introduction to the exquisite and enigmatic art of the Pictish sculptured stones than the little museum at Meigle, just off the arterial A93 trunk-road near Blairgowrie. The museum is a converted schoolhouse which now contains a marvellous collection of twenty-seven locally-carved stones dating from the ninth and tenth centuries: prayer crosses, symbol stones, sculpted cross-slabs with hunting scenes, animal stones, public war-memorials and personal tombstones. Most of them are decorated with the enigmatic shapes and symbols which no one has yet been able to decipher satisfactorily.

One of the last testimonials of the Picts is the majestic sculptured red sandstone monolith known as 'Sueno's Stone', which stands six metres tall at the eastern edge of the town of Forres, on the Moray Firth, in the heartland of the ancient Pictish kingdom.

'Sueno's Stone' was another of the great problems which the Ancient Monuments Board for Scotland had to tackle in the 1980s. It is a magnificent piece of statuary, with a wealth of intricate carving (pictorial as well as stylised) on all four of its faces. The front bears a relief carving of a great ring-headed cross whose shaft is filled with interlace spiral knotwork; the reverse side depicts an immense battle scene in four panels of unequal length. It is an extraordinarily vivid and complex sculptural gallery: the top panel presents the leader and his guard arriving on horseback for the battle. The great central panel shows ranks of warriors fighting on foot, then rows of the decapitated bodies of prisoners (their hands still tied) and the executioner holding a severed head, while the enemy flee in disorder. The third panel shows another pile of ruthlessly beheaded corpses and severed heads, while the fourth, partially obscured by the modern base, shows the dispersal of the vanquished army.

By the 1980s it was becoming increasingly difficult to make out the images on the stone (for instance, the heaps of severed heads were barely discernible to the naked eye without recourse to earlier sketches of the stone). Modern atmospheric pollution was creating galloping erosion, which was eating away at the vulnerable sandstone and blurring the detail of the sculptor's art. Something Had To Be Done: Sueno's Stone either had to be moved into safe housing (the Old Tolbooth at Forres?) or given a protective covering *in situ*. The need for a decision was made urgent by plans to alter the line of the A96 from Inverness to bypass the town of Forres: the new road was going to run just a few metres to the north of Sueno's Stone.

It was not an easy decision. The stone had been discovered, fallen and buried under peat, in 1726, and re-erected in its present position on a new circular pedestal. It had become a prominent part of the landscape of Moray.

Eventually, after much heart-searching, the decision was made to leave the stone where it was, and to give it its own protective canopy of reinforced glass and steel – a bit like Snow White in the Disney film (although no prince was expected to come to the rescue). The glass case was erected in 1992, complete with immaculate landscaping, useful interpretive panels and all the technological gizmos needed to provide an environment which would ensure Snow White's survival. Not everyone liked it – it looks incongruous at first glance – but it grows on you. The glass case makes photography difficult, but Historic Scotland is happy to accommodate anyone with a special interest.

Sueno's Stone is clearly a memorial to some momentous encounter, but there is no 'label' on the stone, and there has been endless speculation about the conflict it was set up to commemorate. The stone cannot be dated, on stylistic grounds, more precisely than the end of the Pictish period (ninth or tenth century); it has none of the characteristic Pictish symbols on it, which suggests that the Pictish sculptors were then working for new masters. The spurious name 'Sueno' was an antiquarian invention of the eighteenth century, referring to some viking leader with the generic name of 'Svein', and cannot give any clue to the battle depicted on the stone. But to me it seems not unlikely that Sueno's Stone does, indeed, celebrate a real battle, probably some momentous victory against the Picts' and Scots' most formidable adversaries, the vikings. According to the *Annals of Ulster* there was just such a battle in the year 909, when the 'men of Alba' (Albanaich), fighting under their miracle-working standard, the crozier of St Columba, won the day. That date falls within the early years of the reign of Ted Cowan's favourite early king of Scotland, Constantin II, and the battle seems to have led to a treaty whereby the Norsemen were confirmed in their control of Caithness in exchange for a promise to leave the rest of Alba alone.

Academic speculation about the provenance of the stone and the battle it was designed to commemorate will doubtless continue. Whatever the truth of it, I like to think that Sueno's Stone is the last recorded signature of the people who left their mark on history by carving it on stone.

Chapter 4

MACBETH (r.1040–57)

... the three old women went and stood by the wayside, in a great moor or heath near Forres, and waited till Macbeth came up. And then, stepping before him as he was marching at the head of his soldiers, the first woman said, 'All hail, Macbeth – hail to thee, Thane of Glamis.' The second said, 'All hail, Macbeth – hail to thee, Thane of Cawdor.' Then the third, wishing to pay him a higher compliment than the other two, said, 'All hail, Macbeth, that shalt be King of Scotland.'

TALES OF A GRANDFATHER, CHAPTER II

The little village of Lumphanan, in Aberdeenshire, lies about fifty kilometres to the west of Aberdeen. It is not as celebrated a name in the Macbeth chronicle as Birnam Wood or Dunsinane Hill in Perthshire, or Forres in Moray, but in fact it is much more significant – because it was at Lumphanan that Macbeth (the historical Macbeth, not the Macbeth of Shakespeare's 'Scottish play') met his death in the year 1057.

What Shakespeare did for Macbeth was to make him perhaps the best known, and certainly the most notorious, character in Scottish history – but at appalling cost to historical veracity. Yet so persuasive is the story, so compelling is the skill of the playwright, so powerful is the characterisation of a noble soul seduced by ambition (and by a ferocious harpy of a wife), that everyone knows it and believes it.

Oddly enough, Sir Walter Scott gave it his imprimatur, too. In his

Tales of a Grandfather he related the Shakespeare version wholesale, with some additional embroidery of his own. The puzzle is that Scott knew perfectly well that it was a travesty of events; indeed, in his *History of Scotland* (1829–30), which he wrote as a spin-off from *Tales of a Grandfather*, he gave a very different and much more soberly accurate account. Yet in the *Tales* he preferred to entertain his grandson rather than to educate him. It is a dilemma which faces every 'popular' historian.

According to Shakespeare (and the *Tales of a Grandfather*), Macbeth was a trusted general of the venerable and much-loved King Duncan I of Scotland. With his fellow-general Banquo, Macbeth quells an insurrection and defeats a major viking invasion in Fife. On his way home, on a 'blasted heath' near Forres, he encounters three witches. The first addresses him as Thane of Glamis (a title which he has just inherited). The second addresses him as Thane of Cawdor (which Duncan has just named him, although Macbeth does not know it yet). The third, ominously, addresses him as 'Macbeth! that shalt be king hereafter!' For Banquo, they promise less in the immediate future but much more to come: 'Thou shalt get kings, though thou be none.'

Soon afterwards, messengers arrive to announce that Macbeth is to receive the title and possessions of the Thane of Cawdor, who had been a traitor in the rebellion and is shortly to be executed. Macbeth is thunderstruck: 'Two truths are told,/as happy prologues to the swelling act/of the imperial theme'.

According to Shakespeare, Macbeth now writes a letter to his wife telling her of his encounter with the witches, and sends notice that the king himself is coming to stay with them at their castle at Inverness. Lady Macbeth works on her husband's latent ambition and incites him to kill the king – which he does, albeit unnerved by the deed.[1] Duncan's two young sons, Malcolm (the Prince of Cumbria) and Donalbain, fearful of suffering the same fate, flee the country.

Macbeth thereupon assumes the crown. Mindful of the witches' prophecy that Banquo will be the progenitor of future kings of Scot-

---

1 Local tradition in Inverness insists that the murdered King Duncan was buried in Culcabock, a village to the east of the town (now a suburb of it). In front of a petrol station on the Old Perth Road, at the junction with Culcabock Avenue, is a stone marked with a plaque which reads: 'Behind is the supposed burial place of King Duncan 1040' – that is to say, underneath the present petrol station. On the opposite side of the road is a 'Duncan's Well' (*Fuaran Dhonnachaidh*). According to this tradition, the king's body was later removed and buried in the royal cemetery on the Holy Island of Iona. In fact, Duncan was killed in battle in Aberdeenshire (see page 60).

land, Macbeth sends hired assassins to kill Banquo and his young son Fleance; Banquo is struck down, but Fleance escapes, and his progeny later become the ruling Stewart dynasty of Scotland.

Macbeth now embarks on a reign of terror. He consults the witches again, and they warn him to beware of Macduff, the Thane of Fife. But they also tell him that 'none of woman born' will ever harm him, and that he 'shall never vanquished be, until/Great Birnam wood to high Dunsinane hill/Shall come against him.'

Before Macbeth has time to act, Macduff, suspecting that he is next on the king's hit-list, flees to England to join Duncan's son Malcolm. In thwarted fury Macbeth sends his assassins to Macduff's castle in Fife and has Macduff's wife and young family slaughtered.

At the English court the Scottish refugees, spurred on by Macduff's arrival, assemble an army with English help and invade Scotland. To hide their advance towards the tyrant's lair at Dunsinane Castle they camouflage themselves with branches cut from Birnam Wood. Macbeth is shaken by the news that the wood seems to be coming to Dunsinane; he is even more dismayed when he faces the vengeful Macduff, who reveals that he was not 'of woman born', but had been 'from his mother's womb untimely ripp'd'. There is nothing left for Macbeth now but to die valiantly: 'Lay on, Macduff; and damn'd be him that first cries, "Hold, enough!"' Macbeth is duly slain by Macduff, who brings the tyrant's head to Malcolm – the future Malcolm III, Malcolm Canmore.

Birnam Wood and Dunsinane

A walkway along the River Tay, known as the 'Terrace Walk', runs between the neighbouring towns of Dunkeld and Birnam. Just behind the Oak Inn of the Birnam House Hotel a sign highlights the presence of the 'Birnam Oak' – a very old, gigantic oak tree, its heavy, brittle branches now propped up on crutches. It is said to be the last remaining tree from the ancient Birnam Wood made famous by the witches' prophecy in Shakespeare's *Macbeth*. It was from this very tree (it is implied), and others like it, that Malcolm's soldiers cut branches to disguise their advance on Macbeth's castle at Dunsinane Hill, in the Sidlaws, some twenty-two kilometres as the crow flies to the south-east, off the Perth to Coupar Angus road (A94).[1] Dunsinane is a low hill which is not difficult to ascend. Its flat summit is crowned by the

---

1 Just for the record (literally), the 'Birnam Oak' stands next to the largest sycamore tree in Britain; it has a height of thirty metres and a girth of eight metres.

impressive remains of a huge prehistoric hill-fort with triple ramparts which are still clearly visible; unfortunately, it could not have been a castle in Macbeth's day. However, from the summit one can look north-west along the Tay Valley towards the woods of Birnam and the beautiful Howe of Strathmore, and (with luck and a little imagination) make out the gap in the hills through which a camouflaged army might have advanced towards Dunsinane. Or so they say.

A few miles to the south of Dunkeld, and now bypassed by the A9 to Perth, the little village of Bankfoot provides a 'Macbeth Experience' as part of a Visitor Centre which was created in a former motor museum in 1993 by an entrepreneurial local couple, Wilson and Catriona Girvan. A spirited multi-media production offers a view of the 'millennium of mystery' surrounding the Macbeth story, or rather two views – the Shakespearean view, and the 'real' view. It presents Shakespeare enthusiastically reading his source material – the English chronicler Ralph Holinshed, who compiled *The Chronicles of England, Scotland and Ireland* in the 1570s – and penning his 'pretty tale' of the witch-ridden, bloodthirsty usurper who lost his head to Macduff when Birnam Wood came to Dunsinane; interwoven with this yarn is the story of what is now considered the 'real' Macbeth.

In this story, Macbeth was one of the great Scottish kings. His name in Gaelic, MacBeathadh, means 'Son of Life'. He was the son of Findlaech mac Ruairdri, *mormaer* (earl) of Moray, who was killed by his nephews in 1020; Macbeth had royal blood in his veins as a member of one of the three kindreds of Dalriada (Argyll) who had extended their power up the Great Glen into Moray. In 1032 Macbeth took vengeance when he burned to death one of his father's killers, Gillacomgain, along with fifty of his men, and was thereby able to assume his father's rank of *mormaer* of Moray. He then strengthened his claim to the throne by marrying the dead man's widow, Gruoch, who was herself descended from the royal line.

In the same vein, Duncan I was not by any means Shakespeare's gentle, much-revered king, rich in years and loved by his subjects. He was, in fact, a rash and militarily incompetent youngster, the grandson of a ruthless and despotic king, Malcolm II, who had appointed him Prince of Cumbria and arranged that he should succeed to the throne in 1034. His succession caused widespread anger: ancient custom favoured succession by election, not *diktat*; besides, Duncan had neither the maturity nor the track-record to merit the throne.

Duncan had clearly inherited his father's ambition, but not his skill: he invaded the north of England and made a disastrous attack on

Durham in 1039; he then made an equally ill-fated attempt to impose his authority in the recalcitrant north of Scotland. Duncan met Macbeth, *mormaer* of Moray, in battle somewhere near the village of Pitgaveny, near Elgin, on the Feast of the Assumption (10 August) in 1040, and was killed.

Macbeth was immediately accepted as King of Scots and crowned at Scone, which suggests that Duncan I's military failures had antagonised his subjects in the south, too. Macbeth went on to reign for seventeen years (1040–57), and the *Chronicle of Melrose* noted that 'in his time there were productive seasons' (a line borrowed from an early Latin poem – *fertile tempus erat*). He drove Duncan's two sons out of Scotland: Malcolm fled to England, where he became a protégé of King Edward the Confessor (r.1042–66); and Donalbain (Donald Bán) fled to the Western Isles.

Macbeth was able to deal effectively with an abortive attempt by Duncan I's father to oust him in 1046. He was less successful in his confrontations with his half-cousin, Thorfinn the Mighty, the Norse Earl of Orkney.

Thorfinn Sigurðarson, nicknamed 'the Mighty', is one of the most compelling figures in the great portrait-gallery of Norse earls presented in *Orkneyinga Saga*. A huge, powerfully-built, swarthy man, ugly and sharp-featured, beetle-browed and with a prominent nose, he was ambitious, ruthless and very shrewd, a born survivor in an age when survival was always precarious. According to *Orkneyinga Saga* Thorfinn was one of the sons of Earl Sigurð Hlöðvisson of Orkney, and (like Duncan I) a grandson of a King Malcolm of Scotland (Malcolm II?). He was created Earl of Caithness and Sutherland by King Malcolm at the age of five in 1014; thereafter he fought his way to control of Orkney (by the 1030s), and by the time he died, at some date between 1057 and 1065, he had extended his realm deep into the heartlands of Scotland and over the Western Isles as well, and was recognised as the most powerful ruler in northern Britain. He was a man of compelling personal authority; after the turbulent years of his early piratical reign, he spent the latter part of his life ruling his realms wisely and benevolently from the palace and church he built on the Brough of Birsay, at the northern end of the Mainland of Orkney. His reign was the high point of the golden age of viking power in the north.

This was the man who represented the greatest threat to Macbeth's authority in the north of Scotland. According to *Orkneyinga Saga*, Macbeth and Thorfinn had several encounters, all of which ended in Thorfinn's favour. But it would say that, wouldn't it?

Macbeth may not have been the most compelling King of Scots in the eleventh century, but he seems to have been a very capable one. He was generous to the Church, which ensured him a good early press (he and Gruoch granted lands in Fife to the Culdees of Loch Leven[1]). Certainly, he felt secure enough to leave Scotland in 1050 and go on a pilgrimage to Rome where, according to the *Chronicon* of Marianus Scottus (1028–83), written in 1073, 'he scattered his money like seed among the poor'.

In the 1050s, however, Macbeth's reign became clouded. Duncan's elder son, Malcolm – the future Malcolm Canmore – was cultivating support in England to reclaim the throne of Scotland. Edward the Confessor seems to have backed his ambitions. In 1054 he sanctioned an invasion of Scotland by Earl Siward, the doughty Danish-born Earl of Northumbria. Siward (probably with Malcolm at his side) invaded Scotland with a mixed army of Anglo-Saxon Northumbrians and Scots. Macbeth seems to have conducted a defensive guerrilla campaign at first; the contemporary English chronicle *Vita Edwardi Regis* claims that the Scots were 'an uncertain race of men and fickle, and one which trusts rather in woods than on the plain, and more in flight than in manly courage in battle'. Siward reached Dundee apparently unopposed, where his army was reinforced by supply ships. Shortly afterwards he brought Macbeth to pitched battle on the Festival of the Seven Sleepers (27 July).

Where was this battle? Was this Shakespeare's final 'Battle of Dunsinane'? It could well have been – there is no documentary evidence either way. But if it was at Dunsinane, it would have been decided on the level ground below Dunsinane Hill, not in the ancient hill-fort on the summit.

Wherever it took place, it was a long and bloody encounter. There were heavy casualties on both sides. The *Anglo-Saxon Chronicle* for 1054 noted:

> *In this year Earl Siward invaded Scotland with a great host both by land and sea, and fought against the Scots. He put to flight their king, Macbeth, and slew the noblest in the land, carrying off much plunder such as none had previously gained; but his son Osbern and his sister's son and numbers of his housecarles, as well as of the king [Edward the Confessor], were slain there.*

---

1 The Culdees (*Cele dei*, 'Friends of God') formed early monastic communities which attached themselves to hereditary secular priests.

'He put to flight their king, Macbeth'. The one historical fact we can be absolutely sure of, *pace* Shakespeare and Walter Scott, is that Macbeth was not killed at Dunsinane in 1054.

For the next three years the records are silent. Siward's victory had not been enough to give Malcolm the throne; Siward had to return to Northumbria to deal with an uprising there, and died soon afterwards. Malcolm seems to have been installed by Edward the Confessor as ruler over Strathclyde and the Lothians, but no more. Macbeth retreated northward, back to his original power-base in Moray. By 1057, however, his support seems to have been draining away, and Malcolm felt strong enough to seek out his enemy on his home ground.

The chronicles say that the fugitive Macbeth was eventually hunted down by Malcolm near the village of Lumphanan, in Aberdeenshire, and killed there in a desperate final stand rather than a pitched battle. His head was then brought to Malcolm, either on a pole or a golden platter.

There is nothing like local tradition to keep historical memory alive, however embroidered it might have become. At Lumphanan, which lies on the A980 between Banchory and Alford, the epicentre of the tradition is the nearby Peel Ring of Lumphanan, which is signposted. The Peel was once a medieval Anglo-Norman fortified motte-and-bailey;[1] now all that remains of it is a large grassy mound surrounded by a swampy moat, with an encircling earthwork. A convenient path offers easy access to the crown of the mound. In the fifteenth century, a local worthy had built himself a stone residence there – Ha'ton House – which was abandoned in the eighteenth century. The Peel has long been linked with Macbeth's last stand; unfortunately, it dates from the early thirteenth century – nearly two hundred years after Macbeth's death.

Other features in the district are traditionally associated with the demise of Macbeth, but it takes a very determined pilgrim to track them down. On Perk Hill on the farmlands north of the village, clearly visible from the road, there lies a ruined Bronze Age cairn girdled by a guard of honour of beech trees. It is known locally as 'Macbeth's Cairn'. The farmer is quite happy to permit access, although he cannot fathom why anyone should want to trek across his fields to visit it.

---

1 'Motte-and-bailey' is the term used for an early Anglo-Norman fortification consisting of a timber tower raised on an artificial mound. The word 'motte' comes from Old French, meaning mound, and the 'bailey' was the fortified courtyard within the surrounding ditch, or moat. In English, 'motte' came to mean the moat rather than the mound.

The site was roughly excavated in 1855 and was found to contain the bones of someone who had died three thousand years earlier. It has nothing at all to do with Macbeth; indeed, the early chroniclers say that Macbeth was buried, like so many Kings of Scots before him, on the holy island of Iona.

There is also an even less accessible 'Macbeth's Stone', unmarked, where the king's head is alleged to have been severed from his body. It is the largest of a group of boulders on top of a grassy slope on Cairnbeathie Farm, on the west side of the disused railway embankment.

And there is (of course!) an unmarked 'Macbeth's Well', at Burnside, near the parish church to the north-east. It is practically invisible – a small and very low stone lintel set into the base of a steep and overgrown bank at the roadside. There is no hope of finding it without a friendly and particularly knowledgeable local guide – the casual visitor would drive or even walk right past it without spotting it. An incongruous plastic hose-pipe now drips into the well. This is where the doomed monarch is said to have quenched his thirst before the final encounter.

Wherever Macbeth died, and wherever his body ended up, his death did not automatically give Malcolm the throne. Macbeth's remaining supporters in the north proclaimed as King of Scots his stepson, Lulach (the son of Gruoch from a previous marriage). Lulach appears in history under the unflattering nickname of 'Lulach the Simpleton'. Simpleton or not, he too was hunted down by Malcolm, and killed in March 1058 in an ambush at Essie (now Rhynie) in Strathbogie, the strategic pass between Moray and Strathdon. Lulach, too, was buried on Iona.

With Lulach dead, Malcolm's hold on the kingdom was at last secure. A month later he was crowned at Scone at the age of twenty-seven, and embarked on his thirty-five-year reign as King of Scots (see Chapter 5).

Shakespeare and Scott

So what were Shakespeare, and Sir Walter Scott following him, playing at? Why did they present such an extraordinarily biased view of Macbeth?

Shakespeare had not simply made it all up; nor had Holinshed in his *Chronicle*. The denigration of Macbeth had started much earlier, by John of Fordun in *Chronica Gentis Scotorum* (Chronicle of the

Scottish People), his proto-version of the *Scotichronicon* around 1380:[1] here Macbeth is portrayed as an evil murderer and usurper. Andrew Wyntoun, prior of St Serf's in Loch Leven and author of the metrical *Orygynale Cronikil of Scotland* in vernacular Scots around 1420, introduced the witches and the advancing Birnam Wood and the theme of 'unnatural birth'. It seems clear that conflicting stories about Macbeth and Malcolm were current soon after Macbeth's reign: pro-Macbeth stories in the heartlands of Moray, and anti-Macbeth stories which were nurtured by the court propagandists of the victorious Canmore dynasty. These were the tales which Holinshed relied upon in his *Chronicle*.

Did Shakespeare believe what he read in Holinshed? For a playwright, it scarcely mattered – he must have found Holinshed extraordinarily convenient. He wrote *Macbeth* in the period around 1606, soon after the Union of the Crowns of 1603 which had brought King James VI of Scotland to London as King James I of England as well. James was the latest of the Stewart dynasty of Scotland, and Banquo (who seems to have been an invented character) was, providentially, the legendary progenitor of the Stewart monarchy. What more flattering than such a theme for a play presented by The King's Men to welcome the new incumbent of the throne? Shakespeare was in no way averse to twisting history for political ends: ten years earlier he had played fast and loose with the story of *Richard III* to celebrate the first of the Tudors, Henry VII, in order to please his demanding royal patron, Queen Elizabeth.

It was also well known that King James VI and I was deeply interested in witchcraft – his book on *Daemonologie*, first published in Edinburgh in 1597, had been republished in London on his accession in 1603. Furthermore, the mere fact that Macbeth had caused the death of a reigning king made him automatically, in Elizabethan eyes, a regicide and a usurper, even though kingship in Macbeth's day was decided by election, not inheritance – as the succession had been in England at the death of Edward the Confessor in 1066.

There was less immediate excuse for Walter Scott, however. Ted Cowan says:

1　John of Fordun (c.1320–84) has often been called 'the Father of Scottish History'. Not a great deal is known about him; he is believed to have been a chantry priest at Aberdeen Cathedral, and may have come from Fordoun in the Mearns. His history was a compilation of (now lost) earlier historical writings on Scotland and took the story down to 1383. His work formed the basis of the *Scotichronicon* of Walter Bower, which was written in the 1440s.

The Macbeth episode in Tales of a Grandfather *has always puzzled me because Scott simply regurgitated the plot of Shakespeare's play. His account gives the impression of Macbeth the usurper, Macbeth the barbarian king, Macbeth the tyrant who would massacre his own subjects, and so on; yet Scott knew that this was far from the historical truth – if there is such a thing as historical truth!*

Scott was perhaps trying to set up a contrast between the disappearing old Celtic world and the wonderful new world of the Normans as portrayed in Ivanhoe *and other novels; he was personifying the dissolution of Celtic Scotland in the figure of Macbeth. That may be all right in literary or artistic terms, but it is certainly not legitimate in strictly historical terms.*

So *Tales of a Grandfather* presents the demise of Macbeth as a happy prelude to the normanisation and ultimate anglicisation of Scotland to come. For pro-Unionist historians like Scott, the denigration of Macbeth reflected a profound distaste for the ancient role of Celtic culture in the Lowland Scotland of his day; for Scott, any relevance it might have had was overshadowed by the emerging Norman (i.e. civilising) influence which was to begin in the reign of Malcolm Canmore. Not that Scott himself would have admitted to any such notion; in his *History of Scotland* he showed clearly that he was aware of the historical inaccuracies of Shakespeare's plot:

> *All these things are now known: but the mind retains pertinaciously the impression made by the impositions of genius. While the works of Shakespeare are read, and the English language subsists, History may say what she will, but the general reader will only recollect Macbeth as a sacrilegious usurper, and Richard [III] as a deformed murtherer.*

It is only in much more recent times that Macbeth has been rehabilitated as the champion of the Men of Moray and the last truly Celtic king of Scotland.

But there was another player in the Macbeth drama whom Shakespeare did not mention at all – Thorfinn the Mighty, Earl of Orkney. The sources about Thorfinn's life (both Icelandic and Scottish) are tantalisingly elusive about his real impact on Scottish affairs – so elusive, indeed, that the eminent Scottish historical novelist Dorothy Dunnett was able to create a brilliantly plausible scenario from them in her novel *King Hereafter* (1982). Her thesis was that Macbeth and Thorfinn were in reality the same person, known as Thorfinn in Orkney and Macbeth in Scotland. It may sound outrageously unlikely, but . . .

Orkneyinga Saga relates that on the Feast of the Assumption (10 August) in 1040 – the very day on which Macbeth defeated Duncan near the village of Pitgaveny in Aberdeenshire – Thorfinn defeated a King of Scots called 'Karl Hundason' in battle at a fortified site the saga called Torfnes, somewhere on the northern coast of Scotland. It is impossible to identify the site with any certainty, but circumstantial evidence suggests that 'Torfnes' may well have been a name for the large and important fortification at modern Burghead, on the north Moray coast, near Elgin. Meanwhile John of Fordun's early version of the *Scotichronicon* relates an old Scottish tradition that after Duncan's death at Pitgaveny in 1040, his body was taken to Elgin; it was this tradition which, two centuries later, in 1235, inspired King Alexander II to found a chapel in the cathedral church in Elgin where masses were sung for Duncan's soul.

In the year 1050, when Macbeth went on his pilgrimage to Rome, *Orkneyinga Saga* tells us that Thorfinn the Mighty went to Rome as well. Was it pure coincidence that these two rulers should choose the same year in which to absent themselves from their respective warring domains for such a long time? Thereafter, according to the saga, Thorfinn maintained good relations with the Scottish court.

There are just as many inconsistencies as coincidences between the stories of Thorfinn and Macbeth, of course. According to *Orkneyinga Saga*, for instance, Thorfinn died peacefully in Orkney and was buried in his beloved minster of Christchurch on the Brough of Birsay; whereas Macbeth, as we have heard, was buried on Iona. But both the saga and the Scottish sources agree that Thorfinn was married to Ingibjörg, the daughter of Earl Finn Arnason of Norway, and that after Thorfinn's death she married Malcolm III – Macbeth's conqueror and successor as King of Scots. Intriguing, isn't it?

Chapter 5

MALCOLM CANMORE AND ST MARGARET

Malcolm III, called Canmore (or Great Head) . . . was a brave and wise prince, though without education. He often made war upon King William the Conqueror of England, and upon his son and successor William, who, from his complexion, was called William Rufus, that is, Red William.

TALES OF A GRANDFATHER, CHAPTER IV

The accession of Malcolm Canmore in 1058 marked the end of what Michael Lynch has called 'the crisis of the mac Alpin succession' (*Scotland: A New History*). It also marked the start of a highly formative period in the development of 'Scotland' as a modern state; in particular, Scotland's boundaries along the lines we recognise today began to take shape now (apart from the later inclusion of the Northern Isles). For the next 230 years, until the death of Alexander III in 1286 (see Chapter 8), the throne of Scotland was occupied by a powerful royal dynasty which is called variously the 'Canmore Dynasty' or the 'House of Dunkeld'. In comparison with preceding centuries, and with what was to come during the 'Wars of Independence', this was to be a period of considerable prosperity and relative peace.

Malcolm III, who reigned for thirty-five years (1058–93), has come down in history with a mixed reputation. Commentators have made much mock of his Gaelic nickname: 'Canmore' is from the Gaelic *ceann mòr*, meaning 'Great Chief', but it is frequently translated as 'Big-head'. Nigel Tranter, in *The Story of Scotland*, called him 'something of a boor, bloodthirsty and without statesmanlike qualities. His one delight was in raiding, pillage, slaughter.' The historical records, however, are too scanty to justify such a sweeping judgement.

Malcolm's chief preoccupation throughout his reign was the consolidation and extension of his kingdom of 'Scotia', or 'Alba'. Thorfinn the Mighty, Earl of Orkney, died some time between 1057 and 1065 (it is, alas, impossible to be sure of the precise date), and with his death his widespread empire in the north, which was said in *Orkneyinga Saga* to have included nine earldoms on the mainland of Scotland, began to disintegrate. Malcolm helped the process by marrying Thorfinn's widow, Ingibjörg; some sources say that Ingibjörg was Thorfinn's daughter, not his widow, but no matter. Before her death, some time before 1069, Ingibjörg bore Malcolm two sons: Duncan (the future King Duncan II) and Donald (d.1085); more importantly, however, the marriage helped to neutralise or at least diminish the insistent pressure on Scotland from the north.

Malcolm's main objective was to seize the perennially debatable lands of Northumbria and Cumbria. At this time there was no recognised border between the kingdoms of 'Scotland' and 'England'; and once again the events in England were to provide an opportunity for an ambitious and energetic King of Scots. After the death in 1055 of Earl Siward of Northumbria, who had helped Malcolm gain a foothold in Scotland in 1054, the new earl was a Wessex warlord named Tostig (the half-brother of the future King Harold Godwinsson who would die at Hastings). During Tostig's absence abroad in 1061, Malcolm launched a major raid into Northumbria. It was the first of no fewer than five incursions into the north of England which he was to make during his reign – none with lasting success, and the last, in 1093, at the cost of his life.

But Malcolm Canmore will always be overshadowed, in Scottish eyes at least, by the woman who became his second queen sometime between 1069 and 1071: Margaret, a princess of the old Saxon royal house, who would become Scotland's only royal saint.

Queen Margaret, the Saint

At the summit of the citadel of Edinburgh Castle stands a tiny, simple building which is the oldest surviving structure in the castle: St Margaret's Chapel. It was built in the 1130s or 1140s by Margaret's youngest son, King David I (see Chapter 6), and dedicated to his mother, who had died in the castle in 1093. It began as a private oratory for the royal family; in the sixteenth century it passed out of use as a chapel and was converted into a gunpowder magazine. Its original purpose was rediscovered in 1845 and it was restored to its present condition. It is now a very popular venue for weddings and christenings: castle guides tell visitors, tongue in cheek, that it is the ideal place for a Scottish wedding, for it only holds twenty people and the bride's father can have the reception in the telephone box on the way down!

The interior is as charming as the exterior is austere. The semi-circular chancel at the east end which housed the altar now has stained-glass windows depicting St Andrew and St Ninian. St Columba is represented, too, as is William Wallace in full battle array. But pride of place goes to St Margaret herself, flaxen-haired and beautiful, flanked by handmaidens at their sewing and holding an open book on her lap.

Margaret arrived in Scotland as a direct result of the Norman Conquest of 1066. She was of the English royal family which was swept aside by William of Normandy. Born in Hungary about the year 1047, she was a granddaughter of Edmund Ironside (half-brother of Edward the Confessor, r.1042–66), who had been killed resisting the conquest of England in 1016 by the Danish king Knút (Canute); she was the daughter of Edmund's son Edward, who had married a Hungarian princess during his long exile in Hungary but died soon after the family's return to England in 1057; and she was the sister of Prince Edgar ('Edgar the Atheling'), whose claims to the throne at the death of the childless Edward the Confessor early in 1066 were passed over in favour of the warrior Harold Godwinsson.

After the Conquest, William the Conqueror treated Edgar and his family well, despite the fact that Edgar had been, rather optimistically, declared king-elect after Harold's death at Hastings. But this cosy state of affairs did not last long, and in 1068, after an abortive rebellion in the north of England which he supported, Edgar tried to escape back to the greater safety of Hungary with his mother and two sisters, Margaret and Christina. Their ship, bound for the Continent, was driven off course by gales to Scotland and made land in Fife in a small bay now called St Margaret's Hope (Inlet).

The story goes that Malcolm Canmore, now a forty-year-old widower, rode from his residence at Dunfermline to welcome the royal refugees to Scotland; he fell instantly in love with the young Princess Margaret, who was then in her early twenties, and within a few months he married her in Dunfermline.

Be that as it may, it was clearly a good political marriage. From Edgar's point of view, it meant becoming brother-in-law to a formidable warrior King of Scots who could provide him with powerful support against the Norman 'usurpers' in England. For Malcolm, Margaret brought not just an alliance with the old royal house of England, but also a significant dowry in the form of the rich treasures which King Stephen of Hungary had given to her mother.

> *She was an excellent woman, and of such a gentle, amiable disposition, that she often prevailed upon her husband, who was a fierce, passionate man, to lay aside his resentment, and forgive those who had offended him.*
>
> TALES OF A GRANDFATHER, CHAPTER IV

Sir Walter Scott's picture of Queen Margaret as a Saxon diamond among Celtic dross is the conventional image of her which has come down in history. Margaret's confessor in Scotland was a chaplain named Turgot (subsequently the first Roman, as opposed to Celtic, Bishop of St Andrews), who wrote a vivid biography of her soon after her death. In Turgot's account she emerges as a determined and saintly woman who dominated her brash but doting husband who was so besotted with her that, although illiterate himself, he would kiss her devotional books and have them bound with gold and jewels.

As is to be expected in a biography which was also a hagiography, Turgot placed huge emphasis on the saintly queen's piety. She enjoyed the rich trappings of royalty, but she also spent many hours in prayer, and fed the poor regularly and washed their feet. Soon after her marriage she attended to the building of a small Romanesque church at Dunfermline, and three Benedictine monks were sent at her request from Canterbury to form the nucleus of a Benedictine priory there. She restored the church on Iona and was a benefactress of St Andrews, where she revived the cult of St Andrew and encouraged pilgrims to go there by giving them free passage across the Forth – the names of South and North Queensferry, on either side of the estuary of the Forth, still carry the memory of this initiative. Her devotion to the Roman Church which had embraced her during her childhood in Hungary was undoubtedly significant in the struggle between the doctrines and formulas of the Celtic Church of Scotland, founded by St Columba, and the established practice of the Universal Catholic Church in which she had been reared.

Apart from the influence she may have had on spiritual matters in

Scotland, Margaret has also been credited with, or blamed for, the anglicisation of the court and culture of southern Scotland:

> *a very great number of the Saxons who fled from the cruelty of William the Conqueror, retired into Scotland, and this had a considerable effect in civilizing the southern parts of that country; for if the Saxons were inferior to the Normans in arts and in learning, they were, on the other hand, much superior to the Scots, who were a rude and very ignorant people. . . No doubt, the number of the Saxons thus introduced into Scotland, tended much to improve and civilize the manners of the people . . .*
>
> TALES OF A GRANDFATHER, CHAPTER IV

Walter Scott never missed a chance to rub in his view that the Scots of medieval times were a decidedly backward people compared with their southern neighbours. But certainly at this time, in the latter half of the eleventh century, Scotland can be seen to be moving from a Gaelic-speaking realm of semi-autonomous princedoms to a much more centralised monarchy on the English and Continental model. If Macbeth was the last truly Celtic King of Scots, as some claim, it is because during Malcolm's reign there was a greater intermingling of the Celtic and Anglo-Norman cultures and *mores*.

It was perhaps on the future of Scotland and Anglo–Scottish relations, rather than on their present, that Queen Margaret had most effect – through the children she had by Malcolm. She gave birth to six pious sons, three of whom would reign successively as Kings of Scots: Edgar (r.1097–1107), Alexander I (r.1107–24) and David I (r.1124–53). She also had two daughters, both of whom married into the English royal house: Edith, the elder, married William the Conqueror's son, Henry I of England (r.1100–35), and became known in England as the Empress Matilda (see below); and Mary, the younger, married Eustace, Count of Boulogne, and their daughter (also named Matilda, or Maud) married Stephen of Blois, who was King of England from 1135 to 1164.

The border issue

Malcolm's marriage connection with a claimant to the English throne may well have added fuel to his ambitions to extend his own kingdom by attacking Northumbria, allegedly on Edgar the Atheling's behalf. His first opportunity came in 1070. Northumbria had fiercely resisted the Norman conquest of southern England, and had been savagely punished by King William. Malcolm launched his own invasion, ostensibly to help the English rebels, but it did little more than add to the cruel devastation of Yorkshire.

King William recognised the danger to the security of England posed by Malcolm's aggression. In 1072 he invaded Scotland with a large, well-organised army, supported by a fleet; it was the first full-scale invasion of Scotland since Roman times. William marched through Lothian and across the River Forth at Stirling, and went on to the River Tay. Malcolm realised that his own forces were no match for the powerful host of Norman knights and men-at-arms, and refused to give battle. Frustrated by Malcolm's delaying tactics, William offered to talk terms at Abernethy on the Tay. The treaty which resulted is known in English sources as the 'Abernethy Submission': Malcolm apparently submitted to William – 'he gave hostages and was his man'. He agreed not to harbour the English king's enemies (for instance, Edgar the Atheling), and surrendered his eldest son, Duncan (by Ingibjörg of Orkney), as a hostage. But was it a formal act of homage by a King of Scots as a vassal of England – or was Malcolm only recognising English suzerainty of the disputed lands of Cumbria and Northumbria? Ted Cowan believes that the idea of the King of Scots accepting the overlordship or 'feudal superiority' of the English king was a later fabrication by English chroniclers, designed to reinforce English claims to be rulers of Scotland; certainly, the 'Abernethy Submission' would remain a bone of contention between English and Scots constitutional lawyers for centuries to come.

Malcolm did not consider himself bound by it in any way. In 1079, when Norman control of the north of England was precarious once more, Malcolm invaded again – but again with no other result than a retaliatory invasion from England, led this time by William's son, Robert Curthose. Malcolm, again, refused battle, and at Falkirk the terms of the Abernethy Treaty (such as they were) were renewed. It also seems that a border was agreed, stretching between the Solway and the Tyne. Certainly, it was immediately after the Falkirk meeting that Robert Curthose commissioned the building of a 'New Castle' on the Tyne. It was a motte-and-bailey, and was the foundation of modern Newcastle. The border was reinforced in 1091, after yet another indecisive incursion against Durham and a counter-incursion into Lothian, this time led by William's successor on the throne of England, his son William Rufus (William II). William II took Carlisle and temporarily robbed the Scots of that part of ancient Cumbria which lay south of the Solway; he consolidated the western end of the 'border' by ordering the building of the first castle at Carlisle.

The death of Malcolm

There was to be one more Scottish invasion of Northumbria. In November 1093 Malcolm Canmore, stung (it is said) by some calculated insult from William II, or irritated by the building of Carlisle Castle, gathered another army and marched south on a last furious raid, accompanied by his eldest son by Margaret, Edward. It was a grievous miscalculation. Near the castle of Alnwick he was ambushed by the Norman Earl of Northumbria, Robert de Mowbray, and was killed, along with his son Edward – by treachery, it was subsequently claimed.

Malcolm had left Queen Margaret on her sickbed in Edinburgh Castle when he set off on his last expedition to Northumbria. According to her biographer, Turgot, she had foreseen that it would have disastrous consequences. For consolation she sent for the 'Black Rood' – a fragment of the True Cross encased in a cross of gold, with an ivory image of Christ upon it, the most precious of the treasures she had brought from Hungary.

The news of her husband's and son's deaths was too much for her, and three days later, on 16 November 1093, she died. Malcolm's death prompted fears of a palace coup. Margaret's body was taken from Edinburgh Castle in great secrecy, through the west postern gate, and ferried across the Forth to Dunfermline, where she was buried in the little church she had founded there.

Standing in the soaring sonorities of Dunfermline Abbey today, it is difficult to visualise the small church where Margaret was first laid to rest. On the floor of the nave are some brass strips which mark the outlines of parts of an early church whose foundations were uncovered during excavations in 1916, and grilles in the floor allow glimpses of the stonework. It was Margaret's youngest son, King David I (r.1124–53), who rebuilt the first church as a major abbey, the most splendid ecclesiastical building of its time in Scotland; it was consecrated in 1150.

Margaret's manifest piety throughout her life soon made Dunfermline a place of pilgrimage after her death. It was clearly of great advantage to the ruling Canmore dynasty to have a saint on its books, and her canonisation was vigorously promoted. It eventually came about in 1250, in time to add lustre to the inauguration of Alexander III the previous year (see Chapter 8), and her body was moved to a new shrine in a chapel specially built to receive it near the High Altar.

Aftermath

After the death of Malcolm Canmore, the Scottish crown was occupied successively by three princes of little power or talent, who seized on the supreme authority because the children of the deceased sovereign were under age.

Malcolm Canmore's death threw Scotland into a virtual civil war. From his refuge in the Western Isles, where he had been living since Macbeth had killed his father Duncan I, came Malcolm's younger brother Donald bàn (Shakespeare's 'Donalbain'), who now, at the age of sixty, claimed the vacant throne and was crowned as Donald III. It was the Celtic backlash against the anglicisation of the court: his accession seems to have been backed by the native aristocracy, who had come to resent the foreign influences associated with Queen Margaret. According to the *Anglo-Saxon Chronicle* entry for the year 1093, 'the Scots drove out all the English who had been with King Malcolm'. Certainly, the surviving children of Malcolm Canmore and St Margaret fled to the English court for safety, led by the eldest son Edgar and including the youngest, the ten-year-old David – the future King David I.

There was another claimant to the throne of Scotland – the royal prince who had been surrendered as a hostage by his father to William the Conqueror at Abernethy twenty years earlier: Duncan, Malcolm Canmore's son by Ingibjörg of Orkney. He had been brought up at the English court, and had been formally released, and knighted, on William the Conqueror's death in 1087. Here was an obvious opportunity for King William II of England to make his presence felt in Scotland again. Duncan was now a fully 'normanised' Celt, a protégé who had sworn fealty to the English king. According to the *Anglo-Saxon Chronicle* for 1093, 'Duncan came to the king, and gave such pledges as the king demanded of him and, with his consent, went to Scotland.' With the help of an English and French army he ousted Donald III and was accepted as King of Scots as Duncan II – but only on condition that he dismissed his alien supporters. It was a fatal promise: before the year was out he had been murdered (November 1094), and Donald III resumed his interrupted reign.

William Rufus was not to be balked, however. He had another claimant to the Scottish throne up his sleeve: Malcolm Canmore's fourth son by Margaret, Edgar, who had fled to his court in 1093. In

1097 William sent Edgar to Scotland as his vassal at the head of another army. This time there was to be no slip-up. Donald III was soundly defeated, hunted down and captured, then blinded and thrown into a dungeon. When he died, he was the last King of Scots to be buried on Iona.

The accession of King Edgar in 1097 heralded a remarkable span of rule by three men of the same generation, the three youngest sons of Malcolm Canmore and Queen Margaret, who gave Scotland's relationship with England a new stability: Edgar, Alexander I and David I.

Edgar was known as 'the Peaceable'. He made no resistance when Magnús Barelegs (*berfœttr*), king of Norway, made a violent onslaught on the Western Isles and confirmed Norwegian sovereignty there, leaving the sacred island of Iona in ruins again. There were no rebellions or uprisings against Edgar's rule. He never married, and had no children; when he died in 1107 he bequeathed his kingdom to his younger brothers Alexander (as monarch) and David (as ruler of southern Lothian and Strathclyde).

In contrast to his 'peaceable' elder brother, Alexander I was known as 'the Fierce', perhaps because of the severity of his suppression of a rebellion in Moray and the Mearns. Apart from that he was a devout man who showed all the signs of his strictly pious upbringing by his mother, Queen Margaret. Like his brother Edgar he was a vassal of the English king, Henry I (r.1100–35); Henry was the youngest (and only English-born) son of William the Conqueror, and the husband of Alexander's sister Edith (Matilda). Alexander I now married his brother-in-law's illegitimate daughter Sibyl, and his vassalage to England seemed to be confirmed in 1114 when he participated in an English campaign in Wales. His reign is particularly remembered, however, for his encouragement of monastic orders. He brought Augustinian canons from England to found priories at Scone and at Inchcolm in the Firth of Forth, and made plans for Augustinian foundations at the ancient Celtic royal centres of Dunkeld and St Andrews. He died at Stirling in April 1124 without legitimate issue, and was buried with his parents in the church at Dunfermline which his mother had founded.

To what extent was Scotland being 'normanised', as England had been? Some commentators have seen the accession of Edgar in 1097 as Scotland's equivalent of England's Norman Conquest. Dauvit Brown disagrees:

There was no Norman Conquest of Scotland, as such. In England, simply and spectacularly, the Normans conquered the kingdom; the native aristocracy were largely dispossessed, or at least fell down a few rungs in the social ladder. In the case of Scotland, however, the Normans came by invitation: the Scottish kings themselves invited the Norman knights into their kingdom, and not necessarily from England – for instance, there were Norman knights fighting in Macbeth's defeated army at the Battle of Dunsinane in 1054. They were given, as grants from the king, positions of authority in some regions or in the court; these Norman knights represented the latest in military technology, and they were an important element in the attempt to consolidate and extend control of the kingdom.

The kings who succeeded Macbeth were trying to do something really new: they were aligning themselves with the major social and cultural forces in western Europe, especially the reform of the Church which was being promoted by the papacy from the middle of the eleventh century. They promoted this in their own kingdom by establishing monasteries staffed by monks and nuns of the brand-new religious orders which were part of the mood of the day.

The other major force in western Europe was the French knightly culture which came to Scotland with the Norman knights. The Scottish kings were themselves part of this culture; they, too, were knights, and in due course the major members of the Gaelic aristocracy, first in the east and later in the west, also became fully-fledged knights.

What was happening in Scotland was not a simple clash between the old, kin-based values of Gaeldom and the new-fangled feudal ideas of the Normans; rather, it was a gradual melding of the old and the new.

The death of Alexander I left the way open for his brother David to ascend the throne at the age of about forty: David I (r.1124–53), the man who could never have expected to become King of Scots.

Chapter 6

DAVID I (r.1124–53)

*David was a most excellent sovereign . . . He founded bishoprics,
and built and endowed many monasteries, which he vested with
large grants of lands out of the patrimony of the kings . . . He
had many furious wars with England, and made dreadful incursions into the neighbouring provinces, which were the more easy
that the country of England was then disunited by civil war.*

TALES OF A GRANDFATHER, CHAPTER IV

The noble remains of four magnificent abbeys punctuate the landscape of the Borders: four great monastic foundations which
survive today only as monastic monuments, piercing reminders of the
transience of greatness and power. They were all founded by one King
of Scots – King David I – and all brought to ruin by the punitive
onslaught on the Borders, known as the 'Rough Wooing', ordered by
King Henry VIII of England in the 1540s (see Chapter 19).

Kelso Abbey is now just a stump – but what an elegant stump it
is. Only the west end of the abbey church survives, with its Galilee
porch islanded by traffic in the middle of the town. It was founded
by King David in 1128 for the Tironensian order of monks (reformed
Benedictines) from Tiron, near Chartres, who had originally been
settled in Selkirk but who wanted to be closer to the formidable royal
castle of Roxburgh on the other side of the Tweed. Kelso became one
of the country's wealthiest religious houses, as well as being one of

the most spectacular achievements of Romanesque architecture in Scotland. It was where the young King James III was crowned King of Scots in 1460, following the untimely death of his father, James II, at the siege of Roxburgh when a cannon burst during a ceremonial firing (see Chapter 15).

Melrose Abbey, the largest and, some would say, the finest of the four, was founded under the patronage of King David by Cistercian monks from Yorkshire in 1136. Even in ruin it is strikingly handsome, and it is still of great importance to the local economy of Melrose – it is one of the most popular visitor attractions in Scotland.

Jedburgh was founded as a priory under the patronage of King David in 1138 and raised to the status of abbey in 1154. It is a graceful and almost entire ruin of an Augustinian abbey, sitting high and proud on a ridge above its associated monastic and domestic buildings. In the course of its history it suffered the usual ransackings due to its strategic position at one of the main gateways to Scotland. It was rebuilt on several occasions, but finally succumbed to the English hammer during the 'Rough Wooing' and was later suppressed by the Scottish Reformers in 1559. It is now served by a splendid new Visitor Centre which explains and illuminates its story with exemplary clarity.

Finally there is Dryburgh Abbey, perhaps the most hauntingly exquisite of the four. It stands in a beautiful sylvan setting on a horse-shoe bend of the River Tweed, with fine parklands sweeping down to the river. It was established in 1150, towards the end of King David's reign. Because of its nearness to the border it, too, was severely damaged on several occasions, and never recovered from the final indignities of the 'Rough Wooing'. It was in one of the chapels of the ruined north transept that Sir Walter Scott was buried in September 1832 (see Chapter 29).

With these four great foundations, and many others besides, so resonant with the echoes of the nation's history, King David I created the fabric of the great period of medieval civilisation which Scotland was to enjoy in the twelfth and thirteenth centuries.

David the king

David was the most 'English' of the three Canmore brother kings, and perhaps the luckiest. He was an attractive person in every sense, well-favoured physically and good-natured; he had spent much of his youth in England, where he was groomed as a Norman knight and 'polished from his boyhood by his intercourse and friendship with us', as an English chronicler put it. His sister's marriage to Henry I of England in 1100 added to his social standing as a prince who, from 1107, was viceroy of the southern half of Scotland. In 1114 he married a wealthy forty-year-old widow, Maud de Senlis, Countess of Northampton and a ward of the king; she was also the daughter and heiress of Waltheof, the Earl of Huntingdon. This brought David the earldom of Northampton and the earldom ('Honour') of Huntingdon, with manors in eleven counties across the Midlands of England, making him one of the greatest barons in the country. Such was the premier nobleman of Norman England who turned into one of the greatest kings of medieval Scotland.

When David succeeded his brother on the throne in 1124 he brought with him to Scotland many of his friends from England who were to help him reshape the organisation and administration of Scotland, both civil and ecclesiastical, and become its new feudal aristocracy. We now meet for the first time the families who were to mould Scotland's future, powerful names like the Bruces, the Balliols and the Stewarts (David's first 'Steward' in Scotland was Walter Fitzalan, originally from Brittany, whose father had acquired lands in Norfolk and Shropshire). To these families David gave huge grants of land to establish their authority: to the Bruces he gave the vast lands of Annandale around the river Annan, which runs from the southern uplands to the Solway Firth; the hereditary 'Stewards' were given land which corresponds to modern Renfrewshire.

David's ecclesiastical foundations were the most spectacular of his reforms. In addition to the four great Border abbeys, he converted the wooden church of Drumselch Forest outside Edinburgh into the Abbey of Holyrood; he promoted the Benedictine priory of Dunfermline to the rank of an abbey, in honour of his mother Queen Margaret; he founded Newbattle on the Esk and St Mary of Cambuskenneth on the Forth. To all the churches and monasteries he founded he gave extensive estates and extravagant benefactions. So generous was he with the royal lands and revenues that he was later to be called 'a sair sanct [sore saint] for the crown' – that is to say, his pious activities cost the crown dear.

But there was prudence as well as religious devotion involved. Abbeys were good for the national economy. The Cistercians were the international wool merchants of their time, for instance; and David's monks engaged in all kinds of business enterprises, in farming, fishing, forestry, coal-working and salt-mining. The fledgling village of Kelso consisted almost entirely of people employed by the monks.

On top of this, David was assiduous in promoting commerce through the granting of royal charters to burghs from which he could collect regular revenues, and many of the towns and cities in today's Scotland date their origin or their first charters to David's reign. The first royal burghs, at Berwick-upon-Tweed and Roxburgh, were fortified with castles: Berwick Castle, standing high above the left bank of the Tweed, was to play a critically important role in Scottish history for centuries; Roxburgh Castle, sited between the Tweed and the Teviot, was to become the strongest bastion anywhere in the border lands. These developments may be seen as the beginning of a fortified 'border'.

All these important innovations were designed to give cohesion and stability to the realm, held together by a feudal system looser than its English model. Norman castles provided royal and baronial authority and security for the king's officers and tax-gatherers. His personal chaplains – well-educated priests all – formed the basis of an administrative bureaucracy, headed by a chancellor (for legal advice) and a chamberlain (for financial control). King David brought Scotland, as a kingdom, into the medieval European mainstream.

Steve Boardman, lecturer in Scottish History at Edinburgh University, says:

> *David is regarded as a pivotal figure in the development of Scotland and the Scottish kingship, because it was during his reign that so many novel and important features begin to develop and all the attributes of a medieval kingdom appear in Scotland. He was a very international figure in terms of Scottish kingship, part of the great cosmopolitan world which embraced Norman Europe. He had first-hand experience of Norman military techniques and tactics. He was part of the fashionable scene in terms of wider developments in Europe. Through David the Scottish kingdom began to develop along the same path as other European kingdoms, along similar lines to the accepted norms in France and England; so, in that sense, his kingship was crucial and has to be seen as extremely important.*

Ted Cowan urges caution in an uncritical use of the term 'feudalism' as it applies to David's Scotland:

> *I think David masterminded, quite brilliantly, a combination of what he wanted from the Norman world and what he perceived as being desirable in the old Celtic world.*

But this question of 'feudalism' is a highly problematical area. Many historians are no longer sure that there was any such thing as feudalism. If it is to be understood at all, it is best thought of simply as a system of landholding, whereby all land is held of the king; the king is the absolute proprietor of all land in the country. This is interesting, because in Celtic law all land was held communally by the clan. There were no absolute proprietors in the Celtic world. So there was a potential conflict there, but it is largely in the way in which landholding is described: the two systems could be accommodated quite well. And David was intelligent enough, and opportunistic enough, to achieve it.

It all suggests a sunshine reign of success and untroubled prosperity. There were rebellions in the Celtic north-east in 1130 and again in 1134, but with southern help David was able to suppress them both and put his own men in place there. At home (which by now, for a King of Scots, meant Edinburgh) David's wife Maud (who died in 1130) provided him with three children. The only one to reach adulthood, however, was Henry (c.1114–52), the heir apparent, who became Earl of Northumberland and Northampton. He was a dashing young man of whom David was manifestly very proud. But not everything was to go David's way.

The Battle of the Standard (Northallerton, 1138)

At the side of the A167 between Northallerton and Darlington, in North Yorkshire, stands a plain stone obelisk, its plinth marked with the simple legend: 'Battle of the Standard: AD 1138'. It also bears a metal shield with a stylised picture of a four-wheeled cart with a ship's mast festooned with banners. The monument marks the site of the most spectacular military event in David's long reign – the crushing defeat of a marauding Scottish army on a stretch of rolling moorland some three miles north of Northallerton on 22 August 1138.

The moorland has long been cultivated for agriculture, but the battle-site is easy to make out. Behind and in line with the monument is a rise in the ground on which sit the buildings of a farm called Standard Hill Farm; this was where the English army took up position around the curious 'standard' which gave the battle its popular name. To the left (i.e. the north) the ground dips and rises again towards another farm (also called Standard Hill Farm), which was where the Scottish force was deployed.

What was the battle about? England at that time was in the grip of a civil war following the death of Henry I in 1135. Henry's daughter Matilda, who was David I's niece, had the most obvious claim to the vacant throne and had been nominated by the late king as his heir. But another claimant stepped in – the king's nephew, Stephen of Blois, a grandson of William the Conqueror and husband of another of David I's nieces. Stephen had sworn fealty to Matilda (as had David I as a baron in England), but no sooner was Henry I dead than Stephen seized the throne for himself. It was to lead to nineteen years of bitter conflict within England; but its chief significance for Scotland was that it gave David I an opportunity to try to push Scotland's boundaries southwards. Claiming that he was supporting Matilda, he moved south in force and seized the English fortresses of Newcastle and Carlisle.

This was his great chance, it seemed, to recover the 'lost provinces'. From all corners of his kingdom he mustered a huge army (twenty-five thousand strong, according to English chroniclers, but this is now considered a substantial over-estimate) and set off in July 1138 towards York, harrying and pillaging on the way. Stephen had his hands full with a baronial uprising near Bristol, and the defence of the north fell to Thurstan, the ageing but militant Archbishop of York. Thurstan called for a 'holy crusade' to repel the Scottish invaders; from every pulpit in the county the call went out for able-bodied volunteers.

The English army – much smaller than the Scottish force – mustered at York and marched north to Thirsk; on Sunday, 21 August King David crossed the River Tees from Durham into Yorkshire. The English army thereupon marched north to stop his advance, and drew up in battle order early next morning just north of Northallerton. They were a motley collection of knights, peasants and priests, led by prelates; and because the resistance was Church-inspired, the English monastic chroniclers of the time took particular interest in what happened. Prior Richard of Hexham, writing in 1154, mirrored the propaganda war which preceded the encounter:

> The king [David] then passing by Durham . . . and according to his usual practice, caused the towns and churches which had previously escaped uninjured to be dismantled, plundered and burnt. Crossing the Tees, he commenced a similar career of violence. But God's mercy, being moved by the tears of innumerable widows, orphans, and victims, no longer permitted such wickedness to remain unchastised.

The rallying-point of the English army was a cart on which had been erected a ship's mast topped by a cross. From the pole hung a silver pyx containing the consecrated host, with the sacred banners of St Peter of York, St Cuthbert of Durham, St John of Beverley and St Wilfred of Ripon.

The Scots army presented a formidable array. In the centre were the lightly-armoured Pictish Galwegians from Galloway (known as Gallgaels), spoiling for a fight; on the left flank David's eldest son Henry led a force of mounted knights and well-equipped men-at-arms from the Borders and Cumbria; the Highland brigades were on the right flank, and King David himself commanded a reserve comprising the men of Moray and the eastern shires in the rear.

The battle was fought with tremendous heroism, and at terrible cost. The Gallgaels, dashing forward in a furious charge with their war-cry of 'Albanaich!', fell in droves under a storm of English arrows, but charged again and again at the English van. As the impetus of the reckless Gallgael attack faltered, Prince Henry charged the English centre with his mounted knights, but found himself isolated and extricated himself only with great difficulty. The Scottish attack stalled, and King David was pragmatic enough to realise that there could be no victory that day. Covered by the mounted reserve, the Scottish troops withdrew from the field. An old tree-lined lane just to the south of the English position, known as 'Scotpit Lane' (now disused and barred), is named after the burial pits into which some of the Scottish dead were thrown.

Surprisingly, after such a defeat in the field, David was able to salvage a great deal from this reverse. Neither Stephen nor the Empress Matilda was in any position to follow up the English victory. By the Treaty of Durham, which was signed in 1139, Stephen granted Northumberland to David's son, Earl Henry of Huntingdon, and to David I he granted Cumberland (with Carlisle) as far as the Ribble. It opened up the possibility, at least, that the Scottish frontier would run on the line of the Tees rather than the Tweed – which was precisely what David had hoped to achieve. Ten years later, in 1149, Matilda's son Henry of Anjou (subsequently Henry II of England) swore that should he become king, he would give David all the land between the Tweed and the Tees, and Cumberland on the west. But by the time Henry of Anjou became Henry II in 1154 he had little compunction about ignoring this promise to make the northern counties of England a part of Scotland for ever.

The Battle of the Standard left another and more enduring legacy.

The invasion brought out all the deep-rooted English prejudices against the Picts and the Scots as murderous barbarians, which Walter Scott reflected so faithfully in his *Tales of a Grandfather*. An English chronicler, Henry of Huntingdon, wrote of David's troops:

> *They cleft open pregnant women, and took out the unborn babe; they tossed children upon the spear-points, and beheaded priests upon the altars ... There was the screaming of women, the wailing of old men; groans of the dying, despair of the living.*
>
> HISTORIA ANGLORUM

What seems to have shocked the English was the fact that one of 'their own', a flower of Norman chivalry like David, should have unleashed such a savage horde to ravage a civilised kingdom. According to the English version, one of David's own Norman-English knights, Robert de Brus (the ancestor of the future King Robert Bruce), whom he had made Lord of Annandale, was so appalled by the Scots' brutality that he went over to the English camp; another of his new Norman friends, Bernard de Bailleul (the ancestor of the future King John Balliol), also deserted him.

Richard of Hexham described David's 'wicked army' as being 'composed of Normans, Germans, English, of Northumbrians and Cumbrians, of men of Teviotdale and Lothian, of Picts (who are commonly called Galwegians) and of Scots'. For Ted Cowan, this list of participants from Scotland tells us a lot about David's kingship:

> *Whether that list is strictly accurate or not, it was a code for saying 'David controlled the whole of his kingdom'. He was the ruler – the first person who ruled all of Scotland; and all its representatives showed up to fight for him against the English in 1138. That is a remarkable testimony to the ability, and probably the ingenuity, of this man.*

David escaped from the potential disaster of the Battle of the Standard with his territorial ambitions unscathed, even enhanced. But what sort of 'Scotland' did he create? To what extent could Scotland be called 'a nation', in the modern sense, in King David's reign? Steve Boardman says:

> *'Nation' is not the right word to use when we look back on the medieval kingdom. Scotland in the eleventh and twelfth centuries*

was a collection of regional lordships, presided over by a man who called himself King of Scots. David issued charters during his reign to his subjects – Scots, French, English – reflecting the different racial, ethnic and linguistic groups which made up the kingdom. The idea of nationhood would have been alien to people in twelfth-century Scotland, because they still belonged to different lordships, they still belonged to different ethnic and linguistic groups. What held Scotland, and indeed all medieval kingdoms, together was allegiance to the king and submission to the king's laws, the king's political authority; so to be a 'Scot' would not have meant what we mean by it today; it would have meant being someone who acknowledged the authority of the King of Scots – and that is not the same thing as identifying yourself ethnically and linguistically as part of a bigger group who are called Scots.

Later Scottish sources were fulsome in praise of David. John of Fordun wrote of him in the *Chronica Gentis Scotorum* in floridly metaphorical terms:

He enriched the parts of his kingdom with foreign merchandise, and to the wealth of his own land added the riches and luxuries of foreign nations, changing its coarse stuffs for precious vestments, and covering its ancient nakedness with purple and fine linen.

King David I reigned for twenty-nine years. He was nearly seventy years old, but had lost none of his vigour, when he died – significantly, in 'his' Carlisle Castle – in May 1153. His only son, Henry, Earl of Huntingdon, had died the previous year, leaving three sons and three daughters from his marriage to Ada, the Anglo-Norman daughter of the Norman Earl of Warenne. These three granddaughters of David I were to play an important role in the dynastic crisis which followed the death of Alexander III in 1286 (see Chapter 9).

In the last year of his life, after his son Henry's death, David designated the eldest of his grandsons, Malcolm, as his successor. In 1153, at the age of twelve, Malcolm was inaugurated on the Stone of Scone as Malcolm IV (r.1153–65). He never married, and was known as Malcolm 'the Maiden'. Sure enough, as David had feared, having a minor on the throne triggered unrest, and there were uprisings against Malcolm in the 'unreconstructed' Celtic west and north. In 1157 Malcolm was summoned to meet the new King of Engand, Henry II, at Chester. Henry forswore the undertaking he had given David in 1149 about Scotland's future frontier; by the Treaty of Chester the young King of Scots gave up Carlisle, together with the rest of Cumberland, Westmorland and Northumberland. He was compensated, however, with the gift of the earldom of Huntingdon. This made him a vassal of the King of England, for that possession at least. Henry II was not slow to press home his advantage; in 1158 he took Malcolm to France as his liegeman to campaign under his standard.

Malcolm was a frail, intensely pious young man who never enjoyed good health. Nonetheless, he showed unfailing courage and determination in dealing with the various uprisings and rebellions which broke out during his reign. He died at Jedburgh in December 1165 at the age of twenty-four, and was succeeded by his twenty-two-year-old brother William, a much more aggressive character: William I (r.1165–1214), later to be known as William 'the Lion'.

Chapter 7

WILLIAM THE LION (r.1165–1214)

William King of Scotland, having chosen for his armorial bearing a Red Lion, rampant . . . he acquired the name of William the Lion . . . William, though a brave man, and though he had a lion for his emblem, was unfortunate in war.

TALES OF A GRANDFATHER, CHAPTER IV

The majestic ruins of Arbroath Abbey, on the Angus coast about thirty kilometres east of Dundee, retain memories of many significant events in the story of Scotland's nationhood struggle: it was here that the Declaration of Arbroath was prepared and signed in 1320 (see Chapter 11), and it was on the foundations of the High Altar that the Stone of Destiny was laid in 1950 after it had been spirited away from Westminster Abbey by four young Scottish Nationalists (see pages 673–80).

On the turf a few metres in front of the High Altar, sheltered now only by the gaunt remains of the east gable wall, an incised slab of red sandstone commemorates the burial, somewhere in that area, of the royal founder of the abbey in 1178: King William I, 'the Lion'.

William the Lion is one of the least known and most disregarded of Scotland's kings. Despite the fact that his was the longest reign by a medieval Scottish monarch (forty-nine years, from 1165 to 1214), he is strangely unknown to the general public compared with his grandfather David I or his successors (his son Alexander II and grandson Alexander III). Indeed, some historians have been scornfully dismissive of him:

> *Of this king little can be told that is creditable to himself, of advantage to Scotland or, indeed, of interest to the reader. He reigned for almost half a century but achieved practically nothing.*
>
> P. AND F.S. FRY, *THE HISTORY OF SCOTLAND* (1980)

But was William really as toothless a lion as that? Geoffrey Barrow, Professor Emeritus at Edinburgh University and an eminent scholar of late medieval Scotland, has stressed that William successfully extended royal authority over the remoter Celtic and Scandinavian areas of the kingdom (the far north and west), and greatly improved the feudal administration of Scotland. His major failure, however – a failure which cost Scotland very dear – was his attempt to recover, as his personal fiefdom, the northern provinces of England: David I had assigned to William's father, Prince Henry, the earldom of Northumberland, but William's predecessor on the throne, his elder brother Malcolm IV, had surrendered it to the King of England.

And therein lies the paradox at the heart of William's reign. Totally committed as he was to consolidating Scotland's independence, he was nonetheless forced to pledge the nation's vassalage to England as a result of his disastrous obsession with the lost province of Northumbria.

Yet when he ascended the throne in 1165 at the age of twenty-two, William must have looked every inch the part of a native Scottish king. He was red-haired and powerfully built, a man of lusty energies and appetites (he fathered six illegitimate children before his marriage in 1186 at the age of forty-three), a reckless young knight who lacked both the political guile of his grandfather David I and the artistic sensibilities of his brother Malcolm IV, a blustering, headstrong fellow, the sort of captain of men who could today win a rugby international at Murrayfield single-handed and just as easily throw away the Calcutta Cup at Twickenham.

The most useful way of assessing his long reign is to divide it into four distinct periods.

The first nine years, from 1165 to 1174, was a time when the new king enjoyed comparative peace. But he quickly signalled his obsession with the earldom of Northumberland by badgering Henry II of England about it at every opportunity – so much so, as reported in a private letter reproduced in Sir Archibald Lawrie's *Annals of the Reigns of Malcolm and William, Kings of Scotland* (1910), that *the mere mention of William's name caused Henry to fly into a violent rage, tearing at his clothes, ripping the covers on his couch and even gnawing at handfuls of straw snatched up from the floor.*

The second period, the fifteen years from 1174 to Henry II's death in 1189, marked the most humiliating period of William's reign – the long and bitter subjection to English overlordship. Disregarding the counsel of his senior advisers, William thought he could take advantage of a rebellion fomented by Henry's sons against their father and recover the northern counties while Henry's attention was distracted. He sent his younger brother, David, the Earl of Huntingdon, south to the English barons as an earnest of his good faith, while he himself mounted an invasion of Northumbria which became (in English minds, at least) a byword for merciless ferocity. But his attempt to bludgeon Henry into agreement failed disastrously. David was quickly made a prisoner; worse still, William himself was captured at Alnwick in July 1174.

There is an air of tragi-comedy about that capture. William's army had failed to capture Newcastle and was now besieging Alnwick. One day William was out riding with a small group of men-at-arms when he detected, through the early-morning mist, a band of cavalry approaching. William thought they were a detachment of his own army; when he realised they were English knights, he charged at them, lance at the ready, shouting, 'Now we shall see which of us are good knights!' Hopelessly outnumbered, he was unhorsed and taken prisoner. His captors retreated swiftly with their royal prisoner and he was taken to King Henry at Northampton with his legs tied under his horse's belly like a common felon. Henry incarcerated him in a dungeon in the castle of Falaise, in Normandy, and kept him prisoner there for five months. Eventually, through the Treaty of Falaise (December 1174), William was forced to pay Henry explicit homage not just for himself but also 'for the kingdom of Scotland and his other lands in England', directly subject to the overlordship of the king of England and his heirs. The implication was clear: Scotland was only held by the King of Scots as a fief from the King of England as his overlord. English garrisons were installed in the castles at Berwick-upon-Tweed, Edinburgh, Jedburgh, Roxburgh and Stirling (all at Scotland's expense), the Scottish bishops were required to make submission to Canterbury (which they resisted successfully), and the sons of important Scottish nobles were taken as hostages.

For fifteen years the Treaty of Falaise remained in full force, and until the day he died Henry II extracted every drop of homage and humiliation he could from William, demanding the scrupulous fulfilment of every letter of the treaty. Perhaps the most humiliating sign of William's subjection to Henry was his marriage in 1186. Not only did Henry choose William's wife for him (Ermengarde, the daughter of a minor Norman vassal, Richard de Beaumont), he gave the new Scottish queen a cheap (for him) and cynical wedding-gift – Edinburgh Castle.

The English stranglehold on Scotland was loosened only when Henry II, brought to bay in France by another rebellion stirred up by his sons, died in the summer of 1189. His death ushered in the third major period of the reign of William of Scotland, from 1189 to 1209 – a twenty-year period of independence and peace with England and comparative prosperity. The new King of England, Henry's eldest surviving son Richard I (Richard Lion-Heart), had already taken a vow to go on the Third Crusade to drive the Saracens out of Palestine, and was desperate for money to finance the expedition. The castles north of the border still in English hands were returned to Scottish ownership, and William and the Scottish nation willingly paid ten thousand Scottish *merks* for the abrogation of all the terms of the Treaty of Falaise, in what is known as the 'Quitclaim of Canterbury' (1189): 'Thus, God willing, he worthily and honourably removed the heavy yoke of domination and servitude from the kingdom of the Scots' (*Chronicle of Melrose*).

No sooner did William get back the unfettered feu of his kingdom, however, than he was riding his relentless hobby-horse to Northumbria again. In 1194, after personally subscribing two thousand *merks* towards Richard's own ransom after his capture by the German Emperor in 1192, William offered fifteen thousand *merks* for Northumberland, more than he had paid for Scotland itself – but Richard would have none of it, if it meant acknowledging Northumberland to be part of Scotland.

But where it mattered – in Scotland – the decade of Richard's tenure of the English throne saw William reach the peak of his predominance at home, building up his military power to deal with domestic insurrection and knitting his kingdom together. From the accession to the English throne of Richard's treacherous younger brother, John 'Lackland', in 1199, it all began to go downhill. As usual, William lodged another claim for Northumbria and, as usual, it was turned down. John was much more skilfully ruthless than William, much better versed in the subtleties of power-politics. Relations between them, which had been strained from the outset, reached breaking-point in 1209 over the building of a new English castle at Tweedmouth, facing the vital sea-port of Berwick, which was then part of Scotland.

This trouble ushered in the fourth and final period of William's reign, from 1209 to 1214. William was a relatively old man by now, in his mid-sixties, and his health was beginning to fail. He had lost the initiative in the power-play with England. In 1204, in an act of blatant provocation, King John had given orders for the Tweedmouth fort to be built where it could menace Berwick. The Scots had responded by levelling the half-built castle to the ground – twice. The two kings held peace talks in Norham Castle, but nothing came of them. In 1209 John returned to Norham with a huge army. William, in response, assembled a force at Roxburgh, and full-scale war threatened. This time, however, William drew back from the brink. By the Treaty of Norham John agreed that the castle would not be completed, but in return for this 'concession', and as compensation for damage inflicted, William had to pay fifteen thousand *merks* 'for having the goodwill of King John'. William also had to relinquish all claim to the northern counties, and to hand over his two elder daughters, Margaret and Isabel, to be married off by John, on the vague suggestion that they would eventually marry John's sons. Nothing came of that, and William would never see them again; in the event they were married off to high-ranking English noblemen many years after his death.

The Treaty of Norham was another grave setback for the Scottish monarchy. The last six years of William's reign became a sort of interregnum: the ageing king was steadily losing his vigour and drive, and the young heir to the throne, the future Alexander II, was barely out of childhood (he was born in 1198, twelve years after his parents' marriage), too young and inexperienced to take over the reins of leadership with any confidence. Little wonder, then, that King John was able to impose himself so aggressively on the Scottish kingdom and its subjects.

William had a year of illness and convalescence in 1213, but was sufficiently recovered by the following year to march north to Caithness to impose the king's peace there. In September he was back in Stirling, where he succumbed to his final illness. He died on 4 December 1214, at the age of seventy-one.

The legacy of the Lion

To be saddled with the sobriquet of 'Lion' (or 'Lion-heart', for that matter) can be a handicap if one's actions are not perceived as being sufficiently leonine. William was never known as 'the Lion' in his lifetime – it was a nickname invented by later historians – and there is little agreement about how or why he acquired the name. In *Tales of a Grandfather*, Sir Walter Scott assumed that it was because of the emblematic lion rampant on his coat of arms. Others have thought it was because of his 'rough and stern countenance'. The most likely explanation, to my mind, lies with the earliest Scottish chronicler to imply the name, John of Fordun in the fourteenth century, who referred flatteringly to William as *leo justitiae*, a 'lion of justice'. Nonetheless, if he really was the first Scottish king to emblazon his standard with the lion rampant, William bequeathed to his nation a symbol of defiance with which generations of Scots have been happy to identify ever since.

Arbroath Abbey was the other major legacy of his reign, and thereby hangs an intriguing tale. William was not greatly renowned for piety or devotion to the Church, as his brother Malcolm IV had been (although towards the end of his life he seems to have achieved a reputation for personal sanctity). But in 1178, three years after his release from Henry's captivity after the disaster at Alnwick, he not only founded Arbroath Abbey but also endowed it so lavishly that it became one of the richest religious houses in all Scotland.

According to the original charter, William founded a monastery and church 'at the place near the mouth of the Brothock Burn in honour of God and of St Thomas à Becket, Archbishop and Martyr'. That should give us pause, for there is more to this than meets the eye. Why should this violently anti-English king choose to dedicate this magnificent Scottish foundation to Thomas à Becket, an Anglo-Norman prelate?

Thomas, in his time, was the most brilliant figure in the court of Henry II, a man of great personal charisma, apparently, an assiduous party-giver, a skilled diplomat and, moreover, well-versed in all the martial arts of chivalry. He became Henry's chancellor in 1155 (the year after Henry's accession), and in 1162 Henry appointed him Archbishop of Canterbury. Almost overnight the sybarite became an ascetic; his former loyalty to Henry was replaced by an unswerving zeal for the Church and its rights against the state. This led to exile, followed by an uneasy reconciliation; but as soon as Thomas returned to Canterbury the old antagonism flared up again, and Henry uttered his cele-brated, impetuous wish to be rid of 'this turbulent priest'. It was as a direct result of these intemperate words that Thomas à Becket was murdered in Canterbury Cathedral on 29 December 1170 by four of Henry's hard-tempered Norman knights. The murder and its circum-stances sent a thrill of horror throughout Europe, and stories soon spread of miracles worked at Thomas's tomb. In 1173 he was canonised and quickly became the most widely venerated of all English saints.

King Henry was nothing if not a pragmatist. Becket's martyrdom had swung the struggle between Church and crown in the Church's favour, and Henry had to swing it back again. After settling some differences in Normandy in the summer of 1174, Henry came back to England to do public penance for the death of Thomas à Becket. On 12 July he submitted himself to be scourged by each one of the eighty assembled clergymen in turn.

A week later, when Henry was back in London, he was brought the news that King William of Scotland had been captured at Alnwick on the previous Saturday – 13 July. Praise be to God! And, in particular, praise be to Thomas à Becket, who had in this way clearly rewarded Henry for his (albeit belated) repentance.

But why, four years later, should *William* wish to thank God and Thomas à Becket for his capture? One can understand his motives, in the middle of the most abjectly humiliating period of his reign, for building Arbroath Abbey in the first place, as a deliberate and defiant statement of his continuing importance and prestige. And perhaps – just perhaps – the dedication to St Thomas was intended as a monu-mental insult to the English royal house, by extolling the man who, both in life and in death, had humbled the crown of England, yet couched in such unassailable piety that none could publicly take offence, not even Henry of England himself. I tend to believe that it was the one truly subtle thing which this blunt and headstrong king ever did.

After his death at Stirling in 1214 the body of King William the Lion was taken to the abbey he had founded and was buried there 'in front of the high altar', according to John of Fordun. But *where* 'in front of the high altar'? For many years there was no monument nor plaque to commemorate his interment, because no one knew the precise spot where his body had been laid. And then, in 1816, a local antiquarian named Dr Stevenson who was poking around with spade and trowel in the ruins, four metres in front of the High Altar, chanced upon an old stone coffin containing some mouldering bones, its lid surmounted by a headless recumbent effigy with its feet resting upon a crouching lion.

We should remember that this period was the heyday of earnest amateur antiquarianism. 1816 was also, by an agreeable coincidence, the year in which Sir Walter Scott published one of his most charming works, his own 'chief favourite among all his novels', as he himself put it: *The Antiquary*. The antiquary of the title, Jonathan Oldbuck, the learned and garrulous Laird of Monkbarns, is an affectionately mocking caricature of all those earnest snappers-up of unconsidered historical trifles – including Walter Scott himself:

> *He had his own pursuits, being in correspondence with most of the virtuosi of his time, who, like him, measured decayed entrenchments, made plans of ruined castles, read illegible inscriptions, and wrote essays on medals in proportion of twelve pages to each letter of the legend.*

Dr Stevenson, the real-life Jonathan Oldbuck, leaped to the instant and uncritical conclusion that he had found a royal tomb – *the* royal tomb, indeed: the tomb of William the Lion. The find created a local sensation; it also created a small fortune for unscrupulous local entrepreneurs who were soon exhibiting and selling bits of bones from the coffin (assiduously replenished whenever stocks ran out). Dr Stevenson himself sent various items of ossified royalty to his fellow-virtuosi and antiquarians, including a tooth ('a royal grinder', as he called it) to a gentleman in Montrose: 'Very few relics are so well authenticated,' he wrote, 'even the most venerated of the Church of Rome.'

But it was all wishful thinking. After more than a century and a half of fierce argument the effigy on the sarcophagus lid was dated, on stylistic grounds, to be that of a wealthy commoner from no earlier than the middle of the fourteenth century – 150 years after King William's death. It was placed for safe keeping in the Abbot's House outside the skeleton walls of the abbey and put on proper display as part of an imaginative Visitor Information system in 1982 (the first to be put in place at a historic monument in the care of the state). Finally, in 1986, to give the vexed issue of William's place of interment a dignified conclusion, the Historic Buildings and Monuments Directorate of Scotland (now Historic Scotland) planted that sandstone memorial slab in the area in front of the High Altar. It marks not the alleged site of the burial, but only the event itself:

WILLIAM THE LION (r.1165–1214)

King William the Lion
King of Scots 1165–1214
Founded this monastery in 1178
In honour of St Thomas of Canterbury,
Archbishop and Martyr,
For monks of St Benedict from Kelso,
Of the family of Tiron.
King William died at Stirling, 4 December 1214,
And was buried in this Abbey Church.

It is symptomatic, ironically, that the burial place of this much mis-prised King of Scotland should still be a matter of mystery and lingering doubt.

Chapter 8

THE THIRTEENTH CENTURY:
ALEXANDERS II AND III

William the Lion was succeeded by his son, Alexander II, a youth in years, but remarkable for prudence and for firmness. In his days there was some war with England, as he espoused the cause of the disaffected barons, against King John. But no disastrous consequences having arisen, the peace betwixt the two kingdoms was . . . effectually restored . . .

Relieved from the cares of an English war, Alexander endeavoured to civilize the savage manners of his own people. These were disorderly to a great degree.

TALES OF A GRANDFATHER, CHAPTER V

The reigns of two Alexanders – Alexander II (r.1214–49), the son of William the Lion, and Alexander's son, Alexander III (r.1249–86) – spanned most of the thirteenth century. That century came to be wistfully remembered by John of Fordun in the 1380s as a golden age of princely stability and prosperity – especially as it was a prelude to tragedy and to the desperate times of the Wars of Independence. But how much of a Golden Age was it? Professor Ted Cowan has his reservations:

This 'Golden Age' was only golden because of what came after. It so happens that the second half of the thirteenth century was a period of prosperity everywhere in Europe. It seems to have just been one of those boom periods, for whatever reason, and Scotland shared in this. This was a period, after all, which is associated with the development of some of our greatest religious architecture, of abbeys and Romanesque churches, and of castle-building. The development of the royal burghs established by David I went on apace. Church organisation was strengthened and a proper parish system was established. So to that extent it was a period of development, prosperity and consolidation. It was also a time of relative peace – and 'peace' is always equated with 'golden age'.

That is not to say that the thirteenth century was uneventful. The 'peace', as Ted Cowan points out, was relative. As soon as Alexander II ascended the throne at the age of sixteen his fledgling authority was challenged by a Celtic uprising in the north, but this was quickly quelled by a loyal lieutenant there. In England the old enemy, King John, was in deep trouble with his barons and was constrained to sign away some of his more arbitrary powers in the Magna Carta at Runnymede on 15 June 1215. Alexander II seized what he saw as a fine opportunity to regain the lost territories in the north of England which had so obsessed his father. It was a misjudgement: King John turned on Scotland with a snarl, 'to chase the red fox-cub back to his lair', as a chronicler put it, and vicious warfare flared on both sides of the border. But now the forces ranged against John were threatening to overwhelm him, and he was fighting for his life: his barons were at war with him and had brought over a French claimant to the throne – Louis, son and heir of King Philippe II of France. In October 1216 the English king was struck down by a mysterious illness which caused his death – from poison, according to some.

The death of King John changed everything. His son Henry, only nine years old, was quickly enthroned at Gloucester as Henry III under the regency of the stalwart old William Marshal, Earl of Pembroke. In England, baronial support for Louis of France melted away and he sailed back home; and in Scotland, Alexander II laid aside his military ambitions in the north of England. Indeed, in 1221 he married Henry III's elder sister, Joan, which did much to stabilise relations between the two countries. This left Alexander free to assert and consolidate royal authority in the ever-recalcitrant north and west of the mainland of Scotland.

In the 1230s Alexander came to realise that he was never going to recover Northumberland as a family possession, and in the autumn of 1237 he signed an amicable agreement (the Treaty of York) whereby he renounced all claims to territory south of the Tweed and the Solway. In recompense he was given tenure (under the overlordship of the English king) of certain lands in Northumberland and Cumberland – though not their castles. The Treaty of York, curiously enough, finds no mention in Scott's *Tales of a Grandfather*, but it was of extreme historical importance in that it established the Anglo–Scottish frontier along a line from the Tweed to the Solway – a line which was to remain unchanged from then on, with the conspicuous exception of Berwick-upon-Tweed. It was an implicit acceptance by England, for the time being at least, of Scotland's right to exist as a free and independent kingdom.

And what of the common people of this independent nation of Scotland, as it could now be called – the people whose manners Walter Scott called 'savage' and 'disorderly' and much in need of civilising? The population of Scotland at this time was only about 300,000. Most of them were poor peasants living in small stone-and-turf houses which they usually shared with any livestock they might have had: subsistence farming – mainly pastoral in the north and west, more arable south of the Forth – with the tenants paying rent to the laird in kind and in labour; but at least the weather conditions were markedly better than they had been in previous centuries. Only a small proportion of the population – perhaps 10 per cent – lived in the trading towns established by David I and continued by the Alexanders as new links were forged with overseas markets; Europeans with commercial and manufacturing skills were encouraged to come and settle in these burghs, of which there were nearly fifty by the end of the thirteenth century.

The Treaty of York gave Alexander II greater freedom of manoeuvre, now that he no longer had to devote so many of his energies to coping with his much larger and more powerful neighbour. In 1238 his wife Joan died childless, and Alexander immediately applied himself to one of the most urgent functions of medieval kingship – producing a male heir to the throne. He turned not to England but to the nobility of France, and in the following year he married Marie de Coucy, a kinswoman of the French king. In September 1241 she duly bore him a son, who was named after his father – the future Alexander III.

There was to be another spat with England, in 1244, when Scottish and English armies eyed one another menacingly across the border. There seems to have been an element of brinkmanship involved, and in the event no battle ensued; but as part of the peace negotiations the infant Alexander was betrothed to Henry III's daughter Margaret, herself only a year older than her future bridegroom. It seemed to adumbrate a future when the two kingdoms would be much more closely allied – perhaps even a Union of the Crowns many centuries before that actually came about in 1603.

Alexander II had consolidated the crown's control over mainland Scotland and welded it into a more cohesive realm than it had ever been. Now the time was ripe to extend this centralised royal authority over the islands to the west – the Hebrides. For long (too long, in thirteenth-century Scottish eyes) they, and the Northern Isles, had been subject to the crown of Norway (see Chapter 3)

Norwegian royal authority in the Western Isles had been waning steadily as the Gaelic-speaking leaders of the warrior Somerled dynasty vied for the title of 'Lord of the Isles'. In Norway, however, there was now a king of great drive and imperial ambition – King Håkon IV (r.1217–64), who has come down in history with the sobriquet Håkon 'the Old'.

Historians seeking to gain a clear picture of relations between Scotland and Norway at this period now look to overseas sources – particularly the medieval Icelandic sagas such as *Orkneyinga Saga* and *Hákonar Saga*, the biography of Håkon the Old written soon after his death by the Icelandic saga-historian Sturla Thórðarson; there are no contemporary Scottish sources for the events, and later Scottish historians were to invent and embellish to fill the gaps.

In 1230, Håkon the Old decided to re-establish effective Norwegian suzerainty over the Hebridean warlords, who owed him revenues and allegiance. He sent a punitive expedition in 1230 which caused considerable havoc. One furious engagement is described in graphic detail in his saga – a three-day assault on Rothesay Castle on the island of Bute, in the Firth of Clyde. The Norsemen finally got in by hacking through the castle's thick circular stone walls with their axes despite cascades of boiling lead and pitch raining down upon them from the battlements. Rothesay Castle, with its unique (for Scotland) circular walls, is now in state care and has been vividly restored by Historic Scotland; romantics like me can persuade themselves that they can still see the marks of the implacable Norse axes which forced an entry.

The Norsemen did not stay long to enjoy their exploit, but the expedition as a whole was considered to have been a success: those whose allegiance to Norway had been suspect were killed or driven out, and new men were put in their place; the Western Isles had been 'pacified' to Håkon's satisfaction.

It was only natural that Alexander II should want to exercise dominion over the Western Isles himself, if only to curb the piratical Islesmen whose galleys menaced the seaways off the western Highlands. Accordingly, he sent embassies to Norway from 1244 onwards to try to negotiate a deal over the islands. The Scottish envoys even indicated that Alexander would be prepared to buy the Western Isles for good silver, to which King Håkon gave a haughty answer: 'He said he was not aware that he was so short of silver that he needed to sell his lands for it.'

The repeated diplomatic snubs from Norway only increased Alexander's determination to deal with this thorn in his western side, by force if necessary, especially after Håkon appointed Ewen, Lord of Argyll and head of the powerful Macdougall clan, as his vassal king over the islands. In the spring of 1249 Alexander mobilised a massive expedition by land and sea to crush this threat to 'the soft underbelly of Scotland', as the novelist Eric Linklater called it.

Alexander's first target was to be Dunstaffnage Castle at the entrance to Loch Etive on the western seaboard; it was the chief stronghold of the Macdougalls and had only recently been built by Ewen of Argyll (or his father). What a fortress it was, and is! It stands proud on a rocky knoll on a promontory some four miles north of Oban. Its massive stone curtain walls, still intact after nearly eight centuries, must have seemed almost impregnable; its lofty battlements command a tremendous view west across the seaway towards the island of Lismore and east into the narrows of Loch Etive towards the looming bulk of Ben Cruachan.

Alexander gathered his great fleet in the Sound of Kerrera, the three-kilometre-long fertile island which shelters the Oban coastline. But as his galleys lay at anchor in Horseshoe Bay, poised to launch the assault on Dunstaffnage, Alexander had an ominous dream, according to *Hákonar Saga*:

> *When King Alexander was lying at anchor in Kerrera Sound he had a dream. In his dream he thought that three men came to him. One of them seemed to him to be dressed in royal robes. He looked very menacing, ruddy of face and rather stout, of medium height. The second man seemed slender in build and gallant-looking, very handsome and of noble bearing. The third man was much the biggest in build and the most menacing of them all. His forehead was quite bald. He spoke to the king and asked him if he were heading for the Hebrides. The king replied*

that this was so: he was on his way to subjugate the islands. The man in his dream asked him to turn back, saying that nothing else would do.

The king recounted his dream, and most of his companions urged him to turn back, but the king refused. Soon afterwards the king fell ill and died. The Scots then dispersed their army and transported the king back to Scotland. The Hebrideans say that the men who appeared to the king in his dream would have been Saint Ólaf, King of Norway, and Saint Magnús, Earl of Orkney, and Saint Columba.

Whether one believes in dreams or not, Alexander II did indeed fall ill in Kerrera Sound. He died there, either on his ship or on land, on 8 July 1249; no cairn commemorates the spot, but a grassy field beside the shore is known to this day as 'Dalrigh' – Gaelic for 'the field of the king'. He was buried in Melrose Abbey, in accordance with his last wishes; his unmarked tomb is in a recess in the wall of the presbytery to the south of the High Altar, but there is no plaque to identify it for visitors, as yet.

With Alexander's death, his army melted away and the great fleet dispersed; but the crown's ambition to annex the Hebrides was only put on hold, not abandoned.

The inauguration of Alexander III

ALEXANDER III, then only in his eighth year, succeeded to his father in 1249. Yet, when only two years older, he went to York to meet with the English King, and to marry his daughter, the Princess Margaret.

TALES OF A GRANDFATHER, CHAPTER V

Scone Palace, hard by the city of Perth in the geographical heartland of Scotland, is one of the stateliest of the country's private homes, the seat of the Earl and Countess of Mansfield. The first house, built at the end of the sixteenth century, was almost totally rebuilt in pseudo-Gothic style in 1802–12 by the third Earl of Mansfield; this huge mansion is a treasury of beautiful *objets d'art* and paintings and furnishings of rare historic interest.

It was here at Scone, seated on the Stone of Scone in what had been the power-base of the old Pictish kingdom of Fortriu (see Chapter 3), that the seven-year-old Alexander III was inaugurated as King of

Scots on 13 July 1249, a week after the death of his father. The boy-king was accompanied to Scone by seven earls and many other leading magnates and churchmen of Scotland. The scene was described, a century later, in John of Fordun's *Chronica Gentis Scottorum*:

> *[They] led Alexander, soon to be the king, to the cross which stands in the churchyard at the east end of the church of Scone. There they set him on the royal throne, which was decked with silken cloths inwoven with gold; and the Bishop of St Andrews, assisted by the rest, consecrated him king, as was meet. So the king sat down upon the royal throne – that is, the Stone – while the earls and other nobles, on bended knee, spread their garments under his feet before the Stone.*
>
> *Now, this stone is reverently kept in that same monastery for the coronation of the kings of Alba; and no king was ever wont to reign in Scotland unless he had first, on receiving the name of king, sat upon this Stone at Scone, which by kings of old had been appointed the capital of Alba.*

It was a solemn and striking occasion. Afterwards a traditional Highland *sennachie* (bard) recited in Gaelic the new king's genealogy far back into the distant mythical past, to the eponymous Scota and Gaedel Glas: 'Hail, king of Alba, Alexander, mac Alexander, mac William, mac Henry, mac David . . .' It was a powerful public recognition of the strength of the living inheritance from the Celtic kingdoms of the past.

It is impossible to be certain where at Scone the ceremony took place. In the thirteenth century there was an abbey where the present palace now stands. The inauguration of Alexander III seems to have taken place in the open air, close to the abbey at a site traditionally known as Moot Hill (Hill of Meeting) directly opposite the palace; the Stone of Scone ('Stone of Destiny') would have been carried from the abbey and decked as a throne. Moot Hill, now half-screened by yew trees, was reduced in height in the nineteenth century. On it today stands a small family mausoleum, all that remains of the church which was built there in 1624 and in which Charles II was crowned in 1651. Outside the mausoleum is a replica of the Stone of Scone; it is as close to actual history as the visitor can get.

The accession of a minor might well have caused a political crisis (as it would do, time and time again, during the Stewart dynasty), but on this occasion Church and nobility closed ranks to protect the crown.

Alexander's kingship was perceived to be blessed by divine grace within two months by the canonisation of the matriarch of the dynasty, Queen Margaret, wife of Malcolm Canmore, in 1250. This was a notable coup which gave the royal line the lustre of a saintly ancestry and which was celebrated in June 1250 by the solemn translation of her remains to a new shrine near the great altar in Dunfermline Abbey.

In December 1251, at the age of ten, the boy-king was taken by his court to York to be knighted by Henry III before being married to Henry's daughter Margaret. It gave the English king an immediate opportunity to raise the dormant question of Scotland's subjection to England; according to the contemporary *St Albans Chronicle*, Alexander was then asked to do homage for the kingdom of Scotland. His advisers must have seen this coming, for the boy replied gravely that he had come to marry, not to answer so difficult a question. That answer helped to defuse, for a time at least, the perennial issue of overlordship.

The years of Alexander's minority in the 1250s had their political tremors as different noble factions and parties within the regency vied for control of the king's person (and therefore the government), with Henry III interfering busily in the background – ostensibly out of concern for his daughter's welfare. The young couple were not allowed to live together as man and wife and were kept under the strict control of tutors or guardians

When Alexander's minority ended in 1259, on his eighteenth birthday, the reins of government were firmly held by pro-king nobles – particularly the powerful Comyn family, who exercised power on behalf of the king in both the north and the south-west – and he was able to hit the ground running, as the saying goes. He showed strength of character and even-handedness in dealing with his quarrelsome nobles. Soon he was resuming his father's attempt to wrest the Hebrides from Norwegian control. In 1261 he sent an embassy to Norway to discuss the Scottish claim to the Hebrides, but King Håkon was in no mood for concessions. In the summer of 1262 news reached Norway of savage raids on the Isle of Skye from the mainland; furthermore, the messengers from Skye reported that the King of Scots had declared openly that he intended to take possession of the Hebrides by force or die in the attempt.

These reports 'caused King Håkon the gravest concern', as his saga puts it, and that Christmas he called on all the regions of his realm to muster the traditional defence levy in Bergen the following spring. He fitted out a royal flagship which had been specially built in Bergen

– a magnificent oaken vessel with snarling dragon-heads fore and aft, gleaming with gold inlay. It was an exceptionally large ship, with thirty-seven pairs of oars, and Håkon had designed it as a troop-carrier for the cream of his soldiers: one half-bench for each oar carried four men, making a total complement of 296, including a retinue of priests and civil servants. According to the contemporary *Icelandic Annals* Håkon's fleet contained 'the largest army which had ever sailed from Norway', and it is clear that Håkon was using his ships as transports laden to the gunwales with troops in case he decided to launch a full-scale invasion of the Scottish mainland and engage the Scottish army in pitched battle.

The fleet set sail from Bergen for Shetland early in July 1263, but things did not go smoothly in mustering more ships in the Northern Isles. Eventually, on 10 August, Håkon set sail westwards through the Pentland Firth and across the Minch to Lewis. He mustered again near South Rona, off Skye, where he was joined by reinforcements from the Isle of Man, and from there the great, glittering fleet passed through the narrow Kyle of Lochalsh at a point which was thereafter named after him: the Strait of Håkon, Kyle-Håkon – Kyleakin.

South they coasted, to Kerrera and Oban Bay, where they were joined by some loyal Islesmen. Here Håkon paused again, and sent off a squadron of fifty ships to plunder in Kintyre, while another fifteen rounded the Mull of Kintyre and attacked the Isle of Bute, where Rothesay Castle was taken again as it had been in 1230. Kintyre and Islay submitted at the first taste of pillage, and the plundering was called off in return for a tax of a thousand head of cattle. After that, with the islands to the west brought to heel, Håkon weighed anchor and sailed south down the coast of Kintyre and rounded the Mull into the Clyde estuary, where he anchored in Lamlash Bay, on Arran, in the lee of Holy Island. It was now September, and Håkon's strategy was clear: the stronghold on the Isle of Bute had been reduced, and he lay poised with a huge army to strike at the mainland at will.

Alexander, meanwhile, had apparently been mustering the Scots army somewhere in Ayrshire. He now sent an embassy of Dominican friars to Arran to make overtures of peace. Håkon responded by sending over a delegation of two bishops 'skilled in the Scots tongue'. When the talks began, Alexander seemed only too willing to come to terms. He said he would think things over and send his delegation back to renew the talks on Arran the next day. Håkon had made up a list of all the islands to the west which he claimed to own; Alexander jibbed over Arran, Bute and the Cumbraes – but that was merely a technicality, he implied. Agreement was just around the corner; a settlement was almost within their grasp – but somehow it remained just beyond their grasp. The saga suggests that the Scots were deliberately spinning things out: 'The Scots had decided to prolong the negotiations, and make sure that a settlement was never quite achieved, as summer was passing and the weather would soon worsen.'

The drift of the Scottish tactics was not lost on King Håkon. In another threatening move he took his fleet much closer to the Scottish coast, to the lee of the Cumbraes just off Largs. More talks followed, but the outcome was always the same: there were still some minor differences to be settled, nothing serious – but meanwhile Alexander allowed the Norsemen a glimpse of his army assembling on the hills inland. Håkon was rapidly losing patience, and now he sent Alexander an ultimatum – that they should meet on land, each with his full army, and talk, and if the talks failed they would fight. Alexander responded that he was not averse to fighting, but gave no definite answer either way.

Håkon was now running out of time and provisions. Abruptly he called off the talks and sent a squadron of sixty ships up Loch Long to Arrochar, where they dragged their ships' boats across a porterage to Tarbet and Loch Lomond and burned and terrorised the islands in the loch and the surrounding Lennox countryside. On their way back, however, the saga relates that ten of their ships were wrecked in Loch Long in a gale.

The same gale was to play havoc with Håkon's main fleet sheltering under the Cumbraes. It struck on the night of Sunday, 30 September, howling in from the south-west. During the night a merchantman was blown against the king's ship; its stays fouled the dragon-head, snapping off the nostrils. As the tempest blew harder, ship after ship dragged its anchors; it took no fewer than eight anchors to hold the king's huge ship steady. By dawn the loose merchantman and three longships had been blown across the sound and lay stranded on the mainland shore below the steep slopes of the Cunninghame hills (hence the name 'Largs', meaning 'slopes'). So ferocious was the storm that many were convinced it had been conjured up by sorcery.

The 'Battle' of Largs (2 October 1263)

Visitors to Largs arriving from the south are greeted by the sight of a tall cylindrical tower standing, like an unlit lighthouse, on a low outcrop of rocks on the foreshore at Bowen Craig, overlooking the modern marina there; constructed of rough whinstone with a sharply conical cap of red sandstone, it rears eighteen metres from the ground and is known, familiarly, as the Pencil. This prominent landmark was built by public subscription in 1912 on the traditional site of the so-called battle, and formally unveiled in appropriately foul weather on 12 July of that year.

The memorial, which cost £290 to build (plus £8 for the ornamental stonework of the doorway), was modelled on the eleventh-century 'Round Towers' of Brechin and Abernethy on the popular misconception that these had been erected for protection against viking raids. The only access is through a padlocked oaken door, two and a half metres off the ground. Inside, there is absolutely nothing, apart from a generous legacy of guano bequeathed by the local pigeons who use the memorial as a convenient dovecote. There were originally four wooden floors which allowed access by ladder to the 'look-out' floor at the level of the small window at the top, but the flooring has long since been removed for safety reasons. Soon after the tower was built, it was locally believed that the vikings themselves had stored their swords and shields in it! In our perceptions of Scotland's history, the sharpened Pencil has often proved mightier than the Sword.

The 'Battle' of Largs which it commemorates was not a proper battle; it was more of a series of skirmishes on the beach. Nonetheless it is celebrated annually at an autumn Viking Festival in Largs which culminates with fireworks at the Pencil and (of course) the burning of a viking boat. For the people of Ayrshire, Largs has much of the significance of Bannockburn itself – a battle by which Scotland was saved from the hordes who threatened the nation's freedom. It may have marked a significant turning-point in history, but it was never quite like that . . .

On the Monday morning after the great gale (1 October 1263) some of the local Scots militia came down to the shore and indulged in some long-range skirmishing with the Norsemen in the stranded longships, but pulled back out of range when Håkon sent some reinforcements ashore during a lull in the weather. Under cover of darkness that night the Scots managed to loot some of the cargo of the merchantman, but on the Tuesday morning Håkon himself landed with a task-force to rescue what was left of the cargo. The work was almost done when the Norwegians sighted Scottish troops approaching. It looked a very large force, and the Norsemen thought at first that it was commanded by Alexander in person. Håkon allowed himself to be rowed back to his fleet, albeit reluctantly; and now hostilities began.

According to *Hákonar Saga* there were an estimated eight or nine hundred Norwegians on land by then. The Scots had up to five hundred knights mounted on mail-clad horses, and a host of foot-soldiers armed with bows and axes. No estimate of their numbers is given. At one stage the saga says that the Norwegians were outnumbered by ten to one; but the context suggests that this refers only to a particular stand made by one group of Norsemen and should probably not be interpreted to mean that the Scottish army numbered eight or nine thousand men – which is hardly credible, particularly in the light of how things turned out.

The fighting was confused and inconclusive, and much of it consisted of desultory exchanges of arrows and stones. The wind now got up again, and Håkon had to sit helplessly on his ship and watch as his beleaguered men fought a grim rearguard action southward along the beach, withdrawing and counter-attacking in turn. As dusk fell the Norsemen mounted another fierce attack and drove the Scots from the beach; in the respite thus gained the Norsemen were able to embark and struggle back to the main fleet. A couple of days later Håkon sent another party ashore to burn the ships which lay wrecked there. There was no opposition: the Scottish army had obviously withdrawn inland and had no intention of engaging again. Nor had Håkon: on that same day his fleet upped anchor and sailed to Lamlash Bay on Arran. The 'Battle' of Largs was over.

It had been neither a famous victory nor a crushing defeat. The numbers given in the saga seem overblown, no doubt on the principle that if you cannot beat them you multiply them. Since the Norwegians had ultimately been left in possession of the beach at Largs, it cannot be said that they lost the day. George Buchanan's magisterial Latin *History of Scotland* (1582) claimed that Håkon had landed a force of twenty thousand men who were routed to the tune of sixteen thousand dead at a cost of five thousand Scottish lives; but that is now recognised by historians as nonsense. It is a nonsense, however, which has died hard.

Yet if the Norwegians did not lose that particular engagement, they certainly lost the campaign: Håkon had failed to secure the islands against future encroachments by Alexander, which had been his original objective.

Håkon now limped away with his battered and mutinous fleet. After a trying voyage, he reached haven in Orkney at the end of October. He took up residence in the Bishop's Palace, whose ruins are such a striking feature of Kirkwall, just across the road from the beautiful rose-red Cathedral of St Magnus. No sooner was he installed in the palace, however, than he fell ill:

> In his sickness, he had Latin books read to him at first; but he found it too much trouble to work out what the Latin meant. Then he had books read to him in Norse, first the sagas of the Saints, and then the sagas of the Kings of Norway all the way from Hálfdan the Black onwards, one after the other, until the saga of King Sverrir [his grandfather] was reached ... Near midnight the reading of Sverrir's Saga was concluded; and just as midnight passed, Almighty God called King Hákon from this earthly life.

His death was big news in Norway. In Scotland, however, the *Melrose Chronicle* displayed a very different order of priorities:

> In this year [1264] upon the Day of St Agnes [21 January], the queen of Scotland gave birth to a son, who, at his father's desire, was named Alexander ... And it happened that on the same day upon which the king of Scotland was informed that God had given him a son, intelligence also arrived that the king of Norway was dead. Rejoiced by these twofold tidings of joy, the king gave thanks to God, who exalts the humble and humbles the proud.

The death of King Håkon was a real turning-point; but the entry in the *Melrose Chronicle* was of particular poignancy, not so much because of what had gone before, as of what was to come.

With Håkon's death the way was now open for Alexander's own territorial ambitions in the Hebrides. Alexander was a young and vigorous man, still only twenty-three years old; he had thwarted the naval might of Norway and seen off a major threat to his own kingdom, and now, with every reason to expect a long and successful reign ahead of him, the future of the realm seemed assured with the birth of an heir to the throne. And so, at first, it seemed.

As far as the Western Isles were concerned, Alexander was now in the driving seat. According to the *Saga of Magnús Hákonarson*, the Norsemen in the Orkneys sent an embassy to Scotland in the spring of 1264 to make overtures for peace, but were brusquely rebuffed. Alexander was not slow to press home his advantage; he was now in a position to pick off the Western Isles one by one, and was clearly determined to do so.

In Norway, Håkon's successor King Magnus (known as 'the Law-Reformer') was realistic enough to recognise that Norwegian suzerainty over the Western Isles dependencies was no longer tenable. In the autumn of 1264 he again sent messengers to Alexander; this time their reception was less chilly, and Magnus was told that treaty terms could be discussed in Scotland the following summer. Eventually, on 2 July 1266, peace was made and sealed through the Treaty of Perth. It was in all respects a sensible and welcome settlement, which King Magnus was able to announce in Bergen on 9 August without loss of face: in return for the cession of the Hebrides and the Isle of Man, the Scots were to pay a lump sum of four thousand *merks* of refined silver in four annual instalments, and an annual tribute of a hundred *merks* in perpetuity. According to the *Melrose Chronicle*, King Alexander paid out the whole sum of four thousand *merks* on the spot; but the annual tribute of a hundred *merks* seems soon to have petered out. From the Norwegian point of view, the most important provision of the Treaty of Perth was a firm guarantee that Scotland would respect Norway's sovereignty over the Orkneys and Shetland; indeed, the Northern Isles remained a Scandinavian preserve until the middle of the fifteenth century, when they were pawned by the impecunious King Kristian I of Norway and Denmark in lieu of a dowry for the marriage of his daughter Margrethe to the future James III of Scotland (see Chapter 16).

Hindsight suggests that it was the right and realistic outcome, and that Håkon the Old had been flying in the face of the inevitable. The Western Isles were too far from Norway to remain an outpost of Scandinavia, physically, socially or culturally; their only ties with Norway in the thirteenth century were those imposed by power-politics, and those bonds were being inexorably loosened.

With this deal, Alexander, at the age of twenty-five, had vastly enlarged the kingdom of Scotland. Only the Northern Isles now remained outside his royal control. Just as his father's Treaty of York had consolidated the southern frontier in 1237, the Treaty of Perth of 1266 extended and consolidated the western frontiers of the kingdom.

For the rest of his reign, Alexander III is said to have managed the government of his realm with justice and fairness, earning the respect and loyalty of his lieges. Through his consolidation and expansion of royal power and administration he welded the disparate regions of the realm into a cohesive nation with one Church, one law and a common language. The hitherto vague concept of 'Scottishness' was developing into a sense of national consciousness, an awareness of national identity which would gain powerful expression in the Wars of Independence to come.

Meanwhile the relationship between Scotland and England remained very close, underpinned by intermarriage between the royal families and many of the leading nobles. Henry III had died in 1272, to be succeeded by his energetic and charismatic elder son, Edward I, whom Alexander found a congenial brother-in-law; they were on excellent terms, and Edward (as prince) and his wife Eleanor of Castile visited the Scottish court in 1268. To be sure, Edward (as king) tried to revive the homage issue: in 1278 he attempted to persuade Alexander to swear homage to him *for the kingdom of Scotland* at a ceremony at Westminster, but Alexander insisted that he would only swear fealty for the lands he held *in the kingdom of England*.

The Norway connection

The death of Håkon IV in 1263, and the Treaty of Perth which ensued in 1266, cleared the political air between Norway and Scotland and helped to create a greatly improved relationship. This was cemented when Alexander's only daughter, Margaret, was betrothed to the grandson of Håkon the Old in the spring of 1281. The bride was nineteen years old, the bridegroom only fourteen; but he was the new king of Norway, Erik II, son of King Magnus the Law-Reformer. The marriage of these two royal youngsters symbolised the new amity across the North Sea and augured well for the future. In the event, however, it was all to end in tragedy, not only for Scotland and Norway but most especially for Alexander III himself; for 1281 also saw the first of a series of crushing family mishaps which were to darken the last years of his vigorous and successful reign.

His wife Margaret, sister of Edward I, had died in 1275, but Alexander saw no cause to marry again. However, in June 1281 his younger son, David, fell ill and died at Stirling Castle; he was eight years old. The mourning weeds had to be shrugged aside to celebrate his daughter Margaret's wedding and coronation in Bergen two months later. But on 9 April 1283, not two years after the marriage, Queen Margaret died at Tönsberg, apparently in childbirth. She was only twenty-two years old, and she left a sickly infant daughter, also christened Margaret, the 'Maid of Norway' who would be Queen of Scots for a brief time (see Chapter 9).

And then, less than a year later, came the third and cruellest blow so far: on 17 January 1284 Alexander's elder son, Alexander the Prince of Scotland, who had been born on the very day twenty years earlier on which news of King Håkon's death had reached his father, died at Lindores Abbey in Fife after a long illness. Young Alexander had been married for just over a year, and died without issue.

The widower king had now lost all three of his children, and Scotland had lost all the immediate male heirs to the throne. But tragedy has to be overcome, and Alexander and his nation set about picking up the pieces. On 5 February 1284 the magnates of Scotland, meeting at Scone, acknowledged the infant Princess Margaret, the Maid of Norway, as heir presumptive to the Scottish throne, failing any further issue of her grandfather. Some of the nobility were unhappy about it, however: not only was she an infant, she was also a girl – and there was no precedent for a female ruler of Scotland. Besides, many of them felt that they themselves had a better claim to the Scottish throne. They comforted themselves with the thought that Alexander, who was still in his early forties, had plenty of time in which to produce another son.

Alexander recognised that he had to marry again. The bride he chose was Yolande, Comtesse de Montford, daughter of Robert IV, Comte de Dreux, a vassal of Edward I of England. They married in Jedburgh Abbey on 14 October 1285. But once again tragedy struck, the worst tragedy of all. Only five months after the wedding, Alexander III's thirty-six-year reign came to an abrupt end.

The death of Alexander III

It is now no less than five hundred and forty-two years since Alexander's death, yet the people of the country still point out the very spot where it happened, and which is called the King's Crag.

TALES OF A GRANDFATHER, CHAPTER VI

On 19 March 1286 the king held a session of his council in Edinburgh. It became a convivial affair. The weather grew boisterous as the evening lengthened, but after supper Alexander insisted on setting out to spend the night with his young wife, who was staying in a royal castle at Kinghorn, on the east coast of Fife. It meant crossing the Firth of Forth in the teeth of a northerly gale heavy with snow, and a hazardous journey on horseback through the stormy dark. The boatman at South Queensferry at first refused to sail, but complied after being taunted with cowardice. When they landed at Inverkeithing on the north shore the king was urged to stay there overnight, but he refused and took horse to ride to Kinghorn.

On the seaward side of the busy A921 coastal road between Burnt-island and Kinghorn there stands a tall memorial, surmounted by a cross, dedicated to the memory of Alexander III. It was unveiled on 19 July 1886 'before a huge concourse of spectators – a red letter day in the history of Kinghorn', according to the *Fifeshire Advertiser* of that week. Today few motorists take advantage of the small lay-by next to it to stop to have a look at the memorial and read its inscription:

> *To the Illustrious*
> *ALEXANDER III,*
> *The Last of Scotland's Celtic Kings,*
> *Who was Accidentally Killed*
> *Near this Spot*
> *March XIX, MCCLXXXVI*

To one side of the road lie the broad sands of Pettycur Bay; on the other stand the shrub-shrouded cliffs along which the king was riding that night. No one knows what happened. The surmise has always been that he became separated from his guides in the darkness, his horse stumbled, and Alexander was thrown and fell to his death at the foot of 'King's Crag', as it was later named, where his body was found next morning. He was buried in the south aisle of Dunfermline Abbey, and all Scotland mourned its king. A scrap of verse, preserved in Andrew of Wyntoun's *Original Chronicle of Scotland* (c.1400), records the profound general sense of loss:

> *Quhen [when] Alexander our kynge was dede,*
> *That Scotlande led in lauche [law] and le [peace],*
> *Away was sons [plenty] of alle [ale] and brede [bread],*
> *Of wyne and wax, of gamyn [sport] and gle [glee],*
> *Our gold was changit into lede [lead].*
> *Crist, borne into virgynyte*
> *Succoure Scotlande, and ramede [remedy],*
> *That stade [placed] is in perplexite.*

Alexander's fatal night-ride is often portrayed as the result of romantic impulse: the ardour of an impetuous lover in the prime of life (he was only forty-four years old) eager to return to the arms of his bride in order to father a son. Be that as it may, his untimely death brought an abrupt end to the mini Golden Age, and plunged Scotland into a fearful constitutional crisis which would lead inexorably to the Wars of Independence with England.

Chapter 9

JOHN BALLIOL – 'TOOM TABARD'

The full consequences of the evil were not visible at first; for, although all Alexander's children had died before him, yet one of them, who had been married to Eric, King of Norway, had left a daughter named Margaret . . .

TALES OF A GRANDFATHER, CHAPTER VI

Rail travellers who alight at Berwick-upon-Tweed are stepping straight into the cockpit of the troubled history of Anglo–Scottish relations; whether they know it or not, they are standing on the threshold of the so-called Wars of Independence led first by William Wallace (see Chapter 10) and then by Robert Bruce (see Chapter 11). The notice above Platforms 1 and 2 explains:

> *This station stands on the site of the Great Hall of Berwick Castle. Here on the 17th November 1292, the claim of Robert Bruce to the crown of Scotland was declined and the decision in favour of John Baliol was given by King Edward I before the full parliament of England and a large gathering of the nobility and populace of both England and Scotland.*

Across from the platforms the gaunt remains of the west wall of the old castle define one side of the station.[1] Not much else is left, apart

---

1 The Great Hall of Berwick Castle, which had fallen into a ruinous state by the seventeenth

from the curtain wall which King Edward built from the castle to the shore of the Tweed below after his savage sacking of the town in March 1296 (see below). A steep path leads down from the station forecourt, past a quatrefoil lily-pond, until you emerge on the shingle foreshore of the broad river. To your right, the noble Royal Border Bridge carries rail traffic rumbling and hooting its way across the Tweed; on the far side of this great viaduct Edward's 'White Wall' crow-steps its way right down to the water's edge.

It is a curiously desolate spot. There is a tang of seaweed in the air, and the melancholy cries of seabirds and waders. The ruined walls and their abandoned defensive works speak sad volumes. And all because a little princess named Margaret, who held the destiny of Scotland in her palm, had died.

The Maid of Norway

The death of Alexander III in March 1286 was a devastating blow for Scotland – but it is only in hindsight that we can see just how devastating it was. The immediate effect was simply a dynastic crisis, because the sole heir of Alexander's body, and the only surviving descendant in the direct line of the MacMalcolm dynasty, was his granddaughter Margaret, the Maid of Norway, who had been acknowledged as heir presumptive in 1284 ('our lady and rightful heir'). To fill the sudden vacuum in the business of government, a committee of six Guardians was elected at an assembly or parliament of the 'Community of the Realm' at Scone the month after Alexander's death; the Guardians comprised two bishops (William Fraser of St Andrews and Robert Wishart of Stirling), two earls (Alexander Comyn, Earl of Buchan, and Duncan MacDuff, Earl of Fife) and two barons (James the Steward and John Comyn, Lord of Badenoch). The Bruces, although a powerful family in the south-west of Scotland, were not represented. The seal which the Guardians created for their use showed the royal arms on one side and the image of St Andrew on his cross on the other, with the legend: 'Andrew be leader of the Scots, your fellow countrymen'.

---

century, fell victim to the building frenzy of the Railway Age in the nineteenth century. In 1844 an Act of Parliament was passed to permit the linking of the North British Railway line from Edinburgh to Berwick and the Great North British Railway line from London to Berwick. The ruined castle, hard by the north end of Stephenson's magnificent Royal Border Bridge over the river, was considered the most suitable site for the station, which was formally opened in June 1846.

It was a sign of the growing political maturity of the nation that its leaders could come to such an effective arrangement, despite threatening rumblings of discontent from some of the leading noble families – especially the two who thought themselves legitimate claimants to the throne: the Balliols (supported by the Comyns) and the Bruces.

The uncertainty over the succession continued for a few months, however; Alexander's young French widow, Yolande, claimed to be pregnant – whether this was genuine or feigned only time would tell – which raised the possibility of the birth of a posthumous heir. Within a few months, however, it became clear that she was not with child, and in October 1286 the Princess Margaret, Maid of Norway, was formally accepted as Queen of Scots.

Meanwhile, embassies were sent to Edward I, the king of England – as a courtesy, at least: Edward was the child's great-uncle, after all, and England had a legitimate interest in the royal affairs of its neighbour. Besides, Edward was by then one of the most powerful and respected kings in Europe. There was also the question of the Maid of Norway's marriage prospects. The obvious candidate for the infant queen's hand, given the ties between the two kingdoms, was Edward I's two-year-old son, Edward, Earl of Caernarvon, the future Edward II. Edward I also had the stature and authority to ensure the stability of the kingdom during Margaret's minority.

Soon after Margaret's birth in Norway, Alexander III had written to Edward hinting at the desirability of a royal marriage between his granddaughter and a member of Edward's family. A marriage between the Queen of Scots and the heir to the throne of England would have profound dynastic significance, and would probably lead to a Union of the Crowns. Not everyone relished that prospect – the Church in Scotland, in particular, jealously cherished its independence from England – but it seems that Scotland in general preferred a 'foreign', English marriage, if only to avoid the tensions which marriage to a Scottish nobleman might produce.

In Norway, King Erik was naturally concerned about his young daughter's prospects, at the mercy of warring factions, perhaps, and he too made a diplomatic approach to Edward of England. There was a serious problem to overcome, however, because the two infants were closely related – Edward of Caernarvon's father and the Maid of Norway's grandmother were brother and sister – and this family relationship was within the prohibited degrees of canon law. Papal dispensation was sought.

The Guardians were determined that Scotland should remain a

The complex of megalithic standing stones at Calanais, on the Isle of Lewis. Astronomical observatory, power-centre or temple? Or all three? Built long before Stonehenge and the pyramids of Egypt, Calanais is the most impressive surviving monument of the Neolithic Age.

Maes Howe, on Orkney, is the finest chambered tomb in north-western Europe. In the twelfth century, Norsemen broke into it and covered its walls with the largest collection of runic graffiti ever discovered.

The broch on the tiny island of Mousa, off the mainland of Shetland, has survived almost intact. Built as a defensive structure in the Iron Age about two thousand years ago, it was used on at least two occasions as a refuge for runaway lovers in the viking age.

The remains of the Antonine Wall at Watling Lodge. The wall, a continuous barrier built by the Romans between the Forth and the Clyde, consisted of a massive turf rampart protected by a deep ditch. It was in use for only twenty years.

The Aberlemno Stone is believed to depict the great victory of the Picts over the Northumbrians at the Battle of Dunnichen (AD 685). The sculpture on the reverse of the stone is subtly coded. The Picts are bare-headed, with long flowing hair, whereas the Northumbrians wear helmets. The Pictish horses are light and sprightly, with long tails; the Northumbrian horses are more heavily built, with trimmed (rather than docked) tails.

In the top tier, a Pictish cavalryman pursues a Northumbrian who is fleeing the battlefield on a Pictish horse. In the middle tier, Pictish infantrymen confront a charging Northumbrian cavalryman with spear levelled. The Picts are drawn up in three ranks: in the lead stands a swordsman carrying a shield with a spiked boss; behind him a comrade wields a long thrusting-spear; and behind him a third infantryman holds a throwing-spear. The Northumbrian horseman holds the reins with one hand, with his shield strapped to his arm, and so has only one arm free to wield his weapons.

In the bottom tier, a Pictish cavalryman confronts a Northumbrian cavalryman. Here the Pictish superiority in horsemanship is emphasised. The Pict controls his horse with his knees, leaving both hands free. The Northumbrian, again, has only his right arm free. In the bottom right-hand corner, an outsize Northumbrian lies dead. The enlargement suggests a special importance – perhaps he is the King of Northumbria (Ecgfrith) himself. A raven tears at the flesh of his unprotected throat.

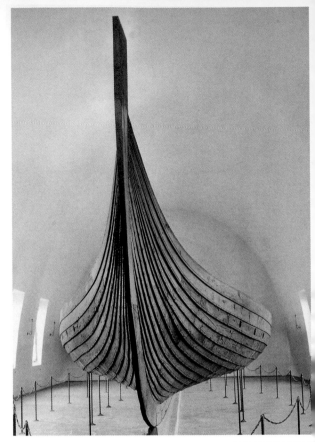

The Gokstad ship, excavated in Norway in 1880 and now on display in the Viking Ship Hall at Bygdøy in Oslo, has been called the most beautiful ship ever built. It has become the most vivid icon of the viking age: flexible, lean and menacing, it is the epitome of viking power.

Macbeth met his death in 1057 in battle against Malcolm Canmore, not at Dunsinane but at Lumphanan, in Aberdeenshire. The grassy mound known as the Peel Ring of Lumphanan conceals the remains of an Anglo-Norman fortified 'motte-and-bailey'. Although it dates from the early thirteenth century, local tradition associates it with Macbeth's last stand.

Jedburgh Abbey was founded as a priory under the patronage of David I in 1138 and raised to the status of an abbey by his grandson and successor, Malcolm IV, in 1154. It was burned during the 'Rough Wooing' by Henry VIII in the 1540s, and further damaged during the Reformation in 1559.

Arbroath Abbey was founded by William 'the Lion' (r.1165–1214) in 1178 and dedicated to Thomas à Becket, mortal enemy of William's captor Henry II. It was to the ruins of the abbey that the Stone of Destiny was returned in April 1951 by four young Scottish Nationalists who had earlier abducted it from Westminster Abbey.

Norham Castle, a mighty fortress on the English side of the Tweed, ten kilometres south-west of Berwick-upon-Tweed, was the venue chosen by Edward I for his arbitration over the succession crisis in Scotland after the death of the Maid of Norway. It was here, in 1291–92, that most of the meetings were held which led to Edward's decision in favour of John Balliol ('Toom Tabard').

The Coronation Chair in Westminster Abbey, specially built by Edward I to hold the Stone of Destiny which Edward removed from Scotland as a trophy of war in 1296. Although the Stone was due to be returned in 1328, it was not formally brought back to Scotland until 1996.

No contemporary likeness of William Wallace has survived. Down the centuries, artists have portrayed him according to the taste of the times: (top left) portrait by the eleventh Earl of Buchan after an unknown artist; (top right) monumental statue in pink stone, carved by John Smith in 1814, erected by the eccentric Earl of Buchan on his estate at Bemersyde, near Dryburgh in the Borders; (bottom left) statue by Tom Church, inspired by the 1995 film *Braveheart*, at the foot of the Abbey Craig on which the Wallace Monument stands; (bottom right) statue on the façade of the Wallace Monument.

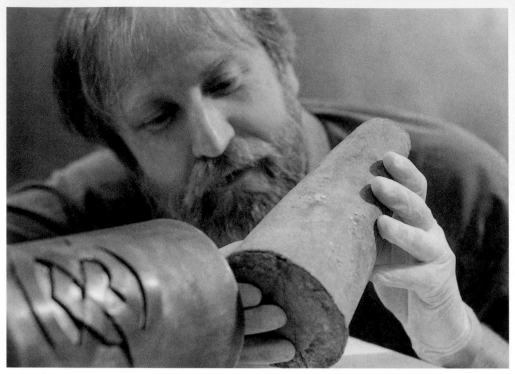

Richard Welander of Historic Scotland places in a new casket the lead cone which is believed to contain the heart of Robert Bruce. Bruce's heart had been taken, at his wish, on a Crusade, and then buried somewhere in Melrose Abbey. The lead cone was found in the abbey during excavations in 1921 and reburied, then rediscovered during new excavations in 1996. In June 1998 it was re-interred at a solemn ceremony: 'A noble hart may have nane ease…gif freedom failye.'

The Monymusk Reliquary (*Breccbennach Chaluim Cille*), a tiny bronze-and-silver-covered wooden casket dating from the eighth century, was said to have contained the relics of St Columba. The Abbot of Arbroath, as hereditary keeper of the casket (*Deòradh*, or Dewar), carried it at the Battle of Bannockburn in 1314.

distinct kingdom in any such dynastic union, and long and painstaking negotiations ensued. At last, by November 1289, all three sides – Scotland, Norway and England – were ready to subscribe to a preliminary treaty, which was confirmed in the Treaty of Birgham, on the north side of the Tweed between Kelso and Coldstream, in July 1290.

The marriage settlement guaranteed that Scotland would remain a separate and independent kingdom. The treaty stipulated that the Scottish realm was to remain 'separate and divided from England according to its rightful boundaries, free in itself and without subjection', and that its rights, laws, liberties and customs were 'wholly and inviolably preserved' for all time. Should Edward and Margaret die childless, her kingdom would pass to her nearest heir 'wholly, freely, absolutely, and without any subjection'.

That was the intention, anyway. But Edward's negotiators added the ominous words: 'Saving always the right of our lord king, and of any other whomsoever, that has pertained to him . . . before the time of the present agreement, or which in any just way ought to pertain to him in the future.' And King Edward, on ratifying the treaty, insisted on appointing the new Bishop of Durham (Anthony Bek) as his 'lieutenant' in Scotland on behalf of the royal pair, and required the Scottish Guardians to obey the bishop (in the event, the appointment seems to have been largely ignored in Scotland).

In May 1290, Edward I sent 'a great ship' from Yarmouth to fetch his future daughter-in-law from Norway, bearing toothsome gifts of sugar-loaves, gingerbread, figs and raisins. King Erik of Norway insisted on using a Norwegian vessel, however, and the English ship returned without her. In September 1290 the Maid of Norway set sail from Bergen, en route for Leith. It was a wild, storm-tossed voyage, and the ship was driven far off course to Orkney (which was still Norwegian territory). Margaret's health, never robust, broke under the strain and she was 'seized with illness at sea', according to the Norwegian bishop accompanying her. She was carried ashore, more dead than alive, and there she died. Her body was taken back to Bergen, where it was 'narrowly examined' by her father and then buried beside her mother in Christ's Kirk in Bergen. She was not yet eight years old, and had been Queen of Scots for four years and six months. With her sad little death the MacMalcolm dynasty came to an end.

Margaret's death created a very real crisis of succession: now there was not a minority to deal with, but an interregnum with a disputed succession. The terms of the Treaty of Birgham were nullified, of course, and all thoughts had to turn to identifying the person who had the best claim to the vacant throne.

Now the figure of Edward I of England suddenly loomed larger, and much more ominous:

> *He was a very brave man, and a good soldier, – wise, skilful, and prudent, but unhappily very ambitious, and desirous of extending his royal authority, without caring much whether he did so by right means or by those which were unjust. And although it is a great sin to covet that which does not belong to you, and a still greater to endeavour to possess yourself of it by any unfair practices, yet his desire of adding the kingdom of Scotland to that of England was so great, that Edward was unable to resist it.*
>
> TALES OF A GRANDFATHER, CHAPTER VI

Edward I, who was to be given the posthumous sobriquet of *Malleus Scottorum* ('Hammer of the Scots'), was the most compelling of the Plantagenet kings of England. In Scotland he has always been regarded as a ruthless despot, intent only on subjugating his little neighbour to his unscrupulous will; but in England his reputation is coloured by a romantic glow. He was the dashing Crusader knight *par excellence*, so devoted to his Spanish wife, Eleanor of Castile, that when she died in 1290 in Nottinghamshire he constructed a series of twelve 'Eleanor Crosses' to mark the places where the funeral cortège stopped on its way to her burial at Westminster.[1]

When the crisis of succession struck Scotland in 1290 Edward was fifty years old, a tall, handsome, forceful, dominating figure, experienced in all the arts of war and peace (he was a great lover of poetry, music and chess), a charming friend and a menacing foe. He was totally committed to strengthening the kingdom he had inherited in 1274. He reorganised the financial system, the army and the feudal holdings of his barons. He also concentrated on extending his western frontier: in two violent campaigns (1276–7 and 1282–3) he annexed north and west Wales. This was the man who would become Scotland's most implacable enemy – but whose enmity, paradoxically, would unite Scotland as a nation.

Fiona Watson, senior lecturer in History at Stirling University and

---

1 An 'Eleanor Cross', erected by Middleton Barry in 1865, stands in the forecourt of Charing Cross Station in London; it is a replica of the original which King Edward put up in the ancient village of Charing.

the author of *Under the Hammer* (1998), makes no secret of her admiration for Edward I:

> *I am absolutely fascinated by him. Despite what has been written about him – whether in England or Scotland or Ireland or France, because he had an impact on all these areas – I think people always tend to admire him, grudgingly or otherwise. He was an incredibly impressive person, and still is to this day, despite any revisionist ideas we might have. From Scotland's point of view it was very unfortunate that we had a dynastic crisis at a time when England had such a dynamic king. I think that is one of the biggest tragedies of the period.*

The Competitors

The succession to the throne of Scotland was wide open. There were no fewer than thirteen claimants – 'Competitors', as they were called; many of them were remote or foreign (they included King Erik of Norway, as father of the Maid of Norway). But there were only two who really mattered: John Balliol (c.1250–1313), Lord of Galloway, and Robert Bruce (1210–95), now in his eighties, the fifth Lord of Annandale and grandfather of the future king.

John Balliol was descended from a Picardy nobleman, John de Bailleul, who had been a landowner in England under William Rufus and whose son, Guy, came to Scotland in the reign of David I. In 1263 his father, John Balliol the elder, had founded Balliol College, Oxford, as an act of penance for assaulting the Bishop of Durham, and his wealthy mother, Devorgilla, Lady of Galloway, had founded the beautiful and romantic Sweetheart Abbey a few miles south of Dumfries in memory of her husband in 1273 – it is his embalmed 'sweet heart' which was buried with her there when she died in 1290.

Robert Bruce was descended from an old Normandy family named de Brus, from Bruis (Brix), who were given lands in north Yorkshire by Henry I; the family came to Scotland in the reign of David I in about 1120, when Robert de Brus was granted the Lordship of Annandale and its attendant castles of Annan and Lochmaben as a military fief in what is now Dumfriesshire.[1] Robert de Brus was the ancestor of a long

---

1 Nothing remains today of Annan Castle. The large oval site of the original wooden motte-and-bailey castle at Lochmaben is now the fourteenth tee of the golf course to the south-west of the modern town; the ruins of the thirteenth-century stone castle which superseded it occupy a promontory at the southern end of Castle Loch.

line of Bruce Lords of Annandale, most of whom were called, rather confusingly, Robert. The fourth Robert Bruce, Lord of Annandale, married into the King David dynasty, as did one of the Balliol family: they married daughters of David, Earl of Huntingdon, the youngest son of King Malcolm IV and a grandson of David I.

Robert Bruce (the 'Competitor') could claim a greater nearness of degree than his rival John Balliol: he was the grandson, on his father's side, of Isabella, the *younger* daughter of David, Earl of Huntingdon. Balliol, the younger of the two men, nevertheless had the senior claim: he was the great-grandson, on his mother's side, of Margaret, the *eldest* daughter of Earl David. The argument would centre on which was the more important, proximity or primogeniture.

The competition for the throne has come to be known as the 'Great Cause'. For a while it threatened to degenerate into civil war between supporters of the two factions. The most powerful family in Scotland were the Comyns, Lords of Badenoch and Earls of Buchan; John Comyn, Lord of Badenoch, who was himself one of the lesser Competitors, was Balliol's brother-in-law, and there was no love lost between the Comyns and the Bruces.

To avert an armed struggle the Guardians approached Edward I to arbitrate between the claimants. Edward was more than willing to undertake the task of honest broker, and summoned the Scots to a parliament to be held on 6 May 1291 at Norham Castle, the great stronghold of the Bishop of Durham on the English side of the Tweed.

The 'Great Cause'

> *Day sat on Norham's castled steep,*
> *And Tweed's fair river, broad and deep,*
> *And Cheviot's mountains lone:*
> *The battled towers, the donjon keep,*
> *The loophole grates, where captives weep,*
> *The flanking walls that round it sweep,*
> *In yellow lustre shone.*
> SIR WALTER SCOTT, *MARMION*

Norham Castle had been chosen with great care by Edward I as the venue for the business at hand. Its romantic ruins still superintend the southern bank of the River Tweed, ten kilometres south-west of Berwick-upon-Tweed along the A698 and up the B6470. It was the most impregnable (for a time, at least) of all the mighty fortresses built to defend the 'debatable lands' on each side of the border, both militarily and diplomatically. Founded by Bishop Ranulph Flambard of Durham in 1121 and greatly strengthened in the 1160s, it was to withstand three prolonged sieges during the Wars of Independence (see Chapter 11).

Today the solid remains of the Great Hall stand open in moated splendour in a green sweep of manicured English Heritage grass. This was where the business of the Great Cause was conducted over seventeen long months. High up on the back wall you can still see the outline of the fireplace of the first-floor chamber where matters of state were discussed and banquets served.

Edward I arrived at Norham in May 1291 in full panoply, accompanied by the northern levies of England, to be entertained by Bishop Anthony Bek of Durham. The Scots stopped just north of the border, wanting King Edward to cross the Tweed and come to them, but Edward would not shift. When the Scots reluctantly sent a delegation across the Tweed they were met with a demand that Edward must first be acknowledged as the Lord Superior of Scotland before he would settle the succession – as judge, not arbiter; they were given three weeks to make up their minds.

The Scots were deeply affronted by this reiteration of old pretensions, and argued that only a sovereign could commit a realm in this way. But Edward had made his point, and within a matter of days one of the leading Competitors, Robert Bruce, accepted his overlordship and his right to sasine (legal possession of feudal property) of the kingdom. Others followed this lead; a few days later, John Balliol was the last of the Competitors to accept the inevitable. On 12 June the Scottish Community of the Realm finally came to Norham, and the lengthy process of adjudication began; as a favour to the Scots, King Edward allowed some of the meetings to be held in Berwick Castle, which was then on the Scottish side of the border.[1]

The adjudication of the Great Cause dragged on, with four lengthy adjournments. The Competitors were whittled down to a short-list of two: John Balliol and Robert Bruce. A panel of 104 arbiters or 'auditors'

---

1 Berwick-upon-Tweed had been given its royal charter by David I in 1120. From then on the town and its castle bore much of the brunt of Anglo–Scottish border conflict. Once Scotland's richest port, it changed hands between Scotland and England no fewer than thirteen times before it was finally surrendered to England in 1482. It was the scene of umpteen sieges and sackings, and especially of the savage massacre of 1296.

was appointed – forty each nominated by Balliol and Bruce, and twenty-four from Edward's council. Eventually, on 6 November 1292, the court adjudicated in favour of Balliol – indeed, twenty-nine of Bruce's own auditors voted for Balliol: primogeniture, it was decided, was more significant than proximity.

Was it a perverse choice? Had Edward somehow manipulated the decision to suit his own ends? Fiona Watson has no doubt that it was the correct outcome:

> The decision of Edward I to choose Balliol as king has gone down in Scottish history as being a travesty of justice – the justice of the Bruce claim to the throne. But historians are no longer prepared to accept that. In terms of the claims of the two men, Balliol had the most obviously straightforward claim because of the way in which the laws of primogeniture had evolved by the thirteenth century. Bruce's big claim was that he was a generation nearer to the previous king, but that was irrelevant; so it would not have come as any surprise to anyone that Balliol was chosen as king.
>
> The argument has been advanced that Balliol was chosen because he was the weaker man, the man who would bend the more easily to Edward's will. In fact it was Robert Bruce the Competitor, not John Balliol, who was the first to accept Edward's claim to overlordship of Scotland, and who did so at every oppor-tunity thereafter.

Two days after the court's verdict was announced, Bruce formally resigned his claim to his son and heirs, so that it would not be lost after his death; he retired to his castle at Lochmaben and took no further part in politics (he died in 1295). His son Robert Bruce, Earl of Carrick, in turn surrendered his earldom to his own son, Robert Bruce (the future king), who was now eighteen years old. The Bruce claim to the throne was anything but dead.

Now, if not before, Edward I must have realised that he had a golden opportunity to interfere decisively in the future of the northern kingdom, perhaps even to fulfil what may well have been a deep-seated imperial ambition – to be king of all the territories of Britain. Ted Cowan says:

> This was Edward's chance. During or just before the Great Cause, when he sat in the court at Berwick and decided who had the best claim, it must have occurred to Edward that he could

manipulate this situation to his own advantage. After all, he had just conquered Wales, and he saw an opportunity of making himself ruler here in Scotland as well, the first ruler of the whole of the British Isles. One can hardly blame him – he was a politician, after all, and a very acute man. Why not exploit the situation to suit himself?

The die was now cast. On 17 November 1292, in the Great Hall of Berwick Castle, Edward formally accepted the decision of the auditors and chose John Balliol as the next King of Scots. Next day, in the chancel of St Cuthbert's Church in Norham, he accepted the homage of Balliol for the kingdom of Scotland.[1]

Three days later, after paying homage to Edward, Balliol left for Scone, where he was inaugurated as King of Scots on the Stone of Scone inside the abbey church on 30 November 1292 – St Andrew's Day. It was to be the last time a King of Scots would sit on the royal Stone at Scone. Within a month Balliol and many Scottish nobles had to travel to Newcastle to swear fealty yet again for his kingdom to King Edward. It was the start of an unhappy four-year reign which ended in humiliation for King John Balliol and disaster for Scotland, and left Balliol with the jeering sobriquet of 'Toom Tabard' (Empty Tunic) with which he has come down in history.

There are few details available of Balliol's reign. It is clear that much of the authority which had been exercised by the Guardians during the Maid of Norway's minority was passed to the Community of the Realm, in the shape of a parliament; and there is evidence that King John tried to carry out the functions expected of a king, despite the implacable enmity of the Bruces. But Edward I was clearly intent on humiliating him at every turn. He usurped the right to hear appeals from Scottish judgements, and King John was even ordered by the Sheriff of Northumberland to appear before a court in London to account for a wine-bill left unpaid by Alexander III. John never had a chance, according to Fiona Watson:

Balliol was not well known in Scotland before he became king, but he did a reasonable job, considering that he was up against

---

1   It comes as a surprise to discover that the solid, Romanesque St Cuthbert's Church at Norham today, set in a huge graveyard which testifies to its antiquity, is the very one in whose chancel Balliol paid homage to Edward I all these centuries ago. Its survival through all the alarums and excursions of the Middle Ages is little short of miraculous.

a king who had the best legal mind in Europe – a man, moreover, who was prepared to use military force to back up his claims. From south of the border, Edward was constantly telling him what to do. I do not think anyone could have stood up to Edward; and anyone who tried would have had to fight a war over it. That was a decision which Balliol took a long time to make – quite rightly, because it would plunge Scotland into a war with a very formidable adversary.

I think John Balliol's reputation is due for serious revision – he certainly deserves much more attention and much more understanding; but that devastating nickname, 'Toom Tabard', is difficult to get round, and it is even more difficult to reach the real John Balliol through the propaganda and vilification engendered by the man who usurped his throne – Robert the Bruce.

In 1294, less than two years after his accession, King John was instructed to raise troops to assist Edward in his war with Philippe IV ('Philippe the Fair') of France over Gascony. That was one demand too many. In July 1295 a meeting of parliament at Scone decided to put the direction of affairs into the hands of a Council of Twelve, made up of four bishops, four earls and four barons – a new form of Guardianship, in effect. John Balliol remained king, but was effectively sidelined: the real power behind the governance of Scotland was in the hands of Balliol's main supporters, the Comyn family.

In October the hard-line Council of Twelve decided to look for help abroad. In Paris that month they concluded a mutual defence treaty with Edward's arch-enemy Philippe IV of France, who was giving Edward as hard a time as Edward was giving Scotland. It was the start of what has become fondly known, in Scotland at least, as the 'Auld Alliance'. In practical terms, the Auld Alliance was little more than a sentimental association between two countries which for a long time shared a certain antipathy towards England. Historians tend to look askance at it. During the Wars of Independence it proved of some value in terms of French political and diplomatic intercession with the papacy or as a potential threat against England; but there was very little in terms of military co-operation. It helped Scotland to maintain a role as a player in European politics, and was an alliance of mutual self-interest, but there is no indication that either of the allies was ever prepared to go to any lengths to support the other at the expense of its own interests.

The 1295 Treaty of Paris guaranteed that Scotland would maintain hostile pressure on England in return for military aid from France should Scotland be invaded. It was to be cemented by a future marriage between John Balliol's son and heir, Edward Balliol, and Jeanne de Valois, niece of Philippe IV (in the event, the marriage never took place). The treaty was ratified by the full Community of the Realm at Dunfermline in February 1296. It was an implicit declaration of war on England; Edward I certainly read it as an open act of rebellion by the country over which he claimed overlordship, and in the autumn of 1295 he had put the north of England on a war footing.

Effectively, the Treaty of Paris was the start of what have become known as the 'Wars of Independence'; to the English they were simply the 'Scottish Wars', but perhaps they could more accurately be described as 'Wars of Preservation'. Buoyed up with the hope of French military assistance, Scotland raised a national army which was ordered to assemble at Caddonlea, the traditional site of a Scottish *wapinschaw* ('inspection of weapons'), four miles north of Selkirk, on 11 March 1296. Significantly, but not surprisingly, the Bruces refused to attend the muster; as a result their Annandale lands were declared forfeit by King John, and granted to his father-in-law John Comyn, Earl of Buchan.

King Edward I was also on the move. He had summoned his feudal host to assemble at Newcastle upon Tyne on 1 March; it was a formidable force, comprising an estimated four thousand cavalry and twenty-five thousand infantry – larger by far than the Scottish army which would assemble at Selkirk on 18 March. By the middle of March, Edward had joined the English army in person as it moved to a new encampment near the village of Brunton, north of Alnwick. He celebrated Easter Day (25 March) at Wark Castle, just south of the Tweed, and here he received renewed pledges of fealty from the Bruces (father and son) and other Scottish barons for their lands in Scotland:

I shall be faithful and loyal, and shall maintain faith and loyalty to King Edward, King of England, and to his heirs, in matters of life and limb and of earthly honour against all mortal men; and never shall I bear arms for anyone against him or his heirs . . .

In his response, King Edward tellingly referred to John Balliol as 'the former King of Scotland' (*qui fust Roy d'Escoce*). The King of Scots was king no more; to the Bruces it could only have meant that the throne was up for grabs again.

It was the Scots who struck the first blow. On 26 March, the day after the ceremony at Wark, a strong Scottish force from the former Bruce fiefdom of Annandale, led by John Comyn the Younger of Buchan, attacked Carlisle Castle, which was held by the dispossessed Lord of Annandale and his son, young Robert Bruce, Earl of Carrick; but Carlisle, with its formidable fortifications, was too strong to be stormed, and the attack was repulsed with little difficulty.

King Edward now unleashed the counter-invasion he had been planning all winter. He moved across the border at Coldstream and on 30 March launched a ferocious assault on the royal burgh of Berwick, which was then the wealthiest commercial town in Scotland. The timber palisade walls of the town offered no defence, and Berwick was sacked with terrible brutality. The inhabitants were massacred without mercy – women and children as well as men. Of the town's 12,500 inhabitants, only five thousand survived the slaughter. The wholesale destruction of Berwick quickly became a byword for savagery, the ultimate war atrocity. The castle held out, however, until the garrison, commanded by Sir William Douglas (who offered himself as hostage), were promised truce and safe conduct from the burning town.

The Scots retaliated with an equally savage raid deep into Northumberland on 8 April, burning villages and abbeys all the way to Hexham. This raid, with English claims of gratuitous cruelty (including the burning alive of schoolchildren in Hexham), became as much of a byword for merciless brutality as the sack of Berwick. Edward I ignored it. He stayed on in Berwick for the next month, supervising the rebuilding of the town and its flimsy defences, and repopulating it with English burgesses; it was now that he ordered the construction of the curtain wall (the 'White Wall') from the castle down to the shore.

The Scots raiding force moved back across the border and up to English-held Dunbar, where the castle was opened to them by the Governor's wife, the Countess of March. Part of the English army, under the command of John de Warenne, the Earl of Surrey (ironically, John Balliol's brother-in-law), was sent north to retake the castle at Dunbar. Surrey laid siege to the fortress on 25 April. Two days later the main body of King John's army, under the command of John Comyn (the 'Red Comyn'), made an attempt to raise the siege, but it was no match for the heavy English cavalry and the disciplined men-at-arms. The Scottish cavalry fled the field, and the foot-soldiers were cut down relentlessly as they scattered. English sources claimed that ten thousand Scots were killed, which seems an impossibly exaggerated figure. Nevertheless the casualties among the Scottish foot-soldiery were heavy. The castle promptly surrendered, and many of the leading barons of Scotland – including Atholl, Ross, Menteith and John Comyn the Younger – were taken captive and sent to the Tower of London.

'Toom Tabard'

Edward defeated the Scottish army in a great battle near Dunbar, and Baliol, who seems to have been a mean-spirited man, gave up the contest.

TALES OF A GRANDFATHER, CHAPTER VI

It was the end of the 'rebellion'. Scottish resistance simply collapsed after Dunbar Castle surrendered. The castles of Roxburgh, Edinburgh, Stirling and Perth followed suit. Scotland lay paralysed and helpless. John Balliol sent a letter to Edward in Perth, suing for peace, but Edward would be satisfied with nothing less than unconditional surrender. On 2 July 1296 Balliol met Bishop Bek of Durham at Kincardine Castle, where he issued his document of surrender:

> ... *seeing that we have by evil and false council, and our own folly, grievously offended and angered our lord Edward, by the Grace of God, King of England ... Therefore we, acting under no constraint, and of our own free will, have surrendered to him the land of Scotland and all its people ...*

A week later, on 8 July, at a humiliating ceremony in Montrose, Balliol formally resigned his kingdom to Edward and was subjected to the ultimate ignominy: he was stripped of his crown, sceptre, ring and girdle, and the red and gold royal insignia were ripped from his surcoat, giving rise to that nickname of 'Toom Tabard'. He and his son were sent into captivity in the Tower of London, along with the last of his supporters still at large, including John Comyn the Elder of Badenoch and the Earl of Buchan. Balliol was soon moved to more comfortable house arrest in Hertford, and after three years he would be released into papal custody and permitted to retire to his family's estates in Picardy in France, where he died in 1313.

Steve Boardman is more sympathetic to John Balliol than Sir Walter Scott was:

I think of Balliol as one of those unfortunate figures who simply gets run over by history. At one stage he tried to assert his own power as Scottish king and to govern effectively, but he was faced with one of the most powerful kings in Western Europe, a massively prestigious figure. Edward I had destroyed the power of the Welsh princes in the 1280s, and in the 1290s he wanted to make his rights in Scotland stick: he wanted to make something concrete of the vague claim to overlordship which previous English kings had occasionally asserted. Edward was in the position and was of the mind to make these vague claims to overlordship a reality in the years after 1292.

In that sense, Balliol was caught in a unique situation: because of the nature of the competition for the throne, he had already acknowledged Edward specifically as the overlord of Scotland. He was dealing with a very powerful adversary, and his own support within Scotland was limited by the disaffection of the Bruces and their supporters. He was simply unable to cope with that combination of circumstances. But that does not mean that when he came to the throne he intended to be any less of a king than any of his predecessors had been; he was, quite simply, hopelessly outgunned.

From Montrose, Edward I made a triumphal progress north as far as the Moray Firth. Then he ransacked the country, systematically and purposefully. The Great Seal of Scotland was ceremoniously broken in two. The Stone of Scone was removed and sent south to Westminster Abbey, where it was placed in the chapel dedicated to St Edward the Confessor. The state archives were packed into fifty-three containers and shipped out of the country. Edward also ordered the removal of the Scottish regalia (the crown, sceptre, sword, ring and royal robe) and the precious relic of Scotland's only royal saint, the Black Rood of St Margaret, which had comforted her on her deathbed; it was never seen in Scotland again.[1]

Dauvit Brown has studied Edward's motives for the looting of the symbols and the raiding of the government archives:

---

1 Tradition has it that it was returned to Scotland as part of the 1328 Treaty of Edinburgh/ Northampton (see page 192), and recaptured at the Battle of Neville's Cross in 1346. A list of relics which arrived at Durham Cathedral after 1346 included 'a silver gilt cross, with part of the middle of black wood'. It disappeared during the Reformation.

The English kings and their government had by this stage become one of the most bureaucratic in Europe. The reason why they took all the Scottish government records was not to suggest that Scotland had never existed as a kingdom, but because Edward I, as the sovereign lord, had taken control of it and because, in order to govern Scotland properly, he needed to have on file all the previous records of the kings.

It was typical of their approach to their task that they did not just throw things into sacks and take them south; they compiled an inventory of what they were taking. There is a lengthy and impressive list of the titles, at least, and brief descriptions of what the documents were. Sadly, the documents were lost en route: they sank with their ship on the way south, which was a great loss. If those records still existed we would have a much more complete set of evidence relating to government in Scotland and many more royal charters and official documents of that kind.

It has been claimed that Edward also ransacked the country for any histories and chronicles which existed and took them away, too – which was why chroniclers like John of Fordun had to start writing Scotland's history from scratch. But, in fact, narrative histories were not listed in the inventory of documents removed; they would not have been part of the government archives.

Edward also clearly believed that taking the Stone of Scone, the inaugural stone of the kings of Scots, was the absolute and final symbol that Scotland had ceased to be a kingdom. But what seems to have happened is that the Stone and its legend became even more famous; references to it as the 'Stone of Destiny' start now, along with the story that wherever the Stone is, the Scots will rule. Edward may have thought that it represented a full-stop and a final statement of Scottish existence; but as far as the Scottish people were concerned, it was the beginning of a new chapter.

That new chapter was still a long way off, however. Before Edward left Scotland, a parliament was held in Berwick on 28 August, at which a compilation was made of more than 1,500 earls, lords, bishops and leading burgesses who had sworn fealty to him and formally recorded their homage to him as King of Scotland. This document has come to be known as the 'Ragman Roll' from the tangle of ribbons which hung from the seals of the signatories.

John Balliol's name is there. So is that of Robert Bruce, son of Bruce the Competitor (who had died in 1295), and of his twenty-two-year-old son Robert, Earl of Carrick. Every notable family, every major landowner, every significant member of the gentry – all were required to make legal acknowledgement of Edward's overlordship. But one name among the lesser gentry is missing: the name of William Wallace.

Only hindsight can claim to know how significant an omission this was. The Comyn-led government of Scotland was discredited, with most of its leaders incarcerated in castles throughout England. Of the aristocratic families of Scotland, only the Bruces were still in favour with the autocratic King of England – but even the Bruces had been contemptuously dismissed. When the older Robert Bruce, father of the future king, importuned Edward about the cherished Bruce claim to the throne, Edward is said (by Walter Bower in his *Scotichronicon*) to have given the withering reply, 'Have we nothing else to do but win kingdoms for you?'

What was the driving force behind Edward's single-minded, ruthless treatment of Scotland? Fiona Watson finds it an enigma:

> *Edward was already embroiled in a bitter dispute with France over Gascony, of which he was Duke. But that made no difference – he simply ditched Gascony (temporarily, in his mind) to go for Scotland. And that makes no sense: Gascony was one of the richest parts of the English empire, and to lose it for a cold, fairly barren northern kingdom is bizarre. But Edward was the sort of man who never gave up: if he wanted something, he went for it, again and again and again.*
>
> *Edward was absolutely determined to subdue Scotland, but one cannot be sure why, other than sheer pride and stubbornness. He did it in the face of mounting protest at home over the expense of his seemingly endless wars and the ever-increasing burden of taxation. So there are some large unanswered questions about Edward's character and motives; but ultimately, to my mind, he was simply an obsessive who refused to be balked from his purpose. That made him very dangerous indeed as far as Scotland was concerned.*

Edward I left his newly acquired kingdom in the hands of the Earl of Surrey as Governor and Hugh de Cressingham as Treasurer. An exchequer was established at Berwick on the Westminster model. English sheriffs and justiciars were appointed the length and breadth of the country. English soldiers garrisoned the major castles. The subjugation was complete; it had taken Edward I only five months to achieve.

> *Perhaps Edward thought to himself, that, by uniting the whole island of Britain under one king and one government, he would do so much good by preventing future wars, as might be an excuse for the force and fraud he made use of to bring about his purpose. But . . . the happy prospect that England and Scotland would be united under one government, was so far from being brought nearer by Edward's unprincipled usurpation, that the hatred and violence of national antipathy which arose betwixt the sister countries, removed to a distance, almost incalculable, the prospect of their becoming one people, for which nature seemed to design them.*
>
> *TALES OF A GRANDFATHER*, CHAPTER VI

King Edward thought he had settled the 'Scottish question' once and for all. There is a story, recorded by Sir Thomas Grey of Heaton (near Newcastle) in his *Scalacronica* (written while he was imprisoned in Edinburgh Castle in 1355–57), that as Edward left Berwick in September 1296 he said to his companions (in French), 'A man does good business when he rids himself of a turd' (*Bon besoigne fait qy du merde se delivrer*). But if Edward thought he was rid of the business, he was very wrong.

Chapter 10

WILLIAM WALLACE

Scotland was, therefore, in great distress, and the inhabitants, exceedingly enraged, only wanted some leader to command them, to rise up in a body against the English or Southern men, as they called them, and recover the liberty and independence of their country, which had been destroyed by Edward the First. Such a leader arose in the person of WILLIAM WALLACE, whose name is still so often mentioned in Scotland.

TALES OF A GRANDFATHER, CHAPTER VII

On the first floor ('Life of Wallace') of the National Wallace Monument, which rears to a height of sixty-seven metres on the top of the eminence of the Abbey Craig near Stirling, a glass case displays the most treasured icon of this shrine to the memory of William Wallace, National Hero of Scotland – 'Wallace's Sword'.

It is a fearsome-looking weapon: a traditional two-handed Scottish broadsword, measuring 1.7 metres from the top of the hilt to the tip of the blade. The information panel proclaims it to be the weapon wielded by Wallace himself, and draws the conclusion that he must have been a giant of a man: 'It is reasonable to assume that, in order to wield a sword of this size, Wallace would have had to be of considerable stature – at least six foot six inches in height.'

Meanwhile, in the 'Hall of Heroes' above, TV broadcaster and weaponry expert Rod McCance from Cambusbarron, near Stirling, gives informal talks on 'Scottish weaponry used from 1291 to 1745'.

He shows groups of spellbound youngsters and adults how the weapons were made and how they were used in the brutal exchanges of the battlefield. Scottish weapons were of notoriously poor quality compared with Continental arms, and soon broke or buckled ('We spent most of our time jumping up and down on our sword-blades trying to straighten them!'); their purpose was to bludgeon rather than to slice, to concuss an opponent and render him vulnerable to a stabbing stroke to the throat or temple.

As for the big weapon labelled 'Wallace's Sword' downstairs, however, Rod McCance has grave doubts. The belief that it is the sword owned and wielded by Wallace is based on tradition rather than on documentary proof – and in that respect it mirrors the current debate about the origin, the deeds and the achievements of William Wallace himself.

The blade of the two-handed sword has no maker's mark, nor any owner's mark – and this is rather disconcerting for weaponry experts: it is impossible to date the metal of the blade scientifically, and they can only make judgements about the sword based on style. The hilt could, perhaps, be in keeping with a renovation made during a visit to Dumbarton Castle in 1505 by James IV, the 'New Golden Age' king who would meet his death at the disaster of Flodden in 1513 (see pages 290–4). An item occurs in the books of the king's Lord Treasurer for 8 December 1505, when the king ordered the sword to be re-hilted:

> For bynding of ane riding sword and rappyer, and binding of Wallas Sword with cordle of silk, and new hilt and plomet, new skabbard, and new belt to the said sword, xxvjsh [26 shillings].

The presence of a 'Wallas Sword' in Dumbarton Castle in 1505, two hundred years after the execution of William Wallace, can be given a plausible explanation: Sir John Menteith, the man who betrayed and captured the outlawed Wallace and sent him in chains to Edward I for trial and summary execution, was the Sheriff of Dumbarton and Constable of Dumbarton Castle. What would be more likely than that he should have kept Wallace's sword and stored it in the castle as a war trophy? And what more likely than that James IV, with his taste for dress and pageantry, should choose to embellish this relic (as well as his own formal court rapier and riding sword) in the bicentenary of Wallace's death?

Rod McCance does not accept that Wallace's stature can be deduced from the size of the two-handed sword. The weapon was not used 'to the fore', like a short-sword; the wielder whirled it around his head, moving his hips and shoulders as when using a hula-hoop or winding up for a hammer-throw. It was strength, not size, which mattered. 'The lower your point of gravity, the better,' McCance says. 'It could be suicidal for a tall man, because his body was totally unprotected against a lance-thrust when the sword was being brandished.' Moreover, the two-handed sword was never carried slung over the back – it was much too long; nor did it have a sheath or scabbard ('You would have needed arms fifteen feet long to draw the thing!').

But is it Wallace's own sword, the sword with which he 'made great room about him' in battle? David Caldwell, curator of Scottish Medieval Collections at the Museum of Scotland and author of *Scotland's Wars and Warriors* (1998), tells me he thinks it could well be the 'ghost' of the original sword, with all its original parts, including the blade, replaced or renewed for display purposes at different times in the past. This would explain why the blade does not have any maker's or owner's markings on it.

Perhaps it does not matter, after all. The sword has become a compelling icon of independence – so much so that it has been stolen (by extremist nationalists, it is alleged) on two occasions, in 1936 and 1972, although it was returned each time after a few months. Like so many saints' relics of yore, the Wallace Sword is something which helps to make legend tangible; and to that extent it is symptomatic of much else concerned with the story of William Wallace. Legend, especially in the way in which it is shaped by succeeding generations, is often a metaphor for the times at which the legend has particular relevance to people. There is, indeed, a very fine line between story and history, between the patriotic legend and the elusive reality of the man who has become enshrined as Scotland's National Hero. As Ted Cowan puts it:

> William Wallace was probably one of the greatest Scots who ever lived – not only for himself, not only for his own lifetime, but for what he became. The mythos of Wallace is just as important as what the man himself achieved.

There are three kinds of sources from which to build up a picture of the life and death of Wallace and his legacy to Scotland's history.

The first is English-based – primarily official government records and contemporary chroniclers; they are, without exception, violently anti-Wallace.

The second is Scottish-based – the *Original Chronicle of Scotland* by Andrew of Wyntoun (c.1355–1422), the *Scotichronicon* by Walter Bower (c.1385–1449), and the *Acts and Deeds of Sir William Wallace* by Blind Harry (?1440–c.1495), popularly known as *The Wallace*; they are all vehemently pro-Wallace.

The third, and for many just as important, is folk-memory – local traditions and stories about Wallace which were endemic in many parts of Scotland for centuries and which are still recalled in scores, hundreds even, of surviving place-names associated with him: trees, stones, hills, caves, roads, wells.

William Wordsworth noted this phenomenon in *The Prelude* when he was contemplating subjects for an epic:

> *Or I would record . . .*
> *How Wallace fought for Scotland; left the name*
> *Of Wallace to be found, like a wild flower,*
> *All over his dear Country; left the deeds*
> *Of Wallace, like a family of Ghosts,*
> *To people the steep rocks and river banks,*
> *Her natural sanctuaries, with a local soul*
> *Of independence and stern liberty.*
> THE PRELUDE, BOOK I

Robert Burns, too, had ambitions to write about Wallace, inspired by a boyhood visit to Leglen Wood, on the Auchencruive estate in Ayrshire, which was reputed to have been one of Wallace's safe havens:

> *As I explored every den and dell where I could suppose my heroic*
> *Countryman to have sheltered, I recollect (for even then I was a*
> *Rhymer) that my heart glowed with a wish to be able to make*
> *a Song on him equal to his merits.*
> LETTER TO MRS DUNLOP, 15 NOVEMBER 1786

Elspeth King, Director of the Smith Art Gallery and Museum in Stirling, is passionately committed to the idea that 'folk-history' enshrines a reality which is every bit as significant as formal, documented history:

> *Memory is an important part of history – it's the only history*
> *which some of the ordinary people of Scotland have, because such*
> *history hasn't been considered as worthy of being written by some*
> *of the historians who have acted on Scotland's behalf; so the*
> *ordinary people have taken the process into their own hands.*

It was this folk-history which the three main Scottish written sources exploited.

In his *Original Chronicle of Scotland*, written in rhyming Scots in the 1420s, Andrew of Wyntoun expressed regret that he lacked 'both wit and good leisure' to write down all the 'great gestes [tales] and songs' about Wallace in 'a great book'.

Walter Bower, in his *Scotichronicon*, written in the 1440s, seems to have had access to traditional oral tales with which he embellished his historical narrative. It is in Bower that the heroic legend of Wallace first emerges: Wallace the great warrior, Wallace the patriot, Wallace the generous friend of the oppressed, Wallace 'the man successful in everything'.

Blind Harry[1] claimed that his own epic, *The Wallace*, was founded on a Latin book (now lost) which had been commissioned shortly after Wallace's death from Wallace's boyhood friend and personal chaplain, Master John Blair, by Bishop William Sinclair of Dunkeld (d.1337); the bishop apparently planned to send it to the Pope – to plead the righteousness of Scotland's cause against England and, per-haps, to promote the case for Wallace's canonisation as a martyr.

Most academic scholars simply do not believe that such a book ever existed. Even if it did, Blind Harry must have taken very considerable liberties with it. It is apparent that most of the epic relied on traditional stories about Wallace which Blind Harry had collected and collated from different parts of the country.

Blind Harry's *The Wallace* is violent, gory, nationalistic and pro-foundly xenophobic – a sustained and bitter polemic against the Eng-lish ('Our old enemies come of Saxon's blood,/That never yet to Scotland would do good'). It struck an immediate chord in the Scot-land of the 1470s, where the unpopular King James III was conducting a policy of rapprochement with England in the face of opposition from his brothers and his court (see Chapter 16). It was one of the first books to be printed in Scotland (by Chepman and Myllar, around 1508, with the blessing of King James IV), and became the text-book

---

1 Little is known about the bard 'Blind Harry', or 'Harry the Minstrel': his name may not have been Harry, and he may not even have been blind. He wrote for the court, and must have been a familiar figure to his audience; the historian John Major (or Mair), writing in 1518, said, 'By recitation of [his works] in the presence of men of the highest rank, he procured, as he indeed deserved, food and raiment.' He seems to have lived from around 1440 to about 1495; he was noted among the great Scottish 'makars' (poets) of the past by William Dunbar in his *Lament for the Makars* in 1505. *The Wallace* seems to have been composed in the late 1470s.

of Scottish patriotism for generation after generation; it went through twenty-three editions before the Act of Union with England in 1707. In 1722, when the old Scots of the original was becoming inaccessible to most readers, it was modernised and adapted by another Scottish poet, William Hamilton of Gilbertfield, near Cambuslang, and became the second most treasured book in Scotland, next only to the Bible.[1] But after the mid-nineteenth century it fell into obscurity, until Elspeth King produced a new edition in 1998.

It was this remarkable and gory epic which inspired the American writer Randall Wallace to create the novel and the screenplay for the film *Braveheart* which took Scotland and the rest of the world by storm when it was released in 1995. The academic establishment was scornful of its portrayal of history; but the film caught the imagination of a people who were then moving towards a new chapter in the long, long story of Scotland's nationhood.

'William Wallace raised his head'

According to the annals of the time, William Wallace sprang on to the stage of history, like Athena from the forehead of Zeus, fully-grown and fully-armed:

> In [1297] the famous William Wallace, the hammer of the Eng-
> lish, the son of the noble knight [Malcolm Wallace], raised his
> head ... When Wallace was a young knight, he killed the sheriff
> of Lanark, an Englishman who was dexterous and powerful in
> the use of arms, in the town of Lanark. From that time therefore
> there gathered to his side [like a swarm of bees] all those who
> were bitter in their outlook and oppressed by the burden of

---

1   Hamilton's version 'poured a Scottish prejudice' into the veins of Robert Burns and inspired his celebrated 'Scots Wha Hae' (Scots Who Have), subtitled 'Robert Bruce's address to his army before the Battle of Bannockburn' – the Scottish equivalent of America's 'Battle-Hymn of the Republic':

> Scots wha hae wi' Wallace bled,
> Scots, wham Bruce has often led,
> Welcome to your gory bed,
> Or to victorie ...
> Lay the proud usurpers low!
> Tyrants fall in every foe!
> Liberty's in every blow!
> Let us do or die!

> *servitude under the intolerable rule of English domination, and*
> *he was made their leader.*
>
> SCOTICHRONICON, BOOK 11, CHAPTER 28

William Wallace, in fact, belonged to one of the minor knightly families which made up the feudal following of the powerful Stewart family which had been granted the lands of modern Renfrewshire by King David I. The Wallaces seem to have come to Scotland with the Stewarts; the name 'Wallace' may be a corruption of 'le Waleys', suggesting that they could have come from the Welsh Marshes.

Little is known about William Wallace's early life – even the date of his birth is uncertain. Most scholars now accept a date of around 1272, which would put him in his mid-twenties when he first 'raised his head' in 1297. The rest comes mainly from Blind Harry. According to him, William was the second son of a small landowner, Sir Malcolm Wallace 'of Ellerslie', but even that place-name is the subject of fierce debate: it could be the town of Elderslie near Paisley in Renfrewshire, or the obscure estate of Ellerslie/Elderslie near Kilmarnock in Ayrshire. Both lay claim to be the birthplace of Wallace, and there are numerous traditions and plaques and trees (both past and present) which purport to back them up.

Wallace seems to have fallen foul of the English regime early, according to Blind Harry. In Dundee he is said to have killed, in a street confrontation, a young man named Selby, the 'overbearing' son of the English constable of the castle there. He managed to make his escape from Dundee, but from then on he was an outlaw, a notorious fugitive with a reputation for lethal brawling. Later, when he was fishing on Irvine Water, he is said to have killed a couple of English soldiers who demanded that he give them his catch.

Blind Harry had many such tales to tell, of violent exploits and brutal encounters, of merciless killings and miraculous escapes. Many are commemorated in the names of woods and caves and other hide-outs all across the south and west of Scotland.

To the English, Wallace was merely a brigand; but his brigandage appealed to a deep-seated Scottish resentment of English domination and of the obeisance of Scotland's leaders to King Edward of England. Legends began to accrete around Wallace's name, and his activities became synonymous with patriotism (not that the word 'patriotism' existed then). What was believed to drive him was a fierce love of liberty for his suffering country, an absolute dedication to the idea of independence for the Scottish nation. It was said that in his boyhood he had learned from his uncle, a priest in Dunipace, a Latin precept which inspired all his achievements: *Dico tibi verum, libertas optima rerum* (I tell you truly, liberty is the best of things).

Wallace was now a fully-fledged guerrilla (or terrorist, depending on your point of view), implacably dedicated to the destruction of the English troops who garrisoned Scotland's towns and castles, with a formidable band of disciplined, battle-hardened followers at his back. He ranged the countryside with his men, murdering Englishmen at every opportunity, attacking and capturing castles apparently at will. He seems to have had all the attributes of a born leader: charisma, bravery, nerve, decisiveness, imagination, the ability to inspire men to follow him and a formidable physical presence. All the Scottish sources – including the immense dimensions of his reputed sword – attest to his exceptional strength and size. The *Scotichronicon* described him thus:

> *He was a tall man with the body of a giant, cheerful in appearance with agreeable features, broad-shouldered and big-boned, with belly in proportion and lengthy flanks, pleasing in appearance but with a wild look, broad in the hips, with strong arms and legs, a most spirited fighting-man, with all his limbs very strong and firm.*

According to Blind Harry's *The Wallace* he was all of seven feet tall (nine quarters of the Scots ell of thirty-seven inches):

> *IX quartaris large he was in length indeid.*
> *Thryd part that length in schuldrys [shoulders] braid [broad]*
> *was he.*

The turning-point in Wallace's spectacular career as a guerrilla fighter came, according to Blind Harry, after he had secretly married a beautiful young heiress named Marion Braidfoot, of Lanark. At the time, Lanark Castle was the seat of an English sheriff, Sir William Heselrig. One day in May 1297, when Wallace was paying a visit in disguise to his wife (who had recently given birth to a daughter), his presence in Lanark became known to the soldiery. He and his followers managed to make good their escape after a typically bloody fight, whereupon Heselrig exacted prompt retribution by having Marion seized and cruelly put to death.

In a murderous fury of grief Wallace struck back at once. That very night he and his men infiltrated the town in ones and twos, then formed up for a surprise attack on the sheriff's residence. They burst into the castle, where Wallace slew Heselrig in his bed; when Heselrig's son rushed to his father's assistance Wallace killed him too, then he and his men went on a rampage of slaughter, cutting down every Englishmen in sight. William Wallace had 'lifted his head' with a vengeance.

News of the killing of William Heselrig and the massacre of his entire garrison sent shock-waves all the way to London. At Wallace's arraignment there in 1305, amid all the general charges of murder, arson and sacrilege, the first specific indictment was that he had attacked, wounded and slain the Sheriff of Lanark 'and, in contempt of the king, had cut the said Sheriff's body in pieces'. In the English sources, the attack on Lanark Castle seems to have been regarded as the trigger for a general revolt against English domination.

Insurrection was now in the air. The 'official' rebellion, known today as the 'aristocratic' or 'noble' revolt, was being orchestrated by two former Guardians – James Stewart (the Steward) and the Bishop of Glasgow (Robert Wishart). Surprisingly, one of the magnates involved was Robert Bruce, the young Earl of Carrick, whose father's request to King Edward had been so cuttingly snubbed (see Chapter 9). The 'aristocratic' revolt soon fizzled out, however, in humiliating circumstances: an English force led by Sir Henry Percy and Sir Robert Clifford crossed the border early in July and surrounded the confederation of rebellious nobles and their followers encamped at Irvine, on the Ayrshire coast. After lengthy negotiations the Scots surrendered without a fight on 7 July 1297, giving hostages for good behaviour on condition that they would not have to go to fight for Edward in France. Among those who renewed their pledges of loyalty to King Edward was Robert Bruce, the Earl of Carrick.

Much more significant was a rising in the north-east of Scotland. It was led by a young man named Andrew Murray (de Moray), son and heir of a leading baron of the Comyn family. Father and son had been captured at the Battle of Dunbar and imprisoned; Murray junior, however, escaped from Chester Castle and made his way back to his father's castle at Avoch, in Ross-shire. In the summer of 1297 he was leading a Comyn rebellion in the north-east; one by one he captured the English-held castles in north-east Scotland – Urquhart, Inverness, Elgin and Banff – and soon he was in control of the whole of Moray and Aberdeenshire.

Wallace himself had not been idle. After a foray into the south-west of Scotland he moved north with a hand-picked body of cavalry to Scone, where the English Justiciar of Scotland, William Ormesby, was holding court and outlawing all those who would not take an oath of fealty. Ormesby's troops melted away at Wallace's approach; the Justiciar fled precipitately to Edinburgh to raise the alarm and thence to the safety of his estates in Northumberland. Scotland was now in a ferment. Bands of armed rebels roamed the countryside, and the English troops withdrew to their forts and castles in a virtual state of siege.

King Edward, still busy with preparations for his expedition to France, decreed that the rest of Scotland now had to be brought to heel; Wallace and his rebels had to be crushed and extirpated. He instructed his two lieutenants in Scotland, the veteran Earl of Surrey (the victor at Dunbar the previous year) and the Treasurer of Scotland, Hugh Cressingham, to raise an army from the north of England; they were to march north to give support to the key fortress in Scotland – Stirling – and to deal with Wallace, who was by now besieging another major English-held castle, at Dundee. With that, Edward set sail for France.

When news reached Wallace that a huge new English army was on the move north he broke off the siege of Dundee Castle and sent word to Andrew Murray in Inverness to come and join him. The rebel forces met up at Perth and together the two young generals led their troops to Stirling, there to await the inevitable confrontation with the approaching English army.

The Battle of Stirling Bridge (11 September 1297)

High above the crest of the Abbey Craig north of Stirling, 226 steps up the circular stone staircase of the National Wallace Monument, the look-out platform offers a breathtaking panoramic view of the surrounding countryside. To the south-west, like a galleon breasting the sea, Stirling Castle stands proud on its dolerite eminence; in between lies the flat carseland through which the stripling River Forth snakes eastwards in a series of huge meanders. For centuries this area was of immense strategic importance as the key to the Highlands, the sole route to the north of Scotland and the scene of many battles; until the opening of the Kincardine Bridge in 1936, Stirling was the last place at which the river could be crossed before it widened into the Firth of Forth.

The Battle of Stirling Bridge took place near the Old Bridge over the Forth which connects the town to the causeway leading west towards Bridge of Allan; that stone bridge, built in the late fifteenth century, replaced the ancient, narrow wooden bridge ('bryg of tre') about which the battle hinged. Recent underwater research has revealed traces of massive stone piers which pinpoint the precise site of the ancient bridge which straddled the thirty-metre-wide river diagonally, only a few metres upstream of the present bridge, in a straight line towards the Abbey Craig.

Wallace and Murray arrived at Stirling before the English did. They took up position near and on the Abbey Craig, which gave them a clear view of the approaching army. It was not a particularly large force, but it was formidable nonetheless; making due allowance for the usual exaggerations of contemporary or near-contemporary accounts, it has been estimated at some two hundred knights and mounted men-at-arms and ten thousand foot-soldiers, against the waiting Scottish force of thirty-six cavalry and eight thousand foot, made up of lesser gentry, burgesses and countrymen.

On the eve of the battle James the Steward and Malcolm, Earl of Lennox, who were (nominally, at least) attached to the English army, volunteered to go and parley with the Scots, but their overtures were brusquely rebuffed. Two friars were then despatched to renew the offers of peace, but once again the offers were refused by Wallace: 'Tell your commander that we are not here to make peace but to do battle, to defend ourselves and liberate our kingdom. Let them come on, and we shall prove this in their very beards.' That evening the Earl of Surrey gave orders for the English army to cross the bridge next morning for a frontal attack on the Scots, and retired for the night to Stirling Castle.

At dawn next morning (11 September) the English infantry began to cross the bridge and were deploying on the marshy ground on the north side of the river when they were recalled: the elderly Earl of Surrey had not risen from his bed, and the action was postponed. When Surrey eventually arrived, he saw the lightly-armed Scottish army arrayed near the slopes of the Abbey Craig half a mile away, and summoned a council of war. Some of the Scottish knights in his army urged caution, arguing that the bridge would be a death-trap because it was so narrow; on the other hand there was a ford farther upstream where cavalry could cross sixty at a time, and could then attack the Scots from the flank while the main army was crossing the bridge. This sensible tactical advice was rejected, but there was still considerable altercation about whether to cross or not. Eventually Cressingham, the hugely obese Treasurer of Scotland, urged Surrey to hurry up, since a flanking movement would probably make the Scots retreat and thus prolong the war, which was costing a great deal of money. And so they began the slow process of crossing the bridge – slow, because no more than two or three horses could ride over it abreast. By midday less than half of the army had reached the other side.

On the north side of the river the Scots can scarcely have believed their luck. All they had to do was wait until a significant (but not too large) part of the English army had crossed on to the marshy meadowland on the north bank. At just the right moment a horn was sounded, and the massed ranks of Scottish spearmen surged down and along the raised causeway (the modern Causewayhead) towards the bridge. The marshy ground was hindering the deployment of the English cavalry, and neither the floundering horsemen nor their supporting infantry could withstand the onslaught. The end of the narrow bridge, quickly surrounded by Scottish pikemen, offered no escape route for the packed mass of panicking troops, and the Scots had a field-day of slaughter. The Earl of Surrey could only watch helplessly as nearly half of his seasoned, powerfully-equipped host was cut to pieces or drowned in the deep waters of the Forth in the space of an hour. Only one group of English knights, led by Sir Marmaduke Tweng, managed to force a way back to the bridge and over it to safety. Surrey thereupon ordered the bridge to be broken and set on fire, to forestall any attempts by the Scots to use it for pursuit, and headed back to Berwick, leaving Tweng to take charge of Stirling Castle.

The rout was spectacular, and total. Cressingham, who had crossed the bridge at the head of the English knights, was an early victim of the carnage. Realising that he was doomed, he charged the massed spears of the Scottish ranks, where he was pulled from his horse and butchered; the English *Lanercost Chronicle* said that his body was flayed and his skin used to make a baldric for Wallace's sword. According to the English chroniclers, a hundred English men-at-arms and five thousand foot-soldiers perished that day. Meanwhile James the Steward and the Earl of Lennox, opportunist as ever, turned their coats and fell upon the retreating baggage train of the English and plundered it of much of its cargo.

It had been a dramatic victory, an achievement of immense psychological importance to the rag-tag people's army of the Scottish resistance. Not one of the powerful Scottish magnates had been present to lead it; they were either languishing in English prisons or had compromised themselves through the oaths of fealty and the hostages they had given to Edward of England. In one frenzied hour the legend

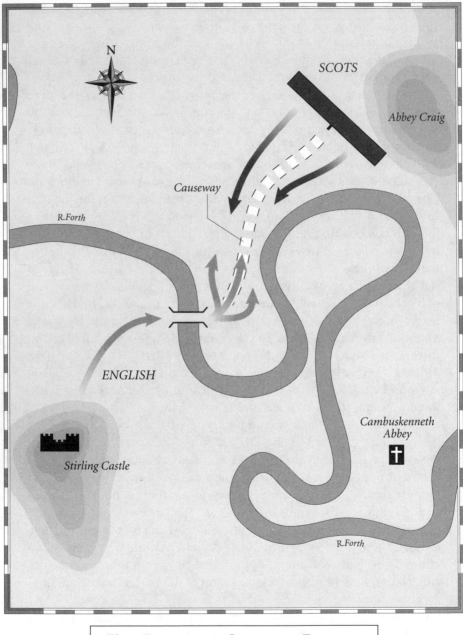

THE BATTLE OF STIRLING BRIDGE,
11 SEPTEMBER 1297

of English invincibility had been broken by the common people of Scotland. It was a great Scottish feat, but it was hardly a great English defeat – indeed, one of the English chroniclers described it as a *confusio*, a battle without a clear result. The Scots had not beaten the full might of the English war machine, one of the most powerful in all Europe; they had not beaten Edward of England himself.

Wallace and his gallant young co-commander Murray were now the *de facto* joint rulers of Scotland, working in the name of John Balliol, the deposed king, and the people all over Scotland rallied to them – including most churchmen, and some at least of the nobility. There was much work to be done, both military and administrative. But the Battle of Stirling Bridge had not been won without cost: Murray had sustained terrible wounds in the fighting, and his life was hanging in the balance. Nevertheless, the work was put in hand. Wallace and Murray sent letters in Latin to Scotland's trading partners in the Hanseatic League, at Lübeck and Hamburg, inviting them to resume trading – 'for the kingdom of Scotland, God be thanked, has been recovered by war from the power of the English'. One of these missives has providentially survived the centuries; it was sent to the merchants of Lübeck on 11 October 1297 by 'Andreas de Moravia and Willelmus Wallensis, commanders of the army of the kingdom of Scotland, and the community of the same kingdom'.

In November, Andrew Murray died of his wounds, and Wallace was left to carry on as the sole ruler of the realm. Some argue that it was Murray who had tempered Wallace's inspiring enthusiasm with strategic and tactical skill, and that his loss was to prove fatal to the Scots when the crunch came in the Battle of Falkirk in 1298 (see below) – but that can only be a matter of speculation.

Meanwhile Wallace built on his victory at Stirling by leading a large and unruly army into Northumbria and Cumbria on an orgy of vengeful pillage which included Lanercost Priory, near Carlisle – which would not have endeared him to the monks there who were writing up the annals of the time. Only fierce snowstorms brought an end to the harrying of the northern shires, and by Christmas the Scots had withdrawn.

Wallace's position in Scotland seems to have been made official when he was knighted by an unnamed earl, according to the *Scotichron-icon*, and gained (or took) the title of sole Guardian; in a Latin charter dated 29 March 1298 he styled himself 'Wilhelmes Wallays, Knight, Guardian of the Kingdom of Scotland and Leader of its armies, in the name of the illustrious Prince, Lord John [Balliol], by the Grace of

God King of Scotland, by consent of the Community of that Kingdom' and 'by consent and assent of the nobles of the said Kingdom'.

It was too much to hope, however, that all the leading magnates of Scotland would acquiesce to being ruled by someone whom they regarded with contempt (not unmixed with jealousy, perhaps, and even guilt) as a low-ranking young upstart. Someone like Wallace, in their eyes, had no business whatsoever to be leading the Scottish army – that was the role of the nobility. Much has been made of the pusillanimity or even downright treachery of many of the Scottish magnates, but they were caught in a difficult and dangerous situation. Most of them had estates in England as well as in Scotland; they owed allegiance as vassals to two overlords, two kings, and were looking to preserve themselves, their estates and their families. In the 1290s they must have felt, pragmatically, that the future lay rather with the powerful King Edward than with the cause of an independent Scotland espoused by Wallace. The concept of 'nationalism' scarcely existed in those days. The Scottish nobility did not, and probably could not, share the stubborn and ferocious resentment which fuelled Wallace's hatred for all things English: Wallace, the extremist partisan leader, could identify with the dispossessed, the abandoned, the perpetual victims of warfare.

The real test was yet to come. The defeat at Stirling Bridge had been a terrible blow to England's pride. As soon as Edward had extricated himself from his war with Philippe the Fair in March 1298, he hastened back to England: it was time to deal once and for all with this brigand who had dared to usurp his authority in Scotland. He moved his capital – exchequer, law courts and all – to York and summoned his magnates to a council of war there in May; the Scottish nobles cannily found reasons not to attend, and had sentences of forfeiture passed on them. The campaign was planned down to the very last detail. Finally, on 3 July, Edward crossed the Tweed near Coldstream and started moving slowly through Scotland with a mighty army: 1,500 mounted knights and men-at arms in four brigades, with twelve thousand battle-seasoned foot-soldiers, including a large contingent of Welsh and English archers.

Despite all the meticulous planning, the logistical organisation of moving and victualling such a huge army through hostile territory broke down. The Lowlands of Scotland were bare – the Scots had devastated their own fields and foodstocks in a scorched-earth policy to deprive the invaders of any sustenance. It was said that in all Lothian the English had been able to find only one skinny cow. The momentum of the march began to falter. The army had to stop at Kirkliston, a few miles west of Edinburgh, to await provisions from ships coming up from Berwick; most of the ships never arrived, because of bad weather, and those which did carried wine, not wheat. Soon the great army was hungry, mutinous and riddled with disease; there were furious drunken altercations between the Welsh archers and the English foot-soldiers, leading to brawls in which many died, including some priests who tried to separate the combatants.

It was now an army in deep trouble. Furthermore, Edward had no idea what the enemy was up to – for all he knew, the Scots army might be planning to mount a massive raid into England in his absence. On the morning of Monday, 21 July, he was on the point of falling back to Edinburgh to try to feed and calm his demoralised troops, when two Scottish earls (Dunbar and Angus) sent word to his camp that the Scottish army had been sighted within striking distance, only twenty-nine kilometres away, lurking in the great forest near Falkirk. 'Praise be to God,' Edward is alleged to have said, 'who has brought me out of every strait. They shall have no need to follow me, for I shall go to meet them and on this very day.'

With that he marched his army westwards towards Falkirk. That night he bivouacked on the Burgh Muir south of Linlithgow, in the fields of the present Burghmuir Farm. In case the Scots tried to surprise them with a night raid, the English lay down in combat readiness, the knights with their huge stallions tethered at their sides. At some time during the night, it seems, King Edward was injured by his charger, breaking two ribs. Alarm spread through the uneasy, wakeful army: was the king dead? To calm his men's fears, the elderly Edward (he was now nearly sixty) hauled himself into the saddle; sitting ramrod straight, he gave the order to break camp at once and move on to engage the enemy.

The Battle of Falkirk (22 July 1298)

Notwithstanding this unwillingness of the great nobility to support him, Wallace assembled a large army; for the middling, but especially the lower classes, were very much attached to him. He marched boldly against the King of England, and met him near the town of Falkirk.

TALES OF A GRANDFATHER, CHAPTER VII

High on a hill to the south-east of Falkirk a mounted patrol of Scottish spearmen caught sight of the English host moving in their direction through the early-morning mist. By the time a detachment of English cavalry had galloped up the hill to engage them, according to the English chroniclers, the Scots had disappeared. Local tradition has it that the leader of the patrol was none other than Wallace himself, perched on a great boulder on a ridge where the village of Wallacestone now stands. The boulder itself has disappeared, but in its place is a tall pillar, erected in 1810, dedicated to the memory of William Wallace.

From that vantage point, Wallace (or whoever else might have been leading the patrol) would have had a commanding view of the surrounding countryside: to his right the English army moving inexorably forward, to his left the Scottish army also, perhaps, on the move – but not, it would seem, yet aware that the English were almost upon them.

We can only speculate about what went through Wallace's mind when he saw, or was told of, the English advance. Had he expected to see the English army on its way back towards Edinburgh, providing his forces with an easy target for harassment and ambush? Or did he welcome the opportunity of a great showdown with an army which, according to intelligence from his spies, was exhausted and demoralised? Or . . . or . . . or?

All conjecture apart, the fact is that on the morning of 22 July 1298, Wallace drew up his army on the slope of a hill somewhere in the Falkirk area, with a forest behind him and a stream with a low-lying boggy meadow in front of him.

What sort of a force had he been able to muster to face the armoured might of England? After his autumn foray into the north of England, Wallace – who now had the authority given to the Guardian of Scotland – had devoted considerable time to enlisting and training a standing army from the Lowlands and Borders for the defence of the realm. The *Scotichronicon* gives details of his conscription policy – a policy which cut right across the customary obligations of feudal duty of a man to his master – and the meticulous chain of command from groups of five right up to the general himself.

The nucleus of this army was based on spearmen: trained infantry equipped with twelve-foot spears and deployed in huge 'schiltrons'. These were, in effect, oval-shaped phalanxes – formations of massed ranks, bristling on all sides with spears like monstrous hedgehogs. Each schiltron might consist of 1,500 to two thousand spearmen. In addition, there was a corps of skilled archers from Ettrick under the command of James the Steward's brother, Sir John Stewart of Jedburgh. Where Wallace's army was sadly deficient, however, was in heavy cavalry, the armoured squadrons of experienced fighting knights which Edward of England could require as a feudal obligation; the Scots horse were more lightly armed – skirmishers rather than cavalry. So when the two armies faced up to one another on the battlefield at Falkirk, there was a very considerable imbalance in military power as well as in numbers.

The site of the battle cannot now be determined with any certainty, alas. The English chroniclers provided a description of the topographical features, but this was general enough to fit a number of candidate places; there are no prominent landmarks, as at Stirling, which would help to pinpoint the spot, and the battle has been sited in various corners of the Falkirk district. However, the course of the battle, when it was joined, seems clear enough from the detailed English accounts.

The Scottish army was drawn up in four (perhaps five) massed schiltrons, each protected by a ring of sharpened wooden stakes roped together. Between the schiltrons were the Ettrick archers, and at the rear was a small force of cavalry provided by the nobility, under the command of Sir John Comyn, the 'Red Comyn' of Badenoch. It has been estimated that the Scots were outnumbered by two to one, at least, by the English host.

Before the battle began, Wallace is said by the English chroniclers to have shouted to his schiltrons, 'I have brought you to the ring – now dance if you can.' As a battle slogan to enthuse an army, it had a curiously resigned ring to it which chimed ominously with the peril of the situation.

The onset of the English attack was a confused business. Apparently the Welsh foot-soldiers, still seething with resentment at the English, refused to advance against the formidable spear-walls of the schiltrons. So the first charge came from two of the English cavalry squadrons. The leading knights galloped forward in an impetuous and disorderly rush and found themselves floundering in the grassy morass which separated them from the schiltrons; after an undignified scramble out of the marsh they wheeled towards firmer ground on the left to attack from the flank. The second cavalry wave was more circumspect, and cantered diagonally to the right before turning to charge into the other Scottish flank.

The schiltrons held firm; the English knights could make no impression on them, and many of their horses were impaled on the deadly spears. Then came an extraordinary turn of events: the Scots cavalry, which should have gone into action to distract the English knights who were thundering in from both sides, simply abandoned the field without having struck a blow. This was so utterly unexpected that no one has been able to explain it properly. The later Scottish sources, desperate to find an excuse for the defeat of their peerless hero, Wallace, blamed it on either cowardice or a plot by the English nobles to ensure that Wallace would be beaten, even killed. Neither explanation carries much conviction. It remains the great mystery of the Battle of Falkirk.

Even without the help of their cavalry the schiltrons stood firm, and the English knights were unable to break their ranks. So the knights turned instead on the Ettrick archers who, now without the protection of the cavalry, were a much easier target. Their commander, Sir John Stewart, leaped from his mount to stand by his men, but after a gallant resistance they were cut down, every one.

Still the schiltrons held, however; so now Edward recalled his cavalry and called instead upon his ultimate weapon – his own Lancashire archers. They were equipped with the new longbows which would later destroy the chivalry of France at Crécy, Poitiers and Agincourt; their iron-tipped arrows could pierce leather and even chain-mail at a range of six hundred metres. With no cavalry to disrupt them the archers fired volley after relentless volley with deadly accuracy into the packed ranks of the schiltrons – and now, at last, the schiltrons began to waver as great gaps appeared in their defences. This was the turning-point. As the schiltrons disintegrated the English cavalry charged in again, and this time there was no keeping them out. The fighting became a slaughter as the spearmen were overwhelmed and the survivors tried to flee to safety in the cover of the woods behind them.

Wallace himself and some of his men managed to escape to fight another day, but the Scottish casualties had been horrendous. Scotland's army had been all but annihilated.

The defeat at Falkirk was as total as the victory at Stirling Bridge had been. Wallace had lost some of his most loyal supporters, like Sir John Stewart. In particular, he had lost his trusted and devoted second-in-command, Sir John de Graham, the local hero of the battle: Grahamston, a district of Falkirk, was named in his memory. His elaborate tomb in the graveyard of Falkirk Old and St Modans Church, caged in an ornate wrought-iron cupola, carries epitaphs in Latin and (later) Scots:

Here lyes Sir John the Grame, baith [both] wight [brave] and wise,
Ane [One] of the chiefs who rescewit [rescued] Scotland thrise [thrice].
Ane better knight not to the world was lent [given],
Nor was gude [good] Grame of truth and hardiment [boldness].

The tombstone and the tomb, with its knightly effigy lying on top and a cast of Graham's sword, have been repaired and restored on several occasions. Graham's memory is still cherished here.

The dust of that grievous battle has still not settled, seven hundred years later. From it emerged a legend which has survived down the centuries against all the evidence to the contrary: the idea that Robert Bruce, the future king, had fought on the English side against his countrymen at the Battle of Falkirk. Such treachery! Indeed, according to the *Scotichronicon* and, later, Blind Harry's *Wallace*, Bruce himself had led the pursuit of the fleeing Scots and had overtaken Wallace, whom he thereupon upbraided for his arrogance in trying to oppose the power of the King of England 'and of the more powerful section of Scotland' – to which Wallace gave this dignified reply:

> *'Robert, Robert, it is your inactivity and womanish cowardice that spur me to the liberation of the native land that is legally yours. And indeed it is an effete man even now, ready as he is to advance from bed to battle, from the shadow into the sunlight, with a pampered body accustomed to a soft life feebly taking up the weight of battle for the liberation of his own country – it is he who has made me so presumptuous, perhaps even foolish, and has compelled me to attempt or seize these tasks.' With these words William himself looked to a speedy flight, and with his men sought safety.*
>
> *On account of all this, Robert himself was like one awakening from a deep sleep; the power of Wallace's words so entered his heart that he no longer had any thought of favouring the views of the English.*

This alleged exchange between Wallace and Robert Bruce, which was featured prominently in the film *Braveheart*, has been dismissed by scholars as a complete fabrication: there is no evidence that Bruce was present at the battle. No amount of imaginative embellishment or partisan justification can disguise the bitter fact that Wallace, the leader who had inspired a whole people to fight for independence and nationhood, had failed in his greatest test – and failed disastrously.

Fiona Watson says:

> *The problem has always been to explain the fact that Wallace could win a stunning victory at Stirling Bridge and then, less than a year later, lose so badly at Falkirk. Personally, I think that Wallace was desperately unlucky. He was without his outstanding military commander, Sir Andrew Murray; and he was up against a new and devastatingly effective weapon – the long-range English longbow. Wallace took a gamble and lost; in 1314, Bruce would take a similar gamble and win. Sometimes you have to take the gamble – otherwise you never can win. And history would be written very differently if the outcomes of these two battles had been different.*

And yet defeat did not bring humiliation. Wallace had given point and pride to popular resistance against English dominion, and despite the shattering outcome of the Battle of Falkirk, that spirit of resistance was not broken. If anything, paradoxically, it was greatly strengthened – and now the nobles who had failed to rally to Wallace would lead the resistance for the next six years.

After Falkirk

> *A large oak-tree in the adjoining forest was long shown as mark-ing the spot where Wallace slept before the battle, or, as others said, in which he hid himself after the defeat. Nearly forty years ago Grandpapa [i.e. Scott himself] saw some of its roots; but the body of the tree was even then entirely decayed, and there is not now, and has not been for many years, the least vestige of it to be seen.*
>
> TALES OF A GRANDFATHER, CHAPTER VII

Oak wood has long been revered in Scotland as a potent symbol of strength, hardness and durability. Until two centuries ago there was a vast oak tree known as 'Wallace's Oak' in the Torwood, a couple of miles north-west of Falkirk. In 1723 it was described as having a girth of thirty-six feet, still bearing leaves and acorns, and 'ever excepted from cutting when the wood is sold'. Fifty years later its girth was measured as twenty-two feet at four feet above the ground by a John Walker, who observed that 'whatever may be its age, it certainly has in its ruins the appearance of greater antiquity than what I have observed in any tree in Scotland . . . it has been immemorially held in veneration and is still viewed in that light.' But, as Sir Walter Scott and others reported, by the end of the eighteenth century no trace of it remained, and efforts to pinpoint the exact site of the tree have been somewhat conjectural.

Tangible relics of 'Wallace's Oak' remain, however. The great tree was ultimately, and literally, loved to death by souvenir hunters. In the 1790s a piece of it was made into a box by the goldsmiths of Edinburgh and presented to George Washington, first President of the United States, as 'the Wallace of America'; this relic does not survive, alas – it was stolen in a stage-coach raid in the 1820s and never seen again. The last of the roots of the tree was excavated to make a snuff box which was presented to King George IV on the occasion of his celebrated Royal Visit to Edinburgh in 1822 (see Chapter 29). Numerous other presentation artefacts (such as mounted quaichs[1] and boxes) were made from the tree, including the frame around the portrait of the eleventh Earl of Buchan, the eccentric Scottish nobleman who erected a huge statue of Wallace on his land near Dryburgh in 1814 (see below). Like the acorns of Torwood, the legend of Wallace had taken root and was flourishing more strongly than ever five centuries after his death.

Unfortunately, there is a tantalising lack of hard evidence – contemporary sources, artefacts, even 'relics' – to match the legend, one way or another, and historians of the Wallace period usually have to fall back on a modicum of opinion, however well-informed, and conjecture.

The defeat at Falkirk presaged the end of Wallace's brief period as the acknowledged leader of the Community of the Realm and the Scottish army; soon afterwards he resigned his position as Guardian of Scotland, and disappeared from all but a very few of the official records which have survived. No one can now be sure of the circumstances of his resignation. Did he jump, or was he pushed? Did he feel that he had lost the authority which only military success could bestow? Could he no longer stomach the jealous politicking of his noble rivals? For whatever reason, whether voluntarily or otherwise, within a few weeks of the battle Wallace had stepped down from his front-line position and dropped out of sight into comparative obscurity.

But it would be wrong to think that the man himself was now a spent

---

1 Shallow, bowl-shaped drinking cups with two projections, or lugs, for handles.

force. Occasional written references, bolstered by persistent legend and folklore, suggest that, in the aftermath of defeat, Wallace still ranged the country with a hard core of surviving troops, inflicting whatever damage he could on the English garrisons left by King Edward to try to enforce his writ. When the king returned to England in October, after distributing among his own followers the estates and titles he deemed had been forfeited by Scottish nobles (including Robert Bruce), he left Scotland nominally under English control; but the control was more apparent than real – the English held and garrisoned the major castles in the southern half of Scotland, but north of the Forth their presence was negligible.

With Wallace gone from the inner circles of power, the leadership of the country was devolved to a series of Guardians working in tandem or troika: John Comyn (the 'Red Comyn', who had succeeded his father as Lord of Badenoch), Robert Bruce (the Earl of Carrick), Bishop William Lamberton of St Andrews and Sir Ingram de Umfraville. The resistance fight was carried on in a number of key areas, with considerable success, but none of the combinations of Guardians worked; the deep-seated rivalries between the Balliol/Comyn and the Bruce factions could not be resolved. In May 1301 a new sole Guardian would be appointed: Sir John de Soules, a veteran patriot and experienced diplomat from Liddesdale with a steady and neutral head on his shoulders. By that time William Wallace had embarked on a new phase of his single-minded pursuit of independence for Scotland and the restoration of King John Balliol to his rightful throne – as an ambassador on behalf of his country.

Ted Cowan says:

> Wallace always claimed that he was fighting for King John Balliol, the man whom Edward I had selected to be king. He was absolutely unwavering in that. He never wanted to be king himself – that would have been completely unthinkable. In the summer of 1299 he was despatched to the Continent, to France, on a diplomatic embassy to try to persuade Philippe the Fair to honour the 1295 'Auld Alliance' treaty and provide military support for the Scots against England. He was not very successful in that, but in the autumn of 1300 he was given a letter of introduction from Philippe to the Pope himself [Boniface VII], to try to persuade him to lean on the English to lay off the Scots. The future was now looking better for John Balliol. Edward had just released Balliol from captivity in England and handed him over to papal

*custody on the Continent, and there seems to have been a move
by the papacy, at the turn of the century, to reinstate John Balliol
as King of Scots. The restoration for which Wallace was working
did not come about; but this, I believe, is when Robert Bruce
said to himself, 'Hey, wait a minute, this is where I should be
making my own bid for the throne. We start now to plan an
alternative strategy.'*

That 'alternative strategy' was soon to become apparent. The 'Scottish
War', as the English called it, was at a stalemate, despite sporadic
attempts by King Edward to force the Scots into subjection. Furthermore, in the autumn of 1301 John Balliol was released from papal
custody and returned to his ancestral estates in Picardy, in France.
The return of Balliol to the throne now seemed much more than just
a pipe-dream.

This must have looked deeply ominous to Robert Bruce: the restoration of Balliol (whom he had never recognised as King of Scots)
would have meant a restoration of Comyn power in the land and the
end of his own hopes to achieve the throne. In January 1302 he
suddenly defected and went over to the English side. His submission
was well received by King Edward, who was equally concerned about
a possible return by John Balliol, and Bruce seems to have been given
a promise – implicit, at least – that Edward would support him in his
claim to the crown if Balliol were restored to the throne.

This was the start of the rot, one might say – the decay of Scotland's
resistance. It was largely due to the withdrawal of French and papal
support for the Scottish cause. In July 1302, Philippe the Fair was
shocked when his mighty army, the flower of French chivalry, was
massacred at Courtrai, in Belgium, by a Flemish army of burghers
who deployed their infantry in schiltrons, as Wallace had done at
Falkirk, but with much greater success. From now on, Philippe was
to have no time to spare for Scotland, and no stomach for supporting
it: in May 1303 he signed a peace treaty with England from which,
contrary to all his previous promises, Scotland was excluded. At the
same time the Pope, who was now at loggerheads with France, was
making friendly overtures to England, and in August 1302 sent a
strongly-worded letter to the Scottish bishops, admonishing them and
commanding them to make peace with King Edward. Scotland now
stood alone, and Edward prepared carefully for an invasion in 1303
which would crush the Scots forever.

William Wallace was now back in Scotland, having returned from his abortive diplomatic missions abroad. There is no evidence that he mustered an army of any strength, although it appears that he took part in some engagements against the English – particularly, it is thought, a successful foray against an expeditionary English force at Roslin in February 1303. But when Edward himself arrived with the main army in May there was to be no respite for the Scots, no famous victories to halt the unstoppable advance of the English military machine. Castles and strongholds fell to Edward all over Scotland – apart from the pivotal fortress of Stirling Castle, which he bypassed on his inexorable way north by using three huge prefabricated pontoon bridges which had been brought to the Forth by an English fleet: he was keeping Stirling, that place of ill-omen for English arms, for a showpiece end to his conquest of Scotland.

Edward pushed northwards past Perth to Brechin, whose castle fell after a severe pounding, then on to Aberdeen and Banff on the Moray coast. At Kinloss Abbey he paused while his forces took Urquhart Castle and tightened the English grip on the north.

Resistance continued in the south, sporadically. The Red Comyn, who had conducted the defence against the invasion in his capacity as Guardian of Scotland (again), still had a small army in the field, and Wallace, it seems, exhorted and supported by the patriotic Bishop William Lamberton of St Andrews, was prominent in several unavailing guerrilla actions. But the Scottish cause was becoming more and more hopeless.

At the end of the summer campaigning, Edward did not return to England, but stayed for the winter at Dunfermline; he was determined to keep up the pressure on the Scots to submit to his authority. For the Scots, the idea of peace (or at least 'returning to the king's peace', as Edward put it) was beginning to look a tempting option after the long and wearisome years of perpetual warfare. After much preliminary parleying and negotiation, the end came on 3 February 1304, when the Red Comyn surrendered on behalf of the Community of Scotland – but not unconditionally. The terms agreed by Edward showed unexpected forbearance: the leading magnates were allowed to retain their lands and positions in Scotland, with one or two token sentences of temporary exile, and some were even appointed sheriffs. Edward clearly felt that he needed the active support of the Scottish nobility in order to ensure acceptance of his government.

One member of the Scottish nobility seems to have been active on the English side throughout: Robert Bruce, Earl of Carrick. His relations with King Edward, however, were wary at best. Then in

March 1304 Bruce's position in life changed significantly: his father, Robert Bruce senior, the Lord of Annandale, died, and now the long-standing Bruce claim to the throne devolved directly on the Earl of Carrick, the new Lord of Annandale. This was to make Robert Bruce's position extraordinarily difficult.

As for William Wallace – King Edward's mercy to the leaders of the Scots resistance stopped short at forgiving Wallace his past sins. There are some indications that Edward offered him some sort of guarantee that his life would be spared if he surrendered himself unconditionally to the king's will but, if so, Wallace can only have refused. In March 1304 the king convened a parliament at St Andrews, at which 129 Scottish landowners took Edward as their liege lord, and a declaration of outlawry was passed on Wallace and his close comrade-at-arms Sir Simon Fraser. Two former Guardians – Sir John de Soules and Sir Ingram de Umfraville – were not to be granted letters of safe-conduct until Wallace surrendered (de Soules, unwavering in his patriotism, made no attempt to return from France, where he stayed until his death).

Now only Stirling Castle remained defiant, held by Sir William Oliphant in the name of King John Balliol – a forlorn cause if ever there was one. Edward made his preparations for the siege with meticulous care. He gathered a huge collection of siege engines and an impressive arsenal of lead, iron, crossbows and bolts, and took lodgings in the town from which the ladies of his court were able to watch the fun in safety. The siege began on 22 April 1304 and lasted for three months. Every day the mighty siege engines, led by a monster named *Warwolf*, battered at the castle walls. Lethal earthenware bombs of 'Greek fire' (sulphur and saltpetre, mixed with pitch and charcoal) showered down on the defenders. Despite all this formidable firepower, however, Stirling Castle was only surrendered, on 24 July, when the garrison ran out of food. Its leaders were publicly humiliated, but their lives were spared.

Before the end of the siege, Sir Simon Fraser put discretion before valour and submitted to King Edward; but at the same time, Robert Bruce was making a move in a very different direction. On 11 June, while he was a bystander at the siege, he slipped away to nearby Cambuskenneth Abbey[1] where he had a meeting with Bishop William

---

1 There is little left today of Cambuskenneth Abbey, which lies a kilometre or so east of Stirling. It was an important Augustinian foundation, and Robert Bruce would use it as the venue for the parliament of 1326 which acknowledged his son (David II) as his heir; it also

Lamberton of St Andrews.[1] What they discussed can only be surmised; but at the end they signed a private bond in which they promised

> *that they should mutually help each other in all their several business and affairs and at all times and against all other persons whatever without any deceit, and that neither of them should undertake any important business without the other of them. They will mutually warn each other against any impending danger and do the best to avert the same from the other.*

The document made no specific mention of Bruce's claim to the throne, but commentators agree that this must have been the motive behind it.

King Edward knew nothing of this private treaty when he left Scotland in triumph in the summer of 1304, and Robert Bruce dutifully took part in Edward's plans for a new administration for Scotland as a province of England. In September 1305 this would be formalised as an 'Ordinance for Government of the land of Scotland' – a new constitution, no less, with an English viceroy (Edward's nephew, the Earl of Richmond), drawn up in consultation with a commission consisting of twenty English representatives and ten Scots.

One piece of important business had been left outstanding when King Edward left Scotland, however: the matter of William Wallace. On the very day after the showpiece siege of Stirling ended, Edward had ordered the people of Scotland, but especially Sir John Comyn, Sir Simon Fraser and others, 'to exert themselves until twenty days after Christmas to capture Sir William Wallace and hand him over to the king, who will watch to see how each one conducts himself so that he can do most favour to whoever shall capture Wallace, with regard to exile or legal claims or expiation of past sins'.

Wallace was now clearly marked as Public Enemy Number 1, the object of an intensely personal and vindictive royal vendetta. In addition to the pressure he had put on Comyn and Fraser, King Edward suborned a number of other Scotsmen with tempting bribes. He also put a price of £100 on Wallace's head. For Edward, Wallace symbolised the spirit of Scotland's resistance which could only be

---

became the burial place, in the fifteenth century, of James III and his queen, Margrethe of Denmark. Today the only substantial survivor of the building is the thirteenth-century free-standing bell-tower, although the foundations of the abbey church can still be seen.

1 Bishop Lamberton would assist at Bruce's coronation in 1306.

finally broken if the Scots themselves turned in the already legendary folk-hero to face the king's punishment.

William Wallace was now on his own, and his capture – and inevitable death – could only be a matter of time.

Capture and death

In Sir Walter Scott's house at Abbotsford, crammed with antiquarian memorabilia, there is a rather special chair. It was made from the wood of the rafters of a barn in Robroyston, a district at the northern rim of Glasgow, and presented to Scott in 1822. This barn, long since demolished, is said to have been the place where William Wallace was captured on 3 August 1305. A tall monument in the shape of a Celtic cross with a great sword embossed on the front was unveiled to mark the spot in 1900; it was restored in 1986, when new housing estates were extending the urban boundaries of Glasgow. It now stands islanded in oak trees beside a quiet stretch of the B812 from Robroyston to Lenzie.

What had Wallace been doing in the months before his capture? Documentary references to him at this time are scanty, but we can safely surmise that he lived an ever more desperate life on the run, perhaps with a handful of fellow-outlaws, a fugitive hiding in caves and forest fastnesses as the net closed in on him. Any resistance to English subjection was now over, and Wallace cannot have found many sympathisers who were willing to risk their lives to help him, however much they had admired his exploits in the past.

In the end, inevitably, he was captured; and, just as inevitably, his capture was effected not by a military action but by a fellow-Scot. Sir John Menteith has come down in history as an arch-traitor, the man who betrayed and delivered into his enemies' hands the great war-hero who had led the Scots in their struggle for freedom and the restoration of their rightful king.

The circumstances of Wallace's capture, like so much else, have been the subject of much embroidery, by folklore and by Blind Harry. Sir John Menteith was a member of the Stewart family, and uncle of the gallant Sir John Stewart who had died with his archers at the Battle of Falkirk. Like so many other Scottish knights he had fought for the Scots at the Battle of Dunbar in 1296 and been imprisoned for his pains, then earned his release by fighting for King Edward on the expedition to France in 1297. When he returned he had joined the Scottish cause, and by October 1301 he was described in English documents as 'the king's enemy'. Again, like so many other knights, he submitted to Edward in the surrender of February 1304, and as part of the king's pardon he was appointed sheriff of Dumbarton and constable of Dumbarton Castle in March 1304.

Blind Harry, predictably, emphasises the presumed treachery: Menteith was a close personal friend of Wallace; Wallace was godfather to two of his children; Wallace trusted him completely; Wallace had no suspicions when another of Menteith's nephews attached himself to Wallace's dwindling band; Wallace was lured to Glasgow by the false promise of a meeting with Robert Bruce; and so on.

What is incontrovertible is that a payment of forty Scots *merks* was made to 'a servant who spied out William Wallace' (*un vallet qui espia Will. le Waleys*), along with a further payment of sixty *merks* 'to be given to the others . . . who were at the taking of the said William, to be shared by them'. The 'taking of William Wallace' happened late on the evening of 3 August. Wallace was lurking in what is now Robroyston when he was surprised by Menteith's men in an isolated building in the forest there. He was overpowered and taken to Dumbarton Castle in fetters. From Dumbarton he was conveyed under heavy escort, secretly and by night, south to Carlisle, where he was handed into the custody of Sir John de Segrave, a professional soldier who had recently been appointed Warden of Scotland south of the Forth.

From Carlisle Wallace was taken on a triumphal seventeen-day journey, his hands bound behind his back and his feet roped beneath his horse's belly. In every town and village the local people turned out to stare and jeer at the shackled ogre who had plagued their king for so many years. The contemporary English *Lanercost Chronicle* was exultant:

> *The vilest doom is fittest for thys crimes,*
> *Justice demands that thou shouldst die three times.*
> *Thou pillager of many a sacred shrine,*
> *Butcher of thousands, threefold death be thine!*
> *So shall the English from thee gain relief,*
> *Scotland! Be wise and choose a nobler chief.*

When the procession reached London the throng was so great, apparently, that it could not reach the Tower, and Wallace was lodged overnight in the house of an alderman in Fenchurch Street. Next morning, 23 August, he was taken to Westminster Hall accompanied by a host of civic dignitaries and soldiers.

Westminster Hall is much the oldest surviving part of the Houses of Parliament, a vast, cavernous chamber which was the largest medieval hall in Europe when it was completed in 1099. In the early days it was used for state feasts and other great events – and for state trials. Sir Thomas More was tried and condemned here in 1535, Guy Fawkes in 1606 and, most famously of all, King Charles I in January 1649: a plaque set into the last step of the second flight of stone stairs at the south end of the hall commemorates that dramatic occasion, and draws the attention of every one of the thousands of visitors who flock into the Hall when Parliament is in recess.

Another plaque, made of brass, is set into the floor of the upper landing and commemorates the 'trial' of William Wallace. It was installed at the instigation of the Labour MP for Bothwell, John Robertson, and unveiled on 31 October 1924 (the idea came from some schoolchildren in his constituency whom he had been showing round Westminster). The inscription is now very worn and difficult to read, and most visitors to the Hall walk right over it or past it without noticing what it says:

> *Near this spot, at the Kings Bench at the South end of the Hall, took place the trial of Sir William Wallace the Scottish Patriot on Monday 23rd August 1305.*

Today Westminster Hall has the feel of a mausoleum, a gigantic echoing cenotaph of memories; but when William Wallace appeared before the Court of King's Bench, mockingly crowned with laurel leaves, the place would have been like a bear-pit. The judges sat at a table on the raised, south-east part of the hall. Below them the floor was crammed with noisy spectators, some of them perhaps seated in specially erected wooden stands. The magnificent hammer-beam roof would not be built for nearly another century, but it would have been an awe-inspiring place nonetheless.

'Scottish Patriot' is not a term which Wallace's judges would have recognised; and 'trial' is not a term we would apply to the proceedings today. They consisted of a recital of the charges, immediate conviction and, inevitably, a sentence of death; no copy of the arraignment for the prisoner, no jury, no defence witnesses, no defence counsel even.

The commissioners appointed by King Edward to conduct the trial were Sir John de Segrave, Sir Peter Mallory (the Justiciar of England), Ralph de Sandwich (Constable of the Tower), John de Bacwell (a judge) and Sir John le Blound, or Blunt (Lord Mayor of London).

Mallory read out the long and sonorous indictment: William Wallace, 'a Scot and of Scottish birth', was charged with treason, murder, spoliation of property, robbery, arson, sacrilege and atrocities and 'horrible enormities' of every kind; he had driven out all the wardens and servants of the Lord King, he had convened Scottish parliaments, he had tried to persuade the Scottish nobles to submit to the lordship of the King of France and to help that king to destroy the realm of England.

The prisoner was not expected to plead. But according to an eyewitness at the trial, although Wallace may have acknowledged most of the crimes with which he was charged (they were public knowledge, after all), he denied that he was guilty of treason, on the irrefutable ground that he had never sworn personal allegiance or done homage to King Edward of England. The court's argument was that John Balliol's surrender of the kingdom of Scotland in 1296 had made all Scots automatically vassals of the English king, whether they had sworn personal oaths of fealty or not.

But argument was irrelevant. King Edward was determined to make a public example of Wallace, and to have him suffer the barbarously brutal execution meted out to traitors. Sir John de Segrave was given the honour of reading out the pre-ordained sentence – for Wallace to be hanged, drawn and quartered:

> ... *That the said William, for the manifest sedition that he practised against the Lord King himself, by feloniously contriving and acting with a view to his death and to the abasement and subversion of his crown and royal dignity, by bearing a hostile banner against his liege lord in war to the death, shall be drawn from the Palace of Westminster to the Tower of London, and from the Tower to Aldgate, and so through the midst of the City to the Elms ...*

'The Elms' were at Smithfield, on the northern edge of the city as it was then.

As soon as sentence had been pronounced, Wallace was taken outside and stripped naked, then bound to a hurdle, face up, and thus dragged through the crowded, jeering streets at the tails of two horses. It was a hideous journey, an especially long, circuitous route of more than four miles in order to expose the prisoner to the maximum insult and indignity.

On the façade of St Bartholomew's Hospital, facing the entrance to

Smithfield Meat Market, is a handsome plaque which was unveiled in April 1956:

To the immortal memory of
Sir William Wallace
Scottish patriot born at Elderslie Renfrewshire circa 1270 A.D.
who from the year 1296 fought dauntlessly in defence of his
country's liberty and independence in the face of fearful odds and
great hardship being eventually betrayed and captured brought to
London and put to death near this spot on the 23rd August 1305
His example heroism and devotion inspired those who came
after him to win victory from defeat and his memory remains
for all time a source of pride honour and inspiration to his
countrymen

On a railing below the plaque bouquets of flowers are usually to be seen. Here Wallace was led up onto 'a gallows of unusual height, specially prepared for him' (according to Matthew of Westminster, an onlooker, in his *Flores Historiarium*). And now the long-drawn-out execution began – the triple death over which the Lanercost chronicler had exulted.

First, 'for the robberies, homicides and felonies he committed in the realm of England and in the land of Scotland', as the death-sentence put it, Wallace was hanged by the neck to the very point of strangulation, before he was cut down, half-alive, from the gallows. After he had regained consciousness the torment continued. His genitals were cut off, and he was 'drawn', like a chicken: his intestines were pulled from his belly, then his lungs and liver and finally his heart, when the long agony would come to an end. His innards were then ceremonially burned by the executioner. That was the second death, 'for the measureless turpitude of his deeds towards God and Holy Church'. Only then was his lifeless body decapitated, for his outlawry – the third death.

What remained of his body was now quartered – butchered into four parts – and the quarters were distributed to different parts of the country for exposure on gibbets in Newcastle upon Tyne, Berwick, Stirling and Perth 'as a warning and a deterrent to all that pass by and behold them'. His head was placed on a spike and hoisted above London Bridge.

Through the very public humiliation of a traitor's death, King Edward must have believed that he would not only exterminate his enemy but extirpate his very existence. He was to be disappointed, for in the event he achieved the very opposite – he created a martyr. Elspeth King says:

> *Edward was determined* not *to create a martyr, and that was why Wallace's body had to be destroyed and dispersed; in order to destroy Wallace's memory totally, Edward had to destroy Wallace's body totally, to desecrate it and be utterly rid of it. There's an exact parallel between that and the treatment of Joan of Arc a couple of centuries later, when she was literally destroyed by the English: her body was burned and the ashes cast away so that no trace of her might remain.*
>
> *But because of the very savagery of the treatment which Edward meted out to Wallace, the people of Scotland wanted desperately to remember him. Officially, Wallace ceased to exist; he was completely written out of Scottish history by John Barbour in* The Brus, *his epic poem about Bruce which was commissioned by the Bruce dynasty in the 1370s [see Chapter 11]. It was not until Blind Harry in the 1470s, a century later, that the stories of Wallace were collected and written down as a quasi-historical epic.*
>
> *These stories were part of what we can call a 'people story', because the people wanted to cling on to his memory, and the way of doing that was through personal, local remembrance in the areas in which Wallace had operated. That is why there are so many Wallace stones in Scotland, so many Wallace trees, so many Wallace wells – there is even a Wallace thumbprint on a rock on Bizzyberry Hill, near Biggar in Lanarkshire. The Irish have a word for this concept – dinnshenchas, the telling and constant retelling of stories around places, and the stories reinforce the identification of these geographical features. These stories grew in the telling; greater and greater deeds were ascribed to Wallace, as they are to heroic warriors all over the world.*

Wallace the hero became the darling of nineteenth-century Scotland. In 1814 the eccentric Earl of Buchan erected a colossal pink-stone statue of him in the grounds of his home at Bemersyde, near Dryburgh.[1] The pinnacle of Wallace-worship was the erection in the 1860s

---

1 It stands, seven metres high on a bluff above the Tweed, frowning fiercely; on the plinth are carved the words 'Great Patriot hero. Ill requited Chief'. Sir Walter Scott utterly loathed

of the Wallace Monument on the Abbey Craig by Stirling. There had been plans to build it on Glasgow Green, and Edinburgh had also expressed interest, but Stirling was selected as the most suitable 'neutral' ground between the two cities for this 'material remembrance of Scotland's independence and individuality'.[1]

Today, more than ever, Wallace is popularly revered as *the* national hero of Scotland, the one man (unlike Robert Bruce) who never compromised with English tyranny. It is noteworthy that a 1996 film, *The Bruce*, made nothing like the impact of the earlier *Braveheart*: it was *Braveheart*, not *The Bruce*, which not only reflected but may well have influenced the growing popular movement for a separate Scottish Parliament. It can hardly be a coincidence that when the referendum which would ratify a new Scottish Parliament was held in 1997, the date chosen for the vote was 11 September – seven hundred years to the day since Wallace's spectacular victory over the English army at Stirling Bridge on 11 September 1297.

---

this statue, and told James Hogg (the 'Ettrick Shepherd'): 'If I live to see the day when the men of Scotland, like the children of Israel, shall every day do that which is right in his own eyes (which I am certain either I or my immediate successors will see), I have settled in my mind long ago what I shall do first. I will go down and blow up the statue of Wallace with gunpowder. Yes, I will blow it up in such style that there will not be a fragment of it left: the horrible monster' (James Hogg, *Anecdotes of Sir W. Scott*).

1   The Wallace Monument project in Stirling was inaugurated on a tidal wave of public enthusiasm at a gathering of thirteen thousand people in King's Park, Stirling, in June 1856. The laying of the foundation stone five years later attracted a crowd of eighty thousand from all over Scotland. The building works led to prolonged acrimony and bickering, however, and the monument was eventually opened at a distinctly low-key ceremony in September 1869.

Chapter 11

ROBERT BRUCE (r.1306–29)

Now, this Robert the Bruce was a remarkably brave and strong man: there was no man in Scotland that was thought a match for him except Sir William Wallace; and now that Wallace was dead, Bruce was held the best warrior in Scotland. He was very wise and prudent, and an excellent general . . . He was generous, too, and courteous by nature; but he had some faults, which perhaps belonged as much to the fierce period in which he lived as to his own character. He was rash and passionate, and in his passions, he was sometimes relentless and cruel.

TALES OF A GRANDFATHER, CHAPTER VIII

On 24 June 1998, the 684th anniversary of the Battle of Bannockburn, the heart of this 'rash and passionate' man, Robert Bruce, was buried in Melrose Abbey for the third time, 669 years after his death. Donald Dewar, the Secretary of State for Scotland at the time (and about to become the First Minister in the new devolved Scottish Parliament), unveiled a circular sandstone marker on the lawn outside the Chapter House of the abbey to mark the reburial of a small lead casket. The stone was inscribed with a legend taken from John Barbour's great vernacular chivalric epic, *The Brus*: 'A noble hart may have nane [no] ease . . . gif [if] freedom failye' (Book I).

The casket had been unearthed two years earlier from under the Chapter House by archaeologists from Historic Scotland. Inside it was another, unmarked lead casket, and a note written by the archaeologists who had dug it up in 1921: 'The enclosed leaden casket containing a heart was found beneath the Chapter House floor in March 1921 . . .'. The casket had been examined, placed inside a larger lead casket and then reburied. Unfortunately there was no indication of *where* it had been reburied, and no one could remember the location. But at least the 1921 excavation had verified that it contained a human heart, and since no other heart is reported to have been buried at Melrose, it could be asserted, with some confidence, that the medieval casket which was found and unearthed again in 1998 did, indeed, contain Robert Bruce's mummified heart. And with that, the last relic of Bruce's earthly remains was laid to its final rest. As Donald Dewar said:

> *We cannot know for certain whether the casket buried here contains the heart of Robert the Bruce, but in a sense it does not matter. The casket and the heart are symbols of the man.*

When Bruce died in 1329 he was buried in Dunfermline Abbey before the High Altar with exceptional reverence. A marble tomb was shipped over from Paris, and his body was wrapped in a shroud of cloth-of-gold and encased in a thin sheet of lead. The inscription on the tomb read:

> *Here lies the invincible Robert, Blessed King. Let him who reads his exploits repeat how many wars he carried on. He led the Kingdom of the Scots to Freedom by his Uprightness. Now let him live in the Citadel of Heaven.*

Over the centuries the old abbey fell into ruin, and the location of the tomb was lost. In February 1818, however, workmen clearing the floor of the choir of the abbey church before rebuilding came upon the vault which contained the royal burial. News of the discovery and official confirmation of its authenticity unleashed an extraordinary wave of patriotism throughout Scotland. The plans for the new abbey were altered to accommodate, below the high pulpit, a railed enclosure for the ornate gilded grave-slab covering the reburied vault.

The skeleton was that of a man about six feet tall. What made identification certain was that the breastbone had been cut to allow the heart to be removed. On his deathbed, Bruce had asked that his heart should be taken from his body and carried to the Holy Land in order to fulfil a lifelong ambition even after death. Obedient to the late king's wish, one of his most loyal supporters, James Douglas (the

'Black Douglas'), had set off for the Crusades with Bruce's embalmed heart. In Spain he was caught up in a campaign against the Moors of Granada, and was killed in battle in 1330. Eventually his body, and the king's heart, were returned to Scotland, and the heart was buried in Melrose Abbey as Bruce had wished.

The ceremony at Melrose in June 1998 marked the end of a long and hazardous journey for the remains of one of Scotland's favourite sons and hero-figures, the man who is credited with having achieved Scotland's independence and nationhood at last. Donald Dewar said:

> *Bruce gave definition to the Scottish crown and the country he ruled. He was himself one of the great leaders of our history. More than that, he shaped the relationship between Scots and their leaders. He fought to protect his people, not to vanquish their enemies.*

It was a judicious and refreshingly unbiased summation. The name of 'Robert Bruce' arouses mixed responses in Scotland, especially in recent years when the role of William Wallace as *the* Scottish Patriot has been more strongly emphasised at the expense of the part played by Bruce in the independence struggle. Bruce has been castigated for not being as 'patriotic' as Wallace, because he changed his allegiance more than once – yet the concept of 'patriotism' did not, and could not, exist in the Scotland of the time. He has been denigrated as a 'Norman' incomer, an alien in Scotland – despite the fact that he was the *sixth* Robert Bruce to be born in Scotland since the first Robert Bruce from Brix, created Lord of Cleveland by Henry I, was granted the lands of Annandale by King David I; and it should be remembered that Wallace, too, was of Anglo-Norman stock – his family seems to have followed the Stewarts to Scotland from Shropshire and perhaps even from Brittany. Bruce has also been blamed for the activities of what we would now call spin-doctors employed later by the Bruce dynasty – notably the poet John Barbour, who air-brushed Bruce's image to the extent of trying to write William Wallace out of Scottish history altogether: there is no mention of him at all in *The Brus*.[1]

---

1 John Barbour was one of the great fourteenth-century Scottish 'makars' (makers of words), and *The Brus* is considered one of the great masterpieces of Scottish literature. He was born sometime between 1325 and 1335 and enjoyed a comfortable rise in the Church hierarchy to become archdeacon of Aberdeen Cathedral. When Robert II became King of Scotland in 1371, Barbour was summoned to court and commissioned to write *The Brus*. Part of the purpose of the epic was not only to remove Wallace from the historical record, but to glorify

ROBERT BRUCE (r.1306–29)

The sixth Robert Bruce was born in Turnberry Castle in 1274, the eldest of ten children. He had four brothers – Edward, Thomas, Alexander and Neil – and five sisters – Mary, Christian, Matilda, Margaret and Isabella (who in 1293 married Erik II, the widower king of Norway and father of the 'Maid of Norway'). In 1295 Robert Bruce married Isabella of Mar. The following year, Isabella died in childbirth; the baby, a daughter, was named Marjory (after Bruce's mother), and she, through her marriage to Walter the Steward (Stewart) in 1315, would transmit the royal succession from the 'Robert dynasty' to the start of the Stewart dynasty through her son, Robert II (see Chapter 13).

The resistance movement led by William Wallace in 1297–98 placed Robert Bruce, the young Earl of Carrick, in a real quandary. Wallace consistently fought in the name of the man he regarded as the rightful King of Scots, John Balliol, who had been deposed by Edward I; the Bruce family, on the other hand, felt that their own claim to the throne had been stronger than Balliol's. Furthermore, King Edward's grip on the south of Scotland was much tighter than on the north: young Robert Bruce was caught in the difficult dilemma of having to reconcile the conflicting demands of being a vassal of the kings of both Scotland and England.

After Wallace's defeat at Falkirk in 1298 it behoved the nobility of Scotland, the 'natural' ruling class, to take up the resistance battle; and the vacuum caused by Wallace's fall as the military and political leader of the nation was filled by the appointment of two Guardians. One was Robert Bruce; the other was John Comyn, Lord of Badenoch, the 'Red Comyn'. This unlikely partnership did not last; but it brought into high relief the simmering tension between two of the most significant noble families in the land.

In terms of political and landed clout the Comyns, loyal supporters of King John Balliol, were pre-eminent in Scotland. They were the government party, and had been throughout the thirteenth century. Their main power-base was well north of the Forth–Clyde axis, in Badenoch and Buchan, but a network of marriage alliances gave them strength and a string of castles all over the country.[1]

---

the Stewart dynasty at the expense of the Comyn family (the Comyns had fought for Scotland's independence while the Bruces had been supporters of Edward I of England). As a reward, Barbour was awarded a pension of £10 a year in 1388. He died in March 1395.

1 The list of Comyn castles and power-bases throughout Scotland at the end of the thirteenth century makes remarkable reading, although few of them survive today. The Great Glen was superintended from Inverlochy Castle in Lochaber to Urquhart Castle at the head of Loch Ness. In Moray they owned Balvenie Castle and the rather sinister island castle of Lochindorb

By comparison the Bruces were rather marginal; apart from their lands in Annandale and Carrick they had an important marriage alliance with the Earl of Mar (husband of Bruce's sister Christian) which gave them a foothold in the north-east. But that was all.

In 1302, when it looked as if John Balliol might be restored to the Scottish throne, Bruce defected to the English side (see Chapter 10). His submission to King Edward was rewarded by a marriage alliance with Elizabeth de Burgh, daughter of the Earl of Ulster; this second marriage would bring him much-needed support in Ireland in later years. The immediate effect of his return to the English fold, however, was to marginalise him further as a force in Scotland; even his traditional supporters, like James the Steward (Stewart) and the Earl of Atholl, lost faith in him. No one could have expected him to make a political comeback.

The submission to Edward of John Comyn of Badenoch (nephew of King John Balliol) and the rest of the Scottish government in February 1304 was a very different matter: it was Comyn who had been the real 'patriot' in the struggle with England, not Bruce. The Scottish army, such as it was, had not been defeated in the field; the Scots had kept the mighty English war machine at bay for eight years, but there had been a haemorrhaging of support, especially in the south, among the leaders of the local communities who were tired of war, tired of harassment, tired of being hammered financially. Fiona Watson says:

> Submission was surely the sensible, pragmatic thing to do. Scotland had been abandoned by France and was isolated internationally. People also realised that King Edward would not live for ever, and that his son Edward was probably not as implacably hostile to Scotland as his father was – so why not submit now and see what happened when Edward died? So they submitted, on reasonably lenient terms, and lived to fight another day.

The brutal execution of William Wallace must have sent a shiver of apprehension through the ranks of the Scottish aristocracy, as a dire warning of the penalty for crossing King Edward. There is no record

---

('Isle of Trouble'), from which the 'Wolf of Badenoch' launched his arson attack on Elgin Cathedral in 1390 (see pages 211–12). Buchan was studded with Comyn fortresses – Cairnbulg, Dundarg, Kingedward, Rattray and Slains. In the central Highlands they held Ruthven Castle in Strathspey (now occupied by the ruins of Ruthven Barracks and Blair Atholl). In the south and south-west (where the Bruce family had their influence) they held Kirkintilloch, Kilbride Cruggleton and Kirkcudbright.

of what Robert Bruce thought about it, but he was aware that he was out of favour with Edward. Edward did not know of Bruce's secret pact with Bishop Lamberton in July 1304, but he was aware of Bruce's ambition to be king, and Bruce had not been favoured with any important administrative post in the new constitution which Edward was preparing for Scotland. Bruce was evidently preparing for a political comeback, but he was playing a highly dangerous game.

Now in his early thirties, Bruce was probably planning ahead to such time as Edward was dead. There are conflicting indications that he made overtures of some kind to the Red Comyn. According to Walter Bower's *Scotichronicon* and John Barbour in *The Brus*, he offered Comyn a choice: that Comyn himself should take the throne (even though the legitimate heir was John Balliol's son, Edward Balliol) and grant to Bruce all his lands and possessions, or that Bruce should become king and Comyn should receive all Bruce's lands. Comyn allegedly accepted the latter proposition, and the bargain was sealed.

The idea of any kind of written compact, however vaguely worded, seems unlikely, for such a document would have been dangerously incriminating if it had fallen into Edward's hands. But there may well have been an understanding of some sort between the two men: Comyn knew that his own claim to the throne was very much weaker than that of Bruce, and Bruce knew that he could hardly hope to be king of a united nation without the wholehearted support of the powerful and patriotic Comyn faction.

But events were to take a dramatic and wholly unexpected turn on 10 February 1306, after Bruce and Comyn had arranged to hold a private discussion in the neutral sanctuary of the Church of the Grey Friars in Dumfries.

He who would be king

> They met in the church of the Minorities in that town, before the high altar. What passed betwixt them is not known for certainty; but they quarrelled, either concerning their mutual pretensions to the crown, or because Comyn refused to join Bruce in the proposed insurrection against the English ... It is, however, certain, that these two haughty barons came to high and abusive words, until at length Bruce, who I told you was extremely passionate, forgot the sacred character of the place in which they stood, and struck Comyn a blow with his dagger.
>
> TALES OF A GRANDFATHER, CHAPTER VIII

There is nothing left now, above ground, of the 'Greyfriars Church' where Robert Bruce murdered the Red Comyn. The killing took place in the church of the old Franciscan priory which had been established in 1262 on the left bank of the River Nith in the centre of the old burgh. Bruce, to expiate his guilt, gave the Franciscans a generous annuity; but during the Reformation the priory disappeared.

The precise spot, masked by a row of glass bus-shelters, is now identified by a plaque on the wall between two windows of the yellow-and-red '£-stretcher' shop at 9–13 Castle Street, almost opposite the present Greyfriars Church. It was erected by 'the citizens of Dumfries and the Saltire Society' in 1951:

> Here stood the monastery
> of the GREY FRIARS where
> on Thursday 10th February
> 1306 ROBERT THE BRUCE
> aided by
> SIR ROGER KIRKPATRICK
> slew THE RED COMYN and
> opened the final stage
> of the war for
> SCOTTISH INDEPENDENCE
> which ended victoriously on
> the FIELD of BANNOCKBURN,
> 1314.
> 'I Mak Siccar'

The words 'I mak siccar' (*I make certain*) are said to have been spoken not by Bruce but by one of his companions, Sir Roger de Kirkpatrick. The story goes that Bruce, after the stabbing, had rushed from the church, saying that he thought he had killed Comyn. Kirkpatrick was appalled that he had not finished the job, and ran into the church where he delivered the *coup de grâce* to the stricken Comyn.

Ironically, that was the one way in which Bruce would not 'mak siccar' his attempt on the throne. Some commentators have claimed that the killing of Comyn was premeditated, in order to get him out of the way of Bruce's ambitions; but Bruce knew that he had to have Comyn support for his bid for the throne – and nothing could have been more disastrous for his chances than to antagonise the most powerful family in the land, not just by murder, but by sacrilegious murder at that.

But the deed was done, and the die was now cast – much sooner than Bruce could have wanted, and in much worse circumstances than he could have envisaged. If he was to have any chance of success he had to act, and act fast. Whatever contingency plans he might have discussed with Bishop Lamberton and others had to be brought forward in a hurry.

There was no time to lose. The Comyn castles in the south-west were seized, while Bruce went to Glasgow to try to make peace with the Church. He made his confession to Bishop George Wishart and received absolution for his sin; in exchange he swore an oath that, as king, he would be obedient to the clergy of Scotland. Then he rode off to be proclaimed king.

Six weeks after the murder, on 25 March 1306, Robert Bruce was inaugurated as King of Scots at Scone. It was a symbolic, simple and obviously makeshift ceremony. There was no Stone of Destiny on which to be enthroned – that had been removed by Edward I as part of his subjugation of Scotland in 1298. There were no royal robes, no sceptre, no royal sword and no bishops (although Bishop William Lamberton arrived two days later to celebrate High Mass for Bruce).

The traditional role of leading the new king to the throne should have been taken by the Earl of Fife, but he was only sixteen years old and still a ward of King Edward; in his place his aunt, Isabella of Fife, the Countess of Buchan, claimed her familial right to enthrone the king. She led Bruce to the throne and set a simple gold circlet on his head. The Earl of Buchan, who was in England at the time, was a cousin of the murdered Comyn, and Isabella's defection to the Bruce cause was a terrible blow to him. It was to cost her dear: when she was captured by the English later that year she was imprisoned for four years in an open wooden cage which was suspended from the battlements of Berwick Castle.

The hurried coronation at Scone was the signal for the outbreak of civil war in Scotland. Bruce did not enjoy much support; he did not represent the Community of the Realm in Scotland and, above all, the rightful king, John Balliol, was still alive, albeit in exile in France. Almost immediately after Bruce's inauguration the Comyns started to gather their strength. Edward I appointed the Red Comyn's able brother-in-law, Aymer de Valence (soon to be Earl of Pembroke), as his special lieutenant in Scotland with wide-ranging powers against Bruce – he was commanded to 'burn and slay and raise dragon', which meant unfurling the dragon standard which proclaimed that the normal conventions of war were in abeyance: captured knights would be treated as outlaws and executed. In addition, King Edward persuaded Pope Clement V to authorise the excommunication of the new King of Scots; this was pronounced by the Archbishop of Canterbury on 5 June 1306.

Bruce moved quickly to consolidate his power-base in the southwest of Scotland. From there he moved north, through Glasgow and via Perth to Aberdeen to raise support in the north – traditionally the chief power-base of the Comyns. He had some initial successes, taking the town of Dundee and the castles of Brechin and Cupar, but soon he came under formidable military pressure. An English army, led by Pembroke and supported by Comyn adherents, recaptured Cupar and the city of Perth. Bruce moved south to meet Pembroke. He had no siege engines with which to invest the city, so instead he issued a challenge to Pembroke to come out and fight, or else surrender. Pembroke apparently accepted the challenge to do battle the following day, while his Comyn allies (according to Barbour) were treacherously planning a surprise attack on the Scots that very night.

Bruce drew off his forces and encamped six miles away in Methven Wood; suspecting no treachery, they laid aside their weapons and set no watch. At dusk their enemies fell upon them, determined to take Bruce dead or alive. After a savage battle the Scots were routed, and many of Bruce's lieutenants were taken prisoner. Bruce himself escaped, however, with some of his light cavalry, and took refuge in the wild hills of Atholl. He had been king for only four months, but was now a fugitive.

Before moving south, Bruce had left his second wife, Elizabeth de Burgh, and his ten-year-old daughter Marjory by his first wife, along with the other ladies of his court, in the care of the Earl of Atholl in Kildrummy Castle on Donside, which was held by his brother Neil. Early in September the castle fell to Pembroke (through treachery, it is said), and Neil Bruce was taken prisoner. The royal ladies, including Isabella, Countess of Buchan, had escaped, however, and were already on their way north with the Earl of Atholl to seek refuge in Orkney; from there they planned to make their way to Norway and the protection of Bruce's sister Isabella, who had married Erik II after the death of his first wife and was now Dowager Queen of Norway. But before they could reach the relative safety of Orkney their party was intercepted at Tain, on the southern shore of the Dornoch Firth, by the Earl of Ross, a Comyn supporter, and they were all were handed over to the English.

The English revenge on the Bruces and their supporters was swift and terrible. Robert's brother Neil was hanged, drawn and quartered at Berwick. His loyal lieutenants the Earl of Atholl and Simon Fraser were taken to London for execution: Atholl was hanged on a specially high gallows before being decapitated and burned, while Fraser had his head impaled on a spike beside that of William Wallace. Bruce's sister Mary was suspended in a cage (like Isabella, Countess of Buchan) from the battlements of Roxburgh Castle where she, too, was to remain for four years. His daughter Marjory was sent to a Yorkshire nunnery. Another of his sisters, Christian, who was married to Christopher Seton (one of those who had been present at the death of the Red Comyn), was sent to a nunnery in Lincolnshire; Christopher himself was hanged, drawn and quartered in Dumfries, and his brother John was put to death in the same barbaric manner at Newcastle. Only Bruce's wife, Elizabeth de Burgh, was treated with anything like leniency; because her father was the Earl of Ulster, who had always been loyal to Edward I, she was imprisoned (albeit in harsh conditions) in a royal manor at Burstwick-in-Holderness.

Robert Bruce's position was now desperate. An English chronicler reported that his queen had prophesied to Bruce that he would only be king for the summer – 'King of Winter you will not be'. That was certainly the way it looked now. In late July he was ambushed in a narrow defile known as Dalrigh (Field of the King), just south of Tyndrum, by John Macdougall of Argyll – son-in-law of the murdered Comyn and owner of Dunstaffnage Castle; he suffered heavy casualties, and only escaped with his life after a heroic rearguard action. With that he disappeared as far as his enemies were concerned, and disappeared, too, from the historical record for the winter.

Bruce and the spider

. . . Bruce was looking upward at the roof of the cabin in which he lay; and his eye was attracted by a spider, which, hanging at the end of a long thread of its own spinning, was endeavouring, as is the fashion of that creature, to swing itself from one beam in the roof to another, for the purpose of fixing the line on which it meant to stretch its web. The insect made the attempt again and again without success; and at length Bruce counted that it had tried to carry its point six times, and been as often unable to do so. It came into his head that he had himself fought just six battles against the English and their allies, and that the poor persevering spider was exactly in the same situation with himself,

*having made as many trials, and been as often disappointed in
what it aimed at. 'Now,' thought Bruce, 'as I have no means of
knowing what is best to be done, I will be guided by the luck
which shall attend this spider. If the insect shall make another
effort to fix its thread, and shall be successful, I will venture a
seventh time to try my fortune in Scotland . . .'*

TALES OF A GRANDFATHER, CHAPTER VIII

The story of the spider which refused to give up is the one thing which
everyone knows about Robert the Bruce. Children are taught it at
school; tourist guides tell it in every 'Bruce's Cave' on their itinerary
– all thanks to Sir Walter Scott. The 'King's Caves' on Arran are a
favourite spot for visitors. Another is the small island of Rathlin, a
few miles off the coast of Antrim in Ireland, where Bruce seems to
have spent at least part of the winter of 1306–7. But any cave will do
– because the spider story simply is not, and cannot be, true. Sir
Walter Scott did not invent it; but he certainly was the first person to
father it on Robert Bruce.

The story had first appeared two hundred years earlier in a history
of the Douglas family written by Hume of Godscroft. According to
him it was James Douglas, the 'Black Douglas', Bruce's greatest captain
and the secondary hero of Barbour's *The Brus*, who saw a spider –
not Bruce. Douglas watched this spider trying to climb a tree (not the
roof of a cave) with its web, and falling to the ground twelve times.
When it tried for the thirteenth time it succeeded. Douglas then told
the story to Bruce while he was a fugitive in the Hebrides, to encourage
him to try, try and try again, even though he had already suffered
twelve reverses in battle: 'My advise [sic] is to follow the example of
the spider, to poush forward your Majestie's fortune once more, and
hazard yet our persones the 13 tyme.' It was a homily, a parable of
leadership – and Scott lifted it and made Bruce, not Douglas, the
central figure.[1]

No one now knows where Bruce spent the desperate weeks and
months on the run in the winter of 1306/7. Some say the Western
Isles. Some say the Northern Isles. Some say Ireland. Some even say
Norway. When spring came, however, he burst into history again,
apparently annealed and tempered by his ordeals, with his determi-

---

1 The first time the Douglas manuscript was put on public display was in an exhibition entitled
'Freedom is a Noble Thing', put on by the Scottish Record Office (now the National Archives
of Scotland) at HM General Register House, Edinburgh, in 1996.

nation to succeed renewed. Perhaps Douglas's story of the plucky spider, if not the spider itself, had revitalised his resolve.

When Robert Bruce emerged from hiding early in 1307, it was as a reinvigorated guerrilla leader; but his renewed campaign started disastrously. His first objective was to try to regain control in the south-west of Scotland. He mounted a seaborne expedition from Ireland, splitting his forces in two. One division, led by two of his brothers, Alexander and Thomas, headed for Galloway in eighteen galleys; but no sooner had they landed at Loch Ryan than they were overwhelmed by a local force commanded by Dougal MacDougall, a Comyn supporter. Bruce's brothers were captured and dragged off to Carlisle, where they were hanged and beheaded.

Meanwhile Bruce himself, with his other brother Edward and James Douglas, landed on the Ayrshire coast near his birthplace, the castle at Turnberry. He found the countryside terrorised by the English occupation, and went to ground in the wild hinterland of Carrick. Bruce's position was now worse, if anything, than it had been the previous autumn. Once again he was a fugitive king, a king whom no one apparently wanted, and his kingdom seemed more out of reach than ever.

Glen Trool

On a rocky eminence at the head of Loch Trool, in front of the rocky Fell of Eschoncan in Dumfries and Galloway, a great granite boulder shaped like a clenched fist stands square and squat on a plinth of rough stones: 'Bruce's Stone', it is called. It is an impressive memorial, relatively easy of access by public road off the A714 between Girvan and Newton Stewart at the village of Bargennan; the carpark provided by Forest Enterprise is much used by hill-walkers heading for the highest hill in the Southern Uplands, the Merrick (844 metres).

The memorial was unveiled in June 1929, on the six hundredth anniversary of Bruce's death; on it is inscribed, in triumphant capital letters:

> IN LOYAL REMEMBRANCE
> OF
> ROBERT THE BRUCE
> KING OF SCOTS
> WHOSE VICTORY IN THIS
> GLEN OVER AN ENGLISH

FORCE IN MARCH, 1307
OPENED THE CAMPAIGN OF
INDEPENDENCE WHICH HE
BROUGHT TO A DECISIVE
CLOSE AT BANNOCKBURN
ON 24TH JUNE, 1314

The stone commemorates a brief skirmish which took place on the opposite side of the loch, and which hindsight has endowed with a pivotal but exaggerated significance.[1] Bruce and his small band of followers, hiding out in the wild mountainous terrain of Glen Trool, were being hunted by an English force of two thousand men based at Carlisle commanded by the Earl of Pembroke. According to Barbour, Pembroke heard of Bruce's whereabouts and decided to send a raiding party to attack him. He despatched a woman dressed in rags to Bruce's camp to beg for food and come back with information about the size and disposition of his forces. Bruce saw the woman wandering about in the camp and soon suspected her of being a spy; when challenged, she quickly told him that Pembroke and 'the flower of Northumberland' were planning to attack him.

Bruce at once prepared an ambush on the narrow track which ran alongside the loch. The English rode straight into the trap and were easily repulsed. There were few casualties on either side. It was not a major battle, nor a significant victory for Bruce; but its propaganda value was considerable. The mere fact of his escape – and many other escapes which Barbour chronicles – began to lend romance and credibility to the king without, as yet, a proper kingdom.

Much more important was another battle, on 10 May 1307, which was the direct outcome of Glen Trool – Loudon Hill, near Galston in Ayrshire, a few kilometres east of Kilmarnock. The Earl of Pembroke had been stung by his reverse at Glen Trool, and by threatening letters from King Edward I accusing him of being dilatory in his efforts to crush the rebellion. Now Pembroke, according to Barbour, issued a challenge to Bruce to come out of hiding and engage in formal battle.

---

1 Confusingly, there are two 'Bruce's Stones' in the area. Some fifteen kilometres to the east as the crow flies, or fifteen kilometres along the A712 from New Galloway, is another 'Bruce's Stone' on Moss Raploch, on the edge of Clatteringshaws Loch; it is a massive boulder which commemorates a skirmish in the spring of 1307: 'Here on Moss Raploch King Robert the Bruce defeated an English army in 1307. It is said that Bruce rested against the stone after the victory.' This memorial was presented by the Earl of Mar and Kellie to the National Trust for Scotland in 1932 – one of its first acquisitions after its establishment in 1931.

Bruce, rather surprisingly for a guerrilla leader, accepted. He chose his ground with care, placing his men on the slope of a hill under the sharp crag of Loudon Hill. In front of them he dug three lines of trenches lined with sharpened stakes, expertly camouflaged, to await the onslaught of the English knights.

Barbour, doubtless exaggerating the figures, claimed that Pembroke brought three thousand men to the field; Bruce's army of fugitives numbered only six hundred. The English knights, magnificently accoutred, came thundering across the level ground. Suddenly – chaos. The galloping ranks of horsemen went crashing down into the trenches, helpless against the Scottish spearmen. The rearguard saw what had happened and promptly took flight, leaving Pembroke to limp back to Bothwell Castle. The humiliation of Methven Wood had been avenged.

It would be misleading to speak of Loudon Hill, or any other engagement, as a specific 'turning-point' in Bruce's fortunes; but it is clear that the tide was beginning to turn. On 15 May 1307 an official at Forfar Castle sent a report to England:

> I hear that Bruce never had the good will of his own followers or the people generally so much with him as now. It appears that God is with him, for he has destroyed King Edward's power both among English and Scots. The people believe that Bruce will carry all before him . . .

Clearly, Bruce's apparently charmed life was having an effect on English morale and on Scottish confidence. He certainly had not 'destroyed King Edward's power'; but he had shown himself capable of defying it – and surviving.

For King Edward himself, this was mortifying news. Bruce's usurpation of the Scottish throne – his treachery, as Edward saw it – had been the last straw. He was more determined than ever to crush the Scots once and for all. Captured rebels were summarily executed, whatever their rank. Despite unrest at home, where the cost of his Scottish campaigns escalated every year, Edward had sent an army into Scotland under his best commanders, led by his son Edward, Earl of Caernarvon. English rule in Scotland had become a reign of terror. What more could Edward do? In the summer of 1306 he himself started moving north: he was not going to be balked of a personal victory over Bruce. By late September he had reached Lanercost Priory, not far short of the border.

Edward was now in his late sixties and his health was deteriorating. He was forced to pause at Lanercost to rest – a rest which would last for nearly six months. Even from his sickbed, however, he tried to direct operations in Scotland, despatching innumerable testy letters to his commanders.

It must have been obvious to everyone that the king had not long to live. Perhaps that was one of the factors which affected the mood in Scotland: if Edward's iron will and implacable hostility were removed, Scotland would surely have a much better chance of freeing itself from English oppression. But early in July the old king rallied. He hoisted himself into the saddle and set off for Scotland once again at the head of a feudal army. He was, however, so frail that his army could move only ten kilometres over the next three days. On 6 July they camped at Burgh-on-Sands, within sight of the Solway Firth and Scotland beyond it. Next morning, 7 July 1307, King Edward I died. Fiona Watson says:

> *Edward I has come down in history as the 'Hammer of the Scots' – and that, without any doubt, is what he was. Yet he died a bitter and, ultimately, defeated man on his way back to Scotland yet again, when he must have felt that he had solved the 'Scottish problem' with the submission in 1304.*

After lying in state in Waltham Abbey, Edward I was buried in Westminster Abbey on 27 October 1307. He had said, 'Do not bury me in fitting state until Scotland is subdued' – and he was taken at his word. In the midst of all the elaborately ornate royal tombs behind the High Altar at the east end of the abbey, Edward's tomb is an unadorned chest of Purbeck marble; within it, his body lies in a coffin also of varnished Purbeck marble.[1] Originally it had a gilded wooden canopy, but this was apparently destroyed during a riot at a funeral! The tomb is one of many which encircle the Chapel of St Edward the Confessor; today it is reached by a creaking wooden staircase from the North Ambulatory, and its relative anonymity takes you by surprise. In Elizabethan times an inscription was painted in gold letters on its side:

---

1 The tomb was opened in 1774 for 'scientific investigation'. The king's body, richly clothed in his royal robes, had been well preserved in waxed linen cloth and was almost entire. The scene was sketched for Richard Gough's book on Sepulchral Monuments; during the course of the examination Gough was spotted furtively pocketing something. He was searched, and was found to have purloined one of the king's fingers. The finger was replaced.

Edwardus primus Scotorum Malleus pactum serva ('Edward I, Hammer of the Scots: keep troth'). It was the first written occurrence of the sobriquet 'Hammer of the Scots'.

It is a commonplace to say that Edward's son and successor, Edward II, was not the man his father was; yet when he inherited the throne he also inherited Edward I's avowed intent to subjugate Scotland to England's will, although in the event he was unable to sustain the impetus of the English effort. As Robert Bruce was being hunted all over the south-west of Scotland by eight hundred men with blood-hounds, Edward II led the waiting army into Scotland – but only to receive the homage in Dumfries of a number of Scottish barons. By the end of August he had had enough, and returned to London. There would be no further military incursion into Scotland for three years – three years during which Robert Bruce took the opportunity to consolidate his position by a series of brilliant military strikes.

As soon as the English army had left, Bruce descended on Galloway in furious retaliation against the Macdougalls to avenge the deaths of his brothers after the landing at Loch Ryan. Then, leaving his brother Edward in Galloway to extort 'protection money' from the Gallovidians and keep the English occupied, he struck north into Argyll and the western Highlands, supported by a fleet of galleys supplied by Angus Og (the Young) MacDonald of Islay. His priority had to be to eliminate his enemies in the north.

Bruce's surge into the lands of the Macdougalls of Lorn set off all the right alarm signals, and John Macdougall of Lorn, lying ill in Dunstaffnage Castle, asked for, and received, a truce. With his rear secure, Bruce's first target was now the formidable Inverlochy Castle, three kilometres north-east of Fort William, guarding the southern end of the Great Glen. It was one of the earliest stone castles to be built in Scotland – a quadrangular castle with high curtain walls forti-fied with round towers and protected by a wide ditch and outer bank. It had been the chief stronghold in Lochaber of the murdered Red Comyn. With the limited forces at his disposal, Bruce could have had no hope of taking the castle by siege or by storm; instead, it fell to him through the treachery of the garrison. This was to be the pattern of the winter campaign which followed. Bruce had no standing army; he relied on a core group of seasoned fighters and gathered reinforce-ments and adherents locally for specific tasks.

It was now November 1307. Bruce swept onwards up the Great Glen. Urquhart Castle on Loch Ness, one of the strongest castles in the north, was taken and destroyed. Inverness Castle was surrendered, and Bruce had it dismantled, to ensure that it could not be retaken and used against him. Nairn Castle was razed to the ground. The Earl of Ross, a key Comyn ally in the north, was frightened into a six-month truce. Elgin Castle was forced to negotiate a truce. At that point Bruce fell seriously ill – so ill that he could neither eat nor drink, and his men feared for his life. The momentum of the campaign was lost, and Bruce and his men withdrew to a defensive position in a wooded bog at Slioch, south of Huntly. At that point, on Christmas Day, John Comyn, the Earl of Buchan, arrived with a strong force. For some reason Buchan's troops were unwilling to do battle, and Buchan withdrew to muster reinforcements; when he returned a week later, Bruce had gone.

That was the turning-point. Bruce, not yet fully recovered, destroyed the Earl of Buchan's castle of Balvenie at Dufftown in March, then Duffus Castle near Elgin, then Tarradale Castle on the Black Isle.

The final showdown came on 22 May 1308. The Earl of Buchan had assembled a large army at Inverurie. Bruce, although he still had to be carried on a litter, determined to meet the threat head-on. Somewhere on the road between Inverurie and Oldmeldrum the two armies met. Bruce was helped into his saddle, where he needed two men to hold him upright. But the mere sight of him on his charger had an electrifying effect. Buchan's men took fright and fled. The Earl of Buchan himself hurried south to England to seek support there.

And now, with the earldom undefended, Bruce laid waste to the Buchan lands from end to end. All Comyn's supporters were put to the sword. Every village was burned. It would be fifty years before the district of Buchan recovered from the terrible harrying carried out by Bruce in the bleak spring of 1308.

The town of Aberdeen was next to fall, in July. The only major force left intact in the north was that of John Macdougall of Lorn, in Dunstaffnage Castle, who had made a truce with Bruce the previous summer. It was now the third week in August: the truce was over, and there was an old score to settle – the mauling which Bruce had received at the hands of the Macdougalls at Dalrigh when he was on the run two years previously. Macdougall decided to try to stop him before he could reach Dunstaffnage.

Bruce's route to the west would take him past Tyndrum and Dalmally to the head of Loch Awe and along the forbidding northern shore of its western arm – the Pass of Brander, the same dramatic route taken today by the A85 and the rail line to Oban. The Pass of Brander allows only a narrow track along the lochside below the steep side of Ben Cruachan, one of the highest mountains in Scotland (1,126 metres). This was where John of Lorn decided to lay an ambush. He hid his forces high on the mountainside, where they could roll boulders down on Bruce's forces as they came along the narrow track and then charge down to finish them off with their swords. John of Lorn himself, still not recovered from his long illness, waited in a galley on the loch to watch.

Bruce was not to be caught by a Macdougall ambush a second time. He sent James Douglas ahead with a detachment of archers to take up position even higher up the mountainside than Macdougall's men. As the Macdougalls began their assault on the main body of Bruce's army they were caught by a storm of arrows from behind. After fierce hand-to-hand fighting the Argyll men fled west towards Dunstaffnage Castle. John of Lorn got away to the south, but Dunstaffnage was surrendered after a short siege. The power of the Macdougalls was broken. The reverse at Dalrigh in 1306, like that at Methven Wood, had been avenged.

Now Bruce began to show his shrewdness as a long-term strategist. He did not slight Dunstaffnage, as he had the castles in the north – he needed it to maintain his control of the area. He himself returned to the north-east to deal with the last of the Comyn supporters there, the Earl of Ross, who had captured his family at Tain and handed them over to the English; but instead of wreaking merciless vengeance, Bruce accepted Ross's submission at Nairn on 31 October 1308 and 'received him into the king's grace'. The agreement was later sealed by the marriage of Ross's heir, Hugh of Ross, to the third of Bruce's younger sisters, Matilda.

For Robert Bruce it had been a remarkable year. He had picked off his domestic enemies one by one. He had made superb use of classic guerrilla tactics – speed, surprise and ruthlessness – to keep his opponents guessing and prevent them from combining their forces against him. Apart from the key fortresses of Dundee, Perth and Stirling he now controlled the old kingdom of Scotia north of the Forth–Clyde line and could justifiably claim to be King of Scots by right of conquest. That autumn he issued his first surviving instruments of government. It was time to start administering the kingdom he had won. The civil war in Scotland was not over – the opposition to Bruce (the remnants of the Comyn-led government) continued to claim to represent the Community of the Realm and to enjoy English support; but that support was more moral than material.

Edward II of England

King Edward II . . . was not a wise and brave man like his father,
but a foolish prince, who was influenced by unworthy favourites,
and thought more of pleasure than of governing his kingdom.
TALES OF A GRANDFATHER, CHAPTER X

Edward II, King of England from 1307 to 1327, the fourth but oldest surviving son of Edward I and Eleanor of Castile, has had an unremittingly bad press, especially in England. He was considered unkingly and weak, an unworthy successor to his great father. He was blamed by English chroniclers for abandoning his father's single-minded crusade to make Scotland a province of England – in effect, he was blamed for 'losing' Scotland to the Scots. In particular, he was castigated for his 'immoderate' relationship with his favourite, Piers Gaveston, with whom he was assumed to be having a homosexual relationship; it was this which provoked the bitter baronial resentment which crippled his actions and destroyed his reign.

Edward was only twenty-three years old when he came to the throne. His character was not as martial as his father's, and he lacked his father's ferocious energy; but he had been schooled in warfare from an early age, and no one doubts his personal bravery. Soon after he came to the throne he contracted, in 1308, a political marriage which was meant to seal an alliance with France; his wife was Isabella, daughter of the wily Philippe IV ('the Fair') of France, but the marriage turned out more disastrously than most such dynastic matches. Isabella had to endure Edward's obsession with Gaveston (who was murdered by the barons of England in 1312), and with his new and equally unacceptable favourites, the Despensers, father and son; eventually Isabella took a lover herself – Roger Mortimer – and fuelled a rebellion which led to the deposition and death (probably by murder) of the king in 1327, in favour of his son, Edward III.

It is hard not to feel some sympathy for Edward II. He had the misfortune to be up against a great and ruthlessly effective war-leader (as King John Balliol had before him), at a time when the English people were becoming increasingly resentful of the demands of the 'Scottish War'. But there is no doubt that his early years on the throne were marked by an inability to act; this eased the task of Robert Bruce in asserting the independence and nationhood of Scotland.

Edward always seemed to be waiting for the right time to strike back in Scotland – but the opportunity did not materialise. He promised his garrisons and allies in Scotland a punitive expedition in 1308, but problems with the English nobility put paid to that plan. In 1309 he agreed a general truce for a year, which gave Bruce a chance to hold his first parliament, in St Andrews in March 1309. Bruce had just been addressed as 'King of Scots' in a letter from Philippe IV of France requesting Scottish aid on a Crusade; the request was politely declined after discussion at the parliament, but it was the first time that a foreign power had formally recognised his kingship. The assembly seems to have been more of a party conference of Bruce's supporters than a parliament: the occasion was used to produce a 'Declaration of the Clergy' in support of Bruce:

> *This people, being unable any longer to endure injuries so many and so great, and more bitter than death, which were being continually inflicted on their property and their persons for lack of a captain and faithful leader, agreed, by divine prompting, on Lord Bruce who is now king.*

In this party manifesto, for the first time, the claim is made that the Bruce claim to the throne had been *unjustly* turned down in favour of the puppet king, John Balliol. It was to become the leitmotif of pro-Bruce propaganda from now on: John Balliol was being written out of Scotland's history.

When an English expedition into Scotland eventually materialised in September 1310, it was a dismal failure. Starved of troops he had demanded from his nobles, Edward could do little more than make a tour of English garrisons in the south of Scotland: come November, he retired to Berwick for the winter. Meanwhile Bruce had withdrawn into the hills, never offering battle but picking off any stragglers from the English columns – guerrilla tactics which caused the English nothing but frustration. When Edward tried to revive the Scottish expedition in the summer of 1311 he was no more successful in raising troops, and retired south to face further unrest at home in July.

Now Bruce started turning the screw. He was determined to extend his control of Scotland south of the Forth. No sooner had Edward left Berwick than Bruce began making punitive raids into the Lothians and extorting tribute in exchange for 'truces'; to finance his military activities, he launched a series of lightning raids into northern England. Their objective was neither vengeance nor slaughter: Bruce was after cattle, and protection money. He also started picking off the English-garrisoned strongholds, one by one. His seasoned guerrillas were not equipped for sieges, so they used surprise, guile and audacity. Perth fell in January 1313 after Bruce and his followers swam across the moat in darkness and used specially-made rope-ladders to scale the walls in silence; a similarly bold attempt on Berwick the previous December had been foiled only by the barking of a dog. In September 1313 Linlithgow was captured by using a haywain as a Trojan horse: it concealed eight Scottish commandos who held the gate until the main force arrived to tackle the garrison.

At a parliament in Dundee in November 1313 Bruce felt confident enough to make a proclamation that any Scots who did not 'come within his peace' within one year would face forfeiture. Edward II sought to hearten his supporters in Scotland by declaring that he would bring an army to Scotland in the summer of 1314. This only added urgency to Bruce's policy of seizing as many English bases as possible before Edward arrived, and in March 1314 the greatest prize of all fell into Bruce's hands – Edinburgh Castle.

Once again, it was achieved by stealth, not by storm. Bruce's nephew, Sir Thomas Randolph, was told by a local man of a secret route up the precipitous north face of the crag. While the main body of the attackers created a diversion by assaulting the East Gate, Randolph climbed the north crag with thirty men, then used rope-ladders to get over the walls and opened the gates. Bruce had the English garrison killed and the defences destroyed.

Only one key castle now remained in English hands – Stirling. It was, by general consent, impregnable. Moreover, it could be easily supplied from the River Forth. Bruce established a blockade, and left the siege to his impetuous younger brother Edward. Edward was known to prefer the excitement of the battlefield to the grinding monotony of a long siege, and when the English constable of Stirling Castle, Sir Philip Mowbray, offered a deal, Edward accepted it with alacrity: the agreement was that if an English army had not arrived to relieve Stirling by Midsummer's Day (24 June), Mowbray would surrender the castle – which made a siege unnecessary.

When Robert Bruce heard of the bargain his brother had made, it is said (in John Barbour's *The Brus*) that he was furious. His strategy had been to frustrate the English by *not* fighting them in a conventional pitched battle – he knew that Scotland's forces could not match the armoured might which England could muster. Edward Bruce had now undone all that: the time and the place for a battle had been pledged. The die was cast for the confrontation which would decide the future of Scotland.

ROBERT BRUCE (r.1306–29)

The Battle of Bannockburn (23 and 24 June 1314)

King Edward the Second, therefore, assembled one of the greatest armies which a King of England ever commanded. There were troops brought from all his dominions. Many brave soldiers from the French provinces which the King of England possessed in France, – many Irish, many Welsh, – and all the great English nobles and barons, with their followers, were assembled in one great army. The number was not less than one hundred thousand men.

TALES OF A GRANDFATHER, CHAPTER X

A magnificent bronze equestrian statue of Robert Bruce stands on a tall plinth near the Bannockburn Heritage Centre on the A872, about three kilometres south of Stirling Castle; the site was selected more than a century ago to mark the area in which the Battle of Bannockburn took place. The statue, by the English-born Edinburgh sculptor C. d'O. Pilkington Jackson, was unveiled by Her Majesty the Queen on the 650th anniversary of the battle: 24 June 1964. It is placed a few metres from a rotunda which was erected by the National Trust for Scotland in 1962 at the spot where, according to tradition, Robert Bruce had his command post at the heart of the battle. Fragments of the original Borestone (a large stone block with a hole for a flagstaff) were built into a pedestal, and there is a memorial cairn.

As a battle memorial it is a curiously uninspiring, anonymous place. The trouble is that the traditional site of the battle has been proved wrong, and the rotunda is nowhere near the carseland where the decisive engagement was fought; furthermore, the landscape has been greatly altered by agricultural developments, and much of it is now submerged under a tide of housing and industrial estates. From the rotunda it is impossible to get any feeling for the battle scene, but the handsome Heritage Centre nearby offers an audio-visual programme which recounts the movements of the opposing armies over those two vital days in June 1314.

In order to preserve his credibility in Scotland – in order to preserve his throne in England, indeed – Edward II had no choice but to accept the challenge of relieving Stirling Castle by Midsummer Day. He had made peace of sorts with his barons after the murder of Piers Gaveston, and for once he was able to depend upon a reasonable response to a military call-up. A summons was issued, requiring attendance at

Berwick-upon-Tweed on 10 June 1314. The size of the English army has been a source of much debate. Modern scholarly estimates suggest a total of at least fifteen thousand men, including ten thousand infantry, more than two thousand cavalry and a contingent of archers – far short of Walter Scott's 'one hundred thousand men' (following Barbour's *The Brus*), but a formidable host nonetheless and probably the largest English army ever to invade Scotland.

Meanwhile, Bruce was assembling a larger Scottish army than he had ever been able to put in the field – six thousand men, at most. His forces had always been composed of hardened guerrilla soldiers who were numbered in hundreds, not thousands; but they were experienced warriors who had become used to winning battles over the years. With the foreknowledge that England was committed to an invasion sometime that summer, Bruce mustered the strongest army he could call up. What's more, he had the luxury of two months in which to train them in warfare. Lacking the feudal cavalry of the English on their huge shire horses (he had only about five hundred light horse under the command of Sir Robert Keith), Bruce relied again on the traditional schiltron of spearmen – steel-helmeted foot-soldiers hefting spears more than three metres long; but he had had time to train them not only to withstand the shock of a cavalry charge but to manoeuvre as mobile offensive units. Men who joined the army late were set aside as a reserve which came to be known as the 'small folk' – farmers, labourers, burgesses and craftsmen, equipped only with home-made weapons and boundless enthusiasm; they numbered perhaps three thousand in all by the time of the battle.

On 17 June 1314 the English host left Berwick and headed for Edinburgh. It made a brave sight, glittering and shimmering as the sun shone on kilometre upon kilometre of burnished armour and embroidered banners. Behind it came a huge wagon train, consisting of 110 wagons drawn by teams of eight oxen and 106 drawn by teams of four horses.

With only a week to go before the deadline of Midsummer Day, there was no time to be lost. On Wednesday, 19 June the vanguard reached Edinburgh, where it paused for two days to take on fresh provisions. Early on the morning of Saturday, 22 June the army moved off again, making a forced march of thirty-two kilometres to Falkirk – still twenty-two kilometres short of Stirling. Next morning they pushed on, and on the afternoon of Sunday, 23 June the forward units emerged from the Torwood which stretched from Falkirk nearly as far as the Bannock Burn. They were on the old high road from Falkirk, built by the Romans as a marching road north from the Antonine Wall. Ahead of them lay the open cultivated Bannock Burn valley, and on the high ground on the far side lay the wooded 'New Park', an enclosed royal hunting preserve. The easiest route to Stirling Castle was the Roman road which continued through this New Park, past the Borestone – and that was where Bruce had deployed his forces.

Bruce was apparently still in two minds about whether or not to offer battle. He had booby-trapped both sides of the Roman road which crossed the Bannock Burn with camouflaged anti-cavalry pits and small triangular spiked 'calthrops' designed to disable any horse which stood on them. The vanguard of his army, led by his nephew Thomas Randolph, Earl of Moray, was in the north of the New Park, closest to Stirling Castle to the north; behind Moray were two divisions commanded by Bruce's brother Edward and James Douglas. Bruce himself, at the rear, was patrolling the point where the Roman road entered the New Park from the south. The 'small folk' were camped well out of sight, guarding the supplies in a hollow behind and west of Coxet Hill. The Scottish army was in an excellent strategic position from which it could either retire safely into broken ground to the west or stand and bar the way to Stirling Castle.

When the English van, led by the Earls of Gloucester and Hereford, emerged from the Torwood late in the afternoon of Sunday, 23 June, they could see the Scots deploying in the southern fringes of the New Park ahead of them. Without waiting for reinforcements, they went straight into the attack with a sweeping cavalry charge across the Bannock Burn. One of the heavily-armoured English knights, Sir Henry de Bohun (Hereford's nephew), caught sight of Bruce in his golden coronet ambling along on a sturdy grey pony, directing the marshalling of his spearmen. Bohun couched his lance and charged at a gallop. Bruce, armed only with a hand-axe, waited until Bohun was almost upon him, then sidestepped the charge on his much smaller but nimbler horse, and as Bohun thundered past he stood up in his stirrups and split Bohun's skull with a single blow of his axe. It was a masterly counter-stroke. As Bohun fell dead, the Scottish ranks surged forward to meet the cavalry attack. The great English horses were already in trouble among the booby-traps; as the attack floundered the Scots were upon them, and after fierce close-quarters fighting the English withdrew. Bruce called off any pursuit, and the disciplined Scots heeded the call and went back up the hill to the New Park.

With the road route to Stirling Castle through the New Park blocked, another large English cavalry squadron, five hundred strong, under Sir Robert Clifford and Sir Henry Beaumont, set off to find and force a way to the castle through the low-lying flat carseland to the east of the New Park. It was not ideal ground for a cavalry army, for it was intersected by small ditches and streams. The intention was to bypass the Scots army altogether and link up with the beleaguered garrison in the castle. This foray was not spotted until perilously late; in the nick of time the Earl of Moray, at the north end of the New Park, marched down from the escarpment with a schiltron of spearmen to block their path. When the English cavalry charged, the schiltron held firm; the knights were thrown to the ground as their horses were impaled on the long spears and the mobile schiltron then moved forward to the attack. Eventually, after a long fight, the English withdrew in disorder, having suffered heavy casualties.

The preliminaries were over. The main English army had not been engaged, but the morale of the Scots had been given a tremendous boost. That evening the English host crossed the Bannock Burn with some difficulty and bivouacked as best they could on the constricted, triangular-shaped carseland between the confluence of the Bannock and the Pelstream. They spent an uncomfortable night there, on the alert for a surprise attack.

Bruce, however, was still apparently determined to avoid risking all in a pitched battle, and was proposing to withdraw westwards at sunrise. But at a dawn conference with his leaders, he realised that the mood of his army was to take on the English there and then.

24 June 1314

At daybreak on Monday, 24 June 1314 (about 3.30 a.m.), Bruce addressed his troops:

> *For eight years or more I have struggled with much labour for my right to the kingdom and for honourable liberty. I have lost brothers, friends and kinsmen. Your own kinsmen have been made captive, and bishops and priests are locked in prison. Our country's nobility has poured forth its blood in war. These barons you see before you, clad in armour, are bent upon destroying us and obliterating the kingdom, nay, our whole nation. They do not believe that we can resist.*[1]

---

1 These words were attributed to him by Bernard de Linton, Abbot of Arbroath and Chancellor of Scotland. He was the hereditary keeper of the *Breccbennach Chaluim Cille*, the tiny

With that, he gave the order to attack. Three of his four battalions of spearmen now moved east out of the New Park and advanced down the slope of the escarpment into the carse where the English army had taken up its cramped position. The English longbowmen launched their customary volleys of arrows, but the schiltrons were no longer sitting (or standing) targets – they were moving forward in the offensive. The English vanguard, under the Earl of Gloucester, charged the leading Scottish schiltron, led by Edward Bruce, but the schiltron held firm, and Gloucester and several other knights (including John Comyn, son of the murdered Red Comyn) fell before the unwavering hedge of spears. The other Scottish brigades, under the Earl of Moray and James Douglas, now launched a general attack on the bunched mass of the English knights. Unable to manoeuvre effectively, the English ranks took a great deal of punishment; it was not until later that a contingent of archers could be brought forward from the rear to attack the now-static Scottish schiltrons. This was what Bruce had been expecting, and he released his light cavalry under the Earl Marischal of Scotland, Sir Robert Keith – five hundred knights and men-at-arms, who charged so fiercely that the English archers broke and fled. From now on the battle became a murderous exchange of blows between the spears and Lochaber axes of the Scots and the swords and maces of the English knights; the English infantry were hardly engaged at all.

With the formidable English archers scattered, the battle now hung in the balance; and at this point Bruce committed his own brigade, largely composed of highlanders and islanders under Angus Og Macdonald of Islay. They had been champing at the bit for hours, and now they threw themselves forward in a great Highland charge. The shuddering impact of their impetus turned the tide, and the English ranks began to waver. The Scottish schiltrons moved forward remorselessly, metre by metre, a terrible and irresistible engine of destruction. The English must have realised now that they were losing the battle they thought they could not lose. And at that moment came another, totally unexpected twist: behind the Scottish schiltrons the untrained, exuberant 'small folk' hidden behind Coxet Hill suddenly appeared,

---

bronze-and-silver-covered 'Monymusk Reliquary' which is one of the greatest treasures of the National Museum of Scotland. This venerable eighth-century casket, a metal-mounted wooden box in the shape of a miniature oratory, is said to have contained the relics of St Columba. As hereditary keeper, or Deòradh (Dewar), of the sacred relics, it was Bernard's task to ensure that the reliquary, the symbol of Scottish independence, was carried with the Scottish army at Bannockburn – a very appropriate role for a Dewar, nearly seven centuries ago!

unbidden, streaming down from the escarpment brandishing their home-made weapons and banners and yelling defiance. To the English they looked like a second Scottish army, arriving fresh and vigorous when they themselves were on the point of exhaustion.

The effect was decisive. The English high command realised that all was lost, and now their priority was to get King Edward safely off the field. Under protest he was led away, with a bodyguard of fifty knights. They galloped to Stirling Castle, where the constable wisely refused them access because it would have meant surrendering Edward to the Scots under the terms of the agreement about relieving the castle. Instead, the fugitive party wheeled west and round the back of the New Park and headed for Dunbar, where the king found an open boat to take him to the safety of Berwick Castle.

King Edward's departure from the field was the signal for a general English flight. The battle turned into a rout, and then a massacre. The Bannock Burn filled with corpses, and the River Forth, meandering lazily past Stirling Castle, took another toll of drowned soldiery. The rich English baggage train fell into the hands of the Scots as plunder to be shared out all over Scotland. As a personal bonus for Bruce, he was able to exchange the captured Earl of Hereford for his queen, Elizabeth de Burgh, his sister Mary and his daughter Marjory.

The battle was over – the most resounding triumph in Scotland's military history. But the victory was not quite complete – King Edward II had escaped, even if only by the proverbial whisker: at one stage his pursuers had come close enough to unhorse him, but he fought them off and got away. Had he been captured, the huge ransom for his release would have put Scotland back on its financial feet, and would undoubtedly have required unconditional recognition of Robert Bruce as King of Scots and of Scotland's independence. As it was, the battle was won, but the War of Independence was not. It would be another fourteen years before it ended, with the Treaty of Edinburgh in 1328.

Steve Boardman says:

I think the significance of Bannockburn has been exaggerated in the Scottish consciousness, but there is no doubt that it was hugely important in terms of its moral and political significance – the defeat of a major English army in open battle. It also, and perhaps more importantly, gave Bruce much greater control of his own kingdom: most of his former opponents now accommodated themselves with the new regime or went into exile as pensioners

*or retainers of the English crown. What Bannockburn did not
do was to deliver independence. The English realm could absorb
one defeat; England could always generate another army which
could reverse the effects of Bannockburn. Bannockburn was an
important staging-post on the route to recognition of Scotland's
independence, but it was not the end of the road.*

The Declaration of Arbroath (6 April 1320)

The Battle of Bannockburn had triumphantly confirmed Bruce's position as King of Scots – in Scotland. But not in England. For the next
few years he hammered his way into northern England time and
again, in an effort to force Edward II to recognise him as king of an
independent Scotland. The devastation was incalculable. In 1315 he
extended the area of war by invading Ireland and having his brother
Edward Bruce declared king there in 1316; Edward only lasted until
1318, however, when he was defeated and killed in battle. In the same
year Bruce at last managed to capture Berwick Castle after several
failed attempts. Now nowhere in the north of England was safe: even
the city of York was menaced by an invasion in 1319. It was sufficient
to wring from Edward II a two-year truce (1319–21), which allowed
Bruce the opportunity to concentrate on the diplomatic front abroad.

The Pope had never lifted the excommunication laid on Bruce after
the sacrilegious murder of the Red Comyn in Dumfries in 1306. For
Scotland to be able to join the comity of nations it was vital that this
ban be lifted, but the elderly Pope John XXII, who had succeeded
Clement V, was too good a friend of England to be disposed to confirm
as King of Scots the man who had unlawfully deposed King John
Balliol. In the autumn of 1317 he had sent two papal negotiators to
broker peace between England and Scotland, in order to set up a new
Crusade, but Bruce respectfully refused to receive a letter addressed
to the 'governor', not 'king', of Scotland. In response the Pope renewed
the excommunication of Robert Bruce and placed the kingdom of
Scotland under interdict.

Scotland's response came in the so-called 'Declaration of Arbroath',
which is now revered as the most important document in Scottish
history. In March 1320 Bruce held a Great Council at Newbattle Abbey,
near Edinburgh, to draft a letter to the Pope asking him to put pressure
on Edward II to recognise him as the legitimate King of Scots. The
resulting address is thought to have been affirmed at Arbroath Abbey,
and the received date is 6 April 1320. Its authorship is traditionally

attributed to Bernard de Linton, Abbot of Arbroath and Chancellor of Scotland, hereditary keeper of the sacred relics (see note, page 184). It was issued in the names of eight earls, thirty-one barons 'and the other barons and freeholders and the whole community of the realm of Scotland'.

The Declaration of Arbroath, couched in articulate and fluent Latin, was an intellectual and ideological *tour de force* of its time. It began by recounting the Origin Myth of the Scots and the 113 kings who had ruled the land in unbroken succession. It referred to the conversion of the Scots to Christianity by one of the leading Apostles, Scotland's patron saint, St Andrew, brother of the blessed St Peter. It spoke of how the Scots were a free and unconquered people whom neither Picts nor Britons nor vikings had been able to subdue. It castigated Edward I who 'came in the guise of a friend and ally' but then revealed himself as an enemy with

> *deeds of cruelty, massacre, violence, pillage, arson, imprisoning prelates, burning down monasteries, robbing and killing monks and nuns, and yet other outrages without number which he committed against our people, sparing neither age nor sex, religion nor rank . . . But from these countless evils we have been set free . . . by our most valiant Prince, King and Lord, the Lord Robert. He, that his people and his heritage might be delivered out of the hands of our enemies, bore cheerfully all toil and fatigue, hunger and peril, like another Maccabeus or Joshua . . . To him, as to Him by whom salvation has been wrought unto our people, we are bound both by law and by his merits that our freedom may still be maintained, and by him, come what may, we mean to stand.*

The text continued with the eloquent and much-quoted paean to freedom; but there was an important caveat:

> *Yet if he should give up what he has begun, and should seek to make us or our kingdom subject to the King of England or to the English, we would strive at once to drive him out as our enemy and a subverter of his own right and ours, and we would make some other man who was able to defend us our king; for, as long as but a hundred of us remain alive, we shall never on any conditions be subjected to English rule. It is in truth not for*

*glory, nor riches, nor honours that we fight, but for freedom
alone, which no honest man gives up except with his life.*

It was splendid, stirring stuff – and it seems to have stirred the Pope,
too. His reply was addressed to 'that illustrious man Robert, who
assumes the title and position of King of Scotland' – a step in the right
direction, at least; in it he temporarily waived the excommunication of
King Robert and promised to exhort the English to make peace. His
efforts were in vain, however. The peace talks held in April 1321
foundered on the obstinate English claim of English suzerainty over
Scotland. As a result the Pope pronounced excommunication afresh,
and the ferocious war of attrition was to flare up again as soon as the
current truce ran out, at the end of 1321.

The Declaration of Arbroath is one of the most remarkable, and
one of the most precious, documents in Scottish history; and not the
least significant aspect of it is that telling caveat about removing the
king from the throne if necessary. Ted Cowan says:

> *Everyone knows the freedom clause, the 'as long as but a hundred
> of us remain alive' bit. But much more significant is the earlier
> sentence, about removing Bruce from the throne and replacing
> him if he fails to live up to expectations – because here we
> have the idea of 'elective kingship', of the contractual theory of
> monarchy: the king is answerable to his subjects exactly as the
> subjects are answerable to the king. This is the first time in
> European history that we have a clear articulation of this view.
> So the Declaration of Arbroath is not only one of the earliest
> manifestations of nationalism – it is also one of the earliest
> manifestations of constitutionalism.*

And yet – astonishingly – there is no reference whatsoever to this
crucial document in Walter Scott's *Tales of a Grandfather*. It is not as
if Scott was unaware of its existence: in his *History of Scotland* (Chapter
XI) he discussed it at length, calling it a 'celebrated document' and 'a
spirited manifesto or memorial'. So why did he ignore it in *Tales of
a Grandfather*? Ted Cowan has an explanation:

> *Scott was the archetypal Tory of his time. He believed in the
> monarchy, and he was not particularly enamoured of the idea
> that the monarchy might be answerable to its subjects. The Dec-
> laration of Arbroath had generated one of the most powerful*

ideas in Western constitutionalism which ran right through to the American Revolution and the French Revolution – both of which filled Scott with horror. He saw the enunciation of these democratic ideas in the Declaration of Arbroath as potentially subversive – so for his impressionable young readers he simply ignored the whole document.

Success – and succession

After the breakdown of the peace talks in 1321, and the end of the two-year truce, the Scots resumed their devastation of the north of England and its fortresses. Once again York, the capital of England's military organisation in the north, came under threat. Bruce's intention was clear: to force the English to recognise his kingship. To that end he tried to capture important political prisoners, even Edward II himself, as bargaining counters – and he very nearly succeeded, at Rievaulx Abbey in 1322.

Bruce's position was strengthening all the time. In 1322 Edward's brother-in-law was crowned Charles IV of France; Charles's hatred of the English king for Edward's treatment of his wife Isabella soon inspired renewed conflict with England and a French treaty with Scotland (the Treaty of Corbeil, in 1326) which renewed the 'Auld Alliance'. Early in 1324 the Pope formally recognised Bruce as King of Scots (but did not lift the excommunication or interdict).

While Bruce prospered, Edward II's troubles were increasing. His queen, Isabella of Hainault, had taken her eldest son, Prince Edward, to France to pay homage to Charles IV for his father's lands in Gascony. This failed to heal the rift between the two kings. Queen Isabella refused to return home, despite the gathering war-clouds. In France she had taken a lover, Lord Roger Mortimer of Wigmore, one of Edward's sworn enemies and now an exile. Together they gathered a group of English dissidents and raised an invasion force which anchored in the Orwell estuary in September 1326. The army advanced on London, which declared for Isabella. Suddenly, any support the king might still have had simply crumbled.

According to the *Lanercost Chronicle* Edward made a last bid to save his throne by writing to the Scots 'freely giving up to them the land and realm of Scotland, to be held independently of any king of England, and bestowed upon them, with Scotland, a great part of the northern lands lying next to them, on condition that they should assist him against the queen, her son, and their confederates'. If such a letter was ever written, it was too late: Edward II was captured in Wales in November 1326 and deposed on 20 January 1327, and on 1 February his fifteen-year-old son was crowned as Edward III. Although he was not, strictly speaking, a minor, he was clearly under the thumb of his mother Isabella and Roger Mortimer.

A change of king in England did not lead to a change in relations between Scotland and England. On the day of Edward III's coronation the Scots sent a small raiding party across the border for a night-time assault on Norham Castle, which very nearly took the garrison by surprise. That summer the fighting flared up again. The young king marched north towards Scotland, while three Scottish columns raided deep into England. As far as the English were concerned, the Scots were everywhere and nowhere – here one day and gone the next, stinging fiercely and then disappearing before the English could land a blow in exchange. In one daring night-raid led by the 'Black Douglas' the Scots infiltrated the English encampment at Stanhope Park in Weardale and reached the royal pavilion; they cut the guy ropes and flattened the pavilion, but the young king was hustled to safety before he could be captured. With that the English abandoned the campaign in despair.

That autumn the deposed King Edward II died in Berkeley Castle – of natural causes, according to the official version. But rumours that he had been murdered – and horribly murdered at that, with a red-hot poker up his anus – spread quickly and roused public opinion against Isabella and Mortimer. They tried to initiate another campaign against the Scots, but parliament refused to grant the necessary funds. In October 1327, Isabella and Mortimer sent envoys to Scotland to sue for peace. The negotiations lasted all winter. On 1 March 1328, at a parliament in York attended by one hundred Scottish envoys, Edward III issued letters-patent which set out the theme of the agreement:

> We will, and grant by these presents, for us and our heirs and successors, by the common counsel, assent and consent of the prelates, princes, earls, barons and communities of our realm assembled in our parliament, that the kingdom of Scotland . . . shall be retained by our dearest ally and friend, the magnificent prince Lord Robert, by God's grace illustrious king of Scotland, and to his heirs and successors, separate in all respects from the kingdom of England, entire, free and quit, without any subjection, servitude, claim or demand. And by these presents we renounce and demit to the king of Scotland, his heirs and successors, what-

soever right we or our predecessors have put forward in any way
in bygone times to the aforesaid kingdom of Scotland.

On 17 March the negotiations ended with the formal signing of a treaty in the King's Chamber of the Abbey of Holyrood, ratified in England by Edward III in parliament at Northampton on 3 May. By the terms of this treaty Edward renounced all claims to English suzerainty over Scotland, recognised Bruce as King of Scots and promised mutual friendship and good will. It was also agreed that the Stone of Scone, the 'Stone of Destiny' which had been removed by Edward I in 1296, should be given back to Scotland; in the event it was not.[1] In return, Bruce agreed to pay Edward £20,000 in war reparations for the sake of peace.

By the Treaty of Edinburgh/Northampton King Robert I of Scotland had achieved, for Scotland and for himself, all the objectives for which he had been striving for twenty-two arduous years. The pact was sealed by a contract for the marriage of Bruce's four-year-old son and heir David and Edward III's seven-year-old sister Joan. The problem of the succession to the Scottish throne had been a matter of concern for many years. When Bruce's queen, Elizabeth de Burgh, had been taken captive in 1306 she was still childless. When she was released from captivity after the Battle of Bannockburn in 1314 no one knew whether she was still capable of child-bearing. In April 1315 the Scottish parliament, meeting at Ayr, enacted a decree that if the king died without a male heir the crown should pass to his brother Edward. If both brothers died without male heirs, the crown would pass to Marjory, Bruce's daughter by his first wife, and her issue; it was also enacted that she should marry with her father's consent. Shortly afterwards she married the husband of his choice, Walter the Steward (Stewart). In March 1316 Marjory died after a riding accident in the last month of her pregnancy, but her child's life was saved by Caesarean section. The child was named Robert, after his grandfather. Then Edward Bruce was killed in battle in Ireland in October 1318; and in December 1318 parliament, assembled at Scone, enacted that, failing legitimate male

---

1   A royal writ issued by Edward III on 1 July 1328, addressed to the Abbot of Westminster, said: 'Whereas it was formerly agreed by us, our council and our last Parliament held at Northampton that the stone on which the kings of Scotland used to sit at the time of their coronation, and which is now in your care, should be sent to Scotland . . . we have ordered the Lords of our City of London that they should carry it to the Queen of England, our very dear dame and mother.' The Londoners, however, prevented its removal from the Abbey.

issue to the king, the heir to the throne was his young grandson, Robert Stewart.

Meanwhile, the queen had given birth to two daughters (Matilda and Margaret). And then, on 5 March 1324, almost ten years after her release from captivity, the longed-for miracle occurred: she gave birth to twin sons, David and John. John died in infancy, but David survived. The direct succession was assured; in 1326 parliament recognised the boy David as heir to the throne.

It soon became all too clear, however, that such a late-born son would probably succeed as a minor, for in 1328 the king's health was failing. He was confined to his bed in the Abbey of Holyrood with a disfiguring skin disease when he signed the Treaty of Edinburgh/ Northampton. Contemporary chroniclers said that he was suffering from leprosy – but 'leprosy' was used as a general term for any kind of skin disease, and the king was never kept in isolation as a leper would have been; nor was there any physiological evidence of leprosy in the skeleton which was located in the royal vault in Dunfermline Abbey in 1818.

Robert Bruce had not long to live. The marriage of his son David and Edward III's sister Joan took place at Berwick in July 1328. Edward stayed away, and so did Bruce – possibly because of illness, or possibly to avoid highlighting Edward's petulant gesture. In October 1328 the Pope, at long last, released Bruce and his kingdom from excommunication and interdict. What is more, he also granted Bruce's request to allow the anointing and crowning of Scottish kings by the Bishop of St Andrews as the Pope's representative; it was the final seal of approval on his kingship but, alas, the bull was not issued until 13 June 1329 – six days after Bruce had died at his country manor at Cardross, by Dumbarton. His life's work was done. He was fifty-five years old.

Epilogue: Scotland's parliament

In the hurly-burly of Robert I's reign, it is easy to overlook a significant development in the concept of a Scottish parliament, in 1326. Before then the King of Scots relied on a small group of nobles (a prototype privy council) for matters of specific policy; the Community of the Realm formed a general council which would discuss (and preferably approve) matters of general application to the rest of the country. 'Parliament' consisted of the two major estates of the realm – the nobility and the Church: the Lords Temporal and the Lords Spiritual. In 1326, however, Robert I decided to ask for a substantial increase in taxation, and for that reason he ordered the burghs to send representatives to parliament. This is the first known example of the 'Third Estate' being involved in a parliamentary system in Scotland which was to become known as the 'Thrie Estaites'.

Chapter 12

DAVID II (r.1329–71)

The young king of Scotland . . . raised a large army, and entering England on the west frontier, he marched eastward towards Durham, harassing and wasting the country with great severity; the Scots boasting, that, now the King [of England] and his nobles were absent, there were none in England to oppose them, save priests and base mechanics. But they were greatly deceived.

TALES OF A GRANDFATHER, CHAPTER XV

King David II was the late-born son of the hero-king, Robert Bruce – and it is never easy to be the son of a hero. He was born in Dunfermline in March 1324; and in July 1328, just after his fourth birthday, he was married to Joan, the seven-year-old sister of King Edward III of England. He and his child-bride took up residence in Turnberry Castle in Ayrshire as the Earl and Countess of Carrick. Less than a year later, in June 1329, he succeeded to the throne as King of Scots. He was only five years old, but his childhood had long been over.

The rest of his minority would be no less eventful. The English under Edward III were waiting for an opportunity to wrest back from Scotland the gains which King Robert I had made at England's expense. For two years they were held at bay; the compensation payments to England specified by the 1328 Treaty of Edinburgh/Northampton were paid on the nail. With the throne apparently secure, young David was crowned and anointed King of Scots at Scone in November 1331. But the situation was much more precarious than it seemed. David II was to have an extremely troubled minority – King Edward III of England saw to that.

Edward III of England

When Robert Bruce – King Robert I – died in July 1329 he had achieved the apparently impossible: Scotland was a free and independent nation, its rights recognised by both England and the Pope; a dynastic betrothal had been agreed which would, it was devoutly hoped, unite the two royal families in harmony and friendship. Scotland was strong and brimming with self-confidence, and its people looked forward to a long period of peace after the years of constant struggle and warfare, both internal and external.

No sooner was Bruce in his grave, however, than the legacy of his spectacular reign began to be undone. All the great loyalists who had supported him through every vicissitude – the Old Guard of his reign – would soon be dead: Sir James Douglas, Walter Stewart (the Steward), Thomas Randolph (Earl of Moray), Bishop William Lamberton of St Andrews. There was a child on the throne, and royal minorities were always fraught with risk; the governance of Scotland would be in the hands of Guardians (the first was the Earl of Moray, until his death in 1332). Furthermore, in England, the Scots now had an opponent almost as implacable and aggressive as Edward I had been – his grandson, Edward III: he would devote the first part of his fifty-year-reign (1327–77) to a relentless reassertion of England's claims to suzerainty over Scotland.

King Edward clearly resented, from the outset, the 1328 Treaty of Edinburgh/Northampton which had been signed in his name, and lost little time in repudiating this *turpis pax* ('shameful peace') on the grounds that it had been arranged when he was under-age, and against his will. In 1330, as soon as he reached the age of eighteen, he deposed his mother, Isabella of France (the dowager queen), and her lover Roger Mortimer in a palace coup at Nottingham; Mortimer was hanged, drawn and quartered, and Isabella was sent into lifelong seclusion in Castle Rising, in Norfolk (she died in 1358). Edward III was now his own man.

As far as Scotland was concerned, there was another dynastic player waiting in the wings to lay claim to the Scottish crown: Edward Balliol, the exiled son of King John Balliol, 'Toom Tabard'. In 1331 he was brought over to England from his family estates in Picardy. With

Edward III's tacit compliance, he gathered support among the dissident Scottish and English nobles who had been deprived of their estates by Robert Bruce – 'the Disinherited', as they were called – and mounted a seaborne invasion of Scotland in eighty-eight ships from the Humber. The expeditionary force made an unopposed landing at Kinghorn, on the coast of Fife, on 6 August 1332 and marched towards Perth. The new Guardian, Donald, Earl of Mar, was ready for them; he had mustered a large army – much larger than the invasion force – to deal with the threat, and took up position on Dupplin Moor on the banks of the Earn, near Perth, to block the advance.

The battle which ensued, at dawn on 8 August, ended in dreadful carnage. The Scots had considerable superiority in numbers, and no fewer than twelve earls in their ranks. But they were fighting uphill in blazing sunshine, and the rebels were able to absorb the first punishing impact of the huge Scottish schiltron. Soon the Scots were clenched in one massive mêlée, into which the English archers poured volley after volley of their deadly arrows. By noon the attack had stalled and turned into a retreat. Balliol now sent in his small mounted reserve to harry the exhausted fugitives. The Guardian was killed, along with two earls, several lesser noblemen, sixty knights and nearly two thousand spearsmen; the rebels lost only thirty men. The *Lanercost Chronicle* gloated:

One most marvellous thing happened: the pile of dead was greater in height from the earth toward the sky than one whole spear's length.

Scotland, it seemed, had fallen at the very first blow. Edward Balliol, now attended by some of Robert Bruce's erstwhile supporters, had himself crowned at Scone as King of Scots on 24 September 1332. The country now had *two* kings – the legitimate David II, and the usurper Edward Balliol. Two months later, at Roxburgh Castle, Balliol swore homage and fealty to Edward III as lord superior of all Scotland, and ceded most of southern Scotland to the English crown, while he himself was to rule the north of Scotland in Edward's name. The eight-year-old King David was a fugitive holed up in the impregnable fortress of Dumbarton Castle. Scotland was right back where it had stood in 1306, a province of England in the grip of civil war.

Scotland was by no means finished, however. The Guardian who replaced the Earl of Mar was Sir Andrew Murray, the son of William Wallace's brilliant general at the Battle of Stirling Bridge and an uncle of David II by marriage (he was the third husband of Robert Bruce's sister Christian). It was Andrew Murray who now led the Scots into the third phase of the Wars of Independence, along with the teenage John Randolph (the next Earl of Moray) and the king's uncle, Robert Stewart (the Steward).

'King Edward Balliol' did not have long to enjoy the crown he had seized – less than three months, indeed. At dawn on 17 December a surprise raid on his quarters in Annan caught him unawares and sent him scurrying across the border to the safety of Carlisle, riding bareback and in his underclothes.

In May 1333 Edward III himself came north to support Balliol; in return, Balliol ceded to him the town of Berwick-upon-Tweed, which had been in Scottish hands since 1318. Edward now laid siege to Berwick Castle, executing hostages (the two sons of the governor) in full view of the defenders. The Scots tried to draw him away by raiding deep into the north of England, but Edward was not to be deflected from his aim. On 12 July the governor agreed to surrender the castle if it were not relieved within a week. The Guardian, Sir Andrew Murray, had been captured and was now in prison in England; but the new Guardian, Archibald, Lord of Douglas (brother of Bruce's great comrade, the 'Black' Douglas), quickly mustered an army to come to Berwick's aid before the deadline: it was the Bannockburn scenario in reverse.

The Battle of Halidon Hill (19 July 1333)

King Edward, with Edward Balliol at his side, took up position on Halidon Hill, to the north-west of Berwick, just inside the present border at the A6105 from Berwick to Duns. The site was as well chosen for both defence and offence as Bannockburn had been nineteen years previously; it commanded the approaches to Berwick, high at the rear, with a slope to the front levelling out into boggy ground at the base. Here Edward deployed his forces into three brigades of dismounted knights and men-at-arms, each flanked by a contingent of archers. The Scots, numerically superior (as the English had been at Bannockburn), came marching down from Duns and on the night of 18 July occupied the high ground at Witches' Knowe, facing the English in three massed schiltrons, each consisting of thirteen thousand spearsmen, alongside a division of 1,200 knights.

Because of the deadline set by the truce, the onus was on Douglas to attack. At noon on 19 July the Scots launched themselves into a disorderly massed charge, but quickly got bogged down in the wet ground below the slope of Halidon Hill. As they struggled to move on up the slope, the practised English archers unleashed their volleys in a deadly crossfire. The charge was spent before the Scots reached the English lines, and at that moment the English knights mounted their great war-horses and crashed down on the wavering Scottish spearsmen. Douglas fell, along with the earls of Ross, Sutherland and Carrick, seventy barons, five hundred knights and thousands of foot-soldiers; the English lost only fourteen men. The annihilation was complete, and terrible – and once again it had been the English archers who had done the damage. It was one of the worst of Scotland's long, sad litany of military disasters. Bannockburn had been avenged. It was the twenty-year-old Edward III's first and only military engagement on English soil.

Edward now occupied Berwick, and Balliol formally handed over the town and its castle to be a possession of the English crown.[1] All the other disputed lands and castles of southern Scotland also fell into English hands. The whole country lay at the mercy of Edward III, now Lord Paramount of Scotland. Edward Balliol was re-installed as Scotland's puppet king. The position of the supporters of the Bruce dynasty was now so perilous that the boy-king and his wife were sent to France for safety.

David and Joan were to stay in France for seven years as guests of King Philippe VI in the fortress of Château Gaillard on the Seine. During that time vast areas of Scotland were devastated and the fortunes of war ebbed and flowed, favouring first one side (the Bruce faction) and then the other (the Balliol faction). The struggle continued under a succession of Guardians – especially Andrew Murray, who was now Guardian again after being ransomed from captivity; under his inspiring leadership the Scots fought back against the Balliol adherents and the might of the English occupation and recaptured and dismantled most of the key fortresses, one by one.

The turning-point in the resistance battle came in the north-east, on 30 November 1335, at the Battle of Culblean, near Ballater on Deeside, which was fought to settle the fate of Kildrummy Castle. Kildrummy, formerly a Comyn stronghold, was still held by David loyalists. Balliol appointed one of the 'Disinherited', David of Strathbogie, son and heir of the Earl of Atholl, as king's lieutenant in the north-east, and

---

1 The understanding was that the surrender of Berwick was to be permanent. It was to remain under English occupation for nearly 130 years, but that occupation was not to go unchallenged.

Strathbogie drove north with a powerful force equipped with siege-engines to establish Balliol's authority in the north-east. He laid siege to Kildrummy, which was on the point of surrender when Murray arrived in the nick of time and destroyed Strathbogie's army in a brilliant guerrilla dawn attack. A monument to the battle, a rugged pillar of granite, stands by the A97 near Loch Kinard.

From then on, the Anglo-Balliol forces found it increasingly difficult to maintain their hold on Scotland, despite annual English campaigns led by Edward III himself.

'Black Agnes' of Dunbar

The countess, who from her complexion was termed Black Agnes, by which name she is still familiarly remembered, was a high-spirited and courageous woman, the daughter of that Thomas Randolph, Earl of Murray, whom I have so often mentioned, and the heiress of his valour and patriotism.

TALES OF A GRANDFATHER, CHAPTER XIV

The story of 'Black Agnes', Countess of Dunbar, and her resolute defiance of the English occupying forces, is the very stuff of balladry and legend. Agnes was the wife of Patrick, Earl of Dunbar and March; more significantly, she was the daughter of the great Thomas Randolph, Earl of Moray (Robert Bruce's nephew), and sister of John Randolph, Earl of Moray, the first Guardian during David II's minority. In her husband's absence it fell to her to defend Dunbar Castle with a small garrison of archers and servants when it was besieged by an English expeditionary force in 1338.

All that is left today of Dunbar Castle is a couple of craggy columns of masonry on separate stacks of rock across the mouth of the Victoria Harbour at Dunbar. It is now in a deplorably precarious state; the original archway between castle and gun blockhouse, carrying the passageway which spanned the rock stacks, fell into the sea in November 1993, and access to the ruins of the tumbled towers has been forbidden by the local council for reasons of public safety.[1] Nesting kittiwakes have taken over the cliff-like walls for courting and breeding.

---

1 I was fortunate enough to be given a tour of the interior and exterior of the ruins by Gordon Easingwood, a local fisherman and enthusiastic member of the Dunbar and District History Society. It meant penetrating the innards of the castle, which until recently housed a fish-hatchery, and making a cautious foray to the grass-grown top of the ruins to sample the

In its day, however, Dunbar Castle was an immense and formidable fortress which had been refortified in 1333, and must have been all but impregnable before the days of artillery; it was eventually demolished, on the orders of the Scottish parliament, in 1567 after Mary Queen of Scots had been taken there by Bothwell before their hasty marriage at Holyroodhouse that year (see Chapter 19).

The English army, led by Montague, Earl of Salisbury, began the siege on 13 January 1338; it was to last until 16 June. There was no way of storming the castle from the landward side. Every assault was repulsed, and Salisbury soon sent for specialised siege-engines. They arrived by sea from the Tower of London and Berwick-upon-Tweed – mangonels (catapults for hurling huge boulders) and a covered battering-ram known as a 'sow'. Black Agnes conducted the defence with a flamboyance which has endeared her to posterity: after each day's bombardment from the mangonels, the countess and her ladies-in-waiting would parade along the battlements and ostentatiously wipe away with their white kerchiefs the debris created by the missiles; when the 'sow' was pushed into position against the walls, she crushed it with vast lumps of masonry from the parapets.

When starvation threatened the survival of the gallant garrison, a daring operation brought relief. Sir Alexander Ramsay, who had been operating successfully as a guerrilla leader, 'borrowed' some fishing-smacks from the little sea-ports of the Forth and loaded them with food and drink. At dawn one morning, apparently engaged in innocent fishing, they emerged from the shelter of the Bass Rock and slipped through the English naval blockade to deliver much-needed provisions and reinforcements through a secret seaward door of the beleaguered castle.

By late spring it was obvious to Salisbury that he was wasting his time and King Edward's money (the siege had already cost the English nearly £6,000, including the hire of two Genoese galleys manned with crossbowmen to patrol the castle's seaward approaches). Andrew Murray now controlled most of Scotland, and Edward was becoming more and more impatient at the escalating cost of trying to subdue

---

impressive view which generations of Dunbar residents had formerly been able to enjoy. As far as I can gather, no attempt has ever been made to stabilise and conserve the castle ruins, and the Society is, quite rightly, determined to have something done about them for the benefit of the town, and of history. No one knows now, for sure, what it looked like in its heyday; but Rennie Weatherhead, a former physics teacher, has created a 'virtual reality' model of the castle as it might have appeared in the fourteenth century. It should be on permanent display.

his rebellious province; besides, his interest had now turned to France, where he believed he had a legitimate claim to the throne through his mother, Isabella of France, daughter of King Philippe IV. In July 1338 he set sail for the Continent with 115 ships and landed at Antwerp for the first of his many assaults on France, and Scotland could breathe a sigh of relief.

The return of the king

Sir Andrew Murray died in the spring of 1338, and the role of Guardian fell to Robert Stewart (the Steward). He was the twenty-two-year-old son of Robert Bruce's daughter Marjory, and was eight years *older* than his uncle, King David II. As David's nephew he was also heir presumptive to the throne. By the time it was deemed safe enough for King David to return to Scotland in June 1341 to start his personal rule as King of Scots at the age of seventeen, Robert Stewart – by then only twenty-five – had become one of the most powerful magnates in the kingdom.

David's return to Scotland in 1341 marked a new stage in Scotland's affairs. The Bruce cause seemed much more secure; Balliol and his dwindling group of supporters no longer posed a major threat; and on the Continent, Edward III was deeply embroiled in his war with France – the start of the prolonged struggle which would become known as the Hundred Years' War (1337–1453).

King David set to work to restore his battered kingdom to normality. He strengthened the administration, restored the royal revenues, and made a few destructive raids into northern England to get his own back on the absent Edward. In October 1346, however, he made one raid too many.

The Battle of Neville's Cross (17 October 1346)

In August 1346 Edward III won a stunning victory over the French at the Battle of Crécy, where the experienced English archers with their deadly longbows destroyed a larger and more heavily armoured French army. He was now besieging Calais, and King Philippe VI called upon France's 'auld ally' to create a diversion by invading England. To the Scots, the call to invade Northumberland seemed an excellent opportunity of safe plunder; they were confident that the north of England would be a relatively easy target in the absence of the bulk of England's fighting men. But they were wrong. The Archbishop of

York (William de la Zouche) and two powerful northern magnates (Lord Ralph Neville and Lord Henry Percy), along with Sir Thomas Rokeby, mustered an army of fifteen thousand men – 'miserable monks and pig-drivers', according to the Scots – to meet the Scottish challenge. The showdown came at Neville's Cross, which is now a district in the western suburbs of Durham.

The stone socket of 'Neville's Cross' itself stands on a plinth in a railed enclosure on the north side of the A690 Durham–Crook road, at the junction with the A167 trunk road which runs between Newcastle and Darlington. This ancient cross has given its name to the battle which was fought on 17 October 1346 and which brought sore embarrassment and dismay to Scotland.[1]

Just to the north of the junction a gaunt pedestrian bridge over the A167 carries an information panel which explains the panoramic view of the site of the battle. The landscape has changed a great deal, of course: in 1346 it was a broad ridge of moorland rough grazing running north–south, with the valley of the River Browney to the west and Flass Vale to the east. Looking north from the footbridge, across the rooftops of the new housing which lines the road, one can catch a glimpse of the Crossgate Moor where the Scottish army formed up in three divisions; a railway line now cuts deeply through the Red Hills part of the ridge where the English army had taken up position, and the A167 bisects it.

The Scottish army, probably rather larger than the English forces, had camped in the grounds of Beaurepaire (now corrupted to 'Bearpark') manor house, near Durham. On the day of the battle the Scots took up position in three bristling schiltrons at the northern edge of Crossgate Moor to the east of the ravine of the winding River Browney: the king's brigade was in the centre straddling the A167, flanked to the left by Robert Stewart, the Steward of Scotland, and to the right by Sir William Douglas beside the River Browney. The English, also in three battalions, faced them on the Red Hill ridge, with Neville in the centre (just where the pedestrian bridge now crosses the A167), the Archbishop of York and Rokeby to the left and Percy to the right.

---

1 The ancient cross was one of a number at which pilgrims to Durham Cathedral would have paused at the town's western boundary. It is not unlikely that Lord Ralph Neville erected a new cross at or near the site of the battle to commemorate the victory. That cross was destroyed in 1589; the present 'cross' is a milestone which was inserted into the socket of the old cross when it was moved to its present position, at the corner of the A690 at St John's Road.

Each of the English battalions had a screen of archers out in front; at the rear, concealed by a fold of the ground, was a cavalry reserve under the command of the resilient Edward Balliol.

The Scots made the first move, with an attack down the right flank by Douglas. Hemmed in by the ravine of the Browney, the Douglas men were forced into a concentrated mass and suffered fearful losses from the longbows of the English archers. The king's division advanced to engage the English centre, with Robert Stewart's division on its left, and Neville and Percy were pushed back by weight of numbers. At that point the English cavalry under Edward Balliol swung into action with a thunderous flank attack which sent Stewart's battalion reeling back in disorder, while Rokeby's troops attacked the surviving Douglas troops on the other flank. The Scottish attack was broken. Stewart withdrew his men from the field, leaving the king's division exposed and stranded. The young king, his men almost encircled, fought on with memorable courage but was cornered under a bridge over the Browney; he had been severely injured by an arrow in the face, but he knocked out the teeth of one of his attackers before he was over-powered. He was carried off to the Tower of London in triumph; he was to remain his brother-in-law's captive in England for the next eleven years.

The rise of the Steward

One great Scottish lord had escaped from the debacle at Neville's Cross, however – Robert Stewart. The Steward made his way back to Scotland unscathed with his own men and a leading supporter, Patrick, Earl of March. Contemporary chroniclers were divided about the Steward's behaviour at the battle: some claimed that he could have done more to rescue the beleaguered young king, instead of running to save his own skin. Stewart's reputation thereafter was always to be shadowed by this apparent abandonment of his king in his hour of need.

In the aftermath of the battle the English overran much of southern Scotland; Edward Balliol was at their head. But there was little support for Balliol in Scotland now; he lingered on in the south-west until, in 1356, he resigned to Edward III personally his claim to the Scottish throne in return for a pension of £2,000. He died, childless, in 1364.

King David II remained a prisoner in England for eleven years, and during that time his nephew, Robert Stewart, ran the government as the 'king's lieutenant'. Stewart used the opportunity to create a formidable network of power through marriage-alliances and territorial deals the length and breadth of Scotland, collecting earldoms and baronies all over the place. He gave one of his daughters, Margaret, in marriage to John, Lord of the Isles, the most powerful magnate in the Gaelic-speaking west; and in 1347 he himself, after the death of his first wife, Elizabeth Mure, married Euphemia, the widowed Countess of Moray.

Throughout his captivity in England, King David's main concern was how to secure his release so that he could take up the reins of kingship again. His first major attempt was in 1350, when he worked out a deal with Edward III which, in effect, pledged the Scottish throne in return for his freedom. The basis of the deal was that David was to be released without ransom if the Scottish parliament would accept a new heir-presumptive – one of the King of England's younger sons who was not an heir to the English throne, John of Gaunt (Shakespeare's 'time-honoured Lancaster'). John of Gaunt was David II's nephew through David's marriage to Joan, the sister of Edward III. In November 1351 David was allowed parole to go to Scotland to try to persuade his subjects to accept this proposal, which included tempting clauses like a thousand-year truce and the restoration to the Scots of English-held castles and lands.

The Scottish parliament met in March 1352. Not surprisingly the main opponent of the proposed settlement was Robert Stewart, who had been appointed heir-presumptive as early as 1318, six years before David's birth; for Stewart, the choice of a new heir-presumptive would put an end to his own hopes of ascending the throne of Scotland. The Steward's allies carried the day: the Scottish parliament rejected the settlement, and in April 1352 King David had to return to captivity in England.

David tried again in 1354, this time with a more limited draft agreement which would obtain his release for a ransom of ninety thousand *merks* (£60,000), to be paid in nine annual instalments, while the Scots were to deliver twenty noble hostages as security. But once again Robert Stewart seems to have been the stumbling block; negotiations broke down abruptly when he committed the Scots to another military initiative against England on behalf of France in 1355. Edward III retaliated with a punitive foray into Lothian in January 1356; it coincided with the Feast of the Purification of the Virgin (2 February), and so destructive was it that it became known as 'the Burnt Candlemas'.

Edward's crushing defeat of the French at Poitiers in September 1356 removed the French card and the last obstacle to David II's release; in October 1357 he returned to his kingdom in exchange for a larger ransom of a hundred thousand *merks* (£66,666), payable over ten years, during which there was to be a truce. His title as king was not formally recognised, however, and parts of his kingdom were still occupied; but the third phase of the Wars of Independence was over, for a time at least.

David II came back at the age of thirty-three to a country largely in ruins, devastated by constant warfare. He was in no position to take on, far less to punish, Robert Stewart for twice blocking his release: the Steward was much too powerful, and another outbreak of civil war was surely unthinkable. So what could David do?

It seems that his policy was twofold: first, to try to diminish some of the Steward's power by promoting his own supporters and favourites into positions of territorial strength, and secondly to try to foil the Steward's royal dynastic ambitions by fathering sons of his own.

King David's wife, Joan of England, had come back to Scotland with him in 1357 after his release, but only briefly; within a few weeks she had gone back to England, where she stayed until her death in 1362. The marriage was childless, and during her absence the king consoled himself with an English mistress, Katherine Mortimer; but Katherine was assassinated in 1360 by 'certain great men of Scotland'.

The king's new mistress was a beautiful widow who had proved her fertility by producing a son; her name was Margaret Drummond, the widow of Sir John Logie. By 1363 it was clear that David, by then a widower, was planning to marry her; he showered her and her family with titles, lands and offices – all at the expense of Robert Stewart and his family.

It was this which prompted what could have become the major crisis of David II's reign early in 1363 – a 'rebellion' started by a coalition of barons who resented the king's relentless promotion of his own favourites. Robert Stewart and his sons were certainly associated with the rebellion but not, it seems, full-heartedly. It started with a resolution in the form of a petition presented to the king, complaining about the misuse of funds which had been levied to pay for his ransom: these funds, it was alleged, had been frivolously diverted to finance the king's pleasures and to reward his favourites. The Steward, however, wily politician that he was, seems to have realised very early on that he was backing a lost cause, and within a matter of weeks he publicly renewed his fealty to David while the king's forces dealt with the other dissident barons one by one.

The rebellion, if such it could be called, was an unmitigated failure, and a serious political setback for the Steward: not only had his bluff been called, but by his submission to the king he had also alienated the support of those of his fellow-barons whom he had deserted.

In the wake of the failed rebellion King David travelled to England in the autumn of 1363 to try to renegotiate the ransom treaty and to secure a permanent peace between Scotland and England. The *quid pro quo* was to be the designation of Edward III himself as heir-presumptive to the throne of Scotland if David were to die without legitimate issue. There was a fall-back position whereby the Scots could revert to the earlier idea of nominating John of Gaunt as the heir-presumptive; but David, newly married to the demonstrably fecund Margaret Drummond, must have felt sure that he could produce an heir himself, which would obviate the need for any heir-presumptive at all.

The Steward's political standing was now at its lowest ebb. Contemporary chroniclers were saying that he had been an ineffective, incompetent and disloyal royal lieutenant, a man not to be trusted with the throne. The idea of an English succession – not through Edward III in person but through his son John of Gaunt – was not all that unattractive to many people in Scotland. In the event, however, the Scottish parliament once again found the English terms too hard to swallow, and the proposed new settlement was rejected in March 1364.

King David now spent heavily on improvements to Edinburgh Castle to provide the crown with a more secure stronghold. He provided a better water-supply (protected by a new Well-House Tower), and in 1367–68 he embarked on a massive L-shaped tower-house crowning the eastern crags above the grassy edge of the Castle Hill – what was subsequently to become known as David's Tower. It comprised a ground-floor strong-room for the Treasury, a private hall on the first floor, and royal apartments on the second floor.[1]

For the rest of his reign King David II seems to have been determined to produce an heir of his own, or to create a new heir-presumptive – anything to stop his nephew, the Steward, inheriting the crown. He relentlessly promoted the interests of his new queen, Margaret Drummond; he insisted on the marriage, in 1367, of Robert Stewart's eldest son, John, to Annabella Drummond, the queen's niece,

---

1 David's Tower was shattered during the siege of Edinburgh Castle by the 'King's Men', supported by English artillery, in 1573, during the captivity of Mary Queen of Scots in England (see Chapter 20), and its position was forgotten. It was 'rediscovered' early in the twentieth century, in a jumble of cellarage underneath the gun-platform of the Half-Moon Battery. Only a part of the ground floor and a stretch of stone curtain-wall to its south remain, entombed within the Half Moon Battery.

to try to ensure a Drummond-Stewart heir who might eventually ascend the throne; and John Stewart was created Earl of Atholl and Earl of Carrick.

It looks as if, after a while, David gave up hope of fathering a son – at least by Margaret Drummond. In 1369 he introduced another twist to the saga by abruptly starting divorce proceedings against her. He had another mistress now – Agnes Dunbar, sister of the Earl of March. She, too, had children from a previous marriage; and David was still in the prime of life, in his mid-forties. Agnes was clearly going to be David's next queen; he put through huge sums of money for her upkeep, and promoted her kinsmen as was now his wont. He also insisted on a marriage between Agnes's brother, John Drummond, and another Stewart daughter: David was still hedging his bets – and the Steward was helpless to stop him.

And then, on 23 February 1371, everything changed: practically on the eve of his wedding to Agnes the king suddenly died in Edinburgh Castle. After all his machinations and manoeuvrings, the man whom he had tried so hard to prevent inheriting the throne had won – simply by surviving. At the age of fifty-five David's nephew, Robert Stewart, became King Robert II, the first of the long and tragically unlucky royal Stewart dynasty of Scotland.

Epilogue

In the last few years there has been a significant change in academic perceptions of David II's achievements. His reign was for long considered lacklustre and feeble, and he was consistently portrayed as frivolous, extravagant and pleasure-loving, an unworthy successor to his heroic predecessor, his father Robert Bruce. In this view, historians were taking a lead from early chroniclers like Walter Bower in his *Scotichronicon*. Modern historians, however, have radically revised this assessment. Michael Lynch writes:

> *The older picture of a worthless incompetent attracted to a procession of domineering women, which was encouraged by the moralising censures of pro-Stewart chroniclers such as Walter Bower, has been replaced by a cooler assessment, based on analysis of the growing activity of the king's administration, of a tough-minded, energetic ruler – a model for later Stewart kings such as James I or II.*
>
> SCOTLAND: A NEW HISTORY

David's reign has been used as a kind of shorthand for a failure of the impetus with which his father had transformed Anglo–Scottish relations in the first three decades of the fourteenth century. Robert Bruce had greatly increased the power of the crown in Scotland, strengthening Scotland's position *vis-à-vis* England; but whereas, in England, royal power was strengthened and extended by Edward III, in Scotland there was decentralisation (and therefore weakening) of royal power. But was that really such a bad thing? And was it the fault of weak, vacillating kings? Perhaps it should rather be seen as a reflection of changing times in Scotland – including a devastating outbreak of bubonic plague in 1349 which caused the death of a fifth to a sixth of the population (perhaps two hundred thousand people out of a million).

Recent research into the reigns of David and his two successors, Robert II and Robert III, has concentrated on trying to understand better the motivations of these three kings in the context of the society of their time. Historians like Steve Boardman (*The Early Stewart Kings: Robert II and Robert III, 1371–1406*) now recognise that David II, despite all the disadvantages of his long absences from Scotland, the wars with England and the massive burden of his ransom repayments, was able to administer law and order capably, and he is now credited with much good legislation and sound fiscal administration.

David II, it seems, was not nearly as bad a King of Scots as he has been painted.

Chapter 13

ROBERT II (r.1371–90)
AND ROBERT III (r.1390–1406)

Robert Stewart . . . was now called to the throne. He was a good and kind-tempered prince. When young he had been a brave soldier; but he was now fifty-five years old, and subject to a violent inflammation in his eyes, which rendered them as red as blood. From these causes he lived a good deal retired, and was not active enough to be at the head of a fierce and unmanageable nation like the Scots.

TALES OF A GRANDFATHER, CHAPTER XVI

They call it, affectionately, the 'Lantern of the North' – Elgin Cathedral, one of the most hauntingly beautiful of Scotland's medieval buildings, and Scotland's second largest cathedral, next only to St Andrews. On 17 June 1390 it fell victim to the fury of the picturesquely-named 'Wolf of Badenoch', who turned it into a real lantern of the north by setting it on fire in an orgy of destruction. This act of sacrilege was mourned in a dignified letter to the king from the Bishop of Moray, Alexander Bur:

My church was the ornament of the realm, the glory of the kingdom, the delight of foreigners and stranger guests: an object of praise in foreign lands.

The Wolf of Badenoch was Alexander Stewart, Lord of Badenoch and Earl of Buchan, the younger and favourite son of one king (Robert II)

210

and the younger brother of another (Robert III). His recumbent effigy, hands clasped in prayer but in full fighting armour, rests on his tomb behind the high altar of Dunkeld Cathedral in Perthshire, where he was buried in 1405.

Alexander Stewart has been portrayed as the stereotype of dissatisfied younger royal sons. He was the third surviving son of the first Stewart king, Robert II, by his mistress (later wife) Elizabeth Mure. In 1371, when his father came to the throne, Alexander was showered with lands and titles in Badenoch and the north-east, which he enhanced by marriage to Euphemia, the widowed Countess of Ross: he was Lord of Badenoch, titular Earl of Moray and Earl of Buchan, and was appointed the King's Lieutenant north of the Moray Firth. By the 1380s he had become much the most powerful magnate in the northern and western Highlands.

His task as king's lieutenant was to enforce justice in an area riven by feuds and fighting. Great Highland chieftains kept large private armies of professional soldiers or mercenaries (*ceatharn,* 'caterans') which they used to enforce their will upon their neighbours. There were indignant complaints to the king's council when Alexander Stewart, too, started to employ a force of caterans himself, and the word 'cateran' became synonymous in the Lowlands with 'Highland bandit' or 'malefactor'.

Throughout the 1380s the Wolf of Badenoch conducted a long and acrimonious dispute with John Dunbar, the lawful Earl of Moray, and with the powerful and aggressive Bishop of Moray over authority in the area. The Wolf wielded the power of his office with a ruthlessness for which he was censured by the king's council in 1388. To cap it all, he was consistently and flagrantly unfaithful to his wife, Euphemia, the Countess of Ross; Euphemia denounced the marriage as a sham and demanded the return of all the Ross lands. This gave the Bishop of Moray an opportunity to censure him again. It was too much for the Wolf of Badenoch to stomach; in late May 1390, soon after King Robert II's death and before the coronation of his successor, he erupted from his lair in Lochindorb with what Andrew of Wyntoun called a band of 'wyld wikkit Heland men' (caterans). He sacked Forres, the second burgh in the earldom of Moray, then wreaked ferocious and symbolic vengeance by burning the cathedral of Elgin, together with eighteen residences of the canons and chaplains.

This ranks in popular perception as one of the most notorious outrages committed in medieval Scotland; but it did not go unpunished. The Wolf was excommunicated by the Bishop of Moray, and as soon as the new king, Robert III (the Wolf's brother), was crowned, the king's council forced the Wolf to pay hefty reparations to the bishop in order to have the ban lifted. The great cathedral was rebuilt in stages, and the present ruins are the result of vandalism and neglect after the Reformation; but they will always be associated with the spectacular depredations of the Wolf of Badenoch.[1]

These acts of destruction had another enduring significance. They symbolised a growing dichotomy between the English-speaking Lowlands and the Gaelic-speaking Highlands. From now on, the Highlanders would be stigmatised as 'a savage and untamed race, rude and independent, given to rapine . . . and exceedingly cruel' (John of Fordun), compared to the civilised, cultured Lowlanders. It was the thin end of what would become a very large wedge in the fabric of the nation.

King Robert II (r.1379–90)

Robert the Steward (Stewart), nephew of David II and first of the royal Stewart dynasty, was crowned King Robert II at Scone on 26 March 1371. He was the son of the powerful west-coast magnate Walter the Steward and Robert Bruce's daughter Marjory.

Robert Stewart was now fifty-five years old, tall and majestic of bearing, a skilled and experienced politician who was all too aware of the problems which a disputed succession could produce; his very first act as king, on the day after his coronation, was to name as his successor his eldest son by his first wife (Elizabeth Mure) – John, Earl of Carrick, who was now appointed Steward of Scotland. Two years later an elaborate Act of Succession was approved by parliament which made careful provision for a *male* Stewart succession; it ordained that, in the event of the failure of the direct male line through John, the crown should pass successively to the male heirs of Robert's four other sons, Robert (Earl of Fife), Alexander (the Wolf of Badenoch), David (Earl of Strathearn) and Walter (Earl of Caithness and, later, Atholl). At this time the heir-presumptive John, Earl of Carrick, who had been married since 1367, had produced two daughters but no son; Robert, Earl of Fife, had a ten-year-old son, Murdoch, who was now second in the line of succession.[2]

---

1 The Wolf of Badenoch was given an undeserved reputation for heroism in 1827 as the eponymous hero of a historical romance by the eccentric author and polymath Sir Thomas Dick Lauder, which enjoyed great popular success.

2 John, Earl of Carrick, and his wife Annabella Drummond eventually produced a son, David, in 1378; their second son James (the future King James I of Scotland) was born in 1394.

The popular perception of Robert II has been even less flattering than that of David II: 'yesterday's man' and 'a pathetically weak personality' are two of the damning verdicts on him. But, as with David II, modern historians see him in a much more positive light.

Perhaps the most realistic way to look at Robert II is to see him as the chairman of the board of a family firm over-stocked with ambitious and self-seeking siblings, like a medieval version of a dynastic soap opera. Certainly, the family was large enough: Robert II, by his two marriages, had five surviving legitimate sons (he had a clutch of at least eight illegitimate sons, too) and seven daughters. Royal offspring were a political resource of immense importance: when he was Guardian of Scotland Robert Stewart had done much to place members of his family in important positions all over Scotland, and in the early years of his reign he did everything he could to encourage the territorial aggrandisement of his extensive family network. Michael Lynch notes:

> By 1377 seven of the sixteen current earldoms were in the family's control, and by the mid-1390s no fewer than twelve. The seven daughters ... played their part: they added a total of eleven sons-in-law to the Stewart nexus.
>
> SCOTLAND: A NEW HISTORY

At the same time, Robert II was making powerful use of public relations to create a favourable image of the Stewart/Bruce dynasty. Less than fifty years after the death of Robert's grandfather, Robert the Bruce, John Barbour, Archdeacon of Aberdeen, was commissioned to extol Bruce's memory in his great chivalric epic *The Brus*, composed between 1375 and 1378. The poem laid great stress on Robert II's descent from the hero-king and on his leadership in the fight for national independence, and the continuity of the dynasty in his own kingship.[1] Furthermore, while John Barbour was creating his epic, an obscure chantry priest in Aberdeen named John of Fordun was compiling, from older (now lost) records, a Latin 'Chronicle of the Scottish People' (*Chronica Gentis Scotorum*) which traced the history of the Scots from their earliest origins to 1383, celebrating the independence of the Scottish kingdom in Robert II's reign.

The French chronicler and poet Jean Froissart (c.1333–c.1404) did much to colour posterity's view of Robert as a weak, cowardly and

---

1 Barbour also composed a (now lost) Stewart genealogy, *The Stewartis Orygenale*, which traced the Stewart line of descent back into the origin myth of the Scots.

ineffective king. He described him, unflatteringly, as having 'red-bleared eyes, of the colour of sandalwood, which clearly showed that he was no valiant man, but one who would rather remain at home than march to the field'. What we are seeing is a propaganda battle between the pro-Douglas faction (supporters of the Earl of Carrick, the heir-presumptive and future king) and the King Robert faction, especially those who supported the king's younger brother Robert, Earl of Fife, who would later become Regent as the Duke of Albany.

The picture of Robert II which emerges at this time is of a cautious conservative, intent on providing continuity of government, a shrewd pragmatist who practised non-confrontational politics as the art of the possible, busily wheeling and dealing with the leading magnates of the country to create a proper balance between crown and nobility. He treated his parliament, or General Council, with unfailing respect. He was also fortunate in the broader circumstances in which he came to the throne. The economy was doing reasonably well: wool exports were booming, and high tax yields enabled him to be generous to his supporters with grants of lands, privileges and pensions. England or English assignees still exercised military control of much of southern Scotland through garrisons in the major castles at Berwick, Jedburgh and Roxburgh; but there was no war with England, nor likely to be for as long as the ageing Edward III remained on the throne (he died in 1377).

In fact, Robert II was not proving to be a lame-duck king by any means. It was only after the first decade of his reign that he began to falter. The traditional view of John, Earl of Carrick, the heir-presumptive, is that he was indolent and uninterested in public office; on the contrary, he was a vigorous and ambitious man. In 1380 he was forty-three years old, impatient to get his hands on the crown; he had established a formidable vice-regal power-base in the south of Scotland and was custodian of Edinburgh Castle. There was growing tension between Carrick and the king and between Carrick and his younger brothers Robert and Alexander.

In the Border lands, hostilities between Scots and English were simmering and flaring as the great Border families (especially the Douglas kin-group), closely associated through marriage-ties with Carrick, campaigned sporadically against the English presence. Cross-border raiding and skirmishing was once again becoming endemic. War drums were sounding along the border throughout the early 1380s, as the policy towards Scotland of the new English government under the young Richard II, Edward III's grandson, hardened. By 1384 it was clear that a full-scale war was in the offing, and that the French were prepared to send an expeditionary force to help Scotland against the English.

It was at this moment, in November 1384, that King Robert II was pushed aside in a palace coup which was endorsed by the General Council. There had been growing political discontent about his ability to administer justice fairly (especially in the north, in the light of the Wolf of Badenoch's depredations as the king's lieutenant) and to conduct a war against England vigorously enough. The sixty-nine-year-old king was persuaded by the council to demit the enforcement of royal justice to his heir, John, Earl of Carrick. Carrick was declared Guardian of the kingdom: the Young Turks of the Border lands were now in the ascendant.

The Battle of Otterburn (19 August 1388)

The great historian Froissart says, that, one other action only excepted, it was the best fought battle of that warlike time.
TALES OF A GRANDFATHER, CHAPTER XVI

The village of Otterburn, in Redesdale in Northumberland, lies fifty kilometres north-west of Newcastle upon Tyne, just south of the Scottish border, on the busy A696 from Newcastle towards Jedburgh. Just beyond the village an avenue of pine trees leads off the main road to a curious standing stone; this is known as 'Percy's Cross', and commemorates a spectacular encounter which took place nearby in 1388 – the Battle of Otterburn.

Otterburn was the last flamboyant flare-up of the Anglo–Scottish war which had threatened in 1384. In June 1385 the French had sent their promised expeditionary force of knights and men-at-arms under a seasoned military commander, Jean de Vienne, Admiral of France, but this had not led to a renewed *entente cordiale*: the French troops complained about their billets, and the Scots complained about French arrogance and indiscriminate foraging for food (something like a hundred French troopers lost their lives after being caught pilfering by irate Scottish farmers). The invasion of England, led by the new Guardian and his Border nobles, followed its usual course: parts of the north of England were put to the sword and the flame, but the Franco-Scots drive was stalled when Richard II approached with a massive English army. Hopelessly outnumbered, the Scots reverted to guerrilla tactics (to the disgust of the battle-oriented French, who wanted the

215

chivalric glory of a pitched battle) while the English host marched unopposed through southern Scotland, burning the abbeys of Dryburgh and Melrose. When it reached Edinburgh it put the city and St Giles' Church to the torch, before returning in triumph to England. The disgruntled French force also left Scotland, vowing never to return except as allies of the English!

The ease with which England had walked into Scotland alarmed the Scots into making a truce for three years. A truce was equally welcome to England, where Richard II (who was still a minor) was now embroiled in a revolt led by his uncle, the Duke of Gloucester. But as soon as the truce period was up, the headstrong Border nobles under the leadership of James, the second Earl of Douglas, brother-in-law to the Guardian, were on the warpath again. In a two-pronged attack they lunged into both Cumberland and Northumberland in the summer of 1388 in the first of a planned series of destructive raids. It was the second raid, in August 1388, which led to the immortalised encounter at Otterburn.

The eastern prong of the Scots incursion was led by James, Earl of Douglas, by now an inveterate opponent of his counterpart in the north of England, Henry Percy, son and heir of the first Earl of Northumberland and better known to history as 'Hotspur'.

Outside the walls of Newcastle the Scots skirmished with the English garrison, led by Hotspur. During the exchanges, the Earl of Douglas contrived to snatch the silk pennon from Hotspur's lance and then withdraw, heading back to Scotland. Hotspur, as dashing as his name suggests, swore that his standard would never leave England, and set off in pursuit with a force of about eight thousand lightly-armed mounted troops. He caught up with the Scots – perhaps three or four thousand strong – in their encampment to the north-west of Otterburn.

At Percy's Cross a display panel in the carpark informs the pilgrim:

> *Tradition has it that on the night of August 19th, 1388, a bloody encounter took place on these fields between Scottish raiders led by James, Earl of Douglas, and an English force commanded by Sir Henry Percy, eldest son of the Earl of Northumberland, which resulted in a defeat for the English forces and the death of James.*

The Battle of Otterburn is remembered in folk-tale and ballad on both sides of the border as one of the most heroic encounters ever staged between Scots and English forces. But there is nothing heroic or grandiose about Percy's Cross. There was once a 'Battle Stone', some 160 metres to the east; it was nothing more than a roughly carved boulder which rested drunkenly in a socket much too large for it. When a new road was being built in 1777, the socket was moved to the present site of Percy's Cross and set into the top of a pedestal base. The original 'Battle Stone' did not survive the move; instead, a slab of lintel from the fireplace at Otterburn Tower was used as the new monument, complete with two of the iron fixtures for holding cooking pots.

Six centuries after the battle, there is some doubt about its precise site. Behind Percy's Cross is another display panel which provides a graphic description of the battle according to the version favoured by English Heritage. It carries a 'Word of Caution', reminding us that other locations have been favoured in the past.[1] The really dedicated pilgrim can walk from Otterburn Hall Farm round the perimeter of the deeply undulating open countryside where English Heritage suggests the battle took place.[2]

There are several accounts of the battle, none of which is precise enough to enable identification of the site with complete certainty.[3] The encounter was also immortalised in two magnificent ballads – *The Ballad of Chevy Chase* in England, and *The Ballad of Otterburn* in the Scottish Borders. All the sources agree that it began in the summer gloaming and that the fierce hand-to-hand fighting went on all night. The Scots had apparently been expecting Hotspur's arrival, but were taken by surprise by the speed of his pursuit.

Hotspur's men were tired and hungry after their long trek from Newcastle. Nevertheless, Hotspur went straight into the attack. He sent a large detachment in a wide flanking movement to the north to

---

1 On a roadside verge on the A68 beside Bennettsfield, two and a half kilometres west of Otterburn and far from the battlefield, is a semi-circular, classical-style stone exedra (now covered with lichen) commissioned in 1888 by Lord Northbourne to commemorate the fifth centenary of the battle and known locally as the Battle Seat at Bennettsfield. One of the weathered inscriptions on it reads: 'In these fields, the Battle of Otterburn was fought, and deeds were done which, in the noblest of English ballads [The Ballad of Chevy Chase], live immortally recorded'.

2 See *Battlefield Walks: North*, by David Clark (Grange Books, 1995).

3 There are two main sources of information about the battle. One is the Scottish version, recorded by Andrew of Wyntoun (*Original Chronicle of Scotland*, 1413–20) and Walter Bower (*Scotichronicon*), who used an anonymous contemporary chronicler; the other is the French version, written by Froissart as part of his popular *Chroniques*, a history of the European wars of his time. Froissart derived his account from a meeting he had with a knight who had been in Douglas's service; and as with Shakespeare's version of the Macbeth story, there is no argument about which is the more memorable account.

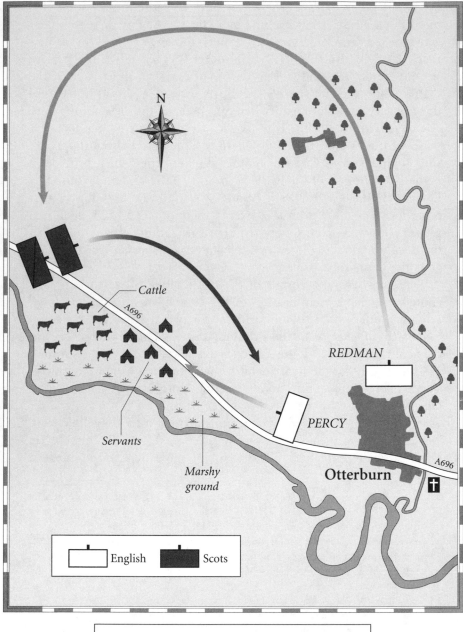

N

Cattle

A696

Servants

Marshy
ground

REDMAN

PERCY

Otterburn

A696

English   Scots

THE BATTLE OF OTTERBURN,
19 AUGUST 1388

attack from the rear; but this detachment got lost in the darkness and never made contact with the Scots. Meanwhile, Hotspur himself launched a thrust straight at the Scottish encampment alongside the River Rede. The advance part of the camp was occupied by serving men and foragers, and their resistance enabled Douglas to lead his main force of mounted men-at-arms in a flanking movement of his own:

The moon was clear, the day drew near,
The spears in flinders [splinters] flew;
But mony a gallant Englishman
Ere day the Scotsmen slew.
THE BALLAD OF OTTERBURN

It must have been a macabre sight: hundreds of men flailing at one another in the fitful moonlight. It soon became too dark for the English to use their most feared weapon, the longbow.

At last the Duglas and the Persè met,
Lyk to captayns of myght and mayne;
The swapte together [they fought] tyll the both swat [sweated],
With swordes, that wear [were] of fyn myllàn [fine Milanese steel].
THE BALLAD OF CHEVY CHASE

Eventually Douglas fell, exhausted by innumerable wounds. He knew he was mortally wounded; but he knew, too, that the battle was almost won. His one concern was that his men should not know that he had fallen:

My wound is deep, I fain would sleep;
Take thou the vanguard of the three,
And hide me by the bracken bush
That grows on yon lily lea.
THE BALLAD OF OTTERBURN

In accordance with his dying wish, Douglas was laid 'by the bracken bush'. His standard was raised again and his men charged back into the fray shouting the war cry 'A Douglas! A Douglas!'[1] As dawn broke,

---

1 A painted silk ceremonial standard of the Douglas family (the 'Cavers Standard'), bearing the traditional Douglas emblem of a heart, is displayed in the National Museum of Scotland

Percy was surrounded and agreed to surrender – but only to the man by the bracken bush. The Scots had won: they had lost only two hundred men, compared with a thousand or 1,500 English casualties; but it had been a Pyrrhic victory.

'*C'est magnifique, mais ce n'est pas la guerre,*' as Marshal Bosquet was to say of the Charge of the Light Brigade at Balaclava. Like the hopelessly valiant charge by the Light Brigade, the Battle of Otterburn has become one of the great chivalric set-pieces of courage and dauntless heroism.

With the death (without issue) of the Earl of Douglas at Otterburn, the carefully-knitted network of alliances created in the Borders by the king's son and heir John, the Earl of Carrick, began to unravel; there was territorial wrangling over the vacant earldom, and Carrick found his regional power-base rapidly eroding. Sometime in 1388, too, he suffered severe physical injury when he was kicked by a horse during a tournament, which virtually incapacitated him. After the humiliation of his virtual deposition by his son in 1384, Robert II was in no mood to show sympathy. When the royal council met in December 1388 the king had his revenge: the council censured Carrick for failing to bring justice to the north and to deal with the English threat in the Borders, and removed him from the Guardianship in favour of his younger brother Robert, Earl of Fife.

Robert, Earl of Fife, was the most capable of Robert II's sons – and he needed to be. Sooner or later (and in all probability sooner rather than later) John, Earl of Carrick, the king's eldest son, would ascend the throne, incapacitated or not; yet the new Guardian not only governed Scotland firmly and well for the rest of Robert II's life, but as Duke of Albany he would succeed in keeping an iron grip on the kingdom for the next thirty-two years as the uncrowned ruler of Scotland.

King Robert III (r.1390–1406)

The eldest son of Robert II was originally called John. But it was a popular remark, that the kings named John, both of France and England, had been unfortunate, and the Scottish people were very partial to the name of Robert ... John Stewart, therefore,

---

in Edinburgh. It is a massive artefact, nearly four metres long, and must have required several strong men to lift it. According to tradition, this was the standard carried at Otterburn, although scientific analysis of the fabric suggests that it could be later in date.

*on ascending the Scottish throne, changed his name to that of
Robert III. We shall see, however, that this poor king remained
as unfortunate as if his name had still been John.*

TALES OF A GRANDFATHER, CHAPTER XVII

Walter Scott expanded his sweeping condemnation of Robert III in
his *History of Scotland* (Chapter XVI):

*He was lame in body and feeble in mind, – well-meaning, pious,
benevolent, and just; but totally disqualified, from want of personal activity and mental energy, to hold the reins of government
of a fierce and unmanageable people.*

Robert II died in Dundonald Castle in Ayrshire in April 1390, soon
after completing an arduous royal circuit of the north-east. He was
seventy-four years old, but was still active in his royal duties, although
his elder sons (John, and then Robert) had latterly exercised executive
power on his behalf under the close scrutiny of the council.

There followed a curious four-month gap between the death of the
old king in April and the coronation of his eldest son, John, at Scone
on 14 August 1390. In the interim it was agreed that John should take
the regnal name of Robert III – 'John', as Scott wrote, had unhappy
associations as a royal name in England and France. More significantly,
a regnal name of 'John II' would retrospectively accord to John Balliol
('Toom Tabard') the formal status of King of Scots as John I. The
Bruce/Stewart faction had consistently denied the legitimacy of Balliol's
claim, and such a move might revive English claims to the Scottish
throne as Edward Balliol, son of John, had resigned his to Edward III
in 1354.

There must also have been a political struggle going on in the
background, between the supporters of the new king and those of his
ambitious younger brother Robert, Earl of Fife, who had taken over
from him the Guardianship of the realm in 1388. In addition, there
was the violent eruption of the third brother, Alexander Buchan, the
Wolf of Badenoch, and his ferocious attack on Elgin Cathedral, a
spectacular power-play against both of his brothers to demonstrate
his dominance of the north of Scotland.

In the event, the Earl of Fife's position as Guardian was confirmed
by the General Council despite the fact that a new king was about to
be crowned. It all made for an inauspicious start to the new reign.
Although he was more than fifty years old, Robert III had shown

himself to be as ambitious, energetic and, if necessary, ruthless as any of his predecessors. His major handicap, apart from his lack of physical health, was that he was less ambitious, energetic and ruthless than his younger brother Robert, Earl of Fife, who had already undermined his credibility in 1388 when he had taken over the Guardianship from him. In addition there was a sharp economic downturn during the 1390s.

The royal succession seemed secure, however: Robert III and his queen, Annabella Drummond, already had a son, David, who was twelve years old and the heir-presumptive; a second son, Robert, had died in infancy, but in 1394 Robert III had another son, James, the future King James I. Robert III's main priorities as king, therefore, were to restore the crown's authority and to safeguard the succession.

Prince David soon became the vehicle for the king's reassertion of royal authority. Robert III carefully created for his precocious son (now Earl of Carrick) a power-base of his own from which he could take part in the conduct of government. In February 1393 the Council terminated the Earl of Fife's appointment as Guardian, and with that the king regained at least nominal control of his kingdom, aided by the increasing political involvement of Prince David, his son and heir.

The major problem which faced Robert III, and would have faced any occupant of the throne, was the 'Highland question'. The Wolf of Badenoch's depredations in the Highlands as the king's unruly lieutenant were only a symptom of it – exceptionally violent, no doubt, but not by any means isolated. The king's younger brother was seen in Lowland eyes as being out of control, despite several determined attempts by the Earl of Fife to undermine his power. Outraged complaints about the lawlessness of the Highland chieftains occupied much of every meeting of the General Council. The longer the king was seen to be impotent to impose authority and justice in the north, the more his political, indeed his royal, credibility was eroded. Walter Bower, in his *Scotichronicon* in the 1440s, would write of Robert III's reign:

> There was a great deal of dissension, strife and brawling among the magnates and the leading men, because the king, being bodily infirm, had no grip anywhere.

It was perhaps in an attempt to restore his credibility that Robert III became involved in one of the most bizarre events of his reign – the infamous Clan Combat on the North Inch of Perth in September 1396. If so, it was a public relations exercise which failed.

The Battle on the Inch (1396)

One of the more serious and long-standing feuds in the Highlands at this time was the enmity between two Gaelic kindreds, Clan Kay and Clan Chattan. To bring the dispute to a decisive conclusion the king ordered a public judicial combat in Perth, where thirty warriors from each side were to fight to the death. The chosen site was the North Inch, a flat, thirty-two-hectare meadow by the River Tay; it is now a recreation area ('the playground of Perth'). A stone-built plinth at the corner of Rose Crescent, looking towards Atholl Crescent, commemorates the combat ('The Battle of the Clans was fought on the North Inch, 1396'), which took place at the southern end of the Inch, level with the magnificent old Perth Academy building in Rose Terrace. Spectator stands were erected (at a cost of £14.2s.11d) to accommodate the great crowd which thronged to watch the battle in the presence of the king and his court and many high-ranking guests; the young Prince David acted as umpire. There can have been little like it since the heyday of the gladiatorial combats in the Colosseum in Rome.

The story of the Homeric contest has been much embellished by legend and folk-tale: one version claims that at the last moment the Clan Chattan contingent found itself a champion short, and that a giant Perth blacksmith, Hal Gow of the Wynd, took his place and tipped the scales of the outcome.[1]

The sixty champions were ushered into the lists to the martial sound of trumpets and bagpipes. They were allowed no body armour, but could carry a sword and a dirk (dagger), an axe and a crossbow with three arrows; their only form of protection was a leather targe (shield). As the signal to start was given, they all loosed their arrows and then flung themselves at one another in fierce bouts of hand-to-hand fighting. No quarter was given, and no one was allowed to retire from the fray. Throughout the long and bloody afternoon they hacked and

---

1 The Battle on the Inch provides the dramatic climax to Walter Scott's novel *The Fair Maid of Perth* (1828). Scott set his story in Perth during a two-month period between St Valentine's Day and Palm Sunday (although the battle took place in September), and telescoped into that short time the political events of the last ten years of Robert III's reign. In the novel, 'Hal Gow' is Henry Smith, the armourer, who loves Catharine Glover, the daughter of Simon Glover; she refuses to accept him until he vows to renounce his fighting ways after the battle. In Curfew Lane there is a charming and much restored seventeenth-century building known as 'Fair Maid's House'; it is thought to have been built as the hall of the Glover Incorporation on the site of the home of Simon Glover, Catharine's father. It is not open to the public at present.

thrust and stabbed at one another, until at last the Clan Chattan men emerged victorious: eleven clansmen (including the 'guest' clansman, the giant blacksmith) were still on their feet, albeit grievously wounded, while the last surviving member of the Clan Kay side took to his heels and plunged into the Tay to make his escape.

The government must have hoped that this parody of a medieval tournament would both get rid of the trouble-makers in the glens and break the fighting spirit of the clans. It did neither. The valour displayed by the clansmen of both sides in this heroic clash only added lustre to the legend of their savage courage, and did nothing to reconcile Lowlander with Highlander.

The rise and fall of Prince David

The rising star on the political scene was now the young Prince David. It was becoming embarrassingly clear that King Robert III – no doubt because of his physical disability – was barely capable of exercising the kind of vigorous royal authority which the kingdom, and especially the recalcitrant Highlands, required. At a ceremony at Scone in 1398, at the age of twenty, Prince David was created Duke of Rothesay (the new title was derived from the ancestral Stewart fortress on the Isle of Bute); on the same day his uncle Robert, Earl of Fife, the former Guardian, was created Duke of Albany (derived from *Alba*, the ancient Gaelic name for Scotland north of the Forth–Clyde axis). These were the first royal dukedoms to be created in Scotland, and they provided the setting for what was to become a life-and-death power-struggle between the two men for the control of Scotland at the end of the fourteenth century.

At first the two new dukes, nephew and uncle, worked in close co-operation. In January 1399 the General Council ended the ageing King Robert III's personal rule because of his incapacity: he was accused of 'misgovernance of the realm and default of the keeping of the common law'. In his place the Council appointed his son David, the Duke of Rothesay, as king's lieutenant for the next three years, 'with full power and commission of the King', guided by a council of twenty-one which was dominated by the Duke of Albany and his allies. This bloodless coup was supported and, some say, inspired by the queen, Annabella Drummond, who clearly saw in her vigorous young son the best way of saving the Stewart monarchy.

Two new factors, apparently unrelated, now came into baleful interplay, however: the deposition of King Richard II in England by Henry IV, and the marital status of the young Duke of Rothesay.

In England in July 1399 Henry Bolingbroke, the son of John of Gaunt (Earl of Lancaster), returned from exile to lead a successful revolt against his cousin, Richard II. Richard was forced to abdicate, and was imprisoned in Pontefract Castle where he died (probably murdered) early in 1400. In Scotland in that year David, the Duke of Rothesay, married into the powerful Douglas family in the Borders; his bride was Mary Douglas, daughter of Archibald 'the Grim', third Earl of Douglas. It must have seemed a sensible move, to ensure alliance with the warlords who defended the Borderlands against England – apart from the fact that David was already married (well, more or less). In 1395 he had gone through a form of marriage with his kinswoman Elizabeth Dunbar, daughter of the influential Earl of March. However, that marriage required papal dispensation, which had not been sought, and was temporarily invalidated: in 1397 the young couple had been compelled to separate, on the understanding that they would be allowed to remarry after a suitable period.

The marriage was never resumed; and when the Earl of March heard of David's wedding to the daughter of the Earl of Douglas his fury at this snub to his daughter knew no bounds. He resigned his allegiance to the Scottish crown and defected to England, to the welcoming arms of Henry IV. Soon Henry was on the march, determined to reassert the lingering English claim to suzerainty over Scotland. The Scots retreated to the relative safety of Edinburgh Castle while a huge English army swept unopposed northwards to Leith. Henry IV did not press home his advantage; he was content to show the Scots that he could march in and take over whenever he pleased, and he withdrew to England without any of the burnings and ravagings normally associated with such military incursions.

David, Duke of Rothesay, had lost a great deal of political 'face' by his failure to stem the English invasion. In addition, he lost a valuable and influential mentor in 1401 when his mother, the queen, died. With the old king still powerless on the sidelines the young duke, freed of parental counsel, seems to have cast off any political restraints on his actions. He began to assert his power as king's lieutenant and heir to the throne much more vigorously, seizing revenues and titles without consultation with his council, and thereby began to alarm and alienate the former Governor of Scotland, his uncle, the Duke of Albany.

Some time towards the end of 1401, apparently out of the blue, Albany struck, and struck hard. As Rothesay was leaving St Andrews, where he had been demanding the keys of the episcopal castle, he was 'arrested' by two of his own councillors and handed over to Albany, who imprisoned him in St Andrews Castle. One of Rothesay's most powerful supporters, the Earl of Mar (the late queen's brother), was similarly thrown into prison. Albany moved equally swiftly to neutralise any opposition from Rothesay's other leading ally, his brother-in-law Archibald, who had succeeded his father as the fourth Earl of Douglas: Douglas was bought off with major concessions and additions to his power in the Borders.

The young prince was now isolated. His father, the king, was impotent (and, some chroniclers implied, unwilling) to help him. For greater security, the royal duke was moved from St Andrews Castle to Albany's own castle at Falkland, wearing russet robes and riding on a mule.[1]

The only question for Albany now was what to do with his nephew. Rothesay was the heir to the throne, and certain to outlive his ailing sixty-five-year-old father; he would undoubtedly seek savage vengeance as soon as he was freed or inherited the throne. Albany can only have come to one conclusion: like Richard II in England in 1400, Rothesay was simply too dangerous to be allowed to live, and had to be eliminated.

David, Duke of Rothesay, died in his uncle's castle at Falkland late in March 1402. He was twenty-four years old. Rumour had it that he died of starvation. A meeting of the General Council in May 1402, however, made no attempt to charge Albany with treason, and asserted that Rothesay had died 'by divine providence, and not otherwise'. Divine or not, it had certainly been providential for Albany. With the king declared incapable of ruling, the heir to the throne dead and the new heir (James) a seven-year-old boy, the council had no alternative but to appoint Albany governor of the realm once again. The boy James would not forget the manner of his brother's death when he succeeded to the throne as James I.

The heir in peril

Young James Stewart, the king's only surviving son, was now the last frail hope for avoiding the abrupt extinction of the senior line of the Stewart dynasty: it would only take one more 'providential' death for

---

1 The russet robes and the mule may have been intended as a disguise, or as a symbol of Rothesay's humiliation. Either way, it was an ominous sign: in England, russet was used for the grave-clothes of poor people, and Richard II had been conveyed to London, after his arrest in 1399, riding on a humble pony.

the crown to devolve upon the Albany family – the male heirs of the king's brother. The king himself now seemed a spent force, confined to his castle of Rothesay on the Isle of Bute, an old man with a long white beard, broken by ill health.

Albany's grip on the kingdom was not quite complete, for his brother Alexander, the Earl of Buchan, the Wolf of Badenoch himself, was still prowling the northlands unchecked with a pack of warlike sons; but Albany's power was sufficient to cause concern for the future of the new heir to the throne.

The old king tried to strengthen his son James's political status as heir to the throne by creating a power-base for him in the south-west of Scotland; in 1404 he made him Earl of Carrick and granted to him the main Stewart lands as his own 'regality' – a 'principality', to be held outside the authority of central government. Meanwhile, for security reasons no doubt, the young prince was sent away to stay in the safety of St Andrews Castle.

And then, early in 1406, James's supporters made a disastrous mistake: they tried to extend his (and their) influence into the Lothians. With a strong force they sallied forth from St Andrews, bringing the young prince as their figurehead, only to be routed by Albany's forces near Edinburgh. The safety of the heir to the throne was now paramount. In a desperate attempt to protect him from Albany, James was spirited away from North Berwick in a rowing-boat with a few members of his household to the relative safety of the fortress on the Bass Rock, a bare, uncomfortable sanctuary in the waters of the Forth estuary. Here he stayed for a month, waiting for arrangements to be made for a ship to take him abroad. Eventually he was picked up by a merchantman from Danzig, the *Maryenknecht*, carrying wool and hides from Leith to France.

Even now luck – or treachery – was to play its part. On 22 March 1406 the *Maryenknecht* was intercepted by Norfolk pirates off Flamborough Head. The young Prince of Scotland was carried off in triumph to the Tower of London into the custody of King Henry IV of England.

The news of his capture hit his father hard. Walter Bower said in his *Scotichronicon*:

> *He was moved inwardly in his heart on hearing the messenger; his spirit failed directly, the strength of his body dwindled, his face grew pale, and in his grief he ate no more food until he breathed out his spirit to his Creator.*

Within a few days of his son's capture, on 4 April 1406, the old king died in his lonely castle on the Isle of Bute, and was buried in the comparative obscurity of Paisley Abbey. His reign had been a sad one. Today he is remembered chiefly for the desolate epitaph he composed for himself (according to the *Scotichronicon*) in reply to a question from his wife about the kind of monument he wanted when he died:

> *Let these men who strive in this world for the pleasures of honour have shining monuments. I on the other hand should prefer to be buried at the bottom of a midden, so that my soul may be saved in the day of the lord. Bury me therefore, I beg you, in a midden, and write for my epitaph: Here lies the worst of kings and the most wretched of men in the whole kingdom.*

With the heir to the throne a captive in England, the Scottish parliament again had no option but to confirm the dead king's brother, the Duke of Albany, as governor and regent of Scotland in June 1406. He was to hold that position, unchallenged, until his death in 1420 at the age of eighty-one.

Chapter 14

JAMES I (r.1406–37)

This King James, the first monarch of the name, was also the
first of his unfortunate family who showed a high degree of talent.
TALES OF A GRANDFATHER, CHAPTER XIX

The most magnificent and visible monument of the Stewart dynasty is Linlithgow Palace, which stands on a promontory jutting into Linlithgow Loch, hard by the M9 motorway from Edinburgh to Stirling – a constant landmark, too, on the rail journey between Edinburgh and Glasgow. It was to be the scene of many significant royal Stewart occasions, but Linlithgow Palace will always be associated in my mind with King James I: it was, above all, *his* palace and *his* achievement.

There had been a royal manor in Linlithgow since the middle of the twelfth century, when King David I gave the burgh its royal charter. It had been transformed into a military stronghold and supply base by Edward I of England in 1302 during the first War of Independence, and then recaptured by Bruce's men after the Battle of Bannockburn in 1314. However, in 1424, the year of James I's return from his eighteen-year captivity in England, it was destroyed in a disastrous fire which razed most of the town of Linlithgow.

James immediately determined to rebuild it – and to rebuild it in the image of the 'new' Scottish monarchy he was intent on promoting. From 1425 to the year of his death in 1437, huge sums of money were spent on building works and luxurious internal decoration – sculptures, moulded ceilings and painted wall-plaster. The grandest of

229

the rooms was the Great Hall on the first floor of the east range of the palace, directly above the old royal gateway.

James I's palace was a striking display of a new cult of chivalry at his court: Linlithgow was rebuilt not as a fortified stronghold but as a glittering, Renaissance royal residence. Standing in the long, roofless Great Hall today it is not difficult to imagine the presence of the most enigmatic of all the Stewart kings.

James Stewart had been born in Dunfermline in 1394, probably in late July. He was the first 'James' in the royal family, possibly named after the day of his birth – St James's Day, 25 July; the name was to have long-lasting consequences for the Stewart dynasty, and give rise to the term 'Jacobite', from its Latin form (*Jacobus*).

He was a late-born child, sixteen years younger than his brother David. Three of his sisters were already married. His father, Robert III, was in his late fifties, and his mother, Queen Annabella, was at least forty. It is possible that he was conceived after the death of the second brother, Robert, in an effort to strengthen the dynastic position of the royal house.

Within weeks of James's capture by the English in March 1406 at the age of eleven, his father's death made him King of Scots – but a king uncrowned. He would have to wait eighteen years before his coronation could be held. For these eighteen formative years he was kept in England, part prisoner and part guest.

The Albany years (1406–24)

For the eighteen years during which James was a captive in England, Scotland was ruled by a governor: Robert, Duke of Albany (1406–20) and then his son Murdoch, second Duke of Albany (1420–24). Robert, Duke of Albany, was second in line to the throne. During the reigns of his father (Robert II) and his brother (Robert III) he had amassed tremendous wealth, and he liked the good things of life: according to the *Scotichronicon* written by his contemporary, Walter Bower, he was 'a man of great expense and munificent to strangers'. His most enduring monument was the building of Doune Castle, overlooking the River Teith near Dunblane, as a grandiose fortress-residence at the end of the fourteenth century – a castle which in its time witnessed 'large tabling and belly cheer'.[1]

---

1   The castle had a massive gate-tower and severe curtain-walls enclosing a courtyard. The Great Hall was flanked by Albany's private lodging above the main entrance into the courtyard, and

Albany was an experienced political veteran by the time he was appointed Governor of Scotland in 1406, and he seems to have been a highly effective regent; working through a General Council, he conducted himself as first among equals in the Scottish nobility, and kept the nation's affairs on an even keel. Although he was generally suspected of having caused the death of his nephew David, the Earl of Rothesay, in 1402, there is no evidence to suggest that he tried to engineer a similar fate for the new heir to the throne, David's brother James; on the other hand there are no indications that he tried particularly hard to have James released from his captivity in England.

The English, under Henry IV (r.1399–1413) and Henry V (r.1413–22), did all they could to undermine Albany's regency, calling him a scheming usurper – not surprisingly, perhaps, because Albany had immediately started trying to rid the castles of southern Scotland of their English garrisons; Jedburgh Castle was recaptured. And early in 1407 the Scots negotiated a renewal of the 'Auld Alliance' with France, with a view to unsettling the English, at least, in the course of their Hundred Years' War with France.

The Battle of Harlaw (24 July 1411)

Much the most spectacular event of Albany's long regency occurred on 24 July 1411: the Battle of Harlaw, some thirty-two kilometres north of Aberdeen – a battle which has become a byword for savagery and valour. It was a ferocious confrontation between the Gaelic-speaking north and west of Scotland, and the forces of the north-eastern Lowlands, and became known in ballad and folk-tale as the Battle of Red Harlaw. The leading protagonists were Donald Macdonald, second Lord of the Isles, and Alexander Stewart, Earl of Mar, eldest cub of the notorious Wolf of Badenoch and nephew of Albany, and by this time the agent of royal policy in the north. At stake, ostensibly, was the rich Earldom of Ross which included the Hebridean islands of Skye and Lewis; in reality, it was about the ultimate control of northern Scotland. It was the fiercest and bloodiest battle ever fought by the Gaels; it was also a battle which nobody won.

Today, the scene of the battle is marked by a large and elaborate

---

by a tower housing the cavernous kitchens and other residential quarters. The Great Hall was extensively reconstructed in Victorian times, complete with an open-timber roof and a minstrels' gallery, hanging banners and a central fire-basket on the flagstoned floor.

monument erected by the city fathers of Aberdeen.[1] It stands on a lofty height beside a minor road off the B9001 north of Inverurie, looking west across the Urie valley towards the jagged fang of Bennachie. The original farming settlement of Harlaw has long since disappeared, but memories of that fabled encounter have never died.

The Lordship of the Isles had been a private fiefdom of Clan Donald for more than a century, ever since the Norsemen had lost control of the Western Isles in 1266. The lordship had long been a potent factor in mainland politics as well: the Macdonalds had backed Robert the Bruce during the Wars of Independence, and their chief, Angus Og, had been one of Bruce's lieutenants at Bannockburn. The Lord of the Isles – *Rí Innse Gall* – based in Dunyvaig Castle on the island of Islay but exercising sway over all the Western Isles and large areas of the western mainland, could muster an army of ten thousand fighting men whenever he wished: a useful ally but also a potential threat to the crown.

At Christmas-time in 1411, Donald, Lord of the Isles, held a great gathering of his clansmen and supporters at his castle of Ardtornish, on the Sound of Mull. There, according to tradition, he selected six thousand of the best fighting men and sent the rest home. He transported this formidable army to the mainland and then marched up the Great Glen to Inverness, brushing all opposition aside. After burning Inverness he was joined by the men of other clans, including the MacIntoshes, the MacLeans, the MacLeods, the Camerons and Clan Chattan. He headed straight for Aberdeen, promising his clan troops – now ten thousand strong – unlimited plunder in the undefended city of Aberdeen.

Alexander, Earl of Mar, refused to be daunted and gathered what forces he could. The Provost of Aberdeen could muster only a few burgesses, but Mar could count on a large company of north-eastern lairds and their followers as well as a host of armoured, battle-seasoned knights.

On the night before the battle, the Highlanders camped on the elevated plateau to the north-east of Inverurie; Mar's forces, numerically inferior but better armed, were gathered at the foot of the slope. As dawn broke, the armies began to close for battle.

There seems to have been little attempt at strategy or generalship:

---

1 The Harlaw monument provoked huge controversy when it was erected in 1914, because its dedication only mentioned the Lowlanders who died, and not those who died on the Highland side.

it was to be a test of individual valour, and the armies simply rushed at one another. Time and time again the ill-protected Highlanders charged with reckless bravery against the massed spearmen and knights of the Lowlanders; time and time again they were repulsed, at fearful cost. By afternoon the battle had become a desperate, confused mêlée of savage hand-to-hand combat.

By nightfall both sides had fought themselves to a standstill. The Lowlanders had held their ground, but the Highlanders had not been vanquished. During the night both sides withdrew, not knowing who had won the day. Donald of the Isles moved back to Inverness, leaving, according to some reports, no fewer than a thousand clansmen dead on the field, including two clan chiefs ('Red Hector' Maclean and the MacIntosh). The Earl of Mar had suffered heavy casualties, too – six hundred men, some say, including the Provost of Aberdeen and many knights of the north-eastern nobility. The city of Aberdeen had been saved. The government hailed it as a national deliverance from the Highland hordes – an ominous sign of the growing division of Scotland into two nations, Lowland and Highland.

The only long-term victor was the regent himself, the Duke of Albany, the 'uncrowned king of Scotland'. Within a year he had manipulated the vacant Earldom of Ross to his own family advantage by bestowing it upon his son John, the Earl of Buchan.

Albany died in 1420, more than eighty years old but vigorous and shrewd to the end. He was succeeded as governor by his son Murdoch, who lacked his father's guile and political touch. At least he did not attempt to block James's release from captivity, as his father seems to have done. But he had already made an enemy of the young king; they had shared captivity in England for a few years, until Murdoch's release in 1416, and James had little love for him, as events were to show.

The captive poet-prince

Some six kilometres along the B734 to the east of Girvan, in Ayrshire, stands Penkill Castle; the original square peel-tower was erected in the fifteenth century by a member of the Boyd family which controlled King James III in the latter years of his minority (see Chapter 16), but it was transformed in the nineteenth century when extensive additions and restorations were made in the fashionably romantic 'Gothic revival' style of the time.

Penkill Castle is an enchanting place, now owned and cherished by

Patrick and June Dromgoole as a family home and an informal shrine of pre-Raphaelitism.[1] Penkill is well known in the annals of British art as a favoured holiday haunt of members of the pre-Raphaelite brotherhood of painters and poets – Dante Gabriel Rossetti, his sister Christina, William Holman Hunt, William Morris, Algernon Swinburne and others; it is less well known as the home of a magnificent sequence of murals painted in the 1860s by the leading Scottish pre-Raphaelite artist William Bell Scott (1811–90) – wall-paintings which have a unique connection with King James I of Scotland.

The castle was inherited in a semi-derelict state by Spencer Boyd in 1827 as the fourteenth Laird of Penkill, who spent a great deal of money restoring and rebuilding the old place. He lived there with his unmarried sister, Alice Boyd; she had met William Bell Scott in Newcastle, where he was master of the School of Design. A friendship developed when she went to him for art lessons, and they became lovers when he visited Penkill in 1860. Spencer Boyd died in 1865, having completed most of the restoration of the castle. William Bell Scott was a married man; so in order to provide a socially acceptable reason for his prolonged visits to Penkill he proposed painting a sequence of murals on the new circular tower linking the original house with a new 'baronial' hall.

Bell Scott was already a valued member of the pre-Raphaelite brotherhood; and Penkill was a perfect vehicle for the pre-Raphaelite dream – 'the Palace of the Sleeping Beauty, in its enchanted and limitless repose', he called it. It is traditionally believed that Christina Rossetti wrote her Christmas hymn 'In the Bleak Mid-Winter' while she was staying at Penkill Castle.

The subject Bell Scott had chosen to illustrate was a long and lyrical medieval love-poem known as *The Kingis Quair* (The King's Book), a charming, romantic work written by the young James I in the 1420s while he was still languishing as a prisoner in England; it is the only one of James's works to have survived, written in a mixture of Scots and Chaucerian English and dedicated to Chaucer. It was apparently composed to celebrate his love for Lady Joan Beaufort, granddaughter of John of Gaunt and cousin to King Henry V. According to the

---

1 Patrick Dromgoole, retired actor and drama producer/director, is a former managing director of Harlech TV; his wife June is Controller of Programme Acquisition at Channel 4. They have succeeded in finding some, at least, of the original furniture made for Penkill by Spencer Boyd, and have garnered a fine collection of pre-Raphaelite works of art with special resonance for Penkill Castle.

literary convention of the poem, James catches sight of his lady-love ('Lady Jane') one May morning from the window of a tower-room in Windsor Castle, where he is being held captive. She is walking in the garden below with her little white lap-dog, and the lonely prisoner, pierced by Cupid's dart, falls in love with her:

> And therewith kest [cast] I doun [down] myn eye ageyne,
> Quhare [where] as I sawe, walkyng under the Toure,
> Full secretely, new cumyn [come] hir [here] to playne [play],
> The fairest or the freschest younge floure
> That ever I sawe, me thoucht, before that houre,
> For quhich sodayne abate [stopped], anon astert [rushed]
> The blude of all my body to my hert.

> And though I stood abaisit [abased] then a lyte [little],
> No wonder was; for quhy? My wittis [wits] all
> Were so ouercome with plesance and delyte,
> Only through latting [letting] of myn eyen fall,
> That sudaynly my hert become hir thrall
> For ever; of free wyll, for of manace [menace]
> There was no takyn [token] in hir suete [sweet] face.

The winding mural at Penkill Castle depicts the dawn reveille at Windsor Castle, the king's first sight of 'Lady Jane', the Garden of the Court of Queen Venus (to whom the lovesick king prays for aid), 'Lady Jane' sending a turtle dove with a message of love, and the king receiving it. In the paintings, 'Lady Jane' is Christina Rossetti, the young king is Algernon Swinburne, two of the guards at Windsor are William Holman Hunt and Bell Scott himself, and the Goddess of Love is (of course!) Alice Boyd.[1]

The true-life romance of King James and Lady Joan Beaufort was to blossom into a close and enduring marriage (see below). But James had more than love on his mind. He had grown up into a studious, sensitive young man. He was also strong and well-built, a keen sportsman, a skilled athlete, archer, horseman and even wrestler. He was a

---

1 The murals are much eroded now, and are in urgent need of expert conservation and restoration. A series of watercolour designs for the murals is in the Dick Institute Museum and Art Gallery in Kilmarnock; they can be viewed by prior arrangement. Dante Gabriel Rossetti was so impressed with the story of *The Kingis Quair* that he was inspired to write a ballad about the death of King James, *The King's Tragedy* (1881).

talented musician as well as an accomplished poet. But he was also deeply scarred by the experiences of his childhood. He had endured a brutal schooling in the exercise of power-politics – the desperate insecurity caused by the humiliation of his father and the death of his brother David, the ignominy of his flight and his capture by English pirates. It was a legacy of fear and bitterness which he was to nurture throughout his captivity, and which would be visited upon his enemies as soon as he was free to ascend the throne.

But when was he going to be set free? Certainly, it suited English policy at the time to hold him in captivity; Henry IV seems to have been prepared to negotiate a release, but after his death in 1413 his charismatic successor, Henry V, preferred to keep James as a diplomatic tool in his campaigns in France. Henry V evidently liked the young prince of Scotland and enjoyed his company, and promoted him to a position of military command in his army. But there was a more sinister agenda: the Scots had answered a call for help from Charles VI of France by sending a contingent of troops. They were helping to defend the French garrison at Melun, to the south of Paris, when it was besieged by Henry V's army. King James, wearing the Scottish royal arms, was forced by Henry to order the Scots to change sides. Their commander refused to do so while the King of Scots was a prisoner. As a result, when Melun fell the Scots were excluded from the terms of surrender and executed as traitors to their king.

A king's ransom

The English government were not unwilling to deliver up James, the rather that he had fallen in love with Joan, the Earl of Somerset's daughter, nearly related to the royal family of England. They considered that this alliance would incline the young Prince to peace with England; and that the education which he had received, and the friendships which he had formed in the country, would incline him to be a good and peaceable neighbour.

TALES OF A GRANDFATHER, CHAPTER XVIII

After the death of Henry V in 1422, negotiations for James's release resumed. One of the factors in the negotiations may well have been the love-affair with Joan Beaufort which James had hymned in *The Kingis Quair*. Joan's father and uncle, half-brothers of Henry IV, were powerful figures in the English Council of Regency for the infant Henry VI, and marriage into the English royal family would have been considered a useful way of breaking, or at least weakening, the Scottish alliance with France.

In Scotland, however, the prospect of the king's release was welcomed less warmly, particularly by the new governor, Murdoch, second Duke of Albany. But eventually a lengthy meeting of the General Council in Scotland in August 1423 authorised a Scottish embassy to seek James's release. The outcome of the negotiations was the Treaty of London, signed in December 1423, which stipulated that James would be released for a ransom of £40,000, to be paid at the rate of ten thousand *merks* a year for six years; twenty-one hostages from the Scottish nobility were to be provided as surety, and these were to stay in England at their families' expense, to be released or exchanged in the course of the payment of the ransom. In addition, a sum of £4,000 was demanded to cover the costs of the king's eighteen years' enforced residence in England. That money was to be paid in five instalments – but the first payment was remitted, to serve as Joan Beaufort's dowry.

Events now moved quickly. In February 1424 James married his Joan in London in a lavish ceremony celebrated by the Bishop of Southwark. The young couple then travelled north with a large retinue to Brancepeth Castle, to the south-west of Durham, where James I was able to entertain and get to know many of his subjects for the first time, including sixty-four nobles. Early in April he finally crossed the border into Scotland to assume the active role of king in his own country.

The key to the castle

On James's very first day in Scotland, at Melrose on 5 April, someone complained to him about the plight of the nation which bad government had caused; it was then, according to Bower's *Scotichronicon*, that James uttered his celebrated statement of intent:

> If God spares me, gives me help and offers me at least the life of a dog, I shall see to it throughout the whole of my kingdom that the key keeps the castle and the thorn bush the cow.[1]
> SCOTICHRONICON, BOOK XVI, CHAPTER 34

James's overriding personal business was to wreak retribution against the Albany Stewarts who had blighted his early life. He was now thirty

---

1 What James seems to mean is that property would be inviolate: castles would be safe from attack, and livestock in enclosed fields would be safe from cattle-rustlers.

years old, a 'king unleashed', a 'king in a hurry'. Without waiting for his coronation he arrested Walter Stewart of the Lennox, the son of the former governor, Murdoch, second Duke of Albany. Albany, who was now in his sixties, was the heir-presumptive to the throne until such time as James I produced a son, but he had surrendered his office of governor without demur as soon as James returned from England. His son Walter Stewart posed a much greater threat, however; he had never concealed his hostility towards the new king. He was sent, with telling irony, to the bleak fortress on the Bass Rock where James himself at the age of eleven had waited grimly for the ship to take him to France in 1406. This was soon followed by the arrest of the Earl of Lennox, Murdoch's father-in-law.

The first blows had been struck, but before he could make any further moves James had to consolidate his position on the throne and the revenues of the crown. His coronation was held at Scone on 21 May 1424. It was attended by all the bishops, prelates and magnates of the kingdom – a deliberate display of restored royal prestige. Murdoch (Albany), in his role as Earl of Fife, himself placed the crown on James's head, despite the fact that his son was now in detention. The next day, in Perth, James summoned a four-day meeting of parliament; it passed a huge agenda of legislation which must make today's parliamentary draughtsmen sick with envy. Laws were made forbidding breaches of the king's peace and decreeing the punishment for 'rebels against the king's person' (forfeiture of lands). Parliament also passed a novel 5 per cent tax on lands and goods (James had learned all about the royal taxation system in England). Export duties were imposed on horses, herring and wool, and customs duties and burgh rents were reserved for the crown. A close season for salmon was decreed, and rooks were to be destroyed to protect the crops. Archery practice was encouraged as a useful sport pertinent to the defence of the realm, while a much more popular but more frivolous pastime (football) was banned – 'Na man is to play at the fute ball, under the payne [pain] of four pennies.'

James waited until the second meeting of parliament, in the spring of 1425, before making his final assault on the house of Albany. On the ninth day of the parliament he suddenly arrested Duke Murdoch, his wife Isabella and his younger son Alexander. He then dismissed parliament, with instructions for it to reassemble at Stirling in the middle of May for the trial of the Albany Stewarts.

Murdoch's youngest son, James 'the Fat', had managed to escape the royal swoop, and was soon fomenting discord in the Lennox area

The replica crannog at the Scottish Crannog Centre at Kenmore, on Loch Tay. Crannogs were inland loch-dwellings built on artificial islands by farmers of the Neolithic Age; some were still inhabited as late as the seventeenth century.

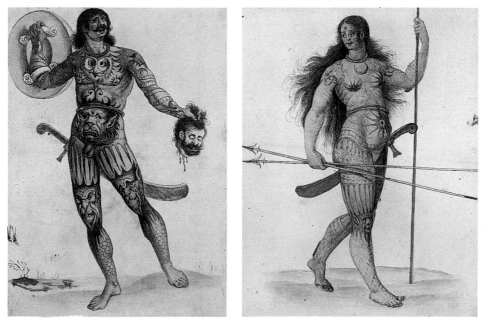

A male and female Pict imaginatively depicted as 'noble savages' by the Elizabethan explorer John White (c.1585), inspired by descriptions in classical sources but coloured by White's experience of Roanooke Indians he had seen on a visit to North America.

According to the medieval origin myths, the original Scots were descended from Scota, daughter of the Pharaoh Ramses II of Egypt, and Gaedel Glas (Gathelos), a prince of Scythia. Scota wandered for two thousand years before bringing to Scotland a sacred keepsake from her homelands – Jacob's stone pillow, the Stone of Destiny. An illustration from Walter Bower's fifteenth-century *Scotichronicon*.

In Shakespeare's play, Macbeth instructs two murderers to kill Banquo: painting by George Cattermole (1800–68). The version of Macbeth's reign served up by Shakespeare (and perpetuated by Sir Walter Scott) is a travesty of the facts.

Malcolm Canmore (r.1058–93) consolidated and extended the kingdom of 'Scotia', while his English wife Margaret (who was later canonised) helped to bring the early Celtic Church into the orbit of the Universal Catholic Church. Illustration in the sixteenth-century *Seton Armorial*.

David I (r.1124–53, left) and his grandson Malcolm IV (Malcolm the Maiden, r.1153–65). Illustration from the charter of 1159 granted to Kelso Abbey, one of the four great Border abbeys founded by David I.

The inauguration of Alexander III (r.1249–86) at Scone at the age of seven. The illustration, in Walter Bower's *Scotichronicon*, accompanies the first full description of a royal inauguration to have survived. Alexander III gained control of the Western Isles from Norway, but his accidental death in 1286 precipitated a succession crisis which led to the Wars of Independence.

John Balliol (r.1292–96), later known as
'Toom Tabard', swears homage to
Edward I in 1292 after being nominated
King of Scots by him. His reign lasted
only four years before Edward invaded
Scotland and deposed him.

Seventeenth-century portrait of Robert Bruce by
George Jamesone.

The earliest surviving depiction of the Battle of
Bannockburn (1314): an illustration in the
Scotichronicon.

David II (r.1329–71) and his first wife, Joan, sister of Edward III of England. They were married as children, and the union was childless. David was captured after the Battle of Neville's Cross in 1346; when he was released in 1357, Joan was discarded in his fruitless attempts with other women to sire an heir for his kingdom. Illustration in the *Seton Armorial*.

On 17 October 1346, King David II made a rash invasion of Northumberland and was captured at the Battle of Neville's Cross, near Durham. This genre painting (1789) by the American artist Benjamin West shows Philippa of Hainault, the queen of the absent Edward III of England, mounted on a white charger and watching the battle.

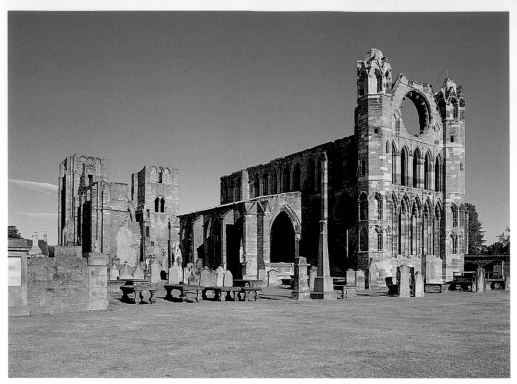

In 1390 Elgin Cathedral, the 'Lantern of the North', was fired by the 'Wolf of Badenoch', Alexander, Earl of Buchan, younger son of Robert II (r.1371–90). Robert II was the grandson of Robert Bruce, and the founder of the royal Stewart dynasty. The Wolf of Badenoch acted as the king's lieutenant in the north.

Robert III (r.1390–1406) succeeded his father Robert II in his fifties. He saw his eldest son, Prince David, Duke of Rothesay, die in 1402 in the custody of his uncle Robert, Duke of Rothesay. To avert a similar fate for his second son, the future James I, Robert III tried to send him abroad for safety – only for the boy to be captured by pirates and imprisoned in England. The news hastened his grieving father's death. Illustration from the *Seton Armorial*.

James I (r.1406–37) succeeded his father Robert III at the age of eleven as a captive in England, but was not released to take up the reins of kingship until 1424. He was murdered in a sewer in Perth by his disaffected nobles. Portrait by an unknown artist, probably sixteenth century.

During his captivity in England, James I fell in love with Joan Beaufort, cousin to Henry V, and composed a lyrical poem celebrating his love, *The Kingis Quair* (The King's Book). The theme was the subject of a magnificent series of murals painted in Penkill Castle in Ayrshire by the Scottish pre-Raphaelite artist William Bell Scott. The first mural, *The Awakening*, depicts the prisoner (James) at his turret window in Windsor Castle at dawn reveille.

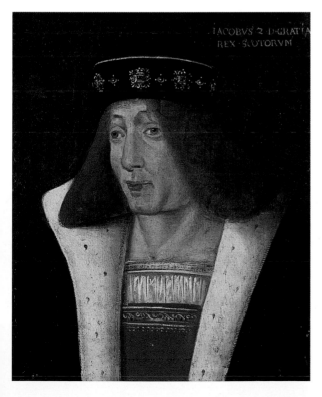

James II (r.1437–60) is best remembered for the manner of his death. He was fascinated by heavy artillery and its potential to give authority to the monarchy, and was killed at the siege of Roxburgh Castle when one of his giant bombards burst its casing. He was known as 'James of the Fiery Face' because of a conspicuous vermilion birthmark which covered the left side of his face, but in this sixteenth-century portrait the offending mark was discreetly omitted.

James III (r.1460–88) gained the Northern Isles of Orkney and Shetland through his marriage in 1469 to Margaret, Princess of Norway/Denmark: her father, the impecunious Kristian I, pledged the islands in lieu of a dowry – and the pledge was never redeemed. To celebrate the marriage, the king commissioned the Flemish artist Hugo van der Goes to paint portraits of himself and his bride as part of an altarpiece for Trinity College Church in Edinburgh (now destroyed), which was founded by the devout Queen Margaret.

James IV (r.1488–1514) was the quintessential Renaissance monarch of Scotland. He married an English princess (Margaret Tudor, daughter of Henry VI), founded the Scottish navy and kept a glittering and highly cultured court. He was killed at the Battle of Flodden in 1514.

in the west of Scotland. He and his supporters attacked Dumbarton, seized the castle and burned the town to the ground. However well-intentioned a protest it was, it simply played into the king's hands: in the light of the 1424 laws on rebellion, James I now had ample justification for a charge of treason against Murdoch and the rest of the Albany family.

When parliament convened in Stirling it set up an assize of seven earls and fourteen lesser nobles to sit in judgement on the Albany Stewarts. The king presided. Within two days he had systematically destroyed the most powerful family in the land. On the first day, 24 May 1425, Walter Stewart was condemned and summarily executed on the 'Heading Hill' in front of Stirling Castle. On the second day Earl Murdoch, his younger son Alexander and his father-in-law the Earl of Lennox were similarly despatched. They were the first state executions for more than a century. Isabella, the Duchess of Albany, was sent into lifelong imprisonment in Tantallon Castle, the formidable fortress which reared up on a rocky headland on the Firth of Forth, looking out towards the Bass Rock.[1] James 'the Fat', the last of the Albany Stewarts, fled to Ireland, where he remained a potential threat to the throne; but he never returned to Scotland.

The House of Albany had been destroyed, and James's long-nursed vengeance was complete. The executioner's axe had delivered three earldoms (Fife, Lennox and Menteith) and their associated territorial rights and revenues. James had been the crowned King of Scots for barely a year, and the 'law-giver king' had shown just how ruthless and uncompromising he could be.

Hindsight suggests that, in modern parlance, the executions spelled the end of the king's honeymoon period with his people. From now on there would be increasing resentment against James's rule. The unrest came not just from the noble families who felt dismayed – and, no doubt, apprehensive – over the calculated vindictiveness of the king's destruction of the Albany Stewarts; it was also apparent among the common people, the burghers and countrymen who had been so heavily taxed in 1424. James was soon to run into parliamentary opposition over his taxation policies.

His energy never flagged, however – for cultural pursuits as well as for masterful government. He found time to take a close interest in the progress of St Andrews University, the first university in Scotland, '

---

1 Tantallon Castle was built in the middle of the fourteenth century as a mighty Douglas fortress. It is one of the most impressive and evocative of Scotland's ruined castles.

which had been founded by Albany during his captivity, in 1413; he even attended some lectures there. He also worked hard to strengthen the machinery of administration and justice. He set up a parliamentary business committee, later known as the Committee of the Articles, to determine and prepare the appropriate measures to be laid before parliament. He instituted a special court, consisting of representatives chosen from parliament, to consider complaints which could not be decided in the local courts, so that justice would be available to all, rich and poor alike; he also tried to ensure that all litigants, whether men, women or children, had access to a form of legal aid. In these enactments we can see the first green shoots of parliamentary government beginning to sprout.

In the north and west the 'Highland problem' remained unsolved, however: Alexander Macdonald, third Lord of the Isles and son of that Donald of the Isles who had fought so hard at Harlaw in 1411, was in open defiance of the king's writ. James decided that the northerners had to be brought to heel. To that end he engineered what was to become a trademark Stewart ploy – the royal kidnapping. In 1428 he summoned the Lord of the Isles and his recalcitrant chieftains to a parliament in Inverness. As they were shown into the Great Hall of the castle one by one, James broke faith and had each of them arrested and imprisoned. Three of them were hanged, but the rest – though not Alexander Macdonald himself – were released after a few 'salutary' months in confinement. It soon became apparent, however, that the scheme had not worked. The Lord of the Isles might be in prison, but his authority was undiminished, and the king saw no alternative but to release him in order to deal with the continued unrest in the Highlands.

If the king thought he had tamed the Lord of the Isles, he was mistaken. In the spring of 1429 Alexander retaliated with an assault on Inverness, the scene of the royal betrayal the previous year. The castle held out, but the town was destroyed by fire. Once again, James I had no choice: he had to be seen to be able to deal with this northern rebellion or lose all credibility as king. He mustered a large royal army – ten thousand men or so – and advanced purposefully into the Highlands. The Lord of the Isles was surprised in Lochaber and fled to Islay; when James launched an expedition to the Isles, equipped with cannon, Macdonald gave himself up. He was taken to Edinburgh where, in front of the high altar of Holyrood Abbey and clad only in shirt and drawers, he was forced to make abject submission to the king. A second period of imprisonment followed this humiliation, but once again it failed in its purpose: the struggles in the north continued unabated, and the parliament which met in October 1431 was reluctant to raise taxes to finance further expeditions. The king felt the stiffening of resistance to his rule and abruptly released the Lord of the Isles again, leaving his lieutenant, the doughty Earl of Mar, to deal with the north.

All the early chroniclers recognised that the 1431 parliament represented a watershed in James I's reign. The aristocracy was becoming increasingly resentful of his arbitrary swoops and attacks on its members; James was ruling through fear rather than mutual respect. The common people were 'murmuring' against him for his constant increases in direct and indirect taxes; for James was spending money on himself and his court on a scale the country had never seen before. During his captivity in England he had witnessed, and no doubt envied, the opulence which went with secure royal authority and which helped to maintain it. He recognised the status and prestige which splendour and display could bestow. The Scottish royal household lived in conspicuous luxury; embassies and missions were received with all possible magnificence. The rebuilding of Linlithgow as a major residence, at the huge cost of £5,000, was designed to show off a new style of monarchy: wealthy, cultured and literally palatial. Ironically, the finances for all this extravagance came from the ransom money collected by James's tax levies – money which he owed to England and showed no sign of repaying.

Dynastic considerations were also uppermost in James's mind. After destroying the threat to the succession posed by the Albany Stewarts, he had to produce a male heir. His devoted queen Joan Beaufort gave birth to daughters to start with; but on 16 October 1430 she gave birth to twin sons: Alexander and James. There was general rejoicing that the male succession had been secured. The anonymous *Book of Pluscarden* noted:

> *Seeing that they were born in the monastery of Holyrood, bonfires were lighted, flagons of wine were free to all and victuals publicly to all comers, with the sweetest harmony of all kinds of musical instruments all night long proclaiming the praise and glory of God for all his gifts and benefits.*

The older of the boys, Alexander, died in infancy, leaving the younger son, James, as the heir to the throne; he was to ascend the throne of Scotland as James II (see Chapter 15).

In 1430 James I had also scored a triumph on the European stage with the betrothal of his eldest daughter, Margaret (who was six years old), to the Dauphin Louis as part of a new treaty of alliance with France. It was less of a triumph for Margaret, however: in 1436, at the age of twelve, she eventually married the thirteen-year-old Dauphin (who would succeed his father as Louis XI in 1461), but he turned out to be a cold and vindictive man. Margaret was known as a poet (although none of her work has survived); for consolation in her loveless marriage she sought the company of poets and writers, sitting up late into the night composing French *rondeaux* and ballads. She was alleged, in a moment of indiscretion, to have kissed the lips of the sleeping poet Alain Chartier as a tribute to his genius; the ensuing scandal broke her spirit and she died, lonely and miserable, at the age of twenty.[1]

James I is often portrayed as the first of the 'real' Stewarts – the man who gave the dynasty its stamp. He stood at the threshold of the European Renaissance; in his reign we see the King of Scots trying to promote the kind of government structure and cultural climate of new learning which can be labelled as 'Renaissance' (see Chapter 17). He wanted to move Scotland on from the medieval modes of the past and to cut a dash on the European stage. Roger Mason, lecturer in Scottish History at St Andrews University, says:

> *The Stewart monarchs, all the way from James I to James V, were very conscious of their own importance, very keen to emulate what was going on elsewhere in Europe – not so much in England, perhaps, as in France and Burgundy, which were the centres of European Renaissance influences. There was a very self-conscious effort to keep up with European trends, and the monarchy was absolutely crucial to that.*

Towards the end of his reign much of the glamour associated with the young James I had worn off. He had lost the charm and graceful athleticism of his youth; in 1435 the Italian diplomat and poet Aeneas Sylvius Piccolomini, who later became Pope Pius II, visited Scotland and described the king as 'thick-set, very fat, greedy and vindictive in nature'.

---

1   Margaret's sisters, who had also inherited their father's literary talents, were luckier in their marriages into prestigious European families: Isabella married Francis, Duke of Brittany, in 1442 and became renowned as a collector of richly-illuminated manuscripts; Leonora married Sigismund, the Archduke of Austria, in 1449, and translated into German a popular French romance, *Ponthus and Sidonia*, which was published in 1483.

When James's daughter Margaret was promised to the Dauphin Louis, part of the marriage treaty involved a renewed Franco–Scottish alliance against England. England still held two major castles in Scotland, Berwick and Roxburgh, and in the wake of Margaret's marriage in 1436 James saw an opportunity of recovering Roxburgh Castle. He mustered a large army, equipped not only with a sizeable contingent of archers but with a formidable artillery train of cannons. The centrepiece was a 'great bombard' named Lion which he had ordered from Flanders. On its barrel were inscribed the words:

> For the illustrious James, worthy prince of the Scots. Magnificent king, when I sound off I reduce castles. I was made at his order, therefore I am called Lion.

The Lion duly roared, but it did not reduce Roxburgh Castle. The siege began on 1 August 1436, but turned into a fiasco. James was not used to military command; the army was apparently rent with division, and when news came that a relieving English force was on the march, the siege was abandoned and the Scottish army ignominiously withdrew. It was yet another severe blow to James's royal prestige. He had now become thoroughly unpopular. At a General Council in Edinburgh in October he made matters worse with another attack on the privileges of the barons on whom he depended for support. For some people, even those closest to him, it was the last straw.

Assassination of the king (21 February 1437)

> The King, while at Perth, took up his residence in an abbey of Black Friars, there being no castle or palace in the town convenient for his residence; and this made the execution of the conspiracy more easy, as his guards, and the officers of his household, were quartered among the citizens.
>
> TALES OF A GRANDFATHER, CHAPTER XIX

For the Christmas season of 1436 the court established itself at Perth (St Johnstone), which James I preferred to Edinburgh as his capital. The king and his immediate household stayed at the Dominican friary at Blackfriars, a fine old building which stood on the northern edge of the town, outside the burgh walls, forming a sort of northern suburb and protected only by a ditch; the other members of the court were lodged within the town. Blackfriars occupied the site of the old wooden castle of Perth which had been swept away by a flood in 1209: the land had been granted to the Black Friars, probably in exchange for providing lodging for the royal household whenever required. The area is now occupied by a new sheltered housing complex, Carpenter Court, at Kinnoull Street; before it was built, the site was excavated in 1983 by the Scottish Urban Archaeological Trust (SUAT), and the remains of some of the foundations of the friary were unearthed; part of the cloisters was identified, as well as the burial ground, and the church of the friary may underlie Christie's public house in Kinnoull Street on the north side of Carpenter Court.[1]

During the day, we are told, the king would play tennis,[2] and in the evening he would play chess, read romances and listen to music. A pleasing, idyllic scene – but behind the festive jollifications there was treachery afoot. A small but determined group had decided that the only solution to what was perceived as the king's tyranny was his removal. The leaders of this conspiracy were Sir Robert Graham and Sir Robert Stewart. Robert Graham was the nephew of Malise Graham, the Earl of Strathearn, who had been sent to England in 1424 as one of the hostages for the king's ransom and who carried a deep grudge against the king; Robert Stewart was the grandson and heir of Walter, the elderly Earl of Atholl, who was Robert III's youngest brother and therefore James I's uncle.

Robert Stewart was chamberlain of the royal household at this time, and a close confidant of the king: according to John Shirley's *Dethe of the Kynge of Scotis* (written in the 1440s) he 'did ever abide yn the kynges presence, full familiar aboute hyme at all houres and most privey'. But the *eminence grise* behind the conspiracy seems to have been the king's uncle Walter, Earl of Atholl. As the youngest brother

---

1 I was taken on a brisk walking tour of the crowded medieval burgh of Perth by David Bowler, Director of SUAT – the type of archaeologist who thinks not only with his hands but also with his feet! He brought to life the hidden results of all the urban excavations which the council has encouraged ahead of redevelopment projects – including the last surviving fragment of the old burgh walls at the northern end of Skinnergate, just inside the ditch ('canal') which surrounded the medieval town and which still flows underneath the modern city.

2 The royal game of tennis was an early instance of a developing court culture in Scotland inspired by the Renaissance; it seems to have been introduced by James I from the French Burgundian court. The earliest surviving 'real' (i.e. royal) court in Scotland is one built at Falkland Palace by James V in 1539, modelled on Henry VIII of England's private tennis court at the riverside palace of Hampton Court. It was a hard game which monarchs would share with their household servants on occasion, a mixture of tennis and fives (it was originally played by hand, not with a racquet).

of Robert, first Duke of Albany, who had been suspected of complicity in the death of the heir to the throne David, Duke of Rothesay, in 1402, Atholl was all too familiar with the politics of royal assassinations.

On 21 February 1437 the conspiracy moved into gear. John Shirley relates that while the king and queen were preparing for bed in the Blackfriars priory that evening, the king's chamberlain, Sir Robert Stewart, laid wooden planks across the ditch surrounding the friary. He also disabled the locks in the house and left the doors of the building unbarred. Just after midnight a small group of conspirators, led by Sir Robert Graham, entered the building and made for the royal apartments. The king heard the noise of their arrival and knew that he was in mortal danger. The windows were barred, but he prised up a floorboard with a fire iron and dropped into some sort of drain or sewer which ran under the floor, leading to an outlet in the wall by the tennis court; as soon as he was inside the drain his womenfolk pressed the floorboards back into place.[1] By a supreme irony of history, however, James had just had the outlet blocked to prevent stray tennis balls rolling into it and getting lost: it was to cost him his life.

The conspirators – perhaps ten of them in all – burst into the royal apartments and in the ensuing scuffle the queen, in her night attire, was wounded. The intruders could not find the king at first, but after ransacking the rest of the house they returned to the bed-chamber; this time they tore up the floorboards and discovered the secret egress to the sewer. The king was cornered. Dressed only in his nightgown and 'furry slippers', he put up a desperate fight. He disabled the first two men who attacked him. Then Sir Robert Graham climbed into the sewer and struck him down with his sword. The others now joined in; when it was over, sixteen deadly wounds were found on the king's body.

Queen Joan had meanwhile fled from the house, bleeding and scantily dressed. The assassins had presumably meant to kill her, too, but they were now in a hurry to make their getaway before the town was aroused, and did not pursue her. In the event, letting the queen escape with her life was to cost them very dear.

The queen's first move was to take possession of the six-year-old Prince James and to head for the security of Edinburgh Castle. The

---

1 It is said that one of the queen's ladies-in-waiting, Catherine Douglas, tried to delay the attackers by thrusting her slender arm through the bar-sockets on the door. When the intruders broke in, her arm was snapped. From then on she was known as 'Kate Bar-lass' or 'Kate Bar the Door'. Alas! it appears that this tale of heroism and devotion is a sixteenth-century invention.

succession was by no means assured, and there were many factions lurking in the wings to take advantage of the chaos and confusion caused by the king's assassination. Possession of the young prince was crucial to the queen's political future: only then could she think of going on the offensive.

In Edinburgh she was safe among her husband's loyal adherents, and could send them to track down the assassins. Sir Robert Stewart was soon captured and put to death with a barbarity which was said to be appalling even by medieval standards: he had to endure three days of public flogging, wearing a red-hot iron crown on his head, before the executioner's axe brought merciful release. This was quickly followed by the arrest of the Earl of Atholl, uncle of the king and grandfather of Sir Robert Stewart.

With the opposition quelled, the coronation of the new boy-king could now take place. On 25 March 1437 James II was crowned in Holyrood Abbey in Edinburgh rather than at Scone (which may have been thought to be too dangerous, being in the heart of Atholl territory); parliament assembled on the same day for the trial of the Earl of Atholl. The result was a foregone conclusion; next day he was taken from the Tolbooth in Edinburgh and beheaded; at least he was spared the hideous tortures which the other conspirators had suffered.

Meanwhile, James I was buried in a tomb surrounded by an iron railing somewhere in the lands of a Carthusian priory – the Charterhouse, known as the 'House of the Valley of Virtue' – which his queen had founded in 1429; it stood to the south-west of the burgh walls in Perth, where the King James VI Hospital stands today. He would be joined there by his wife, Queen Joan, in 1455, followed nearly a century later by another royal consort, Margaret Tudor, the wife of James IV, in 1551. At the complicated intersection of South Street, County Place, Methven Street, King Street and Hospital Street, in a corner of the hospital grounds, is a small, open rose garden tended by the ladies of Soroptimist International of Perth; a slender stone column surmounted by a crown royal commemorates the burials:

> Within these grounds stood the Carthusian monastery founded by King James I of Scotland in 1429. It was the only house belonging to this order in Scotland. In the precincts of the monastery were buried the royal founder, his queen Joan Beaufort and Margaret Tudor, queen of King James IV.

Epilogue

The reign of James I aroused diametrically opposite views among contemporary commentators. Was the poet-prince a martyr for his country, or a bloody tyrant? The best or the worst of the Stewart monarchs?

For Walter Bower in the *Scotichronicon*, James was 'the law-giver king', 'a tower, a lion, a light, a jewel, a pillar and a leader'. He concluded his massive history of Scotland with a florid epitaph, written within ten years of the king's death:

> ... *an ornament made gracious, shining with virtues,*
> *radiant with nobility, illustrious, charming,*
> *rich with merits, upright and cheerful.*
> *He was a patron of peace, a weighty deviser of laws,*
> *a man who disarmed envy, an energetic foster-father of peace.*
> *While he lived, law was available to all; crime was buried;*
> *theft lay low, dishonour never went unpunished.*

A very different view was given by an Englishman, John Slater, in *The Dethe of the Kynge of Scotis*; for Slater, James I was a tyrannous prince who acted out of vengeance and to satisfy his greed.

James's reputation has been a matter of sharply divergent historical assessment ever since. Steve Boardman says:

> *James I used to be regarded as a 'good' king because he gave real*
> *authority and prestige to the Scottish kingship: he brought down*
> *the over-mighty magnates of medieval Scotland, he held lots of*
> *parliaments and he killed lots of people. For earlier historians, a*
> *'good' king was by definition a king who did physical damage to*
> *some of his greatest subjects in an attempt to assert his authority*
> *within his kingdom. The growth of royal power was seen to be*
> *a good thing in itself, and therefore those who stood in the*
> *way of this royal power were standing in the way of the proper*
> *development of society.*
>
> *In recent years, however, people have been asking whether it*
> *was quite as straightforward as that. Historians are now looking*
> *at him more as a man who went through his entire reign in a type*
> *of crisis management, constantly launching pre-emptive strikes*
> *against potential rivals or potential opposition within his realm.*
> *He was acquisitive in terms of land and resources and money,*
> *and he generated a lot of resentment because of his activities.*

Michael Lynch says:

> *I think the jury is still out on James I: whether he was a despicable despot (he would be a wonderful casting in a soap opera – small, fat and ugly!), or whether he set a train for a dynasty, and laid down the patterns which would be amplified, but not changed, over the next century or century and a half.*

Either way, James I remains the most enigmatic – and, some say, the most brilliant – of the early kings of the Stewart dynasty of Scotland.

Chapter 15

JAMES II (r.1437–60)

*When James I was murdered, his son and heir, James II, was
only six years old; so that Scotland was once more plunged into
all the discord and confusions of a regency, which were sure to
reach their height in a country where even the undisputed sway
of a sovereign of mature age was not held in due respect, and
was often disturbed by treason and rebellion.*

TALES OF A GRANDFATHER, CHAPTER XX

In pride of place in one of the vaults off Crown Square in Edinburgh
Castle sits one of the most celebrated guns in medieval warfare:
the 'great bombard', or siege gun, known as Mons Meg. It was the
largest and most advanced cannon of its time – a great brute of a gun
with a twenty-inch bore, weighing more than six tons (6,040 kilograms) and capable of firing gunstones weighing 150 kilograms a
distance of 3.5 kilometres. The muzzle-loading barrel and the breech-
chamber were made from separate parts fixed together. To make the
barrel, long wrought-iron bars were welded together to form a cylinder
at the core, and iron hoops were then shrunk over the bars. The
massive breech-chamber was hammer-forged from several masses of
red-hot iron smelted in separate batches, since no iron furnace was
large enough then to produce so much metal at a single firing.

This giant bombard was manufactured at Mons in what is now
Belgium in 1449 to the order of Philippe the Good, Duke of Burgundy,
by his artillery-maker Jehan Cambier. In 1457 the duke presented it,

along with other ordnance, to King James II of Scotland, whose queen, Marie de Gueldres, was Philippe's niece.

James II was always fascinated by artillery, which meant a great deal to him in his bid to lend authority to the monarchy. But a cannon of the size and weight of Mons Meg was ponderously slow to move around – it could only be trundled about five kilometres a day, and its value was probably more deterrent than actual.

James's obsession with artillery was to be the undoing of him, however. In July 1460 he moved against Roxburgh Castle, near Kelso, which had been in English hands for a century or more. The old castle, the strongest fortress in the Borders, was situated on a narrow strip of land between the River Tweed and a meander of the Teviot, just off the present A699 and immediately above the junction of the two rivers. James's objective was to destroy both burgh and castle and thereby dispose of a major base for hostile forays from England. He took with him a formidable detachment of the artillery he had been amassing for years; it very probably included his magnificent wedding present, Mons Meg.

At the outset, James took the town and levelled it. Then he focused his attack on the castle, deploying his cannons to fire directly at the castle across the Tweed. On Sunday, 3 August the king was 'recreating himself in shooting great pieces, whereof he was very expert'. Unfortunately, one of the big guns – the Lion (see page 243) – burst its casing as it was fired; the king, who was standing right beside it, was killed by a flying chunk of iron.[1]

The traditional site of James II's death is marked by a holly tree in the magnificent grounds of Floors Castle, the palatial mansion at Kelso of the Duke of Roxburghe, which overlooks the remains of Roxburgh Castle across the river. The castle was captured a few days after the king's death, and systematically demolished. Nothing is left of that mighty fortress today except for the high, oblong mound on which it stood, superintended by gaunt fragments of masonry sticking up like tombstone epitaphs to the unfulfilled reign of a formidable young Stewart king.

---

1 One source (the *Extracta E Variis Cronicis Scocie*, which seems to have been based on local traditions) claims that the fatal accident happened when the king was supervising the firing of a salvo in honour of the arrival of the queen at the siege; a piece of metal broke from one of the guns and pierced his leg, mortally wounding him.

JAMES II (r.1437–60)

'James of the Fiery Face'

The six-year-old boy who had been crowned as James II of Scotland in Holyrood Abbey on 25 March 1437 had a conspicuous vermilion birthmark covering the left side of his face; the writer of the *Auchinleck Chronicle* (the only substantial contemporary sources for James II's reign) described him as the king 'that had the fyre mark in his face', and he was known by the nickname of 'James of the Fiery Face'. It was not just his face which was fiery, however: when he came to manhood he would display both a passionate temper and a fierce pride as he stamped his authority on the nation he had inherited.

His accession was not so much a crisis of succession as a crisis of government. With a six-year-old boy on the throne there would have to be a minority government, and James II's mother, Queen Joan Beaufort, as custodian of the king's person, was determined to lead it. But where was she to find the necessary support?

James I's ruthless attacks on the leading magnates of Scotland had left an extraordinary vacuum in the ranks of the traditional leaders of the political community – the earls. Usually there were ten or twelve earls on the Scottish scene; at the time of James's assassination, however, there were only three (Douglas, Angus and Crawford); within two years, the earldoms of Douglas and Angus would be inherited by under-age boys. Two other earls (Sutherland and Menteith) were being held in England as hostages for James I's still unpaid ransom; the remaining earldoms were vacant and already subject to acrimonious disputes.

It was fertile ground for sowing dissension and unrest. Parliament cautiously appointed Archibald, fifth Earl of Douglas, as Lieutenant-General – and now the power-struggle began in earnest. The Douglas seemed to have no stomach for politicking, and remained a figurehead. Into the breach stepped two new families (new to the corridors of power, anyway) – the Crichtons and the Livingstons. Variously described by historians as 'bandits', 'ruffians', 'rascally', 'upstart' and 'opportunist', they began a long feud for control of the young king's person, and thereby control of Scotland.

Sir William Crichton had been a lesser-ranking but rising favourite in James I's court. At the time of the king's death he was Master of the King's Household; he was now appointed keeper of the key royal fortress of Edinburgh Castle, and soon afterwards Chancellor of Scotland. Sir Alexander Livingston of Callendar was a relatively unknown Lothian baron who had played little part in government but who was now, almost out of the blue, it seems, appointed Keeper of Stirling Castle. These two men would play a deadly game of chess in which the young king and his mother were mere pawns on the board of their ambitions.

Queen Joan was deeply concerned about her son's future. In the summer of 1439 she managed to smuggle the young king out of Crichton's care in Edinburgh Castle and take him to Stirling Castle, perhaps hoping that Livingston would prove more biddable than Crichton. At the same time, in order to strengthen her own position, she married again. Her new husband was Sir James Stewart of Lorne, by whom she would have three sons; two of them would later become the earls of Atholl and of Buchan, the third would become Bishop of Moray, and all three would play key roles in the reign of James III (see Chapter 16).

Livingston's reaction to news of the marriage was as sharp as it was surprising: he locked the couple up in a cell in Stirling Castle. Their incarceration was short-lived, however. At the next General Council, four weeks later, Livingston was persuaded to release them, and the dowager queen signed a declaration that Livingston had been motivated only by 'great truth and loyalty'! Crichton responded by kidnapping the young king while he was out riding near Stirling Castle and taking him back to Edinburgh Castle.

While Crichton and Livingston were fighting it out over the king's person, a third family, more powerful than either, was making a decisive move to take over the reins of power – the Douglases.

There were two distinct branches of the family operating in the fifteenth century – the 'Black Douglases' and the 'Red Douglases'. To simplify a complex genealogical tangle, the Black Douglases were Earls of Douglas and the Red Douglases were Earls of Angus. Both lines were descended from the 'good' Sir James Douglas ('the Black Douglas', as he was called, because of his swarthy complexion), the hero-lieutenant of Robert Bruce who had carried the Bruce's heart on Crusade after the king's death. The 'Black Douglases' were descended from an illegitimate son of the 'good' Sir James; the 'Red Douglases' (so-called because of the colour of their hair) from an illegitimate son of James, the second Earl of Douglas and hero of the Battle of Otterburn.

Archibald, the fifth Earl of Douglas, the Lord-Lieutenant, died of the plague in 1439 after only two years in office. He was succeeded as sixth earl by his fifteen-year-old son William, a handsome young man whom later chroniclers would call 'haughty and ambitious'. He had a fondness for the eight-year-old king, who hero-worshipped him in return. The sixth Earl of Douglas was nearly of age, poised to become the greatest magnate in the kingdom with five thousand knights and spearmen at his call. For both Crichton and Livingston, Douglas represented a threat which had to be eliminated.

The 'Black Dinner' (24 November 1440)

Working in concert for a change, Crichton and Livingston invited the young earl to dine with them and the king at Edinburgh Castle on 24 November 1440. Douglas and his younger brother David went there trustingly with only one attendant, and were received with every mark of friendship. At table they 'banquetted royally with all delicates which could be got'. At the end of the dinner, however, a black bull's head was served on a great dish – traditionally a symbol of doom. The youths were seized, despite the king's entreaties, and subjected to a mock trial for treason; after that the brothers and their friend were hustled from the hall into the courtyard, where an execution block had already been set up. Douglas apparently begged for their lives, but his pleas were futile; he then requested that his young brother be executed first, so that the boy might not suffer the added agony of watching him die. The helpless ten-year-old king wept as his friends were beheaded. That grim occasion has been known as the 'Black Dinner' ever since, and was commemorated in a popular rhyme:

> Edinburgh castle, towne and toure,
> God grant thou sink for sinne!
> And that even for the black dinoir
> Earl Douglas gat therein.

The man who succeeded as seventh Earl of Douglas was James Douglas of Balvenie and Abercorn, known as James 'the Gross' because of his obesity; he had been created Earl of Avandale in 1437 after the death of James I. He was the great-uncle of the two murdered boys, but he may well have been party to the conspiracy, for he took no revenge for their murders. From his stronghold at Abercorn Castle by the Forth he extended the territorial power of the Douglases; when he died in 1443 he had become the most powerful magnate in the central belt of Scotland.

His successor, the eighth earl, was his son William, the eldest of a sheaf of vigorous and charismatic sons – James and Archibald (twins), Hugh and John. James, who would become the ninth Earl of Douglas, distinguished himself in 1448 as a champion in the lists, tilting against the legendary Burgundian knight Jacques de Lalain;[1] Archibald became Earl of Moray; Hugh became Earl of Ormond; and John became Lord of Balvenie.

William, eighth Earl of Douglas, quickly became active in government. He exploited the weakness inherent in the self-seeking coalition of Livingston and Chancellor Crichton, joining Livingston in a concerted attack on Crichton, who was toppled from office and forced to give up control of Edinburgh Castle. Douglas then married his kinswoman Margaret, the 'Fair Maid of Galloway', sister of the sixth earl who had been the victim of the 'Black Dinner' in 1440; through her the eighth earl added the province of Galloway to his domains. He now ruled virtually the whole of the south of Scotland. His brothers wielded considerable power in the north and east, his sisters married the high constable and the heads of the houses of Fleming and Wallace. Douglas also now formed an alliance with the Earl of Crawford, the most formidable of the magnates north of the Forth. Very soon the Black Douglases were again the dominant faction in Scotland and were in control of the king in the latter years of his minority.

The Burgundy marriage (3 July 1449)

The dowager queen died in July 1445 and was buried beside her first husband James I in Perth. She had been decisively outplayed in the political turmoil of the king's minority, and her second husband, Sir James Stewart of Lorne, swiftly sought safety in England with their three sons. At the same time, the young king's minority officially ended: a General Council in October 1444 – the month of James's fourteenth birthday – formally declared his majority. But it was not until his marriage in 1449 at the age of eighteen that the king stepped from the wings of history and took over direct control of his kingdom.

Since the marriage of James I's daughter to the Dauphin of France

---

1 This celebrated tournament was held at Stirling in the presence of the king, who acted as referee. Three Burgundian champions were matched against three Scottish knights. Jacques de Lalain was supported by his uncle Simon de Lalain and a Breton knight named Hervé de Meriadec; James Douglas by the Laird of Halket and James Douglas of Lochleven. With lances, axes, swords and daggers they were to fight to the death or until one of the combatants yielded, or the king called a halt. It was a stern contest. James Douglas of Lochleven was given a hard time by de Meriadec and knocked to the ground. James Douglas (the future earl) fought Jacques de Lalain; the Burgundian was unhorsed, and had lost all his weapons except his sword when King James dropped his baton to signal an end to the contest.

in 1436, Scotland had occupied a seat at the high table of Europe, diplomatically and commercially. Its reputation was high in the courts of Europe: others of James I's daughters had married into the European aristocracy in Brittany, the Low Countries and Austria. This paved the way for James II to marry a princess of the house of Burgundy: Marie, daughter of the Duc de Gueldres and niece of Philippe the Good, the immensely wealthy and powerful Duke of Burgundy. It was a hugely prestigious royal match for a Stewart king; it was also of great benefit to the Scottish merchants who were able to establish lucrative new trading links with the Continent.

The wedding was a spectacularly lavish occasion. The bride and her escort sailed for Scotland in a convoy of thirteen ships, bringing three hundred men-at-arms and retainers. Marie was to receive an annuity of ten thousand gold crowns (£30,000 Scots). On 3 July 1449 James II and Marie de Gueldres were married at a glittering ceremony in Holyrood Abbey, and Marie de Gueldres was crowned Queen of Scotland.

After their marriage James was soon concerned to demonstrate that he was now king in his own right. His first act was to launch an attack on the Livingston family, bringing to an abrupt end the ascendancy they had enjoyed during the minority. In January 1450 the Livingstons were forfeited and two of them were executed, apparently for fiscal misdemeanours.

James II now turned his attention to the problem of the Douglas power, which was formidable enough to make any monarch apprehensive. In 1450 William, eighth Earl of Douglas, went to Rome to attend a papal jubilee, parading his magnificent train through the courts of Europe. James was irked by this ostentatious display of power, and while Douglas was abroad he suddenly went on the attack and seized two of his castles. When Douglas returned to Scotland he prudently made formal submission to the king at the June parliament of 1451, and an uneasy truce ensued.

Douglas must have been all too aware of his vulnerability to the king's animosity, and to shore up his position he entered into a bond of mutual alliance with two other noblemen, John, Earl of Ross and Lord of the Isles, and Alexander, Earl of Crawford, according to which they promised to work together for their common good. The king, however, chose to interpret this bond as an act of potential rebellion.

The Douglas murder (22 February 1452)

In February 1452 James invited Douglas to Stirling Castle for discussions, giving him a promise of safe-conduct. After two days of
protracted wrangling he bluntly ordered Douglas to revoke the bond
he had made with his confederates. Douglas said that he could not
and would not. James lost his temper and shouted, 'Since you will
not, I shall!' With that he drew his dagger and stabbed Douglas twice,
once in the body and once in the neck. Others joined in; one courtier
crushed Douglas's skull with a pole-axe and the rest then pushed
forward and stabbed him twenty-six times.

It was a particularly odious crime, for it had violated a royal safe-
conduct. Parliament, however, loyally exonerated the king, acquitting
him of any guilt on the grounds that Douglas had been conspiring
against the crown; the crime had been committed 'in hot blood', which
made it manslaughter rather than the more grievous crime of murder.
In a symbolic act of retaliation the new (ninth) Earl of Douglas, James,
rode into Stirling with his brother Hugh, Earl of Ormond, and six
hundred men. They nailed the dishonoured safe-conduct to a board
and dragged it through the streets at the tail of a broken-down old
horse. Then Douglas plundered and burned the town, formally
renouncing his homage to James II and offering it to England.

Once again, James made peace with the Douglases, after a savage
foray into the Douglas lands in the summer of 1452. But he was only
biding his time. Soon he gathered his forces and descended upon the
Douglas lands with such savagery that the Earl of Douglas submitted.
James accepted his fealty and then secured for him papal dispensation
to marry his brother's widow, Margaret, the 'Fair Maid of Galloway',
which brought Galloway into the Douglas earldom. But it seems to
have been only a feint: by bribery and threats the king neutralised the
earl's allies, and then, in March 1455, launched another attack on
the Douglas lands. He rolled out all the new firepower available to
the monarchy and battered two of the Douglas castles into submission.

The Earl of Douglas fled to England, where he became a pensioner
of the English crown, and the younger Douglas brothers were dealt
with at an encounter at Arkinholm, near Langholm: the Earl of Moray
was killed, the Earl of Ormond was captured and later executed and
the Lord of Balvenie was driven into exile. The Earl of Douglas himself
was (retrospectively) attainted by parliament *in absentia* for treasonable
activities and his estates were forfeited to the crown, adding a welcome
annual income of £2,000 to the king's revenues. To complete his

coup, King James now laid siege to the mightiest of all the Douglas strongholds – Threave Castle on its island on the River Dee near Langholm in Dumfriesshire. The king had with him in his artillery train a 'great bombard' (*magnus bombardus*), a massive iron gun capable of firing large balls of iron and stone huge distances. After a two-month siege, despite the new anti-artillery fortifications which had been added around 1450, Threave Castle surrendered.

That year of 1455 was a watershed in James II's reign. On his twenty-fifth birthday (16 October) parliament announced that he had formally attained his 'perfect majority', when he was freed of any restraints of his minority. He had already made a spectacular impact on his kingdom. He had destroyed the power of the Black Douglases, and in their place had promoted the loyal Red Douglases in the person of George, the fourth Earl of Angus. He had strengthened the crown's links with the hierarchy of the Church. Above all, he had secured the Stewart succession: a male heir, named James, had been born in 1451, to be followed by the birth of a second son, Alexander, in 1455.

Parliament was concerned also to provide the monarchy with a stable foundation of crown revenues in the form of certain lands, lordships and castles with the incomes which went with them; it passed an Act of Annexation which ratified the king's acquisitions from the Douglases and others as inalienable crown lands in order to enable him to 'live on his own' without resort to further increases in taxation. Three of the great Scottish castles – Dumbarton, Edinburgh and Stirling – were set aside as royal residences. New earldoms were created – Argyll (for the Campbells), Erroll, Morton, Rothes and Earl Marischal. James also created a new title for the lesser nobility – 'Lord of Parliament' – which he now bestowed on his favoured supporters; it cost the crown nothing in terms of land or grants, and helped the king to build up a new royalist party. With his queen, Marie de Gueldres, he promoted a deliberate 'cult of monarchy' based on chivalry, artistic patronage and the support of the ecclesiastical hierarchy.

The king's chief counsellor was his kinsman, Bishop James Kennedy of St Andrews, who has become a byword in Scotland for wisdom and humanity. It is said that he would reinforce his advice with parables. In the early 1450s, when the young king was pondering how to deal with the Douglases and their supporters, the good bishop picked up a sheaf of arrows tied with a leather thong and invited the king to break them; when he could not, the bishop showed him that although his enemies were irresistible in combination, they could be broken, like the arrows, one by one. As chancellor of St Andrews University, Bishop Kennedy founded the College of St Salvator there in 1450. Not to be outdone, only a few months later the king supported the foundation of Glasgow University, in 1451.

The crown now had unprecedented power and prestige; the king's new high-tech artillery from the Low Countries had made him the master of his barons' castles. For the last five years of his reign James was able to govern his country in relative peace. Parliament passed several acts which were designed to improve rural husbandry: land-owners were required to plant woods and hedges (fences were for-bidden), and arable farming was encouraged. Justice, law and order were enforced more rigorously. The parliament of 1458 which enacted these measures was bold enough to address the king forthrightly about his duties and responsibilities; it enjoined him and his ministers to promote 'the quiet and common profit of the realm' and to see to it that justice was kept among his lieges. Furthermore, parliament

> with all humility exhorts and requires His Highness to be inclined with such diligence to the execution of the statutes, acts and decrees above written, that God may be pleased with him, and all his lieges, spiritual and temporal, may pray for him to God, and give thanks to Him that sent them such a prince to be their governor and defender.

England: the Wars of the Roses (1455–87)

The year 1455 also saw the outbreak of the sporadic and disjointed civil war in England known as the 'Wars of the Roses' between two lines of the royal family – the ruling House of Lancaster (red rose) and the House of York (white rose). It was a complex and (to Scottish eyes, at least) confusing conflict; but its varying outcomes would have a direct effect on the fortunes of Scotland over the next three decades.

The rival claims of the Lancastrians and the Yorkists went back to John of Gaunt, Duke of Lancaster (the third surviving son of Edward III), and to Edward's fourth surviving son, Edmund Langley, Duke of York, both of whom had been uncles of the Plantagenet King Richard II.

The Lancastrians had seized the throne from Richard in 1399, and three Lancastrian kings followed: Henry IV (r.1399–1413), Henry V (r.1413–22), and Henry VI, who succeeded to the throne as a nine-month-old infant in 1422. Henry VI's minority, when England was governed by a Protector (his uncle the Duke of Gloucester), was good news for Scotland, which was left alone while England was steadily losing its possessions in France. Henry VI, who was a cultured and intensely pious young man[1] (diametrically opposite to his martial father, Henry V), married the strong-minded Margaret of Anjou in 1445; in 1447 the Duke of Gloucester was executed and in the ensuing chaos the Yorkists began to build up their claim to the throne.

Poor Henry VI was subject to bouts of insanity, and in one of his mental lapses, in 1454, Richard, Duke of York, was appointed Protector. The Lancastrians and Yorkists came to blows at St Albans in May 1455. It was the first of the battles of the Wars of the Roses; the Lancastrians were defeated, and Henry VI fell into the hands of the Yorkists. But the first real encounter came at Northampton in July 1460; the king was defeated and taken prisoner again. After a further series of battles he was formally deposed and the twenty-year-old Duke of York assumed the crown as Edward IV (r.1461–70, 1471–83).

Not unnaturally, James II of Scotland saw the turmoil in England as an opportunity to recover the two major Scottish strongholds which were still in English hands – Berwick and Roxburgh. He made a couple of feints at Berwick-upon-Tweed; but when Henry VI was humbled at Northampton by the Yorkists on 10 July 1460, James was ready to make a decisive move. Within two weeks he had mustered a huge army from all over Scotland. The English were expecting another assault on Berwick and concentrated their defences there; but James's target was Roxburgh Castle. It was here that the accidental bursting of one of his cherished guns brought his reign to a sudden and untimely close. He was only twenty-nine years old.

He left his wife (and the nation) with a family of five – two daughters (Mary and Margaret) and three sons. The youngest, John, Earl of Mar, was three years old; Alexander, Duke of Albany, was six. The eldest, James, Duke of Rothesay, was nine years old: Scotland had yet another Stewart boy-king on the throne.

---

1   Henry VI, who was to become known as the 'royal saint', founded Eton College in 1440 and King's College, Cambridge, in 1446.

Chapter 16

JAMES III (r.1460–88)

The minority of James III was more prosperous than that of his father and grandfather. The affairs of state were guided by the experienced wisdom of Bishop Kennedy. Roxburgh was . . . taken and destroyed. Berwick, during the dissensions of the civil wars of England, was surrendered to the Scots; and the dominions of the Islands of Orkney and Zetland, which had hitherto belonged to the Kings of Norway, were acquired as the marriage portion of a Princess of Denmark and Norway, who was united in marriage to the King of Scotland.

TALES OF A GRANDFATHER, CHAPTER XXII

On 10 July 1469 King James III of Scotland married Margrethe, Princess of Norway/Denmark, at a ceremony in Holyrood Abbey; the groom was eighteen years old, the bride only ten. It was a happy and auspicious occasion for Scotland's young king, but even more so for Scotland; for with that marriage the kingdom of Scotland finally gained the last territories which make up Scotland today – the Northern Isles of Orkney and Shetland.

It had all started two centuries earlier. When Alexander III signed the Treaty of Perth in 1266, by which Norway ceded the Western Isles to Scotland for a yearly payment of one hundred *merks* in perpetuity (the 'annual of Norway', as it was called), the status of Orkney and Shetland as possessions of the Norwegian crown was secured. The payments had seldom been made, and had stopped altogether after

1426. The Northern Isles had become heavily Scotticised by now, and the status of Norway, too, had changed considerably.[1] The new King of Denmark/Norway, the impecunious and improvident Kristian I, was not one to overlook any source of revenue, and in the 1450s, during the reign of James II, he began to make complaints about the non-payment of the 'annual of Norway'. James, however, had no intention of paying up; he had another agenda – he was determined to force King Kristian to give up Orkney and Shetland. In 1460 he sent an embassy to a meeting arranged by King Charles VII of France between the Scots and the Danes.

The intention was to discuss a marriage contract between James's heir (the future James III) and Kristian's only daughter, the pious Princess Margrethe of Denmark. The Danish envoys were taken aback when the Scots audaciously demanded, as part of any marriage settlement, not only the remission of the 'annual of Norway' but the relinquishment of Orkney and Shetland as well. The negotiations broke down, and were abandoned at the death of James II in August 1460.

The discussions were renewed in 1468 when the new king, James III, was of age to be married. A marriage treaty was drawn up in Copenhagen on 8 September. By its terms, Princess Margrethe would receive the Palace of Linlithgow; she would also receive, as a hunting lodge and country retreat, the magnificent Doune Castle near Dunblane, built by the first Duke of Albany. Her dowry included the ending of the 'annual of Norway' and a quitclaim for all arrears; the rest of the dowry was to consist of sixty thousand florins of the Rhine (guilders) in cash. The first instalment of ten thousand florins was to be paid before the wedding; the remainder was to be secured by mortgaging Orkney until such time as Kristian could redeem the pledge. When the time came for the wedding in 1469 the king could only raise two thousand florins, so he mortgaged Shetland as well for the eight-thousand-florin balance.

King Kristian doubtless had every intention of redeeming his pledges; it was a meagre sum, after all – in five years' time, for instance, he would borrow twenty-five thousand florins to go on a pilgrimage to Rome. By then, however, the five centuries of Norse rule in Orkney and Shetland were effectively over. In 1470 James III made a shrewd

---

1   Since the Union of Kalmar in 1397, Norway had been part of a triple Scandinavian monarchy comprising Denmark, Norway and (albeit reluctantly) Sweden. In 1448 the throne was given to the twenty-two-year-old Kristian of Oldenburg, who married his predecessor's childless widow, Dorothea of Brandenburg.

bargain with the Sinclair family of Roslin, who had got their hands on the earldom of Orkney: the king acquired the rights and lands of the Northern Isles while the Sinclairs got the castle and lands of Ravenscraig, newly built by his mother, Marie de Gueldres. By an Act of Parliament in 1472 the islands were annexed and united to Scotland. Until the eighteenth century kings of Denmark would make recurrent attempts to open negotiations for the return of the islands, but the Scots simply refused to discuss the matter. Geography and politics had come together in irresistible combination: the boundaries of the kingdom of Scotland had at last been brought to their fullest extent.

The minority of James III

After James II was accidentally killed outside the walls of Roxburgh Castle on 3 August 1460, the queen urged the army to complete the capture and destruction of the castle, which fell to the Scots five days later. On Sunday, 10 August, exactly a week after his father's death, the nine-year-old Prince James was crowned in nearby Kelso Abbey as James III of Scotland.

The early years of James III's minority were dominated by two powerful characters: the king's mother Marie de Gueldres (the dowager queen), and Bishop William Kennedy of St Andrews. The first parliament of the new reign, meeting in Edinburgh in February 1461, appointed Marie Guardian of the King's Person, with a Regency Council made up of prelates and nobles headed by Bishop Kennedy.

Marie de Gueldres was a lively, talented and passionate woman. She was also a very wealthy one, with huge revenues from her widow's dower. She improved the amenities at Stirling Castle and Falkland Palace, built Ravenscraig Castle in Fife (the first castle in Scotland to be designed specifically for the use of artillery), and founded Trinity College Church in Edinburgh.[1]

She also played an active part in the Wars of the Roses. When the

---

1 The original Trinity College Church no longer exists. It was built in the valley between the Old Town and the Calton Hill, but the site was bought by the North British Railway in 1848 to create access for its lines to Waverley Station. The building was demolished and the stones, carefully numbered, deposited on the Calton Hill. The church was rebuilt on its present site in Chalmers Close (between the High Street and Jeffrey Street) in 1872, but many of the stones had been pilfered by then. The altarpiece in the original church included separate portraits of James III and his bride, Princess Margrethe of Denmark, commissioned from the Flemish artist Hugo van der Goes on the occasion of the king's marriage in 1469; the paintings are now in the Scottish National Portrait Gallery.

Yorkists came to power late in 1460, Marie had a welcome for the Lancastrian Henry VI's wife, Margaret of Anjou; and when Edward IV consolidated the Yorkist hold on the crown after a bloody victory at Towton, in Yorkshire, in March 1461, Margaret of Anjou found sanctuary in Scotland again, this time with the deposed Henry VI and their son, Prince Edward. In return for this hospitality and the possibility of Scottish military support, the Lancastrian exiles surrendered Berwick-upon-Tweed to Scotland,[1] and also promised to cede Carlisle.[2]

Bishop Kennedy, on the other hand, had Yorkist sympathies. He was kinsman to King James III (his mother had been a daughter of Robert III), and an experienced courtier; he was also a brilliant scholar who had been made Bishop of St Andrews at the age of thirty-one. He had a taste for splendour and ostentation – both in life and in death: he built a great ship, the five-hundred-ton *Salvator* (familiarly known as 'the Bishop's Barge'), and a tomb for his own interment in the chapel of St Salvator's College, each of which was reputed to have cost as much as the college itself.

Bishop Kennedy found the queen mother's politicking not only meddlesome but dangerous. Scotland, he claimed, was threatened with perdition because of her actions. What seemed to scandalise him even more than Marie's politics was her private life. She had an affair with the Lancastrian Duke of Somerset while he was in exile in Scotland. She lived openly with Adam Hepburn, the Master of Hailes, who was already married. She then switched her support to the victorious Yorkist side, and even discussed with Richard Neville, Earl of Warwick (the future 'Kingmaker'), the possibility of marriage to King Edward IV!

Marie de of Gueldres died in December 1463. Her death allowed Bishop Kennedy to take control of government policy; he was able to negotiate a fifteen-year truce with the Yorkist government of England, and accepted an annual pension from Edward IV (no doubt to ensure

---

1   The Scots were exultant over the recovery of their 'natural' frontier with England in the south-east. They were to hold Berwick for the next two decades.

2   From her sanctuary in Scotland, Margaret of Anjou travelled to France to persuade Louis XI to send an army to the north of England. Only a small force arrived, which was soon dealt with by the English Warden of the Marches. Undeterred, Queen Margaret went back to France in 1463 to seek more effective support. She returned with a much larger force which landed near Bamburgh and occupied Alnwick Castle. Edward IV promptly marched north with a sizeable army, and Queen Margaret had to be hastily evacuated back to Scotland in a French ship. She was nothing if not persistent, however, and later that year she entered Northumberland again, only to see her army decisively defeated and dispersed near Hexham. She fled to France, and remained there.

that Henry VI would not be allowed into Scotland again). But the good bishop did not have long to enjoy the fruits of his diplomacy. He died in May 1465, having achieved for Scotland blessed relief from the attentions of its troubled southern neighbour.

James III was now thirteen years old. There was not much time for another faction to take control of the king's person before he reached his majority; but as with James II, when the Livingstons and the Crichtons seized power during his minority, another family was ready to step into the power-vacuum – the opportunist Boyds of Kilmarnock.

In July 1466, while the fourteen-year-old king was out hunting near Linlithgow Palace, he was seized and abducted in an audacious *coup d'état* led by Robert, Lord Boyd of Kilmarnock. The boy was taken to Edinburgh Castle, whose governor, Sir Alexander Boyd, was Lord Boyd's brother; he was also Chamberlain of the Royal Household, and had been the king's instructor in military matters. At a parliament in Edinburgh in October the king was somehow induced to say that what had happened had been done with his consent; parliament accordingly approved a charter whereby Robert, Lord Boyd, was named as Governor of the King's Person and Keeper of the Fortresses of the Kingdom. The Boyds now embarked on a whirlwind campaign of self-aggrandisement: Lord Boyd's son Thomas was created Earl of Arran, and married the king's elder sister, Lady Mary. It is said that the king wept during the wedding ceremony; it was not the last time that he would resort to tears in times of stress.

The Boyds did not last long on the political stage. Even before his marriage to Princess Margrethe of Denmark in July 1469, King James III had 'conceived a great hatred for the Boyds'. It was the Earl of Arran who went to Denmark to escort the princess to Scotland for her wedding. When the vessels docked at Leith, his wife (Lady Mary, the king's sister) was waiting for him with a warning of the king's growing displeasure. After Princess Margrethe had gone ashore with her attendants, Arran promptly hoisted sail and went straight back to Denmark with his wife. It was a prudent move. In November 1469 parliament heard charges of treason against the Boyds 'for having traitorously abducted the king from Linlithgow on 9 July 1466'. The Earl of Arran was already in exile in Denmark; his father, Lord Boyd, now fled to England. Sir Alexander Boyd, however, was still in Scotland and was executed for the sins of the family. The Boyds' lands were forfeited, to the considerable advantage of the royal exchequer.

JAMES III (r.1460–88)

Majority and maturity

James III began his personal reign at the time of his marriage to Margrethe of Denmark in July 1469. He was to rule Scotland for nineteen years, until his murder in mysterious circumstances after the Battle of Sauchieburn on 11 June 1488 (see page 272).

At least the kingdom was at peace – unlike England, where the Wars of the Roses had flared up again. In August 1469 the powerful Earl of Warwick ('the Kingmaker') made Edward IV a virtual prisoner; when Edward managed to escape, Warwick sailed to France where he made an alliance with Margaret of Anjou, Henry VI's queen, and invaded England in September 1470. Edward IV fled abroad to Burgundy, and Henry was released and restored to the throne under Warwick's tutelage. In March 1471, however, Edward returned with a Burgundian army; he defeated the Lancastrian forces at Barnet in Hertfordshire on 14 April (where Warwick was killed) and at Tewkesbury in Gloucestershire on 4 May (where Prince Edward was killed). Margaret of Anjou was captured. Edward IV went straight back to London; that very night Henry VI was murdered in the Tower, and Edward IV resumed his interrupted reign.[1]

In Scotland, James III's foreign policy was focused on consolidating good relations with the Yorkist dynasty in England. Edward IV's attitude towards Scotland was ambivalent, to say the least, and James III took the precaution of investing heavily in more artillery. At this early stage in his reign, James was displaying considerable confidence and even aggressiveness, just like his warrior father.

The chance of a more binding relationship with England came in March 1473, when Queen Margrethe of Scotland gave birth to a son, James, Duke of Rothesay (the future James IV), to be followed by two other sons. When little James was a year old a marriage was arranged for him with Lady Cecilia, the three-year-old daughter of Edward IV. The formal betrothal was solemnised in the Blackfriars of Edinburgh in October 1474. Cecilia's dowry was set at twenty thousand English marks; a first instalment of two thousand marks was paid immediately, followed by annual instalments of two thousand and one thousand marks.[2]

---

1 Margaret of Anjou was ransomed by Louis XI and retired to France, where she died in 1482.
2 In the event the marriage never took place: it was cancelled by Edward IV after the abortive invasion of Scotland by the Duke of Gloucester and the Duke of Albany in 1482 (see below). James eventually married Margaret Tudor, the eldest daughter of Henry VII, in 1503.

It was good business for Edward IV, for the contract neutralised any threat from Scotland and left him free to concentrate on France, where he still harboured designs on the throne; he invaded France with a huge army in July 1475, and allowed himself to be bought off by Louis XI for an annual pension of fifty thousand crowns.

In Scotland, however, James III's policy of amity with England did not go down well. Indeed, the king was losing support where it mattered – among the nobility, especially in the Borders, where sporadic warfare with England had become a way of life. Parliament had occasion to chide the king (very respectfully, of course) for his lack of interest in the minutiae of government and the administration of firm royal justice; he seldom left Edinburgh, and never travelled to attend the local justice 'ayres' (circuits) in person.

James was also criticised for what was perceived as his avarice: he was thought to be amassing money for his personal use – a 'black kist' (chest) stuffed with treasures with which to finance his extravagant outlays on ornaments and clothing for himself, his queen and his court. At a time when the country was suffering from 'famine, inflation and feud', the king's increasingly demanding methods of raising money to pay for his personal excesses was not a recipe for respect. To increase the royal revenues he also progressively debased the currency by introducing cheap copper coins with a high face-value – 'black money', they were contemptuously called. The fact that the coins were stamped with the king's face did nothing to increase his, or their, popularity.

Be that as it may, there can be no doubt about James's benevolent impact on the arts in Scotland. He encouraged the development of a native school of literature which would reach its peak under the patronage of his successor, James IV. Many poets whose works are now lost are mentioned in contemporary treasurers' accounts as having received pensions from the king. Chief among those whose writings still survive was Robert Henryson (see page 284). The most popular poet of the day, however, was the minstrel known only as Blind Harry, the author of the *Acts and Deeds of Sir William Wallace*, which provided a barbed contrast between the heroic, anti-English patriotism of Wallace and the pro-English policies of James III.

The king was also perceived to be surrounding himself with favourites who crossed the class barriers, but whom later chroniclers would accuse of being 'low-born'. He called them his 'familiars', and many of them were cultivated men whose society was attractive to a king who had intellectual and artistic interests. One of them was William Roger, an accomplished English musician, who founded the musical tradition in the Chapel Royal at Stirling. Another was William Scheves, who started as a shirt-maker for the king and ended up as Archbishop of St Andrews. The most notorious was Thomas Cochrane, who is said to have been a stonemason (he was at one time thought to have been responsible for starting the construction of the Great Hall of Stirling Castle).

Cochrane has been cast as the major problem where the king's reputation was concerned. He acted as James's trouble-shooter in the north-east, trying to sort out the endemic feuding there, but only succeeded in infuriating the powerful local nobility. He is said to have exercised inordinate influence over the king in matters of state; he controlled access to James and charged heftily for the privilege of seeing him.

The real trouble may have been that the king's 'familiars' also included a crowd of hangers-on: physicians and apothecaries, esquires who were rewarded with extensive lands and baronies, a fencing master (Torphichen), a royal tailor (James Hommyl), a royal shoemaker (Leonard) and a renowned astrologer (Dr Andreas). These 'familiars' were accused of supplanting the king's privy council with what would nowadays be called a 'kitchen cabinet'. It may not have been entirely true, but there certainly seems to have been a grain of truth in it.

The traditional version of James III's reign (Robert Lindsay of Pits-cottie's *Scotland*, written in the sixteenth century) states that the king 'lost the hearts of many of his lords . . . and also of their sons and brethren who fain would have served the king's grace except that they could not reach him for this Cochrane and his company'. As a result the king's nobles looked to his adult brothers – Alexander, Duke of Albany, and John, Earl of Mar – for the smack of firm government. They, at least, *looked* like hero-kings, extrovert and masculine: Albany was said to be a great horsemen, with 'a very awful countenance', and Mar was tall and handsome, a mighty huntsman and an excellent archer.

King James must have been aware of this threatening development. Thomas Cochrane (of course!) was believed to be poisoning his mind against his brothers, and sometime in 1479–80 the king had them arrested and thrown into prison. The Earl of Mar died in Craigmillar Castle in rather suspicious circumstances – he is said to have been bled to death in a bath. The Duke of Albany, however, contrived to escape from Edinburgh Castle and took refuge in Dunbar Castle, which he garrisoned and munitioned; when the king besieged the castle, Albany escaped again and made his way to France. But France, it seemed, was in no position to forward his ambitions in Scotland, and from there he would go to England, to become a client of King Edward IV.

Meanwhile, the king's assiduous cultivation of English friendship was running into the buffers. While Edward IV was still paying the instalments on his daughter's dowry for her marriage to Prince James, James III was organising another marriage alliance, this time between his younger sister, Lady Margaret, and Edward IV's brother-in-law, Anthony Woodville, Lord Rivers. Unfortunately, when the time came for the young lady to be escorted to England for her wedding in November 1479, it turned out that she was pregnant by another man, and the marriage was cancelled. Everything James had worked for was wrecked, and border skirmishing broke out once again.

The Lauder lynchings (July 1482)

War was now inevitable. In 1480 Edward IV demanded the return of Berwick and Roxburgh, and insisted that young James, the Duke of Rothesay, should be delivered to England by the end of May so that his promised marriage to Lady Cecilia could take place. A hostile English fleet was sent to patrol the Firth of Forth.

This was the Duke of Albany's chance. In the spring of 1482 he went to England and signed a covenant with Edward IV at Fotheringhay, promising to do homage to the King of England when he won the crown of Scotland for himself and signing himself 'Alexander R, King of Scots' (by the King of England's gift); he promised also to surrender Berwick and most of the south of Scotland to England. In return, Edward IV committed himself to a full-scale invasion of Scotland, to overthrow the existing regime north of the border. The invasion army was to be led by Edward's brother Richard, Duke of Gloucester (the future Richard III).

As a massive English army mustered in the north of England, the danger to Scotland was very real and very stark: this was the greatest crisis of James III's reign. He was obliged to muster an army to meet the invasion, and turned to his nobles for support. The senior nobles in the land were now his three half-uncles (his father's half-brothers): John Stewart (Earl of Atholl), James Stewart (Earl of Buchan) and Andrew Stewart (Bishop-elect of Moray); but the call to arms triggered a remarkable family conspiracy in which, it is thought, even James's queen, Margrethe of Denmark, was personally involved.

In July 1482 the Scots army assembled on the Burgh Muir of Edinburgh and the king marched south with it to Lauder in Berwickshire.

The English army had already moved into Scotland, taking the town of Berwick on the way but bypassing Berwick Castle. At Lauder, the Scottish nobles found themselves faced with a huge invasion army only forty-eight kilometres away. Their reaction to the crisis has become the subject of much hearsay and legend. It was said by later chroniclers that the nobles learned that the hated Cochrane had been given command of the artillery. They held a meeting in Lauder kirk to discuss the position; the ringleader seems to have been Archibald, Earl of Angus, who was married to a daughter of Lord Boyd. It was decided to present the king with an ultimatum: either the 'familiars' were dismissed from positions of command, or the army would not move another step. But who would confront the king? Who would bell the cat? One of the lords volunteered – the impetuous young Archibald, Earl of Angus, who thereby earned the nickname of Archibald 'Bell-the-Cat'. The earl went to the royal tent, but King James flatly refused to dismiss his 'familiars'.

The lords now decided to take the law into their own hands. They invited Cochrane to meet them in the kirk. When he appeared, he was wearing gold-painted armour with a heavy gold chain round his neck 'worth 500 crowns'. The Earl of Angus snatched it off, saying that a common rope would suit him better. Cochrane was held there, while a lynching party went to the king's tent and arrested five others of the 'familiars'; they then hanged them all from the parapet of the bridge over the Leader Water.

Having apparently achieved their object, the army leaders now made no attempt to face the English invasion; instead they seized their king, placed him under arrest and marched straight back to Edinburgh. Perhaps the arrest of the king, rather than the lynching of his household, had been their intention all along. In Edinburgh James was imprisoned in the castle in the keeping of his half-uncles, the earls of Atholl and Buchan.

The English army now swept into Edinburgh unopposed. But here the Duke of Gloucester faced a quandary. The king he had come to depose was a prisoner in his own fortress, and inaccessible without a major siege (for which Gloucester was unprepared and which he could not afford); the king's uncles had the royal seals in the castle, and the would-be usurper, Albany, now seemed to be in two minds about his promised homage to Edward VI. It is impossible to know what Albany's real agenda was, but it is unlikely that he planned the death of his brother, for the king had legitimate heirs with much better claims to the throne; possibly he only wanted to run a Regency Council for his young nephew, Prince James. Be that as it may, Richard of Gloucester made the best of an impossible position: he extracted a bond for the repayment of Lady Cecilia's dowry and went back home, pausing only long enough to capture Berwick Castle. Berwick-upon-Tweed thus became part of England again, and has remained so from that time forward.

The *coup*, if *coup* it was, had gone off half-cock, but it remains another of the great enigmas of James III's reign. After protracted and secret negotiations, which involved the queen in Stirling Castle and may also have involved her heir, James, Duke of Rothesay, the king was triumphantly released (ostensibly by his brother Albany) with the help of the burgesses of Edinburgh. James and Albany were apparently reconciled, and Albany was appointed the king's lieutenant-general. By 1483, however, Albany was in disgrace again, exposed in another conspiracy with England, and left the country. He made a final, quixotic return to Scotland in 1484 but was beaten up by an angry crowd at a fair in Lochmaben. That was enough for the king's frustrated brother; he went straight into exile in France, where he died the following year, mortally wounded in a tournament.

Death at Sauchieburn (11 June 1488)

King James III had survived the crisis of confidence in his reign – but only just. His position was strengthened, however, by the turmoil which engulfed England after the death of Edward IV in April 1483 and the usurpation of the throne by his brother Richard III. In 1485 King James took advantage of England's distractions by besieging and capturing Dunbar Castle, thus ending a long English occupation. The new English king who defeated Richard III at Bosworth in August 1485 – Henry Tudor, Henry VII – was not deterred from negotiating a three-year truce with the Scots.

The respite on the cold front with England did not extend to domestic affairs in Scotland. James's nobles in the Borders grew ever more restless and resentful, demanding reforms. The country was fragmenting into royalist and anti-royalist factions – and the anti-royalists were growing stronger all the time.

Even within James's own family circle, problems were looming. In July 1486 his wife, Margrethe of Denmark, died in Stirling Castle; she was only thirty years old, and had won the hearts of her subjects with her manifest devotion to the Church (there were even moves afoot to have her canonised). The king and his queen had been living apart for some years, and rumours (in all probability quite untrue) spread that she had been poisoned by one of James's trusted counsellors. Margrethe had borne him three sons: James, Duke of Rothesay, who was now thirteen years old; another James, Marquis of Ormonde and Duke of Ross, who was ten; and John, Earl of Mar, who was seven.

The king's attitude to his eldest son in the latter years of his reign was strangely hostile. Perhaps he associated him (and his mother) with his humiliation in 1482. At any rate he ignored his heir-apparent and favoured his second son, James, the Marquis of Ormonde. James III was still determined to make marriage alliances with England, especially after Henry VII succeeded to the English throne; but this time it was his second son, Ormonde, who was contracted to marry a daughter of Edward IV, and the widower king himself who was to marry Edward IV's widow, Elizabeth Woodville. Neither of these fanciful proposals bore fruit; but they were enough to suggest to the young Duke of Rothesay that his own future, perhaps even his life, was no longer safe. On 2 February 1488 he left Stirling Castle without the king's knowledge or permission, and went to ground. By now the anti-king nobles, too, had had enough. The fifteen-year-old heir to the throne was exactly what they needed to provide a figurehead for revolt. This time the rebellion was to be conclusive.

In the early months of 1488 James III realised that he was losing control of his kingdom. Suddenly he started spending lavishly from his private treasury, throwing money at potential supporters to raise troops for him; his oldest half-uncle, the Earl of Atholl, for instance, received two full chests of money. But the king's spending spree came too late to save his throne.

Early in June 1488, James III left Edinburgh Castle with as many supporters as he could muster – mainly Highlanders and burghal levies. His son and heir was back in Stirling by now, and the king's plan was to seize him and thereby put an end to the rebellion. The young prince emerged from Stirling Castle with a small rebel force and was put to flight near Stirling Bridge, the scene of Wallace's great victory in 1297. Prince James escaped, however, and joined up with the main army of Border rebels farther to the south.

On 11 June the second and final encounter took place south of Stirling somewhere between the Sauchie and the Bannock Burns (later to be known as Sauchieburn) – ironically, the site of the battlefield of Bannockburn. The king, symbolically, was carrying the sword of Robert Bruce. Here the final tragedy was enacted. The rebels seemed to have the larger army and their leaders, confident of victory, all swore an oath before the battle that they would not harm the person of the king. The encounter itself was not so much a set-piece battle (no artillery was involved) as a series of running skirmishes in which the rebels soon got the upper hand.

And now fact and fiction become hopelessly intertwined. One story goes that the king left the field, unaccompanied, abandoning the sword of Robert Bruce and a treasure chest of £4,000 Scots in gold coin. He was mounted on a great grey charger, presumably heading for the safety of a ship in the River Forth. He got as far as the mill of Bannockburn, but when his horse tried to jump the burn, James was thrown. The miller and his wife found him lying on the ground in his heavy armour, dazed and in pain, and carried him into a nearby stable. They asked him who he was, and he replied, 'I was your king this day at morn.' He asked for a priest to shrive him. The miller's wife ran outside and found a passing stranger who claimed to be a man of the cloth (an alternative version says that she met a posse of pursuing rebel knights). Whatever the truth, some person or persons unknown entered the stable and stabbed the king to death.

The circumstances of James III's death remain a mystery, like so much of his reign. The subsequent parliamentary inquiry could only come to the conclusion that the king 'happened to be slain', despite offering a reward of a hundred *merks* of land for the identity of his killer.

Whoever wielded the sword which killed the king, the death of James III was another watershed in the history of Scotland: it marked the end of an era, the end of the Middle Ages and the flowering of the Renaissance in Scotland with the prince who had helped to bring down his own father. That prince was crowned at Scone as James IV fifteen days later, on 26 June 1488.

Epilogue

James III may, or may not, have been the least attractive of the Stewart kings of the fifteenth century; but he was certainly the worst served by 'history'. Just as the Tudor historians of the sixteenth century turned Richard III ('Crookback') into a monster of depravity, so the Scottish chroniclers of the sixteenth century presented a portrait of James III as feckless, idle, erratic, vindictive and deeply unpleasant.

It is beyond doubt that James became extremely unpopular among his subjects during his reign. He was relentless about raising revenue for the crown, through arbitrary forfeitures and annexations of lands and titles, through levying extraordinary taxes and debasing the coinage for his personal profit. It may be that he had an inflated concept of monarchy which required ever-increasing revenues to enable him to keep up with the lavish lifestyles of other European rulers; yet he spent little on accepted royal activities such as building castles and palaces or acquiring artillery to strengthen his military capacity. Similarly, his assiduous pursuit of peace and alliance with England, including many and fruitless marriage negotiations, cost him the respect and support of his southern magnates, for whom hostility to England had become second nature and border warfare a way of life.

James spent most of his time in Edinburgh, which became the parliamentary and legislative centre for government business – the capital, in effect. This centralisation meant that the king was seldom seen by his subjects elsewhere in the country, and was generally considered to be a recluse (which he certainly was not). Ultimately, perhaps, the trouble lay in the personality of the king himself. He heaped rewards on the unworthy and failed so signally to reward loyalty that his natural supporters turned away from him. He broke faith with too many people, too often. Above all, he had a morbid distrust of members of his own family – rightly or wrongly – and in the end it was a close kinsman, his eldest son, who became the indirect instrument of his miserable, lonely death.[1]

---

1 For a penetrating and compelling summary of James III's personality defects and failures, see the 'Conclusion' to Norman Macdougall's excellent *James III: A Political Study* (1982).

Chapter 17

JAMES IV (r.1488–1513) AND
THE RENAISSANCE

*Besides being fond of martial exercises, James encouraged the
arts, and prosecuted science, as it was then understood. He studied
medicine and surgery, and appears to have been something of a
chemist . . . His authority, as it was greater than that of any king
who had reigned since the time of James I, was employed for the
administration of justice, and the protection of every rank of his
subjects, so that he was reverenced as well as beloved by all classes
of his people.*

TALES OF A GRANDFATHER, CHAPTER XXIII

On St Andrew's Day 1999 – 30 November – Her Majesty the
Queen unveiled the gloriously refurbished Great Hall of Stirling
Castle. The First Minister, Donald Dewar, called it 'a second birth' for
one of the finest surviving buildings from the Renaissance period in
Scotland. He might well have called it a second renaissance – for
Stirling's Great Hall, the most sumptuous ever built in Scotland, sym-
bolises all the glittering state glamour of the reign of Scotland's Renais-
sance king, James IV.

The restoration of Stirling Castle and its Great Hall has been a long
and expensive business – costing some £22 million in all. Away back
in 1984, when I was chairman of the Ancient Monuments Board for
Scotland, I had the privilege of switching on the first phase of the
floodlighting scheme which turned the castle into a stately spotlit

galleon sailing serenely across the night skies – and what a breathtaking spectacle it made. Fifteen years and £8.2 million later the castle makes an even more impressive sight, with the newly restored Great Hall glowing in the radiant finish of its original lime-yellow exterior – 'King's Gold', as it was called.

The interior has been transformed into an exact replica of what it was like when James IV built it around 1500 as the largest hall in his kingdom. The marvellous hammer-beam roof, which had been removed in the 1790s when the Great Hall was converted into a barracks, was recreated from 350 oak trees without a single iron nail or screw (only doweling rods). The stonework was renewed where necessary. New heraldic stained-glass windows were installed. The five great fireplaces were reconstituted. A replica of James IV's Cloth of Estate, which was displayed whenever the king was dispensing justice, was hand-stitched by members of the Embroiderers' Guild from around Scotland.

It was a magical transformation for the castle which has been the guardian gateway to the Highlands since prehistoric times and which, five hundred years ago, was the setting for the reign of the most charismatic of all the Stewart kings.

Yet few monarchs could have had a less auspicious start to their reign. James IV had been the figurehead of a rebellion by a small group of magnates against his father, James III, which had resulted in the king's murder. James was now a prisoner of his supporters and of his own remorse: whatever the rest of the country may have thought, he believed himself to have been responsible for the murder of his father, and for the rest of his life is said to have worn next to his skin an iron chain-belt to which he added a link every year.

James IV was crowned at Scone, somewhat hurriedly, on Wednesday, 24 June 1488, the day before his father's funeral at Cambuskenneth Abbey. He was the first Stewart monarch to be crowned at Scone since his great-grandfather James I in 1424. Despite the haste, it was a self-conscious and showy occasion: the chosen day was the anniversary of Robert Bruce's victory at Bannockburn. The king rode to his coronation dressed in satin doublet on a horse caparisoned in velvet, and no effort was spared to make the ceremony as impressive as possible, in order to emphasise the legitimacy of the new king and of the new government of rebel nobles and clerics who were placing the crown upon his fifteen-year-old head.

The minority government had two urgent priorities. The first was to track down and requisition as much as possible of the treasure which James III had hoarded throughout his troubled reign; ultimately more than £24,000 Scots was recovered – a huge sum, but even that was believed to be only a fraction of the total. The second priority was to confirm a government which had been responsible for regicide: however unpopular the late king might have been in many quarters, the circumstances of his death were unacceptable to the Community of the Realm. The rebels had to justify their takeover and to consolidate their position against those who had supported the previous regime.

They did this by seizing the 'commanding heights' of the administration – the principal offices of the state and the royal household – and by arraigning ten of the late king's leading supporters for treasonable negotiations with England. Two new families quickly came to the fore – the Hepburns, and their kinsmen and neighbours in the south-east, the Humes. Patrick Hepburn (Lord Hailes) became Earl of Bothwell, Master of the Household, Keeper of Edinburgh Castle and Admiral of Scotland; and Alexander Hume of that ilk became Lord Hume, Warden of the East Marches, Keeper of Stirling Castle and Chamberlain for life.

Not all the treason trials ended in forfeiture, and none in state executions. Nevertheless, in 1489 an insurrection by supporters of the late king broke out against the new regime: the rising in the north-east was led by Alexander Gordon, Master of Huntly, and supported by the Earl of Lennox in the west. The regime responded by laying siege to the Lennox stronghold of Dumbarton Castle at enormous cost, using huge artillery pieces like Mons Meg, but the castle did not fall. Meanwhile the rebels joined forces and advanced on Stirling Castle, where the young king was in residence; but the attack was beaten off in a long-running engagement which was less than an overwhelming victory.

The rebels presented a petition to the king against the injustice of the new regime. The government had been alarmed by the scale and spread of the rebellion, and appeasement and pardon were now the watchwords. A parliament which met early in 1490 rehabilitated many of the supporters of James III, to form a more broadly-based political administration. It elected a new privy council, made up of a more balanced representation of magnates from all over Scotland and limiting the power of the regime. The new privy council annulled many of the previous forfeitures. It included, for instance, William Elphinstone, Bishop of Aberdeen and founder of Aberdeen University, a noted educationist who had been James III's Chancellor; he was now reinstated as Keeper of the Privy Seal and would be one of James IV's closest advisers and ambassadors throughout his reign.

Some commentators refer to the 1490 parliament as the 'healing parliament'. From now on the reconstituted government achieved acceptance from the whole Scottish political community, and was able to operate in a much more even-handed way. It was a lesson in politics which was not to be lost on the young king during his minority.

From minor to major

The minority of James IV was to last until his twenty-first birthday – 17 March 1494 – when he was able to start his personal rule. During the intervening years we catch fascinating glimpses of the sort of person he was becoming. Exchequer records, which record several large payments of pocket-money which he spent playing cards, suggest that he was addicted to gambling. He was deeply fond of hawking and the chase, and of formal tournaments. He had received, and was still receiving, an excellent formal education and was proficient in several languages: Latin and French, of course, but also Flemish, German, Italian, Danish and a little Spanish; he also spoke Gaelic.

James was a handsome, virile young man who had many *amours* both before and after marriage. As a teenager during his minority he was 'fed' a succession of lovers by those in power who saw political advantage in encouraging his sexual intrigues with their relatives. His first recorded affair was in 1492 with Marion Boyd, niece of Archibald Douglas, Earl of Angus, a close confidant and card-playing companion of the king. The affair was to last three years, during which the Earl of Angus rose high in royal favour (he was made Chancellor in 1493) and Marion bore King James his first two illegitimate children: Alexander Stewart, who would be appointed Archbishop of St Andrews at the age of eleven, and a daughter, Catherine. The affair came to an end in 1495, when the king married Marion off to someone else.

The second royal mistress was Margaret Drummond, daughter of the first Lord Drummond, one of the royal justiciars. This affair lasted for two years. King James made the liaison public by installing her in Stirling Castle, where she bore him a daughter also named Margaret, but in 1497 he sent her back home to her father, suitably rewarded. There is a story that the two were secretly married and that Margaret and her sisters were deliberately poisoned in 1502 by those who wanted the path cleared for an alliance with the House of Tudor, but this seems to have been no more than a legend invented by the Drummond family long after her death.

Margaret Drummond was succeeded in 1498 by the third and most durable of the king's lovers – Janet Kennedy, daughter of John, Lord Kennedy, and mistress of Archibald, fifth Earl of Angus; indeed, there are indications that Angus fell out of favour with the king over Janet – he was dismissed as Chancellor and put under house arrest on the Isle of Bute for ten years. In 1501 Janet bore the king a son, James, Earl of Moray. The king's womanising continued after his marriage in 1503: between 1508 and 1512 royal gifts were showered on the last of his public mistresses, Isabel Stewart, daughter of James, Earl of Buchan, who bore him a daughter, Janet.

These alliances, despite their production of a number of illegitimate offspring, were only a sideline: the important political question was – whom should the king marry?

Diplomatic efforts to find a suitable bride for James IV had begun as early as October 1474, when James was only a year old and his father, James III, had negotiated a marriage contract for the little prince with Cecilia, daughter of King Edward IV of England; this fell through during the crisis of 1482, when England invaded Scotland and James III was imprisoned by his nobles in Edinburgh Castle. Another English bride for the boy was negotiated in 1484 with Richard III of England – Anne de la Pole, one of Richard's nieces; but Richard's defeat and death at the Battle of Bosworth in the following year put paid to that scheme, too.

Given the anti-English sentiment of the government which seized power in Scotland after James III's death in 1488, an English marriage alliance was out of the question. In 1492 an embassy was sent to France to seek both a treaty and a bride; other diplomatic overtures were made for alliances with Spain and the Low Countries, but without success.

Meanwhile, relations with England were uncomfortable, to say the least. In 1495 Scotland not only harboured but welcomed the pretender Perkin Warbeck – who claimed to be the younger of the two murdered 'Princes in the Tower', the sons of Edward IV – as 'Prince Richard of England'. King James even gave Perkin a daughter of the Earl of Huntly as a bride. Poor, deluded Perkin Warbeck was used as a pawn in the international rivalries of the 1490s as Henry VII struggled to consolidate the Tudor hold on the English throne against a Yorkist comeback; Scotland's token espousal of Warbeck's 'cause' was no more than a cynical manoeuvre in James IV's diplomatic and military offensive against England.

The outcome, paradoxically, was a royal English bride for King James after all. James used Warbeck as an excuse to raise the stakes in the war of attrition with England; in September 1496 he assembled an army and all his heavy artillery and moved into England, where he spent a fortnight plundering in Northumberland. When an English army started mustering at Newcastle, James withdrew, having made his point.[1] Henry VII responded by declaring war on Scotland; but before he could invade he was faced with a crisis – an armed insurrection of men from Cornwall and Devon who were marching on London at alarming speed. Henry had to divert his forces to deal with the threat, which he did near Guildford in Surrey, only thirty-two kilometres from London. James took advantage of Henry's discomfiture by going on the attack again. In 1497 he trundled all his artillery (including the mighty Mons Meg) to the border, where he bombarded Norham Castle for a week before returning home. To James's disappointment, the bombardment had no effect on the castle's defences.

It had been a war of gestures as much as anything else. But James IV of Scotland had proved himself as a bold (and very popular) warrior-king who was not afraid to take on the military might of England, and who had expunged the shame of the humiliation of 1482. He could claim to have fought Henry VII of England to a frustrated standstill, and had taken his place at the top table of European diplomacy. Henry VII was now prepared to negotiate a treaty which would include the marriage of his eldest daughter Margaret to James IV, King of Scots, with a dowry of £10,000 sterling (about £35,000 Scots).

The Marriage of the Thistle and the Rose (8 August 1503)

> *The good policy of Henry VII bore fruit after a hundred years had passed away; and in consequence of the marriage of James IV and the Princess Margaret, an end was put to all future national wars, by their great-grandson, James VI of Scotland and I of England, becoming King of the whole island of Great Britain.*
> TALES OF A GRANDFATHER, CHAPTER XXIII

The magnificent hammer-beam roof of the Great Hall of Edinburgh Castle, which was completed by James in time for his marriage, rests on a series of carved stone corbels. Some of them carry the royal cipher of James IV – 'IR4', for *Iacobus Rex quartus*; one of them depicts a bowl in which a rose nestles between two thistles – symbols of the marriage on 8 August 1503 of James IV of Scotland to Margaret Tudor,

---

1   Perkin Warbeck was left to his fate; he was captured in Hampshire in 1497 and executed at Tyburn in 1499.

daughter of Henry VII of England.[1] Contemporaries called it the Marriage of the Thistle and the Rose, which had been sealed by a Treaty of Perpetual Peace between the two nations in 1502. This was a fateful moment in Anglo–Scottish relations, for although nothing had been further from the minds of the treaty-makers at the time, it was eventually to lead to the union of the two crowns exactly a century later, when a great-grandson of the marriage, James VI of Scotland, became James I of England as well in 1603 (see Chapter 21).

The wedding occasioned what has been called the greatest display of pomp and pageantry in the annals of pre-Reformation Scotland. It took place at Holyrood, expensively refurbished for the occasion, and the king did not stint on expenditure – the cost was a prodigious £6,125.4s.6d. The music for the Chapel Royal was provided by Robert Carver, now recognised as one of the greatest composers of masses and motets in his day. The festivities went on for five days with a succession of banquets, pageants, dancing and merry-making, and the courtyard of Holyrood Palace rang to the sounds of jousting and tilting in a tournament which lasted for three days.

The marriage failed to secure more than a brief honeymoon peace with England; it also very nearly failed to produce a son who could inherit the Stewart throne. James IV's first legitimate child, another James, was born in February 1507. Both queen and infant were very ill, and James IV set off to make an arduous eight-day pilgrimage on foot to the shrine of St Ninian at Whithorn, in Galloway, 190 kilometres from Edinburgh; even this spectacular act of piety failed to save the life of the child, who died a year later. In 1508 the queen gave birth to a daughter who died shortly afterwards. In 1509 she had a second son who was christened Arthur, but he too died the following year. At last, on 10 April 1512, another son – again named James – was born. He would survive to become James V, but only with difficulty.[2]

---

1   The use of the thistle as the national emblem of Scotland is very old, but no one knows precisely how old. A thistle was first stamped on Scottish coinage by James III in 1470 – perhaps in response to the white and red rose emblems of the warring houses in England's 'Wars of the Roses'. The Scottish emblem was self-consciously aggressive, reinforced by the royal chivalric motto *Nemo me impune lacessit* – 'Let none assail me with impunity'. One tradition suggests that the thistle earned a special place in history when marauding vikings on a surprise night attack accidentally trod on the prickly plants and cried out in pain, thus giving the game away. Naturally, I would like to think this is true!

2   There was to be a second daughter, who died early in 1513; and in the summer of 1513 the queen was pregnant again: seven months after the Battle of Flodden, she gave birth to a boy, Alexander, Duke of Ross, who lived for only two years.

The Renaissance prince

An experiment made under his direction, shows at least the interest which James took in science, although he used a whimsical mode of gratifying his curiosity. Being desirous to know what was the primitive or original language, he caused a deaf and dumb woman to be transported to the solitary island of Inchkeith, with two infant children, devising thus to discover what language they would talk when they came to the age of speech. A Scottish historian [Robert Lindsay of Pitscottie], who tells the story, adds, with great simplicity, 'Some say they spoke good Hebrew; for my part I know not, but from report.' It is more likely they would scream like their dumb nurse, or bleat like the goats and sheep on the island.

TALES OF A GRANDFATHER, CHAPTER XXIII

This entertaining anecdote from Lindsay of Pitscottie (in *The Historie and Chronicles of Scotland*), which he dated to 1493, is surely apocryphal: a similar experiment is attributed to the Emperor Frederick II in the thirteenth century. But it is typical of the extraordinary eruption of intellectual curiosity and experimentation which is known, loosely but usefully, as the Renaissance. But just what is, or was, 'the Renaissance'? Roger Mason, lecturer in Scottish History at St Andrews University, says:

Literally, the Renaissance means 'a rebirth'. What was being reborn, initially in Italy and then in France and in northern Europe more generally, was an awareness of the classical literature of Rome and Greece. In the course of the fifteenth century and into the sixteenth century, more and more classical Roman and Greek writings were being rediscovered and studied, over and over again, and this new learning changed people's perceptions, not only of the ancient but also of the contemporary world. It had an enormous impact in almost every dimension of the cultural and political life of fifteenth- and sixteenth-century Europe. It was hugely significant.

It is impossible to be precise about when the Renaissance started in Scotland, or, for that matter, when it ended. The Renaissance was a process rather than an event: a gradual move forward from the 'medieval mode' of the Middle Ages, which influenced all aspects of intellectual life in different ways and at different times – ideas in philosophy, education, literature, art, science, technology, architecture and, just as significantly, politics and the governance of nations.

In Scotland, the reign of James IV represents the fullest flowering of Renaissance ideas – the Golden Age of the Stewart monarchy – and James himself is cast as the quintessential Renaissance prince. To the poet and civil servant Sir David Lindsay of the Mount, author of the play *Ane Plesant Satyre of the Thrie Estaites* (1540), James IV was 'the glory of princely governing' – popular, vigorous and enlightened. The outstanding Dutch scholar and humanist Desiderius Erasmus, who tutored James's brilliant illegitimate son Alexander, had nothing but praise for the king:

> *He had wonderful powers of mind, an astonishing knowledge of everything, an unconquerable magnanimity and the most abundant generosity.*

Don Pedro de Ayala, the Spanish ambassador to London who spent a year in Scotland in 1496–97, wrote an account of his impressions of the country in a long despatch to King Ferdinand and Queen Isabella. His description of James IV, who had clearly made a great impression on him, portrayed him as the epitome of the intelligent, energetic, charismatic Renaissance prince:

> *He is courageous, even more so than a king should be. I have seen him often undertake most dangerous things in the last wars … He is not a good captain, because he begins to fight before he has given his orders. He said to me that his subjects serve him with their persons and goods, in just and unjust quarrels, exactly as he likes, and that, therefore, he does not think it right to begin any warlike undertaking without being himself the first in danger. His deeds are as good as his words. For this reason, and because he is a very humane prince, he is much loved.*

James kept a large and colourful court which conversed in at least six languages – an immensely learned, cosmopolitan and expensive household which cost a great deal of money to sustain as it moved around Scotland. He was fond of organising impressive jousting tournaments, and kept a menagerie of lions and other exotic wild beasts. It was all part of the Renaissance ideal of conspicuous royal expenditure. Early in the sixteenth century one of James's court poets, William

Dunbar, addressed a complaint to the king ('Schir, Ye have Mony Servitouris') in which he described the bustling crowd of people with whom James surrounded himself:

> *Schir [Sir], ye have mony servitouris,*
> *And officiaris [officials] of dyvers curis [responsibilities]:*
> *Kirkmen, courtmen and craftsmen fyne,*
> *Doctouris in jure [law] and medicyne,*
> *Divinouris, rethoris [rhetoricians] and philosophouris,*
> *Astrologis, artists and oratouris,*
> *Men of armes and valeyeand knychtis [valiant knights]*
> *And mony other gudlie wychtis [goodly people],*
> *Musicians, mentralis [minstrels] and mirrie singaris,*
> *Chevalours, cawandaris [hurlers] and flingaris [flingers],*
> *Cunyouris [coin-makers], carvouris and carpentaris,*
> *Beildaris [builders] of barkis [boats] and ballingaris [ships],*
> *Masounis lyand [masons lying] upon the land,*
> *And schipwrichtis hewand [hewing] upone the strand,*
> *Glasing wrichtis [glaziers], goldsmythis and lapidaris [jewellers],*
> *Printouris, payntouris and potingaris [apothecaries] . . .*

One of James IV's more eccentric court familiars was the Italian scholar and abbot of Tongland in Galloway, John Damian de Falcusis – the 'French leech', as he was called. He was given a laboratory in Stirling Castle in which he carried out researches in alchemy in an attempt to find the 'quintessence' – the elixir of life – and tried to change base metal into gold. He also experimented with aeronautics. His most celebrated exploit, in September 1507, was an attempt to fly from the battlements of Stirling Castle all the way to France on a huge pair of home-made wings. The experiment was a bit of a fiasco. Damian was said to have been attacked by flocks of outraged birds which tore at his feathers during his brief flight; instead of soaring upwards he plummeted to earth and landed in a dung-heap. Fortunately he suffered only a broken leg, and excused his failure on the grounds that his wings, which should have been made only of eagles' feathers, included some from hens, which 'covet the myddying [midden] and not the skyies'. William Dunbar, who bitterly resented Damian's intimacy with the king, wrote a sneering account of the adventure, entitled 'A Ballat of the Abbot of Tungland', and the failed flight is regularly re-enacted at Stirling for the entertainment of tourists. But lying behind the failure was the intense intellectual excitement of the time: Damian knew all about Leonardo da Vinci and his experimental work in aeronautics, and was trying it out for himself in the true, questing spirit of the Renaissance.

Dunbar, a dazzling wordsmith, was one of the Scottish 'makars' (poets) whom the king rewarded generously (although Dunbar was always complaining about his lack of preferment). James IV's patronage of the arts encouraged a creative outburst in vernacular literature – Dunbar, in his 'Lament for the Makars', mourned the death of more than twenty Scottish poets, most of whose work has not survived.

Apart from constantly pestering the king for more money, Dunbar satirised the more earthy side of court and human life with Rabelaisian humour. He could be witty and melancholy by turns, grotesque and moving, dignified and outrageous. One of his most delightful poems is a long, bawdy satire called 'The Treatise of the Twa Merrit Wemen and the Wedo', in which he exposes the hypocrisies of conventional married life and the failings of men to meet the desires of women.

Literature was central to the Renaissance, and Dunbar was the great poet of the Scottish Renaissance. Ronnie Jack, Professor of Scottish and Medieval Literature at Edinburgh University, says:

> Dunbar was the master craftsman of his age, a man of superb literary virtuosity. You need only listen to the clashing syllables and tolling rhymes of 'Ane Ballat of Our Lady', his hymn to the Virgin Mary, to recognise his extraordinary vernacular ability. In his 'Lament for the Makars' he speaks in simple, understated tones, while every stanza ends with a phrase which tolls like a funeral knell: timor mortis perturbat me – 'the fear of death distresses me'. They are both masterpieces, each in its very different way.

Before Dunbar came Robert Henryson (c.1430–c.1500), a learned Dunfermline schoolmaster and public notary who was one of the greatest of Scotland's early poets. He had a tremendous range, encompassing animal fables, moralities, lyrics, satires and epics like *The Testament of Cresseid* (a supplement to Chaucer's *Troilus and Criseyde*) and a reworking of the classical legend of Orpheus and Eurydice. After Dunbar came the churchman Gavin Douglas, a younger son of Archibald 'Bell-the-Cat' Douglas, fifth Earl of Angus; Gavin Douglas is best known for his translation of Virgil's *Aeneid* into Scots verse. He dedicated to King James an erudite, almost encyclopaedic poem, 'The Palice of Honoure', which explored in an allegorical framework the duties of a Renaissance courtier. After James IV's death, Douglas became Bishop of Dunkeld and tutor to the young James V (see Chapter 18).

In addition to supporting the writers at his court, James IV was involved in setting up the first printing works in Scotland. In 1507 he granted a patent to two Edinburgh burgesses, Walter Chepman and Andrew Myllar, to import and establish a printing press in the Cowgate. It was originally intended for official books – the masterpiece of their press was the *Aberdeen Breviary* and its lives of eighty-one Scottish saints (printed at the instigation of Bishop Elphinstone) – but it also produced popular reading such as Blind Harry's *The Wallace* and poems by Henryson and Dunbar, as well as Gavin Douglas's translation of the *Aeneid* just a few days before the fatal field of Flodden (see below) – a unique collection of early Scots poetry.

Education was another subject in which King James took a keen interest. He tried to extend the benefits of education in order to create a more broadly-based educated class for the future. In 1496 his parliament passed Scotland's first compulsory 'education act': all his barons and freeholders of substance were ordered to put their eldest sons to grammar school from the age of eight or nine, to remain there until they had acquired a basic education and mastered Latin, and then to spend three years studying art and law – on pain of a £20 penalty. He sent his own illegitimate sons Alexander and James to study at Padua, and later at Siena under Erasmus.

Opportunities for higher education were widened with the foundation in 1495 of King's College in Aberdeen, created by Bishop William Elphinstone with the king's support; it had a pioneering foundation for teaching medicine. James took a great personal interest in medicine and frequently looked in on surgical operations; in 1506 he granted a royal charter to a college of surgeons which had just been instituted by Edinburgh's town council.

Roger Mason says:

> The Scots were very cosmopolitan and very willing to travel abroad to be educated; and just as importantly, many of them came back, either to serve in the Scottish court, to serve in the ecclesiastical bureaucracy or to teach at the Scottish universities themselves. There is no reason to think that Scottish intellectual education institutions were on the periphery of Europe in anything other than a geographical sense. These institutions were plugged in, in a very real sense, to European learning, and the

Scottish intelligentsia was a very cosmopolitan one. There is plenty of evidence that Scottish libraries were full of the latest works of Continental learning; Scots had no trouble in ordering books from the Continent and having them brought home to Scotland.

King James was also much given to building at vast expense, as we have seen: in addition to the Great Halls of the castles in Stirling and Edinburgh he initiated a programme of palace-building in all the principal royal residences in his kingdom. Every area of national activity came under his energetic scrutiny. Lawlessness and disorder were preoccupations, and he made strenuous efforts to deal with them, attending circuit courts ('justice ayres') and meting out summary justice for serious crimes. In his reign, too, the concept of a central court of justice was developed, which was later to evolve into the Court of Session. James IV was very much the king who brought justice and peace to his country.

The Great Michael: *a navy for Scotland*

Traditionally, Henry VIII of England is regarded as 'the Father of the Royal Navy'; but James IV of Scotland has every claim to be considered for that title, too. He was quick to recognise the importance of having a fleet of warships available for the protection of his realm, and during his reign he built or bought or hired or seized for the crown no fewer than thirty-eight vessels.

In his father's lifetime James had seen the menace of an English fleet in action against Scotland. In 1481 John, Lord Howard, had raided ports in the Firth of Forth, only to be beaten off by the gallant Captain Andrew Wood of Largo in his *Yellow Carvel*. In the following summer the invasion army which the Earl of Gloucester and James III's perfidious brother the Duke of Albany brought to Scotland was supported by a sizeable fleet, led by the massive *Grace Dieu*, which was able to sail unopposed into Leith.

These attacks had highlighted the vulnerability of Scotland's capital to attacks by sea as well as by land. In 1491 parliament agreed to build a fortress on the island rock of Inchgarvie, at the narrows of the Firth of Forth by Queensferry. Soon after the turn of the century, James IV made the construction of a Royal Scottish Navy a principal policy objective – at huge cost to the exchequer. He built two new naval dockyards on the Forth – at Newhaven and, nineteen kilometres further upriver, near Stirling, at Pool of Airth – which were capable of accommodating the largest ships. He imported shipwrights from France and shipped in two massive timber keels which could not be procured in Scotland.

The first of these keels was used for the pride of James's early fleet, the *Margaret*, named after the king's bride and launched from a new dock in Leith in June 1506. She was a very large ship indeed (five or six hundred tons), took two years to build and cost some £8,000 – more than a quarter of the king's annual income. Her main armament consisted of one large cannon and four smaller guns called 'falcons'. But James's most memorable achievement was his flagship, the *Great Michael*, which took four years to build under the supervision of French shipwrights and was launched from Newhaven in October 1511.

The *Great Michael* was the largest and most powerful warship afloat at the time. She was between forty-five and fifty-five metres long (by comparison, Nelson's *Victory* is fifty-six metres long), weighed about a thousand tons and cost a staggering total of about £30,000. She was armed with twelve bronze cannon on either side and three massive 'basilisks', one for'ard and two aft, and carried a crew of three hundred. According to Lindsay of Pitscottie she was so large and took so much timber that she 'wasted all the wood in Fife, which was oakwood'.

In the course of his reign James IV spent something like £100,000 – a colossal sum for those days – in building and equipping a navy in what became an arms race with England (Henry VIII launched his ill-fated *Mary Rose* in 1509 to match James's *Margaret*, and his *Great Harry* in 1512 to match the *Great Michael*). How much good such conspicuous naval expenditure did for Scotland is debatable; but it helped to reinforce the prestige of the Scottish crown on the international stage, and to add lustre to the persona of James IV as a great warrior-king.

The Battle of Flodden (9 September 1513)

> Tradition, legend, tune and song,
> Shall many an age that wail prolong:
> Still from the sire the son shall hear
> Of the stern strife, and carnage drear,
> Of Flodden's fatal field,
> Where shivered was fair Scotland's spear,
> And broken was her shield.
> WALTER SCOTT, MARMION, CANTO VI

A dignified monument just off the B6353 near the village of Branxton marks the site of this 'calamitous event in Scottish history' – the Battle of Flodden. From a roadside carpark a path leads upwards to a neat enclosure which surrounds the monument, a stone cross on a granite plinth with the simple inscription:

> *FLODDEN*
> *1513*
> *TO THE BRAVE OF BOTH NATIONS*
> *ERECTED 1910*

A display board gives a clear interpretation of the battle which was fought in the marshy valley below. Standing in the centre of what was the English position, looking across to the Scottish position on the eminence of Branxton Hill, it is not difficult to imagine the dreadful carnage of that day on 9 September 1513; but the real tragedy of Flodden, apart from the death of James IV and the other appalling losses involved, was that it was a battle which need not, and should not, have happened.

How *did* it happen, then? The answer to that lies buried in the bewilderingly complicated political situation of Europe at the time. The fragile Treaty of Perpetual Peace which had been signed in 1502 as part of James's marriage contract with Margaret Tudor did not last after the death of her pacific father, Henry VII, in 1509, and the accession of her bellicose brother, Henry VIII. The key problem was the growing and disproportionate strength of France under Louis XII, and of Spain under Ferdinand and Isabella, which caused acute concern in every other chancellery in Europe. Scotland, allied by marriage and treaty to England, was still deeply involved in an even longer-standing alliance with France: the 'Auld Alliance' – not that it had ever done Scotland much good.

In 1511, Henry VIII of England joined a 'Holy League' against France formed by Ferdinand and Isabella of Spain, Pope Julius II and Venice. To counter this threat, Louis XII of France prevailed upon James IV to renew the 'Auld Alliance' and for each to come to the other's aid if one were attacked.

In May 1513 Henry VIII invaded France, and King Louis invoked the terms of the Scottish alliance, sending an envoy with money, arms and experienced captains to help James to train a Scottish army. James probably did not want war – after all, he was married to Henry's sister, Margaret Tudor, and peace had brought prosperity. But he must have been tempted by the chance to demonstrate Scotland's importance in the international power-politics of the day. His sense of chivalry was also aroused by the gift of a gold-and-turquoise ring from the Queen of France and a letter calling him her champion and appealing to him to 'take but three paces into English ground and break a lance for my sake'. It was not meant to be a full-blown invasion of England but a diversionary tactic to take the pressure off France. James also lent his fleet, including the *Great Michael*, which Scotland would never see again.[1]

On 26 July 1513 James IV, in accordance with his concept of chivalric conduct, sent envoys to Henry VIII giving notice of his intention to invade Northumberland. To counter the Scottish threat during his absence in France, Henry entrusted his northern command to the veteran Thomas Howard, Earl of Surrey; he was seventy years old, and a highly experienced professional military commander. Compared with the Earl of Surrey, James was a military amateur. What is more, he had no particular strategy except to create a disturbance in the north of England.

The army which James mustered was the best-equipped ever to have invaded England, and numbered at least twenty-five thousand men. Some 7,500 Highlanders were by his side, as his ability to speak Gaelic had made him genuinely popular among them, and he had also mustered the flower of his nobility, including fifteen earls, twenty barons and hundreds of knights.

On 22 August, after Henry VIII had rejected an ultimatum from James, the Scottish army crossed the Tweed at Coldstream and encamped on English soil. James had brought an enormous artillery train: seventeen heavy siege-guns pulled by 363 oxen and seven horses with ninety-five drivers (and 216 labourers to clear a route across the moors with picks and spades), two culverins, four sakers and six demi-culverins. His first action was to lay siege to Norham Castle on the Tweed; five days later his cannon pounded it into surrender. The Scots now turned their attention to nearby Etal Castle, which surrendered at once, and Ford Castle, where King James stayed for a few days (legend would later claim that he wasted time there on a dalliance with the daughter of the lady of the castle, Lady Heron).

By 4 September the Earl of Surrey had assembled his army at

---

1 The *Great Michael* had an inglorious end. In 1514, after James IV's death, she was sold to the French for forty thousand francs (about £18,000 Scots). She never saw action, and rotted away in harbour in Brest.

Alnwick, nineteen kilometres away. It was inferior in numbers to that of the Scots – some twenty thousand men, perhaps – but it included 1,200 marines from the English fleet which had been brought to him by his eldest son Lord Thomas Howard, Admiral of England, and twenty-two artillery pieces.

Surrey was concerned that the Scottish army, having created the required diversion, would slip back into Scotland without giving battle. He appealed to King James's well-known sense of chivalry and challenged him to fight by 9 September at the latest. James accepted the challenge, but moved his troops to Flodden Edge, an impregnable feature rising above the bleak and windswept Millfield plain to a height of about 150 metres, and fairly steep-sided to the north and east. It was a natural fortress, and Surrey realised that it could not be stormed from the south. He now sent a herald with another challenge, for James to leave Flodden Edge and join battle on more 'indifferent' ground; James refused, retorting haughtily that 'It ill befits an earl to tell a king what to do.'

On 8 September, therefore, the Earl of Surrey struck camp at Wooler and crossed the River Till, then marched north-eastwards in a sweeping arc past Doddington and round the Scottish flank, bringing him to the north of the Scottish position. It was an audacious move and seems to have caused some indecision in the Scottish camp: next morning, when Surrey recrossed the Till at Twizel Bridge to take up position on Piper's Hill, the Scots made no attempt to interfere when the English were at their most vulnerable. Instead, they redeployed along the ridge of Branxton Hill and waited while the English grouped into battle formation on the other side of the low-lying stretch of boggy ground between the two armies.

On the Scottish side, the king was in the centre; to his left was a division led by the earls of Crawford, Erroll and Montrose with, farther out, the Borders division led by the Earl of Huntly and Lord Home. On the right of the Scots line were the Highland division led by the earls of Lennox and Argyll. The Earl of Bothwell kept a division in reserve at the rear.

At 4 p.m. the battle began with a concentrated artillery exchange. The Scottish gunners were less experienced than their English counterparts and were unable to depress their guns sufficiently, while the English cannonade, despite having to be fired uphill, was devastatingly effective. Soon the Scottish guns fell silent and the English cannon methodically raked the ranks of standing Scottish spearsmen.

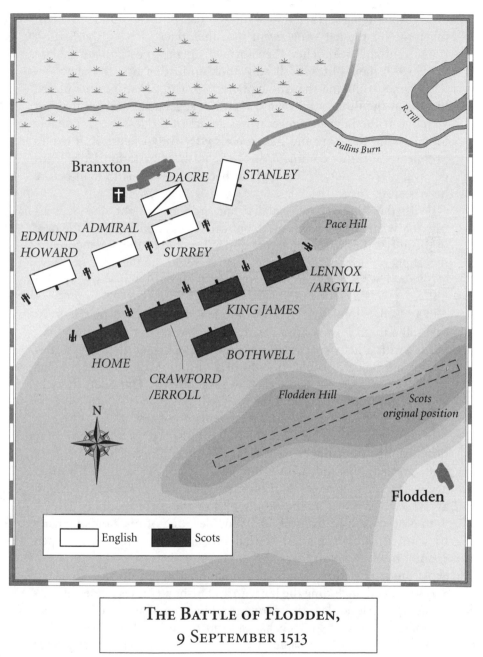

Branxton

DACRE   STANLEY

EDMUND   ADMIRAL
HOWARD   SURREY

Pace Hill

LENNOX
/ARGYLL

KING JAMES

HOME   BOTHWELL

CRAWFORD
/ERROLL   Flodden Hill   Scots
                                        original position

N

Flodden

English   Scots

THE BATTLE OF FLODDEN,
9 SEPTEMBER 1513

To avoid being scythed down, the Scottish Borderers under the Earl of Home on the left wing swept into the attack, driving the English right from the field. They then formed up in a position to menace the English flank but, inexplicably, took no further part in the action. King James, thinking that the battle was practically won, now placed himself at the head of his own division of spearsmen and led them in a charge at the English centre. It was an act of reckless, unpardonable folly, leaving his army and his generals effectively leaderless: it makes prescient the earlier comment by the Spanish ambassador, Don Pedro de Ayala: 'He is not a good captain, because he begins to fight before he has given his orders.'

With the king in the lead like an ordinary knight, the Scottish infantry went charging downhill, but came to a muddy halt at the base of the hill. With their momentum gone, they had to start lumbering up the slippery slopes towards the English ranks in the face of heavy artillery fire. And now another weapon came into play – the English bill.

The Scots were armed with immensely long, 7.3-metre Swiss pikes; the English were armed with much shorter 2.4-metre bills (halberds), with a hefty spearhead and an axe-like blade. At close quarters the English halberds could chop the heads off the Scottish pikes, leaving the Scots defenceless. Soon they were encircled. The Scottish right under Lennox and Argyll and the reserve division under Bothwell were scattered by a surprise cavalry attack from the flank.

King James and his beleaguered infantry divisions were now doomed, but they fought on with desperate courage. There is a story that, towards the end of that bitter day, the king launched himself against the banner of the Earl of Surrey and fell only a spear's-length away, scythed down by the deadly bills of the earl's retainers. He fell with a deep gash in his neck and shoulder, one of his hands hanging by a shred of skin; his last wound was an arrow through his open mouth, fired at close range.

At dusk, after three hours of furious fighting, up to five thousand Scots lay dead, including the king, an archbishop (James's eldest illegitimate son, Alexander, the young Archbishop of St Andrews), two bishops, eleven earls, fifteen barons and three hundred knights. The English losses were estimated at 1,700 men. Surrey was rewarded for his victory with the dukedom of Norfolk.

The body of James IV was so mutilated that it was not recognised until the following day. Some say it was never recognised, and that the king had been spirited away to safety by four noble horsemen who

rode off with him into the realms of legend and everlasting hope.[1]
Steve Boardman says:

> *Flodden represents, in the minds at least of subsequent historians,*
> *a watershed in the history of late medieval Scotland, in that it*
> *seems to bring to an end the most successful kingship, the most*
> *successful reign, of the late medieval period. James IV stands as*
> *the culmination of Stewart kingship, which had started off in*
> *such shaky fashion in 1371. He was a remarkably confident*
> *figure, who presided over something which may be regarded as*
> *a Renaissance court. And the disaster at Flodden, with the king*
> *and so many of his noblemen and his prelates dying, is taken as*
> *emblematic of a failure of that type of Scottish self-confidence in*
> *government and its place in Europe.*

Michael Lynch says:

> *James IV led his army into Flodden. He had done this a number*
> *of times before. In contrast to his father who had pursued a policy*
> *of coming to terms with England, James had deliberately staged*
> *confrontations at the frontier: from the late 1480s onwards, Mons*
> *Meg and other big cannons were trundled down to the English*
> *border almost every year – not along the coast road but over the*
> *Lammermuirs, fifty to seventy miles down to the English castles*
> *at Norham and Wark which were very vulnerable. There they*
> *loosed off perhaps only a dozen rounds, because it took at least*
> *forty-five minutes to reload these things. Then they were trundled*
> *back again. This was a king defending his realm! So in one sense*
> *Flodden was simply one of these border raids which went wrong:*
> *the battle itself was not intended – it was a mistake. It was also*

---

1   In reality, the king's body came to an obscenely humiliating end. It was taken to Berwick-
upon-Tweed, where it was embalmed and sent down to Durham and then York. There it
was encased in lead and despatched to London, and later placed in the monastery of Sheen
in Surrey. Henry VIII's queen, Catherine of Aragon, sent the dead king's blood-drenched
surcoat to her husband in France, adding that she would have liked to send the head as well.
After the Dissolution of the Monasteries in the sixteenth century the body was dumped in
a lumber-room; here the head was cut off by some workmen and used as a football. Later
it came into the possession of Lancelot Young, Queen Elizabeth's master-glazier, who kept
it as a curio and conversation-piece in his house in the City of London. It was eventually
thrown into a grave in the churchyard of St Michael's Church in Wood Street (now the site
of an insurance company building).

a mistake because the portable cannon, James's best firepower, were on his fleet in France, helping the King of France. James was not ready for a pitched battle. Flodden was a battle which should never have taken place.

At Flodden, it is said, Scotland 'lost a civilisation and gained a song' – a lament known as 'The Flow'rs o' the Forest':

I've heard of a liltin' at the ewe-milkin',
Lasses a-liltin' before dawn o' day.
Now there's a moanin' on ilka [each] green loanin' [pasture] –
The Flow'rs o' the Forest are a' wede away [all carried off].[1]

Perhaps Flodden showed the Scottish people that they could never again expect to defeat their mightier neighbour. Flodden was the climax of two centuries of war with England. The tragic loss of the king and much of the nation's manhood should have meant an end to battle; unbelievably, even after two centuries of war, the fight was far from over.

---

1   The words of 'The Flow'rs o' the Forest' were written long after the event by Miss Jean Elliot (1727–1805), the sister of Sir Gilbert Elliot of Minto, in Roxburghshire. They were composed around the middle of the eighteenth century, and first published, anonymously, in 1769. The melody is much older, and may even predate Flodden; the oldest extant tune-variant, in the Skene MS (c.1630), was first published in 1838.

Chapter 18

JAMES V (r.1513–42)

Margaret, the Queen Dowager, became Regent of Scotland, and guardian of the young King, James V, who, as had been too often the case on former similar occasions, ascended the throne when a child of not two years old.

TALES OF A GRANDFATHER, CHAPTER XXV

On Twelfth Night (5 January) in the year 1540 King James V and his French queen, Marie de Guise, accompanied by the whole court and council, attended the première of a remarkable morality play in Linlithgow Palace, midway between the royal strongholds of Edinburgh and Stirling. The event was designed to celebrate the formal opening of the new royal apartments in the palace. The king had been born there twenty-eight years previously, in 1512; his daughter Mary, the future Queen of Scots, would be born there in two years' time, in 1542.

James V was the greatest royal patron of architecture of all the Stewart monarchs. He transformed the physical environment of the Stewart court on a scale which even his father, James IV, had never achieved with his own extensive programme of royal works. James V drew his ideas directly from the Renaissance opulence of the French court, and took a close interest in the transformation he ordered for the palaces at Holyrood, Linlithgow, Falkland and Stirling. New façades were added to the existing structures of James IV and enriched with Renaissance ornament by French craftsmen – especially at Falkland Palace in Fife, the favourite 'hunting-palace' of the Stewarts, which has been described as 'a display of Renaissance architecture without parallel in the British Isles'.

Today, Linlithgow Palace is a magnificent, roofless ruin in the care of Historic Scotland; it was burned by the Duke of Cumberland's Hanoverian troops in 1746 as the '45 dragged to its dismal conclusion at Culloden (see Chapter 28). Even as a shell it is still an extraordinarily impressive place, and enough remains to show the scale and skill of James V's renovations. He added significantly to the existing buildings, creating a great, dramatic courtyard bounded by four ranges, with a tower at each corner. In the centre of the courtyard he erected an elaborate Gothic fountain – 'the King's Fountain', thought to have been a wedding gift to his second wife, Marie de Guise. He created a new main entry on the south side facing the town, decorated with armorial carvings of the insignia of the four orders of knighthood to which he belonged: the Garter of England, the Thistle of Scotland, the Fleece of the Holy Roman Empire and St Michael of France. Marie de Guise diplomatically declared Linlithgow Palace to be the most princely home she had ever looked upon outside the châteaux of the Loire. Alas, none of the floors of the queen's apartments survives.

It was in this 'princely home' that the royal theatrical première was held in 1540. The play was entitled, in full, *Ane Plesant Satyre of the Thrie Estaites in Commendation of Vertew and Vituperation of Vyce* – in short, *The Thrie Estaites* – and had been written by the poet and civil servant Sir David Lindsay of the Mount (c.1486–1555). It was an extremely lengthy occasion: the play took nothing short of eight hours to perform, and was a sprawling, rip-roaring attack on the abuses of power, wealth and morality in the three estates (the lords spiritual and temporal, and the burgesses) of sixteenth-century Scotland, full of biting invective and coarse humour. The chief character was a representative of the common people, the subversive John the Commonweal. King James greatly enjoyed the play's acid wit and its forceful plea for the rights of the common man; but above all (according to the French ambassador, who saw the performance) he enjoyed its sardonic lampooning of 'the noughtines in Religion, the presumpcioun of Bisshops . . . and mysusing of Priests':

> Our Bishops, with their lovely vestments white,
> They flow in riches, royally, and delight,
> Like paradise are their palaces and places,
> And lack no pleasure from the fairest faces.
> Also, these Prelates have great prerogatives.

For why? They may even leave their wives,
Without any correction or damnage,
Then take another wanton, without marriage.[1]

At the end of the performance the king called upon the Bishop of Glasgow (his Chancellor) and all the other bishops, 'exhorting them to reform their fashions and manners of living, saying that unless they did so he would send six of the proudest unto his uncle of England [Henry VIII]'. James's humour (if humour it was) was grim: to the Scottish Church in 1540, Henry VIII, arch-enemy of the Pope, was a nightmare bogeyman.

David Lindsay of the Mount came from a family of landed gentry and had attended James IV's court as a youth; he acted in a play performed for the king in 1511, and early in 1513, not long before Flodden, he was appointed an usher to the baby Prince James. After James IV's death, Lindsay found himself charged with the task of amusing the baby king, carrying him around on his back during the day and comforting him in bed at night:

When thou was young I bore thee in my arme
Full tenderlie, till thou began to gang [walk];
And in my bed oft happed [wrapped] thee full warm
And, lute in hand, sine [then] sweetly to thee sang.[2]

---

1 *The Thrie Estaites* was the smash-hit of the 1948 Edinburgh International Festival, in a vigorous and racy modernised version by the Edinburgh dramatist Robert Kemp; it starred the great Glasgow actor Duncan Macrae, wonderfully ingratiating as Flatterie, while a young Stanley Baxter made his professional stage debut with a one-line part as Divine Correctioun's Varlet. The musical score was composed by Cedric Thorpe Davie. It was spectacularly staged by Sir Tyrone Guthrie in the Assembly Hall on the Mound, the home of the General Assembly of the Church of Scotland (and the temporary home of the new Scottish Parliament in 1999).

2 In 1522 David Lindsay married Janet Douglas, the king's seamstress, and in 1524 he inherited his ancestral estate, The Mount, near Cupar in Fife. When the king assumed personal rule in 1528, Lindsay was employed as a royal herald for an annual salary of £20; in 1542 he was knighted and appointed Lyon King at Arms, and undertook many diplomatic missions to Denmark, France and England. His other principal literary achievements were *The Dreme* (1528), an allegorical lament on the condition of Scotland and an exhortation to the young king, his own master at last; *The Complaynt to the King* (1529), which looked back with affection to the king's childhood; and *The Testament and Complaynt of our Sovereign Lord's Papyngo* (1530), an allegory put into the mouth of a dying parrot (papyngo) addressing its follow avian courtiers with a homily on good kingship. It also contained a panegyric to the Golden Age of James IV, that 'glory of princely governing'.

The infant king

On 21 September 1513, twelve days after his father had died at Flodden, Prince James was crowned James V at Stirling; the ceremony was conducted by James Beaton, Archbishop of Glasgow.[1] The new king was barely seventeen months old. Despite the calamitous destruction of the flower of Scotland's nobility, the nation had not disintegrated. Steve Boardman says:

> Flodden knocked a huge hole in the political and social structure of the Scottish aristocracy, and this may have caused disruption and instability during the minority of James V. But such losses tended to be replaced reasonably quickly; I don't think that Flodden should be regarded as a dramatic watershed in the history of the kingdom.

Indeed, the burgesses of Edinburgh responded to the emergency by ordering the women to go to the churches to pray, and the men to take up arms, and began to build a new city wall – the 'Flodden Wall', of which only fragmentary and barely visible traces now remain.[2] Fortunately for Scotland, Henry VIII had his sights fixed on France and made no attempt to follow up the victory at Flodden with a full-scale invasion of Scotland.

According to the terms of James IV's will, his widow Margaret Tudor (who was the sister of Henry VIII) was to be the child-king's guardian for as long as she remained unmarried; this did not automati-

---

1 James Beaton (c.1480–1539) was the first of a powerful family dynasty of prelates who would play a key role in the ecclesiastical politics of Scotland in the sixteenth century. The son of a minor landowner in Fife (John Beaton of Balfour), James Beaton enjoyed the favour of King James IV and had a rapid rise – Abbot of Dunfermline (1504), Treasurer of Scotland (1505–9), Archbishop of Glasgow (1510) and (during the minority of James V) Archbishop of St Andrews (1522) and Regent of Scotland. One of his nephews (a son of his older brother) was Cardinal David Beaton, Archbishop of St Andrews, who was murdered in 1546 by vengeful Protestant Reformers (see Chapter 19). Cardinal Beaton's own nephew, James Beaton, became Archbishop of Glasgow in 1551 but fled to Paris after the Reformation in 1560, where he set up the Scots College as a Scottish Church-in-exile; he died in 1603 – the year of the Union of the Crowns of Scotland and England.

2 The 'Flodden Wall' enclosed the suburbs of the Grassmarket and the Cowgate. It consisted mainly of fortifying the walls of existing houses and incorporating new garden walls, with bastions at the corners to provide a martial flourish. Part of the crenellated south-west bastion survives in the Vennel; there are traces of crosslet gunloops here and there. The most substantial fragment is in Drummond Street.

cally make her regent, however, and a month after the coronation a Council of Regency was nominated to act with the young queen mother, who was only twenty-five years old. The council consisted of James Beaton (Archbishop of Glasgow and Chancellor of Scotland); Alexander Gordon, Earl of Huntly, the most powerful magnate in the north; the Earl of Arran (grandson of James II); and Archibald Douglas, the young Earl of Angus and leader of the 'Red Douglases'. The Scots were wary of Margaret Tudor from the outset, no doubt because she was Henry VIII's sister, and eyes soon turned elsewhere in the search for a more suitable guardian for the king and governor of the country.

The man who was favoured for the task was John, Duke of Albany (1481–1536), son of James III's brother Alexander, who had been forfeited in 1480 and had made a failed attempt to depose James with English help in 1482 (see Chapter 16). Alexander had thereafter gone into exile in France, where he died in 1485, his son John becoming the new Duke of Albany. John's mother was French, and he grew up in France; he served in the French army and spoke no English; but although he was a French subject, as James II's grandson and James IV's cousin he was also next in succession to the Scottish crown after King James V. In the autumn of 1513 a General Council agreed that Albany should be invited to come to Scotland as governor, with the backing of French soldiers and munitions, and that the 'Auld Alliance' should be renewed. Albany arrived in Scotland in May 1515 and took up residence in Dunbar Castle where, according to the terms of his regency, he was entitled to keep a French garrison.

In 1514, within a year of James IV's death and soon after the birth in April of her short-lived second son, Alexander, Margaret Tudor suddenly married the twenty-four-year-old Archibald Douglas, sixth Earl of Angus – 'for her pleasour', as hostile chroniclers would later claim – thereby invalidating her claim to be the young king's rightful guardian; she was forced to yield to Albany the custody of James and his baby brother. The couple moved to England, but the marriage, which had seemed capricious enough at the time, soon broke up in a long and acrimonious public separation.[1]

For the next few years the course of Scottish politics was to be punctuated by squabbles over the custody of the person of the young king, and opinion polarised into a choice between those magnates and

---

1 Margaret Tudor and the Earl of Angus had a child during their brief marriage: Lady Margaret Douglas, who was to be the mother of Lord Darnley, the second husband of Mary Queen of Scots and father of James VI.

prelates who favoured closer alliance with France and those who saw more safety in an accommodation with England. The political situation in Europe was complex, with France and Spain vying for supremacy, and Scotland was always in danger of being sidelined. It was Scotland's relations with France, and with England, which would largely motivate the country's leaders during the king's minority.

The main stabilising influence in these confused years was the Duke of Albany, who served as governor for two periods – 1515–17 and 1521–24. As an 'outsider' he was able to make the most of the residual stability of the nation through a representative cross-section of the nobility in the General Council; he thereby ensured that the government of the nation continued through the work of committed magnates and ecclesiastics who were experienced and loyal civil servants in the service of the crown. He proved himself to be both resolute and tolerant, and played a skilful diplomatic hand at the European table. In 1517 he negotiated a renewal of the 'Auld Alliance' with the Treaty of Rouen, although the Scots were understandably chary of committing themselves to further military adventures against England in support of France. In 1522 and 1523 Albany brought a large French expeditionary force to Scotland, but in the event these manoeuvres turned into posturing rather than active hostilities, despite the fact that English raiders had burned Kelso and Jedburgh: the Franco-Scottish army advanced to the border, but the Scots (no doubt remembering Flodden) were unwilling to risk another full-scale invasion of England.

In May 1524 Albany returned to France, taking the French troops back with him. He was never to return. Margaret Tudor, who had been allowed back into Scotland on the promise of good behaviour as an honest and loyal Scotswoman, now regained the guardianship of her son, the king. She quickly contrived a ceremony called the 'Erection' of the king, and at the age of twelve James V was invested with crown, sword and sceptre, attended by a bodyguard of two hundred men-at-arms sent by his uncle, Henry VIII of England. But Margaret's eventual divorce from the Earl of Angus in 1527 caused a rift with her brother, Henry VIII, who at that stage still disapproved of divorce.[1] Henry VIII now busied himself with building up a pro-England party in Scotland, led by his sister's estranged husband, the Earl of Angus; Margaret Tudor was marginalised, especially when she

---

1 It was not until 1534 that Henry's divorce from his first wife, Catherine of Aragon, was enacted, a year after his private marriage to Anne Boleyn.

married for a third time – a minor knight named Henry Stewart (later Lord Methven).

James V's minority officially ended in April 1526, on his fourteenth birthday, but his stepfather the Earl of Angus gained control of the young king's person by an audacious and effective *coup d'état*. A sensible scheme had been devised whereby his safekeeping was to be entrusted to four groups of magnates in a rotating regency, three months at a time. The first group was led by the Earl of Angus, along with his kinsman the Earl of Morton and young James's tutor, Gavin Dunbar, Archbishop of Glasgow. The scheme quickly fell apart, however, as the Earl of Angus simply refused to hand over the young king when the time came to pass him on to the second group.

Since the king was now officially of age, he was technically able to exercise royal authority – and his first act, directed by the Earl of Angus, was to annul the provisions of parliament's scheme for his own protection! Angus promptly appointed himself as Chancellor and his uncle as Keeper of the Privy Seal, and packed the royal household with his own relatives to ensure that the king would be kept under constant close supervision. James remained in the custody of the Earl of Angus for two years, a virtual prisoner, despite a failed attempt at a rescue outside Linlithgow, during which the Earl of Lennox was killed.

James V's 'imprisonment' continued until the summer of 1528, soon after his sixteenth birthday. Later chroniclers like Robert Lindsay of Pitscottie tell of a dramatic escape from Falkland Palace, when the young king slipped his supervisors and rode all night to Stirling Castle, which was then in his mother's keeping. The escape story may well be a later embellishment; but however it happened, a group of leading noblemen – including the earls of Argyll, Arran, Bothwell, Eglinton, Montrose, Moray and Rothes – closed ranks around James in June 1528, in open opposition to the Earl of Angus. Angus was dismissed as chancellor and replaced by Gavin Dunbar, Archbishop of Glasgow. In July 1528 the king and his supporters rode into Edinburgh with a bodyguard of three hundred spearsmen. The Earl of Angus withdrew to Tantallon Castle, on the Lothian shore, and fortified it. James V was now ready to assert his personal rule.

Personal rule (1528–42)

It had been a strange childhood for the young king. His father, James IV, would hardly have been even a memory. He had lost a baby brother, Alexander (there was a malicious rumour that the infant had been poisoned by Albany). He had been caught up in an endless and unseemly tug-of-war between his mother and his stepfather, the Earl of Angus (whom, it seems, he did not like very much). He had endured the familiar trauma of emotional neglect amid grand surroundings which is so often the lot of royal children. Whether a 'prisoner' of the Earl of Angus or not, he had certainly suffered considerable constraint on his movements and action during the latter years of his minority (1526–28).

The first act of James V's personal rule was to get parliament to arraign his stepfather for treason, along with several of his closest kin – including the earl's sister, the Countess of Glamis. After a flurry of raids on other Angus strongholds, King James laid siege to Tantallon Castle (see note, page 239) in October. The siege went on for three weeks but failed to force a surrender. The Scottish parliament now negotiated a five-year truce with England in order to isolate Angus from his English support. In April 1529 Angus surrendered Tantallon Castle and was allowed to retire into exile in England, where he became a pensioner of King Henry VIII, his estates forfeited and all his Douglas kinsmen in disgrace.

The Guidman of Ballengeich versus Johnnie Armstrong (July 1530)

James V ... had a custom of going about the country disguised as a private person, in order that he might hear complaints which might not otherwise reach his ears ... When James V travelled in disguise, he used a name which was known only to some of his principal nobility and attendants. He was called the Goodman (the tenant, that is) of Ballengiech [sic].

TALES OF A GRANDFATHER, CHAPTER XXVII

Walter Scott tells a number of entertaining and edifying tales about the king's penchant for travelling among his people in disguise, like the eighth-century caliph Harun al-Rashid in the *Arabian Nights*, to find out what they thought.[1] On one occasion James was set upon by a gang of robbers at Cramond Bridge, near Edinburgh; he was rescued by a farm-worker named John Howieson, who took him home and washed his wounds. When asked what he wanted as a reward, Howie-

---

1 Scott took these tales from a contemporary chronicler, Adam Abell, author of *The Roit and Quheill of Tyme* (National Library of Scotland).

son revealed that he had always dreamed of owning the farm on which he worked, Braehead; his wish was granted, on condition that he and his successors should always be ready to wash the monarch's hands in Holyrood or at Cramond Bridge.[1] On another occasion, in 1536, the king is said to have visited the Duc de Vendôme's court in France in disguise. Such stories helped to establish for James a reputation as 'the poor man's king', the monarch who was determined to provide justice for all.

This image was greatly enhanced by an expedition which King James V made in 1530, when he descended in force on the lawless debatable border lands of the West Marches, which had been the cause of endless contention between Scotland and England. His main target was the notorious border reiver (raider) Johnnie Armstrong of Gilknockie. Seasonal cross-border raiding had become a way of life for many Borderers, and the Armstrongs of Liddesdale had been a law unto themselves for many years; they were said to have boasted that they acknowledged the authority of neither the King of Scots nor the King of England.

The story of the swoop on Liddesdale and the manner of Armstrong's death became the subject of a poignant Border balled, 'The Ballad of Johnnie Armstrong', which claims that the king enticed Armstrong to a peace-meeting at Caerlenrig with fifty unarmed followers and then broke his word by having them arrested. The refrain in the ballad is the king's granite response as Armstrong accuses him of perfidy and pleads for his life:

> *'Away, away, thou traytor strang!*
> *Out of my sicht thou mayst sune be!*
> *I grantit nevir a traytor's lyfe*
> *And now I'll not begin with thee.'*

Johnnie Armstrong and most of his accomplices were taken outside and summarily hanged. Only half a dozen were spared. The royal justice had been swift and terrible.[2]

---

1 The story of John Howieson is enshrined in one of the royal ceremonial roles still held by his descendants – 'Washer of the Sovereign's Hands'. The present holder of the title is Peter Houison Craufurd, twenty-eighth Laird of Craufurd Castle, Kilmarnock. He and his sons are expected to wash the sovereign's hands (from a silver pitcher and ewer) only once in a reign.

2 The execution of the Armstrongs of Liddesdale was the subject of John Arden's play *Armstrong's Last Goodnight: An Exercise in Diplomacy*, which was first performed at the Glasgow Citizens' Theatre in 1965 and revived at the 1994 Edinburgh International Festival.

During his reign, James V was ruthless in his imposition of order throughout his kingdom – even in the Highlands and Islands. He regularly attended the circuit courts ('justice ayres'), where his 'dread' presence was enough to ensure visible and merciless punishment of lawless behaviour. In 1532 he founded the Court of Session as the supreme court for civil cases in Scotland.[1] In 1540 he felt confident enough to make a leisurely cruise round his kingdom: with a fleet of twelve well-armed ships he set sail from the Forth and visited Orkney, Lewis, Skye, Mull and Islay before rounding the Mull of Kintyre to end his tour at Dumbarton on the Clyde.

The burning of the Countess of Glamis (July 1537)

James V had failed to deliver the killer-blow against his stepfather the Earl of Angus, his former 'jailer', who had been allowed to escape with his life to England. Many of Angus's kinsmen and supporters who had been arraigned with him for treason were granted remissions for their 'crimes' – 146 people in all were pardoned for 'art and part assistance'; but some of them were not to escape so lightly.

During the personal rule of James V three individuals were executed for the treasonable crime of conspiring to kill the king: John, the Master of Forbes; Sir James Hamilton of Finnart; and, most notoriously of all, Janet Douglas, Countess of Glamis (one of the four sisters of the forfeited Earl of Angus, and sister-in-law of the Master of Forbes), who has come down in history as a horrific victim of royal vindictiveness – and royal greed.

The Master of Forbes, who had been in constant trouble with his neighbouring landowners, was found guilty of a patently trumped-up charge of plotting to shoot the king and was hanged, drawn and quartered on 14 July 1537 – an English form of execution previously unknown in Scotland. His extensive lands, of course, were forfeited to the crown.

---

1   The present Court of Session is in Edinburgh's Parliament House, behind St Giles' Cathedral. Access to it is through Parliament Hall, which once served as the meeting place of the Scottish parliament and the Outer House of the Court of Session (it is still used as a meeting place for lawyers and their clients). The Great Window in the south wall (installed in 1868) is a striking stained-glass representation of the institution of the Court of Session in 1532. It shows James V presenting the Charter of Institution, and Confirmation by Pope Clement VII, to Alexander Mylne, Abbot of Cambuskenneth, who became the first Lord President of the Court and who is kneeling before him. Enthroned on the right of the king is the queen mother, Margaret Tudor, widow of James IV.

Sir James Hamilton of Finnart was the illegitimate son of the first Earl of Arran, and thus tainted by his connection with the Douglas clan. More importantly, he was a key member of the royal household and principal Master of Works – the royal architect, in effect. He supervised the building works at Falkland Palace, Linlithgow Palace, Edinburgh Castle and Stirling Castle; but his contribution to Scottish architecture did not save him from the scaffold when he too was convicted, on 16 August 1540, of treasonable conspiracy to assassinate the king; he was executed on the same day. His real crime may well have been his wealth, which the king appropriated.

The case of Janet, Countess of Glamis, has always excited pity and horror – and not simply because she was a young woman, and an uncommonly beautiful one at that, by all accounts. She had originally been charged (with 'art and part assistance' to her Douglas brothers) in 1528, during the first 'Douglas purge' in the first year of the king's personal rule, but was granted remission. She was then charged with having poisoned her first husband, John Lyon, Lord Glamis, in 1532, but once again the prosecution case was dropped. Janet then married again (her second husband, Lord Lyon, was a kinsman of her first husband) and resumed her title to the Glamis estates.

But the king had not forgotten her: on 17 July 1537 the thirty-three-year-old countess was charged and convicted on two points of treason: conspiring to poison the king (as well as her husband!), and assisting her brothers. Immediately after being sentenced she was taken out to the Castle Hill in Edinburgh, where the execution was carried out. She was chained to a stake, with barrels of tar packed round her, and burned to death. Next day her husband, trying to escape from the castle, plunged to his death on the rocks.

Historians agree that the charge of attempting to poison the king was totally spurious. Why, then, was the Countess of Glamis put to death? It is perhaps sufficient to note that her forfeited estates brought the crown a total of £5,770 from 1538 until the end of James V's reign in 1542.

Love and marriages

Like so many of the Stewart monarchs, James V had a powerful sexual appetite. He is known to have had at least seven mistresses: Lady Margaret Erskine (the wife of Douglas of Lochleven), Elizabeth Beaton, Elizabeth Stewart, Elizabeth Shaw, Elizabeth Carmichael, Euphemia Elphinstone and Christina Barclay. By them he had a number of illegitimate sons: James senior (born in 1530, to Elizabeth Shaw), another James (James *secundus*, the future Earl of Moray and Regent of Scotland – see Chapter 19 – born in 1531 to Lady Margaret Erskine), John, Robert senior, another Robert and at least two others. The sons were appointed commendators, or titular abbots, of Kelso, of Melrose, of St Andrews, of Coldingham, of the Abbey of Holyroodhouse – the very abuse of ecclesiastical preferment which Sir David Lindsay of the Mount highlighted in *The Thrie Estaites*. The appointments were highly advantageous for James V, because the profits from these foundations went straight into his pocket.

For many years the king's marital status was the object of some interest in the courts of Europe; although Scotland was only a minor player on the European stage, a marriage alliance with the King of Scots always had potential diplomatic advantages, and from Scotland's point of view a bride with a handsome dowry would bring welcome financial relief to the crown.

By the Treaty of Rouen negotiated by the Duke of Albany in 1517 the five-year-old James had been promised a French princess as a bride, but in the shifting alliances of the time François I of France was reluctant to commit himself to such an anti-English stance. Henry VIII had then tried to woo the Scots away from the 'Auld Alliance' by offering the hand of his daughter, Mary Tudor. Scotland engaged in an intriguing round of proposals and counter-proposals over the years to put pressure on France, and various possibilities were publicly explored: a sister of the Emperor Charles V, a daughter of the King of Denmark, even a Medici ward of Pope Clement VII himself.

In 1536, after long negotiations, a contract was made for a French marriage. The bride was to be Marie de Bourbon, daughter of the Duc de Vendôme. She was not the most beautiful of women, and after seeing her portrait James asked for a pension of twenty thousand *livres* in addition to her dowry of a hundred thousand *livres*. His conditions were accepted, and in September 1536 he sailed to Dieppe with an escort of some five thousand men in order to inspect Marie de Bourbon for himself; when he saw the poor girl in the flesh, however, he was so displeased by her appearance that he broke off the match.

Instead he turned to King François I of France with an offer for his daughter, Madeleine de Valois. Madeleine was in delicate health, and her father was reluctant to let her go; in the end he agreed, however, and on 1 January 1537 James married Madeleine at Nôtre Dame in Paris; the wedding was celebrated in great splendour, and the bride brought a dowry of 150,000 *livres* and the annual interest on 125,000 *livres* (£10,000 Scots). James duly received papal approval for the marriage in the form of a papal hat and sword, and the title of Defender of the Faith. Madeleine fell ill in March, but in May the couple sailed for Scotland; in a touching gesture, Madeleine knelt and kissed the ground as she arrived. Alas, within two months her health had broken down, and on 7 July 1537 she died at Holyrood Palace.

But a French bride was still what James wanted, and negotiations soon began for his marriage to another princess. While he was in France he had met Marie de Guise, who had been adopted by King François I; she was the wife of the Duc de Longueville when James first met her, but the duke had died a few weeks before Madeleine's death, and there was now no obstacle to her marriage with James. Henry VIII, too, had been interested in her: having divorced Catherine of Aragon, beheaded Anne Boleyn and lost the real love of his life, Jane Seymour, Henry was by now a serial widower. His offer had been refused, and a marriage with James V was arranged by proxy. In June 1538 Marie de Guise came to Scotland.

Marie de Guise was a remarkable and admirable woman. She was the sister of François, Duc de Guise, and of Charles, Cardinal of Lorraine, which made her a member of the most powerful noble house in France, perhaps in all Europe. She was highly intelligent and well-versed in the subtle intricacies of high politics, both domestic and international, and was to play a tremendously important and impressive part in the governance of Scotland as queen regent after the birth of her daughter, Mary Queen of Scots (see Chapter 19).

To celebrate his new bride's arrival in Scotland, James V had extensive alterations made to Falkland Palace in Fife. He had already beautified the palace for Madeleine: a painter had been engaged for eleven weeks redecorating the ceilings of the royal apartments with 'azure and vermilion and rose of Paris, with white lead and verdigris and indigo of Badeas, and with much fine gold'. For Marie de Guise, however, James embarked on a much more ambitious building programme. Masons were imported from France to remodel the south range of the palace to include a magnificent Chapel Royal which now, superbly restored, is the only surviving interior of James V's palace.[1]

---

1 The French workmen had to be accommodated (to their disgust) in neighbouring hamlets, especially the nearby village of Freuchie, which was then little more than a huddle of insanitary hovels on the verge of a marsh: 'awa' tae Freuchie' ('away to Freuchie') became a dismissive phrase from those early days. Freuchie achieved a much more salubrious kind of renown when its cricket team won the national Champion Village Team title at Lord's in September 1985.

On the inner façade of the courtyard the French master mason Nicholas Roy carved the date 1539, the Scots thistle and the French fleur-de-lis, and the initials of James and his second queen: IRSDG (*Iacobus Rex Scotorum Dei Gratia*) and MARIA RDG (*Maria Regina Dei Gratia*).[1] Marie de Guise was crowned in a lavish ceremony in the Palace of Holyroodhouse on 22 February 1540. Three months later she gave birth to her first son, Prince James.[2]

Marie had brought with her another dowry of 150,000 *livres*. The money was of huge importance to James V. Like so many of his predecessors, he was determined to improve the finances of the crown. Apart from making lucrative marriages, the other major source of new finance lay in the Church. Upon a promise to defend 'the see of Rome and the Holy Church', James received the Pope's permission in 1531 to draw an annuity of £10,000 from the Church for the maintenance of a supreme civil court – a College of Justice, consisting of fifteen salaried clerics and learned laymen. The prelates, desperate for the king's support for the Roman Catholic Church against the growth of critical and 'heretical' opposition, settled for paying the crown a total of £72,000 in four instalments. They raised the money by evicting many of their tenants (which did little for the king's popularity) – but there is scant evidence that any of the money went to the college.

Curtains for a king (12 December 1542)

'It came with a lass, and it will go with a lass.' With these words, presaging the extinction of his house, he made a signal of adieu to his courtiers, spoke little more, but turned his face to the wall, and died of the most melancholy of all diseases, a broken heart. He was scarcely thirty-one years old; in the very prime, therefore,

---

1 Falkland Palace is now in the care of the National Trust for Scotland. The main restoration work was undertaken by John Patrick Crichton Stewart, the third Marquess of Bute (1848–1900), who bought the estate of Falkland in 1887 and spent a fortune on saving the palace from total dereliction. He lavished particular care on the Chapel Royal. It still had its original sixteenth-century carved-oak entrance screen with its slender hand-turned pillars; Lord Bute reconstructed the old royal pew and the pulpit from fragments he found, dark with age but still showing the red and gold paint of the royal livery of Scotland. He also restored the great panelled oak screen behind the altar (the so-called 'chancellery wall') and rebuilt the cross-house containing the king's bedchamber, recreating all the old walls which determined its original position and proportions.

2 Prince James lived for less than a year. A second son, Arthur, Duke of Albany, was born in 1541, only to die a few days after his baptism.

of life. If he had not suffered the counsels of the Catholic priests
to hurry him into a war with England, James V might have been
as fortunate a prince as his many good qualities and talents
deserved.

TALES OF A GRANDFATHER, CHAPTER XXVIII

King James V's last words in 1542, suitably anglicised by Walter Scott,
are remembered as the most celebrated deathbed saying in Scottish
history. They have always been cited as the heartbroken utterance of
a king who had been driven by his churchmen into fighting a Holy
War against 'heretic' England, and had then been betrayed by his
disloyal nobles. James V was the firm and ruthless king against whom
his people had finally turned.

That has for long been the received wisdom about the end of James's
reign. But was it really like that? In *James V: The Personal Rule, 1528–
1542* (1998) the late Jamie Cameron presents a very different picture,
showing how the common verdict of history has been based entirely
on English sources – especially the biased information sent by English
spies in Scotland and the 'spin' put on it by early Protestant reformers
like John Knox (see Chapter 19).

The background to the last years of James V's reign was the growing
wave of protest in many countries of Europe against the corrupt medieval order of Western Christendom – especially against the power and
manifest faults of the papacy and its churchmen. In Germany Martin
Luther, a monk who had married a former nun in flagrant breach of
papal authority, had thrown down the gauntlet against papal
supremacy by drawing up a list of ninety-five theses on the sale of
pardons for ordinary people and their forebears – 'indulgences' –
(especially to raise money for the building of St Peter's Basilica in
Rome) and nailing them to the church door at the University of
Wittenberg on 31 October 1517. The watchwords of his spiritual
rebellion were 'justification by faith alone' and the priesthood of all
believers: it was the individual conscience which mattered, not the
ecclesiastical hierarchy.

In Scotland the first of the 'heretic martyrs' of the nascent
Reformation had been burned in 1528, during the last year of the
king's minority, for 'teaching opinions of Luther and wicked heresies':
a young and talented theologian named Patrick Hamilton who had
studied at Paris and Wittenberg where he had absorbed the doctrines
of Lutheranism. Hamilton, a great-grandson of James II, preached
these principles openly when he returned to Scotland in 1523. He was

exiled for heresy, but came back to continue his work; Archbishop James Beaton (who was a distant kinsman) could not overlook this affront to his authority and had him arrested and tried. On 29 February 1528 Patrick Hamilton was found guilty of heresy and burned in front of St Salvator's College in St Andrews. He was the first known Scot to die at the stake for his beliefs, and the effect of his teaching and his martyrdom was to have far-reaching effects on the spread of Protestantism in Scotland. Ten other Protestant intellectuals were to go to the stake in the 1530s, but many others fled Scotland to continue their academic careers abroad

In England, the Dutch scholar Desidarius Erasmus had sown the seeds of humanism during his tenure of the chairs of Divinity and Greek at Cambridge University (1509–14) and had influenced many of the foremost intellectuals in the country, including Thomas More, the future Chancellor of England under Henry VIII. Henry himself, who had been pious in his youth and had been trained for the priesthood, usurped control of the Church in England in 1534 for reasons which were as much political as religious: it enabled him to divorce and marry almost at will, and provided both crown and the nobility with rich revenues from the ensuing dissolution of the monasteries.

The political implications of the growing movement for Reformation were profoundly important. Henry VIII, under threat from both François I of France and the Holy Roman Emperor, Charles V, had negotiated a 'Perpetual Peace' with Scotland in 1534, but he was constantly anxious lest Scotland joined in a European alliance against him; ever since the 1534 alliance he had been angling for a 'summit meeting' of the 'Big Three' – England, France and Scotland – but nothing had come of this proposal. In 1536 Henry was further embarrassed by unrest in the north of England which erupted into an abortive uprising in Yorkshire known as 'the Pilgrimage of Grace'.

In Scotland, James V took shrewd advantage of the anxiety felt by Scotland's leading prelates about the threat from the Reformers, and was able to blackmail the Pope, in the politest possible way, into allowing him to extract enormous sums of money from the Church. After James's marriage to Marie de Guise, Henry VIII was even more concerned about the 'Auld Alliance' between Scotland and France, and increased his diplomatic overtures to Scotland.

The Battle of Solway Moss (24 November 1542)

In 1541, as the crisis in the Church deepened, Henry VIII's policy was more than ever aimed at trying to persuade his nephew James V to make the same break with Rome that he had made. James was accordingly invited to meet Henry at York to discuss their theological and religious differences. James did not formally accept the invitation, but Henry seems to have assumed that he would, and expected to meet him at York during a royal progress to the north of England that summer. James probably saw no point in meeting his uncle at this stage: he was quite happy to preserve the *status quo* regarding the Scottish Church for as long as it was providing so much income for the crown, and he had the support of both the King of France and the Pope.

Henry VIII waited at York until the end of September, when it had become obvious that James was not coming. But, contrary to the received wisdom, he was not enraged: he sent a letter to James in February 1542 forgiving him for his non-attendance. In the devious diplomacy of the time, Henry was even now planning to join the Holy Roman Empire in a war against France – which he did in July 1542 when François I and the Emperor Charles V went to war.

With France otherwise engaged, Henry now felt able to deal with Scotland without fear of French intervention. Late in July he put the north of England on a war footing. James V responded in August by sending George Gordon, fourth Earl of Huntly, to Kelso as royal lieutenant to organise the defence of the Borders. After a flurry of raids and counter-raids, the English sent a force of three thousand men under Sir Robert Bower to harry the lands of the Merse. This force was scattered by a smaller force of two thousand men under Huntly at the Battle of Hadden Rig at the end of August, leaving hundreds of English prisoners in Scottish hands.

Before the news of this reverse reached Henry VIII, however, he had already commissioned the Duke of Norfolk to prepare to invade Scotland in October. On 22 October the English army left Berwick-upon-Tweed and proceeded to burn Kelso Abbey and Roxburgh Tower; a week later it returned to Berwick. It had been at least twenty thousand strong – formidable enough to deter Huntly from trying to intervene with his small force – but Norfolk complained that he had been desperately short of supplies and could not sustain a longer or deeper incursion into Scotland.

Henry VIII now declared war officially. He resurrected the ancient

English claim to suzerainty over Scotland and recommended that the full invasion should be launched in June 1543.

James V responded to the Norfolk incursion in October by ordering a general mobilisation for a twenty-day campaign, in the belief that Norfolk, supported by an English fleet, was planning to attack Edinburgh. Elements of the army, some ten or twelve thousand men, backed by artillery pieces and led by James himself, were at Lauder by 31 October, but they were too late; it was apparent that the English were safely back in Berwick. Faced with the bad weather and the same shortage of supplies which had hampered Norfolk, James was in no position to mount a punitive raid into England at that stage, never mind a full-scale invasion. The army was stood down and James returned to Edinburgh to rethink his strategy.

The new strategy involved spreading a good deal of deliberate misinformation for the benefit of English spies. James feinted an assault to the south-east, but at the same time was planning an assault through the Merse in the west. To that end he summoned a muster of his army to meet him at Lauder on 20 November; meanwhile, another force was mustering farther to the west, in Peebles. The plan seems to have been that after an attack in the west, a smaller force would escort a group of bishops across the Tweed on to English soil, where they would find a church and pronounce a papal interdict against Henry VIII.

There was nothing wrong with the plan – only with its execution. King James left Lauder and moved rapidly to Peebles to meet his 'western army'; but the English had been alerted in the nick of time: in Carlisle, Sir Thomas Wharton, deputy Warden of the March and a veteran of Border warfare, mustered a force of two thousand men, including a small contingent of three hundred mounted 'prickers' (light cavalry). James had promised his wife not to take part personally in any fighting, and departed for Lochmaben; and at dawn on 24 November a large raiding party of Scots under the command of Lord Maxwell, the Scottish Warden of the West March, and containing several prominent Scottish nobles, moved to the mouth of the Esk, leaving the main bulk of the army in reserve.

The geography of the Battle of Solway Moss which ensued is confused, in that the English reports contradict one another; there are no contemporary Scottish accounts of the battle, and the scale of the fighting is in dispute – was it a real battle, or merely a brawl? It seems, however, that after Maxwell crossed the River Esk on to the vast wastes of Solway Moss he stumbled into trouble. He found himself boxed in

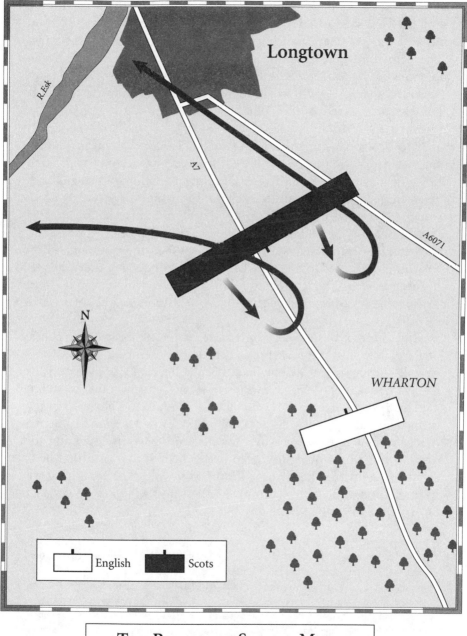

Longtown

R. Esk

A7

A6071

N

WHARTON

English	Scots

THE BATTLE OF SOLWAY MOSS,
24 NOVEMBER 1542

between the mire of Solway Moss and the estuary of the Esk, with the English force shadowing him menacingly. As the Scots tried to regroup to ford the Esk again the English prickers charged their right flank. The Scots put up a fight but were in a hopeless position and began to suffer casualties. Opinions differ as to how heavy these were – from 'several hundreds' down to only seven! Whatever the truth, the Scots quickly surrendered, or fled. What had been intended as a preliminary raid had ended in a débâcle.

Later Scottish historians would claim that the Scottish magnates who surrendered at Solway Moss did so because they secretly harboured Protestant sympathies and were unwilling to fight against England. There seems to be no realistic evidence to justify this view.

James V returned disconsolately to Edinburgh, his military strategy in tatters. Many of his nobles had been captured at Solway Moss, and further raids into England were clearly out of the question. From Edinburgh he issued instructions for strengthening the Border defences to meet any English attempts to follow up their victory; then he went to Linlithgow, where his queen, Marie de Guise, was about to give birth.

James himself was unwell by then. He retired to his favourite palace of Falkland, where he took to his bed on 6 December.[1] He was now very ill – it seems that he may have been suffering from dysentery, or cholera. He was only thirty years old, a strong, sturdy young man, but cholera in particular was a deadly disease. At Falkland he heard of the birth of his daughter, Mary, at Linlithgow on 8 December; but the news brought him no pleasure, for he must have been hoping for another son who would survive to be his heir. It was then that he is said to have uttered his gloomy deathbed saying: 'The De'il gang wi' it. It will end as it began. It cam' wi' a lass and will gang wi' a lass.'[2] On 14 December 1542 he died.

---

1   The 'King's Bedroom' which can now be seen at Falkland Palace is a complete reconstruction. The shell was recreated by the third Marquess of Bute (see note, page 308). The designs were drawn in 1952 by Schomberg Scott (architectural historian for the National Trust for Scotland) and carried out by the Scottish artist David McLure. The ceiling and shutters were painted in the rich colours which all the Stewart monarchs loved, to create what Schomberg Scott called 'what King James V would have recognised and accepted as a royal bedroom for the King of Scots'. The magnificent bed which forms the centrepiece of the chamber, however, known as the 'Golden Bed of Brahan', dates from the early seventeenth century and was brought from abroad as a sumptuous gift for the Earl of Seaforth.

2   James seems to have been referring to the Stewart royal line, which had come into being through the fortuitous marriage of one of Robert Bruce's daughters, Marjorie, to Walter

The baby was a weak, sickly child; but she survived to become one of Scotland's most celebrated monarchs – the ill-fated Mary Queen of Scots.

Epilogue

More than any other Stewart monarch, James V seems to have been unfairly treated by the verdict of history – history written initially by the triumphant Protestant Reformers in Scotland who portrayed him almost as an anti-Christ.

'History' meant something different in the sixteenth century to what it does now. In the culture of the Renaissance, equal place was to be given to vernacular as to classical languages, and the introduction of printing would start to bring 'popular' historical works (albeit written by clerics) to the public for the first time. Michael Lynch says:

> History in those days was not produced to give an accurate account of events; it was written to produce a morally authoritative view which would provide good thoughts in its readers. History, in other words, was not analytic – it was didactic; the search for truth was a kind of cleansing of the reader's mind rather than an exposé or a questioning of the evidence.

James V may not have been particularly likeable (but which Stewart monarch was?). His reign had ended with a humiliating failure – although not as disastrous a failure as Flodden had been. But does he deserve the opprobrium which has been heaped on him? In his posthumously published *James V: The Personal Rule 1528–1542*, Jamie Cameron strongly disagrees with the popular assessment of James's reign.

Perhaps the real problem is that James V died such an untimely death. Had he lived longer, Scotland's later history would have been very different. James was a young and vigorous king in full control of his kingdom, facing an ailing English king who was approaching the end of his controversial reign. Had James lived, Marie de Guise might well have produced the son and heir who would have secured an adult

---

Steward; having lost two sons already in infancy, perhaps he had no faith that this newborn girl would survive. In the event, the dynasty lasted until 1714, when it 'went with a lass' on the death of Queen Anne, the last of the Stewart monarchs of the United Kingdom.

Stewart succession free of the crises brought on by the accession of the infant Mary Queen of Scots.

For myself, the early death of James V at Falkland Palace in 1542 was every bit as disastrous for Scotland as the death of Alexander III at Kinghorn in 1286. Historical 'what-ifs' apart, it is high time that history's hindsight verdict on James V is reassessed in the light of Jamie Cameron's careful researches.

Chapter 19

MARY QUEEN OF SCOTS: 1 – REIGN AND THE REFORMATION

The evil fortunes of Mary Stewart, who succeeded her father to the crown of Scotland, commenced at her very birth, and could scarce be considered as ceasing during the whole period of her life. Of all the unhappy princes of the line of Stewart, she was the most uniformly unfortunate.

TALES OF A GRANDFATHER, CHAPTER XXIX

Deep in the heart of Westminster Abbey, with its unmistakable twin towers – arguably the most important historic building in England – sits the ornate tomb of Mary Queen of Scots. It is much the most magnificent of all the royal tombs in the abbey, situated in the south aisle running alongside Henry VII's Chapel behind the high altar, and is conspicuously more elaborate and imposing than the joint sepulchre of her royal cousins Elizabeth of England and Mary Tudor, who lie together in the North Aisle.

Mary's monument was commissioned by her son, James VI of Scotland and I of England, in 1607 (at a cost of £2,000), just after he had seen to the joint interment of Elizabeth and Mary Tudor (at a cost of only £765). In 1612 the tomb was ready to receive the queen's body, which had been buried, since her execution in 1587, in Peterborough Cathedral. The white marble effigy of Mary lies on a sarcophagus under a sumptuously decorated black-and-white canopy, her hands clasped in everlasting prayer; serenely beautiful (a true likeness, modelled in all probability from her death-mask), she wears a close-fitting coif, a laced ruff and a long mantle fastened by a brooch; at her feet the crowned lion of Scotland snarls ferociously. King James went out of his way to demonstrate his belief that his mother had been unjustly treated by Elizabeth of England, and deliberately gave her a higher status in the soaring necropolis of royalty and fame that is Westminster Abbey.[1]

Thus was laid to her final rest this tall, vivacious, beautiful, thrice-married, thrice-widowed, infinitely controversial and infinitely unhappy queen whose storm-tossed life and ill-starred end have held the world's imagination in thrall ever since.

More has been written about Mary than about any other monarch in Scotland – perhaps in the world. Over the centuries staid scholars have worked themselves into frenzies of passion either 'for' or 'against' her. Her decisions and actions have been endlessly debated, her personality and motives endlessly dissected. Queen Elizabeth of England, taxed beyond endurance by the mere fact of Mary's life, referred to her as a 'daughter of debate' – a studied understatement if ever there was one.

It is a challenge for the historian to present the complicated background to Mary's life clearly, without over-simplification, and to allow the events to speak for themselves dispassionately, without polemics. The cast of characters is enormous – friends and foes, husbands and lovers, politicians and preachers, Catholics and Protestants, lords and ladies, loyalists and 'traitors', champions and belittlers and, above all, the common people of Scotland. Modern scholars have done much to give historical objectivity to the events of her reign; ultimately, however, one's view of Mary, and of the Protestant Reformation which revolutionised Scotland during her reign, will always, I suspect, remain largely a personal matter.

---

1   Mary Queen of Scots' lead coffin was found in 1867 in a bricked-up vault underneath her tomb. The vault contained a huge and haphazard clutter of coffins and urns of all shapes and sizes. They contained the remains of many of Mary's descendants, including the first ten offspring of James VII & II (and an illegitimate son attributed to him, 'Lord Darnley') and all of Queen Anne's seventeen stillborn babies as well as her only child to survive infancy, the young Duke of Gloucester. On top of Mary's coffin lay that of her niece Arabella Stewart (1575–1615), who had been one of her companions during her English captivity. No attempt was made to open Mary's coffin to inspect her remains.

'In my end is my beginning'[1]

Mary Queen of Scots' end had all the inexorability of classical Greek tragedy; her beginning promised little better. Six days before the death of her father, James V, Mary was born on 8 December 1542 in the queen's apartments in Linlithgow Palace, where her father had himself been born thirty years earlier.[2]

Linlithgow was the great royal palace which James V had refurbished so spectacularly for Mary's mother, Marie de Guise. All that remains of the royal bedroom where the future Queen of Scots was born is a four-panelled window high in the floorless and roofless north-west tower overlooking the site of the palace gardens. A few days after her father's death, the infant queen was christened in the nearby Kirk of St Michael, now distinguished by a controversial gold-coloured cross-shaped steeple erected in 1964.

Mary was nursed in Linlithgow Palace for the first nine months of her life. Then she was moved to the greater security of Stirling Castle; and in the Chapel Royal there, sitting on her mother's knee, the baby was solemnly crowned Queen of Scots on 9 September 1543 – the thirtieth anniversary of the Battle of Flodden.

These first nine months had already provided a grim foretaste of the politico-religious manoeuvrings which would haunt the rest of her life. Two factions immediately started struggling for power through custody of the person of the infant queen. Scotland's Protestant Reformers favoured an alliance with the England of Henry VIII, who had already (in 1534) made a decisive break with the papacy and appointed himself head of the Church of England; he was also Mary Queen of Scots' great-uncle. The other faction, supporters of the Roman Catholic Church, looked towards the 'Auld Alliance' with France: the dowager queen was of the French royal house; with a Catholic Scots monarchy, France and the Church could expect Scotland to side with them against Henry VIII.

The obvious choice for regent or governor was James Hamilton, second Earl of Arran, who, as the eldest surviving descendant of James II's daughter Mary, was heir presumptive after the infant queen (he

---

1 *En ma fin est mon commencement:* these pious words, Mary's personal motto, were embroidered by her on the chair of state which accompanied her in her captivity, probably during her time in Sheffield Castle (1570–73). Like so much else relating to her life and death, the sentence is given added poignancy by the circumstances of her death.

2 Marie de Guise had already given birth to two sons in that chamber, but both of them had died in infancy.

was her second cousin once removed).[1] But the first move was made by Cardinal David Beaton of St Andrews, an inveterate persecutor of 'heretics';[2] immediately after the king's death he produced a document, purportedly drawn up and signed by the king and dated on the day of his death, nominating a regency consisting of the cardinal, the Earl of Huntly, the Earl of Argyll and the Earl of Moray (the queen's uncle, James Stewart). The Earl of Arran was pointedly excluded from this list, and Cardinal Beaton appointed himself Chancellor of Scotland on 10 January 1543.

The response came when Henry VIII repatriated a dozen of the nobles who had been captured at Solway Moss the previous year. They were amply provided with funds, and formed the core of a new pro-English faction led by James V's stepfather and former custodian Archibald Douglas, Earl of Angus and second husband of the previous dowager queen, Margaret Tudor: Angus had now returned to Scotland for the first time since he had been ousted by James V at the start of the king's personal rule in 1528. The pro-English nobles arrested Cardinal Beaton for allegedly forging the late king's will, and deposed him as chancellor. In March 1543 the Scottish parliament declared the Earl of Arran to be 'Second Person in the Realm' and appointed him regent and governor for the infant queen.

Parliament also made the first moves towards ecclesiastical reform, and sanctioned the universal ownership and reading of the Scriptures in the vernacular ('in the vulgar tongue') – in effect, William Tyndale's English translation of the New Testament Bible, which had been printed in the 1530s and now started to circulate widely in Scotland. This was a crucial breakthrough, not only for the humanist reformers but also for the growing body of people who were not necessarily 'Protestant heretics' but who nonetheless felt the need for some sort of reform of the Church.

Soon the Scots embarked on talks with the English about a marriage

---

1 The Hamiltons had come to the fore during the reign of James II. The first Lord Hamilton (Sir James Cadzow) had sided with the Black Douglases during the king's minority, but defected to the king's cause in 1455, just before the final Douglas downfall, and was rewarded with extensive lands and sheriffdoms in Lanarkshire. After James II's death, James, Lord Hamilton, was the second husband of James III's sister Mary. Their son, another James Hamilton (c.1477–1529), was awarded the Earldom of Arran for his prowess in a tournament held to celebrate the wedding of James IV and Margaret Tudor; their grandson, the second Earl of Arran (c.1516–75), succeeded to the earldom in 1529.

2 Cardinal David Beaton (c.1494–1546) was the nephew of Archbishop James Beaton; he succeeded his uncle as Archbishop of St Andrews in 1539.

between the infant Queen of Scots and Henry VIII's five-year-old son and heir by Jane Seymour, Prince Edward. From Henry's point of view it made a lot of sense: Mary had a strong claim to the English throne through her grandmother, Mary Tudor, wife of James IV and Henry's sister. If the Tudor line failed with Henry VIII, the Stewart dynasty would inherit. A fruitful marriage between Mary and Henry's heir – a 'golden and godly marriage', as Henry put it – would ensure the future of the House of Tudor, and the House of Stewart (and Scotland, too) would be subsumed into it.

But Henry VIII was an inveterate haggler. He set down his bargaining position: he demanded that Scotland renounce the 'Auld Alliance' and surrender the castles of Dunbar, Dumbarton, Edinburgh, St Andrews, Stirling and Tantallon, and that the infant queen should be sent to England to be brought up as soon as she was weaned. The Scots found these terms unacceptable; they insisted that Mary be brought up in her own realm, and that Scotland should retain its independence. Henry backed down, and two treaties were drawn up at Greenwich in July 1543. One of them was a formal peace treaty. The terms of the other declared that Mary Queen of Scots was to be formally betrothed to Prince Edward; the two were to be married in 1552, when Mary would be ten years old and Edward fifteen, and Mary would live thereafter in England. If they produced a child, that child would inherit the two kingdoms. A Union of the Crowns was becoming a tantalising possibility.

Much damage had been done to the pro-English cause, however, by Henry's high-handed attitude over the future of his infant Scottish great-niece. The parallel with 1290, when Edward I used his position as the Maid of Norway's great-uncle to try to browbeat the Scots into submission to him, was all too obvious. Many Scots began to have second thoughts about closer relations with an England which was still thinking in terms of Scottish subjection, not equal partnership. At this point two prominent nobles who had been living in voluntary exile in France came back to Scotland at the urgent request of Cardinal Beaton. One was the Earl of Arran's older half-brother, John Hamilton, who had been appointed Abbot of Paisley and would become Archbishop of St Andrews.[1] The other was

---

1 John Hamilton (c.1511–71), an illegitimate son of the first Earl of Arran, was the ablest of the Hamilton family. As a churchman and politician he had a colourful and chequered career, falling foul of the Catholic and Protestant parties in turn. He remained loyal to Mary Queen of Scots after her fall from power, imprisonment and escape to England (1567). In 1571 he was summarily tried for alleged complicity in the murder of Darnley (see pages 356–8) and hanged in his episcopal vestments.

twenty-six-year-old Matthew Stewart, the fourth Earl of Lennox, who was still unmarried and was second in line to the throne after the Earl of Arran. Lennox was to prove, in Michael Lynch's graphic description, 'a dynastic time-bomb'.

The arrival of these two exiles revived the pro-French faction. Cardinal Beaton was released from imprisonment; and on 26 July 1543 the queen mother took matters into her own hands and removed the baby queen from Linlithgow to the fortress of Stirling Castle, escorted by an army of 2,500 cavalry and a thousand infantry. Thus Mary Queen of Scots made her first royal progress across her kingdom for her coronation.

The Earl of Arran had initially been a supporter of the marriage alliance with England; now he was clearly siding with the pro-French faction. His behaviour as regent during these critical months of Mary's infancy has often been called into question. Was he merely weak and vacillating? Or was he working to an agenda of his own? As next in line to the throne after the infant Mary, he had a powerful motive for keeping Scotland independent. Also, it was rumoured that he was a secret Protestant; but he seems to have made little secret of the fact that, if the marriage negotiations with England broke down, his eldest son, James, the Master of Hamilton, would make an excellent husband for Mary – it would be a union between the reigning queen and a future heir presumptive. Henry VIII tried to regain Arran's support by offering his own daughter, the Princess Elizabeth (the future Queen of England), as a bride for the Master of Hamilton; Arran agreed enthusiastically to the proposal, but was eventually persuaded to turn the offer down.[1] On 8 September he was given absolution for his 'Reformist' sins and formally received back into the Catholic Church. Next day it was Arran who bore the crown at the coronation of Mary Queen of Scots.

By December the English parliament had failed to ratify the Treaties of Greenwich; so the Scottish parliament seized the opportunity of

---

1 James, the Master of Hamilton, was to become the third Earl of Arran when his father became Duke of Châtelherault in 1548. He was rather a tragic figure. After the betrothal of Mary Queen of Scots to the Dauphin François he went to France, where he distinguished himself as commander of the Scots Guards in French service. He became a Protestant and fled to Geneva. In 1559 he returned to Scotland under an assumed name and joined the Lords of the Congregation in their uprising (see below). In 1560 the Scottish parliament proposed him as a suitor for Elizabeth of England, but Elizabeth was 'indisposed to marry at present'. He was already showing symptoms of mental aberration, and in 1562 he was pronounced insane and was confined until his death – still unmarried – in 1609.

repudiating the agreements; it reasserted the alliance with France and appointed Cardinal Beaton as chancellor. Under pressure from the cardinal, parliament also renewed the penal laws against heresy. The regent, Arran, was placed under an advisory council of sixteen, headed by the queen mother and Cardinal Beaton; and instead of marrying the heir to the throne of England, the idea now was that the child-queen should marry that 'dynastic time-bomb', the young Earl of Lennox.

Denied the immediate prospect of uniting the two kingdoms under his son Prince Edward, Henry VIII now decided on more direct methods of pressing his heir's suit.

The 'Rough Wooing'

The exploits of the English leaders might gratify Henry's resent-
ment, but they greatly injured his interest in Scotland, for the
whole kingdom became united to repel the invaders; and even
those who liked the proposed match with England best, were, to
use an expression of the time, disgusted with so rough a mode
of wooing.

TALES OF A GRANDFATHER, CHAPTER XXIX

It was Sir Walter Scott who first coined in print that telling phrase, the 'Rough Wooing', to describe Henry VIII's furious reaction to the Scots' repudiation of the proposed marriage treaty. This was more than merely an 'episode' in Scotland's history; it was a long and appallingly destructive Anglo–Scottish war (1544–49), a series of sporadic but interlocking military clashes which would culminate (but not end) with the slaughter at the Battle of Pinkie (1547). Much of the country would be left in ruins, tens of thousands of Scots would be killed and thousands of families devastated or dispossessed. But at the end of it, Scotland would have kept its hard-fought independence.

In May 1544 one of England's most formidable veteran soldiers, Edward Seymour, the Earl of Hertford (Jane Seymour's brother and Prince Edward's uncle), made an amphibious landing at Newhaven on the Firth of Forth with sixteen thousand men, while an even larger army crossed the Tweed and advanced overland. The land army laid waste to every town and village in its path, and burned the great Border abbeys of Dryburgh, Jedburgh, Kelso and Melrose. Meanwhile the Earl of Hertford destroyed the port of Leith and attacked the capital, Edinburgh. For two days the south side of the city burned while the English troops massacred and raped its inhabitants. Holyrood Abbey, where King James V lay buried, and the Palace of Holyroodhouse were sacked, although Edinburgh Castle held out.

It looked as if the next target would be Stirling Castle, where the child-queen was in residence. Her mother, Marie de Guise, the dowager queen, moved her to Dunkeld in Perthshire for greater safety. But Hertford turned away when only nine kilometres from Stirling and returned to England, leaving the south-east of Scotland in ruins, and instructed his lieutenants in the north of England, Sir Ralph Eure and Sir Brian Layton, to continue the devastation of the Border lands. It was the first act of the 'Rough Wooing'; but it was also designed as a deliberate diversionary tactic to keep the Scots from threatening northern England while Henry VIII was campaigning in France.

The pro-English faction in Scotland was also busy on Henry's behalf. The Earl of Lennox, mortal enemy of the Earl of Arran, changed sides, went to London and made a formal agreement with Henry VIII. He was appointed lieutenant for the northern counties of England as well as the whole of southern Scotland, with the promise of becoming governor of Scotland in the future. In exchange he surrendered Dumbarton Castle and the Island of Bute for use as an English base. As a sweetener, Lennox, who had earlier been touted as a possible husband for the young Mary Queen of Scots, was given the hand of Henry VIII's niece – Lady Margaret Douglas, the daughter of Margaret Tudor (Henry's sister) by her second husband, the Earl of Angus.[1] Lennox was not alone in his treachery: hundreds of what the English called 'assured Scots' were bribed or bullied into taking an oath of allegiance to King Henry as their liege lord – a dangerous fifth column at the heart of Scottish society.

The calculated violence of the 'Rough Wooing', and the treachery of so many of Scotland's leading magnates, served only to accentuate Scotland's antagonism towards England; they added to the stature and influence of the queen mother, Marie de Guise, while Cardinal Beaton was blamed for the devastation which had been wrought by the English. It even made Archibald Douglas, sixth Earl of Angus and stepfather of James V, for long a pensioner of the English crown, change sides. When a five-thousand-strong English army of mercenaries under Sir Ralph Eure and Sir Brian Layton again desecrated Melrose Abbey, in

---

1 The 'time-bomb' duly exploded when a son was born to Lennox and Lady Margaret Douglas on 7 December 1545 – Henry, Lord Darnley, who would become the second husband of Mary Queen of Scots in 1566.

the heart of the 'Douglas country', the Earl of Angus was stirred into action. With a force which was only half the size of the English army he surprised the raiders on Ancrum Moor, hard by the banks of the Teviot a few kilometres from Jedburgh, on 27 February 1545. The English rushed into the attack against the rays of the setting sun but were stopped in their tracks by the bristling ranks of Scottish pikemen. When the Earl of Angus ordered an advance, the English centre disintegrated. Some eight hundred of the English army fell, and a further thousand were taken prisoner. Both Eure and Layton were killed.

In the autumn of 1545 the Earl of Hertford returned to the eastern Lowlands to continue the 'Rough Wooing', while the Earl of Lennox ravaged Ayrshire and Renfrewshire in the west. This time Hertford restricted his activities to the systematic destruction of that year's harvest before returning to England.

In Scotland the nascent Reformation cause was given a boost by another bloody event – the assassination of Cardinal Beaton in May 1546. The cardinal was a career ecclesiastic who had become a Renaissance prince of the Church through nepotism and his skills as an international diplomat; he had also become an object of loathing in many quarters for his greed and venality even by the standards of a Church which was by now conspicuously and scandalously materialistic and corrupt: he held three rich livings, had amassed a huge personal fortune and indulged in concubinage on a grand scale (he had fathered no fewer than twenty illegitimate children, many of whom were supported by rich Church livings). The revulsion came to a head over the death of a charismatic young Protestant theologian named George Wishart, who had been openly preaching the gospel of reform for eighteen months to packed congregations of sympathisers in several Scottish towns – landed gentry and common people alike. To Cardinal Beaton, Wishart was nothing but an English agent; Wishart was arrested in Haddington and arraigned at a lengthy show-trial in St Andrews Cathedral in February 1546. So eloquently did he defend himself, however, that the authorities cleared the court before delivering their foregone guilty verdict. Wishart was judicially strangled just short of death, then burned in the forecourt of St Andrews Castle in March 1546; to make the spectacle more spectacular, he had bags of gunpowder sewn into his clothes in order to make a fireworks display of his death for Cardinal Beaton's invited audience of nobles and clerics.

The response to Wishart's death was savage. A group of Protestant lairds in Fife entered the castle disguised as stonemasons on the night of 29 May and broke into the cardinal's chamber. The cardinal, who was in bed with his current mistress, Marion Ogilvy, was dragged from the room and butchered. His mutilated corpse, with his genitals stuffed into his mouth, was dangled from the window of the castle from which he had watched Wishart burn, and was then pickled in a barrel of brine and deposited in the castle's notorious Bottle Dungeon. The Protestants took over the castle, where they were joined by many supporters, but soon found themselves stranded there. The ailing Henry VIII sent them no help, despite constant appeals.

King Henry VIII died on 28 January 1547, and was succeeded by his nine-year-old son, Edward VI. Two months later, François I of France died, to be succeeded by his eldest son, the powerful and ambitious Henri II. The new French king's advisers were the Guises, and they moved to assist their niece, the young Scots queen: a French naval force was sent to Scotland to bombard St Andrews Castle, and on 31 July 1547 the Protestant 'Castilians', as they were called, surrendered. The most prominent of the rebels ('the gentlemen') were imprisoned in France, but the less important were sentenced to be galley-slaves.

One of the commoners was a zealous young preacher named John Knox, who in 1546 had attached himself to George Wishart at Haddington, carrying a great two-handed sword for show as well as for protection. When Wishart was arrested on the orders of Cardinal Beaton, the sword was not put to use: 'No, no, return to your bairns, and God bless you,' said Wishart. 'One is enough for sacrifice.' Knox had joined the 'Castilians' in St Andrews Castle as a volunteer defender in the spring of 1547; when the castle fell in July 1547, he was one of those condemned to the galleys. It would be two years of toiling at the oars, and another six years living abroad and in England, before he returned to Scotland to work for the establishment of the Protestant Church there, briefly in 1554–55 and finally in 1559 (see below).

The new monarchy in France was much more interested in a marriage alliance with Scotland than François I had been. Henri II had a baby son, François, a year younger than Mary, and negotiations were opened for a possible marriage between the two children in return for French military support to defend Scotland when necessary.

Henry VIII's 'Rough Wooing' had not produced the desired results. By the time he died in January 1547, it had cost the English treasury £350,000. But neither his death nor the alarming costs altered the thrust of English policy towards Scotland: the new king's uncle, the Earl of Hertford (now elevated to Duke of Somerset), became the Lord

Protector of England, and he was as resolute for a marriage alliance between Mary and Edward VI as Henry had been. So the 'Rough Wooing' continued.

The Battle of Pinkie (10 September 1547)

In the late summer of 1547 the Duke of Somerset made another fierce assault on Scotland – and this time his intent was conquest rather than punishment. On 1 September he left Newcastle with a massive, largely professional army of twenty-five thousand men, including three thousand cavalry, 1,800 musketeers, fifteen heavy guns, sixty lighter pieces, a thousand wagons and 1,400 artisans and sappers; a large English fleet kept pace with him all the way, carrying munitions and supplies and providing floating artillery batteries. Somerset marched unopposed up the east coast, bypassing Tantallon Castle. By Friday, 8 September he had reached Longniddry; then he pushed forward to the coast, east of the River Esk, and there, at Pinkie near Musselburgh, he found the Scottish army awaiting him.

The Scots, under the Earl of Arran, had mustered an impressive army of thirty-five thousand men. They knew that this was to be another crucial showdown with England, perhaps on a par with Bannockburn itself. To meet the advancing English the Scots had marched out of Edinburgh and were drawn up in a strong defensive position on the steep western banks of the Esk, dug in behind carefully-prepared breastworks. The Earl of Huntly, Lord Chancellor of Scotland, was on the left flank, supported by three thousand clansmen under the Earl of Argyll, who commanded the only bridge across the river. Arran himself was in the centre, on Edmonstone Ridge, while the right was held by the Earl of Angus supported by 1,500 light cavalry under Lord Home. The weak point in the Scottish array was the cavalry, which was lighter and much less numerous than the English horse – that, and a lack of heavy artillery.

On Saturday, 9 September Somerset brought his fleet to the mouth of the Esk, where his heavy naval guns could bombard the Scottish left flank at will. He was faced with the prospect of having to make a frontal assault on the formidable Scottish defences; instead, he waited patiently for the Scots to come down from their strong position and make the first attack. Sure enough, the Border horsemen, eager for the fray, came splashing across the Esk to taunt the English ranks. Somerset held back until all the Scots horsemen were across the river on their nimble garrons, then gave the order to charge. For once the little garrons were not agile enough to make their escape, and were caught by the full force of a thunderous heavy charge. Lord Home himself was captured. The Scots were now left without an effective cavalry arm.

On the morning of Sunday, 10 September Somerset ordered the advance. He moved his ponderous heavy artillery into a broad loop of the Esk confronting Edmonstone Ridge and opened fire on Arran's left flank as the naval guns began their bombardment. Arran, concerned that his men would be cut to pieces, ordered a counter-attack. Huntly and Argyll sent their lightly-armed troops across the Esk in a dense, tightly-packed phalanx. As they tried to come to grips with the enemy they suffered fearful losses from the ships' guns, but still they marched on. Somerset, who had lined up his guns to rake the Scottish centre, now slewed them to face the oncoming Scottish pikemen, while the English horse charged and recharged at their flank. In the end the press of dead bodies slowed the Scottish momentum: the great phalanx stumbled to a halt, unable to go any farther. At last it broke, and the survivors headed for the Esk, pursued by the triumphant English cavalry. Very few made it: fourteen thousand men died on the east bank of the river, while the English losses barely exceeded 250, mostly cavalrymen. Arran, closely accompanied by the Earl of Angus, managed to escape to Edinburgh among the fugitives streaming away from the centre and right of the Scottish line.

Somerset now occupied Leith and ravaged Holyrood Abbey, but despite his overwhelming victory at Pinkie he made no attempt to attack the castle. The purpose of his invasion had been to place full-time English garrisons in strategic strongpoints as an army of occupation. He sent his fleet to bombard Dundee, which was almost destroyed. Fife was harried. Kirkcudbright was attacked. Dumfries was taken. A strong force was stationed at Eyemouth to build a new fort. By the time Somerset returned to London to the plaudits of parliament and the thanks of his nephew, King Edward VI, the eastern Borders of Scotland had been virtually turned into an English shire.

Meanwhile, the infant queen was on the move again. On the day after the military disaster at Pinkie she was taken from Dunkeld and transported for safety to the priory of Inchmahome on a wooded island on the Lake of Menteith, in the Trossachs, where she stayed for nearly three weeks.[1] As soon as Somerset marched south with the bulk

---

1 Inchmahome Priory is now a ruin, tranquil in its attractive island setting. Much of the thirteenth-century church survives, but only the foundations of the cellar of the priory house in which Mary stayed remain. The priory is in the care of Historic Scotland.

of his army, Mary was taken back to Stirling Castle, on 29 September 1547. Here she was struck down with an attack of chickenpox which confined her to bed for several weeks. What a childhood! – hounded from place to place, her future a bargaining card in the complexity of allegiances of ambitious politicians.

Early in 1548 another English army invaded Berwickshire and seized Haddington, only thirty kilometres south of Edinburgh; a huge new fort was built there, specially designed to withstand a siege and housing an English garrison two thousand strong. Haddington controlled the main route to the south-east and provided the headquarters for the English occupation of southern Scotland.[1] The young queen was moved yet again, on 21 February 1548, to the safety of Dumbarton Castle on the Clyde.

Now her immediate future had to be decided. Scotland had proved itself unable to withstand the brutal military pressure from England. In November 1547 the Scottish Privy Council sent an appeal to France for aid, and a few weeks later a group of fifty French 'military advisers' arrived in Scotland. In February 1548 the Scottish parliament agreed to betroth Mary Queen of Scots to the Dauphin of France, François, the eldest son of King Henri II, in return for armed French help. Mary was to go to France as soon as possible to be brought up there (she was now recovering from an attack of measles); and the Earl of Arran was given a bonus – the French duchy of Châtelherault, a title still proudly borne by the Hamilton family.

On 16 June 1548 the promised French aid arrived at Leith in a fleet of more than a hundred ships carrying a large and well-equipped army of six thousand French, German and Italian veterans, including artillery experts and two experienced squadrons of light infantry. They quickly laid siege to Haddington, and in a nearby nunnery on 6 July the Scots signed the Treaty of Haddington which sealed the marriage agreement. Haddington itself proved harder to crack, and eventually the French had to retire to their barracks in Leith when an English army arrived to relieve the beleaguered fort. But this was to prove to be the high-point of English success in Scotland. Although a surprise

---

1   One of the casualties of the siege was St Mary's Church in Haddington, which had its bells looted. Four and a half centuries later the congregation of St Mary's raised £70,000 to buy a replacement set, with the help of a £46,000 grant from the Heritage Lottery Fund – the first church in Scotland to break the Kirk's strict anti-lottery policy. The eight bronze replacement bells were the King George V bells of Dunecht House, near Aberdeen. At noon on New Year's Day 2000 the new bells rang out for the first time to welcome the new millennium.

night-time assault on Haddington failed, by the summer of 1549 the English garrisons were more or less prisoners in their strongholds. As the costly war of attrition in Scotland dragged on, the Earl of Somerset lost favour in England; his standing was further eroded when Henri II of France unleashed a tremendous assault on English-held Boulogne. Haddington and the other English-held forts were abandoned in September 1549; and with that, England made peace, first with France in March 1550 and then with Scotland in June 1551.

The cost to the English Exchequer of the Scottish war – some £600,000 – had bankrupted the country, and with it came the end for Somerset; in October 1549 he was deposed and imprisoned by John Dudley, Earl of Warwick, and in January 1552 he was executed. By then, however, Mary Queen of Scots – and Scotland itself – had long been committed to the 'faith and credit' of the King of France.

Mary Queen of Scots in France (1548–61)

In 1548 the future of Scotland – and its infant queen – had still been in the balance. In that fraught summer, King Henri II sent a French fleet (with his personal galley) to Dumbarton to take the five-year-old Queen of Scots abroad to safety. The queen mother, torn between the desire to be with her daughter and the need to stay in Scotland to protect her daughter's inheritance, finally decided to remain in Scotland. On 29 July little Mary took a tearful farewell of her mother and boarded the royal French ship. For nine days the fleet was weatherbound in the Firth of Clyde, and when it managed to sail on 7 August it had a stormy and dangerous voyage before Mary was able to step on to French soil at Roscoff, a fishing port near Brest, in Brittany, on 13 August 1548; the little Chapel of St Ninian there is said to mark the spot where she landed. Four of her young maids-of-honour were to become famous as the 'Four Maries': Mary Beaton, Mary Fleming, Mary Livingston and Mary Seton.[1] The child-queen and her four Maries were not to see Scotland again for thirteen years.

---

1 A costume tableau of the queen and her Four Maries is on display in Smailholm Tower, which rises conspicuously on a rocky eminence between St Boswells and Kelso. Mary Beaton was a distant relative of Cardinal David Beaton and his brother, the future Archbishop James Beaton; Mary Fleming was the daughter of Queen Mary's governess, Lady Fleming; Mary Livingston was the daughter of Lord Livingston, Queen Mary's guardian at Stirling Castle and Dunkeld; and Mary Seton was the daughter of the sixth Lord Seton and his French wife, who had come to Scotland as a maid of honour to Marie de Guise. It should be noted that the 'Ballad of the Queen's Maries', with its haunting refrain of 'Yestre'en the queen had four

The sophisticated French court was captivated by the bright, vivacious five-year-old Scots girl who arrived in Paris in October 1548. The dauphin's mother, Catherine de' Medici, said, 'This small Queen of Scots has only to smile in order to turn all French heads.' By contrast with the tall Scottish princess, the dauphin was small, puny and delicate. Mary cosseted and mothered him, and soon a genuine affection developed between them.

Even in the nursery, Mary enjoyed every luxury. As the royal household moved from palace to palace, from Fontainebleau to Blois, from Saint-Germain-en-Laye to Chambord, a huge retinue of servants was always at hand. Mary had her own chaplain who carried her personal communion vessels from place to place for the celebration of Mass every single day. Her wardrobe included dresses of gold damask, bonnets of silver thread, embroidered caps with trimmings of fur and velvet, and deerskin gloves. Her education was carefully planned, with lessons in Spanish, Italian and the classics; she also studied drawing, singing, dancing and playing the lute, and learned to ride expertly. She was soon speaking perfect French, and French was to be her preferred language for the rest of her life (she would always sign herself as 'Marie Stuart').

As the children grew up, the cross-currents of international politics swirled and eddied around their young heads. The prospective marriage was of acute importance not only to Scotland but also to France and England. Mary Queen of Scots was being blatantly used as a vehicle for Henri II's grandiose designs on England as well as on Scotland: as early as 1550 he had advanced Mary's claim to the English throne, and his plans included the eventual total absorption of Scotland into a greater French monarchy.

In March 1558 a parliamentary delegation from Scotland went to France to discuss the terms for the marriage. The Queen of Scots pledged herself to uphold her realm's ancient freedoms, liberties and privileges. It was agreed that the dauphin should, after the marriage, bear the title of King of Scots, and that on his accession to the throne the two kingdoms were to be united under one crown, with dual nationality for all citizens of both countries; if the marriage produced

---

Maries', does not refer to Mary Queen of Scots: the Maries of the ballad are named 'Mary Beaton, Mary Seton, Mary Carmichael and me' (Mary Hamilton). The song was inspired by a tragic scandal at the court of Peter the Great of Russia in the eighteenth century, when a Scots maid of honour (Mary Hamilton) was executed for the murder of her illegitimate child by the tsar: Queen Mary's 'Four Maries' were simply grafted on to that story.

issue, the eldest surviving son would inherit both crowns, while the eldest surviving daughter would inherit the Scottish crown only. If the marriage turned out to be childless, Henri II would uphold the succession to the throne of the nearest legal heir, who was at that time the Duke of Châtelherault (the former Earl of Arran). It was even agreed that the Scottish crown would be sent to France so that the dauphin could be crowned with it as King of Scots (although, in the event, it was never sent).

The formal betrothal between the two youngsters was accordingly solemnised on 19 April 1558 in the Great Hall of the Louvre (at that time a royal palace), and five days later, on Sunday, 24 April, Mary Queen of Scots was married to François, Dauphin of France. She was fifteen years old, he was fourteen; despite the terms of the marriage treaty, no one really expected the union to prove fertile.

The wedding was celebrated with spectacular pomp and ceremony in Paris in the cathedral of Nôtre Dame. Processions of prelates and princes of the Church preceded a long line of royal guests. The bride, tall and stately, was sumptuously attired in white and blue velvet robes studded with jewels, with a long train and wearing a golden crown encrusted with sapphires, pearls and rubies. After the wedding the new queen-dauphine and her diminutive husband were carried through Paris on a golden litter in a grand royal cavalcade.

Before the marriage, however, Mary had been persuaded to sign a secret protocol which put the glamour of the wedding into a much more realistic context. In the first clause, she agreed that should she die without issue, the crown matrimonial of Scotland would pass to her husband, the dauphin; in effect, Mary was bequeathing the throne of Scotland to France. In addition, she assigned her 'rights and claims' to the English throne to the King of France. In the second clause, the realm of Scotland was mortgaged to the French crown until all the sums spent on her education and on French military aid to Scotland were reimbursed; and in the third Mary repudiated, in advance, any agreement made by the Scottish parliament which might contradict the terms of the protocol. The existence of this agreement did not stay secret for long, and did nothing to reconcile Scotland to France's suspected imperial ambitions.

In November of that year (1558) Queen Elizabeth ascended the throne of England. In Catholic eyes she was illegitimate – Henry VIII's divorce from Catherine of Aragon had never been recognised by the Catholic Church, so his marriage to Elizabeth's mother, Anne Boleyn, had been void. Consequently, Mary Queen of Scots, as a great-granddaughter of Henry VII, was regarded as the rightful heir to the English throne. Henri II of France reflected this by repeating his claim that his new daughter-in-law was the rightful Queen of England as well – which did little to endear Mary to her cousin Elizabeth.

In July 1559 the political position changed again – drastically: Henri II died from wounds he sustained while jousting at a tournament, and François became King of France as François II, with the sixteen-year-old Mary as his queen-consort. The coronation took place in Rheims Cathedral. Their reign was to last barely seventeen months. Late in 1560 the sickly François II – *le Petit Roi*, as his subjects called him – contracted an infection in his left ear. The infection (apparently a mastoid abscess) spread to his brain, and after much suffering he died on 5 December 1560. Mary was heartbroken, for she had been devoted to her little husband and childhood companion.

The death of François II brought an end to the power which the house of Guise had exercised through Mary as queen-consort. François was succeeded by his ten-year-old brother, as Charles IX; his mother, Catherine de' Medici, seized the opportunity to oust the Guise family from power and had herself appointed regent.

At once, envoys of various suitors for Mary's hand were on their way to see her: the King of Sweden, the Archduke Charles of Austria, the third Earl of Arran (former Master of Hamilton, who had been elevated to his father's title) and Don Carlos, the heir to the Spanish throne, with Mary's brother-in-law Charles IX of France as a longer shot. But Catherine de' Medici was resolute against either a Spanish or a French marriage.

Mary's position in the French court became more and more disagreeable. Her mother, Marie de Guise, died in the summer of 1560. Her mother-in-law's earlier fondness for her turned to downright hostility after the death of François, and it was soon clear that Mary had no alternative but to accept parliament's invitation for her to return to her native Scotland and take her rightful place on the throne.

But what had been happening in Scotland during her absence? To what sort of realm would she be returning?

The queen mother: Marie de Guise and the Reformation

The infant Queen, being thus transferred to France, her mother, Mary of Guise, the widow of James V, had the address to get herself placed at the head of affairs in Scotland.

TALES OF A GRANDFATHER, CHAPTER XXIX

When Mary had left for France in the summer of 1548 the south of Scotland was under English military occupation as a result of the 'Rough Wooing'; but as part of her marriage treaty, French troops had arrived to give much-needed support to Scotland's hard-pressed war effort. Within a year the position had been totally changed: the English had abandoned the 'Rough Wooing' and withdrawn their occupation forces, but the French army had remained to support the pro-French Catholic party which now held power. The Earl of Arran's half-brother, John Hamilton, who had been appointed Archbishop of St Andrews in succession to the murdered Cardinal Beaton, was more prepared to make compromises with the reformers than his predecessor had been; he went some way towards satisfying the demands for Church reform without altering its ecclesiastical structure. Three councils of the Scottish Church passed legislation to curb abuses in the Church system; a new Catechism made some concessions to the Lutheran teaching of 'justification by faith alone'; and endowments were made for the better education of priests. It was a start – but in the event it was too little and too late.

The queen mother, Marie de Guise, had been working hard in the background to look after her daughter's realm.[1] She was a handsome, charming woman 'of majestic stature' who spoke broken English with an attractive French accent. Throughout her daughter's early years she had steered a careful political course with great courage and skill. Now, as the 1550s dawned and the English occupation ended, she came into her own. In 1550 she took to France a distinguished company of Scottish notables in order to dazzle the waverers with a sight of the successes and brilliant cultural achievements of Renaissance France. The mission had the desired effect. When Mary Queen of Scots legally came of age in France in 1554 she was entitled to choose her regent in Scotland; not surprisingly, she chose her mother, and the Duke of Châtelherault (Arran) was cajoled and bribed into resigning.

As queen regent, Marie de Guise had already gained widespread respect and acceptance among the Scottish political community. In religion she was neither a zealot nor a persecutor, and she now did

---

1 Marie de Guise had her residence (variously described as a 'palace' or a 'mansion') in the lee of Edinburgh Castle; it no longer exists, alas. After the burning of the Palace of Holyroodhouse and much of the Royal Mile in 1544 during the 'Rough Wooing', she moved her household into new quarters off the Lawnmarket; the building was pulled down in 1845 to make room for the new Free High Church (now New College) at the top of the Mound, next to the Assembly Hall (from James Grant, *Old and New Edinburgh*, Vol. 1, Cassells, 1882.)

everything she could to conciliate the conflicting interests of the people of Scotland. Pastors of the Lutheran persuasion were allowed to preach without hindrance and, during the ferocious Counter-Reformation years of rule by Mary Tudor ('Bloody Mary', r.1553–58) in England, the queen regent allowed English Protestant refugees to find sanctuary in Scotland.[1] But she was the head of a court which was predominantly French; most of her senior officials were French; the professional standing army which reinforced her authority was French. Despite all her efforts to create harmony, her Frenchness undermined all her careful work: the Scots feared that Scotland was becoming a mere satellite province of France, and the Reformers now became associated with patriotism and liberty – they became the party which opposed foreign domination and occupation. Gradually the queen regent's popularity waned, especially after she tried to raise additional taxation to pay for military fortifications.

The Reformation

In December 1557 a handful of Protestant nobles of Scotland, who came to be called the 'Lords of the Congregation of Christ', met in Edinburgh to sign a covenant known as the *First Band* [Bond] *of the Protestant Congregation in Scotland*. In this document, they swore to 'apply our whole power, substance and our very lives to maintain, set forward and establish the most blessed word of God and his Congregation'. The main signatory was Archibald, fourth Earl of Argyll; one of the others was James Douglas, fourth Earl of Morton, who would later play a key role in the quagmire of changing loyalties during the crises of Mary's personal rule in Scotland, and would act as regent during much of the time she was imprisoned in England.[2] A third was

---

1   Scotland had very few Protestant martyrs compared with England and the Netherlands. In England, more than 350 men and women (including five bishops) died in the fires of Smithfield and Oxford during the reign of Mary Tudor; all the deaths were meticulously recounted in John Foxe's *History of the Acts and Monuments of the Church* (1563, popularly known as *Foxe's Book of Martyrs*), which became a best-seller in Elizabethan England. In the Netherlands, almost thirty thousand people were executed for their faith in the 1530s and 1540s. In Scotland, in the thirty years between the burning of Patrick Hamilton at St Andrews in 1528 and the revolt of the Lords of the Congregation of 1559–60, 'only' twenty-one people (including one woman) were executed for heresy.

2   James Douglas, fourth Earl of Morton (c.1516–81), succeeded to the earldom through his wife in 1550. When the Angus Douglases were banished by James V in 1528, young James Douglas remained in Scotland under an assumed name, and worked as a farm foreman in the north of Scotland. He became Chancellor of Scotland under Mary in 1563, but was

Patrick Lindsay, Lord Lindsay of the Byres, a doughty warrior who would be one of Mary Queen of Scots' most implacable enemies.

This open espousal of the Protestant cause has long been seen as a major turning-point in the story of the Reformation in Scotland, but it was more of a glimmer than a real dawn. Few of Scotland's nobles declared themselves, and the covenant attracted little support. It was not sufficient to alarm the queen regent. In April 1558 Marie de Guise went to France to attend Mary's wedding to the Dauphin of France; but four days later an elderly Protestant schoolmaster named Walter Mylne was burned as a heretic at St Andrews. It signalled a major change in policy: Protestantism was no longer to be tolerated.

But now, once again, events in England had a decisive effect on events in Scotland. On 17 November 1558 Mary Tudor, the Catholic Queen of England, died childless, and was succeeded by her Protestant half-sister, Elizabeth, the daughter of Anne Boleyn and the last surviving child of Henry VIII. Elizabeth was twenty-five years old, and still unmarried, and her safety and survival on the uneasy throne of England was going to depend not only on her political skills but also on the support of a Protestant England – and of a Protestant Scotland.

The accession of Protestant Elizabeth in England, and the revival of the Reformation there, brought fresh hope to the Scottish Reformers. The queen regent reversed her policy of religious toleration: Protestant preachers were commanded to present themselves before her, on pain of banishment; none came and all were outlawed.

John Knox, who had ventured into Scotland for a few months in 1555, now returned to Scotland from exile to start his ministry. And what a start! In St John's Church in Perth, on Thursday, 11 May 1559, he preached a sermon so 'vehement against idolatry' that the congregation ('the rascal multitude', as it would later be called) was roused to violent action. Church ornaments and furnishings were destroyed, and the monasteries of the Black and Grey Friars, and the Carthusian Charterhouse monastery, were sacked. It was the spark for the civil war which had been threatening for several months.

The queen regent mustered an army and marched with it towards Perth on 22 May, but Protestant supporters flocked to the town and an armistice was signed on 29 May. One important member of her

---

dismissed after the murder of Rizzio and, after being pardoned, was involved, however marginally, in the murder of Lord Darnley. During Mary's imprisonment in England he was one of her fiercest enemies. He was regent from 1572 to 1580. In 1581 he was executed for being an accessory to Darnley's murder.

forces defected to the Protestants and joined the Lords of the Congregation – James Stewart *secundus*, illegitimate son of James V and therefore half-bother to Mary Queen of Scots and soon to be ennobled as the Earl of Moray; he was to play a major role during his half-sister's short reign.[1] He was one of the signatories of the *Second Band of the Congregation*, which was drawn up in Perth on 31 May 1559.

The reinforced Lords of the Congregation mustered an 'Army of the Congregation of Christ' at St Andrews. The queen regent's forces fell back towards Edinburgh, and the Army of the Congregation was able to occupy Perth (where the mob got out of control and sacked the abbey of Scone) and Stirling, 'purging' churches and friaries as they went, before marching on Edinburgh. The queen regent withdrew to Dunbar, and the Army of the Congregation took possession of the capital. From Edinburgh they issued a decree deposing the queen regent and setting up a Great Council in the name of the absent queen.

The queen regent was now suffering severely from dropsy; but she hung on in Dunbar until reinforcements arrived from France to help her recapture Leith and Edinburgh. Until now, Elizabeth of England had refrained from direct intervention in Scotland; the arrival of the French troops, however, prompted her to send an English fleet to blockade the Firth of Forth in January 1560, and in the following month she signed a treaty with the Lords of the Congregation at Berwick which brought in an English army to besiege the French garrison in Leith.

The fighting between the Protestant English besiegers and Catholic French defenders lasted all spring, while the queen regent lay dying in Edinburgh Castle. Her death, on 11 June 1560, came as a merciful release from agony; John Knox greeted it with obscene rejoicing. By now, however, the envoys of France and England were already discussing peace; and in July 1560 the Treaty of Edinburgh secured French recognition of Queen Elizabeth's right to the English throne and the withdrawal of both French and English troops from Scotland. It marked the effective end of the 'Auld Alliance' which had been estab-

---

1 Lord James Stewart, Earl of Moray (1531–70), was a son of James V by his mistress Lady Margaret Erskine. He was appointed Commendator of St Andrews Priory at the age of seven, in 1538. At seventeen he distinguished himself in the field against the English in south-east Scotland and then accompanied the five-year-old Mary Queen of Scots to France in 1548. He went to France again in 1550 on Marie de Guise's mission, and in 1558 he was one of the eight Scottish commissioners who represented Scotland at Mary's wedding to the dauphin.

lished in 1295, and heralded the effective start of the Reformation in Scotland.[1]

The Lords of the Congregation party was now acting as if it were a provisional government. In August 1560 the Scottish parliament – the 'Reformation Parliament', as it is called – passed a series of acts in the name (but without the authority) of the queen. It authorised a new *Scots Confession of Faith* – twenty-five articles, written quickly and vigorously in the vernacular by John Knox and five others, the 'six Johns' (Knox, Willcock, Winram, Spottiswoode, Row and Douglas). It abolished the Pope's authority in Scotland and forbade the celebration of the Latin Mass, on pain of death for a third offence. On the other hand, parliament did not at that time consider the other major document of the early Reformation, the *First Book of Discipline*. This was the basic 'mission statement' of the fledgling Kirk. It dealt with reform of the organisation of the Kirk and its congregations and the election of ministers and elders, and a compulsory education system designed to give the Kirk a proper supply of ministers as well as making learning freely available to everyone.

So what kind of Reformation was it? The present Historiographer Royal in Scotland, Christopher Smout, has pointed out that the reformed Church of Scotland which broke to the surface in 1560 did not, at that point, assume all the characteristics which we now associate with it:

> For the next 130 years it went on changing and developing, twisting in its ecclesiastical policy first to one side and then to another to accommodate differing shades of religious opinion until finally, in 1690, it emerged as the classic Presbyterian Church of the eighteenth and nineteenth centuries, with its elders, deacons and ministers, its kirk-sessions, presbyteries, synods and General Assembly, its frequent but not invariable association with sabbatarianism and puritanism, and its convictions of ecclesiastical parity.
>
> A HISTORY OF THE SCOTTISH PEOPLE 1560–1830,
> CHAPTER 2.2

---

1 Despite the formal end of the 'Auld Alliance' the close relationship between Scotland and France continued through the seventeenth and eighteenth centuries. In the rue du Cardinal Lemoine in Paris, the Scots College (Collège des Ecossais) is an abiding memorial to the Alliance. On the first floor is a chapel dedicated to St Andrew, containing memorials to its original founder, David, Bishop of Moray; Archbishop James Beaton (nephew of the murdered cardinal); James VII & II, who lived in exile at Saint-Germain-en-Laye until his death in 1701 (his brain is said to be preserved in a casket in the chapel); and his son, the Old Pretender, James Stuart.

Nor did it 'happen' everywhere overnight. Michael Lynch says:

> *For many people the Reformation is the central event of Scottish history; it was the point at which they can claim their birthright as a Protestant nation. For them, the Reformation was a kind of 'big bang' – everything happened overnight. In some places it did. In St Andrews, on 11 June 1559, the citizens went to bed as Catholics and woke up as Protestants, because overnight the Lords of the Congregation – the Protestant army, with John Knox among them – had come into the town, had gone into the parish church and ripped down all the Catholic ornaments, whitewashed the walls and turned it into a Protestant church. That 'big bang' did not happen like that in many places.*

In popular perception, the real 'big bang' of the Reformation happened when John Knox preached his inflammatory sermon in Perth in May 1559 and aroused 'the rascal multitude' to sack the monasteries in the town. For many the name of John Knox is practically synonymous with the Reformation – the single-minded zealot and spellbinding orator who 'created' the Reformation, single-handed, by his celebrated theological disputes with Mary Queen of Scots (see below). These disputes, in fact, had little effect on the course of history (except, perhaps, to drum up hatred against the young Catholic queen), for the Reformation was already a *fait accompli* by the time she returned to Scotland in 1561; but Knox's name is writ so large in the annals of the nation that we should pause here to consider him. Who was he? And what was he about?

John Knox (c.1512–72)

Superintending the quadrangle outside the nineteenth-century Assembly Hall of the Church of Scotland on the Mound in Edinburgh – the temporary first home of the new Scottish Parliament in 1999 – towers a handsome bronze statue of John Knox, sternly bearded to the chest like an Old Testament prophet. His left hand and arm cradle a Bible; his right arm is raised heavenward, palm open to the sky. The statue was sculpted by John Hutchison in 1895; the legend on the plinth reads:

John Knox
1514–1572
Erected by Scotsmen who are
mindful of the benefits conferred
by John Knox on their native land
1896

Knox has for long been cast as the key figure in the story of the Protestant Reformation in Scotland, either baleful or benign, depending on one's point of view.[1] Yet he was never the leader of the Reformation movement, nor was he ever the political leader of his country. He had a hand in drawing up three key early documents of the Reformation: the *Scots Confession of Faith* (1560); the *First Book of Discipline* (1561), which adumbrated the religious and educational organisation of the country ('a school in every parish'); and the service book he had used with the congregation of English refugees in Geneva became the authorised *Book of Common Order* of the Kirk. But his impact on the Reformation is now considered by many historians to have been more apparent than real.

John Knox was born in 1512 or 1514 in Haddington, East Lothian, of English stock. He probably attended the grammar school there and then the University of St Andrews; if he went to St Andrews he could have been influenced by the teachings of the humanist historian John Major, Provost of St Salvator's College, author of a Latin *History of Greater Britain* (printed in Paris in 1521) and a strong advocate of Anglo–Scottish friendship and even union. Little is known for certain about Knox's early life, except that he was ordained as a Catholic priest in 1536. He did not serve a parish, however; he acted as a notary and as a tutor in the family of a local laird.

Soon he became a Reformer. His first appearance on the public scene was in 1546, when he attached himself to the Protestant martyr George Wishart who was burned at the stake at St Andrews. After the capture at St Andrews Castle in July 1547 and his eighteen months' hard labour chained to an oar on a French galley, Knox was released under an amnesty in February 1549. He went to England, where he was appointed to a pastoral charge in Berwick; here he married an

---

1 *Plain Mr Knox*, by Elizabeth Whitley, wife of the then minister of St Giles' (Harry Whitley), which was published in 1960, presented a persuasively positive view of Knox as a man of principle and compassion who articulated the deepest spiritual feelings of the common man. Other, more recent, commentators have been less sympathetic.

Englishwoman, Marjorie Bowes, daughter of the captain of Norham Castle, by whom he had two sons. He became a chaplain to King Edward VI, who had succeeded his father, Henry VIII, in 1547. Knox was offered the bishopric of Rochester, but his political instincts ('the foresight of trouble to come') warned him to decline it: Edward VI was a sickly child, and Knox realised that the next monarch (who would be Edward's half-sister, Mary Tudor) would be the instrument of a Counter-Reformation which would lead to much bloodshed and suffering for Protestants.

As soon as Mary Tudor acceded to the throne in 1553, John Knox – unencumbered by an episcopate – was one of the hundreds of Protestants who fled to the Continent for safety. He found congenial refuge at first in Frankfurt and then in Switzerland, where he settled as minister to a congregation of English exiles in Geneva. Here he met the French reformer John Calvin, in what he called 'the most perfect school of Christ that ever was on earth since the days of the Apostles'. He returned to Scotland for a few months on a secret mission in 1555–56 for discussions with Protestant sympathisers. Scotland was a comparatively safe haven at the time (no heretic had been put to death there for five years) and Knox was in no great danger, but he did not care to stay too long, and soon returned to Geneva.

In Geneva he published a series of thunderous tracts – in particular his celebrated *First Blast of the Trumpet against the Monstrous Regiment* [Government] *of Women* (1558). His targets were the women rulers who were resisting Protestantism: Mary Tudor in England and Marie de Guise in Scotland, of whom he wrote that her appointment as regent was 'as unseemly a sight as to put a saddle on the back of an unruly cow'. Knox did not mince words in his opening paragraph:

> *To promote a woman to beare rule, superioritie, dominion or empire above any realme, nation or citie, is repugnant to nature, contumelie to God, a thing most contrarious to His reveal'd will and approved ordinance, and finallie it is the subversion of good order, of all equitie and justice.*

His invective against 'Bloody Mary' was understandable, but it did little to endear him to Elizabeth of England, who came to the throne in November 1558 soon after his trumpet-blast was printed. When Knox wanted to return to England with the other Protestant refugees he was refused entry.

He therefore decided to wait for a propitious moment to sail directly to Scotland. Late in April he set off from Dieppe and landed on 2 May 1559. Nine days later he preached his celebrated sermon in St John's Church in Perth which sparked the first mob riots against Catholics. Soon he was preaching in Edinburgh, and on 7 July 1559 he was appointed minister of St Giles', only to withdraw to Fife when the queen regent, Marie de Guise, made her comeback.

When Mary Queen of Scots returned to Scotland in 1561 Knox berated her for her religion, her plans to marry a Roman Catholic, and the behaviour of her court, which he considered scandalously indecorous. He applauded the murder of David Rizzio (see below), but when the murderers failed to gain power he left Edinburgh for Ayrshire and then spent some months in England, returning only after Mary's overthrow and in time to preach at the coronation of her son, James VI. He was in high favour with the government carried on by James VI's regents, but was driven from Edinburgh when the castle there was held by adherents of the imprisoned Mary, and took refuge in St Andrews from May 1571 to August 1572.

John Knox made his last public appearance in the pulpit of St Giles' in November 1572. He died on the twenty-fourth of that month, and was buried with national mourning in the old churchyard beside St Giles'; it is now a tarmacadamed parking area for lawyers, and the site of his burial is marked only by a small square of yellow paint on Parking Lot 44 in front of the Court of Session in Parliament Square. The original grave-marker has been placed on the floor by the pews in the Moray Aisle of the cathedral, and a life-size bronze statue of Knox (cast in 1904 by the sculptor Pittendrigh MacGillivray), which used to be outside the cathedral, now stands inside the nave against one of the pillars near the entrance. It is symptomatic, perhaps, of the subtle downgrading of John Knox's role in Scotland's history which has been going on for several years now.[1]

In recent times John Knox has been made the scapegoat for every pathological trait in the Scottish *persona* – bigotry, cruelty, masochism, melancholy, misogyny, narrow-mindedness – you name it, Knox is to blame for it. But what was John Knox *really* like?

He was short of stature, long-bearded, with piercing eyes and a gift for powerful oratory. He was a man with a vision, not only for Scotland but for Christendom, of a Church and society under the rule of God,

---

1 In 1879 several tons of bones were removed from the St Giles' graveyard and taken in twenty boxes to Greyfriars kirkyard, which had been opened up by Mary Queen of Scots to ease pressure on St Giles'. It is assumed that the bones of John Knox were among them.

to whose divine will all monarchs and menials alike were equally subject. He was a theological 'revolutionary for God', prepared to envision the taking of action by a godly people against idolatrous rulers, and he had all the single-minded fanaticism and the self-righteousness of a man convinced that he alone knew what God was saying. He hated Mary Queen of Scots – not only because he saw her as a real danger to the success of the Reformation but also, perhaps, because he could not tolerate the thought of being opposed (and sometimes worsted in argument) by a woman. But he was certainly not a misogynist in the sense of being against all women: he married twice, the second time in 1564 when he was fifty years old and his bride was a sixteen-year-old girl (Margaret Stewart, the daughter of Lord Ochiltree), by whom he would have three daughters. Knox has been blamed for all the less joyful aspects of Calvinism in Scotland, which were actually the result of more Puritan influences in the following century. He was certainly not a killjoy or a bigot, as some have painted him – he liked the theatre (he had a hand in writing the text of a pageant), he enjoyed music, and he allowed Sunday-opening of taverns except during the hours of church services. He even told Mary Queen of Scots that he was 'not utterly against' dancing. Equally certainly, he had no wish to be a martyr to his faith. He was easily persuaded by George Wishart not to follow him to the stake. Whenever trouble threatened (after the murder of David Rizzio, for instance) he made himself scarce. As a politician, he could be called 'prudent' or 'cowardly', according to taste.

Ultimately, it cannot be claimed that John Knox was a great Scottish patriot, in the narrow sense; his vision was always theological rather than nationalistic. On the contrary, he was an important agent in the anglicisation of Scotland, both in its politics and in its culture. In the Reformed Church the Bible, the Psalter, the service books and all the official documents were written in English. His first wife, Marjorie Bowes (who died in 1560), was English, and their two sons were educated in England.

Knox's popular renown rests largely on his violent and often coarse antagonism to Mary Queen of Scots, and on the four disputations he conducted with her and which he described in his *History of the Reformation of Religion in the Realm of Scotland* – a history in which he cast himself in the starring role (it was completed only after his death and published in 1586). The confrontations between Knox and Mary did not 'decide' the course of the Reformation in Scotland; but there was a telling symbolism about their respective characters –

Calvinist zealot *versus* Catholic monarch, dour moralism *versus* charismatic Renaissance brilliance – which has held people's imagination for many centuries and has strongly coloured popular views of the Reformation in Scotland to this day.

Mary: the Scotland years (1561–67)

Her youth, for she was only eighteen when she returned to Scotland, increased the liveliness of her disposition. The Catholic religion, in which she had been strictly educated, was a great blemish in the eyes of her people; but on the whole the nation expected her return with more hope and joy, than Mary herself entertained at the thought of exchanging the fine climate of France and the gaieties of its court, for the rough tempests and turbulent politics of her native country.

TALES OF A GRANDFATHER, CHAPTER XXX

The Protestant Reformation had utterly transformed the political situation in Scotland and the position of its Catholic monarch. No one was more aware of this than the most intelligent and astute of the Scottish royal officials, William Maitland of Lethington (now known as Lennoxlove), who was nicknamed 'Mitchell Wylie' (a corruption of the Italian 'Macchiavelli'). Maitland had latterly been private secretary to the queen mother, and secretary of state, but he had joined the Protestant faction in November 1599 as the queen mother's hold on power was slipping. Despite the political divisions in Scotland brought about by the Reformation, the leading members of the new regime, advised by Maitland, were prepared to give their allegiance to their queen.

In April 1561 two very different Scottish delegations went to France to prepare the ground for Mary's return. One had been sent by the volatile Earl of Huntly, a Catholic, promising her an army of twenty thousand men with which to reduce the kingdom to subjection if she arrived at Aberdeen; this offer was rejected. The other, an official Protestant delegation led by Mary's half-brother, Lord James Stewart, went in a spirit of compromise and reconciliation. The Reformation was there to stay, he urged, and his advice to her was: 'Above all things, madame, for the love of God do not press matters of religion, not for any man's advice on earth.' This was the moderate counsel which Mary was shrewd enough to accept. She was determined that her religion should not, and would not, become an occasion for strife, and she was prepared to recognise the Protestant Church in Scotland as long as she was allowed to attend Catholic services in private.

On 14 August 1561, Mary Queen of Scots set sail from Calais on the great white galley which was to take her to Scotland. She was eighteen years old. She would be a stranger in her own realm but not, she hoped, an unwelcome one. After a swift journey, shadowed by English ships, she landed at Leith on the morning of Tuesday, 19 August. Her arrival was deliberately low-key; she was dressed in mourning black, and was accompanied only by a small retinue of friends and attendants (including her beloved 'Four Maries'). Her ship had not been expected so soon, and there was no official welcoming party on the quayside. But word of her return quickly spread. By the time she had lunched in the home of a local dignitary, the nobles of her court had arrived to greet her, and the road to the palace of Holyroodhouse was packed with bystanders, cheering wildly. The warmth and enthusiasm of her reception delighted her. That evening, and every evening for the rest of the week, the Edinburgh crowds serenaded her beneath the windows of the queen's apartments on the second floor of the north-west tower (the James V Tower). In his *History of the Reformation*, even John Knox admitted (albeit grudgingly, one feels) that:

> *fires of joy were set forth at night, and a company of most honest men with instruments of music, and with musicians, gave their salutations at her chamber window.*

The elation and gaiety changed abruptly on Mary's first Sunday morning, when she and her household attended Mass in the royal chapel at Holyrood. A small crowd (led by Lord Lindsay of the Byres) gathered in the forecourt and attacked a servant who was carrying altar candles to the chapel. Lord James Stewart had promised that Mary could attend Mass in private; now, true to his word, he stationed himself at the chapel door against the demonstrators while two of his brothers protected the terrified priest. That evening the crowds which gathered in the forecourt of the palace were in no mood to sing: this time there was angry shouting.

Next day the queen issued her first royal proclamation. It announced that with the advice of her parliament she would shortly make a final order (which she hoped would please everyone) to pacify the differences in religion; in the meantime she forbade anyone, under pain of death, to attempt any 'alteration or innovation of the state of public religion' current in her realm, or to molest her servants in the practice of their religion.

It was a sensible and statesmanlike placatory move, designed to damp down any stirrings of sedition. But it failed to placate John Knox. On the following Sunday he preached a vehement sermon from the pulpit of St Giles', denouncing the Mass and Mary's private services: 'One Mass is more fearful than ten thousand armed enemies landing in any part of the realm.'

Mary decided that she had to grasp this nettle firmly. She summoned Knox to Holyroodhouse for a private audience on the following Thursday morning (4 September). In a spirited speech she accused him of inciting her subjects to rebel against their rightful monarch; Knox replied that subjects had no duty to obey a monarch who was ungodly. They argued theology for hours, with Mary seemingly giving as good as she got, but without (of course!) coming to a resolution. Mary was clearly offended that anyone should speak to her, a queen, in such a brusque and condescending manner. By the end Knox had made one small, oblique concession towards the spirit of tolerance, quoting Scriptural authority: 'I am as well content to live under your Grace as Paul was to live under Nero.' But the battle-lines had been drawn; and after the audience he told his waiting friends at the gates of Holyroodhouse, 'If there be not in her a proud mind, a crafty wit and an indurate mind against God and His truth, my judgement faileth me.' He had at least recognised that Mary was an opponent of great spirit and even greater charm, which made her a much more dangerous adversary than he had feared. His extremist views were not shared by all the Reformers, however. Lord James Hamilton, for instance, was soon not on speaking terms with Knox; and in 1564 the General Assembly of the Kirk was to censure Knox severely for his unrelenting hostility towards the queen.

Despite the strident enmity of Knox and some of the other Reformer preachers, Mary embarked on her personal rule with much energy and common-sense. She made several royal progresses – to Fife, to Aberdeen, to Inverness, to Argyll, to Ayrshire, to the Borders – overcoming all the difficulties of travel and terrain with tireless gaiety. Everywhere she went, the people were enchanted by her vivacious charm – merchants and farm-workers, Highland lairds and Lowland washerwomen alike. Tall, athletic, graceful and dazzlingly beautiful with her almond-shaped hazel eyes and auburn hair, she looked every inch a queen.

In these early years, ably advised by her half-brother Lord James

Stewart (whom she made Earl of Moray in 1562) and her secretary of state, Maitland of Lethington, Mary governed with great circumspection and intelligence. She did not ratify the Reformation Acts of 1560 (which made them, technically, illegal), but she made no attempt to revoke them. She was scrupulous in showing no favouritism to her fellow-Catholics. She continued to practise her Catholic religion in private, but she sanctioned the prosecution and imprisonment of several priests who had publicly celebrated Mass. She endorsed a decision by her Privy Council that a third of the revenues from the old benefices would be divided between the Kirk and the crown, and some of it was to be devoted to hospitals and schools. Former opponents, like Lord Lindsay of the Byres, were reconciled and became her fervent supporters.

In the summer of 1562 Mary went with Lord James Stewart on a campaign against the most powerful Catholic family in Scotland, the Gordons of Huntly; George Gordon, the fourth Earl of Huntly (the 'Cock of the North', as he was called) and one-time Chancellor of Scotland, died of apoplexy after being captured at a skirmish at Corrichie in October.[1] His embalmed corpse was solemnly convicted of treason, and later Mary had to witness the bungled beheading of one of Gordon's sons, who had tried to abduct her. The scene reduced her to hysterical tears.

At home, however, the royal court was once again a focus for the cultural life of the kingdom, a glittering, cosmopolitan Renaissance court in the style of Mary's father and grandfather and her French in-laws. It was crowded with scholars, poets, artists and musicians. There was much dancing and merry-making, much playing of billiards and cards and dice late into the night, and much riding and hunting during the day. But it was not all frivolity. Mary's personal library of three hundred books contained volumes in many languages, histories of many countries, poetry in Scots, Italian and French, the classics, books on chess and music and a number of theological tracts. She read Latin a great deal, often with the humanist scholar George Buchanan, who wrote Latin masques for the entertainment of the court.[2]

---

1   A tall granite pillar on the B977 marks the site of the battle.

2   George Buchanan (1506–82) was one of the finest scholars in sixteenth-century Scotland, and was hailed by fellow-humanists all over Europe as the greatest Latin poet of his age. He spent much of his life on the Continent, teaching in humanist colleges. When he returned to Scotland in 1561 he was made welcome at Mary's court; but he was alienated from her by the murder of her second husband, Lord Darnley, and became one of her bitterest and most bigoted enemies.

She played the lute and the virginal, and busied herself and her 'Four Maries' with embroidery.

The glamour of Mary's court, which bewitched so many of her nobles and friends, only intensified John Knox's disapproval of her. She endured further tirades from him (in one of which she resorted to tears), and even though the only record of these sessions came from Knox's biased pen it does not appear that he got the better of her. Wearisome they may have been for her, but they were marginal to her activities – and to the political thrust of her reign. Michael Lynch says:

> The figures of Knox and Mary are often used as a kind of symbolic shorthand to illustrate the great clash of the Reformation: a clash of ideas, of culture; a bridge that could not be crossed. But there was no inevitability about the victory of Knox and the fall of Mary. In France, the crown was able to ride out the crisis of Protestantism in the 1560s through various agreements and through compromise. That was what Mary was trying to do in Scotland; she became patron of both the old Catholic Church and the new Protestant Church. And, arguably, she came very close indeed to pulling it off.

What caused Mary's failure was not John Knox, nor Protestant revulsion at her Catholicism. The direct cause of her ruin was a disastrous misjudgement by Mary herself – her marriage, in 1565, to her first cousin Henry Stewart, Lord Darnley.

Lord Darnley

> Young Darnley was remarkably tall and handsome, perfect in all external and showy accomplishments, but unhappily destitute of sagacity, prudence, steadiness of character, and exhibiting only doubtful courage, though extremely violent in his passions.
> TALES OF A GRANDFATHER, CHAPTER XXX

Deep under the foundations of the Old Quad of Edinburgh University, fronting the South Bridge at the corner of South College Street, lies the site of one of the great unsolved murders in the history of Scotland's monarchy – a building known as Kirk o' Field. This was where Henry, Lord Darnley, the second husband of Mary Queen of Scots, met his end in mysterious circumstances during or after a huge explosion which tore the building apart in 1567. Often, when I was Lord Rector of Edinburgh University for three years during the 1970s, I idly wondered where precisely Kirk o' Field had stood; everyone seemed to know that it was somewhere in the vicinity, but there was no marker, no signpost, no wall-plaque anywhere to guide the pilgrim. It was only when I was researching sites for this book that I realised I had been literally sitting on it for those three years: the site of Kirk o' Field is right under the first-floor corner chamber in the Old Quad in which I used to preside over meetings of the University Court. It is a pity that there is nothing at all to commemorate the spot, because it saw the crucial moment in the eventual downfall of Mary Queen of Scots.

The question of Mary's marriage had been uppermost on the European political agenda virtually since the day she was born: possession of her person meant possession of her kingdom, and there were many who aspired to both during her lifetime. The potentates of Europe, locked into their religious wars, had a keen interest in finding for the beautiful young widow a second husband who would secure Scotland's allegiance or at least its neutrality. This was an unmarried queen's ultimate trump card. Mary's cousin, Elizabeth of England, was a skilled player in this game of power-politics. She made it clear that she would never recognise Mary's claim to succeed her on the throne of England unless the Queen of Scots married a suitor who had Elizabeth's endorsement – and Elizabeth even proffered as a suitable husband her own somewhat shop-soiled favourite, Robert Dudley, Earl of Leicester, a man who was suspected of having murdered his wife so that he could marry Elizabeth himself.

Ultimately, Mary Queen of Scots made her own choice, but not for political reasons. She fell passionately in love with her tall, handsome, 'lusty' cousin, Henry, Lord Darnley, and determined to marry him whatever the consequences.

Henry Stewart, Lord Darnley (1546–67), was the elder son of the fourth Earl of Lennox and Margaret Douglas, the daughter of Margaret Tudor (the widow of King James V) by the Earl of Angus; both he and Mary Queen of Scots were great-grandchildren of Henry VII of England, and they both had Tudor and Stewart blood in their veins. Darnley was born and brought up in England. His mother was a Catholic and his father a Protestant; young Darnley had been brought up as a Catholic but conformed to the Protestant Church of England. He had a close claim to the English throne in succession to Queen Elizabeth, and a more distant one to the throne of Scotland.

He was a rank outsider in the marriage stakes until 1565. His father had been outlawed twenty years previously for siding with the English during the 'Rough Wooing'; in September 1564, however, he was pardoned and allowed to return to Scotland, and in the following February his son Henry, Lord Darnley, with express permission from Queen Elizabeth, was allowed to go to Scotland to join him. Mary had met Henry on two occasions in France. When she met him again, on 17 February 1565, she was favourably impressed by his manners. Soon he had become a member of her entourage, and struck up a close friendship with one of her staff, the Italian musician David Rizzio, who dealt with her French correspondence.[1]

Darnley was an exceptionally good-looking youth, eighteen years old, slender and very tall – he was an inch or two over six feet, taller even than the queen herself. He was fond of music and writing verse, and shared Mary's love of hunting and other outdoor recreations. Events would indicate, however, that his beauty and courtly accomplishments were only skin deep, for he was to show himself to be shallow, vain, weak, indolent, selfish, arrogant, vindictive and irremediably spoilt.

Mary's liking for Darnley seems to have been no more than that for a couple of months. Then, early in April 1565, he fell ill at Stirling Castle, where Mary was in residence: it seemed to be only a cold but it turned out to be an attack of measles. Mary felt sorry for him and comforted him at the start of his ailment, but soon she had become his devoted nurse, spending all day and evening at his bedside. Before she knew it, she had fallen in love with her handsome young invalid – totally and tumultuously.

Mary Queen of Scots, four years older than Darnley – politically prudent Mary, worldly-wise Mary – now threw all caution to the winds. This was the man she was determined to marry, and even Queen Elizabeth's reported hostility (real or feigned) had no effect on her wild infatuation. In May she created him Earl of Ross. On Sunday, 22 July, the day on which the banns for the marriage were called, she created him Duke of Albany. On Saturday, 28 July, although parliament had not been consulted, heralds at the Mercat Cross in Edinburgh proclaimed that when Mary married 'Prince Henry' he would be styled 'King of this our Kingdom'. The couple were within the 'forbidden

---

1 Rizzio (or Riccio) had come to Scotland in the train of the ambassador of Savoy. He was swarthy and apparently unprepossessing, but had a quick wit, a clever intellect and a flattering tongue. He was also a highly accomplished musician, with a pleasing bass voice; he had formed a sort of 'barbershop quartet' with three other valets of the bedchamber before he became Mary's secretary.

degrees' of consanguinity, but Mary was unwilling to wait for permission to be granted by the Pope. At dawn on Sunday, 29 July 1565 Mary married Darnley in her private chapel at Holyrood in a Catholic ceremony. As a widow, she wore mourning black. Darnley was not a practising Catholic, and did not stay to hear Mass.

Mary had married against the counsel of her closest advisers (and the unsolicited advice of John Knox); but there was nothing at the time to presage the disaster which the marriage would become. It created an independent monarchy, untrammelled by either England or France. It certainly did not affect Mary's popularity with her adoring public. On the other hand, it lost her much of her political support. Those of her advisers who had worked hard to foster an understanding with Elizabeth of England over the succession to her throne found their policy thwarted; and Darnley's family, the Lennoxes, had many private enemies among the nobility.

Before and after the wedding the Earl of Moray (Mary's half-brother) refused to attend court, and was immediately outlawed – 'put to the horn', it was called. Moray then made a rare political misjudgement. With the support of Châtelherault (Arran) he tried to muster forces at Ayr. Mary promptly raised an army of her own. Leaving Edinburgh on 26 August, riding as fearlessly and tirelessly as a man at the head of her troops, she set off to beard the rebels. For several weeks the two armies chased around the Lowlands without ever meeting in combat – a lively episode which became known as the 'Chaseabout Raid'. By October, the Earl of Moray realised that his cause was hopeless and slipped across the border to seek refuge in England.

Mary was now at the peak of her success as Queen of Scots. But the love match with Darnley soon turned sour. Darnley's behaviour became more and more erratic and dissolute; he would roam the streets of Edinburgh at night with low-life companions in search of women. He seldom appeared at Privy Councils, whose decisions needed his signature as well as that of the queen (eventually Mary made an iron stamp of his signature to apply to official documents). Meanwhile, he was developing his own court circle of sympathetic lords – men like Patrick Ruthven (third Earl of Ruthven and hereditary Sheriff of Perth), Lord Lindsay of the Byres and, most importantly, the Earl of Morton.

It was all too quickly becoming clear that Mary's immature and petulant husband was not going to be a fit consort for her, let alone a fit King of Scots. Despite the title of 'king' she had bestowed on

Darnley, Mary was having second thoughts, and deliberately withheld the crown matrimonial from him, to his unbridled fury. Their estrangement had begun.

The first major crisis of their relationship occurred on the evening of 9 March 1566 when David Rizzio was murdered in Holyroodhouse, in or near Mary's presence, in a plot with which Darnley was closely involved. Mary was then six months pregnant.

The murder of Rizzio (9 March 1566)

Much of Mary's troubled reign is associated with the Palace of Holyroodhouse, at the foot of the Royal Mile in Edinburgh. She lived there for only six years, but it was her principal home during the years of her personal reign (1561–67). The palace had been greatly extended by her father, James V, to provide a fitting residence for his wife, Marie de Guise; and when Mary returned to Scotland in 1561 she chose to live in the apartments on the second floor of the north-west tower which had been prepared for her mother, and not the apartments on the first floor reserved for the monarch. Today, the 'James V Tower' is the only part of the palace of Mary's time to have survived in identifiable form; Holyroodhouse would be extensively transformed in the reign of her great-grandson, Charles II, into one of the finest examples of baroque architecture in Scotland. It is now the official Scottish residence of the monarch.

Mary's bedchamber opened off a large audience-chamber at the head of the main staircase. The bedchamber was connected by a small newel stair to the king's apartments below. Two small rooms led off the bedchamber. One was a closet for Mary's clothes. The other was a small ante-room hung in crimson and green, and measuring less than four metres square; Mary used it as an informal supper-room. This is the room which excites more visitor interest than any other in the palace, because it saw the murderous attack on Mary's favourite, David Rizzio. The newel stair is no longer there, and the floor level of the ante-room was raised during Charles II's renovations; but this did not inhibit the official guides of former years from dramatically pointing out a brass marker which indicated the very spot where Rizzio was assassinated, and even the alleged bloodstains on the floor. The brass marker has now been removed, and the guides provide a more sober account of the event.

The motives for the murder were complex, and the background was one of desperate conspiracy. The disaffected lords who had lost influence after the 'Chaseabout Raid' focused their discontent on the person of David Rizzio who, they claimed, was a secret agent of the Pope and had usurped their proper place in the intimate counsels of the queen. It was an easy matter to persuade the gullible Darnley to believe (or pretend to believe) that Rizzio, his former friend, was cuckolding him with the queen – even though the notion of a sexual liaison between Mary and Rizzio is highly implausible.

Darnley was ready enough to agree to anything which would satisfy his 'honour' publicly and get rid of Rizzio. The murder was also much in the interests of the Earl of Moray and his discredited accomplices of the 'Chaseabout Raid': on 12 March 1566 parliament was due to pass a bill of attainder against them for treason. Darnley was persuaded to enter into a written bond with these men, whereby they would be pardoned and allowed to return to Scotland. In exchange, he would receive the crown matrimonial, and would become king in his own right if Mary died without issue. The first phase was to be the murder of Rizzio. Astonishingly, many people had foreknowledge of the plot: by mid-February the English ambassador, Sir Thomas Randolph, had informed Queen Elizabeth that Darnley was plotting to seize the crown, and that Rizzio would be murdered.

On the evening of Saturday, 9 March, Mary was in her ante-room, enjoying a private supper with a handful of intimates, including David Rizzio. The conspirators had laid their plans with care: the Earl of Morton secured the approaches to Holyrood, while Lord Lindsay occupied the palace of Holyroodhouse with 150 men. Darnley appeared in the ante-room unexpectedly, having come up the private newel staircase to the queen's bedchamber. Suddenly the Earl of Ruthven also appeared at the door of the supper-room, wild-eyed and haggard from a fever, wearing armour under his cloak and brandishing a dagger.

'May it please Your Majesty,' he shouted, 'that yonder man David come forth of your privy-chamber where he hath been overlong.' Five others now came bursting in. Rizzio clung to the queen's skirts, screaming for mercy. While Mary pleaded with Darnley, with a pistol pressed to her belly, Rizzio was dragged from the room, through the bedchamber and the audience-chamber to the head of the main staircase, where he was done to death with more than fifty stab-wounds; Darnley's dagger, deliberately used by one of the murderers, was left protruding from his body.

Thus, with no attempt at secrecy, Rizzio was despatched. But Mary believed that she herself had been the real target – that she was to have been killed in the mêlée or, at the least, that the shock would cause her to miscarry her unborn child. Meanwhile the alarm had been raised and Edinburgh was in an uproar. Darnley went to the balcony of the queen's apartment to speak to the crowd which had gathered in the forecourt of the palace. Mary wanted to join him, but Lord Lindsay coarsely threatened to 'cut her in collops' if she tried.

The following day, a Sunday, Darnley discharged the imminent parliament. That evening Moray and the other Protestant exiles rode triumphantly into Edinburgh from Newcastle, confident that they would be in power. But the attempted *coup* failed – primarily due to Darnley's fecklessness. Having survived the ordeal, Mary knew that she was still in mortal danger. On the Monday morning Darnley was in a panic, realising that he too might be in danger, and begged Mary for forgiveness. She seized the opportunity of winning him over and detaching him from his allies, and started making plans to escape; she knew that if the conspirators got hold of her, they would hold her until the child was born and then imprison her for life. Mary now showed all her courage and coolness. The conspirators requested a meeting, which she granted on the Monday. They demanded that she pardon them all. Desperately playing for time, Mary feigned a sudden pain – the onset of labour, perhaps? – and retired to bed, knowing that they would never try to move her from Holyroodhouse if they thought the child was on the way.

There was now no time to lose. That night, after midnight, Mary and Darnley crept down the newel staircase and down to the servants' quarters, to the back of the palace. Arthur Erskine, her equerry and the brother-in-law of one of her 'Four Maries', was waiting there with horses. They galloped all night to Dunbar Castle, forty kilometres away. It was an exhausting ride for the pregnant queen, but it is recorded that when they arrived in the castle, Mary calmly cooked breakfast for them.

Now another major player in the drama of Mary's reign made a telling entrance on the scene – James Hepburn, fourth Earl of Bothwell. He was a committed Protestant, but as hereditary Lord Admiral of Scotland had loyally supported the queen regent, Marie de Guise. He had been imprisoned in 1562 for allegedly plotting to kidnap Mary Queen of Scots on behalf of the love-struck Earl of Arran, but had been pardoned and appointed lieutenant-general (commander-in-chief of Scotland's armed forces) at the time of Mary's marriage to Darnley. In February 1566 he had married the wealthy sister of the Earl of Huntly, Lady Jean Gordon. Bothwell was considered a very rough diamond indeed: a Borderer, he was a bluff, brave soldier but a notorious adventurer with scandalous liaisons in half the courts of Europe. Now he rushed to Mary's aid in Dunbar, bringing a force of four thousand soldiers. Mary returned to Edinburgh in triumph on 18 March and the conspirators fled. John Knox, who had welcomed the murder of Rizzio, prudently retired to Ayr and, later, to England.

Mary was once again in charge of affairs. Not fully aware of Moray's part in the conspiracy she exonerated him, but the other plotters were exiled. Bothwell, whom she regarded as her saviour at her time of greatest need, stood high in her favour and became her main adviser; for Darnley she felt nothing but contempt and mistrust.

On the morning of 19 June 1566, in the security of Edinburgh Castle, Mary was delivered of a son, Charles James, after a long and difficult confinement. The tiny room in which she gave birth, opening off the chamber now known as Queen Mary's room, is a high point for visitors to the castle.[1]

Mary was understandably anxious to make it clear, in public, that the child was legitimate. She had Darnley summoned to her bedside immediately after the birth and said to him:

> '*My Lord, God has given you and me a son, begotten by none but you. Here I protest to God, and as I shall answer to Him at the great day of judgement, that this is your son and no other man's son. And I am desirous that all here, both ladies and others, bear witness: for he is so much your own son, that I fear it will be the worse for him hereafter . . . This is the son who I hope shall first unite the two kingdoms of Scotland and England.*'
> LORD HERRIES, *HISTORICAL MEMOIRS*

The birth of a male heir to the throne was greeted with much public rejoicing. The castle's guns fired, and five hundred bonfires were lit all over Edinburgh. Mary had a spell of serious illness that autumn, but planned the baptism ceremony in Stirling Castle with elaborate

---

1 In 1830, workmen found some human bones which had been bricked up inside the wall of an old chamber in Edinburgh Castle; they were soon rumoured to be those of a child. This gave rise to the extraordinary story that Mary's child had died at birth and had been substituted by a child born to the Countess of Mar. In her biography *Mary Queen of Scots* (p.321n), Antonia Fraser disposes conclusively of this imaginative notion: the skeleton was wrapped in a woollen cloth (not in a cloth of gold with a royal cipher on it, as has been suggested), and there is no contemporary evidence that it was even a child. If it was a child, 'it is far more likely to be the sad relic of a lady-in-waiting's peccadillo than a queen's conspiracy'.

care. She was determined to make it an unforgettable display of the power and stability of the Stewart monarchy; to that end, all the guns in the artillery parks of Edinburgh and Dunbar castles were shipped up the Forth under cover of darkness to demonstrate the state's firepower. It was also to be an occasion for national reconciliation, between Catholics and Protestants, between queen and consort. Darnley had reverted to his petulant ways, however, and when the child was christened (in a Catholic ceremony, of course) on 17 December in the Chapel Royal of Stirling Castle, he sulked in his chamber and ostentatiously refused to attend. It made no difference to the celebrations, which closed with a spectacular fireworks display and a lavish Renaissance allegorical pageant on the castle esplanade, featuring an enchanted castle under siege.[1]

Darnley's behaviour had been causing grave concern. Earlier that winter, when Mary was staying at Craigmillar Castle on the outskirts of Edinburgh to finalise plans for the baptism, there had been talk among her leading nobles – Moray, Maitland, Argyll and Bothwell (and, later, Morton) – of an annulment of the royal marriage. Mary is said to have agreed to a divorce provided it did not prejudice the legitimacy and succession of her heir. There was also, apparently, darker talk of getting rid of Darnley by 'other means', which Mary refused to countenance. Even more ominously, there were rumours of a Lennox plot to remove Mary from the throne and make Darnley regent for the infant prince. Alarmed for the child's safety, Mary had him brought from Stirling to Holyrood.

The murder of Darnley (9/10 February 1567)

Early in 1567 Darnley fell ill, either from smallpox or, as is now more generally believed, from syphilis. Mary went to Glasgow to visit him, and on 1 February he was brought back to Edinburgh on a horse-litter for his convalescence – but not to Holyroodhouse, lest his disease (whatever it may have been) affected the baby prince. Instead he was lodged in the upper floor of the stone-built Provost's House attached to the old collegiate church of St Mary's-in-the-Field, now known as Kirk o' Field.

---

1 Mary had to borrow £12,000 from Edinburgh merchants to pay for this three-day extravaganza. The final dinner was served from a moving stage; it was said that 'the first two courses were served by nymphs and satyrs, the third by a conduit, and the fourth was preceded by the recitation of a verse by a child who, like an angel, was lowered in a globe from the ceiling.'

It lay just within the city wall, with an adjoining orchard and garden.

The queen spent much of her time with him, soothing him as she had done during the attack of measles when she had nursed him and fallen in love with him. She spent a couple of nights sleeping in the chamber below his. It seemed as if a reconciliation between the estranged couple was on the way – or that, at least, may have been what Darnley was being promised.

On Sunday, 9 February Mary attended a wedding breakfast at Holyrood to celebrate the marriage of one of her French staff to one of her ladies-in-waiting. Later she attended a formal reception to welcome a new ambassador. Then she rode the short distance to Kirk o' Field with her court entourage to visit Darnley, who would be moving to Holyroodhouse the next day. It was assumed she would be staying the night at Kirk o' Field, but late that evening she was reminded that she had promised to attend the wedding masque to celebrate the day's marriage ceremony. Darnley sulked, but the queen blithely departed nonetheless, accompanied by Bothwell and others of her entourage.

Meanwhile, however, some person or persons unknown had been packing the cellar of the house with enough gunpowder to blow it to smithereens. At two o'clock in the morning, when the queen was safely in bed in Holyroodhouse, the Kirk o' Field building was demolished in a huge explosion which was heard and felt all over Edinburgh. Nothing was left of the building; but in the adjoining garden, near a pear tree, Darnley's corpse was found, clad only in a nightgown. He was unmarked by any sign of the blast, but had apparently been strangled or smothered; nearby lay his manservant, Taylor, also dead and also unmarked. A kitchen chair, a quilt, a dressing gown and Taylor's belt and dagger were scattered around them. If the explosion had not caused their deaths, it seems that they may have woken during the night for some reason; perhaps they saw shadowy figures surrounding the house and, fearing that it was about to be set on fire, tried to make a run for it just before the explosion. In that scenario, they must have been intercepted in the garden and despatched before they could escape.

The murder of Henry, Lord Darnley, 'King of Scotland' and father of the heir to the throne, is one of the great unsolved mysteries of Scottish history. Had the plot originally been conceived by Darnley himself, then hijacked by some other plotters? Had it been directed only at Darnley, or had the queen herself been the real target? Had the intention been to blow up the whole court? Virtually every one of the magnates in the long cast of *dramatis personae* in the 'Mary drama' had some motive for killing Darnley and has been fingered, individually or collectively, by contemporary or later historians. It is unlikely that the truth will ever be known.

There can be no doubt, however, about who was suspected at the time. Within days of the murder, anonymous placards and handbills were being posted in Edinburgh accusing Bothwell of having engineered the crime. Within days, the queen herself was being implicated in a placard explicitly portraying her as Bothwell's whore. Mary, still in deep shock, offered a reward of £2,000 for information about the perpetrators, but took no further action. Her chief advisers, many of whom were probably involved in the conspiracy (among them Moray, who had conveniently distanced himself from Edinburgh), seemed paralysed. Rumours flared in the streets and alleyways of Edinburgh and were rehearsed and doubtless relished in the courts of Europe. It was not until the end of the forty official days of mourning that the queen was stirred to action: on 24 March she agreed to allow the Earl of Lennox, Darnley's father, to charge Bothwell before parliament for the murder of his son.

The 'trial' of Bothwell, when it took place on 12 April, was a travesty. As a Privy Councillor, Bothwell was one of those who arranged the proceedings. He had been packing the city with four thousand of his tough Border adherents for days; Lennox, who was permitted by law to bring only six supporters, marched from Glasgow with a body of three thousand men but turned back when he was challenged at Linlithgow by Bothwell's men. As a result there was no accuser in court. After hearing seven hours of rigged evidence, the jury had no choice but to acquit Bothwell of the charge of being 'art and part of the cruel, odious, treasonable and abominable slaughter' of the king.

Marriage to Bothwell

The horrible murder of the unhappy Darnley excited the strongest suspicions, and the greatest discontent, in the city of Edinburgh, and through the whole kingdom. Bothwell was pointed out by the general voice as the author of the murder; and as he still continued to enjoy the favour of Mary, her reputation was not spared.

TALES OF A GRANDFATHER, CHAPTER XXXII

Despite the 'not guilty' verdict, few people believed that Bothwell had not had a hand in Darnley's murder. Bothwell, for his part, faced the criticism with his usual flamboyance and pugnacity: he plastered Edinburgh with handbills proclaiming his innocence and challenging any accusers to single combat. There were no takers. And now Mary Queen of Scots made the second, and fatal, political mistake of her personal rule: she married James Hepburn, the fourth Earl of Bothwell.

With all the advantages of hindsight over the centuries we might well wring our hands and ask, 'What on earth possessed her? Why did this intelligent, politically aware young woman jeopardise, by one calamitous misjudgement, everything she had worked so hard to achieve?' There is no easy answer. Many writers have referred, in a rather condescending way, to Mary's 'woman's frailty', or her 'unrequited sexuality' or even her 'unbridled passions'. But there are other considerations. We have to remember the position in which she found herself after Darnley's murder. She had been forced to come to terms with the unpalatable fact that the crime had been planned, or committed, or condoned, by one or several of her nobles, the chief men in her kingdom. Whom could she now trust? On whom could she now rely? In the political power-game which was being played around her, the man of the hour was undoubtedly Bothwell, who was emerging as the strongest noble in the kingdom – a man who could help to give Scotland firm and stable government. He had proved his unswerving loyalty to her in all the confused alarms of the previous year, and had undoubtedly shown signs of his admiration for her as a person and not just as his sovereign. Mary was not to know that Bothwell, for some time, seems to have been working to a secret agenda which saw himself on the throne beside her as the next King of Scots. He had been married only recently, but was already taking steps to have his marriage dissolved.

What is clear is that, both before and after the 'trial', Bothwell was high in the queen's favour. When she rode to the opening of parliament a few days after the acquittal, it was Bothwell who carried the sceptre before her. By now he was set on the biggest gamble of his life. On the evening of 19 April, the day the parliamentary session closed, he invited a party of twenty-nine lords and prelates to a private supper at Ainslie's Tavern in the Canongate; it was an extraordinary group of powerful and influential men, and included ten earls, eight bishops and eleven lords. There they all signed a bond endorsing Bothwell's qualifications to marry the newly-widowed queen and promising to favour his marriage to her – the 'Ainslie bond', as it is called.

Bothwell now had the ammunition he required. He went to see Mary, accompanied by Maitland of Lethington, who had married one of the queen's 'Four Maries', the Catholic and alluring Mary Fleming, the previous month. Bothwell showed Mary the bond signed by her leading nobles, and made a formal proposal of marriage; but the queen, according to her own later account, refused it on the grounds that there was too much scandal about her husband's death, despite Bothwell's legal acquittal. She then went to Stirling Castle to spend time with her ten-month-old son; she was not to know that it was the last time she would see him.

On Wednesday, 21 April Mary started back for Edinburgh with only a small retinue, which included Maitland of Lethington and the fifth Earl of Huntly. Next morning, at Almond Bridge just outside Edinburgh, she was met by Bothwell with a force of eight hundred troopers. He seized her horse's bridle and announced that he was taking her to the castle of Dunbar, for her safety. Mary made no effort to resist. She allowed herself to be conducted past Edinburgh and on to Dunbar Castle, still accompanied by Maitland and Huntly; and there, according to her own account, Bothwell not only pressed his marriage proposal but took her by force. Mary Queen of Scots later described the episode, somewhat obliquely, in a letter:

> So he ceased never, till by persuasion and importunate suit, accompanied not the less with force, he had finally driven us to end the work begun at such time and in such form as he thought might best serve his turn.

Did he or didn't he? Was Mary a willing accomplice in the 'abduction' but then a victim of 'rape'? We shall never know. Suffice to say that her political credibility as well as her honour were now irredeemably prejudiced, and she seemed to recognise that she had no alternative but to legitimise the carnal association, unwilling or otherwise, by consenting to marriage with Bothwell as soon as possible.

One can speculate endlessly about this. Bothwell was not the most prepossessing of men: he was seven years older than the queen, and six inches shorter; he was powerfully built, with a worn face and a pugilist's broken nose. But he was highly-educated and extremely well-read, was fluent in several languages – and had a blazing bravura which for years had broken the hearts of women all over Europe. Mary may well have been only the latest, and last, of his conquests.

Mary stayed in Dunbar Castle with Bothwell for nearly two weeks. She made no attempt to escape. Meanwhile Lady Bothwell started proceedings for a Protestant divorce, alleging her husband's adultery with one of her servants, and Bothwell applied for an annulment. The divorce was granted on 3 May, Bothwell's Catholic annulment came on 7 May.

Events were now moving fast. On 6 May, Mary and Bothwell returned to Edinburgh. In order that the banns could be read on 11 May the Lord Justice Clerk issued a document, signed by Mary, to the effect that she had been neither kept captive nor ravished. On the following day she created Bothwell Duke of Orkney and Lord of Shetland, placing the ducal coronet on his head with her own hands. On 14 May she signed a marriage contract, with Maitland and the Earl of Huntly (Bothwell's ex-brother-in-law) as witnesses. And on 15 May she married Bothwell according to Protestant rites in the Great Hall in the Palace of Holyroodhouse. This time there was no public rejoicing, no list of important guests, no celebration. It was a strained, tense ceremony, and the bride wore an old black gown hurriedly refurbished with gold braid for the occasion – a far cry from the trousseau of thirty glamorous new gowns she had ordered for her wedding to Darnley.

The cliché is irresistible: the die was now well and truly cast. Mary was clearly ill, exhausted by the strains and stresses of the past months, all her vivacity and self-confidence gone. Far from being a radiant bride she seemed to be in a state of shock, drained and distraught. Everyone (including, it would seem, Mary herself) seemed to know that the marriage was doomed from the start. A wave of popular revulsion sparked rebellion, and the couple were forced to take refuge in Bothwell's own fortresses, first Borthwick Castle south of Edinburgh and then, for greater safety, Dunbar.

Meanwhile, the nobles who had signed the 'Ainslie bond' were clearly having second thoughts. At Stirling on 1 May a confederacy of lords (including many of those who had signed the bond) signed another, this time pledging themselves to 'rescue' Mary from Bothwell's 'captivity'. The confederates, led by the Earl of Morton and Lord Lindsay and including Maitland of Lethington, took to the field to confront Mary and Bothwell, who had emerged from Dunbar for a showdown with a force of about a thousand men. On the morning of Sunday, 15 June, a month to the day after the wedding, the two sides came face to face at Carberry, near Musselburgh.

Today a dignified stone column, headed 'MR 1567', marks the site on Carberry Hill where Mary stood with Bothwell facing the Confederate Lords. But no battle ensued. All day, intermediaries passed to and fro. The Confederate Lords said that they would restore Mary to her rightful position if she abandoned Bothwell and delivered herself up to them. Bothwell wanted to settle the issue in single combat with the formidable Lord Lindsay, but Mary stopped him. The day wore on;

Bothwell was hoping for reinforcements from Huntly from the north and the Hamiltons from the west, but instead his own troops began to melt away. That evening, at the end of a long, hot, exhausting day, Bothwell realised he did not have the armed strength to give battle, and Mary realised that the only way out was to accede to the demands of the confederacy and send Bothwell away. He was assured of a safe-conduct, and Mary promised him a parliamentary commission which would investigate the murder of Darnley (and, no doubt, exonerate him completely); after that they could be together again. At last Bothwell went on his reluctant way and rode off to Dunbar and into historical oblivion; it was the last time he and Mary would ever see one another.[1]

Mary now surrendered herself, with dignity, to the Confederate Lords. If she thought she would be received honourably, like a queen, she was in for a dreadful shock. As she approached the rebels' camp the soldiers jeered and shouted coarse insults at her. She was taken to Edinburgh under armed guard, separated from her servants, her clothes and hair in disarray. As the cavalcade entered the city there was a huge crowd awaiting her, shouting 'Kill the whore!' and 'Drown her!' Instead of being taken to Holyrood, as she expected, she was lodged overnight in the house opposite the Mercat Cross in the High Street. It belonged to the Provost of Edinburgh, who was Maitland of Lethington's brother-in-law.[2] Armed soldiers stayed on guard in her bedchamber all night.

---

1   Bothwell spent the next few weeks energetically but unavailingly trying to drum up armed support for the queen's cause. Eventually he was outlawed and forced to flee to Orkney, where he hoped to muster forces in his new earldom. But his pursuers were hard on his heels, and he barely managed to keep out of their clutches by taking ship to Norway. Here he encountered some kinsmen of one of his discarded mistresses (Anna Throndsen), who had him arrested and thrown into jail. For the next eleven years he was incarcerated, without trial, in appalling conditions, culminating in the forbidding royal Danish fortress of Dragsholm, in the north of Zealand. Here, suffering from gangrene from an old wound, and tethered like a wild animal, he died insane in 1573. His mummified body was displayed in a glass-lidded casket in the crypt of Faarevejle church, near Dragsholm, until it began to disintegrate; it was given a proper burial in a new oak coffin in 1976. It is impossible not to feel sympathy for Bothwell in his tormented, demented end.

2   On the wall of one of the arched entrances to the City Chambers in the High Street a tablet, 'erected by the Lord Provost, Magistrates and Council of Edinburgh' in 1894, marks the site of the house to which Mary was taken: 'On this site stood the lodging of Sir Simon Preston of Craigmillar, Provost of the City of Edinburgh in 1566–67, in which lodging Mary Queen of Scotland after her surrender to the Confederate Lords at Carberry Hill, spent her last night in Edinburgh, 15th June 1567. On the following evening she was conveyed to Holyrood and thereafter to Lochleven Castle as a State prisoner.'

Next day she was seen at her window, dishevelled and hysterical, her spirit broken, screaming for help before being dragged back into the room. It was the last sight of Mary the people of Edinburgh would ever have. Soon she was hustled down to the Palace of Holyroodhouse for a meal; but before it was finished she was brusquely ordered to prepare for departure, in the unsympathetic care of two of the toughest and most ruthless of Morton's followers – Lord Ruthven (the son of Rizzio's murderer) and Lord Lindsay of the Byres. She hoped she was being taken to Stirling Castle, where she would see her baby son; instead, her destination was the royal fastness of Lochleven Castle, in Kinross. It was the first humiliating stage of Mary's journey into her long years of imprisonment and eventual death.

Chapter 20

MARY QUEEN OF SCOTS: 2 – IMPRISONMENT AND CIVIL WAR

*Elizabeth, therefore, considered the Scottish Queen not as a sister
and friend in distress, but as an enemy, over whom circumstances
had given her power, and determined upon reducing her to the
condition of a captive.*

        TALES OF A GRANDFATHER, CHAPTER XXXII

The island castle of Lochleven, at the border of Fife and Kinross,
is a pleasant place to visit nowadays. Its roofless ruins stand on
the second largest of the four islands at the western side of the loch
opposite the town of Kinross – the 'Castle Island', as it is called. In
Mary's time, however, the island was only a quarter the size it is now,
because the level of the loch was much higher then. The castle had
been a royal stronghold for centuries; since it was remote and on an
island, it was comparatively secure and escape-proof. Mary knew it
well. She was related to the Douglases of Lochleven and had stayed
there on several occasions (in April 1563 she had summoned John
Knox to an audience with her there). The keeper of the castle was Sir
William Douglas, half-brother to her own half-brother, the Earl of
Moray, and cousin to James Douglas, Earl of Morton, who had been
one of those involved in the conspiracy to murder Darnley.

But now her former friends were her jailers – and unfriendly jailers,
at that. Mary was confined in two rooms on the third floor of the
lofty fourteenth-century tower house, and had to share her bedroom

with Lady Douglas to ensure continuous surveillance. She was allowed to walk in the high-walled courtyard, but spent much time on her needlework (she was constantly asking for thread and clothing to be brought to her from Holyroodhouse). One consolation for her was that the embrasure of the east window had previously been modified to serve as a place for prayer: an altar shelf had been inserted with a basin (*piscina*) and a small wall cupboard.

Within a month of her arrival at Lochleven Castle, Mary had a miscarriage and gave birth to stillborn twins (presumably sired by Bothwell, but there is no knowing when). On 24 July she received a visit from Lord Ruthven and Lord Lindsay: the Confederate Lords had decided to remove her from the throne. Ruthven and Lindsay presented her with a blunt alternative: abdication or death. The threat was real. That day, exhausted and ill, Mary Queen of Scots signed away her throne. Without even reading them she put her signature to the Deeds of Abdication, whereby her infant son, Charles James, would assume the crown, and the Earl of Moray would become regent (with Morton as his deputy until Moray's return from abroad).

Five days after his mother's deposition, on 29 July 1567, Charles James was crowned King of Scots as James VI in a Protestant ceremony in Stirling; not in the castle where he had been baptised (as a Catholic) but in the nearby parish church of the Holy Rude. He was thirteen months old. Few of Scotland's nobility were present. The crown was too heavy for the child's head and was held above it, not placed upon it. The coronation oath was taken on the king's behalf by the Earl of Morton, who swore to rule in the faith, fear and love of God, and to maintain the Protestant religion. John Knox, who had by now returned from England, preached the sermon.[1] The English ambassador waited outside, because Queen Elizabeth of England did not wish to be publicly associated with the act. At Lochleven Castle, Sir William Douglas fired his cannons in celebration and lit bonfires. It was two years to the day since Mary had set out on the road to ruin with her marriage to Henry, Lord Darnley.

The Confederate Lords were now in control of the government of

---

1 The theme of Knox's coronation sermon was a chilling justification of regicide – the Old Testament story of Joash and Athaliah, from the Second Book of Kings. Athaliah was the daughter of Ahab and Jezebel; and when Jehu had slain her son Ahaziah, she usurped the throne of Israel and tried to exterminate the whole royal line. But her baby son, Joash, was hidden away until he was seven years old; then he was brought forth and crowned king by the captains of Israel. The evil Athaliah was put to death, all the temples and priests of Baal were overthrown and the true religion was restored to the land (2 Kings, 11).

Scotland, with the Earl of Moray as regent. Parliament refused all Mary's appeals to be allowed to appear before it; instead, an Act of Parliament in December declared that Bothwell had been 'the chief executioner of the horrible murder' of Darnley, and that Mary had been his accomplice, 'inasmuch as it was clearly evident both by her letters, and by her marriage to Bothwell, that she was privy, act and part of the actual devise and deed of the forenamed murder of the King her lawful husband'.

Mary did not lack friends and chivalrous sympathisers, however, and her escape was uppermost in their minds. One of them was George Douglas, younger brother of the keeper of Lochleven Castle; he was a handsome young man, nicknamed 'Pretty Geordie'. Another young man on the island, Willie Douglas, an orphan who was thought to be the keeper's illegitimate son, became an enthusiastic conspirator in escape attempts. The first effort, in March 1568, failed when Mary, disguised as a laundry-woman, reached a boat but was given away at the last moment by the whiteness and delicacy of her long hands.

On 2 May 1568 a more ambitious cloak-and-dagger plan succeeded: Mary was smuggled on board a boat through a postern gate while the household was distracted by a traditional May Day masque arranged by Willie Douglas, with himself cast as the 'Abbot of Unreason'. She was rowed across the loch, allegedly throwing the keys of the castle into the water to hinder any pursuit, and on the shore was met by an armed bodyguard led by George Douglas and Lord Seton, the father of one of her 'Four Maries'. It was the start of fourteen days of liberty.[1]

From Loch Leven Mary crossed the Firth of Forth via Queensferry and rode on to Niddry Castle, near Winchburgh, one of Lord Seton's strongholds. News of her escape flew everywhere, and she was elated to see people coming out of their houses to cheer their queen. Next morning she rode to Hamilton, where she was met by Lord Claud Hamilton, younger son of the Duke of Châtelherault and brother of the unfortunate Earl of Arran, who was now confined to a madhouse. At Hamilton, Mary issued a proclamation in which she revoked the

---

1 The Armoury at Abbotsford displays a bunch of keys, said to be those to Lochleven Castle, 'taken by the young Douglas when he assisted Mary Queen of Scots to escape, 1568'. Sir Walter Scott was fascinated by the romantic enigma of Mary, as was every other writer in Europe: the historical setting for one of his Waverley novels, *The Abbot* (1820), was the period of her imprisonment in Lochleven Castle, from her 'abdication' in July 1567 to her escape and subsequent defeat at Langside in 1568. The hero of the novel is the spirited, hare-brained young Roland Graeme, who became one of Mary's attendants during her captivity and helped her to escape.

The Declaration of Arbroath, couched in fluent Latin and signed in Arbroath Abbey in 1320, was a passionately intellectual argument for Scotland's freedom and independence. It is one of the most significant documents in Scottish history.

Mons Meg, now housed in Edinburgh Castle, is one of the most celebrated siege-guns in medieval warfare: a huge bombard with a twenty-inch bore, capable of firing 150-kilogram cannonballs a distance of 3.5 kilometres. It was manufactured at Mons (Belgium) as a wedding present in 1457 for James II by the Duke of Burgundy, uncle of the bride, Marie de Gueldres.

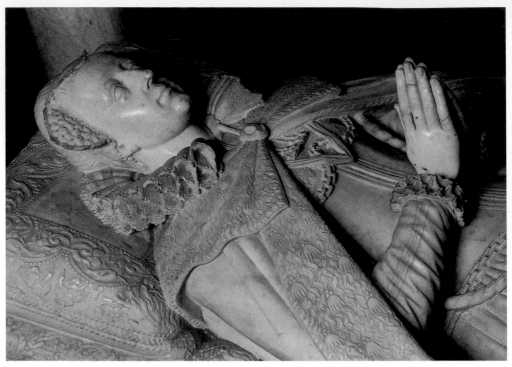

Mary Queen of Scots (r.1542–67) lies buried in the most magnificent of all the royal tombs in Westminster Abbey. It was commissioned by her son, James VI & I, and the queen (who had been buried in Peterborough Cathedral after her execution in 1587) was re-interred in 1612. Her sarcophagus lies under a sumptuously decorated black-and-white canopy; her white marble effigy was modelled from her death-mask.

Dumbarton Castle, on the north side of the Clyde estuary, was one of the most formidable fortresses in Scotland. Mary Queen of Scots stayed there as a five-year-old girl to escape the 'Rough Wooing' of Henry VIII, and sailed from there to France in 1548 as the betrothed of the Dauphin. It was to the security of Dumbarton Castle that she was heading after her escape from Loch Leven, only to be defeated at the Battle of Langside in 1568.

The Palace of Holyroodhouse was the home of Mary Queen of Scots during her brief reign in Scotland after her return from France, a widow, in 1561. On her first evening on Scottish soil, huge crowds flocked to the palace to serenade her outside the royal apartments in the west front of the palace.

John Knox, the Reformer, was Catholic Mary's implacable antagonist. He held four celebrated disputations with her; Mary was appalled by his coarse and violent language, but held her own, albeit resorting to tears on occasion. The confrontations did not decide the course of the Reformation in Scotland, but made Mary's policy of religious conciliation increasingly difficult to sustain. Painting by Samuel Sidley.

In 1565 Mary married her first cousin Henry, Lord Darnley. He was a tall, handsome eighteen-year-old (four years younger than her). Darnley was involved in the murder of Mary's confidant David Rizzio in 1566.

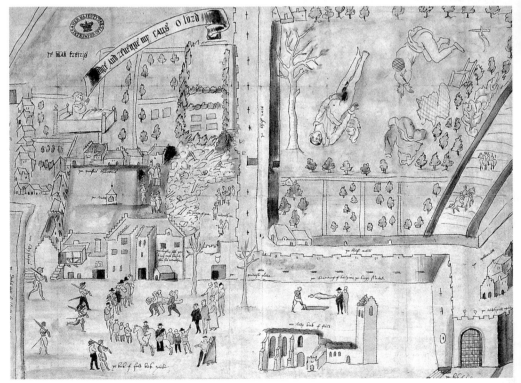

On the night of 9–10 February 1567 Lord Darnley was found dead after a huge explosion had destroyed the house of Kirk o' Field in Edinburgh, where he had been brought by Mary to convalesce after an illness. Immediately after the murder, a rough sketch of the scene was sent to William Cecil in London. It shows the house as a pile of rubble (centre); in the adjoining garden to the right lie the magnified bodies of Darnley and his valet (who had been killed by strangulation). In the top left-hand corner the infant James (the future James VI & I) sits up in his bed, praying for his father's soul.

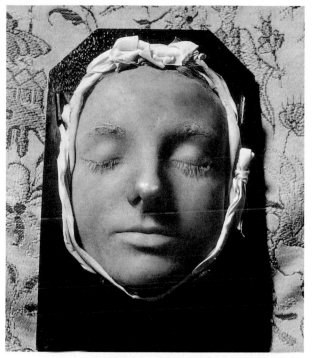

Mary Queen of Scots was executed at Fotheringay Castle in February 1587. Her death-mask is displayed at Lennoxlove, the East Lothian home of Scotland's premier duke, the Duke of Hamilton.

In 1568, after her flight to England, Mary was put on 'trial'. The most incriminatory evidence was a sheaf of letters contained in a casket which she had been given as a wedding present by her first husband, the Dauphin of France. The letters themselves have not survived, but are believed to have been forgeries, or at least 'doctored'. The original casket is on display at Lennoxlove.

James VI of Scotland inherited the throne in 1567 at the age of fourteen months after the enforced abdication of his mother, Mary Queen of Scots. He grew up in the turbulent times of the Reformation, a pawn in the power-games of potentates and prelates. James was a sensitive child and proved to be a brilliant scholar. He was painted at the age of eight with his pet falcon by Arnold van Bronckorst.

King James's first favourite was his cousin Esmé Stuart, Earl of Lennox, a handsome, sophisticated émigré from France. James was thirteen years old; Stuart was thirty, and married. The young king, starved of love throughout his childhood, developed an extravagant affection for Stuart and lavished honours and titles upon him until Stuart was forced to leave Scotland in 1582. Portrait by an unknown artist.

One of the most bizarre episodes in James VI's reign was the so-called 'Gowrie Conspiracy' in August 1600. The king was lured to Perth, to Gowrie House on the bank of the Tay, where he claimed he was attacked by the Master of Ruthven and his brother, the Earl of Gowrie. Gowrie House was pulled down in 1807; the scene of the drama was painted by Alexander Douglas in the late nineteenth century, showing the king shouting for help from a turret window.

In 1589 James VI married Anne, a tall, strapping, blonde Danish princess. They had seven children, including (in 1600) the future Charles I. Portrait attributed to Adrian Vanson.

In 1638 a National Covenant was drawn up which renounced popery and episcopacy, defended Presbyterianism and demanded free parliaments and assemblies. It was circulated throughout Scotland and attracted thousands of signatures. There are nearly seventy copies of the Covenant still extant.

abdication she had signed under duress, and condemned the 'ungrateful, unthankful and detestable tyrants and traitors' who had deposed her.

Mary had two choices facing her – parliament or battle. Either she could make for Edinburgh and try to advance her cause by constitutional means, or head to Dumbarton Castle to consolidate her strength in the west of Scotland. Supporters were flocking to her cause. On 8 May an influential group of nine earls, nine bishops, eighteen lairds and a hundred others signed a bond declaring for her. She knew she could put an army of more than five thousand men in the field – larger than any force the Confederate Lords could muster. So Mary chose the western option – to make for Dumbarton Castle, the almost impregnable fortress on the Firth of Clyde which was now one of the only remaining strongholds in Scotland where she could be sure of support and safety. It was a do-or-die decision. In the event, it proved to be the wrong one.

The Battle of Langside (13 May 1568)

The Battle of Langside
was fought on 13 May 1568 between
the forces of Mary Queen of Scots
and the Regent Moray and marked
the Queen's final defeat in Scotland.
This monument was erected in 1887.

Islanded by traffic in the middle of a busy intersection named Battlefield Place, on the edge of Queen's Park in Glasgow, stands a tall, elaborate memorial column surmounted by a lion. It looks like a miniature Trajan's Column. The lion stares south-east down Battlefield Road, past the cluttered sprawl of the Victoria Infirmary, towards the heights of Mount Florida. This was where Mary's forces gave battle in a desperate gamble to save her throne, and her life: the Battle of Langside.

The regent, the Earl of Moray (the queen's half-brother), was in Glasgow when he received the news of Mary's escape from Loch Leven, and he quickly started mustering troops. News came that Mary's army was marching westward along the south bank of the Clyde, clearly heading for the fortress of Dumbarton. Her troops were making a wide swing to the south round the town of Glasgow, through the old royal burgh of Rutherglen and on to the village of Langside – the only passable route over the marshy ground to the south of the Clyde.

The village of Langside has long since been swallowed up within the urban sprawl of Glasgow; in the sixteenth century it was only a straggle of cottages lining a low ridge bisected by the road which had been worn into a sunken way lined with thick hedges (today's Battlefield Road). The battle memorial stands in the middle of what was once the main street of the village.

Moray was a veteran military commander; he knew the ground well and decided to bar Mary's progress at Langside. His forces were inferior in numbers to those of Mary, but his troops were experienced and he had seasoned commanders at his side – particularly Sir William Kirkcaldy of Grange.[1] Kirkcaldy of Grange was despatched with a flying column of cavalry to secure the hamlet of Langside, each rider, it is said, carrying a musketeer as pillion. Behind the thick hedgerows he posted the musketeers, who would be able to fire concentrated volleys into the lane. The cannons were placed in Langside village, with the cavalry behind them. Moray himself took up a commanding position on the high ground of Camphill (the site of an old Roman camp) in what is now Queen's Park.

From Rutherglen, Mary's forces had marched to what is now Mount Florida, a ridge from which the ground sloped gently upwards towards Langside. Mary's commander was the Earl of Argyll (Moray's brother-in-law!), whom she had appointed 'Lieutenant of the Kingdom' even though he had no military qualifications. She herself wanted to go forward with her troops, but was persuaded to stay back on the eminence of Mount Florida where she would have a clear view of the engagement.

The battle started with a thunderous, if largely ineffectual, cannonade, neither side suffering any serious casualties. To break the deadlock Argyll sent Lord Claud Hamilton forward at the head of a body of foot-soldiers to force a passage up the road to Langside (today's Battle-

---

1   Kirkcaldy of Grange (c.1520–73) was one of the most spirited Protestant Reformers of his time. As a young man he had led the Fife lairds who had infiltrated St Andrews Castle in 1548 to assassinate Cardinal David Beaton, and he had fought the French forces who had occupied Scotland under the queen regent, Marie de Guise. He gave his allegiance to Mary Queen of Scots when she returned to Scotland in 1561; but he disapproved of her marriage to Darnley and commanded the Confederate horse at Carberry Hill. He was responsible for the pursuit of Bothwell, and almost caught him in Orkney; but he was shocked by the queen's treatment after her surrender at Carberry. He nonetheless fought beside Moray at the Battle of Langside, but was later to join the Queen's Party while she was imprisoned in England.

field Road). The musketeers posted by Kirkcaldy of Grange held their fire until the last moment, then raked the exposed column to deadly effect. Hamilton's men reeled back in disorder, re-formed and pressed forward again, but the massed fire was too much and they fell back, leaving the lane choked with their dead and dying.

At this crucial point Argyll's nerve failed, and the main body of Mary's army remained immobile. As the Hamilton contingent broke up in disorder, Argyll's men turned and fled from the field. With the advantage of holding the higher ground, the regent's men were now able to settle the issue with a crashing cavalry charge. The battle was over: the royalist army had been overwhelmed by a much smaller force, with a loss of more than a hundred dead and several hundreds captured.

Mary had gambled everything on reaching Dumbarton Castle, and had lost. There was no hope of reaching Dumbarton now. Accompanied by Lord Claud Hamilton and a handful of retainers she galloped from the stricken field, heading back east and then veering south for the Solway Firth. It was a nightmare journey over difficult terrain; Mary described it in a letter to an uncle in France:

> I have endured injuries, calumnies, imprisonment, famine, cold, heat, flight not knowing whither, 92 miles across the country without stopping or alighting, and then I have had to sleep upon the ground and drink sour milk, and eat oatmeal without bread, and have been three nights like the owls.

On the morning of 15 May 1568 Mary reached refuge at Terregles Castle, on the outskirts of Dumfries. What to do now? Her companions urged her to sail to France, where she had estates and powerful friends and could raise forces for a counter-attack against the regent. But Mary was adamant: she was determined to go to England and throw herself upon the mercy of her cousin and rival, Queen Elizabeth. Next day she rode in disguise to Dundrennan Abbey in Galloway; from there she walked down to the little port at the mouth of the Abbey burn and boarded a small fishing smack with a handful of loyal followers, Lord Claud Hamilton and the love-struck George Douglas among them. During the sail across the Solway her companions begged her to change her mind and make for France; but by then it was too late – the wind and the current were taking her inexorably to the Cumbrian coast. At seven o'clock on the evening of Sunday 16 May, after only fourteen days of liberty, Mary stepped on to English soil at

Workington. It was to be the start of eighteen long years of captivity which would end only under the executioner's axe at Fotheringhay.

In England, Mary was received with cautious courtesy at first. She was escorted to Carlisle Castle while Queen Elizabeth pondered what to do with her unexpected – and unwelcome – guest. Mary's presence was both an embarrassment and an opportunity: the embarrassment was having a Catholic royal claimant or heir-presumptive to the throne of England on English soil; the opportunity was to have a Protestant Scotland as a docile neighbour, heavily dependent on English support. There could be no question of allowing Mary to go to France to seek French armed aid for an invasion of Scotland; the crucial question was whether (and, if so, how) she would be allowed to return to Scotland. This was a matter of acute importance to the future of both Scotland and England. For several months, during a constant flurry of diplomatic activity, Elizabeth played a characteristically cautious game of deliberate political inactivity; Mary was moved south to the greater security of Bolton Castle in Yorkshire, under the care of the courtly Sir Francis Knollys. Knollys formed a high opinion of Mary and her character, and told Queen Elizabeth so; but Bolton was far from the Scottish border, and Mary soon came to realise that she was more of a captive than a guest.

The 'trial' of Mary Queen of Scots (1568)

Elizabeth's solution was to use the precedent set by King Edward I nearly three centuries previously, after the death of the Maid of Norway: she took upon herself the self-appointed role of arbitrator in the dispute between Mary and the rebel Confederate Lords who had deposed her, saying she could not possibly receive Mary at court until the accusations against her had been cleared up. To that end she set up an inquiry (a 'conference', it was formally called) to examine Mary's charges against Moray and Moray's charges against the queen he had deposed. It was to be a tripartite inquiry, where Mary's commissioners and Moray's commissioners would meet a board of English commissioners chaired by the Duke of Norfolk.

Mary raged against the manifest injustice of having to answer charges of murdering Darnley, which were being brought by men who had been closely implicated in the murder themselves. She also questioned the constitutionality of Elizabeth's action, setting herself up as the judge over the sovereign of another state. But to no avail. Moray was happy to go along with Elizabeth's plan, realising that she was unlikely to want to restore Mary to the Scottish throne whatever the outcome.

The inquiry opened in York early in October 1568. It reconvened at Westminster on 25 November with additional English commissioners, and met for its final sessions at Hampton Court on 16 December. Mary was not allowed to attend in person, although Moray was there to present his own case. Gradually the emphasis shifted from Moray's acts of rebellion against his queen to Mary's alleged complicity in the murder of her husband. Moray now formally accused Mary of murder; his case had been prepared by George Buchanan, Mary's former friend and mentor who had become alienated from her at the time of Darnley's murder and was now the principal propagandist of the Reformation.[1]

To bolster his case, Moray produced a silver-gilt box, blazoned with the monogram of François II, Mary's first husband, which contained, he said, damning evidence of her guilt. Inside it were two marriage contracts, a long French poem of 158 lines written by Mary, and the so-called 'Casket Letters' – eight coarsely explicit love-letters allegedly written by Mary to Bothwell at the time of Darnley's illness in Glasgow, which it was claimed showed collusion between Mary and Bothwell in planning Darnley's death. This was the first time that these letters had surfaced, although Moray maintained that he had had them in his possession since just after Carberry Hill. They were never shown to Mary. There seems no doubt now that these documents were either forged or heavily doctored, but they are no longer in existence: they were appropriated by King James VI in 1584 and never seen again. Only incomplete and incoherent copies of copies of them remain.

However incriminatory they were meant to be, the 'Casket Letters' carried little weight with the commissioners (although they have been the source of impassioned debate ever since). On 16 January 1569 Elizabeth delivered her judgement. The findings were ambivalent, to say the least. Nothing had been said which impaired Moray's honour

---

1 George Buchanan, the chief scholarly ornament of Mary's court, became her most virulent detractor – more virulent even than John Knox. He was elected moderator of the Kirk's General Assembly (the only lay moderator in the history of the Kirk) in 1567, the year of Mary's deposition. For the purposes of Elizabeth's court of inquiry he compiled a *Book of Articles* to blacken Mary's name; he later expanded this into a venomous tract, *Ane Detection of the Doinges of Marie Queene of Scottis* (1571), which was full of ludicrously implausible tales of Mary's sexual debauchery. When he was appointed tutor to the young James VI, Buchanan would tell the boy-king that his mother was a murderous whore (see Chapter 21).

and allegiance, and he was to return to Scotland 'in the same estate' as before – as regent. As for Mary, nothing had been said to induce Elizabeth to think ill of her or to show that she had been involved in Darnley's death, but she was to remain in England – for the time being. The 'verdict' was 'not proven', on both sides.

It was a subtle judgement, dictated by English political imperatives and inspired by the cunning of Machiavelli if not the wisdom of Solomon. It gave heart and substance to the 'King's Party'[1] in Scotland led by Moray (who went back home after an audience with Queen Elizabeth with the generous loan of £5,000 in his pocket); but it did not entirely alienate the 'Queen's Party' led by the Hamiltons, for there was still a prospect that Mary might be restored if she played her hand carefully enough. In reality, the ambivalent decision of the court of inquiry marked the irreversible turning-point in Mary's fortunes in England: immediately after the verdict was delivered, she was moved to a new and insalubrious prison, Tutbury Castle.

In Scotland, the King's Party now seemed firmly in control of the government. It won over some of Mary's wavering supporters, but the Queen's Party was still formidable. Its ranks had been augmented by Maitland of Lethington (who had repented of his betrayal of her) and Kirkcaldy of Grange (who was appalled at her imprisonment in England). The 'Marians', as they were called, held Dumbarton Castle in the west and Edinburgh Castle (through Kirkcaldy of Grange) in the east. What seems to have motivated them was a desire not so much for the restoration of the queen as for the downfall of the regent.

Civil war in Scotland (1570–73)

The downfall of the regent came, brutally, after only a year. On 23 January 1570, as the Earl of Moray was riding through the main street of Linlithgow, he was shot in the stomach by a Hamilton laird (James Hamilton of Bothwellhaugh) who had hidden himself behind a line of washing at an upstairs window. The house belonged to John Hamilton, the Catholic Archbishop of St Andrews, a kinsman of the assassin and a Marian. The archbishop took refuge in Dumbarton Castle after the assassination, but was eventually to pay with his life; when the castle was taken in April 1571 he was hanged in his episcopal vestments at Stirling after a summary trial.

---

1 The 'King's Party', or 'King's Men', were the supporters of the child King James VI. Mary's supporters were known as the 'Queen's Party', or 'Queen's Men'.

For six months after Moray's assassination Scotland was without a regent until, on 12 July 1570, the Earl of Lennox, father of the murdered Darnley, was appointed to the post on the recommendation of Queen Elizabeth. During the interregnum support had been growing for the Queen's Party. The Queen's Men set up a rival parliament, and at a session in Linlithgow on 12 July Mary's supporters declared that they would never acknowledge Lennox as regent – they knew all too well how much he hated his daughter-in-law. Kirkcaldy of Grange openly declared for Queen Mary. The Earl of Huntly assembled forces and marched south, but was defeated by Lennox at Brechin. Gradually Lennox began to stamp his authority on Scotland by force of arms. In February 1571 he defeated a Hamilton uprising at Paisley; and on 2 April one of his lieutenants succeeded in capturing the formidable stronghold of Dumbarton after scaling the sheer face of the castle-rock in the dead of night.

In May, Lennox turned his attention to Edinburgh, where Kirkcaldy of Grange held the castle against him. Lennox fortified an area of the Canongate and held a parliament within it. It was dubbed the 'creeping parliament' because it adjourned after less than an hour under heavy bombardment from the guns of Edinburgh Castle; but it had made its point.

Edinburgh was now a divided city. It had two town councils and two kirk sessions. John Knox prudently withdrew to St Andrews. The King's Men set up a complete government-in-exile in Leith, which was besieged by the Queen's Men for fifteen increasingly bitter months. The rival parliaments spent much time sentencing their opponents to death and forfeiting their lands. Violence became endemic: prisoners were executed without mercy, houses destroyed at random.

At the end of August 1571 the King's Party held a parliament in Stirling. It was graced by the presence of the five-year-old King James, wearing a makeshift crown because the royal regalia were still held in Edinburgh Castle.[1] Kirkcaldy of Grange now attempted an audacious *coup d'état*: on 3 September he sent a raiding party of four hundred commandos to Stirling to seize the King's Lords and, if possible, the

---

1 The boy-king made a short speech on the steps of the throne: 'My Lords and other true subjects, we are convened here, as I understand, to do justice, and because my age will not suffer me to do my charge by myself, I have given my power to my grandfather and you to do; and you will answer to God and to me hereafter.' Later in the day he noticed a beam of sunlight coming through a chink in the ceiling of the Great Hall, and said loudly, 'I think there is a hole in this parliament.' Out of the mouths . . .

king himself. They entered Stirling by night and succeeded in capturing many of the nobles, including the regent. The Earl of Mar, captain of the castle, came rushing down to their aid and freed them, but in the resulting mêlée the regent was stabbed or shot in the back and died the next day. The 'hole in this parliament' which the boy-king had noticed had opened.

Lennox was quickly succeeded as regent by the more conciliatory figure of John Erskine, first Earl of Mar.[1] His first act was to proclaim the Earl of Morton as lieutenant-general of the King's Party forces, and from then on he allowed Morton to make all the running against the Queen's Party. The war of attrition between the two sides in Edinburgh dragged on until July 1572, when a truce was called. The Leith brigade violated the truce, however, and marched into Edinburgh where they reclaimed power, although Kirkcaldy of Grange and Maitland of Lethington were still holding Edinburgh Castle against them. It was the last bastion of the Marians.

The Earl of Mar died of a sudden illness in October 1572, to be replaced by Morton as regent on 24 November. On that same day, John Knox died. He had been recalled to Edinburgh at the time of the truce in July, to preach again in St Giles' Cathedral, although he was now so frail that he could scarcely stand or be heard. Earlier that year he had seen, and approved only with the greatest reluctance, a concordat signed between the Kirk and the Privy Council which allowed the crown to nominate bishops to vacant sees, on the English model. Knox lived long enough to hear the appalling news of the Massacre of St Bartholomew's Eve in France on 24 August 1572; he dragged himself to St Giles' to denounce the outrage with something like his old fire and vehemence. At his funeral, the new regent said of him, 'Here lieth a man who neither feared nor flattered any flesh.'[2]

---

1   The Earl of Mar (c.1510–72) was one of the more moderate of the King's Men. He had consistently supported Mary Queen of Scots (who created him Earl of Mar in 1565) until the murder of Darnley. He was one of the Confederate Lords at Carberry Hill and was appointed Captain of Stirling Castle, entrusted with the care of the infant Prince James there. He carried James to his coronation in June, and was one of the King's Men at the Battle of Langside.

2   It is believed that Knox spent the last weeks of his life in the old building with overhanging gables halfway down the High Street in Edinburgh – one of the oldest surviving buildings in the city. It is now known as John Knox House, and is run by the Church of Scotland as a museum dedicated to the life and times of the great Reformer. This was not the formal manse of St Giles', however, which was opposite the church and had been requisitioned during the siege of Edinburgh Castle); 'John Knox House' belonged to a goldsmith named James Mossman (the son of the jeweller who had refashioned the Crown of Scotland for

Knox's death was the symbolic end of an era: new men, like George Buchanan and, soon, Andrew Melville (see Chapter 21), were leading the reformed Church of Scotland.

Morton, the new regent, was determined to wipe out the last remnants of opposition to the King's Party, and was in no mood for negotiations. In April 1573 Queen Elizabeth sent troops and siege artillery to help him to deal with the beleaguered castle in Edinburgh. Guns were placed on the steeple of St Giles' and soldiers dug trenches across the top of the High Street. On 21 May Morton started a furious bombardment of the castle. After a week the two hundred battered defenders surrendered. Kirkcaldy of Grange and his brother were hanged at the Mercat Cross; Maitland of Lethington died in suspicious circumstances – either by poison or his own hand – before sentence on him could be carried out. The civil war was over. For the next seven years, until the downfall of Morton in 1580, Scotland would be at peace (or would be pacified, at least) as the regent imposed his rough authority on the land.

The real turning-point, however, had come nearly two years previously – not through force of arms, but through Mary Queen of Scots herself. Mary had not been inactive during her imprisonment. She had succeeded in capturing the imagination of the most powerful nobleman in England, the widowed Duke of Norfolk who had presided at the court of inquiry, and in 1569 there were plans that they would marry, although they had never met; Mary even sent messengers to Rome to seek an annulment of her marriage to Bothwell. Meanwhile a group of northern Catholic nobles formed a conspiracy to liberate Mary by force; in November 1569 they raised the standard of rebellion and marched south, but the rebellion disintegrated before battle was joined. The Duke of Norfolk was sent to the Tower but later released without trial.

In September 1571 a plot to bring in Spanish troops to support a Catholic rising, organised on the Duke of Norfolk's behalf by a Florentine banker named Roberto Ridolfi, was uncovered. Mary Queen of Scots was falsely implicated by a go-between under threat of torture. Once again Norfolk was sent to the Tower, and this time he did not escape – he was executed for treason in June 1572. Mary was universally

---

James V) who had been appointed by Mary as Assayer of the Mint, with an official residence in the castle. During the civil war Mossman had stayed in the castle and continued to mint gold coins with Mary's head on them on behalf of the Queen's Party; he was executed when the castle fell in 1573.

deemed guilty by association, and the English parliament demanded her head as well. Queen Elizabeth felt magnanimous enough to deflect parliament's demands ('she could not put to death the bird that had flown to her for succour from the hawk'), but it was the last straw: there was now no realistic prospect of Mary ever being allowed out of custody.

In Scotland, support for Mary began to melt away: her cause was now irretrievably forlorn, and there was nothing left to fight for. From now on, the fall of Edinburgh Castle in May 1573 was a foregone conclusion. To all intents and purposes, there was no hope that Mary would ever be restored as Queen of Scots.

Tutbury Castle: 'the winds and injures of heaven'

On 3 February 1569, soon after Elizabeth's court of inquiry had reached its ambiguous 'not proven' verdict, Mary was moved from Bolton Castle to Tutbury Castle in Staffordshire, a dank and depressing old building looking out over an evil-smelling marsh. Tutbury was at that time leased from the crown as a hunting lodge by George Talbot, Earl of Shrewsbury, the wealthiest magnate in England, and it was he who was now entrusted with the responsibility of guarding Mary Queen of Scots. Elizabeth's instructions to him were brief and to the point: 'Use her honourably but do not allow her to escape.'[1]

Mary was to stay in Shrewsbury's care for sixteen years. She was kept at Tutbury for the best part of seven years in all, but there were frequent transfers to other residences for various reasons. Tutbury had to be thoroughly cleaned every now and again, and Mary's large entourage put a severe strain on the resources of the locality; she was also moved whenever her health failed. She was to be held for longer or shorter periods in many places – Wingfield Manor in Staffordshire (the Earl of Shrewsbury's own house), for instance, or Chatsworth (which Bess of Hardwick had inherited from her second husband, Sir William Cavendish), or Sheffield Castle; but whenever evidence was found of any suspicious communications between Mary and the outside world, she was sent back to the greater security of Tutbury. Tutbury, with its leaky roof and damp, draughty rooms, was her punishment – and

---

1   The Earl of Shrewsbury was the fourth husband of the spirited Bess of Hardwick, who was one of Queen Elizabeth's ladies of the bedchamber (they had married in 1567). Elizabeth Hardwick came of minor Derbyshire gentry but, through four judicious marriages, became one of the richest women in England.

how she hated it: 'sitting squarely on top of a mountain in the middle of a plain, as a result of which it was entirely exposed to all the winds and *injures* of heaven', she wrote in one of her letters.

Tutbury Castle had been built by John of Gaunt on the site of an ancient fortified hilltop. The ground slopes steeply away from the castle on all sides down to the once-marshy flat land which surrounds it. Mary complained incessantly of the vile smells which arose from the marsh, about the draughts, about the 'stinking middens' which passed for a drainage system, about the persistent damp. The castle was almost falling down – a process which has continued to this day. Mary and her ladies-in-waiting were confined to two apartments on the first floor of the South Tower; here Mary slept, ate and spent much time in her early years of captivity doing embroidery with Bess of Hardwick, who had become an intimate friend.[1] The spiral staircase leading to the now floorless apartments is still accessible, thanks to the unflagging work of the custodian, Barry Vallens, who has worked single-handedly for twenty-one years to keep the castle from falling into further decay. The empty doorways to the rooms are barred for safety, but the fireplace of Mary's room can still be seen, and the recessed window where she would sit at her needlework.

It is a sad place today, Tutbury Castle; but it was even sadder when it was inhabited in Mary's day. Nothing brings home more keenly the degradation and discomfort of her years of captivity in England. Tutbury was to be her last place of incarceration before Fotheringhay. Before then, however, there were long periods of relative quiet and comfort, broken only by occasional crises of confidence. Mary became, to all intents and purposes, the forgotten queen. Shrewsbury was a devoted public servant, and paid the heavy costs of the upkeep of Mary's substantial household out of his own pocket (albeit complaining constantly); but he was under continual pressure from Queen Elizabeth to impose a stricter regime on his royal prisoner.

During her years of captivity Mary's health, which had long been delicate, deteriorated. But she found real consolation in the company of her small niece Arabella Stewart, the daughter of a romantic marriage in 1574 between Bess of Hardwick's daughter Elizabeth Cavendish and Darnley's younger brother Charles Stewart. The father died soon after Arabella's birth in 1575, and the child was brought up by her grandmother, Bess of Hardwick. Mary became deeply fond of the little

---

1 Some of Mary's embroidered panels were presented to Queen Elizabeth; surviving examples are to be seen at Hardwick Hall and at Oxburgh Hall in Norfolk.

girl, enfolding her in all the maternal love she was unable to lavish on her own child, King James.[1]

In the 1580s Mary's position worsened abruptly. The Earl of Shrewsbury and his wife Bess started to have problems with their marriage. Bess, unforgivably and nonsensically, complained to Queen Elizabeth that her husband was having an affair with his royal prisoner. Mary retaliated by writing a letter to Elizabeth retailing all the scandalous gossip about Her Majesty which Bess had gleefully passed on to Mary. It meant a bitter and abrupt end to the friendship with Bess of Hardwick which Mary had valued so highly.

Worse was to come. In 1569, Elizabeth's chief minister William Cecil had (unofficially) appointed Sir Francis Walsingham to set up a secret service for the protection of the realm. Walsingham had quickly built up an extraordinarily efficient espionage system. His first success was unravelling the Ridolfi plot in 1571, which had so greatly damaged Mary's standing in Scotland. Since then his avowed aim had been to bring about Mary's demise by uncovering (or manufacturing) further plots against Queen Elizabeth which would prove that Mary was too dangerous to be allowed to live. Now, in the 1580s, he stepped up his efforts. In 1583 his agents uncovered the 'Throckmorton Plot', which involved a half-baked scheme for a Spanish invasion – and which aroused a fever of popular indignation against Catholics and, in particular, Mary. In 1585 came the 'Parry Plot' – an alleged scheme to assassinate Elizabeth by a Dr Parry who had connections with Mary's assistant secretary, a double-agent named Thomas Morgan.

Walsingham's unscrupulous use of *agents provocateurs* had its effect. Mary was installed in Tutbury Castle again and given a new jailer – a harshly austere Puritan named Sir Amyas Paulet. The conditions of her incarceration became much stricter. All communication with the outside world, except through the French ambassador, was cut off. The English parliament warned Mary that she was now living on borrowed time: in future she would be liable to execution if any plot

---

1 Arabella Stewart had a sad life, despite (or because of?) her royal lineage. In 1610, at the age of thirty-five, no doubt despairing of ever finding a good match, she accepted the advances of the twenty-three-year-old William Seymour, grandson of the Earl of Hertford and Lady Catherine Grey, and a future Duke of Somerset. Her cousin, King James VI & I, was infuriated – any issue from such a marriage could endanger the succession of his own family. The lovers were thrown into the Tower, but when they were released they married in secret and tried to elope to France. Seymour got there safely, but King James sent a ship in pursuit of Arabella, who was caught and brought back to London. She was once again lodged in the Tower, where she died in September 1615, ill and half-demented.

on her behalf were discovered, whether she knew anything about it or not. Worst of all from Mary's point of view, her son, King James VI, signed a treaty of alliance with Elizabeth which made no mention of Mary whatsoever.

Mary was being ruthlessly entangled in the meshes carefully spun by Walsingham as he masterminded her downfall. It only needed one further *coup* to deal what would be the *coup de grâce*. It came through a complex series of machinations known as the 'Babington Plot'.

Anthony Babington (1561–86) was a young and impressionable Catholic who had been devoted to Mary since childhood, when he had served as a page to the Earl of Shrewsbury. In 1586 he started conspiring with other Catholic friends to kill Elizabeth, liberate Mary and put her on the throne of England; meanwhile, another plot was apparently being brewed, to bring in an invasion army from Spain. In January 1586, Walsingham had infiltrated an agent, Gilbert Gifford, into Mary's coterie of French connections. Gifford set up a local brewer who was willing to act as a courier for Mary's letters; from then on, every letter she received and every letter she wrote to friends in France was intercepted by Gifford, decoded and sent on to Walsingham before being taken to the French embassy in London. In June, when Babington was concocting his fantasy scheme to kill Elizabeth and had been told by Walsingham's double-agents of the Spanish invasion plan, he wrote to Mary with details of the whole complicated plot. Mary wrote a long letter implying approval. When Walsingham's agent had deciphered it, he passed it on to Walsingham with a gallows scrawled on the outside. With that letter, Mary had signed her own death-warrant: her fate was now sealed.

On 11 August 1586 Mary, to her surprise and delight, was invited by her jailer, Paulet, to go deer-hunting with him. It was a hot, sunny day, and the ride was exhilarating. Suddenly she saw a group of horsemen galloping towards her. For a moment she thought it was Babington riding to the rescue. It was not: the riders had come to arrest her for conspiring against the life of Queen Elizabeth. It certainly could not have been Babington: he was already in hiding, but was arrested on 14 August and thrown into the Tower. Soon he was to be hanged, drawn and quartered in an execution of exceptional barbarity.

On 21 September Mary was escorted, heavily guarded, to Fotheringhay Castle in Northamptonshire, which was frequently used as a state prison. It was to be her last journey on earth.

Fotheringhay: Mary's execution (8 February 1587)

Thus died Queen Mary, aged a little above forty-four years. She was eminent for beauty, for talents, and accomplishments, nor is there reason to doubt her natural goodness of heart, and courageous manliness of disposition. Yet she was, in every sense, one of the most unhappy Princesses that ever lived, from the moment when she came into the world, in an hour of defeat and danger, to that in which a bloody and violent death closed a weary captivity of eighteen years.

TALES OF A GRANDFATHER, CHAPTER XXXIII

Nothing is left today of the castle in which Mary Queen of Scots was tried in October 1586 and executed on 8 February 1587, thus ending her eighteen years of imprisonment in England. After her execution the castle gradually fell into decay and its stones were systematically robbed by local builders. The site where it once stood is not a national monument; it is now nothing more than a large grassy mound. At the end of a farm-track lies a random heap of masonry, enclosed within anonymous railings.

On 15 October 1586 the Great Hall of Fotheringhay was crowded with English peers and court officials for Mary's trial. She was allowed neither lawyers nor defence witnesses; she was not allowed to consult any of her papers. For two days she strenuously denied being guilty of any attempt to encompass Queen Elizabeth's death, and insisted that the court had no right to try her because she was a monarch. She disdained to appeal for mercy. The privy councillors returned to London and on 25 October they reassembled in the Star Chamber at Westminster to announce their verdict: guilty of 'compassing and imagining since June 1st diverse matters tending to the death and destruction of the Queen of England'.

Both Houses of Parliament now presented a petition to Queen Elizabeth calling for Mary's execution. Elizabeth was in a dreadful quandary: to execute a fellow-monarch would set a drastic and dangerous precedent. She had first to ensure that Mary's son James VI would do nothing to jeopardise the alliance with England. Then, and only then, she resolved her dilemma with characteristic sleight of hand: on 1 February 1587 her secretary handed her a pile of papers to sign. Buried among them was the execution warrant. Pretending not to notice, Elizabeth casually signed it.

On the evening of 7 February, the Earl of Shrewsbury went into Mary's room and read out her death warrant. She took the news with serenity. Next morning she was led to the Great Hall, where a scaffold had been erected overnight. There were some three hundred people waiting inside, in absolute silence. Mary was wearing a long black dress over a red petticoat; beneath her gown, unseen by the guards, trotted one of her pet dogs, a little Skye terrier. On the scaffold she announced proudly, 'I am settled in the ancient Catholic Roman religion, and mind to spend my blood in defence of it.' Her gown, cap and veil were removed. One of her ladies-in-waiting bound a gold-embroidered cloth over her eyes and round her head. With that she knelt and calmly placed her head on the block. She commended her soul to God, loudly and often. After two strokes of the axe she was dead. To paraphrase Shakespeare, nothing in her life became her like the leaving of it.[1] When the executioner picked up the severed head by the hair, it fell from his grasp, and the onlookers saw that she had been wearing an auburn wig over her own greying hair.

A huge security clampdown was imposed. The castle was sealed, and only one trusted courier was allowed out to ride to London with the news. Every scrap of Mary's clothing was burned, every spot of blood was scoured away, every devotional artefact belonging to the dead queen was destroyed – everything possible was done to forestall the creation of any future 'holy relics' or curios.[2]

In London, there was general rejoicing, while Queen Elizabeth displayed every sign of distress and grief and blamed everyone except herself for the execution. In Scotland, Mary's son, James VI, broke off diplomatic relations with England, but only for a few days.

For several weeks, while Mary's household continued to be kept in close confinement, her body, embalmed in a heavy lead coffin, remained unburied, locked away in the precincts of the castle. Eventually, on Sunday, 30 July 1587, the coffin was transported to Peterborough Cathedral at dead of night and interred, with all due ceremony and dignity but with a Protestant service, in a vault in the south aisle. It would remain there for twenty-five years, before her son had her re-interred in the magnificent tomb in Westminster Abbey.

---

1 *Macbeth*, I, iv: Malcolm (the future Malcolm I of Scotland) describing the execution of the rebel Thane of Cawdor.

2 Despite all these rigorous precautions, 'Mary relics' became a roaring trade. Sir Walter Scott owned 'a crucifix reported to have been carried by Mary Queen of Scots at her execution', which is now on display in the library of Abbotsford House, along with a piece of one of her gowns. And although the executioner's block was burned, a marble butcher's block alleged to be the 'real thing' was acquired by the Duke of Hamilton's housekeeper early in the nineteenth century, and then displayed at Holyrood for a few years as the altar at which Mary and Darnley had been married!

Chapter 21

JAMES VI AND THE UNION OF
THE CROWNS (1603)

*The breath had no sooner left Elizabeth's body, than the near
relation and godson of the late Queen, Sir Robert Carey, got on
horseback, and, travelling with a rapidity which almost equalled
that of the modern mail-coach, carried to the Palace of Holyrood
the news that James was King of England, France and Ireland,
as well as of his native dominions of Scotland.*

TALES OF A GRANDFATHER, CHAPTER XXXIII

Queen Elizabeth of England died in the early hours of Thursday,
24 March 1603, in the Palace of Richmond. She was sixty-nine
years old, and had resolutely refused to name an heir to the throne.
For the previous two years, however, her principal secretary of state,
Sir Robert Cecil, had been in secret correspondence with King James
VI of Scotland. He had told James that his dearest ambition would
be realised – his accession to the English throne was assured.

Accordingly, when the English queen died, her ambassador, Sir
Robert Carey, leapt on to his horse at noon and galloped all the way
from Richmond to Edinburgh, changing horses at every stop. He slept
the first night in Doncaster, the second in Widdrington in Northumberland. On the third day he was thrown by his horse and kicked
as he was leaving Norham. He arrived at the Palace of Holyroodhouse
late on the evening of Saturday, 26 March, 'be-bloodied with great
falls and bruises', and was carried up to the king's bedchamber, where

James was in his dressing-gown. Sir Robert kneeled before him and hailed him as 'King of England, Scotland, France[!] and Ireland'. James was thirty-six years old, and had been King of Scotland for thirty-five of them.

The cradle king

James VI had been born on 19 June 1566 in a tiny room in Edinburgh Castle after a long and difficult labour. His mother, Mary Queen of Scots, had felt it necessary to make public proclamation of his legitimacy as the son of her husband, Henry Stewart, Lord Darnley. He was baptised as a Catholic in a lavish ceremony in Stirling Castle on 17 December 1566, and crowned king, after his mother's enforced abdication, in an austere Protestant ceremony in the parish church of Stirling on 29 July 1567. He was thirteen months old, and had already endured a foretaste of the many perils of Jacobean kingship.

For the next eighteen years James would be a pawn in the pitiless power-games of potentates and prelates who had their own designs on the throne of Scotland. During his childhood he was almost as much a prisoner in Stirling Castle – or a hostage to fortune, perhaps – as his mother was during her long detention before her execution in England.

In Stirling, James was under the guardianship of the Erskine family – John Erskine, Earl of Mar (who was hereditary keeper of Stirling Castle, but who died in 1572 after a brief spell as regent of Scotland), and his formidable countess (whom James called 'Lady Minny'). The leaders of the Reformation regime wanted his education to be directed towards creating an exemplary Protestant ruler. It was a grim and loveless process, for the most part. At the age of four James was put under the tutelage of the sixty-three-year-old classical scholar and reformer George Buchanan, author of scurrilous tracts against Mary Queen of Scots, who now poisoned the boy's mind against his mother, calling her a 'murderous whore'. But Buchanan, a relentless disciplinarian, also subjected James to a gruelling educational regime which left him – surprisingly, perhaps – with a profound love and knowledge of a variety of subjects: Greek, Latin, French, history, cosmography, geography, composition, arithmetic, rhetoric and theology (especially Biblical studies). By the age of eight the child had become a prodigy of learning, a precociously clever child of very considerable intellect, according to the English ambassador Sir Henry Killigrew, in a letter to Sir Francis Walsingham in June 1574:

*He speaketh the French tongue marvellous well; and that which
seems strange to me, he was able extempore (which he did before
me) to read a chapter of the Bible out of Latin into French, and
out of French into English, so well, as few could have added
anything to his translation.*

James's other tutor was a much younger and much kindlier academic
– Peter Young. It was Young who assembled the six hundred books
required for James's education (the basis of the present Royal Library).
He worked by stimulating the boy's intellectual curiosity, and was to
become the king's favourite counsellor and the tutor of the future
Charles I. Other members of the Erskine family were deputed to coach
James in various manly sports, including riding, hunting, archery and
golf.

The young James could think for himself: he absorbed all George
Buchanan's scholarship, but repudiated his political theories on kingship. Buchanan, as the propagandist of the Reformation, required
ideological justification for the overthrow of Mary, the rightful monarch of Scotland. To that end he argued that, since time immemorial,
kingship had depended on a contract between king and people: the
people, who appointed one of their number as ruler, retained their
inalienable rights to life, liberty and property. So Buchanan advocated
the case for limited contractual monarchy which made sovereigns
answerable to the people.[1] It was an early manifestation of republican-
ism, which would be echoed in the American Declaration of Independence in 1776 – but it also reflected the sentiments of the Declaration
of Arbroath of 1320, which had proclaimed the possibility of deposing
King Robert Bruce if he did not act in the best interests of his people.[2]

Meanwhile, beyond the thick walls of his classroom in Stirling
Castle, the child-king's realm was in turmoil, as his adherents ('the
King's Men') fought a brutal civil war with the supporters of Mary
Queen of Scots. During James's minority, four regents ruled Scotland.
The first was his uncle, the Earl of Moray (half-brother of Mary Queen
of Scots, who had defeated her at the Battle of Langside); he was

---

1   Buchanan expounded his philosophy of kingship in a Latin tract, *De Iure Regni apud Scotos*
    ('On the Right of Kingship Among the Scots'), which he wrote soon after Mary's deposition.
    It was published in 1579, and enjoyed considerable and lasting popularity.
2   James was to write his own counter-blast to this political theory in two vigorous philosophical
    works expounding the Divine Right of Kings in two important books – *The True Law of
    Free Monarchies* in 1598 and *Basilikon Doron* (Greek for 'The Kingly Gift') in 1599 – which
    stressed the king's responsibility to God alone and his subjects' duty of obedience.

assassinated in Linlithgow in January 1570. The second was James's grandfather, the fourth Earl of Lennox (father of Lord Darnley); he was mortally wounded in a skirmish in Stirling in 1571. He was succeeded by John Erskine, the Earl of Mar, who died of natural causes in 1572. The fourth regent, the Earl of Morton, then ruled Scotland with a strong, authoritative hand for several years (1572–78).

King James's formal education ended in March 1578, shortly before his twelfth birthday, when he 'accepted the government of Scotland'; it was two years before the official majority of a King of Scots. With the onset of puberty, the boy-king was no longer a boy.

In the autumn of 1579 a Stewart cousin arrived in Scotland from France. His name was Esmé Stuart (the French spelling of 'Stewart'), seigneur d'Aubigny. He was a nephew of Matthew Stewart, fourth Earl of Lennox (the regent who had been killed in Stirling in 1571), and Lennox had been the father of Lord Darnley, so Esmé Stuart was descended in the Lennox line from James II. He was a handsome, sophisticated man in his mid-thirties, married to a French woman and with several children, and had come to Scotland ostensibly on business connected with the Lennox estates. The young king met Esmé Stuart and his French entourage in the Great Hall of Stirling Castle on 15 September 1579 and was bowled over by him. In a few days' time King James rode to Edinburgh to make his first visit to the capital, with Esmé Stuart at his side. From then on they were practically inseparable.

There has been much speculation about their relationship. Many commentators have suggested, or implied, a homosexual element: a teenager, long starved of affection, falling for an older man who shrewdly manipulated the boy's desperate need for love. Certainly, contemporaries commented on the king's extravagantly demonstrative displays towards Esmé Stuart, and the gifts and honours he showered on him. In rapid succession Stuart was appointed commendator of Arbroath Abbey, Earl of Lennox, first gentleman of the king's bedchamber, master of the wardrobe, governor of Dumbarton Castle, privy councillor and Lord Chamberlain of Scotland.

Esmé Stuart used his new-found power to bring down the former regent, the Earl of Morton, who was still the prime lord of the council. His henchman in this plot was a swashbuckling adventurer named Captain James Stewart of Bothwellmuir,[1] who dramatically interrupted

---

1 Stewart had been the brother-in-law of the Reformer John Knox: his sister, Margaret Stewart of Ochiltree, was Knox's second wife.

a meeting of the Privy Council and accused Morton, in the king's presence, of having been 'art and part' in the murder of the king's father, Lord Darnley. Morton was duly arrested and arraigned. At his trial he denied *participation* in the Darnley murder, but admitted *foreknowledge* of the plot. He was executed in June 1581 on a contraption macabrely called 'The Maiden' – a primitive form of guillotine which he himself had recently introduced to Scotland.[1]

The leading men in the *coup* against Morton were all suitably rewarded by the king. Esmé Stuart was created first Duke of Lennox; Captain James Stewart was given the Hamilton earldom of Arran (although the lawful Earl of Arran was still alive, confined in a madhouse); and the Lord Treasurer, Lord Ruthven (the son of Rizzio's murderer and one of Mary Queen of Scots' guards at Lochleven) became the Earl of Gowrie.

The new Duke of Lennox's hold on power was precarious. He was deeply suspect in some quarters not only for his 'unhealthy' influence on the king but for his Catholic leanings – was he a papal agent whose real purpose was to promote the restoration of Mary Queen of Scots? To allay these suspicions, Lennox converted to Protestantism. Then King James and Lennox signed a document, the 'King's Confession' (popularly known as the 'Negative Confession'), which abjured the Church of Rome and all doctrines which did not conform to the Confession of Faith. But it was all to no avail. The Protestant lords and the Protestant leaders of the Kirk alike were resolved to be rid of Esmé Stuart.

The 'Ruthven Raid' (August 1582)

In August 1582, when the sixteen-year-old King James was on a hunting trip in Atholl, in Perthshire, he was intercepted by Lord Gowrie with an offer of hospitality at the nearby Gowrie stronghold of Ruthven Castle. The king did not know that Gowrie had changed sides and joined the ultra-Protestants, and readily accepted the invitation. When he reached Ruthven Castle, however, he found himself a prisoner. His captors, who called themselves rather grandiloquently 'the Lords Enterprisers', included a childhood friend, John Erskine of Mar, who had shared his schooling in Stirling Castle and earned the nickname of 'Jock o' the Slates' for his assiduity at arithmetic. When the new

---

1 'The Maiden' was a much more efficient and humane method of execution than the headsman's axe. It is now on display in the National Museum of Scotland.

Earl of Arran (Captain James Stewart) boldly rode alone to Ruthven Castle to demand the king's release, he was promptly detained too. James VI was forced to sign a proclamation declaring himself to be a free king and ordering the Duke of Lennox to leave the country.

For months Lennox prevaricated; but at last, in December 1582, he accepted the inevitable and left Scotland for France; he died there the following year, and bequeathed to the king his embalmed heart. It was a poignant end to their friendship, and the young king was grief-stricken; he wrote a long poem of lament for Lennox (*Ane Metaphoricall Invention of a Tragedie called Phoenix*), and would look after the interests of Lennox's children for the rest of his life. His grief only reinforced his determination to escape, and to avenge himself on the enemies who had insulted his sovereignty; these included the leaders of the Kirk, whose General Assembly had wholeheartedly endorsed his abduction and imprisonment as 'an act of reformation' which had 'delivered the true religion from evident and certain dangers'.

James remained a prisoner for ten months, but in June 1583 he contrived to escape from his captors. With patience and artful dissimulation he had persuaded them that he was resigned to remaining in their power, and had been moved to the greater comfort of Falkland Palace. From there he was allowed to go on a visit to St Andrews for a feast, having arranged that his supporters should be gathered there. Once behind the walls of St Andrews Castle he was safe: the 'Lords Enterprisers' threw in the towel and submitted themselves to his mercy, which was granted – for the time being at least.

The political vacuum left by Lennox's departure was quickly filled by the new Earl of Arran, who was appointed chancellor in 1584. When the 'Lords Enterprisers' tried another *coup* in April 1584 by seizing Stirling Castle as a prelude to further action, Arran and the eighteen-year-old king marched against them with an army of twelve thousand troops. The castle was tamely surrendered, and most of the failed 'Lords Enterprisers' went into exile in England. The Earl of Gowrie, however, could expect no mercy this time, and was executed for this new treason: one of the insults against the king's sovereignty had been avenged.

James had now begun to assert himself; and his next objective was to stamp his authority on the Kirk after its endorsement of the 'Ruthven Raid'.

Kirk and state

After the death of John Knox in 1572, the Reformers found a new leader: Andrew Melville (1545–1622), who is considered the real founder of Scottish Presbyterianism. Melville, the youngest son of an Angus laird, had entered St Mary's College, St Andrews, in the Reformation year of 1559 and then studied in Geneva under Calvin's successor, Theodore Beza. He returned to Scotland in 1574 to claim the post of Principal of Glasgow University.

Melville was a very different kind of Reformer to Knox. Where Knox had been a firebrand fundamentalist preacher, Melville was an educationist and a scholar with an international reputation; he became as much a thorn in the flesh of the regent, the Earl of Morton (who took over on the day of Knox's death), as Knox had been to an earlier regent, the Earl of Moray. Morton's government was decisively committed to Protestantism, but only on its own terms: indeed, at one stage Morton told Melville that 'there will never be quietness in this country till half a dozen of you be hanged or banished.'

Melville led a committee of thirty Kirk ministers who produced the *Second Book of Discipline*, which was approved by the General Assembly in 1578 as its new programme for the further reform of the Kirk. Morton had set up a quasi-episcopal system, whereby bishops were nominated by the crown but 'chapters' of ministers could veto the nominations; the *Second Book of Discipline* rejected the notion of royal supremacy and insisted on the political autonomy of the General Assembly of the Kirk. Kirk and state were to form 'Two Kingdoms'; but whereas there should be no interference in the Kirk's affairs by the secular authority, ministers should be able to 'teach the magistrate his duty'. In effect, the Kirk claimed to be empowered to direct the secular head of state in accordance with the will of God.

King James, however, was determined to be a 'universal king', which meant a monarch subordinate to no one – especially not to the Kirk. After James escaped from the clutches of the 'Lords Enterprisers' of the Ruthven Raid, Melville was summoned before the Privy Council for preaching a seditious sermon, but prudently took refuge in England. A parliament was now summoned, which met in May 1584 in the Tolbooth of Edinburgh. Melville's supporters were forced out of town during the four-day parliamentary session, which passed a series of statutes, the so-called 'Black Acts', designed to curb radical Presbyterianism. They declared the king head of both Kirk and state, confirmed the authority of bishops within the Kirk against that of 'pretended presbyteries', and issued dire warnings against criticism of the king's person, his parents or his predecessors. The king also banned all the books of his domineering tutor George Buchanan, who had died in 1582 – not only the scurrilous attack on his mother, *Ane Detection of the Doinges of Marie Queene of Scottis* (1571), but also his *History of the Reformation* (1582).[1]

The Kirk was now in disarray. The king was in the driving seat, and he was not slow in exploiting his advantage. He was served by an extremely able civil servant – John Maitland of Thirlestane, the younger brother of Mary Queen of Scots' former secretary of state, William Maitland of Lethington. Kirk ministers all over Scotland were coerced into subscribing to the new laws, and recalcitrant burghs which made objection were forced to toe the royal line.

When Andrew Melville returned to Scotland at the end of 1585 he had to start rebuilding Presbyterianism almost from scratch. The king made this as difficult as possible by ordering him to go to the north of Scotland to look for Jesuits and to 'travail to reduce them to the true and Christian religion' – just to keep him quiet. Politics also came into play, as usual; James was beset by the possibility of a Roman Catholic rising and needed the support of ultra-Protestant Presbyterians like Melville. In 1592 parliament passed the so-called 'Golden Act' which restored many of the former privileges of the Kirk; but the time and place of all ecclesiastical assemblies, including not only presbyteries but also the General Assembly itself, required the assent of the king and parliament. This enabled the king to move meetings of the General Assembly from Edinburgh, which was a hot-bed of 'Melvillian' ministers, to other towns and cities like Perth or Montrose where Melville's Presbyterian ideology commanded less support.

There was still considerable antagonism between Melville and the king. In October 1596 they had a confrontation at Falkland Palace where Melville famously declared:

> *Sir, I must tell you, there are two Kings and two kingdoms in Scotland. There is Christ Jesus the King, and His Kingdom the Kirk, Whose subject King James the Sixth is, and of Whose kingdom not a king, nor a lord, nor a head, but a member.*

---

1   The king was himself well aware of the power of printed propaganda. In 1585 he published his explanation and justification for the 'Black Acts' in a pamphlet entitled *Declaration of the king's majesty's intention and meaning towards the late acts of parliament.*

Melville also called the king 'God's silly vassal' (God's simple servant). James was not insulted, because he certainly considered himself to be God's lieutenant in Scotland; but he had no intention of being Melville's 'silly vassal'.[1]

Personal rule (1585–1603)

In November 1585 the king had lost his anti-Presbyterian 'iron chancellor', the dashing Captain Stewart, Earl of Arran. His policies had never been popular with the Protestant lords who had resented his spectacular rise to power. Elizabeth of England, perverse as ever, had encouraged their dissidence, and in the autumn of 1585 she arranged the release of the exiled 'Lords Enterprisers' to launch another *coup d'état*. This time they had widespread support among the nobility and the Kirk. On 2 November they mustered an army with which to lay siege to the king and the Earl of Arran in Stirling Castle. Arran, with his gambler's instinct, realised that the game was over and that the king had no option but to part company with him. He was stripped of his title and the chancellorship and was banished from the court. It was the end of the Arran administration.[2]

At the age of nineteen, King James now embarked fully on his personal reign. He still had John Maitland of Thirlestane at his elbow as secretary of state; and he had already learned many valuable lessons in statecraft – especially the importance of guile in doing business with England and its queen.

James's overriding objective was to achieve official recognition as heir-apparent to the English throne. Elizabeth surely knew that this was unavoidable, but any formal assurance from her would imply a recognition of Mary Queen of Scots' legitimate position in the succession, for Mary's claim to the throne preceded James's own; and

---

1   James was to get the better of Melville in the long run. His Scottish bishops became servants of the crown, and the king gradually prevailed over the General Assembly. In 1604, when James had ascended the English throne, he suspended all meetings of the General Assembly, and in 1606 he summoned Melville and a group of Presbyterian ministers to London, ostensibly for consultations. Melville poured scorn on the elaborate furnishings of the Chapel Royal and the 'Romish rags' of the Archbishop of Canterbury; he was imprisoned in the Tower for three years and then exiled to the Continent, where he ended his life in 1622 as a professor of theology at the Huguenot seminary of Sedan, in France.

2   As plain Captain James Stewart again he spent the rest of his life wandering in Ireland, Ayrshire and the Highlands. In November 1596 he was murdered by a nephew of the Earl of Morton, the former regent whom he had brought to the scaffold in 1581.

Elizabeth was determined to resist that claim for as long as Mary remained an unwelcome prisoner in England. It meant that James VI had to ingratiate himself with the Queen of England as much as he could, without concern for his mother's fate. To that end, in July 1596 he signed a treaty of alliance with England – the Treaty of Berwick – which gave him a welcome English pension of £4,000 a year, and gave Elizabeth considerable control over his future policy.

Much has been made of James's 'unfeeling' attitude towards his mother and her predicament in England. An earlier Stewart monarch, it is argued, would have mobilised an army and marched into England to rescue the imprisoned queen. But Mary was no longer Queen of Scots. She was now, in fact, a dangerous liability whose continued existence threatened the stability not only of England but of Scotland as well. It should also be remembered that James did not know or remember his mother at all (nor, indeed, his father, Lord Darnley); he had not seen her since her downfall in 1567, when he was still an infant. Not only had his mind been poisoned against her in his childhood by George Buchanan, but all her attempts to write to her son and send him gifts had been blocked by her English captors. Furthermore, Mary was all too easily implicated in various Catholic-inspired intrigues to liberate her and place her on the throne of either Scotland or England, or both. The last straw was the revelation of her complicity, however peripheral, in Anthony Babington's ill-considered scheme to dethrone and assassinate Queen Elizabeth in 1586. Mary's eventual fate was sealed.

His mother's latest and most disastrous indiscretion placed James in a dilemma. If he was ever to succeed to the English throne he had to dissociate himself from any suspicion of having approved of the conspiracy against the English queen; but conventional honour and decency – and public opinion in Scotland – required him to make some effort of intercession to save his mother's life.

'Some effort' is what he made. In his letters to London before and after Mary's trial, it is clear that James did not fully realise how intent England was on having his mother executed. He reminded Queen Elizabeth of the tragic results of the beheading of her own mother, Anne Boleyn, by her father Henry VIII, and implied that he would sever diplomatic relations with England if his mother were executed. When the deed was done, Elizabeth sent him a personal letter, trying to explain that Mary's death had been a terrible mistake, a 'miserable accident'. James's response was a cleverly neutral reply in which veiled reproach was balanced by an equally veiled expectation of future favour – the letter not so much of a grieving son as of a master diplomat:

Madame and dearest sister, whereas by your letter and bearer, Robert Carey, your servant and ambassador, you purge yourself of yon unhappy fact: as, on the one part, considering your rank and sex, consanguinity and long professed goodwill to the defunct, together with your many and solemn attestations of your innocence, I dare not wrong you so far as not to judge honourably of your unspotted part therein, so, on the other side, I wish that your honourable behaviour in all times hereafter may fully persuade the whole world of the same. And, as for my part, I look that you will give me at this time such a full satisfaction, in all respects, as shall be a means to strengthen and unite this isle, establish and maintain the true religion, and oblige me to be, as before I was, your most loving – James R.

The drama was over. Any other response would have been pointless (whatever James's personal feelings) and would only have jeopardised his own prospects of succeeding Queen Elizabeth on the throne of England. The alliance with England also survived the crisis of the attempted invasion of England by the Spanish Armada in 1588, despite suspicions that James had been trailing his coat to Spain and hedging his bets about the outcome of the hostilities.

Marriage to Anne of Denmark (1589)

Princess Anne of Denmark, younger daughter of King Frederik II and Sophie of Mecklenbergh-Schwerin, was a tall, strapping blonde of fourteen when the twenty-three-year-old King James picked her to be his bride. She was a Lutheran (good for Scottish politics), she was Scandinavian (good for Scottish trade prospects) and she came with a large dowry of £150,000 (good for the royal treasury).

The choice of a bride for the king had long been a matter of considerable political concern, both within and beyond Scotland. Queen Elizabeth of England had favoured an alliance with Arabella Stewart, granddaughter of Lord Darnley's younger brother. Others preferred the Calvinist Princess Catherine of Navarre, 'a wise, staid woman'. But Catherine was eight years older than James, and extremely plain. Finally, after fifteen days of devout prayer, James decided on the Danish match.

Once his mind was made up on marriage, whatever his private sexual preferences might have been, James soon worked himself up into a lather of romantic ardour. On 28 August 1589 the princess was married to him, by proxy, in Denmark. She set sail for Scotland on 1 September, but the Danish fleet which escorted her ran into severe storms – so severe that the girl was nearly killed when three cannons broke loose from their fastenings and careered all over the deck of her ship. The Danish admiral reached the conclusion that the storm had been conjured up by witches, and turned back for shelter in a fjord in Norway.

King James was distraught. He could think of nothing but the impending consummation of his fairy-tale love. Impulsively he decided to sail to Oslo himself to fetch his bride. His closest aides were sworn to secrecy about his planned escapade. Before he left, he distributed government offices to those who would run the kingdom in his absence. The heir-presumptive, Ludovic Stuart, second Duke of Lennox (eldest son of Esmé Stuart), was appointed President of the Council; his deputy was to be the Admiral of Scotland, Francis Stewart, fifth Earl of Bothwell, the nephew of the third husband of Mary Queen of Scots; Bothwell was the godson of Mary, who had named him after her first husband, the Dauphin François. King James also composed a proclamation to his subjects, to be published after he had gone, explaining the reasons for his action and exhorting them to be of good behaviour during his absence.

On 22 October 1589 the king left the British Isles for the only time in his life and sailed for Oslo with a flotilla of five ships. The weather was still tempestuous, but the contrary winds which had thwarted his bride now served to blow him quickly to the shores of Norway. At their first meeting the king was in an ecstasy of love. Although they had already been married by proxy, the couple were married in person in Oslo, and the marriage was solemnised again with Lutheran rites in the presence of the Danish royal family in the castle of Kronenberg, in Denmark, in January 1590. The honeymoon in Scandinavia lasted for six months of what seems to have been unalloyed conjugal bliss. On 1 May the couple arrived at Leith, and on 17 May Anne of Denmark was crowned Queen of Scotland in the Abbey Church of Holyrood.

The queen turned out to be suitably fecund, and bore her husband seven children: Henry Frederick (1594), Elizabeth (1596), Margaret (1598), Charles, the future Charles I (1600), Robert (1601), Mary (1605) and Sophia (1607). Of the seven, only Henry, Elizabeth and Charles survived the perils of childhood. The eldest son and heir, Henry, who was greatly loved, died of typhoid in 1612 at the age of eighteen. Elizabeth married the German Prince Frederick, Elector

Palatine of the Rhine, in a glittering ceremony in 1613.[1] By then, however, the initial romantic ardour of the king's marriage had long since cooled. Anne was not an intellectual match for her husband, and soon they were privately, if not publicly, estranged. Within a decade she had become a political liability, by becoming a convert to Catholicism in 1599. Their paths continued to diverge, leaving James free to indulge himself in whatever ways pleased him best. She would die, unlamented by her husband, in 1619.

There was one other side-effect of the royal marriage – the extraordinary witch-hunt which the king instigated soon after his return from honeymoon in 1590. It all started with the allegation that witchcraft had been used to raise the storms which had prevented Anne of Denmark's ship from reaching Scotland. When another storm beset the couple's homeward journey in the following spring, apparently singling out the king's ship for special attention, James determined to discover whether the black arts had been employed against him. Investigation uncovered an alleged witches' gathering at North Berwick kirk, with a congregation of more than a hundred. Six of them were men. Those present included a schoolmaster from Prestonpans, the daughter of a judge, the wife of an Edinburgh burgess, and a midwife from Humbie. They had gathered to prevent James's safe return from Denmark, and the devil himself had addressed them from the pulpit. They tried all the usual sorceries – venom of toads, wax dolls and so on – but only succeeded in raising the storm when they threw cats into the sea after swinging them three times widdershins around their heads.

Several of the putative witches were executed after fearful tortures which extracted agonised confessions. One of the victims confessed *in extremis* that the leader of the North Berwick congregation – the devil incarnate – was none other than the Lord Admiral of Scotland, the Earl of Bothwell.

Not surprisingly, the king took a compulsive interest in the out-

---

1 Princess Elizabeth's marriage was a great love-match, but events turned against the happy couple. In 1619 the Protestants of Bohemia revolted against Austria and gave their crown to Frederick. When he was threatened by the Holy Roman Emperor his father-in-law King James, pacific as always, refused to support him, but offered to mediate. The mediation was unsuccessful and Frederick was defeated at the Battle of the White Hill outside Prague in 1620. The Palatinate was overrun, and Frederick of Bohemia and his 'Winter Queen' fled into exile and poverty. Elizabeth died in 1662; she was the mother of the dashing Prince Rupert of the Rhine (who would lead the Royalist cavalry in the English Civil Wars) and of Princess Sophia, mother of the first Hanoverian King of Great Britain, George I.

comes of the trials. In 1597 he published a remarkable tract on witch-craft and Satanism, entitled *Daemonologie*. It may seem no more than a literary curiosity now, but in its time it had a horrifying effect: it was the start of a Scottish witch-hunt which over the next century would claim more than a thousand victims, 80 per cent of whom were women.

But one man never went to the stake for his supposed part in the North Berwick doings: the Earl of Bothwell. A consequence was one of the most celebrated slayings of Scottish story: that of the 'Bonnie Earl o' Moray'.

The 'Bonnie Earl o' Moray' (February 1592)

> *Ye hielands and ye lowlands,*
> *O whaur [where] ha'e ye been?*
> *They ha'e slain the earl o' Moray*
> *And laid him on the green,*
> *He was a braw [fine] callant*
> *And he rid [rode] at the ring,*
> *And the bonnie earl o' Moray,*
> *He micht ha'e been a king.*
> *O lang will his ladie look*
> *Owre the Castle Doune*
> *Ere she see the earl o' Moray*
> *Come soundan [sounding] thru' the toun.*

This melancholy ballad is one of the best-known and best-loved in Scotland. It gives a popular version of the events which led to the slaughter of James Stewart, second Earl of Moray, by the Earl of Huntly on 7 February 1592 – although he had been forbidden to do so by King James VI:

> *'Noo wae [woe] be tae ye, Huntly,*
> *And wherefore did you sae?*
> *I bad ye bring him wi' ye,*
> *But forbade ye him to slay.'*
> *He was a braw callant*
> *And he played at the glove,*
> *And the bonnie earl o' Moray*
> *He was the queen's true love.*

What really happened to the 'Bonnie Earl o' Moray'? And why did it happen? The story is not nearly as romantic as the ballad implies.

James Stewart, second Earl of Moray, was a handsome and dashing young nobleman. He had inherited the earldom by marrying the elder daughter of Mary Queen of Scots' half-brother Lord James Stewart, the regent who became her bitter enemy. Moray was an ambitious but feckless opportunist who aimed to make himself the greatest lord in the north-east at the expense of his powerful neighbour, George Gordon, sixth Earl of Huntly; Huntly, too, was young and handsome, and was married to Lady Henrietta Stuart, eldest daughter of the king's late and much-loved favourite, Esmé Stuart, Duke of Lennox. The Huntly family also had a claim on the Moray earldom.

Moray played his hand foolishly. He formed an alliance with his dangerously unstable and feckless kinsman, the Earl of Bothwell. It was an unfortunate choice, for Bothwell was an unpredictable man with an alarming propensity for violence. In April 1591 he had been charged with having been the leader of the North Berwick witches and imprisoned in Edinburgh Castle, but he managed to escape in June 1591 and eluded his pursuers to become an outlawed terrorist in the Borders. Six months later he was back in Edinburgh, like a bogeyman who would not go away. On 27 December he mounted an outrageously daring raid on the Palace of Holyroodhouse in which he almost captured the king. Once again he managed to escape.

By now the king was seriously frightened. He became obsessed with the need to deal with the demented earl and his supporters – one of whom was the 'Bonnie Earl o' Moray'. James gave the Earl of Huntly an open-ended commission to hunt them down; meanwhile he sent a promise of a pardon to Moray if he would dissociate himself from Bothwell.

Moray was delighted. He installed himself in Donibristle Castle, in Fife, which belonged to his mother, Lady Doune, and happily awaited a summons to appear before the king. Instead, on the morning of 7 February 1592 he received a visit from the Earl of Huntly with a strong armed force. There was no doubt about Huntly's intentions. After an exchange of shots, he set fire to the castle. Story has it that some of Bothwell's friends created a diversion by making a suicidal break-out through the front door, while Moray slipped out of a back door and ran down to the shore. He tried to hide among the rocks, but was found by Huntly's men and slaughtered. Story has it, again, that it was Huntly himself who struck him first, with a dagger to the face – whereupon the 'Bonnie Earl o' Moray' said, 'You have spoilt a better face than your own.' Such is the stuff of legend and balladry. There is no evidence whatsoever that Moray ever found favour with James's queen, or was 'the queen's true love'.

In an attempt to mobilise public sympathy, the earl's mother, Lady Doune, had a macabre painting made of the body of her murdered son, showing the gashes inflicted by his killers; it still hangs in the ancestral seat of the Moray family in Darnaway Castle, near Forres. She had his corpse embalmed, and refused to allow it to be buried; in 1598 the Privy Council lost patience and insisted on a proper burial.

Huntly was punished with a mere slap on the wrist from the king: he was placed under house arrest for a week. The Earl of Bothwell remained at large to wreak further havoc: in July 1593 he popped up again from nowhere and forced an entry into the king's bedchamber in the Palace of Holyroodhouse, where he defiantly laid a naked sword at the king's feet – and then escaped. In the spring of 1594 he made a wild raid on Leith. Later that year he fled abroad, where he scraped a living as a fortune-teller before dying in Naples in 1624.

The death of the 'Bonnie Earl o' Moray' was, in many ways, an aberration. Throughout the 1590s the king and his administration succeeded in imposing a much greater degree of law and public order than Scotland had known for a very long time. Life for the ordinary people became much less violent and hazardous – except for one extraordinary occasion where the king's own safety was apparently concerned.

The Gowrie Conspiracy (August 1600)

The Sheriff Court in Tay Street in Perth, on the west bank of the River Tay, stands on the site of a turreted courtyard mansion which played a role in the most bizarre episode in the life of James VI: Gowrie House. An ornate panel, with a representation of the house, fills one of the front windows:

> Within the gardens bounded by the Tay, near this spot stood Gowrie House, noted for the historical event called the Gowrie Conspiracy on 5 August 1600. Built in 1520, taken down 1807.

This is how the story goes. On the early morning of 5 August 1600 the king assembled a party of friends at Falkland Palace to go hunting. Before the hunt began he was approached by Alexander, the Master of Ruthven, the younger brother of the third Earl of Gowrie (son of the earl who had been executed after the 'Ruthven Raid'). The Master of Ruthven told him that he had come across a man trying to bury a pitcher of gold coins in a field outside Perth. This man might well be a papal agent, a Jesuit spy, and Ruthven invited the king to come to Perth to see the stranger and to claim the money for the crown as buried treasure.

King James was constantly aware of the crown's poverty; besides, the crown owed the Gowrie family some £80,000 for previous services. So he agreed to go with the Master of Ruthven after the hunt. Accompanied by his courtiers he rode to Perth (then called St Johnstone), where he was entertained to a makeshift dinner at Gowrie House. After dinner his courtiers were shown into the garden to partake of the cherries, while the king was ushered upstairs by the Master of Ruthven to a turret room where, he was told, he would meet the man who had been found with the gold. Instead, he found a stranger dressed in armour. The Master of Ruthven turned on the king, drawing a dagger, and told him he was to die for the execution of his father, the Earl of Gowrie. The king rushed to the turret window and shouted, 'I am murdered! Treason! My Lord Mar, help me!'

His courtiers ran into the house and up the turnpike stairs to the turret room, headed by a young man named John Ramsay. They found the king struggling with the Master of Ruthven. Ramsay sprang at him and stabbed him in the neck, whereupon the others despatched him. Ruthven's brother, the second Earl of Gowrie, who had told the courtiers that the king had already left the house, came running up the turnpike stair, and he too was killed by John Ramsay.

That, it should be said, was the king's version of what happened, which he quickly published in a pamphlet.[1] More than 350 innocent Perth residents were interrogated with varying degrees of brutality, and at the end of August the bodies of the Earl of Gowrie and his brother were given a 'trial' before a session of parliament. The 'stranger in armour' was produced; his name was Alexander Henderson, the earl's chamberlain, and he claimed in evidence that he had been forced into his role but had taken no part in the affray. The corpses were solemnly pronounced guilty of treason, and then hanged, drawn and quartered. Henderson was subsequently granted a pension and lands in Perthshire. John Ramsay, the 'rescuer', was knighted for his bravery and later created Earl of Holderness.

---

1 *Gowries Conspiracie: A Discourse of the Unnaturall and vyle Conspiracie, attempted against the Kings Majesties Person, at Sanct-Johnstoun, upon Twysday the Fifth of August, 1600* (Edinburgh, printed 1600, cum Privilegio Regis).

Not everyone was convinced by the king's account, and speculation has abounded ever since. Had the Gowries been 'set up' in order to obliterate the crown's £80,000 debt to them? It seems unlikely that the king would have risked his own person in such an intricate plot. Had the king made an improper sexual advance which Ruthven had rejected? That seems even less likely – James could attempt liaisons with young men in much more comfortable circumstances, if such was his wish. Whatever the truth, the fact remains that royal vengeance against the Gowries – who had murdered Rizzio, helped to murder Lord Darnley and maltreated Mary Queen of Scots – had finally been achieved. James ordered the ministers of Edinburgh to offer public thanksgiving for his deliverance, but one refused point-blank and was banished to the north of Scotland. Every year for the rest of James's life, thanks were given on 5 August. As a conspiracy against the king's person, however (if that is what it was), the 'Gowrie Conspiracy' never took root in the public imagination as the 'Gunpowder Plot' of 1605 was to do.

Three years after the 'Gowrie Conspiracy', James VI of Scotland prepared to go south to London to ascend the English throne as James I of England. He had achieved a formidable reputation as an immensely successful King of Scots, and ruled a country which was more peaceful and prosperous than it had been for generations. Indeed, when he was installed in London, he felt able to make a proud boast in a speech before the English Parliament in 1607:

> This I may say for Scotland, and may truly vaunt it: here I sit
> and govern it with my pen; I write and it is done, and by a Clerk
> of the Council I govern Scotland now, which others could not do
> with the sword.

Everything was set fair for an equally successful reign as King of England.

The Union of the Crowns (1603)

When Sir Robert Carey had galloped north to bring the breathless news of King James's accession to the English throne, the king was immediately caught up in a flurry of hasty arrangements for his first visit to his new realm. There was no time to waste, for royal accessions could be fraught with unexpected crises. Yet he found time to write an affectionate letter of moral precepts to his son, the nine-year-old Prince Henry, who was being educated in Stirling Castle:

*Let not this news make you proud, or insolent; for a King's son
and heir was ye before, and no more are ye yet. The augmentation
that is hereby like to fall unto you, is but in cares and heavy
burdens. Be therefore merry, but not insolent; keep a greatness,
but* sine fastu *[without haughtiness]; be resolute but not wilful;
keep your kindness [maintain your mutual friendships], but in
honourable sort; choose none to be your play fellows but them that
are well born, and above all things give never good countenance to
any but according as ye shall be informed that they are in esti-
mation with me. Look upon all English men that shall come to
visit you as upon your loving subjects, not with that ceremony
as towards strangers, and yet with such heartiness as at this time
they deserve . . .*[1]

On Sunday, 3 April 1603, James VI of Scotland and I of England
attended morning service in the High Kirk of St Giles' in Edinburgh.
After the sermon he made a warm speech in which he took formal
leave of his subjects in Scotland, promising to return every three years
(in the event, he only returned once, in 1617). With that, he set off
on his leisurely journey southwards to assume his new throne. He left
behind not only his kingdom but his wife, Anne of Denmark (who
was pregnant), and their three young children.

His journey through England was a sustained triumphal procession.
Everywhere he stopped on the way there was public rejoicing, public
orations and pageants, public adulation. When he reached York he
was met by Sir Robert Cecil, now anxious to ingratiate himself with
his new sovereign (he was shortly created first Earl of Salisbury). All
the monarch-worship which had so marked the reign of Elizabeth had
been switched effortlessly to the person of the new king. James knighted
dozens of local worthies on his way: indeed, in the first four months
of his English reign he was to bestow no fewer than 906 knighthoods
– more than the total bestowed by Elizabeth in her entire forty-five-year
reign.

By the time King James I of England was ready for his coronation
in Westminster Abbey on 25 July 1603, he was immensely popular. It
was, perforce, a muted occasion, because the capital was in the grip
of a devastating visitation of the plague, which claimed thirty thousand
lives out of a population of three hundred thousand. There was no

---

1 This letter, in James's hand, is in the British Library (Harleian MS 6986, fo. 65). I have
anglicised the spelling.

procession, no pageantry, no cheering crowds. The sombre coronation, indeed, would mark the end of James's euphoric honeymoon with his new subjects in England.

Could he have done more to retain his popularity? He saw himself, in all sincerity, as a 'universal king'. It was meant as a metaphor for kingcraft, not a dynastic reality; but he certainly wanted to be king of a genuinely universal Great Britain – indeed, in October 1604 he adopted the title of 'King of Great Britain, France and Ireland'. He believed that there would now be an end to conflict between his two countries, and one of his first acts was to stand down the garrisons at Berwick and Carlisle. He wanted the Union of the Crowns to be a full Union of the Kingdoms, a single country called *Magna Britannia* – Great Britain – with one parliament, one set of laws, one national Church and a unified economy. At the first meeting he attended of the English parliament he made an eloquent argument for a 'union of love' between the two kingdoms:

> *Hath not God first united these two Kingdoms both in language, religion and similitude of manners? Yea, hath He not made us all one island, encompassed with one sea, and of itself by nature so indivisible as almost those that were borderers themselves on the late Borders, cannot distinguish, nor know, or discern their own limits? These two countries being separated neither by sea, nor great river, mountain, nor other strength of nature, but only by little small brooks, or demolished little walls, so as rather they were divided in apprehension rather than in effect; and now in the end and fullness of time united, the right and title of both in my person, alike lineally descended of both crowns, whereby it is now become like a little world within itself, being entrenched and fortified round about with a natural and yet admirable strong pond or ditch, whereby all the former fears of this nation are quite cut off.*

But the English parliament was not ready for a full incorporating union. Perhaps it feared that England would be swallowed up by its smaller neighbour, just as many Scots, although mindful of the potential advantages of union, were apprehensive of losing their identity.[1] The proposal was decisively rejected by the English parliament in 1607;

---

1   The most thoughtful diagnosis of the dilemma facing Scotland – and its solution – was written by a distinguished Scottish feudal lawyer, Sir Thomas Craig of Riccarton (1538–

it would be precisely another century before it came about, in 1707 (see Chapter 26). Ted Cowan says:

> When I was at school we got very little Scottish history, but we certainly got the union of the crowns, because our teachers, like Walter Scott, thought this was the beginnings of Scottish greatness. Later, I was surprised to discover that most Scots felt profound anxiety about the meaning and the implications of the union of the crowns. When James went south he reassured the English they had nothing to worry about because the greater must always attract the lesser. James had a scheme for the amalgamation of Scots law and English law, which would mean the demise of Scots law. He wanted to amalgamate religious practice in both countries. And he had an idea for a fully incorporated United Kingdom, not just a personal union of the crowns. This was rejected by both the Scots and the English; but the Scots, in particular, feared that their identity would be engulfed by the much stronger and wealthier kingdom to the south.

King James had done all he could to create a 'British atmosphere'. Michael Lynch says:

> After 1603 new emblems of a British identity were created: a wave of British histories, seals, flags and coinage engulfed James's subjects on both sides of the border. No detail was too small to be overlooked; a new design for the King's Great Seal conjoined not only the English and Scottish seals but also those of Cadwallader and Edward the Confessor, respectively the last undisputed kings of Celtic Britain and Anglo-Saxon England. The elaborate

---

1608), in a Latin treatise entitled *De Unione Regnorum Britanniae Tractatus* (1605, but not published until 1909). Craig had gone to London with King James in 1603, and in 1604 he was a commissioner for the projected union of the two kingdoms. In his treatise, he was in favour of the concept of union, but warned that Scotland could be the loser: the greater would inevitably attract the lesser, future monarchs would be English and live in England, London would become the capital of the whole island and the best Scottish brains would gravitate towards it. For union to be successful, the two kingdoms would have to be put on an equal footing: Scots law and religion would have to be preserved, each parliament must retain its status and authority. Above all, the written annals of the two countries should be revised, in order to expunge 'errors and irritating expressions' – a new history of Britain should be written with the utmost regard for accuracy.

balance struck on the Great Seal was symbolic of the fact that
perfect union had at its heart the notion of a genuinely dual
monarchy; James VI & I was probably the first and last exponent
of it ever to sit on the British throne.

Perhaps King James misinterpreted the undoubted warmth of his reception in England when he first rode south in 1603. He saw it as a genuine English wish for union, rather than as relief that the succession from the tired reign of the last of the Tudors had been achieved without strife. England had a male monarch at last, after fifty years of rule by women (Mary Tudor, 'Bloody Mary', had acceded to the throne in 1553), and a king who would ensure, in his person and his published ideals, the security of moderate Protestantism. It was seen as a new dawn for a kingdom exhausted by war with Spain, and James himself was supremely confident, intellectually, in his ability to rule, and to rule well. The fact that he was Scottish rather than English apparently made no difference – at least, to start with. He had not reckoned on the hatred and contempt which the English had been schooled for centuries to feel for their irrepressible northern neighbours.

In his court appointments James did his best to be even-handed in his dealings with his two principal kingdoms: four in ten of the appointments in the court at Whitehall went to Scots; one in five of the privy council were Scots; and eight Scots noblemen were installed as Knights of the Garter alongside twelve Englishmen. But there was a larger Scottish influx to contend with. Hundreds of Scots followed James south and settled in London. The English disliked these 'hungrie Scottis', these Scots on the make. One of them was a young butter-merchant from Edinburgh named Thomas Dalyell, ancestor of the present-day Labour MP Tam Dalyell of The Binns, near Linlithgow. Thomas Dalyell had done well for himself, organising the import of butter from Orkney to Leith, and in 1601 became the son-in-law of Edward Bruce, first Baron Kinloss, who was Master of the Rolls to King James in Scotland. Edward Bruce took his son-in-law with him to London as deputy Master of the Rolls. In that position Thomas Dalyell became a senior member of the king's private civil service with immense powers of patronage, buying and selling offices and no doubt creaming off a good commission for himself in the process. By 1612 he had made enough money to return to Scotland and become a member of the landed gentry: he bought 'the lands of Bynnis and Croceflattis with the manor place thereof', rebuilt The Binns and settled to a new life as a country laird.[1] Thomas Dalyell was only one of many. The most spectacular example of a Scot who made good in London was the man who came to be nicknamed 'Jinglin' Geordie'.

'Jinglin' Geordie'

If the English nation were at first delighted to receive King James as their sovereign, the Scottish people were no less enchanted by the prospect of their monarch's ascent to this wealthy and pre-eminent situation. They considered the promotion of their countryman and prince as an omen of good fortune to their nation; each individual Scotchman expected to secure some part of the good things with which England was supposed to abound . . .

TALES OF A GRANDFATHER, CHAPTER XXXV

The handsome Renaissance 'palace' of George Heriot's School, facing Edinburgh Castle from the north side of Lauriston, is the largest and most enduring monument of the Union of the Crowns. Its foundation stone was laid in 1628, although it was not opened until 1659; but its metaphorical foundations were laid in the London Goldrush which was inspired by the departure of King James VI to the south in 1603.[2] One of the Scots in the Goldrush was an Edinburgh goldsmith named George Heriot, who became the most successful of Scotland's London-based merchants. He amassed such a fortune that his pockets always jingled with money, and he was accordingly nicknamed 'Jinglin' Geordie'.[3]

'Jinglin' Geordie' was born in Edinburgh in 1563. His father was

---

1 In 1944 the House of the Binns became the first historic house in Scotland to be presented to the National Trust for Scotland, although Tam Dalyell and his heirs retain the right to live in it.

2 The Scottish influx to England became so heavy that even King James found it a burden. In 1614 he appointed a Scots adventurer named William Alexander as 'Master of Requests for Scotland'. It was a euphemistically-entitled post: Alexander was, in effect, head of immigration control, and his task was to fend off the hordes of needy Scots who showered the king with petitions for good jobs in England. Later, in 1621, Alexander dreamed up a scheme for absorbing surplus Scots by trying to establish a Scots colony in western Newfoundland – 'Nova Scotia'. It was incorporated into the kingdom of Scotland, but in 1629 was surrendered to France.

3 'Jinglin' Geordie' is vividly portrayed in Walter Scott's novel *The Fortunes of Nigel* (published in 1822), which chronicles the adventures of young Nigel Oliphaunt, Lord Glenarvon, who travels to London in an endeavour to recover from James VI & I a sum of forty thousand marks which had been advanced to the king at a crisis in his fortunes by Nigel's father.

well-to-do: a skilled goldsmith, a member of parliament and Deacon Convenor of the Incorporated Trades of Edinburgh. 'Jinglin' Geordie' became apprenticed to his father, who set him up in a business of his own in a shop next to the High Kirk of St Giles' when he married in 1586. The quality of his work soon attracted approving notice and, although he was a commoner, in 1597 he was appointed goldsmith to James's Queen Anne. She loved the exquisite jewellery he fashioned, and in 1601 he was appointed goldsmith to the king as well. He knew all about the value of gold plate and jewellery and became unofficial banker to the royal household, lending money on the security of their jewels; and in 1601 he was appointed to a commission set up to issue a new currency.

When the king went to London in 1603 Heriot stayed in Edinburgh to deal with the flow of royal orders for rings and pendants. Soon he realised that the real market was in London, and later in the year he too moved south; it was a harrowing journey, during which his two sons died. When his wife died in 1608 he returned to Scotland, where he married a sixteen-year-old girl, Alice Primrose, the daughter of James Primrose of Carrington (grandfather of the first Earl of Rosebery). He went back to London in 1609 and his business, and his fortune, expanded steadily. There were occasional setbacks, especially when the royal couple were unable to pay their bills (at one time he was owed £15,000 by the crown); by the time of his death in 1624, however, Heriot was an extremely wealthy man, owning extensive property in London as well as in Edinburgh.

His second wife had died in 1612. He had no living kin apart from two acknowledged illegitimate daughters from liaisons in London after his wife's death. In the year before his death he drew up a will, leaving his London properties to his two daughters and bequeathing the remainder of his fortune – £23,000 – to the Town Council of Edinburgh to found a hospital (a school, in effect) in imitation of Christ's Hospital in London. It was to be dedicated to the nursing, upbringing and education of 'poor orphans and fatherless children of decayed burgesses and freemen of the said burgh, destitute and without means'.

The first thirty boys were admitted in 1659, as soon as Oliver Cromwell's troops vacated the city (see Chapter 22). For nearly 350 years the sons (and now daughters) of widows have been educated free. The 'Hospital' was converted into an independent fee-paying secondary school in 1886, but there are still some seventy 'Foundationers' in the roll of 1,500 pupils. Heriot's is one of the great schools of Scotland, and certainly the most handsome – all thanks to 'Jinglin' Geordie', the Edinburgh goldsmith with the Midas touch.

The 'other' Scotland

King James may have seen himself as the 'universal king' not only of a dual monarchy but of a united nation. But there was one large area of his Scottish kingdom which was hardly part of it at all – the Highlands and Islands. For most Lowland Scots (and, no doubt, for all Englishmen), the Highlands and Islands were the cause of nothing but alarm, inhabited by an uncouth, barely-civilised, warlike race whose only interest was war and whose main occupations were feuding and thieving. No matter that the Gaels of the north and west were descended from one of the most ancient strands in the ethnic make-up of the Scottish nation: they were now considered an alien people.

The court of James VI had little sympathy for Gaeldom; if anything, it was afraid of Gaelic culture. There was nothing new about that. The last King of Scots who had been able to speak Gaelic was James IV, who died at Flodden in 1513. Throughout the sixteenth century there had been a developing sense of the Highlands as 'a problem', and a growing hostility towards Gaeldom and the Gaelic language and culture. The process was accentuated by the revival of classical learning inspired by the Renaissance; it made the Gaelic-speaking fringes of the kingdom look even more barbaric than ever, a blot on the civilised Scottish landscape. James VI represented the culmination of this hostility. In his *Basilikon Doron* (1598) the king characterised his Gaelic-speaking subjects:

> As for the Highlands, I shortly comprehend them all in two sorts
> of people: the one that dwelleth in our main land, that are
> barbarous for the most part, and yet mixed with some show of
> civility; the other, that dwelleth in the Isles, that are utterly
> barbarous, without any sort of show of civility.

The kind of policies James had begun to pursue in the 1590s were designed to extirpate all traces of Gaelic culture from Scotland. He had never set foot in the Islands himself, although he seriously considered making a law-and-order expedition on more than one occasion. Instead, he hit upon a curious scheme of Lowland colonisation, or plantation, of the Islands. The Isle of Lewis, the base of the Macleods, was chosen for the pilot scheme. The island was described as if by an exceptionally imaginative estate agent as being 'enriched with an incredible fertility of corn and store of fishings and other necessaries, surpassing far the plenty of any part of the inland'. An Act of Parliament was passed in 1597, leasing the island to a group of Lowland entrepreneurs known as the 'Fife Adventurers', headed by the Duke of Lennox. They were authorised for 'slaughter, mutilation, fire-raising or other inconveniences' – anything necessary to 'root out the barbarous inhabitants'.

Not surprisingly, the 'barbarous' islanders responded with vigour. The adventurers were kept under constant attack, their ships harried, their camps destroyed, their garrisons slaughtered. By 1599 the whole enterprise had collapsed. In 1605, and once more in 1607–8, the adventurers tried again, and failed again, on Lewis. It was an echo of English policies in Ireland between the 1530s and 1570s. Michael Lynch says:

> By 1609 almost any means – blackmail, kidnapping or legal sharp practice – was legitimate, as part of an official policy to 'bring the Highlands and Islands to civility'.

In one view, the problem was really to do with the crown itself. It had been the crown which had dissolved the Lordship of the Isles in the reign of James IV; and every reign in the sixteenth century would see a rising in the Islands against the crown. The crown, in that view, had destabilised the Highlands and Islands – and then blamed the Highlands and Islands for it.

King James was more successful in 1609 with a policy which would now be called cultural genocide. Using Andrew Knox, the Bishop of the Isles, as his mediator, he lured nine influential clan chiefs on to a naval vessel which brought them to Edinburgh; they were released only on condition that they went to the Holy Island of Iona to attend a conference. There they were induced to pledge themselves to the 'Statutes of Iona', which stigmatised what they called Gaelic manners, dress and customs; the carrying of firearms was banned; bards were forbidden to glorify warfare and martial feats; and anyone who owned more than sixty head of cattle was required to send his sons to be educated on the mainland, safely removed from 'barbarous' influences, where they would be taught to speak, read and write in English. The Statutes of Iona proved ineffective as an instrument for peace, but they dealt a devastating blow to the Gaelic language.

Although the 'Plantation' of the Isle of Lewis had failed, the idea was to work elsewhere, with bitter results which have lasted to this day. In 1609 King James issued an invitation to his Scottish subjects to participate in a new Plantation Scheme – the Plantation of Ulster. More than seventy Scottish nobles, burgesses, lairds and merchants took up holdings and settled there. Ireland was to be forced to be a part of Protestant Europe; by the end of James's reign more than eight thousand Scots capable of bearing arms had settled in Ulster. In 1611 King James said proudly of his Ulster Plantation:

> The settling of religion, the introducing of civility, order and government amongst a barbarous and unsubdued people, [are] acts of piety and glory, and worthy always of a Christian prince to endeavour.

The Powder Treason Plot (1605)

A wooden plaque on a wall of a shop called 'Booksale' (formerly Blackwell's bookshop) in Stonegate, in York, marks the site of the house in which one of the most notorious characters in Jacobean history was born and brought up:

> GUY FAWKES
> Hereabouts lived the
> parents of Guy Fawkes
> of Gunpowder Plot fame,
> who was baptized in
> St. Michael-le-Belfrey
> Church in 1570.

England's beleaguered Catholics, who had been severely persecuted during the reign of Queen Elizabeth, had been much reassured by the accession of King James.[1] In Scotland he had shown conspicuous

---

1 Ever since Spain had tried to invade England with the Armada in 1588, Catholicism had been proscribed. Everyone over the age of sixteen had to worship at an Anglican church every Sunday or face a fine of one shilling for each Sunday they missed, and £20 a month if they still refused to attend. They could be jailed for owning rosary beads or Catholic prayer-books. The children of Catholics could not be baptised in their faith; they had to be baptised in Anglican churches before they were a month old. Their weddings had to be in Anglican churches, and when they died they were forbidden the last sacrament. Nonetheless, many Roman Catholics who went to Anglican services also went to secret Catholic masses in people's homes. Babies were baptised in secret as Catholics; there were secret Catholic weddings and priests were smuggled to the bedsides of the dying to give them the last rites. Catholics who owned large houses made secret places in them in which priests could hide; they could be fined or imprisoned for this or for helping priests in any other way. The priests themselves could be exiled, fined, imprisoned or even executed as traitors if they were caught conducting masses.

tolerance of Catholics, even of Jesuits; there was thus a general assumption that James, the son of a 'martyred' Catholic queen and married to a queen who had recently become a Catholic convert, would rescind the anti-Catholic laws. But his English subjects, deeply prejudiced against Catholicism in all forms, rejected James's well-meaning policy of toleration and demanded persecution; in 1604 he reluctantly accepted the necessity of re-enacting the penal laws. The English Catholics felt bitterly disappointed and, indeed, betrayed. Even before his coronation as James I on 15 March 1604 there were two half-baked plots against him;[1] but the Powder Treason Plot was much the most spectacular and, potentially, much the most dangerous.

Guy Fawkes was born in York in April 1570, and was baptised in the parish church of St Michael-le-Belfrey, next to York Minster. His father, Edward Fawkes, a well-to-do lawyer, was an Anglican; his mother, Edith, was a Catholic. Guy was brought up in the Anglican faith, but when his father died and his mother married a Catholic, he became a Catholic too. Many of his school-mates were Catholics. Two of them were John and Christopher Wright, whose mother had spent years in prison for her faith; their sister was married to Thomas Percy, a Catholic neighbour of Guy's stepfather.

When Guy left home to earn his living he went to the Netherlands as a soldier. One of his tasks was to 'undermine' the walls of towns in Spanish hands, which developed his experience of gunpowder. In the late 1590s, however, he left the English army to join a Spanish regiment, in which there were several English Catholics, including its commander, Sir William Stanley, and Thomas Wintour, from Worcestershire. Stanley noticed Fawkes's ability as a sapper and promoted him to ensign. He then took him (he was now calling himself 'Guido', the Spanish for Guy) and Thomas Wintour to Spain in 1598 to petition Philip III to help the Catholics in England by sending another invasion force. Philip received the three English Catholics politely but gave them no encouragement. However, they remained determined to bring about a Catholic revolution in England – especially after James VI

---

1   The two early attempts are known as the 'Bye' plot and the 'Main' plot. The 'Bye' plot had been designed to capture the king and force him to make concessions to Catholics; three men were executed as a result. The 'Main' plot was more serious but equally unrealistic: it envisaged a Spanish invasion which would depose James and place Lady Arabella Stewart on the throne. Sir Walter Raleigh was obscurely connected with both plots; he was found guilty at a trial which was patently rigged, but was reprieved from the scaffold by King James at the last minute. He was to spend the next thirteen years in the Tower before being executed for treason in 1616.

came to the throne as James I and failed to promote greater tolerance for Catholics.

In May 1604 Guy Fawkes went to London, where he attended a secret meeting in the Duck and Drake inn in the Strand; the meeting had been called by Robert Catesby, a devout Catholic. He had summoned two of his relatives, Thomas and Robert Wintour, but Thomas could not attend because of illness. Catesby's friend John Wright was there, with his brother-in-law Thomas Percy. The five men swore an oath of secrecy upon a prayer book and Catesby unveiled an audacious plan to blow up the House of Lords on the opening day of parliament the following February.

The plotters found a suitable apartment near Parliament House. Thomas Percy rented it because he had a reason to be in London which would not arouse suspicion: his relative the Earl of Northumberland had just made him a gentleman pensioner (one of fifty royal bodyguards). Guy Fawkes lived in the apartment as 'John Johnson, caretaker', because his face was not known in London. Catesby had bought about thirty-six barrels of gunpowder, saying that it was for the English army in the Low Countries, and stored them in his lodgings in Lambeth, just across the Thames from the Houses of Parliament.

The conspirators' apartment had a store-room which ran beneath the House of Lords. In July they began to bring the barrels of gunpowder in rowing boats across the Thames from Lambeth. They hid them under piles of coal and wood in the store-room. Nobody would notice, because the room was full of bits of stone, wood and other rubbish. It became known as 'Guy Fawkes's cellar'.

By this time, rumours were spreading among Catholics about a plot to destroy the government. The conspirators had even made plans about who should rule after King James died in the explosion. His elder son, Prince Henry, would probably die with him. Next in line to the throne was his younger son, Charles, who was only four years old and very sickly. They planned to kidnap the king's elder daughter, the nine-year-old Princess Elizabeth, and have her brought up as a Catholic. She would be crowned queen.

Meanwhile there was a change in the planned date for the opening of parliament. Because of fears of a renewed outbreak of plague in London the opening date was moved to 3 October. By the end of July there was still plague in the city, and it was decided to open parliament on Tuesday, 5 November 1605.

By the end of October all the gunpowder was in place in the store-room beneath the House of Lords. The plan was for Guy Fawkes to light the fuse and to escape by boat across the Thames; then he would sail to Europe. But rumours of a plot had reached the king's chief minister, Robert Cecil, the Earl of Salisbury. He learned more on the evening of 25 October: his friend Lord Mounteagle was holding a dinner party at his home in Hoxton, north of London, when a messenger brought him an anonymous letter. It warned him not to go to the opening of parliament because 'they shall receive a terrible blow this Parliament'. Mounteagle sent the letter straight to Lord Salisbury.

On 1 November Salisbury told the king about the letter; the following day Salisbury told the Privy Council. By that time many of the lords had heard the rumours of a plot against the king and parliament. They decided that, on the day before the opening, the lord chamberlain (Thomas Howard, first Earl of Suffolk) should take a walk around all the buildings of the Houses of Parliament to ensure the king's safety. At 3 p.m. on 4 November the lord chamberlain, Lord Mounteagle and others strolled into the cellar. They pretended they were looking for some missing property. They found Guy Fawkes, and asked him about all the wood and coal there. He told them that it belonged to Thomas Percy, and that he was Percy's caretaker.

That night, the cellar of the House of Lords was searched. Guy Fawkes was discovered, dressed for travel, in a cloak, hat, boots and spurs. When he was arrested he gave his name as 'John Johnson'. The other conspirators fled on horseback when they heard what had happened. Fawkes was taken to the Tower of London, where he was questioned. He admitted that he was going to blow up the House of Lords, saying that 'the devil and not God' caused the plot to fail. He would not reveal his real name or the names of the other conspirators. On 6 November the king gave the order to torture 'Johnson' to make him talk. On 7 November Guy Fawkes confessed his real name and, the next day, the names of five of the other conspirators. Two days later he revealed the names of the other seven.

Four of the conspirators were killed by the men who were sent to capture them. The others, including Fawkes, were sentenced to be hanged, drawn and quartered. On 31 January 1606, Guy Fawkes mounted the scaffold; he asked the king to forgive him, said a prayer and made the sign of the cross. His neck broke as he was hanged, so he was dead before he was drawn and quartered.

The first 'Bonfire night' was held on 5 November 1605, the day after Guy Fawkes was arrested. It was the start of an annual fire-festival which has lasted to this day.

The Hampton Court Conference (1604)

Even before the Powder Treason Plot was hatched, King James had embarked on an ecclesiastical conference designed to establish the religious foundations of his reign: the Hampton Court Conference, which convened for the first of its sessions on 14 January 1604. It was essentially a conference of bishops of the Church of England, but many others were admitted. The king's purpose was quite clear: he was seeking conformity throughout the Church, not confrontation, and he was happy to engage in intellectual discussion, even with the Puritan divines who had plagued Elizabeth's reign with their hard-line resistance to 'Popish' ceremonies and usages. James debated with the Puritans with good humour and tact, and was prepared to make concessions to their feelings. But he was not going to have any truck with Presbyterianism. He told the opening session of the Conference, with unconcealed anger:

> If you aim at a Scottish Presbytery, it agreeth as well with monarchy as God and the Devil. Then Jack and Tom and Will and Dick shall meet and censure me and my Council ... My Lords the Bishops, if once you were out and they in, I know what would become of my supremacy, for No Bishop, No King. I will make them conform themselves, or else I will harry them out of the land, or else do worse.

Overall, however, the Hampton Court Conference was a model of thoughtful consideration and compromise, and James earned much credit for his intellectual grasp of theology, his skills as a debater and his patience as a benign chairman. But the major outcome of the Conference for posterity was the decision to produce a new translation of the Bible into English, to be undertaken by a commission of fifty-four scholars. King James, who had himself tried his hand at Bible translation (he had translated the Psalms of David into verse), seized on the suggestion with great enthusiasm.

This was the origin of the Authorised Version, or King James Version, of the Bible. Formal work on it began in 1607. Based largely on the translation by William Tyndale almost a century earlier, it was published in 1611 and 'Appointed to be read in Churches' (hence 'Authorised'). Despite the archaisms and inaccuracies which later scholars and editions have laboured to correct, the King James Bible is still revered by many as the best-loved and most widely-read translation of the scriptures ever made. Stylistically, it ranks with the works of Shakespeare as one of the great glories of English literature; linguistically, it gave the English language a central coherence which it was never to lose.

James's relations with the Kirk in his native Scotland were much less agreeable, however. Much impressed with the ordered and compliant nature of the Church of England, he had increased the number of bishoprics in Scotland to eleven and created two archbishoprics. Two Courts of High Commission had been erected to help the bishops enforce ecclesiastical law based on the English mode; and James was still determined to break the grip of Presbyterianism in Scotland and to unify the religious observance of the two countries.

The royal visit to Scotland (1617)

James remained extremely desirous to obtain at least an ecclesiastical conformity of opinion, by bringing the form and constitution of the Scottish Church as near as possible to that of England. What he attempted and accomplished in this respect, forms an important part of the history of his reign, and gave occasion to some of the most remarkable and calamitous events in that of his successor.

TALES OF A GRANDFATHER, CHAPTER XXXVI

When King James had left Scotland for London in 1603 he had promised to return every three years. Events, and considerations of expense, had prevented him from doing so. But in the autumn of 1616 he finally decided to go, willy nilly:

We are not ashamed to confess that we have had these many years a great and natural longing to see our native soil and place of our birth and breeding, and this salmon-like instinct of ours has restlessly, both when we were awake, and many times in our sleep, so stirred up our thoughts and bended our desires to make a journey thither than we can never rest satisfied till it shall please God that we may accomplish it.

LETTER TO THE SCOTTISH PRIVY COUNCIL,

15 DECEMBER 1616

James rode north with a large entourage on 15 March 1617, retracing the route of his first triumphal procession in 1603. His reception in

Scotland was tumultuously enthusiastic, and he must have been deeply moved by the spontaneous rejoicing with which he was welcomed to his other capital. But the rejoicing was not shared by the Presbyterians of the Kirk, for James had Kirk business to attend to, as well: as part of his vision of a unified realm he wanted a uniform Church, a Church with no sectional differences in worship or liturgy

The king had brought with him a chamber organ from the Chapel Royal in Windsor for use in the Palace of Holyroodhouse, along with a choir and a large supply of candles. To some Calvinists this was the thin end of the wedge of Popery. Furthermore, James wanted to make certain changes to practice and worship in the Kirk. He wanted Scots, like the English, to receive Holy Communion kneeling; he wanted the Kirk to celebrate Christmas and Easter as religious festivals; he wanted new communicants to be confirmed by bishops, not by ministers; and he wanted private baptism and private communion to be permitted in cases of grave illness.

Having produced his scheme for liturgical 'improvements' King James left Edinburgh in August 1617, for the last time. The royal requirements he had issued became known as the 'Five Articles'; in November a meeting of the General Assembly at St Andrews rejected them. The king was furious, and in January 1618 the Privy Council declared, on royal warrant, that Christmas, Good Friday, Easter Sunday, Ascension Day and Whitsunday should henceforth be holidays. Later that year the General Assembly met again, in Perth; there was vehement opposition once more, but eventually a majority was mustered in favour of the 'Five Articles'. Several diehard ministers refused to put them into practice, and a dozen were deprived of their livings. King James angrily banned further meetings of the General Assembly, but the damage had been done; from now on, any proposed alterations to the liturgy would be viewed with profound suspicion as a move towards Anglicanism. It was the start of a protest movement which would explode into rioting in the High Kirk of St Giles' under Charles I in 1638 (see Chapter 22).

Decline and death (1625)

In the prime of his kingship in Scotland, King James had written a book on kingship, *Basilikon Doron* (1598), which became a European best-seller when it was published in London in 1603. In it, he distilled for the benefit of his son his belief in the Divine Right of Kings – and the divine responsibility of kings:

First of all things learn to know and to love that God, whom-to
ye have a double obligation; first, for that he made you a man;
and next, for that he made you a little God to sit on his throne,
and rule over other men ... Being content to let others excel in
other things, let it be your chiefest earthly glory to excel in your
own craft [the craft of kingship].

In his declining years, James ceased to work at his kingcraft. He had been slowly losing contact with his subjects in Scotland, losing not only their affection but their respect; and the alienated Scots were beginning to look to the Kirk, rather than the crown, to represent and symbolise their national identity. Also, his health was deteriorating (it has been suggested that he suffered from porphyria, the 'royal malady' which, it has been claimed, destroyed the health of George III). James had arthritis, gout and piles, and all his teeth were gone. Gradually, he withdrew from active involvement in the affairs of state. There was constant friction with the English parliament. The king became careless of his royal dignity. He scandalised his court, and foreign visitors, with his blatant favouritism for handsome young men like Robert Carr (whom he made Earl of Somerset) and George Villiers (whom he made Duke of Buckingham), and his extravagantly expressed fondness for them.[1] Nonetheless, when he died after a massive stroke on 27 March 1625, he was genuinely mourned. He was nearly fifty-nine years old, and had been a king for all but one of them. He was given a lavish state funeral by his son Charles, and his embalmed body was buried in Westminster Abbey on 7 May 1625.

The abiding picture of James's failing years is a caricature of a king. It was drawn by an English courtier named Sir Anthony Weldon, one of the clerks of the green cloth who were responsible for keeping the accounts of the royal household. He had accompanied the king on the royal visit to Scotland in 1617 and penned some very scurrilous views about the country. When the work was discovered, Weldon was dismissed on the spot; he was to exact cruel revenge with a vitriolic

---

1   Both Carr and Villiers came to grief. Robert Carr (c.1587–1645) lost favour after he fell in love with Frances Howard, Countess of Essex, whom he married after a rigged divorce; the couple were subsequently charged with complicity in the murder of one of the principals in the case, Sir Thomas Overbury, and imprisoned in the Tower (1616). During their imprisonment they came to hate one another, and on their release they were forced to live together under house arrest – an even worse punishment. George Villiers (1592–1628) rose to extreme wealth and power, but caused his own downfall by failed military adventures against Spain and then France; parliament tried to have him impeached, but eventually he was assassinated by a disgruntled subaltern.

character-study of the king which was published in 1651 as anti-Royalist propaganda after the Civil Wars:

> *He was of middle-stature, more corpulent through his clothes than in his body . . . his clothes ever being made large and easy, the doublets quilted for stiletto-proof . . . He was naturally of a timorous disposition . . . his eyes large, ever rolling after any stranger that came into his presence. His beard was very thin; his tongue too large for his mouth, which ever made him speak full in the mouth, and made him drink very uncomely, as if eating his drink, which came out of the cup at each side of his mouth. His skin was as soft as taffeta sarsnet [silk], which felt so because he never washed his hands, only rubbed his finger-ends slightly with the wet end of a napkin; his legs were very weak, having had, (as was thought), some foul play in his youth . . . that weakness made him ever leaning on other men's shoulders; his walk was ever circular, his fingers ever in that walk fiddling about his codpiece . . .*
>
> THE COURT AND CHARACTER OF KING JAMES, 1651

It would be unjust to allow this vindictive portrait of a king in his dotage, self-indulgent and dissipated, to colour the overall view of James's reign and achievements. Yet many commentators have done so down the years. Walter Scott was condescending about him to the point of contempt:

> *He possessed all that could be derived from learning alloyed by pedantry, and from a natural shrewdness of wit, which enabled him to play the part of a man of sense, when either acting under the influence of constraint and fear, or where no temptation occurred to induce him to be guilty of some folly. It was by these specious accomplishments that he acquired in his youth the character of a wise and able monarch, although when he was afterwards brought on a more conspicuous stage, and his character better understood, he was found entitled to no better epithet than that conferred on him by an able French politician, who called him 'the wisest fool in Christendom.'*
>
> TALES OF A GRANDFATHER, CHAPTER XXXV[1]

---

1 In *The Fortunes of Nigel* (1822), Scott portrayed King James as a pedantic middle-aged fogey, sitting in his study surrounded by a dusty disorder of books and papers – 'notes of unmercifully long orations and essays on king-craft' and 'miserable roundels and ballads' in his own hand (Chapter 5).

Modern historians have re-evaluated James as monarch, with the result that he has emerged as a man of high ability and intelligence, as a king who deeply respected monarchy as an institution ordained by God, and as a dedicated advocate of European peace. His personal motto was *Beati Pacifici* – 'Blessed are the Peacemakers' – and he did his best to live up to it.

The succession

On 6 November 1612, Prince Henry, Duke of Wales and heir to the throne, had died after a long illness, probably connected with typhoid. It was a terrible blow to James and his queen: Henry, newly turned eighteen, was a handsome, genial, charismatic young man, the apple of his father's eye and the darling of the crowds. He was manly and athletic and, quite unlike his father, addicted to martial sports; also unlike his father, he was moderate in his drinking and his language (he kept a 'swear-box' in each of his three homes, the contents of which were given to the poor). As King James's personal popularity waned, Prince Henry's increased: already the nation was looking forward to the accession of 'King Henry IX'.

The death of Henry thrust his younger brother Charles unwillingly into the succession. Charles was the youngest of the family to survive infancy, and his father had always called him 'Baby Charles'. He was created Prince of Wales in 1616, at the age of fifteen. A small, slim, sallow man, he was a good scholar, cultured and artistic; but he could never endear himself to the populace as his brother had done so effortlessly. He was determined to be a good king – the 'little God' of the *Basilikon Doron* – and had dedicated himself to the task of being king as soon as his brother died; but he had none of his father's instinct for kingcraft, whether in European peace-making or in handling religious affairs. In the reign of Charles I, much of the good work done by James VI & I would be undone, with disastrous results.

Chapter 22

CHARLES I AND THE
NATIONAL COVENANT

*The rash and fatal experiment was made, 23rd July, 1637, in
the High Church of St Giles, Edinburgh, where the dean of the
city prepared to read the new service before a numerous concourse
of persons, none of whom seem to have been favourably disposed
to its reception.*

TALES OF A GRANDFATHER, CHAPTER XLI

At morning service in St Giles' Cathedral on Sunday, 23 July 1637
an elderly but muscular vegetable-seller named Jenny Geddes
made a dramatic entry on to the stage of story, if not history. She is
said to have thrown a stool at the Dean of St Giles', James Hannay,
as he tried to use a new Book of Common Prayer authorised by Charles
I, King of England, Ireland and Scotland.[1]

Jenny Geddes was known as the 'Princess of the Tron Adventurers',
the street traders of the market place at the Tron, just a few metres
from St Giles'. She was one of the women who were customarily hired

---

1   Inset into the floor of St Giles' Cathedral, not far from the entrance, a metal plaque commemorates the event: 'Constant oral tradition affirms that near this spot a brave Scotchwoman
Janet Geddes on the 23 July 1637 struck the first blow in the great struggle for freedom of
conscience which after a conflict of half a century ended in the establishment of civil and
religious liberty.' Another plaque, on a pillar near the pulpit, commemorates James Hannay
(1634–39): 'He was the first and the last who read the Service Book in this church. This
memorial is erected in happier times by his descendants.'

to arrive early to keep a place for their employers by sitting there on their folding stools. According to legend, Jenny yelled out, 'Deil colic the wame o' ye! Daur ye say mass at my lug?' [The devil take your belly! Do you dare to say Mass in my ear?] Whether or not it was Jenny Geddes who flung the first stool, St Giles' was soon in an uproar.[1] Stools, sticks, stones and Bibles went flying towards the dean. The Bishop of Edinburgh, David Lindsay, went to the pulpit to remonstrate with the women, but he too was driven back by the hail of missiles. Guards were summoned to restore order, and the 'rascal multitude' of women was forcibly ejected; but for the remainder of the service they stood outside the church, shouting and hammering at the doors and hurling stones at the windows.

The riot in St Giles' showed every sign of having been carefully orchestrated, because riots quickly broke out in other churches up and down the land. It was the start of a resistance movement against Charles I's ecclesiastical policy which would lead to bloody revolution.

How had matters come to such a pass?

'The wee king with big ideas'

King Charles I, the third surviving child of King James VI & I and Queen Anne, was a very small man in stature – only five feet (152 centimetres) tall. He had been born in Dunfermline on 19 November 1600, a sickly child who suffered from rickets which stunted his growth; he was too frail to accompany his father on his triumphant journey to London in 1603. Throughout his childhood he was the runt of the family; he was a slow developer, he stammered painfully and his thin legs were too weak to allow him to walk or stand unsupported. As he grew older he forced himself to learn to ride a horse (and thereby strengthened his legs greatly), and applied himself to tennis and other sports, but was constantly overshadowed by his brilliant older brother, Prince Henry, and his beautiful and vivacious older sister, Elizabeth. Where Henry was extrovert and popular, Charles was withdrawn and secretive; where Henry was athletic and militaristic, Charles was studious and a keen patron of the arts.

After Prince Henry's death in 1612, Charles became heir to the

---

1 There is no evidence, other than tradition, that 'Jenny Geddes' was the woman who threw the first stool – but it's a great yarn! The only historical record of a Jenny Geddes is from 1660 when, at the restoration of King Charles II to the throne, she celebrated by burning her stool 'and all her creels, baskets, creepies and forms'.

throne, but without having had the schooling in statecraft which Henry had been given. He was only three years old when the royal family moved from Scotland to England on his father's accession to the English throne in 1603, and by the time he succeeded his father he had no personal experience of the Scots or Scottish affairs; he had even been excluded by his father from the royal visit in 1617 – King James's only visit to Scotland after he moved to London. The main policy (although it was a matter of conviction rather than a policy) which Charles inherited from his father was the concept of absolutism and the Divine Right of Kings – a belief which was to prove fatal for him and for countless thousands of his subjects.

King James VI & I died on 27 March 1625. At the age of twenty-four, Charles I succeeded him as 'the little God on the throne' and was crowned King of England; he would not be crowned in Scotland for eight years.

Marriage (1 May 1625)

Charles's closest friend at court had been his father's last favourite, the handsome George Villiers, Duke of Buckingham, who consequently wielded considerable power and influence. Buckingham became a surrogate elder brother to the young prince.

As Charles approached his twenties, and his father's health began to fail, the question of marriage became important. King James had made a strong gesture towards the Protestant cause in Europe by marrying his daughter Elizabeth to the Elector Palatine of the Rhine; now he wanted to gain credibility in the Catholic camp as well by a match which would demonstrate his neutrality. The bride he favoured for his son was Maria, the Infanta of Spain, daughter of King Philip III (who died in 1621) and sister of King Philip IV. When formal diplomacy failed, Buckingham and Charles resolved on a madcap, romantic scheme of their own in 1623 – to visit Spain themselves to press the suit. They decided to go *incognito*, wearing absurd false beards and using unrealistic assumed names (Jack and Tom Smith). By the time they reached Paris everyone in Madrid knew that they were on their way. Despite their incompetence, the mission very nearly succeeded. They spent several months in Madrid, during which Charles fell in love with the Infanta Maria, and a treaty of betrothal was agreed: Prince Charles would respect the Infanta's religion and allow any children of their marriage to be brought up as Catholics. The Infanta, however, did not return his passion (indeed, she said she would rather take the veil as a nun than marry a 'heretic'). During his journey back to England, Charles changed his mind and abruptly repudiated the betrothal, to his father's despair.[1]

After the failure of the proposed Spanish match, attention turned to another Catholic princess: Henrietta Maria, the fifteen-year-old daughter of King Henri IV of France. This time the negotiations were concluded without a hitch. King James's death in March 1625 delayed the ceremony; but on May Day 1625 Charles was married, by proxy, to his tiny French bride. There was friction in their marriage to begin with; but after the assassination of Buckingham in 1628, Charles grew to love his wife with single-minded devotion. As the crises of his reign developed he discovered in Henrietta Maria a toughness he had never suspected, and found great comfort in his family life. They were to have nine children, six of whom survived into adulthood: Charles (the future Charles II), Mary (the future wife of William II of Orange and mother of William III), James (the future James VII & II), Elizabeth, Henry (Duke of Gloucester) and Henrietta Anne.

Coronation in Scotland (1633)

King Charles did not visit Scotland for eight years after his accession, governing his Scottish realm by remote control from London through courtiers like William Alexander, Earl of Stirling, and James, Marquis of Hamilton. The Scottish Privy Council was staffed by the king's placemen, and it was not long before the Scots began to feel that they were being governed by a king who knew little about them and cared even less. For several years Charles put off his Scottish coronation; the Scots felt that he should have chosen to be crowned in Scotland first, and his failure to do so was regarded as a slight to his native kingdom. Costly preparations were put in hand for a coronation in 1628, and again in 1631, but still the king did not come. What compounded the trouble, however, was not the king's neglect of Scotland but his manifest determination to bend Scotland to his personal royal prerogative.

In 1633 Charles I at last made a royal progress to Scotland for his belated coronation. It was his first visit to the land of his birth since he had become king. William Laud, his Archbishop of Canterbury, was in attendance. The coronation service was held in the Chapel Royal, the old abbey church beside the Palace of Holyroodhouse, with

---

1 The Infanta Maria eventually married the son of the Holy Roman Emperor, the future Emperor Ferdinand III.

full Anglican liturgy. Charles had commanded the officiating clergy to wear surplices, and it is said that Archbishop Laud found one of the Scottish bishops 'deficient in vestments' and sent him out. To celebrate the coronation Charles decreed Edinburgh a new diocese and elevated the High Kirk of St Giles' into St Giles' Cathedral.[1] With his reverence for the office of bishop he also tried to give John Spottiswoode, the Archbishop of St Andrews, precedence in the procession over the lord chancellor; when the nobles refused to accept this, Charles took the first opportunity of appointing Spottiswoode as lord chancellor, in 1635. He was intent on using bishops as his instruments of royal policy, and gave them great power in the mechanism of choosing the effective executive committee of parliament, the 'Lords of the Articles'.

By the mid-1630s Scotland was smouldering with a general sense of discontent. King Charles had increased the levels of taxation to pay for his sabre-rattling activities on the Continent, and for the building of a new church at the Tron and of Parliament House in Edinburgh.[2] He had also issued, in 1625, a sweeping Act of Revocation which would enable him to claw back all the awards of Church lands and tithes since the Reformation, ostensibly to return the revenues to the Church; the security of Scotland's secular land-holders would thus be threatened. But it was Charles's religious policies which caused the greatest resentment, for they were clearly designed to assimilate the practices of the Presbyterian/Episcopalian Church in Scotland with those of the Anglican Church in England.

The first stirrings of revolt began in 1636, when the king issued a Code of Canons (Church law) designed to bring the Kirk into line with the more Catholic practices of the Anglican Church under Archbishop Laud. The Code of Canons assumed 'Royal Supremacy in Causes Ecclesiastical', which had never been established in Scotland; it restricted *extempore* prayer and ordered ministers not to preach in other parishes (thereby curtailing their independence), and made no reference to kirk sessions, presbyteries or General Assemblies. But what put the country in an uproar was the publication of a new Book of Common Prayer for Scotland in 1637.

---

1 At the same time he granted the burgh a city charter, and formally designated it as the capital of the kingdom.

2 Parliament House, built on the site of the manse and glebe of the ministers of St Giles', was designed by the king's master of works, Sir James Murray, and begun in 1632. Parliament Hall, with its impressive oak hammer-beam roof, served as the meeting-place of Scotland's parliament from 1639 to 1707.

On the face of it, the new Prayer Book was fairly non-controversial – indeed, it had been revised by the Scottish bishops, who had made every effort to make concessions to Scottish practice. What really angered the Scots was its introduction on the authority of the crown alone, with the consent of neither parliament nor General Assembly. It was thus a constitutional as well as a religious issue. It was the introduction of the new Prayer Book which led directly to the orchestrated eruption of riots which began in St Giles' Cathedral on 23 July 1637.

In the aftermath of the Prayer Book riots, the Privy Council received petitions from many parts of the country asking the king to get rid of the hated liturgy. The petitioners appointed four 'Tables' (committees) to represent the four orders of noblemen, lairds, burgesses and ministers – an informal parliament, in effect. One of the four representatives of the nobility elected to the 'Tables' was a sophisticated and gallant young man whose name would be writ large in the annals of the Civil Wars to come: James Graham, fifth Earl (and later first Marquis) of Montrose.[1] In December 1637 the 'Tables' presented a joint petition in which they demanded not only the withdrawal of the liturgy but the removal of all bishops from the Privy Council. The petition was brusquely rejected by King Charles, who threatened the petitioners with charges of treason.

In reply to this royal rebuff the 'Tables' presented a formal protest and, to demonstrate the strength of their position, set about preparing a 'National Covenant' which they would invite the whole nation to sign.

The National Covenant (1638)

This engagement was called the National Covenant, as resembling those covenants which, in the Old Testament, God is said to have made with the people of Israel. This covenant . . . was sworn to by hundreds, thousands, and hundreds of thousands, of every age and description, vowing, with uplifted hands and weeping eyes, that, with the Divine assistance, they would dedicate life and fortune to maintain the object of their solemn engagement.

TALES OF A GRANDFATHER, CHAPTER XLI

---

1 The Marquis of Montrose (1612–50) is one of the most romantic and evocative names in Scotland's history. A staunch Royalist, he nonetheless opposed the king's high-handed ecclesiastical policies for Scotland to begin with. Later he would split with the Covenanters and fight for the king with conspicuous gallantry and flair.

The National Covenant was in three parts. The first part repeated the *Confession of Faith* of 1581 – the so-called 'Negative Confession' signed by James VI and the Duke of Lennox – which renounced Catholic beliefs and practices and pledged to uphold Presbyterianism. The second part contained a long list of the various statutes and Acts of Parliament by which the Presbyterian Church had been established. The third part called for free (that is to say, not rigged by the king) parliaments and assemblies, and pledged its signatories to disregard Charles's recent innovations and to defend the Reformed religion 'against all sorts of persons whatsoever'.

On 28 February 1638 the National Covenant was ready for signature. At 2 p.m. the nobles and barons convened in Greyfriars Church. After a sermon and a presentation of the document, the signing began; it went on until 8 p.m. One of the first to sign was the Marquis of Montrose. Next day the burgesses and ministers had an opportunity to sign. Then it was the turn of the people. Copies of the Covenant were despatched by mounted messengers all over the country, and everywhere (apart from Aberdeen, which was a bastion of episcopacy, and the Gaelic-speaking north-west) crowds flocked to sign the document.[1] The number of signatures soon ran into thousands. It was perhaps the most remarkable expression of national unity Scotland had seen in all its history. The Covenant did not simply indicate opposition to the king and distrust of England; it showed that the Scots were looking to their national Kirk as the surest and purest repository of their national identity.

Despite its moderate tone and its appeal to the rule of law, the National Covenant was fundamentally a radical manifesto against the personal rule of Charles I and his arbitrary use of the royal prerogative. It carefully called for 'the maintenance of religion and the King's Majesty's authority, and for the preservation of the laws and liberties of the kingdom, against all troubles and sedition', but for many of the Covenanters it was much more than that – it was an apocalyptic vision. One of the two authors, a brilliant young Edinburgh lawyer named Archibald Johnston of Wariston, hailed its signing as 'the glorious marriage day of the kingdom with God': Scotland, like Israel, was God's chosen land, and its people, like the Israelites, were God's chosen people.

---

1 There are more than sixty specimens of the Covenant still extant: in the National Library of Scotland, in the National Museum of Scotland, in New College, in the Free Church College, in St Giles' Cathedral, in Dunblane Cathedral and many other places.

So what was the real significance of the National Covenant? Ted Cowan considers it one of the great inspirational moments in Scottish history – an attempt to turn the world upside down:

> *I find the National Covenant, and the whole question behind it, profoundly moving. The first covenant in the Bible was that between God and Noah, when God promised Noah that there would never be another Flood. So a covenant was a promise, or a contract, entered into for eternity. The Scots, instead of just paying lip service to the idea of a covenant, actually created a document, and copies thereof, which they signed, some of them allegedly in their own blood.*
>
> *This was another supremely important radical departure, not only in Scottish history but conceivably also in European history; because here you had people taking responsibility for their own actions by signing their names on a contract which said:* We undertake to defend both our Church, the Presbyterian establishment and our King. *That's what it said in the document which was subscribed in Greyfriars. It was a totally new exercise in civic humanism.*
>
> *The Covenant was one of the great disjunctures in Scottish history. It marked, in a very real sense, the end of the medieval world.*

Underlying this 'disjuncture' was a blurring of the distinctions between ecclesiastical and political issues – a 'transposition of political and national realities into an ecclesiastical key'.[1] The Covenanters had an acute sense of God's active involvement in the affairs of both the divinely ordained state and the divinely predestined human soul: social justice was as important to them as justification by faith. William Storrar, Professor of Christian Ethics and Practical Theology at Edinburgh University, says:

> *With such an exalted sense of the role of religion in national life, it became increasingly hard to distinguish between the cause of true religion and the pursuit of Scotland's national interests in the complex world of politics and statecraft. This tendency to transpose national questions into an ecclesiastical key was to find*

---

1 Ian Henderson, *Power Without Glory* (London, 1967).

its clearest expression in the 'godly government' of the radical
Presbyterian Covenanters in the 1640s [see below].

Meanwhile, the king issued various royal proclamations against the Covenanters; they replied that they would rather die than renounce the Covenant. The king's response was equally intransigent: 'I will rather die, than yield to those impertinent and damnable demands.'

The breach between king and Kirk was now very deep. Charles sent his lord high commissioner, the Marquis of Hamilton, to Scotland to offer terms of truce; but his private instructions to Hamilton told a different tale: 'I give you leave to flatter them with what hopes you please . . . your chief end being now to win time till I am able to suppress them.'

As part of his hidden agenda, Charles agreed to a meeting of the General Assembly of the Church of Scotland. It was the first such meeting for twenty years; they had been banned by James VI & I in 1618 after the dispute over the 'Five Articles'. The General Assembly met in Glasgow Cathedral on 21 November 1638, and sat for a whole month behind locked doors. The Covenanters had packed it with nobles and land-owners as 'elders', and thereby fixed all the nominations and elections. One of the new recruits who declared for the Covenanting party was the red-haired, squint-eyed Archibald Campbell, who had recently succeeded his father as eighth Earl of Argyll; the bitter enmity between Argyll and Montrose would colour much of the lurid canvas of the Civil Wars of the 1640s.[1]

The Marquis of Hamilton, the king's lord high commissioner, tried to dissolve the meeting of the General Assembly. He was voted down, and stalked out. The Assembly then proceeded to annul the 1636 Code of Canons and the 1637 liturgy of the new Prayer Book, to depose the bishops (eight of them were solemnly excommunicated for drunkenness, ignorance and neglect) and to abolish episcopacy. This was the start of the Scottish revolution; those who had continued the session of the General Assembly in defiance of the royal will were rebels against the crown.[2]

---

1 Archibald Campbell, eighth Earl of Argyll (1607–61), has been called 'the greatest politician of his age' (Edward Cowan, *Montrose: For Covenant and King*). The rivalry between Argyll and Montrose was likened by contemporaries to that between Julius Caesar and Pompey – 'the one would endure no superior and the other would have no equal'. He was created Marquis of Argyll by King Charles in 1641.

2 The parallel has often been drawn between the refusal of the General Assembly of the Church of Scotland to be dissolved, and the similar resistance of the French National Assembly in 1789. Both events led to the same end – the execution of a king.

It was tantamount to a declaration of war. But where were the troops to withstand an assault from England? There were hundreds of able young Scots soldiering under foreign flags on the Continent – men who had failed to achieve advancement with their king in London and had emigrated to make a living as mercenaries. The Scots now sent urgent word to Sweden to a veteran Scots soldier, Alexander Leslie, who had risen to the rank of field-marshal in the army of King Gustav II Adolf, the 'Lion of the North'.[1] Leslie returned to Scotland immediately to take over as commander-in-chief, bringing with him a cadre of experienced officers and a corps of battle-hardened troops.

King Charles was confident that he could deal with this nuisance in the north fairly easily, but he realised that he would have to mount a military assault with troops from England. He was already preparing his own strategy for defeating the Covenanters. He held Edinburgh Castle, and had the Royal Navy at his disposal to blockade the Firth of Forth or to land troops to bolster his supporters in the north-east; he held Dumbarton Castle, which would provide a secure base and anchorage for troops shipped in from Ireland or western England; and he had support in the north-east of Scotland led by the Catholic Marquis of Huntly, and among many of the clans in the Highlands and Islands. Meanwhile, he would muster a full English army at Berwick-upon-Tweed, whose defences were being strengthened, and smash his way through the Lowlands to Edinburgh.

But that is not how it turned out.

The 'Bishops' Wars' (1639–40)

The 'Bishops' Wars' is the name which was applied to the first military activities in the revolution against King Charles I. It is an illusory nickname, because most of the fighting took place between feuding Scottish families; but it demonstrates how people of the time interpreted the conflict. A better title would be the 'Wars of the Covenant' – and they would last for more than ten years.

Charles himself had no experience of war, and quickly ran into

---

1 Gustav II Adolf (formerly known as Gustavus Adolphus) was the outstanding champion of Protestantism in the Thirty Years' War (1618–48); he was King of Sweden from 1611 to 1632. He made considerable use of Scots mercenaries in his army, putting great value on their bravery and toughness. The oldest of the British Army's line infantry regiments, the Royal Scots (1st Regiment of Foot), was raised in France in 1633 by Sir John Hepburn, who had spent many years fighting for Gustav II Adolf.

difficulties when he tried to put his strategy into effect. For ten years he had ruled England successfully without a parliament, but parliament was the only body which could raise the money for war. Now he found that there was no enthusiasm in England to fight the Scots: his English subjects did not see this as a patriotic call to arms – indeed, many of them sympathised with the Scots and their grievances against the king. Charles managed to rally an army at York from the militia of the northern counties of England, some twenty thousand men, but their quality was poor and their equipment even worse. He sent the Marquis of Hamilton to the north-east to stiffen the Royalist support there; and he ordered the Earl of Antrim in Northern Ireland to raise an army of five thousand Gaelic warrior kinsmen and clansmen to attack the Campbell strongholds in Argyll, while Thomas Wentworth, first Earl of Strafford, the iron-fisted Lord Deputy of Ireland, raised an army of ten thousand in Dublin to invade Scotland *via* the stronghold of Dumbarton Castle.

As a war, the First 'Bishops' War' in 1639 lasted for only five weeks. The only fighting was in the north-east of Scotland, where the Marquis of Huntly crossed swords with the Earl of Montrose. The naval expedition under the Marquis of Hamilton failed to make a landing and returned home. Aberdeen was taken and retaken by the Covenanters; Huntly was captured by the Covenanters and carried off to Edinburgh; and when Huntly's second son, James, Viscount Aboyne, attempted a counter-attack, his men were scattered by Montrose and his Covenanters at the Brig o' Dee on 19 June 1639. Meanwhile, King Charles's Grand Strategy was unravelling. The two-pronged invasion from Ireland failed to materialise. The king himself led his army from York to Berwick-upon-Tweed and took up position at the Birks on the south bank of the Tweed, some five kilometres west of Berwick. Meanwhile, on 5 June, the main army of the Scots, under Alexander Leslie, twenty thousand strong, made camp at Duns Law, on the north side of the Tweed, eighteen kilometres from Berwick. The king realised that he was in no position to offer battle, and saw no option but to negotiate a truce on 18 June – the 'Pacification of Berwick'.

In the autumn the Scots held another General Assembly, and a 'free parliament'. Both meetings confirmed the decisions of the Glasgow General Assembly. The king reluctantly convened his own parliament in April 1640 in order to raise money, but he failed to gain its support and dissolved it three weeks later – the 'Short Parliament', as it was called.

Another outbreak of hostilities was now inevitable; but the Second

'Bishops' War' was even shorter than the first – it lasted only ten days. In England, the Earl of Strafford (who was also President of the Council of the North) was put in charge of raising another army – the so-called 'New Army', consisting of eight thousand foot and a thousand horse. In Scotland, the Covenanters seized the initiative, besieging and capturing Edinburgh and Dumbarton castles, and the Earl of Argyll took dom-estic advantage of the situation by wading into the pro-Royalist clans in the west. On 20 August 1640, with Montrose in the lead, Leslie crossed the Tweed at Coldstream with his main army and drove the English army back towards the River Tyne; after a sharp action at the ford at Newburn on 28 August the Scots entered the undefended city of Newcastle upon Tyne. The war was virtually over. Caerlaverock Castle, which had been held by the Royalist Earl of Nithsdale against a destructive thirteen-week siege by a Covenanting army, was ordered by the king to surrender on 26 September.[1] On 26 October a truce was signed at Ripon: the king agreed to pay the Scots £850 a day for the costs of quartering their army in the north of England!

The Scots had called King Charles's bluff, and had won. In the autumn of 1641 Charles made a visit to Edinburgh (14 August–17 November). He addressed parliament in an emotional speech, claiming that he had come to 'settle their religion and liberty'. No one believed him. Instead, he had to acknowledge the 'free parliament' which had met the previous year, and to ratify the radical constitutional changes it had promulgated, based on the National Covenant: parliament would have the right to vet nominations to the Privy Council and the judiciary, and parliament was to meet every three years at least, with or without the king's permission. He scattered honours and peerages freely (Alexander Leslie was created Earl of Leven, and Argyll was made a marquis), but by the time he left Edinburgh he had gained neither popularity nor trust.

The façade of royal strength had crumbled; worse, the three-headed British state (England, Ireland and Scotland) had been destabilised. The Scottish revolt of 1639–40 was the precursor to an outbreak of Catholic rebellion in the north of Ireland in October 1641, which was

---

1   After the siege the castle was partially dismantled by the Covenanters and subsided into a romantically picturesque ivy-grown ruin, a Mecca for painters and writers (like Robert Burns in 1776, who left his mark on the south wall of the hall in the gatehouse). Caerlaverock Castle, with its dramatic triangle-shape within its moated water, had stood sentinel over the Solway Firth for centuries. Today it is in the care of Historic Scotland; the ivy has all gone, but the structure has been consolidated to permit safe public access to the ruins.

only quelled with the help of a large Scottish army sent to defend Protestantism and the Protestant settlers in Ulster. More crucially for the king's fate, however, it led to the outbreak of civil war in England in 1642.

The First Civil War in England (1642–46)

King Charles was in desperate straits – so desperate that he had no other recourse than to recall his English parliament in order to raise finances to pay off the Scots, as had been agreed under the Treaty of Ripon. This parliament, which assembled at Westminster on 3 November 1640, was to last for thirteen years and earned the nickname of the 'Long Parliament' (1640–53). Led by two radical Puritan politicians, John Pym and John Hampden, it quickly flexed its muscles by impeaching Strafford (who was executed in May 1641) and Archbishop Laud (who would go to the block in 1645). But it was not enough simply to remove the king's chief 'evil' advisers: wrongs must be righted by due legislative process, civil liberties were to be guaranteed, and the Church of England must be stripped of any traces of Popery. Most importantly, it was decreed that parliament could not be prorogued or dissolved without its own consent. Charles seethed with rage, but had to agree. His autocratic attitude to government, however, did not change.

Nor did the tension between the king and his English parliament lessen. In November 1641, parliament narrowly passed a Grand Remonstrance on the respective positions of parliament and king. It was too much for King Charles. He decided to prosecute five of his principal opponents for high treason – including, of course, Pym and Hampden; but he hesitated too long, and when he descended on the House of Commons on 4 January 1642 with a force of four hundred swordsmen (the original 'Cavaliers'), he found that 'the birds had flown'.

In panic, Charles fled London for Hampton Court. His administration was in ruins. He had no civil service, no judiciary, no army and no money. Parliament wanted him to surrender his sovereignty over Church and state, but he obstinately refused. Curiously enough, the king now started to gain support: the growing and strident radicalism of his parliamentary opponents (including the 'Levellers', who were pressing for universal adult male suffrage) was alarming many people of substance. A 'Cavalier' movement developed, to counter the 'Roundhead' movement (so called after the pudding-basin haircuts of the London apprentices in the mobs orchestrated by Pym and his followers).

On 22 August 1642 King Charles raised the royal standard at Nottingham as a symbol of armed opposition to the powers claimed by the English parliament. It is the great paradox of the Civil War in England that the king had not been deposed. He was not fighting a rebellion. It was Charles who was rebelling against the *de facto* government of the country.

Hindsight suggests that the king was doomed from the start – outgunned, out-generalled and outnumbered. But that is not how it seemed at the time. The names of the battles which ensued after the raising of the standard at Nottingham are by no means a litany of Royalist reverses. The first engagement at Edgehill in Oxfordshire in late October 1642 was inconclusive, although the king was able to claim victory. He decided not to try to storm London after he had come as close as Brentford in mid-November, but thereafter the Royalist forces scored victory after victory, securing the West Country, Wales and the north of England for the king. The parliamentarians, clinging on in the south-west, were in trouble: the war was becoming increasingly unpopular, and people were agitating for peace.

The turn of the tide began with the Battle of Newbury, in Berkshire, in September 1643, when the Royalists failed to defeat the pikemen of London in a long and bloody engagement. Within weeks the parliamentarians were reinforced by a Scottish Covenanting army of twenty-one thousand men invading from the north (see below); and on 2 July 1644 the parliamentary army, reinforced by the Scots, inflicted a crushing defeat on the Royalists at Marston Moor in the cruellest battle of the Civil War.

One man saw clearly that the parliamentary army needed reorganising if it was ever to bring the war to a decisive conclusion. That man was Lieutenant-General Oliver Cromwell, Member of Parliament and the greatest military strategist of his day. In November 1644 he told parliament bluntly that it could not win the war with the army in its present undisciplined form. Parliament agreed, and the 'New Model Army' was born. Sir Thomas Fairfax was appointed general, and Cromwell was made general of horse. On 14 June 1645 the New Model Army met the full Royalist army at Naseby, in Northamptonshire, and won a sweeping victory.

Naseby was the climax but not the end of the hostilities. Many months of marching and skirmishing and besieging lay ahead, with enough minor Royalist successes to keep hope still flickering; but

Naseby presaged the end of effective resistance to the parliamentarians, the end of the First Civil War. King Charles clung on for the winter in Oxford, watching his cause collapse around him. Most of his family had escaped to safety. His heir, Charles, Prince of Wales, had slipped the parliamentary net to reach the Scilly Isles. His queen, Henrietta Maria, was ensconced in the palace of Saint-Germain-en-Laye, near Paris, whence she would bombard her husband with ardent letters of well-meaning advice.[1] On 27 April 1646, disguised as a servant and with only two companions, the king slipped out of Oxford and galloped across country towards Newark-on-Trent, where the Covenanting army was besieging the town. On 5 May he went to the Scottish headquarters in the old Saracen's Head hostelry in nearby Southwell, and surrendered his person to the Scots. It was the end of the First Civil War, and the end of the king's liberty.

The Solemn League and Covenant (1643)

When the Civil War broke out in England, the Scots were in a position of great strength. For one thing they now had, in effect, a professional standing army. The Scots had ended their occupation of Northumberland in August 1641, and were paid £300,000 by the English parliament to cover their costs. The Scottish army was scaled down, but not disbanded; and the rebellion in Ireland, when the English parliament sponsored the intervention of ten thousand Covenanters, financed the continuation of the professional core of the Scottish army. It was this national army, well trained and well organised, which would set the example for Cromwell's New Model Army.

But the Covenanters had fallen out with one another. The Marquis of Argyll, who had become more and more radical in his views, wanted to drive home the advantage and depose the king; he argued that it was the overriding duty of the nobility of Scotland to protect the nation's people by investing its parliament with all the authority of the state. The Earl of Montrose was much more moderate; he was alarmed at the political extremism of Argyll's godly and fiercely nationalistic faction – he wanted only to restrain the office of monarchy, not the person of the king. In August 1640 a score of nobles, led by Montrose, had met in Cumbernauld House in Dunbartonshire, where they signed the 'Cumbernauld Bond' to support the king. The Covenanting party was riven in two. Montrose was imprisoned in Edinburgh

---

1 Henrietta Maria was never to see King Charles again.

Castle during Charles's visit in 1641, charged with having had covert dealings with the king; he was released only after Charles had left, by which time he had become marginalised. From then on, the ultra-Presbyterian Covenanting party under Argyll was to hold the reins of government in Scotland for eleven years, and create what amounted to a theocracy, a 'godly state' governed in God's name by a Committee of the Estates (see Chapter 23).

At the end of 1642, when the Civil War in England was at a stalemate following the Battles of Edgehill and Brentford, both sides (parliament and king) sought the assistance of Scotland and its powerful standing army. The appeals divided opinion in Scotland. At first the Privy Council voted by a narrow majority that only the appeal from Charles should be considered, on the grounds that the Scots should do nothing to prejudice the king's honour or the peace of Scotland. The Covenanters in the General Assembly of the Kirk would have none of that. In June 1643 they summoned a Convention to discuss giving military aid to the hard-pressed parliamentarians in England. Commissioners from England arrived in Edinburgh early in August to make a personal plea for help, and a meeting of the General Assembly endorsed this plea.

The Scots realised that they were now in the driving seat: they had a golden opportunity of exporting Presbyterianism and bringing English worship and ecclesiastical order into harmony with those of Scotland. On 17 August 1643 they presented the English commissioners with the draft of a 'Solemn League and Covenant' which was as much a religious treaty as a military and civil pact. In exchange for Scottish intervention in the Civil War – the Scots would attack the strong Royalist positions from the north – the English parliament would guarantee the preservation of the religious settlement in Scotland, reform religion in England and Ireland 'according to the Word of God and the example of the best reformed churches', extirpate popery and prelacy, and confirm the 'firm peace and union' of Scotland and England. This was the ultimate Covenanting dream – a single Presbyterian Church on the Scottish model which would unify religious practices in the three kingdoms.

The English accepted the military part of the Solemn League on 25 September: it was agreed that eighteen thousand foot-soldiers and three thousand cavalrymen would serve the English parliament (at a cost of £30,000 a year). Accordingly, on 19 January 1644, a huge Scottish army crossed the border under its veteran commander-in-chief Alexander Leslie (now the Earl of Leven), with the cavalry under another veteran of the Swedish wars, his nephew Major-General David Leslie. The Scots failed to capture Newcastle, but Leslie's cavalry, in particular, was to play a crucial role in the parliamentary defeat of the powerful Royalist forces at Marston Moor in July 1644.

That was the easy bit; the religious aspect of the Solemn League was less clear-cut. The English commissioners knew that many of their countrymen were as much against presbytery as they were against episcopacy. An assembly at Westminster had been appointed by the English parliament to reform the English Church; now its membership was increased by eight Scots 'observers' while the problem of unifying Church government, doctrine and worship in the three kingdoms was discussed. The Scots, although they were only observers at the Westminster Assembly, were allowed to participate in all the discussions. They accepted an accord between their Churches (the Westminster Confession of Faith) and made a number of concessions over their own cherished usages, and the English parliament eventually agreed to sign a modified form of the Solemn League and Covenant.

John Simpson, former senior lecturer in Scottish History at Edinburgh University, says:

> The Covenanters had many arguments for signing the Solemn League and Covenant. People in the seventeenth century in general believed that the Apocalypse was not far away; they thought that the events of the Reformation had been, in themselves, so remarkable that they could surely only be the prelude to something even more remarkable: the second coming of Christ and the end of the world. The Kirk had a missionary role here, to try to ensure that Christ's Word was established before His return.
>
> To that end it was essential to keep the king under control to prevent him from jeopardising all the gains which the Reformation had made so far. That was why it was necessary to enter the Civil War on the side of the English parliament.

The English parliament had pledged itself to accept the principle of Church unification; but there were many in Scotland who doubted the parliament's good faith. One of them was the Earl of Montrose. He suspected (rightly, as it turned out) that the English were cynically using the Scots' Presbyterian crusade for their own political ends – the prime concern of the English parliamentarians was to ensure, at all costs, that the Scots were on their side in the Civil War.

Montrose, the moderate Covenanter, was by birth and instinct a

Royalist. He still owned his Covenant, but he could not bring himself to disown his king. In February 1644, a month after the Scottish army had crossed the border into England, King Charles made Montrose a marquis and appointed him lieutenant-general of the Royalist forces in Scotland. The Civil War had reached Scotland.

'The Great Marquis'

He either fears his Fate too much,
Or his Deserts are small,
That puts it not unto the Touch,
To gain or lose it all.
JAMES GRAHAM, MARQUIS OF MONTROSE,
'MY DEAR AND ONLY LOVE' (1642)

In the Chepman Aisle of St Giles' Cathedral, beside the organ, a white marble effigy of James Graham, first Marquis of Montrose, lies on an ornate tomb. Montrose was executed on 21 May 1650 and his dismembered body was distributed for display; eleven years later his remains were exhumed from a felon's grave and interred with great ceremony in St Giles'. The elaborate memorial was erected in 1887 – the final act of his rehabilitation. A framed copy of the National Covenant stands vigil over his remains

In March 1644 Montrose had started his campaign in Scotland by capturing Dumfries with a small force of only two thousand men; but he failed to make further progress. A royalist uprising in the north-east led by the Marquis of Huntly was put down by a Covenanting force under the Marquis of Argyll. It seemed that the Royalist threat in Scotland had fizzled out.

A new impetus for the Royalists arrived that summer in the giant and fearsome form of an Irish adventurer named Alasdair McColla MacDonald, already a heroic legend at the age of twenty-one. A close kinsman of the Earl of Antrim, he was the son of MacDonald of Colonsay, and was known as Kolkitto (from *Coll Ciotach*, 'left-handed'); he had scores to settle with the hated Clan Campbell. In August 1644 he landed on the Ardnamurchan peninsula with an expeditionary force of two thousand battle-hardened, well-armed troops from Ireland, and was quickly joined by a thousand Highlanders. Off they went, rampaging through the Campbell territories of Argyll, burning and looting wherever they went. The Marquis of Montrose had meanwhile slipped into Perth with a couple of companions, disguised as Covenanter troopers; late in August, Montrose and Mac-Donald met up at Blair Atholl. It was the start of an *annus mirabilis*, one of the most remarkable military campaigns in British history.

The Year of Miracles (1644–45)

...a man of high genius, glowing with the ambition which prompts great actions, and conscious of courage and talents which enabled him to aspire to much by small and inadequate means. He was a poet and scholar, deeply skilled in the art of war, and possessed of a strength of constitution and activity of mind, by which he could sustain every hardship, and find a remedy in every reverse of fortune.

TALES OF A GRANDFATHER, CHAPTER XLI

The Royalists now had a formidable army in the field, with two inspired commanders of tremendous dash and tactical skill. On 1 September they fell upon a much larger Covenanting force under David Wemyss, Lord Elcho, at the village of Tippermuir, five kilometres west of Perth. Lord Elcho had seven thousand men, with cannons and seven hundred cavalry, shepherded by coveys of attendant ministers. MacDonald's Irishmen had developed a devastating new battle-tactic – the 'Highland charge': the infantry, armed with muskets, advanced to within a hundred metres of the enemy, fired a single volley, then dropped their muskets and charged with their broadswords. Elcho's raw levies broke under the savagery of the onslaught and hundreds were killed. Montrose now made a triumphant entry into Perth, which was systematically plundered for two days. Next he headed for Aberdeen, where another numerically superior Covenanter army was overcome. Aberdeen lay defenceless, and the Irish and Highland troops now indulged in a three-day orgy of looting, raping and killing. It was a 'Black Friday' for the innocents of Aberdeen who were slaughtered – but also for Montrose, whose reputation for chivalry and gallantry was irredeemably besmirched.

Alasdair MacDonald soon departed to drum up more support from his MacDonald clansmen in the west, leaving Montrose with a much-depleted force of 1,500. And now danger was at hand: the Marquis of Argyll was on the warpath, thirsting for revenge. Montrose quietly withdrew from Aberdeen. For eight weeks he outmarched the pursuing Campbells; he was brought to bay at Fyvie Castle, but fought off the attackers in a sporadic two-day engagement. Eventually Argyll called off the chase and in the middle of November he headed for home – Inveraray Castle.

The Royalists, although unbeaten, were apparently down if not out. But they were not to be underestimated. Montrose led his tired and hungry survivors to Blair Atholl, where he was joined by Alasdair MacDonald with fresh reinforcements of five thousand clansmen, mainly MacDonalds but also MacLeans from Morven and Mull, Stewarts from Appin and Farquharsons from Braemar.

Despite the onset of winter, the two commanders resolved to launch a surprise attack on the Campbell heartlands of their inveterate enemy the Marquis of Argyll, who was in Edinburgh at the time. In early December, guides led them through the high mountain passes into Campbell country. When Argyll learned of the impending invasion he gleefully hastened from Edinburgh, convinced that he would soon be picking off his enemies as they starved or froze in the mountains. He was in Inveraray when his scouts arrived with the incredible news that Montrose and his men were advancing down Glen Shira, near the head of Loch Fyne and only a few kilometres from Inveraray. Argyll prudently slipped away to safety down Loch Fyne in his galley, leaving Inveraray and his clansmen to their fate. For several weeks the Mac-Donalds plundered and burned Campbell properties, slaughtering nine hundred Campbells of arms-bearing age.

When the orgy of killing and looting was over, Montrose and his troops withdrew northwards up the west coast. It was a hazardous march, through narrow glens where a hundred men could have stopped them indefinitely: north up Glen Aray to Loch Awe and through the Pass of Brander to the narrows of Loch Etive, where the Prior of Ardchattan bought immunity for his lands by providing Montrose with ferry-boats to cross the loch. From there they marched through Benderloch, past the head of Loch Creran and over into Appin, following the hill-tracks down Glen Fiddich to Ballachulish. After crossing Loch Leven there, they could feel relatively safe in Loch-aber as they marched along Loch Linnhe to the medieval fortress of Inverlochy by Fort William, where they rested and regrouped. Some of Montrose's Highlanders slipped off to their homes, replete with Campbell booty, but other clan leaders sent men to reinforce him.

From Inverlochy, Montrose set off up the Great Glen, apparently heading for Inverness. When he reached Kilcumin (now Fort Augustus) at the foot of Loch Ness, he learned that George Mackenzie, second Earl of Seaforth, was advancing down Loch Ness at the head of a government force. He also heard that the Marquis of Argyll, who had recovered his nerve and assembled a sizeable army, was hot on his heels and had reached Inverlochy. Montrose was now in danger of being caught in a pincer movement.

Montrose, the master of surprise tactics, once again did something completely unexpected: he decided to attack. On the evening of Friday, 31 January 1645 he set off on a forced march which took his men south-west at Culachy, across the mountains in knee-deep snow, fording waist-high streams and rivers, and down through steep-sided Glen Roy to the lower slopes of Ben Nevis at Roy Bridge, where the Roy meets the Spean. It was an epic feat of unbelievable mobility, daring and stamina – fifty kilometres in thirty-six freezing hours in the depths of winter. On the morning of Sunday, 2 February Montrose's force materialised out of the mist at Inverlochy and fell upon the astonished Campbells.

Once again the Royalists were outnumbered; but again they won the day. The Lowland levies disintegrated at the first Highland charge. The Campbells fought desperately but could not match the ferocity of the MacDonalds. Some 1,500 Covenanters – mostly Campbells – died, including their commander, Sir Duncan Campbell of Auchinbreck; the Royalists lost only four, but two hundred were wounded. The Marquis of Argyll, seeing the debacle developing, fled in his galley again. The Earl of Seaforth withdrew to the safety of Inverness. Montrose was now able to range the north and north-east at will. Aberdeen was occupied again. Brechin was put to the torch. Dundee was sacked.

The Covenanters realised that they were in real danger of losing the Civil War in Scotland. Regiments were detached from the Covenanter army in England to strengthen the military opposition to Montrose and his army of wild, wily and apparently invincible guerrillas. A new Covenanter army headed north, resolved to wipe Montrose off the face of Scotland. It was to lead to the bloodiest encounter of the war – the Battle of Auldearn.

Auldearn is a village three kilometres east of Nairn. On the evening of 8 May 1645 Montrose camped there with a force of 1,700 men, planning to push on next day towards Covenanter-held Inverness, some thirty kilometres to the west. A Covenanter army, four thousand strong, had mustered outside Inverness. Its commander, Lieutenant-Colonel Sir John Hurry, took a leaf out of Montrose's own book of tactics: that night he force-marched his troops through the hours of darkness in torrential rain in order to fall upon Montrose's forces at Auldearn in a surprise dawn attack.

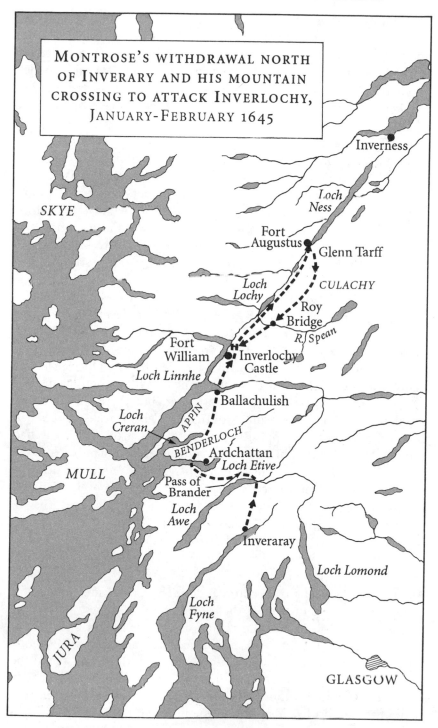

MONTROSE'S WITHDRAWAL NORTH
OF INVERARY AND HIS MOUNTAIN
CROSSING TO ATTACK INVERLOCHY,
JANUARY–FEBRUARY 1645

Montrose was very nearly taken unawares (unlike most good guerrilla leaders he was surprisingly neglectful of gathering intelligence about the enemy). The Royalists were saved by the noise of musket-fire from the Covenanter troops who were trying to clear the sodden powder from their weapons before the attack. Montrose and Alasdair MacDonald hastily deployed their forces into defensive positions. The Irish took the brunt of the first onslaught and fell back, but in good order. They had run out of ammunition, but quickly re-formed to make a heroic counter-attack with broadswords only against superior numbers. It gave Montrose enough time to mount an assault with his own division. Cavalry clashed with cavalry, foot-soldiers with foot-soldiers, and in the end the Royalists, fighting with a fury which had seldom been seen before, carried the day. Some two thousand Covenanter troops – half the Covenanter army – were killed on the field or in the rout which ensued, at a cost of two hundred Royalist casualties.

A few weeks later, after further sparring, the armies clashed again, on 2 July 1646, near the village of Alford, in Aberdeenshire. For once the opposing forces were almost equal in strength – around two thousand men on each side. Montrose was able to lure the Covenanters out of a strong defensive position by feigning retreat. Once again the Royalists won the day, but this time at heavy cost to both armies.

The 'Year of Miracles' was almost over; but there was one last, resounding victory to be won. Montrose and his Royalist forces had eliminated any serious opposition north of the Firth of Tay. He had thrashed every army sent to oppose him in the Highlands. Now the central Lowlands lay open to him. With a greatly reinforced army of five thousand he confronted a Covenanter army of seven thousand troops on 'the field of the desperate battle' at the village of Kilsyth, halfway between Stirling and Glasgow, on 15 August 1645. Accounts of the battle are confused, but Montrose seems to have been able to absorb the initial thrusts by the Covenanters; he then launched his inevitable counter-attack with a combined assault by his cavalry and Alasdair MacDonald's Irish commandos. The Covenanter forces collapsed, and three thousand of them died.

The Marquis of Montrose now appeared to be master of Scotland. The rich cities of the Lowlands submitted to him. Glasgow welcomed him, apprehensively, as a conquering hero, and Montrose spared the city the pillaging which Alasdair MacDonald's men had eagerly expected. Edinburgh submitted, and surrendered its castle. Montrose set up the Royalist headquarters in the burgh of Bothwell, in Lanarkshire, and organised the release of all his Royalist supporters who were languishing in Covenanter dungeons. In a letter to Montrose, the scholar and poet William Drummond of Hawthornden (1585–1649), no friend to the Covenanters, exulted: 'The Golden Age is returned; His Majesty's crown is re-established, the many-headed monster near quelled.'

But Montrose's hold on Scotland, and on power, was precarious in the extreme: it was based solely on military success – it had no political muscle behind it. Notwithstanding his professed adherence to the principles of the National Covenant, the people of Scotland distrusted and feared Montrose for having used Catholic Irish troops to slaughter his own countrymen. The Covenanter regime had not been toppled. Alasdair MacDonald, having slaked his thirst for Campbell blood, marched off with his Irish troops to terrorise the west again, and then returned to Ireland, where he would be killed in a skirmish in 1647.

Despite the stunning success at Kilsyth, the tide was turning against the Royalists. The devastating Battle of Naseby had been fought, and lost, two months before Kilsyth, on 14 June 1645. The pressure was off the Covenanting army in England, and Major-General Leslie was able to detach his veteran cavalry regiments and bring them back to Scotland to deal with the 'invincible' Montrose. He reached Berwick-upon-Tweed on 6 September.

Montrose was now in the Borders, marching in triumph towards England to join up with the Royalist forces there; but his hopes of over-whelming support from the Border potentates had been disappointed. On 13 September 1645, Leslie came across Montrose encamped (carelessly, as usual) near Selkirk on the banks of the Ettrick Water at Philiphaugh and launched an immediate dawn attack through the morning mist. There was no time for Montrose to deploy his troops effectively. Bravely as they fought, the disordered Royalist infantry stood little chance against the crashing charges of Leslie's disciplined, experienced cavalry – especially after their own outnumbered cavalry detachments had been swept from the field. A second, flanking assault across the Ettrick by Leslie's foot-soldiers caught the survivors in a deadly cross-fire. Montrose himself had to be dragged from the ensuing bloodbath by his surviving officers, and escaped on horseback. Hundreds of his men died on the field. The camp-followers – cooks, boys, women and children – were butchered. The fifty Irish soldiers who were taken prisoner were lined up in batches against a wall and shot, at the insistence of the inevitable cohorts of ministers who had accompanied the Covenanter army: the Lord's work had to be seen to be done.

Montrose was now a spent force in Scotland. Many of his officers and closest associates were hanged for treason by the vengeful Covenanters. For a year he laboured to regroup and consolidate, but the cause was lost. When King Charles surrendered to the Scots Covenanter army at Newark on 5 May 1646 he refused to repudiate Montrose, for the marquis was the only potential, slender hope remaining to him. Under further pressure the king was persuaded that Montrose represented a danger to any possible peace, and agreed to order him to disband on condition that he was given leave to go into exile. On 2 June Montrose received a letter from the king:

> You must disband your forces and go into France, where you shall receive my further instructions. This at first may justly startle you, but I do assure you that if, for the present, I should offer to do more for you, I could not do so much . . .

Montrose now had nothing left for which to fight: on 3 September 1646 he left Scotland, disguised as a servant, and set sail for Norway and exile on the Continent.

Defeat and death

Montrose spent four years in Europe, where he was fêted as a hero of the Royalist resistance. In 1649 he learned of the execution of King Charles. He retired to his chamber for two days, overcome with grief. When he emerged, he had written a scrap of poetry which ended:

> I'll tune Thy Elegies to Trumpet sounds,
> And write Thy Epitaph in Blood and Wounds!

Montrose must have suspected that Charles's execution would mean his own death, too.

Armed with a personal royal commission to invade Scotland on behalf of Charles I's son, who had been proclaimed King Charles II in Scotland immediately after his father's execution, Montrose managed to assemble a force of five hundred Danish and German mercenaries, and in March 1650 he sailed from Sweden to Orkney. He supplemented his forces with a thousand enthusiastic but totally untrained Orcadians, and in April he ferried his little army across the Pentland Firth in a flotilla of fishing boats. If he expected an unreserved welcome in Caithness, he was disappointed: sympathy for the Royalist cause had ebbed in the north. Undaunted, he marched southwards, pausing to seize and garrison a few keeps on the way.

The Covenanter government was not going to give him time to muster support in the Highlands. As soon as news came of his landing, the government charged an experienced and ruthless Covenanter soldier, Colonel Archibald Strachan, based in Inverness, to harass Montrose's advance through Sutherland while a larger infantry force moved up from Brechin. Strachan was an impatient man, however; he had no intention of waiting for reinforcements.

Montrose had called a halt on 25 April at Carbisdale, above the tiny village of Culrain, to await reinforcements from the Royalist clans. None came. Two days later Colonel Strachan caught up with him at Carbisdale. The site is well marked today. About a kilometre south-west of Carbisdale Castle (now a Youth Hostel), a path leads to a wooden platform in a thicket of Scots pine and birchwood overlooking the Kyle of Sutherland, towards Bonar Bridge. A viewing panel gives a graphic description of the battle.

Montrose was well dug in behind trenches, and unassailable from any frontal assault; moreover, he had a force of 1,200, whereas Strachan had only three hundred. Strachan quickly sized up the position, and tried the oldest trick in the military manual: he sent a small group of men forward uphill, hoping to lure Montrose out into the open – and, astonishingly, it worked. Montrose abandoned his strong defensive position and pursued the troopers downhill, straight into a devastating ambush. It was all over in a matter of minutes. Montrose's Orcadian levies, who had never been in action before, instantly broke and fled. The Danish and German contingent stood their ground, but were overwhelmed. The Royalists lost four hundred dead and 450 captured; Strachan lost only one man. Montrose and his bodyguard fought with reckless courage. His horse was shot from under him, but he managed to escape with a few survivors, wounded and exhausted.

He hauled himself through Culrain, reputedly dumping his armour in a small lochan (now partly filled in). From there he swam the Kyle of Sutherland to Invershin, before moving north into Strath Oykel. In the wilderness there he and his companions became separated. Montrose struggled on alone, on foot and in pain. He had a price of £25,000 on his head.

For two days and three nights, disguised as a shepherd, Montrose eluded capture, until he reached the northern shore of Loch Assynt. On a slender spur of rock was a keep called Ardveck, now in ruins. It was owned by a man named Neil Macleod of Assynt, who was away from home at Dunbeath. His wife, Christian, gave the starving fugitive a welcome and ushered him down into a basement room for food and rest. The basement was, in fact, a dungeon. Meanwhile she sent word to her husband, and runners to Tain to summon troops to take this valuable visitor into custody.

It was the ultimate betrayal of Highland hospitality. The captive marquis was taken south to Edinburgh, past many of the scenes of his former triumphs – what Ted Cowan has called 'a kind of eerie pilgrimage through his own career',[1] his feet bound under the belly of a little Shetland pony. When he arrived in Edinburgh on Saturday, 18 May his arms were tied behind his back and he was borne on a tumbrel up the Royal Mile to the Tolbooth. The crowds which lined the street, usually so ready to mock the condemned, were silent and tense. The tumbrel passed Moray House, where Lord Lorne, the son of the Marquis of Argyll, was celebrating his wedding to the daughter of the Countess of Moray; the wedding party came out on to the balcony to jeer at Montrose, and it is said that Argyll watched from behind a half-closed curtain and that their eyes – briefly – met. The following day, Montrose was interrogated by a panel of Covenanting ministers. A public letter from Charles II, ordering him to disband his troops, was read, as well as another one in which Charles exculpated himself from Montrose's actions on his behalf. The king had abandoned the marquis to his fate.

Montrose had already been attainted for treason *in absentia* in 1644, so there was no need for a trial. On Monday, 21 May 1650 he was taken to Parliament House where formal sentence was passed: he was to be hanged like a common criminal for three hours in public, then his body was to be beheaded and quartered. His head was to be impaled on the Tolbooth in Edinburgh, and his legs and arms were to be displayed at the town gates of Aberdeen, Glasgow, Perth and Stirling.

On the morning of his execution (Tuesday, 22 May) the Marquis of Montrose carefully combed and curled his long, Cavalier-style hair and dressed himself in a black suit, a scarlet cloak embroidered with silver, white gloves, carnation silk stockings, garters and ribboned shoes – 'like a bridegroom', it was said. It was only a short distance to the towering scaffold which had been erected in the Grassmarket. Montrose walked there. His arms were pinioned, but he mounted the scaffold 'in a very stately manner', theatrical to the last.

On the eve of his execution he had written his last poem:

---

1 *Montrose: For Covenant and King*, p.291.

Let them bestow on ev'ry airt [direction] a limb;
Open all my veins, that I may swim
To Thee my Saviour, in that crimson lake;
Then place my pur-boiled head upon a stake;
Scatter my ashes, throw them in the air:
Lord, since Thou know'st where all these atoms are,
I'm hopeful, once Thou'lt recollect my dust,
And confident Thou'lt raise me with the just.

Montrose's truncated body was buried in a box on the Burgh Muir. Two days later the box was disinterred and his heart removed, to be embalmed in a golden casket. Eleven years later, in 1661, after the Restoration, Charles II would try to assuage his feelings of guilt for 'betraying' Montrose by ordering for him the most splendid state funeral which Scotland had ever seen. His bones were disinterred, and his body lay in state at Holyrood before it was carried by fourteen Scottish lords in a magnificent procession up the Royal Mile to St Giles' Cathedral. 'The Great Marquis', the flawed genius of the battlefield and the man who had sacrificed his life (but not his honour) for a more deeply flawed king, deserved no less.

Charles I: the last years

This tablet marks the spot where
Charles Stuart King of England
stood before the Court which sat
pursuant to the ordinance for erecting
a high court of justice for his trial
which was read the first, second &
third time & passed by Parliament
on the 4th January 1648–9

The Court met on Saturday the 20th,
Monday the 22nd, Tuesday the 23rd,
& on Saturday the 27th January 1648–9,
when the sentence of Death
was pronounced upon the King.

On the lower flight of stone steps at the south end of Westminster Hall, just below the plaque for William Wallace, a brass tablet commemorates another momentous occasion: the trial of King Charles I in January 1649, charged as 'a tyrant, traitor and murderer, and a public and implacable enemy to the Commonwealth of England'. The great hall was crammed with people, separated from the court area by a stout wooden barrier lined with armed soldiers. The presiding judge, John Bradshaw, wore an armoured hat, just in case. Charles repeatedly challenged the authority of the court – any court, indeed – to try a king. But however eloquently and movingly he spoke, however profoundly his dignity and demeanour impressed the crowd, the result was a foregone conclusion; after a trial lasting two and a half weeks, sentence of death was pronounced on 27 January 1649.

The execution of the king had for long been inevitable. When Charles I delivered himself to the Covenanting army besieging Newark-on-Trent on 5 May 1646 he was not giving up the struggle; on the contrary, he was trying to prolong it by other means – by playing off the Scots against the English parliamentarians. The religious settlement which would have brought England and Ireland into Presbyterian conformity with Scotland, enshrined in the Solemn League and Covenant, was already unravelling: the English parliamentarians were showing no signs of fulfilling their part of the bargain. It was this growing Scottish bitterness and disillusionment which King Charles was hoping to exploit.

The Scots had been exultant: they reckoned that, in the king's person, they now held the trump card in British politics. They called off their siege of Newark and withdrew with their royal hostage to Newcastle upon Tyne. The king, however, refused to make any concessions: he still would not accept the National Covenant or the Solemn League and Covenant. The English parliamentarians, furious at what they saw as underhand dealings with the king, threatened military action against the Covenanters if they did not leave English soil.

What were the Scots Covenanters to do? If they took the king back to Scotland, his very presence could breathe fresh life into the Royalist movement which Montrose, although defeated, was still striving to uphold. The Scots' solution was to transfer Charles to the parliamentarians and to leave England – at a price. The price was payment of £200,000 towards the massive costs of the Scottish contribution to the Civil War in England. On 30 January 1647 the Scots army marched out of Newcastle, leaving the king in English custody. It was a deal which would indelibly taint the reputation of the Scottish Covenanters: they had sold the representative of Scotland's royal Stewart dynasty to his English enemies.

In June 1647 the king, who had been ensconced by the English parliament in comfortable quarters in Holdenby House in Northamptonshire, was abducted at dawn by a detachment of soldiers and taken south. The New Model Army under Cromwell was growing steadily stronger than parliament, which was causing much concern in Scotland about the king's ultimate fate. A split now developed in the Covenanting party: the moderates, who wanted to renew contacts with King Charles and were alarmed by the dictatorial and egalitarian aims of the Kirk, won control of the government in Scotland and opened negotiations with the king, who was now imprisoned in Carisbrooke Castle on the Isle of Wight. These negotiations led, in December 1647, to a secret agreement known as 'The Engagement'. This compact promised that the king would be returned to London 'in safety, honour and freedom', where he would establish Presbyterianism in England for a trial period of three years and allow the Scots full participation in the commercial privileges of English subjects. In exchange, the Scots would work in alliance with Royalist sympathisers in England and mount an invasion to rescue Charles from captivity and restore him to the throne.

It may have seemed a good idea at the time, but the result was a disaster. On 8 July 1648 the army of 'The Engagement', twenty thousand strong but ill-equipped and ill-trained, marched into England as part of a short-lived Second Civil War (1648–49). It started in Wales, where a rebellion was crushed by detachments of Cromwell's potent army. The Scots fared no better. As they straggled down through Lancashire, the hoped-for Royalist uprisings in the south of England were broken by Cromwell and his invincible Ironsides. Then Cromwell turned on the Scots, and in an engagement at Preston which spread over two days (17–18 August) the Scottish army was destroyed. At least two thousand men were killed, and more than eight thousand captured.

The Engagement party in Scotland was totally discredited by this reverse. A revolution ensued. A large group of radical Covenanters from all over the south-west of Scotland, two thousand strong, took up arms late in August 1648 and marched on Edinburgh. This was the curiously-named 'Whiggamore Raid' which preceded a *putsch* for what became known as the 'Kirk Party'.[1] While the battered remnants

---

1 There is some doubt about the derivation of the word. It seems to come from 'whig', to spur on, and 'more', for a mare, and is said to have been a derogatory slang term for the mounted drovers of Galloway who brought their cattle to the annual sales in central Scotland. 'Whiggamore' gave rise to 'Whig', which became a term of abuse for any adherent to the Presbyterian cause in seventeenth-century Scotland.

of the 'Engagement' army were straggling back to Scotland, the 'Whig-gamores' occupied the capital and seized power, with the Marquis of Argyll in charge once more. The leading 'Engagers' slipped away into exile. Here, perhaps, was the most radical revolution of the Reformation: extreme, populist and fuelled not just by religious fanaticism but by blazing social protest. Their short-lived regime (1648–50) would come down in Covenanting legend as the 'Rule of Saints' (see Chapter 23).

The 'Whiggamores' hoped to come to an understanding with Oliver Cromwell, who was now virtually the dictator of England and had crossed the border with his army after the Battle of Preston. When he was invited into Edinburgh for talks with the Kirk Party on 4 October he was hailed as a liberator, rather than as the man who had vanquished Scotland. Cromwell was doubtless just as devout as the Kirk men were, but in his own way: as a soldier and as a politician he saw himself as doing 'God's work', and he did it, single-mindedly, in God's name. It is difficult to pin a label on the kind of religion he practised, except that he favoured an 'independent' or congregational form of Church organisation. He was against High Anglicanism and Catholicism; but he wanted no truck with Presbyterianism either. Instead, he insisted that the Scots parliament should ban from holding any public office (national or local) all prominent 'Engagers' and outright Royalists.

Cromwell departed on 7 October, leaving three English regiments for the protection of the Kirk Party; parliament dutifully passed an 'Act of Classes' to put the purge of Royalists into effect. Burgh councils were purged, as was the army, over and over again, leaving just a rump of the 'godly'. It was a self-defeating ordinance which would deprive the nation of the services of some of its most experienced men when they were most needed.

However, it was the problem of the king's future which prevented the possibility of any accommodation between the two sides. Cromwell was resolved: the king must go. He had decided that Charles's abuse of royal power amounted to high treason; the king had become a menace to the stability of the state. Cromwell now conducted a purge of the English parliament, too: his army took control of London and Colonel Thomas Pride, one of his veteran officers, descended on the House of Commons early in December 1648 with a regiment of soldiers and expelled 140 of its less radical members; he also shut down the House of Lords. 'Pride's Purge', as it was called, left only sixty hard-core members sitting in the resulting 'Rump Parliament'; it was this parliament which voted to put King Charles on trial for his life.

The decision to try the king led to vigorous protests from the Scottish government. They might agree with Cromwell's analysis of the problem – that Charles was not to be trusted with his liberty – but they were horrified at its implications. There was little doubt about what the end result would be – the execution of the king; but the King of England was also King of Scotland: it would be impossible to cut off his head without cutting off the head of Scotland's king, too. The Scots had been happy to protest against Charles's abuse of the royal prerogative – but deliberate regicide was a different matter entirely. And what would happen to Scotland if England abolished the monarchy? Would the Scots proclaim the young Prince of Wales as Charles II? The English republicans were unlikely to tolerate a king in Scotland – especially the son of the man they had just executed.

In spite of furious Scottish protests the king was convicted and sentenced to death. In the early afternoon of 30 January 1649, King Charles I stepped out of one of the windows of the Banqueting House at the Palace of Whitehall on to the high, black-draped scaffold which had been erected in the yard outside. It was a bitterly cold day, and the king wore two shirts in case he shivered and gave the impression of being afraid. With a single stroke of his axe the masked executioner severed the neck of the king of both kingdoms. A 'terrible groan' came from the crowds who witnessed the dignified death of the first monarch in Christendom to be overthrown, tried and judicially executed by his own subjects:

> *This tragic spectacle was far from accomplishing the purpose intended by those who had designed it. On the contrary, the King's serene and religious behaviour at his trial and execution excited the sympathy and sorrow of many who had been his enemies when in power; the injustice and brutality which he bore with so much dignity, overpowered the remembrance of the errors of which he had been guilty; and the almost universal sense of the iniquity of his sentence, was a principal cause of the subsequent restoration of his family to the throne.*
>
> TALES OF A GRANDFATHER, CHAPTER XLV

A few weeks later, in March, the monarchy was formally abolished by the English parliament, and England became a republic. In Scotland, however, within a week of the execution, on 5 February 1649, the chancellor, the Earl of Loudoun, went to the Mercat Cross in Edinburgh and proclaimed the eighteen-year-old Prince of Wales the new sovereign as Charles II, King of Great Britain, France and Ireland. However, the Scots were resolved not to admit him to power until he gave assurances for the religion, unity and peace of the kingdoms.

Chapter 23

CHARLES II AND THE
COVENANTERS (1649–85)

*The ceremony of the coronation was performed with such solem-
nities as the time admitted, but mingled with circumstances which
must have been highly disgusting to Charles.*

TALES OF A GRANDFATHER, CHAPTER XLVI

On 24 June 1650, in the tiny village of Garmouth, on the estuary
of the River Spey in Morayshire, the proclaimed but still
uncrowned King Charles II set foot for the first time in his kingdom
of Scotland. A granite slab in the wall of a house named 'The Brae'
in Spey Street, Garmouth, commemorates his arrival (although the
date is incorrect):

> *Here*
> *King Charles II*
> *signed*
> *the Solemn League and Covenant*
> *June 23 1650*

Garmouth, an old Burgh of Barony, was once a busy fishing village,
before the course of the River Spey was altered to accommodate logs
being floated downriver all the way from Rothiemurchus, in the Cairn-
gorms. The royal landing is still part of the living traditions in the
village: the Spey was navigable right up to Garmouth then, and the

king was carried ashore from a rowing boat on the back of a local boatman named Milne, whose descendants were known as 'King Milnes' thereafter. He was then escorted by the Laird of Innes up the brae and along Spey Street to 'The Laird's Toft' (now 'The Brae'), where he enjoyed his first meal in Scotland. Local historians have long claimed that it was in this house that Charles II duly signed the Solemn League and Covenant.

King Charles had sailed from Amsterdam on the Dutch ship *Schiedam*. It had been a stormy twenty-three-day voyage, and in the Pentland Firth he had narrowly eluded an English fleet which had been sent north to intercept him: a morning fog shrouded his approach long enough for his ship to make land.

The nineteen-year-old king must have been delighted by his reception when he landed in Scotland. He was fêted all the way south to Falkland Palace in Fife by adoring crowds. The people of Scotland had not seen their king – any king – for nearly twenty years, since the coronation of Charles I in 1633. No doubt Charles II found the enthusiastic welcome a happy change from the constant hectoring, lecturing and sermonising he had endured from the Scottish Presbyterian commissioners with whom he had sailed from Amsterdam.

Charles had been proclaimed king by the Scottish parliament on 5 February 1649. All Scotland, including even the most anti-monarchist of the Covenanter ministers in Edinburgh, had been shocked at the news of the execution of his father, Charles I, five days earlier. The proclamation of Charles II had been almost a knee-jerk reaction to the outrage of regicide; besides, the Scottish people felt that the killing of their king had been tantamount to an attack on themselves. But the parliament was also determined that Charles would not ascend the throne of Scotland until he had accepted and signed the Solemn League and Covenant and promised to implement it in England as well as in Scotland.

The young king

Charles was a rather engaging young man. He was very tall (well over six feet), athletic and striking-looking, with a dark, unfashionably saturnine complexion and black eyes and hair. He was genial, quick-witted, cynical and cool, with an ironic sense of humour but a natural sense of dignity – what would now be called unusually laid-back (for a king). In 1646, as a sixteen-year-old, he had escaped from England to the Scilly Isles and on to Jersey, where he enjoyed various adventures (some of them romantic). He then spent two years with his mother, Henrietta Maria, in Paris in the stifling formality of the palace of Saint-Germain-en-Laye, before joining his sister Maria and her husband, Prince William of Orange, in The Hague. There the shattering news of his father's execution was brought to him early in February 1649.

When he heard that he had been proclaimed king by the Scottish parliament, Charles's first reaction was one of reluctance. He had little reason to like the Scots, who, he felt, had betrayed his father by handing him over to the English and had then done nothing to save him from the scaffold. Although he no doubt wanted the throne from which his father had been deposed, he was taken aback by the severity of the conditions which the Scots were laying down before they would install him on it. In March 1649 a delegation of Scottish commissioners met Charles in The Hague. They told him bluntly that he would have to promise to establish Presbyterianism in all three of his kingdoms. Two months later he agreed to sign the National Covenant, but not the Solemn League and Covenant – i.e. he would give no assurances about Church government in England and Ireland. The talks were called off: the Solemn League was central to the international missionary vision of the Kirk Party.

Charles was not dismayed. He had hopes of support both in Ireland and in Scotland. His expectations in Ireland, where the Catholics had risen in rebellion, were soon to be extinguished, however: Oliver Cromwell launched a punitive expedition which culminated swiftly in the appalling massacre of the three thousand inhabitants of Drogheda, north of Dublin, in September 1649, followed by another bloodbath at Wexford, on the south-east tip of Ireland, in October.

That left the Scottish Royalists as the last prospect for a successful Restoration by armed force. In February 1650, while Charles was still negotiating with the Scottish parliament, he appointed the exiled Marquis of Montrose as Lieutenant-General of Scotland and commissioned him to invade Scotland on his behalf. When the invasion failed, Charles disowned him.

Charles now had no alternative but to come back to the negotiating table with the extreme Scottish Presbyterians. Another round of talks was held at Breda, in Holland, starting on 26 March 1650. Charles's advisers told him that only his physical presence in Scotland could break the deadlock. The Scots, for their part, were even more adamant for the Solemn League; they were also determined that Charles should repudiate the gallant Marquis of Montrose, who was even then invading the north of Scotland with a small expeditionary force. Charles, seeing no hope of achieving the throne by any other means, began to waver. By the end of May, knowing that Montrose's last desperate gamble had failed, he said he would sign the Solemn League as soon as he reached Scotland. On the voyage from Amsterdam the Scottish commissioners turned the screw tighter and tighter: Charles was not to be allowed any other form of worship than Presbyterianism in his private household. They castigated the sins of his father and the Catholic religion of his mother. By the time the ship was in Scottish waters the voyage had been stormy in more senses than one. But there could now be no turning back for Charles, and on 23 June, while his ship lay at anchor off Garmouth, he finally put his signature to both Covenants. It was tantamount to a declaration of war on the non-Presbyterian England of Oliver Cromwell.

Charles II was now accepted as the Covenanted King of Scotland, but there was wariness on both sides. No one believed that he had really been converted from Episcopalianism to Presbyterianism; the Kirk men trusted him no more than he trusted them, and Charles – still uncrowned – was kept under surveillance, day and night. It was a time of unmitigated gloom and depression which would leave him with a lifelong repugnance for Scottish Presbyterianism and a detestation of most other things Scottish. There was to be an even rougher journey before a coronation could take place, and it was not going to be a glittering occasion fit for a king. Politics – and Oliver Cromwell – would see to that.

The 'Rule of Saints' (1648–50)

Since the defeat of the 'Engagement' in September 1648, power in Scotland had been wielded by the Kirk Party, the revolutionary offspring of the 'Whiggamore' *putsch*. The party did not have the support of the mass of the laity, or of many of the aristocracy, but relied on the corporate power of the ministers: it was essentially a clerical oligarchy which barred all 'ungodly' elements from power, insisted on the direct management of the army, and was prepared to use execution as the disincentive to opponents or backsliders.

The Kirk's presbyteries and General Assembly dictated all policy to parliament. It was a policy infused with radical ideals of social justice. Lay patronage in the Kirk was abolished, depriving lairds of their lucrative right to choose the local parish minister. Responsibility for the care of the poor and the sick was passed to Kirk sessions. Church attendance was made compulsory. Every parish was to have a school, paid for by local landowners. Merchants were forbidden to trade with Catholic countries, lest they be subjected to 'religious contagion'. There was also a resurgence in witch-hunting as, according to the ministers, the practice of witchcraft 'daily increaseth in this land' – a throwback to the witch-hunts of the reign of James VI & I.

John Simpson says:

> Some historians have depicted the 'Rule of Saints' as a totalitarian, almost Stalinist, state, but that is probably going too far. It was certainly a bad time for anyone, high or low, who indulged in sexual misdemeanours, or was suspected of witchcraft, however arbitrarily. On the other hand, for many Scots, clergy and laity alike, the 'Rule of Saints' represented the high point of the Reformation, when Kirk and state were purged of impurities. Indeed, in the period after the Restoration (and on into the eighteenth century), the people who saw themselves as the spiritual descendants of these revolutionary Covenanters always harked back to this as a Golden Age: they claimed that the only people who were unhappy in Scotland at that time were sinners, because they were so discouraged from going on sinning.

Such were the Presbyterians who forced Charles II to submit to their stern demands. But the days of the 'Rule of Saints' were numbered: Oliver Cromwell was on the warpath again, and he had Scotland in his sights.

From 5 February 1649, the day on which the Scots had proclaimed Charles II as 'King of Great Britain', war between Scotland and England had been unavoidable. The English had just got rid of one king, and had absolutely no wish to have another; yet Scotland was committing itself to imposing one upon them. The Union of the Crowns had been smashed: Scotland and England were two completely separate nations again – neighbours bound only by mutual animosity, as they had been for centuries. That animosity was now given additional depth by a religious zeal which was impervious to both logic and political and military reality. The faithful of the Kirk Party were enthusiastic for battle, because they *knew* that God was on the side of His chosen, godly people – the Scots – and would never let them lose. To make divine assurance doubly sure, they carried out yet another politico-religious purge of thousands of officers and men – 'Malignants' – in the army, just as the army of Gideon had been cleansed in the Old Testament (*Judges*, 7: 1–8).

On 24 June 1650 (the very day on which Charles had set foot on Scottish soil at Garmouth) the English Council of State met to plan a pre-emptive strike against any Scottish attempt to install Charles II on the English throne by force. The Lord General of the New Model Army, Lord Fairfax – himself a Presbyterian – refused on grounds of conscience to command the invasion of a neighbour and ally, and resigned. Cromwell was appointed Lord General in his place.

The declaration of military call-up was published on 4 July, and a muster of troops was ordered at Newcastle. There Cromwell promoted one of his officers, Colonel George Monk, a veteran of his devastating Irish campaign of 1649, to the command of a new regiment which would later become famous as the Coldstream Guards.[1] On 22 July, Cromwell crossed the Tweed with an army of seventeen thousand troops, with a supply fleet cruising alongside. After a wary progress up the east coast in torrential rain he made camp in Musselburgh on 29 July. He had no doubt whatsoever that what he was doing was right:

I have not sought these things. Truly I have been called unto them by the Lord, and therefore am not without some assurance that He will enable His poor worm and weak servant to do His will and fulfil His generation.

The Scots had mustered an army which was numerically superior to Cromwell's – some twenty-two thousand men in all, although it was still being purged of its ungodly elements. It was under the command of the experienced David Leslie, veteran of the Covenanter army which had fought alongside Cromwell in England, and the victor over Montrose at Philiphaugh. After the purges, however, it was no longer a professional army but a host of ill-trained religious zealots armed, above all, with unbounded faith in their God of Battles – 'ministers' sons, clerks and such as who hardly ever saw or heard of any sword but that of the spirit'. It was a new 'Army of the Kingdom', doing

---

1 George Monk, or Monck (later created first Earl of Albemarle), was a paradigm of the shifting loyalties of the time. He was born a Royalist (the second son of minor Devon gentry), and fought on the king's side in the First Civil War until he was captured. He was imprisoned in the Tower of London, where he married his laundress (Ann Clarges) and wrote a treatise on military theory. He then joined the parliamentary side 'as the only alternative to chaos' and became one of Cromwell's most effective professional officers. He would be Cromwell's deputy in the conquest, and military governor of Scotland from 1654; but in 1659 he would be instrumental in the Restoration of Charles II.

battle with the English republicans under a new banner – 'For Religion, King and Kingdome'.

The Scots army under Leslie lay entrenched behind a secure, heavily fortified line between Leith and the Canongate in Edinburgh, only five kilometres from the English forces. Cromwell marched and wheeled, probing for a chink in the Scottish defence, while Leslie moved his troops to repulse assaults anywhere along the line, counter-attacking at every opportunity. On 3 August Cromwell addressed a final appeal to the General Assembly:

> *Your own guilt is too much for you to bear: bring not therefore upon yourselves the blood of innocent men, deceived with bitter pretences of King and Covenant, from whose eyes you hide a better knowledge. I am persuaded that divers of you, who lead the people, have laboured to build in yourselves these things wherein you have censured others, and established yourselves upon the Word of God. Is it therefore infallibly agreeable to the Word of God, all that you say? I beseech you, in the bowels of Christ, think it possible you may be mistaken . . . There may be a Covenant made with death and Hell.*

The appeal fell on deaf ears. It was countered, indeed, by a Declaration of Repentance which specifically denounced Charles's father, mother and grandfather James VI & I, their lives and works – and the papacy for good measure. Charles, who had paid a brief morale-raising visit to his troops before being hustled back from the front lines, signed the Declaration of Repentance with a weary sigh.

The Battle of Dunbar (3 September 1650)

Off the A1 on the A1087 to Dunbar, a Battle Stone stands in a walled alcove. On it are inscribed the words of Thomas Carlyle: 'Here took place the brunt or essential agony of the battle of Dunbar.' Carved on the pedestal are the war-cries of the respective armies: 'The Covenant' and 'The Lord of Hosts'. On the opposite side of the road a signposted path leads to the top of Doon Hill; it offers a magnificent panoramic view to the north-east, towards Dunbar and the site of the stern battle which opened Scotland to the English Conquest.

At the end of August 1650, as the rain continued relentlessly, Cromwell's troops were suffering severely from dysentery and other diseases, and he fell back on Dunbar, fifty kilometres east of Edinburgh, where he could replenish his supplies and ship his sick and wounded back to England. His army had been reduced to about eleven thousand fit troops. Leslie followed him, and took up an impregnable position on the steep edge of Doon Hill, on the northernmost edge of the Lammermuirs, overlooking Dunbar from the south-west. He had eighteen thousand troops under his command.

Cromwell, now effectively trapped between the North Sea and the Scots army camped on Doon Hill, realised that he could not win against such overwhelming numbers 'without almost a miracle', as he put it. The miracle duly came: Leslie would have been content to let Cromwell evacuate his depleted army and make a humiliating retreat from Scottish soil; but the religious commissars who were superintending operations insisted that the Scots forsake their high position on Doon Hill and descend to the plain for a Biblical pitched battle – what they called 'going down against the Philistines at Gilgal'.

On the evening of 2 September, Cromwell watched as the Scots made their slippery descent to the lower slopes of Doon Hill in preparation for an attack across the Brock Burn the following morning. He was exultant: 'The Lord hath delivered them into our hand!' he exclaimed. Immediately, he drew up his plans for a pre-emptive strike, moving his cavalry to the low ground at the Brock Burn, while the artillery was manhandled into position to fire into the Scots flank. It was a stormy night of lashing rain; the Scots had no tents in which to bivouac, and the few billets in the area had been appropriated by their officers.

At 4.30 a.m., just before dawn, when Cromwell sounded the attack, six cavalry regiments and three foot regiments of the New Model Army moved forward and crossed the Brock Burn. Simultaneously, an artillery barrage pounded the Scots cavalry from their right flank. The Scots struggled into battle order despite the alarm and confusion, and put up stiff resistance to the onset of the Ironsides; but as dawn broke, Cromwell threw in all his reserves and suddenly the Scots army was broken. By mid-morning it was all over: some four thousand Scots lay dead or wounded on the sodden ground; ten thousand were taken prisoner, and only a rump of four thousand men escaped to the safety of Stirling with their commander, David Leslie. The Scottish prisoners were marched south to slavery in the salt-mines in England or in the new plantations overseas. Hundreds died of disease and starvation on the way.

For Cromwell it was, of course, a God-given victory: 'They were made by the Lord of Hosts as stubble to the sword.' For the Kirk men

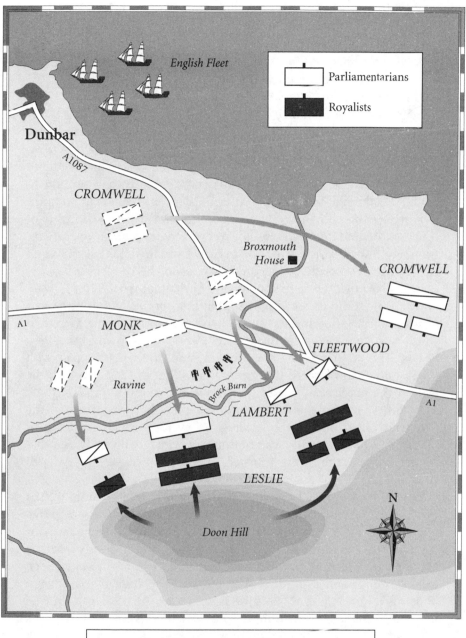

English Fleet

Parliamentarians

Royalists

Dunbar

A1087

CROMWELL

Broxmouth
House

CROMWELL

A1

MONK

FLEETWOOD

A1

Ravine

Brock Burn

LAMBERT

LESLIE

Doon Hill

N

THE BATTLE OF DUNBAR,
3 SEPTEMBER 1650

the defeat was God's proper punishment for the misdeeds of the Stewart dynasty; the Reverend Robert Douglas, a prominent member of the General Assembly, wrote to Charles blaming him for 'the controversy that God hath against you and your family, for which His wrath seems not yet to be turned away'.

The Dunbar debacle presaged the end of the supremacy of the Kirk men and their unquestioned hold over the king. Cromwell himself certainly believed so; on the day after the battle he said, 'Surely it is probable the Kirk has done their do. I believe their king will set up upon his own score now; wherein he will find many friends.' Cromwell marched into Edinburgh, where he had one of his chaplains preach a sermon in St Giles' Cathedral, to the fury of the ministers. He seemed in no hurry to complete the military subjugation of Scotland – there was plenty of time for that, and the weather was not conducive to military operations. Edinburgh Castle surrendered by agreement on Christmas Eve 1650, and the English army had consolidated its grip on the Lowlands; besides, Cromwell himself was very ill that winter in Edinburgh.

The Kirk soon showed signs of splitting, between the moderates (known as the 'Resolutioners') and the extremists of the west and south-west, the original 'Whiggamores', who were known as the 'Protesters'. The 'Resolutioners' were for king and Covenant in a pact with the Royalists, and wanted to tone down the 'Act of Classes' which the Scottish parliament had passed (at Cromwell's behest) in January 1649. The 'Protesters', on the other hand, were for the Covenant and the Covenant only; indeed, they wanted an even more severe purge of 'Malignants' in the army. The Marquis of Argyll, who had been dismayed by the antics of the ministers at Dunbar, became the leader of the moderate 'Resolutioners'.

Nevertheless, on 3 October 1650 the king was told of more purges on the way, including one of his own household. That was one purge too many for Charles. On 4 October he made a sudden dash for freedom from his ultra-Presbyterian courtiers, whom he regarded as his 'captors'. He rode out of Perth, alone, as if going hawking, then galloped north-east towards Kirriemuir. It seems he had some vague hopes of joining up with Royalist sympathisers in the north, but he failed to make contact with them. Next day he was caught by officers who had been sent to track him down, and was hauled back to Perth for yet another lecture. This escapade came to be known as 'The Start', and certainly it was the start of a new boldness, a new overt defiance, on the king's part as the power of the Kirk men dwindled.

In the General Assembly of December 1650 the moderate 'Resolutioners' carried the day. With half of Scotland under military occupation, the decision was made that the king should be crowned. A coronation might well help to inspire some kind of national unity, and would certainly help to enhance the status of the King of Scots abroad.

Coronation (1 January 1651)

On New Year's Day 1651 Charles was crowned in the little Presbyterian church which stood on the Moot Hill beside the palace at Scone.[1] He was the last Scottish monarch to be crowned at that historic royal site; indeed, it was to be the last coronation held in Scotland. It was a strange, hybrid ceremony: the king was crowned, but not anointed (anointing was considered a 'Popish ritual'). Considerable effort was made to give the ceremony a veneer of magnificence. A wooden platform was erected to accommodate a makeshift throne under a canopy of crimson velvet. Charles was mantled in a plush robe of purple cloth. The train-bearers were the young sons of Covenanter nobility. Charles was presented with the 'Honours of Scotland' – crown, sceptre and sword – together with a pair of spurs; the crown was placed on his head by the Marquis of Argyll. Thereafter a leading 'Malignant' soldier, General John Middleton, who had been purged from the army but now wanted to be readmitted to the Covenanter fold, was brought on stage wearing sackcloth to do penance for his sins.

If the ceremony was not as grand as earlier coronations at Scone had been, it was certainly no shorter. The king was treated to a lengthy sermon from Robert Douglas, now the Moderator of the General Assembly, on the precariousness of kingship: 'The sins of former kings have made this a tottering crown ... A king, when he getteth his crown on his head, should think, at the best, it is but a fading crown.' Charles then duly swore the Coronation oath:

> *I, Charles, King of Great Britain, France and Ireland, do assure and declare by my solemn oath, in the presence of Almighty God, the searcher of all hearts, my allowance and approbation of the National Covenant and Solemn League and Covenant above written ... and I shall observe these in my own practice and family, and shall never make opposition to any of these, nor endeavour any alteration therein.*

---

1   The church was built in 1624 with stones from the abbey church, which had been wrecked during the Reformation. It is now a family mausoleum.

The king was then 'shown to the people' in the church, and they acclaimed him. After the ceremony there followed a lavish banquet, and King Charles II set about the business of winning hearts and minds to the Royalist cause. He made a series of progresses in the northern parts of his realm which were still free of English occupation. Wherever he went – Perth, Stirling, Dundee, Aberdeen, St Andrews, Pittenweem – he was accorded an enthusiastic welcome. The coronation gamble seemed to have paid off.

The moderate 'Resolutioners' now moderated the Act of Classes, and those 'Malignants' who had fought for Charles I were eligible to fight again. General Leslie found men flocking to join him at Stirling, to invigorate the shattered survivors of the defeat at Dunbar. As Leslie's army grew larger and stronger at Stirling, Cromwell (now recovered from illness) moved into action. Reluctant to tackle the Scots army with another frontal assault on an entrenched position, he marched to Linlithgow, on to Glasgow, and back again towards Edinburgh to try to tempt the Scots from their position; but this time Leslie stayed put. While Scots eyes were on Cromwell as he manoeuvred near Linlithgow, a flying force under General Monk crossed the Firth of Forth in flat-bottomed landing-craft and landed in Fife. A Scots detachment sent to meet the English thrust was decisively beaten at Pitreavie, near Inverkeithing, on 20 July 1651. To protect his flying force, Cromwell moved north to attack Perth.

Cromwell's long-term strategy seems to have been to encourage the Scots army to move into England, where he was sure it could be overwhelmed. By moving to Perth, he deliberately left the route to England open. King Charles, he knew, would take the bait and try to raise the Royalist standard in England again, for his only hope of winning back the throne of England was by force of Scottish arms. It was a desperate gamble, but Charles took it. Thus, on 31 July 1651, the Scots army started to move southwards, while Cromwell captured Perth, as planned.

On 5 August, King Charles (hoping to be welcomed as a liberator) crossed the border at Carlisle with an army of nearly thirteen thousand men. Cromwell left his generals to mop up in Scotland and went after him.

The Battle of Worcester (3 September 1651)

From this house
King Charles II
escaped his enemies
after the Battle of Worcester
September 3 1651

The medieval house in Worcester which proudly displays this plaque stands in New Street; it is the most visible surviving evidence of the fierce battle which raged in the meadows outside the walls of the city and through its streets. The house was where the king lodged during his stay in Worcester; according to legend, he escaped through its back door as the parliamentary troops hunting for him broke in at the front.

King Charles had reached the city of Worcester on 22 August. The road south led through Lancashire towards Warrington and then on to Wolverhampton, but hardly a single English Royalist joined the invaders. Town after town declined to welcome the king or recruit for him. Instead, the Scots found their heels nipped by English harriers all the way; they also knew that they were being shadowed by English forces. By the time they reached Worcester they were tired and dispirited. Charles worked hard to galvanise his men into action, to prepare for a last-ditch defence.

Cromwell was in no hurry to make his assault. He had gathered an army of twenty-eight thousand men, but he took his time. He was approaching from the north, from Nottingham, but he wanted to attack from the south in order to prevent a Scottish break-out towards London. Worcester lay in fine rolling countryside in a good defensible position: the key to success lay in control of the Severn and its tributary, the Teme, which joined it near Powick Bridge. As Charles was relying on the rivers to protect him, he ordered the four vital bridges guarding access to the city to be blown up; but one of Cromwell's generals succeeded in seizing the Severn Bridge at Upton, and Cromwell was then able to push up towards Worcester along both banks of the Severn. Charles concentrated the bulk of his soldiers inside the city walls, but placed three regiments to guard the confluence of the rivers in the meadows below the city. He positioned the cavalry under General Leslie at St Martin's Gate to the north, to guard the escape route if one should become necessary.

The assault began on 3 September 1651, the first anniversary of Cromwell's 'providential' victory at Dunbar. As the initial bombardment began, Charles climbed the tower of the fourteenth-century cathedral from which he could watch the battle and observe Cromwell's military strategy unfolding. Cromwell, having assembled twenty boats farther downstream, now towed them upstream to act as bridges across the Teme and the Severn. A troop of horse forded the Teme near Powick Bridge to create a diversion while the makeshift bridges were put into place, and Charles's men found themselves under furious assault and were forced back towards the city.

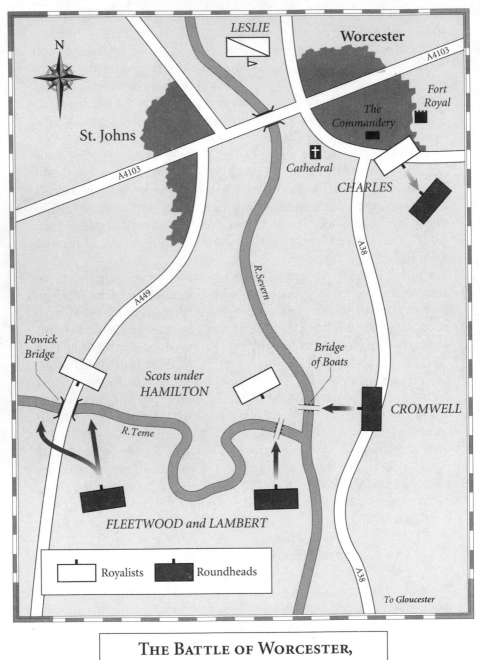

THE BATTLE OF WORCESTER,
3 SEPTEMBER 1651

Charles then saw Cromwell himself crossing with his regiment from the east to the west bank of the Severn, and for a moment the right flank of the English advance was exposed. Charles quickly ordered a dramatic charge out of the Sidbury Gate under cover of a barrage from the guns of Fort Royal. With the king in the lead, the Scots fell upon the remaining Roundheads on the west bank. The English, caught off-guard, reeled back in confusion. Charles called for a supporting cavalry charge from Leslie, which would surely have cleared the east bank of the river, but, inexplicably, Leslie made no move. In the nick of time Cromwell recrossed the river and forced the Royalists back through the Sidbury Gate and into the city.

The Scots were now all but surrounded within the city walls, and the gates were soon breached. Vicious hand-to-hand fighting raged in the narrow, winding streets. The king fought beside his men, on foot, with conspicuous bravery. Leslie's cavalry hovered and hesitated, fatally, before taking the escape road to the north. As dusk fell, the king realised that all hope was gone. More than two thousand of his men had been killed; another nine thousand had been captured. Now it was imperative for him to escape, rather than be captured. This is when he is reputed to have paid a last visit to his lodgings before getting out of the city through St Martin's Gate, to the north, in the company of a small entourage.

Cromwell called Worcester his *dies mirabilis* – his 'miraculous day'. Only one thing cast a shadow over his success – the king had got clean away.

The Royal Oak of Boscobel

Charles, after beholding the ruin of his cause, and having given sufficient proofs of personal valour, escaped from the field, and concealed himself in obscure retreats, under various disguises.
TALES OF A GRANDFATHER, CHAPTER XLVI

Charles II's escape from Worcester and his tribulations as a fugitive in disguise for six fraught weeks, before getting away from England on 15 October, make a great yarn. The king, after dictating the story to Samuel Pepys on board ship as he approached England on the eve of the Restoration in 1660, told it so often that his courtiers would flee the room whenever he embarked on it again. Walter Scott featured a highly fictionalised version of it in one of his Waverley novels, *Woodstock* (1826).

The enduring popular interest in the story of Charles's escape has for long focused on a fine oak tree which grows in Boscobel Wood (from the Italian *bosco bello*, 'beautiful wood'). It stands in the grounds of Boscobel House, thirteen kilometres north-west of Wolverhampton in the Midlands, on an unclassified road between the A5 and the A41.[1] The surrounding woodland has long since disappeared, and the oak (it is actually a descendant of the original tree) stands in solitary glory some 150 metres from Boscobel House, surrounded by an iron paling.[2] In its spreading branches the king spent an uncomfortable day with another fugitive while Roundhead soldiers scoured the woods for him. After the Restoration, Charles's birthday (29 May) was designated Oak-Apple Day, and it remained a public holiday until the middle of the nineteenth century; it is still celebrated as 'Founder's Day' by the Chelsea Pensioners in London.

King Charles owed his liberty, and probably his life, to the loyalty and courage of what might be called the Royalist and Catholic underground. Although there was a huge price of £1,000 on his head as a 'malicious and dangerous traitor', not a single person involved in his escape, high or low, tried to claim the reward.

Charles was practically unknown by sight, but the description of him which was circulated throughout England made him vulnerable to recognition: 'a tall black man, over two yards high', dark-faced, black-haired and black-eyed. He had his luxuriant curly black hair shorn off. He got rid of all his fine clothing and all his money. His face and hands were treated with walnut juice, in an attempt to make his complexion paler. And he took his leave of all his companions – if he was to survive, it had to be on his own. Then he disguised himself as a woodman – 'Will Jones' – in green jerkin, grey cloth breeches, leather doublet and floppy hat. The major problem was his feet, which were enormous, and it was impossible to find a pair of shoes to fit

---

1 Boscobel House, which is now in the care of English Heritage, stands 'in the middle of nowhere'; nonetheless, it attracts more than twenty thousand historical pilgrims a year.

2 The original 'Royal Oak', like 'Wallace's Oak', was literally loved to death by souvenir hunters from the 1660s onwards. Pieces were hacked from it to make snuff-boxes and tobacco-stoppers, and even the roots had gone by the end of the eighteenth century. However, by 1700 a sapling from one of its acorns was growing close to its side, and this was protected from visitors until it reached its full size. One of the brass plates within the enclosure, dating from 1875, refers to the tree as the original 'Royal Oak'; it replaced an earlier plaque which described it as being descended from the original. As the guide-book explains, the 1875 plate was erected in response to a new wave of pilgrimage inspired by the publication in 1872 of Harrison Ainsley's romance *Boscobel, or the Royal Oak*.

him. He would say afterwards that of all the torments he suffered during this time, none was worse than the agonising chafing of boots which were too small.

Throughout his weeks on the run, Charles was handed from one 'safe house' to another, from one secret hiding-place to another. Many a day and night he spent crouched in a cramped 'priest-hole' while soldiers searched the house. The houses belonged, in the main, to Catholics who were by no means militant (they had learned through bitter experience to keep their heads down) but who still cherished a deep-seated sense of loyalty to the crown.[1] There were government troops everywhere, and narrow squeaks a-plenty. On one occasion, in the house of Abbot's Leigh near Bristol, the servants' quarters were agog with talk about the fugitive king; one of the men claimed to have served in the king's own regiment of guards, and Charles made a hasty retreat to his own room. In an inn at Bridport, crowded with soldiers, an ostler remarked that Charles's face looked very familiar; it took a lot of nerve for the king to talk his way smoothly out of that one.

The original plan was for Charles to seek passage abroad from one of the Welsh ports; but all the approaches were blocked by Cromwell's troops. Devon and Dorset hummed with military activity as the commonwealth prepared to invade the Channel Islands. The little port of Lyme (later Lyme Regis) was the king's next target: he went there riding double with a young lady on a pretended elopement, and a boat was engaged for the voyage to France that night, but the captain did not turn up (he had been locked in his bedroom by his wife, who suspected that he was up to no good). After Lyme it was on to Bridport, but after the encounter with the ostler, the king and his party hastened away while rumours spread through the town.

On 14 October the fugitive reached Brighton, where he lodged in the George Inn in West Street. A local merchant had been bribed to procure a boat in nearby Shoreham; it was named the *Surprise*, a coal-boat from Pittenweem in Scotland. At 4 a.m. on Wednesday, 15 October 1651, the *Surprise* set sail, heading for the French coast, and King Charles II was on his way to safety at last; at Fécamp, near Rouen,

---

1 They were all to be specially honoured and rewarded by the king after his Restoration – at least sixty people who had helped him at considerable risk to their lives, and who had kept the secret. One of them was the Jesuit Father John Huddleston, who kept Charles company during several hazardous vigils. When the king was on his deathbed in February 1685, it was Father Huddleston who was smuggled into his chamber and who received him into the Roman Catholic Church. When the dying king saw Father Huddleston at his bedside he cried out with pleasure and said, 'You that saved my body are now come to save my soul!'

he was carried ashore on the shoulders of the ship's mate, a Quaker named Carver.[1]

The great adventure was over. Charles was twenty-one years old, a king without a kingdom. For the next eight years he would wander from one European court to another, an impecunious supplicant for political favours which were often promised but never delivered.

The Interregnum: Cromwell's Scotland (1651–60)

In Scotland, the English campaign of subjugation had continued relentlessly under General Monk. While King Charles was still marching towards Worcester, Stirling surrendered to Monk on 14 August 1651, and the public records of Scotland fell into English hands.[2] On 29 August, at Alyth in northern Perthshire, Monk captured the members of the Committee of Estates (the executive committee of parliament) and of the Commission of the General Assembly. On 1 September, two days before the Battle of Worcester, Dundee was stormed and sacked and hundreds of citizens massacred. By late 1651 the whole eastern half of Scotland, from Edinburgh to Orkney, was under English control, superintended by a chain of English garrisons. Only one Royalist redoubt remained – Dunnottar Castle, perched on a rocky promontory just below Stonehaven, south of Aberdeen. It was blockaded at the end of September, and held out for eight long months before lowering its colours on 26 May 1652; and thereby hangs a dramatic tale – the escape of the Scottish Regalia.

The Honours of Scotland

After the coronation of Charles II at Scone, the regalia were in as much danger from Cromwell's vengeance as was the king himself. Edinburgh Castle, where they were normally kept, was now held by Cromwell's troops, so the Scottish crown jewels were sent to Stirling for safety. In the summer of 1651, however, the English army was on the march into the heartlands of Scotland. On the last day of the parliament held in Perth (6 June), the king ordered the earl marischal William Keith, hereditary keeper of the crown jewels, 'to transport the said Honours to the House of Dunnottar, there to be kept by him

---

1   The *Surprise* was later converted into a yacht and renamed the *Royal Escape*.
2   The records were taken to London; they were later sent back to Scotland by sea, but the ship carrying them was wrecked and they were lost.

until further orders'. The earl marischal was a prisoner in the Tower of London at the time, but his son, John Keith, removed the Honours to Dunnottar Castle; when Cromwell's men entered Perth on 2 August, the Scottish Regalia had gone.

Dunnottar Castle was held in the earl marischal's name by its governor, Captain George Ogilvie of Barras, with just forty men, two sergeants and a lieutenant. It was a difficult place to overcome by frontal assault: the only access was by a sagging tongue of land, like a drawbridge, involving a precipitous descent from the mainland and a perilous climb up to the gates of the castle.

There are various stories of how the Regalia were saved. The chief players were women from the household of James Granger, the minister of nearby Kinneff church. According to one story, Christian Granger, the minister's wife, obtained leave from the commander of the English besiegers, Colonel Morgan, to enter the castle to visit the governor's wife. When she left the castle she had the Regalia in her possession. She concealed the crown and sceptre under her clothes, while the sword and scabbard were broken in two and hidden in bundles of flax carried by one of her maids.[1] There was a momentary panic, however, when Colonel Morgan gallantly helped her to mount her horse. (In another version of the story, the Regalia were lowered by rope over the cliffs, where they were retrieved by a waiting girl who was gathering seaweed and brought to the manse in a creel of dulse.) The Honours were hidden first at the bottom of the minister's bed in the manse until such time as they could be buried in a more secure place. Their final resting place was in the church. At the dead of night the minister and his wife prised up a paving slab just in front of the altar and hid the smaller regalia in a hole they dug underneath it; the sword was buried between the two front rows of pews.[2]

After Dunnottar Castle surrendered in May 1652 it was ransacked by the English troops, but no trace of the Regalia was found, of course; the story was spread that they had been spirited away to the Continent. At the Restoration they were disinterred from their hiding-places in Kinneff church and taken in triumph to Edinburgh Castle; but there was never to be another coronation in Scotland at which the crown

---

1 The marks which are now apparent on the sword and scabbard are said to date from this occasion.
2 The old church at Kinneff was demolished in 1738 and replaced by the present church. It contains memorials to the Grangers and to Sir George Ogilvie of Barras.

could be used.[1] At the Union of the Parliaments in 1707 the Regalia were placed in a large oak chest and locked away in a room in the castle. For many years their location was forgotten – until Sir Walter Scott was instrumental in finding them again for the state visit of King George IV in 1822.

The 'incorporation' of Scotland

Scotland was now a conquered country. But what was England to do with it? A peace treaty was impossible as long as the Scots king was at liberty and claiming the English throne – there could be no peace between a Royalist state and its republican neighbour. The only practical solution seemed to be annexation, and soon after Worcester the English parliament considered a Bill 'asserting the right of England to Scotland'. But it jibbed at full annexation. In December 1651 the parliament passed a Bill whereby Scotland was to be incorporated into 'the free state and Commonwealth of England'.

On 4 February 1652 the 'Tender of Union', as it was called, was proclaimed at a bizarre ceremony at the Mercat Cross in Edinburgh. Eight trumpeters sounded a fanfare, and a town-crier shouted 'Oyez! Oyez! Oyez!' at an apathetic crowd which had never heard this English word before. The 'Tender of Union' was addressed to the thirty-one shires and fifty-eight royal burghs which made up the eighty-nine parliamentary constituencies of Scotland. Eventually, after considerable arm-twisting (Glasgow had to have a regiment quartered on the city before the corporation agreed), seventy-three of the constituencies assented to the Tender.

At a stroke Scotland had lost its parliament. The Privy Council was replaced by a group of English-appointed commissioners. The Scots were allowed to return a mere thirty members to a united parliament at Westminster, but the county and burgh elections attracted few voters and few candidates of worth. After they were elected, the MPs found themselves with neither power nor influence: they were expected merely to rubber-stamp policies for Scotland over which they had no control. The judiciary was also abolished; in its place came committees staffed by able Cromwellian soldier-administrators, who delivered justice fairly and firmly.

---

1 One item of the Regalia was not smuggled out to Kinneff church, but was retained by Captain George Ogilvie as a memento – the elaborate sword-belt. It was accidentally discovered in 1790 in a garden wall of Ogilvie's home at Barras. It was returned by a descendant of the family in 1892 and reunited with the sword in the Crown Room of Edinburgh Castle.

This 'incorporation' of Scotland, although it was carried out by *force majeure*, was a relatively mild process. The Cromwellian army in Scotland, under General Monk, was highly disciplined. After the horrifying sack of Dundee, there was to be no more destruction nor slaughter. Soldiers who looted were brought before courts martial and fined or imprisoned. Any local resistance, however, was promptly quelled. Firearms could only be carried under licence; travellers needed passes to move from one part of the country to another; the number of horses anyone could keep was regulated; and a ban was put on public meetings 'of any persons for the exercise of any jurisdiction other than such as is or shall be from the Parliament of England'.

The English occupation was consolidated by the creation of large garrisons at strategic sites. Huge sums of money were spent on the building of bastioned forts at Ayr, Inverness, Inverlochy, Leith and Perth, as well as twenty smaller forts. Law and order prevailed everywhere. The cost of all this law and order, and of the administrative machine behind it, was formidable. When General George Monk was appointed Military Governor of Scotland he was expected to raise £6,000 a month in taxation from the Scots to defray the costs of the occupation – but there was still an annual deficit to the English treasury of £130,000 a year.

During the period of the 'incorporation' there was only one serious Royalist revolt on behalf of the exiled king. It flared up in the Highlands in 1653, led by a Lowland aristocrat, William, ninth Earl of Glencairn; from Europe, King Charles sent a little support and a professional soldier, General John Middleton, to lead the rebellion, but it was fragmented and riven by internal quarrels and collapsed the following year.[1] For the most part, however, the Scots simply accepted the occupation with resignation.

But what of the religious Reformation for which so many Scots had fought and died over so many years? What of the National Covenant, and the Solemn League and Covenant?

The Kirk and the aristocracy were the main losers in the 'incorporation'. The English in the age of Cromwell were the enemies of hierarchy in all forms, in Church as well as government; they were intent

---

1 John Middleton (1608–74) was the 'Malignant' soldier who had been paraded in the sackcloth of repentance at Charles's coronation at Scone. A bluff, hard-drinking soldier, he had been both a Covenanting and a Royalist officer. He was captured at the Battle of Worcester but escaped from the Tower of London the following year and joined the king in exile. He would be ennobled as Earl of Middleton in 1656, and appointed one of Charles's Commissioners for Scotland after the Restoration.

on bypassing both the aristocracy and the Kirk theocrats. They wanted Scotland to be run by the middle classes, the gentry. In the Kirk the split between the 'Resolutioners' and the 'Protesters' widened. The dissenting ministers could not stomach the religious toleration of the English: full toleration was granted to 'ministers of spiritual ordinances according to the order of the Scots churches'; it was also granted to 'others who, not being satisfied in conscience to use that form, shall serve and worship God in other Gospel ways' – apart from papacy and prelacy. This 'general and doubtsome toleration' threatened the discipline of the Kirk and its authority to speak for the nation.

The Cromwellian regime allowed kirk sessions to meet, but not General Assemblies. The 'Resolutioners' accepted the situation and were soon working with the English occupation. The 'Protesters', however, held an illegal General Assembly in St Giles' in July 1653. A company of soldiers broke into the church and forced them out at gunpoint; the ministers were herded out of the burgh and banished from Edinburgh on pain of imprisonment.

The Scots showed no desire to throw off the clerical yoke and the stern restrictions of Presbyterianism; the ideals of the Covenant were not forgotten. They were only driven underground, and would flourish again, powerfully and tragically, in the 'Killing Time' ahead.

Oliver Cromwell, Lord Protector, who had refused (albeit after much hesitation) the offer of the crown, died on 3 September 1658, the anniversary of his victories at Dunbar and Worcester. He had turned England into a powerful nation with an embryo empire, a nation respected (and feared) in the chancelleries of Europe. He was succeeded by his son, Richard Cromwell, but Richard's grasp of the reins of government was feeble and he was soon deposed. Once again a constitutional crisis loomed, and once again it fell to the military to sort it out.

In Scotland, General Monk realised that the Commonwealth could not last, and that a return to monarchy was inevitable. He summoned his officers to Greyfriars Kirk in Edinburgh and called for volunteers to march south with him 'to restore order'. They all offered their swords. General Monk gathered his army of seven thousand men – the army which he had been using to keep Scotland in subjection – and marched it to Coldstream, on the border. He learned enough from his intelligence sources in England to be sure that no one would stand in his way if he marched on London. On New Year's Day 1660 he took the most momentous step of his long and distinguished career as a soldier: he crossed the River Tweed into England, intent on restoring the Stewart monarchy to the throne.

The Restoration (1660)

Of Charles the Second, who thus unexpectedly, and as it were by miracle, was replaced on his father's throne in spite of so many obstacles as within a week or two of the event seemed to render it incredible, I have not much that is advantageous to tell you.

TALES OF A GRANDFATHER, CHAPTER XLIX

On 25 May 1660 King Charles sailed from Holland on board the *Royal Charles* and landed at Dover to reclaim the throne of his fathers. The beach was crammed with excited, cheering crowds. As soon as the king was rowed ashore he knelt and praised God. The Mayor of Dover presented him with a huge, richly-bound Bible. Waiting, too, was General George Monk, who offered his sword to the king with a symbolic gesture: his men were ordered to lay down their weapons and to consider themselves disbanded; then Monk ordered them to shoulder arms again and to fall in as soldiers of the king.[1]

Monk's march south early in 1660 had been a slow, canny business. He halted often, holding consultations, increasing his support with every stop. In London he summoned Parliament (effectively the old 'Long Parliament'), which recalled the king and then dissolved itself.

Monk had brought with him to London various petitions from the commissioners of shires and burghs urging that the Union should be maintained, but on better terms for Scotland. He had also brought a diligent and clever Scottish clergyman, James Sharp, the minister at Crail, in Fife, who had been nominated to act as the spokesman for the Kirk. When Monk sent a delegation to Holland to negotiate the king's return, Sharp was one of the party who went to Breda to look after the Kirk's interests.

James Sharp (1618–79) was to play a significant role in the events of the Restoration period. A native of Banffshire, he was a Royalist and a moderate 'Resolutioner'. He was one of the ministers captured at Alyth in 1651 and shipped to London, but he was released after a few months and became a Kirk intermediary with Cromwell. To the

---

1 Monk was created first Duke of Albemarle on 7 July 1660, and became an elder statesman and captain-general of the army. He died on New Year's Day 1670.

hard-line 'Protesters' he was Judas incarnate, the man of God who betrayed his Church for personal advancement; to the 'Resolutioners' he was a skilled and astute negotiator who did all he could to moderate the king's anger against Presbyterianism but in the end was defeated – and joined the enemy instead. He would come to be regarded as the evil genius of the eventual Church settlement, and would pay for it with his life.

On 4 April 1660 the king had signed the Declaration of Breda, in which he handed the interim administration of government to an English Convention Government. The government in London proclaimed him king on 8 May. In Edinburgh on 14 May he was proclaimed king of all three of his kingdoms. There was wild popular rejoicing. Cannons thundered from Edinburgh Castle, public fountains ran with claret. But Charles II made straight for London from Dover, arriving on his birthday – Oak-Apple Day – on 29 May to a frenzied and tumultuous welcome. The king remarked, with wry humour:

> It must surely have been our own fault, that we have been so long absent from a country where every one seems so glad to see me!

But he made no attempt to test his welcome in the country which had first proclaimed him, in 1649. He had no wish ever to set foot in Scotland again, and never did so.

Charles was now thirty years old, an intelligent, worldly and easy-going young man. He disliked the fussy pomposity of court ritual, was keen on sailing and passionately interested in horse-racing; he enjoyed the theatre and music, loved fine art and was deeply interested in science (he granted a royal charter to the Royal Society in 1662 and founded the Royal Observatory at Greenwich and Chelsea Hospital). He was also irresistible to women (or irresistibly attracted to women), and his sexual appetite became legendary: the celebrated actress and former orange-seller Nell Gwyn was only one of his innumerable mistresses. He fathered at least fourteen illegitimate children (six of whom were made dukes), but none with his wife, the devoutly Catholic Catherine of Braganza, the Infanta of Portugal, whom he married in 1662. The diarist John Evelyn summed Charles up as 'a prince of many virtues, and many great imperfections'.

'The Restoration' is frequently associated with saucy images of the Merry Monarch and notable moral laxity after the stern years of the Commonwealth. But politically it was not just a Restoration of the monarchy: it was also a restoration of the nobility of Scotland. There was a rush for political power – jobs for the noble boys. The land-owning classes had been excluded from power during the Interregnum, and their aristocratic members were either in exile, in English prisons, or cowed into impotence by English fines and confiscations; the aristocracy was now determined to reclaim control of the levers of power and patronage.

Scotland, apparently, regained its independence; but there was no royal proclamation, no formal dissolution of the Cromwellian 'incorporation'. In June, the old Committee of Estates whose members Monk had captured at Alyth in 1651 was resurrected to form a provisional government until such time as a parliament could be assembled; and two weeks later Charles decided on his Scottish ministers. The Earl of Middleton was made Commissioner to the Scottish parliament; he, of course, had a personal score to settle with the Presbyterians – they had forced him to do public penance at Charles's coronation at Scone. The Earl of Glencairn was made Chancellor of Scotland.

As Secretary of State for Scotland, the king appointed John Maitland, the second Earl of Lauderdale.[1] He was a large, uncouth-looking man with red hair, a hard drinker, like Middleton, but (unlike Middleton) well-versed in the classics and Hebrew. Lauderdale had once been a Covenanter, and was a moderate Presbyterian. He had been captured at the Battle of Worcester and spent nearly ten years in English captivity before being released in the spring of 1660.

But before the business of government began, King Charles II had some personal scores to settle. The corpse of Oliver Cromwell was removed from its coffin in Westminster Abbey and drawn through the streets on a hurdle to Tyburn. There it was hanged for twenty-four hours and the head impaled on a prominent spike; the remains of his body were then flung on to a dunghill. Of the sixty men who had signed King Charles I's death-warrant, only twenty were still to be found, nine of whom were executed for treason. But the king did not stop at that.

---

1 Lauderdale came from a long line of civil servants. He was a grandson of John Maitland of Thirlestane (secretary of state to James VI & I) and a grand-nephew of William Maitland of Lethington (secretary of state to Mary Queen of Scots).

The king's revenge

For many years, Charles had nursed a deep hatred for the men who had browbeaten, coerced and humiliated him during his eighteen months in Scotland (1650–51). First on his hit-list was the Marquis of Argyll. Argyll had placed the crown on his head at his coronation at Scone; the king had promised him a dukedom, and £40,000. Argyll had also for a time pressed the claims of his daughter, Lady Ann Campbell, as a suitable wife for Charles. After the defeat of Scots Royalist hopes at Worcester, Argyll had submitted to the Cromwellian regime ('my duty to religion, according to my oath in the Covenant, always reserved'), and had then retired from active politics to his estates at Inveraray.

In July 1660 Argyll went to London to make peace with his king, but Charles refused him audience and had him arrested instead. He was thrown into the Tower, before being shipped back to Scotland at Christmas 1660 with other 'enemies of the king', and incarcerated in Edinburgh Castle. He was put on trial before parliament in Edinburgh, and for a time his hopes of acquittal were high, until General Monk produced some damning letters which implied a pledge of support for Cromwell. These letters sealed Argyll's fate. He was found guilty of collaborating with the Cromwellian regime, and on 27 May 1661 was guillotined by 'the Maiden'. His head replaced that of the Marquis of Montrose on a spike on the Tolbooth in Edinburgh. He was later given an ornate memorial in St Giles' Cathedral, diagonally opposite that of Montrose. His recumbent marble effigy – almost a copy of that of Montrose – carries the legend: 'I set the Crown on the King's Head: he hastens me to a better Crown than his own.' Posthumous point-scoring, indeed!

Five days later it was the turn of one of the chief leaders of the ultra-Presbyterians, the Reverend James Guthrie, minister of Stirling. Guthrie had preached vehemently against the king during his stay in Scotland, and had written a pamphlet, *Cause of God's Wrath*, which excoriated the Stewart monarchy and the king himself. He had welcomed Charles's return in 1660 with a letter reminding him that he was a Covenanted king, and that God would punish him if he failed to live up to the Covenant. Now an example was to be made of Guthrie. Charged with high treason, he was happy to plead guilty. He was sentenced to be hanged on 1 June 1661, and used the scaffold as a pulpit from which to deliver a last Covenanting sermon: 'The Covenants! The Covenants shall yet be Scotland's reviving!'

Some of Charles's intended victims escaped his vengeance, however. One of them, Neil Macleod of Assynt, who had betrayed the Marquis of Montrose after the Battle of Carbisdale in 1650, was brought to Edinburgh for trial. He was held in custody in the Tolbooth, which he somehow managed to turn into a place of revelry where fashionable Edinburgh caroused and danced the nights away. Whether or not it had been the intention, at the height of the wassailing Macleod escaped.

The last prime target for Charles's revenge was Archibald Johnston of Wariston, co-author of the National Covenant. He had, surprisingly, in the latter stages of Cromwell's Commonwealth become a leading figure in the government of Scotland as a commissioner for the administration of justice and a member of the Council of State for the Commonwealth. When a royal warrant was issued for his arrest he fled to Rouen. In his absence he was condemned to death, and the French obligingly extradited him in 1663. Johnston was now a sorry figure, senile and wretched. He wept piteously at his trial, but on the day of his hanging, 23 July 1663, he had recovered his composure. He apologised to the crowd for being unable to remember the long speech he had prepared, and died with dignity.

Parliament

With the revenge blood-letting done, Charles now got on with governing the Scottish part of his realm. The new Scottish parliament was summoned to meet in January 1661, and the Earl of Middleton, as Commissioner to the Scottish Parliament, was sent north to open it. He landed at Musselburgh at the end of December 1660 and led a military parade into the capital. On New Year's Day he rode with the Committee of Estates and the Honours of Scotland in full panoply up the Royal Mile to Parliament House for the opening of parliament. Contemporary observers reported that he was drunk the whole time. Within a week, on the king's instructions, the remains of the dismembered body of the Marquis of Montrose were given a state funeral in St Giles' Cathedral.

The first fruits of the substantive work of the first parliament appeared on 28 March – a sweeping Rescissory Act which annulled every law that had been passed by all its predecessors since 1633, the year of Charles I's coronation in Edinburgh. It quashed the constitutional settlement of 1639–41, restored the royal prerogatives and gave the king sole power to call and dissolve parliaments and to name his councillors and judges. The Covenants were declared illegal.

Office-bearers had to swear an oath of allegiance to the new order. Noblemen got back their heritable jurisdictions, ended by Cromwell, and the gentry their rights of patronage in the kirks, lost under the Covenant. For good measure, Charles II was voted a large annuity. All this the parliament passed in its first session after the Restoration. Power had been transferred firmly back to the crown and Scotland would increasingly be controlled from London.

The other major proposal was to restore episcopacy. Lauderdale (with Sharp in attendance) argued against it; he favoured an as-yet undefined Presbyterian system, and reminded the king that the attempt to impose bishops on Scotland had been the downfall of both his father and his grandfather; yet many Scots had supported the king during the Civil Wars, provided that he did not offend their religion. To Charles, however, monarchy and Presbytery were totally incompatible, and Middleton was authorised to reintroduce episcopacy. A royal proclamation was issued on 6 September 1661 restoring episcopal government to a Restored Church of Scotland. James Sharp was consecrated at Westminster as one of the first four Scottish bishops; three months later he was appointed Archbishop of Aberdeen and Primate of Scotland.

All the ground which the Kirk had gained so painfully since the Covenant of 1638 was lost. In June 1662 parliament passed an Act of Presentation and Collation which declared vacant all those parishes whose ministers had been appointed since 1649, and that such ministers would have to seek the patronage of the local laird and confirmation from the bishop of the diocese. The Act was designed to root out a few of the most prominent 'Protesters', but nearly three hundred ministers (including at least forty 'Resolutioners') were deprived of their charges for non-conformity; these were mainly in the west and south-west of Scotland, and represented almost a third of the total ministry. In the political crisis which ensued, Middleton was deposed and replaced by John Leslie, the seventh Earl of Rothes, another one-time Royalist soldier.[1]

The deprived ministers were replaced by placemen contemptuously dismissed as 'king's curates', and the congregations refused to attend church to hear them. Instead, they and their homeless former ministers created new places of worship in the fields, in the woods, in barns or private houses. These clandestine meetings for worship were known as 'conventicles', and the government grew increasingly concerned:

---

1 Middleton was posted off to be Governor of Tangier, which had been part of Catherine of Braganza's dowry. He died there in 1674 as a result of a drunken fall downstairs.

there was a thin line between dissension and rebellion. John Simpson says:

> The weather in Scotland at many times of year is not suitable for worshipping in the open air – especially if you are in constant fear of soldiers appearing. But the conventicles, with all the suffering and heroism which came to be associated with them, captured the imagination of later generations. Robert Louis Stevenson, for instance, wrote a haunting poem during his last months in Samoa, saying that he hoped he would see again the Pentlands where 'about the graves of the martyrs, the whaups [curlews] are crying'.

The conventicles were soon outlawed. Ministers like John Welch, John Blackadder and Donald Cargill acquired almost legendary reputations as they flitted about the country in disguise to preach at large open-air conventicles. The Reverend Alexander Peden ('Prophet Peden') was another.[1] The 'common people' who refused to attend church services ('recusants') were fined. Recalcitrant districts had troops quartered in them, and these troops were used to break up the conventicles and hunt down the people who worshipped at them. To counter the constant threat of interruption by armed dragoons, the Conventiclers took up arms, ready to defend themselves. Confrontation was inevitable, and it came with what has become known as 'the Pentland Rising'.

The Pentland Rising (November 1666)

On 13 November 1666 four fugitive Conventiclers were passing through the village of St John's Town of Dalry, in Galloway, when they came upon some soldiers beating up an old farmer who had failed to pay a fine for non-attendance at church. The Conventiclers went to his rescue, and the soldiers were overpowered after a struggle. The 'rebels' hurried to a conventicle which had gathered at nearby Balmaclellan, and gathered support; the Rising was under way.

The Covenanters marched on Dumfries, the headquarters of the

---

1   Peden (1626–86), minister of New Luce in Galloway, was perhaps the most charismatic and inspirational of them all. His uncanny skill at evading arrest earned him the nickname of 'Prophet Peden'. Despite his reputation for prescience he spent much time in prison, but unlike most of his contemporaries he survived to die in his bed in 1686 – still a fugitive.

government troops, where they captured the commander, Sir James Turner, in his nightgown. They then decided to make a protest march to Edinburgh to present a petition to the Privy Council – perhaps they were hoping to emulate the 'Whiggamores Raid' of 1648. They all swore their allegiance to both king *and* Covenant, and set off, via Ayr and Lanarkshire, for Edinburgh. They were not a particularly warlike force – some three thousand countrymen, armed only with pitchforks, scythes and clubs, straggling along in wretched weather. During the long march their numbers dwindled to about 1,100. The government, convinced that a full-scale rebellion was under way, made preparations to crush it. The city gates of Edinburgh were closed, and the militia mobilised.

When the protest march reached Colinton, on the southern outskirts of Edinburgh, in driving sleet and rain, it was met by a vigilante force of Edinburgh Fencibles, and was refused permission to send a delegation to meet the Privy Council. Deeply dispirited, the marchers retreated a few miles southwards to Rullion Green, on the slopes of the Pentland Hills. There they were caught, on 28 November, by the government troops under the command of General Tam Dalyell of the Binns, son of the Thomas Dalyell who had made his fortune in London in the heady days of the Union of Crowns.[1] General Dalyell had a force of 2,500 infantry and six troops of horse. Although the insurgents stood their ground and repelled the first charges, they were eventually overwhelmed and fifty of their number killed. Only gathering darkness prevented greater slaughter as the survivors broke ranks and fled. Some eighty were taken prisoner, including thirty women and children. General Tam promised them quarter, but none was given. Archbishop Sharp wrote to the king: 'This rabble should be extirpated as traitors.' The prisoners were packed into 'Haddo's Hole', at the back of St Giles' Cathedral, where some of them were tortured in 'the Boot', an evil contraption which mashed a victim's foot and lower leg as iron wedges were hammered into it. Ten of the prisoners were hanged in Edinburgh, eleven more in Ayr, Dumfries, Glasgow

---

1   General 'Tam' Dalyell (1615–85) was a lifelong Royalist. He fought in Ireland in the 1640s, was captured at Worcester in 1651 and imprisoned in the Tower, but contrived to escape (one of the few people who ever succeeded in doing so) and took refuge on the Continent. He came back to take part in the failed Highland rebellion in 1653–54, but managed to make his way back to the Continent with a price of £200 on his head. He then soldiered as a mercenary for the Tsar of Russia. In 1666 Charles II summoned him to Scotland as commander-in-chief of the government army, charged with dealing with the dissident Covenanters of the conventicles.

and Irvine. General Dalyell was so outraged by this violation of his quarter that he resigned his commission.[1]

In London, on 4 December 1666, Samuel Pepys was delighted to hear of the outcome of the Pentland Rising:

> *And so to bed – with more cheerfulness than I have done a good while, to hear for certain the Scots rebels are all routed, they having been so bold as to come within three miles of Edinburgh, and there given two or three repulses to the King's forces, but at last were mastered – 300 or 400 killed or taken . . . (they having all taken the Covenant a few days before and sworn to live and die in it, as they did) and so all is likely to be there quiet again . . .*

But Pepys was very, very wrong.

The gathering crisis

The ferocious brutality with which the Pentland Rising had been crushed caused embarrassment even in government circles. Consequently, the Earl of Lauderdale now embarked on a policy of measured conciliation, known as 'The Accommodation': licences were to be issued to ousted ministers who took a bond of peace. This showed the first, albeit limited, toleration of non-conformity. In 1669 Lauderdale was sent north as Commissioner to the Scottish Parliament, and in June 1669 his 'First Indulgence' restored forty-two dissident ministers to their parishes in return for a bond promising good behaviour. Unlicensed ministers and their congregations would be fined or transported to the colonies, baptism could only be performed by lawful ministers and illegal ordination was punishable by imprisonment. In the teeth of opposition from the episcopal establishment, Lauderdale issued a 'Second Indulgence' in 1672, which allowed another ninety ministers to preach; at the same time, field-preaching was made a capital offence.

The irreconcilable Conventiclers were not prepared to accept any concessions from the state, however, and the conventicles spread further into the heartlands of Scotland. The government started harrying them again. Field-preachers who were caught were incarcerated in a dank new state prison which had been built on the Bass

---

1 His retirement proved temporary. In 1679 he accepted a commission again, at the king's request, as commander-in-chief in Scotland during the 'Killing Time'.

Rock, in the Firth of Forth. But still the conventicles grew in number and size. One held on Skeoch Hill in the Irongray parish near Dumfries attracted fourteen thousand adherents: these huge conventicles were beginning to look more like armies than assemblies of worshippers.

As the 1670s drew on, the prospects of a *real* rebellion (unlike the Pentland Rising) seemed to grow more and more imminent in the eyes of the authorities in Scotland. England had suffered a series of severe blows: the Great Plague of 1665 had killed seventy thousand Londoners, and the Great Fire of 1666 had devastated the capital. There had been a disastrous war against Holland, which ended in humiliation when the Dutch fleet sailed up the Medway and towed away the king's flagship with impunity in 1667.

England was also becoming obsessed with fears of a Catholic revival – and not without reason, for the royal family was becoming conspicuously Catholic. The king's wife, Catherine of Braganza, was a Portuguese Catholic. His brother and heir-apparent James, Duke of York, the future King James II & VII, had converted to Roman Catholicism in 1672 and in 1674 had taken a Catholic Italian princess, Mary of Modena, as his second wife.[1] The king himself was believed to have been secretly converted to Catholicism – there were rumours that the Treaty of Dover with France in 1670 had a secret clause in which Charles had promised to declare himself a Catholic. Anti-Catholic feeling was running high.[2] It was not surprising that England fell for the fictitious 'Popish Plot' (1678) invented by Titus Oates; purporting to be a Roman Catholic scheme to assassinate the king, this caused a panic and led to the execution of thirty-five Roman Catholics. It also led to the temporary banishment of James, Duke of York, to Holland in March 1679.

Holland was now ruled by a man of considerable standing, the

---

1 His first wife, a Protestant, had been Anne Hyde, the daughter of Charles II's most trusted minister, Edward Hyde, first Earl of Clarendon. She was a lady-in-waiting in the household in the Netherlands of Princess Mary (sister of James, Duke of York, and widow of William II of Orange). James met Anne there and seduced her, and when he discovered that she was pregnant, in the spring of 1660, he secretly married her. This royal marriage to a commoner caused scandal and opposition (not least from Anne's father), but James insisted on the marriage being recognised. Anne bore him seven children, but only two of them survived infancy: Mary (b.1662) and Anne (b.1665).

2 The classic, and enchanting, paradigm is the occasion when Nell Gwyn, the king's mistress, had her carriage stoned in 1681 in Oxford by a mob which thought that it carried one of the king's *French* mistresses. She lowered the window and pleaded with the crowd: 'Pray, good people, be civil. I am the *Protestant* whore!'

martial William of Orange (the future King William III).[1] He had made his reputation as the heroic defender of the Netherlands against the expansionist aims of Louis XIV of France, and was now the champion of Protestantism in Europe. In 1677 he had married the fifteen-year-old Princess Mary, elder daughter of James, Duke of York, by his first wife, Anne Hyde.

The Scottish dissident Presbyterians found a ready haven in the Netherlands after the Pentland Rising, as the government cracked down hard on the conventicles which were mushrooming over the south of Scotland. Little wonder that the government in Scotland was becoming jittery, haunted by the fear of Dutch aid for another Scottish rising. Besides, the government was in disarray. Lauderdale (who had been elevated to a dukedom in 1672) had been losing authority as his policies became more and more arbitrary; he was now in failing health, culminating in a stroke in 1679. No one was in real control of Scotland.

The gathering tension was to come to a head with the assassination of the man whom the Covenanters had, for long, cast as the arch-enemy of the Presbyterian Kirk: Archbishop James Sharp.

The murder of Archbishop Sharp (1679)

On the afternoon of Saturday, 3 May 1679, Archbishop Sharp was completing a leisurely journey from a meeting of the Privy Council in Edinburgh to his home in St Andrews. He was travelling with his daughter Isabel in a coach and six, with five servants in purple livery, lumbering along the rutted track from Strathkinness over the bleak moorland of Magus Muir down to St Andrews. Just after he had driven through the village of Magus a band of men came clattering through the village in pursuit. Within sight of home the postillion noticed the band of riders galloping hard in pursuit. The coachman whipped up his horses and made a run for it, but the pursuers soon caught up with the coach, slashed through the harness of the horses and forced it to a stop.

These were no ordinary highwaymen. They had been lying in ambush for William Carmichael, the Sheriff of Fife, who was in charge of the military occupation of Fife by troops engaged in the vigorous suppression of conventicles. The sheriff (perhaps forewarned) had not

---

1 William of Orange (1650–1702) was the posthumous son of William II (Stadtholder of the United Provinces of the Netherlands) and his wife Princess Mary, the eldest daughter of Charles I.

gone out that day: instead, the ambushers found that an infinitely richer prize had fallen into their hands – James Sharp, the hated Judas of the government policy towards the Kirk.

They dragged the archbishop out of the coach, stabbing him in the kidneys as they did so. Two of them hustled Isabel aside and disarmed the postillion and the other servants. Grovelling on his knees, Sharp begged hysterically for mercy. In a frenzy of fury his attackers fell upon him, hacking at his arms and head until he fell down dead. They paused only long enough to search Isabel and ransack the luggage, then rode off the way they had come.[1]

A large stone pyramid on Magus Muir marks the site of the assassination. But who were they, these murderous highwaymen? Their leader was a local laird, John Balfour of Kinloch, who later claimed to have 'received a call from God' to commit the murder; his brother-in-law, David Hackston of Rathillet, was another of them; the rest consisted of local farmers, a weaver and a deprived minister. They had spent the previous night in a barn at Baldinny. When they came upon the archbishop, the nature of their mission changed drastically: instead of teaching a lesson to a tough professional soldier, they were now engaged in the assassination of a man who was not only a Privy Councillor but also the Primate of Scotland. God had delivered up to them the man whom they blamed for all the sufferings of the Covenanters, and their divine duty, as they saw it, was to destroy him.[2]

It was the start of the Covenanter Rising which culminated in what has become known as the 'Killing Time'.

The Covenanter Rising (1679)

In the Lanarkshire town of Biggar there stands a restored seventeenth-century farmhouse which has been converted into a Covenanting museum by the Biggar Museum Trust. The Greenhill Covenanters'

---

1 Sir Walter Scott gave a dramatic account of the murder of Archbishop Sharp in one of his early Waverley novels, *The Tale of Old Mortality*, in 1816. In his house at Abbotsford Scott installed in the baronial stone fireplace in the entrance hall an old basket grate which, it was said, had belonged to the archbishop.

2 Archbishop Sharp was buried in the Church of the Holy Trinity in New Street, St Andrews. A beautiful marble memorial, erected by his son in the south transept, features a life-size carving of the archbishop kneeling to receive the crown of martyrdom. Below a lengthy Latin inscription is a powerfully-modelled bas-relief of the assassination on Magus Muir. The tomb itself is empty: in 1725 it was rifled by 'certain ryotous and disorderlie persons', and the body was never recovered.

House contains period displays and relics from the 'Killing Time'; yet it is little known outside Biggar, and attracts fewer than a thousand visitors a year. This lack of interest is symptomatic of a curious blind-spot in the national consciousness, a strange neglect of one of the most remarkable, inspiring and tragic periods in Scotland's history.

Historians now point out, reasonably enough, that the total number of Covenanting 'martyrs' who died in the 'Killing Time' after the battles of Drumclog and Bothwell Brig (see below) was comparatively small – perhaps two hundred in all, far fewer than the number of witches who were burned in the Restoration period (for instance, three hundred witches were put to death in 1661–62 alone). Even so, there was a quality about the way in which the Covenanters faced their persecution which compels profound respect and humility.

It is fashionable, nowadays, to talk of the Covenanters as being 'fundamentalists', in the way in which we call some modern Islamic regimes 'fundamentalist'. But how useful a description is that? Louise Yeoman of the National Library of Scotland says:

> *All religion in the seventeenth century was 'fundamentalist', in our terms. All the religious denominations, Catholic and Protestant, took the Bible as being infallible. They might come up with different interpretations of it, but they were seriously worried about being sent to Hell: they thought that gay people, for instance, or adulterers, were going straight to Hell. Protestants and Catholics alike, they all thought in this way. They were all modern-day fundamentalists.*
>
> *The truth is that Covenanting religion was a religion of the heart. People say that Calvinism was a purely intellectual concept; but when you look at ordinary people's spiritual diaries of the time, you find that they were not concerned with politics: they were examining their feelings, they were having the most incredible emotional experiences in prayer. At the same time they were very strict – they said that having wonderful rapture in your spiritual life should not mean distracting yourself from your everyday concerns; so you had to be active in the world as well as having a deep spiritual life. They were certainly not mad – they were very well-adjusted people. They were people with a particular form of piety which says that you can know that you are one of God's elect, and unconditionally loved by God, by*

examining your heart, by looking for the breathings of the spirit in your heart. This gave people a marvellous independence: what do you care what the laird thinks, when you are having these fantastic experiences of God's love for you? People became very, very attached to the forms of the Church whose teaching led to these marvellous experiences; and that was why ordinary people were prepared to fight for the Covenanting ideals.

There was not much fighting to do – only one splendid victory, at Drumclog, and one devastating defeat, at Bothwell Brig. But for nearly ten years the Covenanters resisted the authorities bravely, fervently, desperately and, ultimately, hopelessly, as they were mercilessly hunted down. Their leaders were always prepared to sacrifice their lives for the joy their faith had brought them, and which they were not prepared to forswear. When they were caught they were sometimes tortured, sometimes imprisoned, sometimes hanged; but whatever their fate they met it with incredible heroism, with a psalm in their hearts and a prayer on their lips. There are scores of sad, proud and often neglected monuments and headstones all over Scotland commemorating the martyrs to the Covenant during the 'Killing Time'.

The Covenanters of 1679 knew all too well that retribution would be on the way after the gruesome murder of Archbishop Sharp. The murderers fled to the west of Scotland, where they joined a party of militant Conventiclers led by Sir Robert Hamilton. On 29 May – the king's birthday and the anniversary of the Restoration – Hamilton and eighty armed followers rode into the royal burgh of Rutherglen. There they made a flamboyant gesture of defiance: they burned copies of all the oppressive Acts of Parliament on the birthday bonfires, then nailed to the Mercat Cross in Rutherglen's wide Main Street a 'Declaration and Testimony' denouncing every violation of the Covenant over the past twenty years.

Meanwhile John Graham of Claverhouse, a thirty-one-year-old Royalist soldier who had been recalled from Europe, was hastening north from Dumfriesshire with his dragoons to put down any rising which might erupt. He was soon in full pursuit of Hamilton and his men, but they eluded him. Claverhouse now heard that a huge conventicle was assembling on Loudoun Hill, near the village of Darvel in Ayrshire. That was his next target.[1]

---

1 John Graham of Claverhouse (1648-89), later created first Viscount Dundee (1688), was a distant kinsman of the 'Great Marquis' of Montrose. He has an extraordinarily contrasting

The Battle of Drumclog (1 June 1679)

The battle which ensued is known by the name of Drumclog, a conspicuous volcanic hump at Loudoun Hill to the north of the A71 from Strathaven to Kilmarnock. Here, on 1 June 1679, Claverhouse came upon the conventicle. It was an enormous assembly, several thousands strong, including whole families. When the minister was warned of the approach of the dragoons he concluded his sermon and snapped his Bible shut: 'Ye have got the theory – now for the practice,' he said. He supervised the withdrawal of the women, children and the very old, and now the conventicle became a host of 1,500 men on Drumclog Moor armed with a variety of pikes and swords, plus a few firearms and fowling pieces. Under the direction of a young divinity student on holiday from St Andrews University, a born soldier named William Cleland,[1] they formed up at the foot of the hill behind a ditch and marsh of deep peat with miry ground beyond, extending around the flanks. They outnumbered Claverhouse's dragoons by about four to one.

Claverhouse realised that a cavalry charge would not get far on that terrain; he ordered his dragoons to dismount, and advanced them in a skirmish line facing the Conventiclers across the ditch. The battle was not to be decided by tactics, however. As the dragoons worked their way forward to the ditch, firing ragged volleys from their carbines, the mass of Covenanters moved forward. Singing their metrical psalms they waded fearlessly across the ditch and attacked the dragoons at close quarters.[2] As the dragoons reeled back, Claverhouse's horse was gashed in the belly and bolted. His men, thinking that their leader had fled, broke and followed him. By the time Claverhouse had found himself another horse and returned to the battlefield it was too late to save the day. Thirty-six soldiers were killed, and seven taken prisoner. Claverhouse and his routed dragoons had to force their way through

---

reputation in Scotland: to the Covenanters he was 'Bluidy Clavers' for his assiduous work in suppressing them; to the Jacobites he was 'Bonnie Dundee' for his dashing feats on behalf of the deposed James VII & II after the accession of William and Mary in 1688 before his death at the Battle of Killiecrankie (see pages 515–16). He was a handsome, debonair, devil-may-care cavalier, and a superb horseman; he rode a magnificent coal-black charger named 'Satan'.

1 William Cleland (1661–89) was one of the most charismatic of the Covenanter military leaders. He was only twenty-seven years old when he met his death in a heroic action in Dunkeld in 1689 (see pages 518–19).

2 Among the first Covenanter casualties was William Dingwall, one of Archbishop Sharp's assassins.

the narrow streets of Strathaven, pelted with stones and refuse, before they could flee to join up with reinforcements in Glasgow.

The Covenanters were in pursuit, but by the time they reached Glasgow the troopers had had time to throw up makeshift barricades. The Covenanters swarmed into the city and up the Gallowgate, but ran into withering fusillades of musket-fire and were eventually forced to abandon the assault.

The Battle of Drumclog was an extraordinary event, and an extraordinary victory. It was the high-point of the Covenanting Rising. But Drumclog was to be the one and only set-piece battle won by the Covenanters against government forces during the Restoration period.

The Battle of Bothwell Brig (22 June 1679)

The victorious Covenanters now mustered in an encampment near Hamilton at Bothwell Brig over the River Clyde, just south of the village of Bothwell. Over the next three weeks Conventiclers flocked to their standard, from the south-west, from Stirling, from Fife, from the Lothians, from Perthshire. But these crucial three weeks were spent not in arming and drilling the raw recruits to the 'army', but in arguing about the uncompromising wording of the 'Rutherglen Declaration'. It became apparent that there were now deep and irreconcilable divisions within the Covenanters' ranks.

There were three distinct factions. The most extreme was the 'Cameronians', associated with a young exiled schoolteacher and field-preacher, Richard Cameron: they advocated unrelenting pursuit of the Solemn League and Covenant, and refused to recognise an uncovenanted government or even to work with anyone who did. They saw the 'indulged' ministers who had returned to the Kirk as a greater menace than even the government's dragoons.[1]

The second faction, and the largest, was led by the Reverend John Welch; they represented a broader, milder strand of Presbyterian opinion, which was quite prepared to accept the 'indulged' ministers into the fold.[2] They wanted a free Presbyterian Kirk, a lawful king, a

---

1   The Cameronian Regiment, one of the most distinguished in the British Army, derives its name from the followers of Richard Cameron. It was originally raised in 1689 by the Marquis of Angus and immediately distinguished itself at Dunkeld in a fierce action against the Jacobite army which had won at Killiecrankie (see Chapter 25). The regiment was finally disbanded in 1968.

2   John Welch (d.1681) of the parish of Irongray, north-west of Dumfries, was a great-grandson of John Knox. He was 'deprived' in 1662 and became involved in the Pentland Rising of

free parliament and General Assembly. And they nailed their own Declaration to the Mercat Cross at Hamilton on 13 June.

The third, and much the smallest, faction was associated with the pacifist views of the Reverend John Blackadder of Troqueer, near Dumfries; he advocated passive resistance.[1]

The old split between 'Resolutioners' and 'Protesters' had dramatically sprung to life again.

While the Covenanters argued, the government hastily gathered a new army to deal with them. To command it they were given the eldest and most attractive of King Charles II's illegitimate sons: James Scott (or Crofts), Duke of Monmouth.[2] Monmouth – handsome, athletic and licentious like his father – was married to Anne, Countess of Buccleuch, and was therefore a Scottish magnate, but had never set foot in Scotland before.

On 22 June, Monmouth reached Bothwell Brig, where the Covenanters were to make their stand. They had about four thousand footsoldiers and perhaps two thousand men on horseback, drawn up a kilometre or so from the bridge on rising ground known as Little Park. Although they looked a formidable host, they were ill-armed, under-officered and still squabbling. They had only one precious piece of artillery, a little brass cannon they had picked up somewhere. On the other side of the Clyde, across Bothwell Brig, stood fifteen thousand government troops under a team of experienced officers (including Claverhouse) headed by the Duke of Monmouth. At the last minute the Covenanters sent a delegation to propose a truce. Monmouth refused to negotiate while the Covenanters remained in arms, but promised that if they were prepared to surrender he would intercede on their behalf with the king.

These terms were refused, and Monmouth attacked. For two hours

---

1666. He escaped from the debacle at Rullion Green to become a leading field-preacher, with a price on his head, but his views became less intransigent as the years went by. After the Battle of Bothwell Brig he escaped to England, where he died.

1 John Blackadder (1615–86) was another of the ministers who were 'deprived' in 1662; he took to the hills with his family and became one of the most celebrated of the Covenanting field-preachers, ministering at some of the largest conventicles in the 1670s. He was outlawed for field-preaching in 1674, but escaped to Holland. He returned to Scotland in 1679 but was soon arrested, and died in the prison on the Bass Rock.

2 The Duke of Monmouth (1649–85) was the son of Charles II's first mistress, Lucy Walters, whom he had met and seduced in Jersey and, according to persistent rumour, secretly married. After Charles's death in 1685 Monmouth would launch an invasion of England as a claimant to the throne, only to be defeated at Sedgemoor and executed.

the government artillery laid down a devastating bombardment of the Covenanter positions. The defenders at the bridge held on stubbornly, until a fresh barrel of gunpowder for their little brass cannon turned out to be full of raisins! At that, they were forced to pull back. The dragoons now poured across the bridge, followed by their own guns, and the battle became a massacre. The Covenanter 'infantry', who had run out of power and shot after the first volley, stood helplessly as their ranks were scythed down by a ceaseless rain of round-shot. They held out for a long time before they broke, and then the rout began. The pursuit was indiscriminate, ferocious and bloody, as Claverhouse avenged his humiliating reverse at Drumclog. Monmouth tried his best to restrain the slaughter: he would not, he said, have men killed in cold blood – that was the work of a butcher. By the end, however, some eight hundred Covenanters had been killed, and 1,400 were taken prisoner.[1]

Next day, General Tam Dalyell arrived in the government camp with a commission to succeed Monmouth as commander-in-chief. He roundly abused Monmouth for his attempts at clemency, declaring robustly that if he had been there the previous day, 'the rogues should never more have troubled the king or country'.

With that, in effect, the Covenanter Rising ended: Bothwell Brig represented the last coherent attempt by radical Covenanters to act as a national armed force. According to the standards of the times, Monmouth now showed considerable leniency despite the strictures of General Tam. He had failed to capture the Covenanter leaders; but as revenge for the assassination of Archbishop Sharp he ordered a symbolic hanging on Magus Muir – five prisoners, chosen at random, from Bothwell Brig. Not one of them had been in any way involved with the murder. Their bodies were left dangling there on the moor, conspicuously, to rot in their chains.

The other prisoners were kept for several months in open cages in the churchyard of Greyfriars Kirk in Edinburgh, where the Covenant had been signed twenty-one years earlier.[2] Those who agreed to sign a bond for future good behaviour were released. The others – 340 of them – were sentenced to transportation to Barbados. Some 250 of

---

1 An obelisk stands on the west bank of the River Clyde at Bothwell Bridge, a few hundred metres from the M74.

2 In the south-west corner of Greyfriars Kirkyard there is now a walled enclosure, open to the skies but barred by an iron gate; it is labelled the 'Covenanters' Prison', and commemorates the place where the caged Covenanters were kept.

them were herded on board the *Crown of London* and packed into the hold. The ship, which sailed from Leith on 27 November 1679, was completely unseaworthy, and on 10 December it was driven on to the rocks at the Mull Head of Deerness, on the extreme eastern coast of the mainland of Orkney. All but fifty of the prisoners, who had been battened below hatches, perished.[1]

Monmouth now issued a fresh Indulgence to Presbyterian ministers, and even legalised conventicles if they were held inside private houses. But the respite in the suppression of the Covenanters proved brief: Monmouth was relieved of his command. The problem was – who should replace him? King Charles was determined that the Covenanting crisis should be defused before it became any worse. To that end, he recalled from 'exile' in the Netherlands his brother and heir-apparent to the throne, James, Duke of York (and Duke of Albany in Scotland); and in late 1679 James was appointed as the king's viceroy in Scotland.

Scotland under James, Duke of York (1680–82)

On the Duke of York's arrival in Scotland, he was received with great marks of honour and welcome by the nobles and gentry, and occupied the palace of Holyrood, which had long been untenanted by royalty.

TALES OF A GRANDFATHER, CHAPTER LII

James, Duke of York, arrived in Scotland on 24 November 1679 with his wife, Mary of Modena, and the best of intentions. He was seen as a worthy man (if rather humourless), and he took pains to be friendly to everyone. He wrote to his brother, the king:

I live as cautiously as I can, and am careful to give offence to none and to have no partialities, and preach to them laying aside all private animosities and serving the King his own way.

James established a glittering court at the Palace of Holyroodhouse which was remembered with wistful nostalgia for many years. He was also concerned to promote the economic development of the nation

---

1 A tall memorial to the drowned prisoners, erected by public subscription in 1888, stands at Scarva Taing, on Deerness, where the bodies were buried. It is the most northerly Covenanting monument in Scotland.

as best he could. He introduced protectionist legislation in 1681 'for encouraging Trade and Manufacturies' to help domestic industry, lifting the taxes on the import of raw materials and on the export of manufactured goods; Glasgow became a manufacturing boom town. To open new markets abroad which could send exotic goods home, James encouraged the Scots Covenanters to found colonies overseas – Perth in New Jersey in 1682 (which lasted until 1702), and Stewart's Town off the coast of South Carolina in 1684 (which was promptly destroyed by a Spanish force in 1686).

But the fundamental issue in Scotland was religious, not economic. At James's first meeting of the Privy Council he had refused to take the Oath of Allegiance because it contained a declaration against Roman Catholicism. He restored the medieval nave of Holyrood Abbey as the Chapel Royal for Catholic worship, and Mass was heard at Holyrood for the first time in more than a century; to accommodate the displaced congregation, he commissioned the building of Canongate Kirk nearby. But James's Catholicism was not a real problem in Scotland – it was the fact that he was still trying to reconcile the moderate Presbyterians with the idea of episcopacy. This only infuriated the radical Covenanters, who would not tolerate any form of episcopacy whatsoever. James's response was to step up repressive measures against them.

The 'Killing Time' (1682–85)

The divisions in the Covenanting party which had become apparent in the weeks before the Battle of Bothwell Brig had widened even further in defeat. After the battle, Richard Cameron, the spiritual leader of the 'Cameronians', returned to Scotland from Holland to stir things up. He was implacably opposed to any compromise with the state and to anyone who accepted the government's Indulgences.

The violence of his preaching at the few open-air conventicles which were still operating dismayed the moderate Presbyterians no less than it alarmed the government. On 22 June 1680, the anniversary of the Battle of Bothwell Brig, Cameron declared himself against the king and government of Scotland. He descended on the Ayrshire village of Sanquhar with a band of armed zealots (the 'Society Folk', as he called his group) and nailed to the Mercat Cross a defiant Declaration 'as the representatives of the true Presbyterian Kirk and covenanted nation of Scotland':

We for ourselves do by their presents disown Charles Stewart, that has been reigning (or rather tyrannising as we may say) on the throne of Britain these years bygone, as having any right, title to, or interest in the said crown of Scotland for government, as forfeited several years since by his perjury and breach of covenant both to God and His kirk . . .

Also we, being under the standard of our Lord Jesus Christ, Captain of Salvation, do declare a war with such a tyrant and usurper and the men of his practices, as enemies to our Lord Jesus Christ, and His cause and covenants.

This flamboyant declaration of war did not lead, as Cameron had hoped, to a popular rising. Instead, he and his followers became marked men. On 22 July 1680, a detachment of 120 dragoons caught up with Cameron and sixty of his men at Airds Moss, just west of Muirkirk in Ayrshire. There was a fierce battle, and more dragoons than Cameronians fell, but eventually the Cameronians were overwhelmed. Cameron and his brother were killed, along with seven others. John Simpson says:

Richard Cameron has been described as 'the Lion of the Covenant'. He was not regarded with favour, even by some of the Presbyterians, because he was thought to have gone too far. His Declaration of Sanquhar, in which he personally deposed the king, was an extravagant act of defiance which sealed his death sentence; but as an act of defiance against a tyrannist government, I would regard it as one of the high points of Scottish history.

The survivors were rounded up and taken to Edinburgh, where they were tortured in 'the Boot'. One of the prisoners was David Hackston of Rathillet, a leader in the assassination of Archbishop Sharp; he was executed after his hands had been cut off. James, Duke of York, took a keen interest in the interrogations, and was present at many of them. Although this earned him a reputation for sadistic cruelty it was in fact the case that he frequently called a halt to the torture when he saw that no amount of pain would persuade the victims to forswear their faith in the Covenant. He wanted no more martyrs, and had the dissidents transported to the colonies instead.

The policy worked – but only for a time. In 1681 James summoned a parliament (the first for nine years) to help him deal with the problem. He wanted to ensure control of every level of society, and he induced parliament to pass the Test Act of 1681; this required every office-holder to swear an oath of loyalty to the king, accepting royal supremacy in all spiritual and temporal matters, and abjuring all political or religious reforms.

One of the nobles in Scotland who found themselves in difficulties with the Test Act was Archibald Campbell, ninth Earl of Argyll, son of the Argyll who had been executed by Charles II in 1661.[1] He had always opposed the repression of the Covenanters; when he was called upon to swear the Test Act oath he prevaricated: he could only take it 'as far as it is consistent with itself and the Protestant religion'. James, enraged by this quibbling, had Argyll imprisoned in Edinburgh Castle.[2]

By the spring of 1682 James felt that his work in Scotland was accomplished, and the king allowed him to return to London; James resumed his place on the Privy Council, where he was able to exercise indirect control over government policy in Scotland through a secret committee of the Privy Council. The effect of the Test Act, however, had been to criminalise large swathes of the population. Once again violence was unleashed as government troopers roamed the country forcing anyone and everyone to 'take the Test'. Smouldering embers of revolt in the radical south-west burst into flames again. The leadership of the radicals was assumed by the Reverend Donald Cargill, who had been wounded at Bothwell Brig but had escaped to Holland. He returned to Scotland after Richard Cameron's death at Airds Moss and preached his funeral sermon. Two months later, in October 1680, at Torwood near Falkirk, he excommunicated the whole government – king, viceroy, ministers and all. For this treason a price of five thousand *merks* (£3,333) was put on his head; he was captured at Covington Mill and beheaded at the Mercat Cross in Edinburgh on 27 July 1681.[3]

The Cameronian movement of radical Presbyterians was now driven completely underground. The few surviving Cameronians (reduced now to only a few hundred extremists) formed themselves into 'Praying Societies', which held their first quarterly Convention in Logan House near Lesmahagow on 15 December 1681. Afterwards they published

---

1 Archibald Campbell, ninth Earl of Argyll (1629–85), had been allowed to succeed his father to the earldom, but not the marquisate: his father was the first, and only, Marquis of Argyll.

2 Argyll was found guilty of treason; but rather than wait for his execution he escaped from the castle wearing women's clothing, and fled to Holland.

3 The bed in which Cargill was hiding when he was captured is on display in the Greenhill Covenanters' House in Biggar.

The Great Hall of Stirling Castle, built around 1500 by James IV, was the largest hall in his kingdom. It has now been sumptuously restored by Historic Scotland at a cost of £22 million. The exterior has been given the radiant finish of its original lime-yellow exterior – 'King's Gold', as it was called.

James V (r.1513–42) succeeded to the throne at the age of barely seventeen months, and became the greatest royal patron of architecture of all the Stewart monarchs. He refurbished Falkland Palace and rebuilt the royal apartments of Linlithgow Palace for his cultured second wife, Marie de Guise, whom he married in 1538. A week before James's death, Marie de Guise gave birth to the future Mary Queen of Scots.

In 1567 Mary Queen of Scots made a disastrous third marriage to the Earl of Bothwell, a tough adventurer who had given her loyal support, and who was probably responsible for the murder of her second husband Lord Darnley; he was newly married, but quickly got rid of his wife in order to marry Mary (allegedly after raping her).

Mary Queen of Scots was executed in Fotheringay Castle on 8 February 1587 on the orders of her cousin Elizabeth of England. A strict security clampdown was imposed on all news of the execution. This sketch is by an unknown artist.

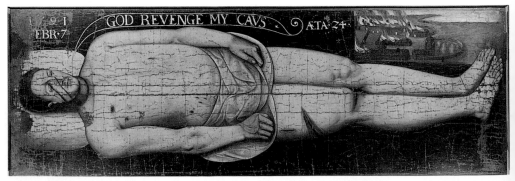

The most macabre portrait in Scotland: the 'Bonnie Earl o' Moray', killed in February 1582. His grieving mother, Lady Doune, commissioned the painting of her murdered son, showing the wounds inflicted on him. It still hangs in the ancestral seat of the Moray family in Darnaway Castle, near Forres. Lady Doune also had her son's corpse embalmed and refused to allow it to be buried, but in 1598 the Privy Council lost patience and insisted on a proper burial.

At the Union of the Crowns in 1603, James VI of Scotland became James I of Scotland, England and Ireland. He had been king of Scotland since his mother, Mary Queen of Scots, was deposed in 1567. He was painted in 1610 at the age of forty-four by De Critz.

Charles I (r.1625–49) was an absentee king as far as Scotland was concerned – he only paid two visits to the country, for his coronation in 1633 and to try to gain support against his English parliament in 1641. He married the Catholic Henrietta Maria, daughter of Henri IV of France; this family portrait (1632) by van Dyck shows the royal couple with the future Charles II (born in 1630) and Mary (the future mother of William III) in her mother's arms.

Oliver Cromwell, Lord Protector of England, invaded Scotland after the Scots proclaimed Charles II King of Scotland and England in 1649. After his 'miraculous' victory at the Battle of Dunbar in September 1650, and his defeat of a Scottish army under Charles II at Worcester exactly a year later, Cromwell incorporated Scotland into the Commonwealth, abolished its parliament and proclaimed a full union of Scotland and England. Miniature by Samuel Cooper, c.1650.

Charles II might have been expected to hold Scotland in special affection – in 1649, a few days after his father's execution, the Scots proclaimed him Charles II of Scotland and England, and crowned him at Scone in 1650. But he never forgot or forgave the months of hectoring and browbeating to which he was subjected by Scotland's ultra-militant Presbyterian ministers. After his escape following the Battle of Worcester, and the Restoration in 1660, he never set foot in Scotland again. The brooding portrait by John Michael Wright depicts him in parliamentary robes, sitting before a tapestry representing the judgement of Solomon.

James VII & II (r. 1685–88) was the last Stewart king of Britain; his reign lasted only four years before he was deposed in the 'Glorious Revolution'. As Duke of York he had been viceroy of Scotland in the early 1680s and had been popular there, despite his second marriage to a Catholic (Mary of Modena), but his policy of religious toleration alarmed those who feared a reversal of the Reformation. This family portrait (1674) by Peter Lely and Benedetto Gennari shows the Duke of York with his first wife, the Protestant Anne Hyde, and their two daughters, Mary (the future Queen Mary, wife of William III) on the left, and Anne (the future Queen Anne).

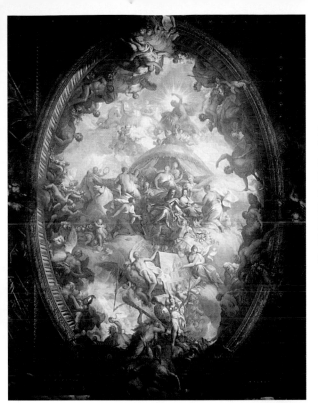

The Apotheosis of William and Mary. This extraordinarily grandiose scene was painted on the ceiling of the Lower Hall of the Royal Naval College at Greenwich to celebrate William and Mary's reign after the 'Glorious Revolution' of 1688. For Scotland, however, their reign was anything but glorious.

The United Parliament of Great Britain was established by the 1707 Act of Union. The House of Commons in session was painted by Peter Tillemans in 1710.

Prince Charles Edward Stuart, the 'Young Pretender': his charisma and dash helped lure the reluctant clans to his standard at the 1745 Rising. Portrait by G. Dupré.

The Duke of Cumberland, son of George II, had not proved himself a particularly able commander, having been decisively defeated by the French at the Battle of Fontenoy in 1745. But at the age of twenty-five he proved more than a match for the Jacobites at Culloden in 1746. Portrait by the studio of David Morier.

The escape of Prince Charles from Scotland after the disaster on Culloden Moor in 1746 has become the stuff of legend. One brief, eleven-day episode during his months on the run has caught the romantic imagination of the world: his journey from North Uist to Skye disguised as the maid ('Betty Burke') of Flora Macdonald. A sentimentalised depiction of their leave-taking, painted by George William Joy in 1891, has adorned countless tins of shortbread over the years.

'Bonnie Prince Charlie' became not so bonnie in the years following his escape to France after the debacle of Culloden. He was painted at the age of sixty-four by Hugh Douglas Hamilton; by then he had become a melancholy figure, a drunkard and wife-beater, shunned by the courts of Europe.

Abbotsford was Sir Walter Scott's dream home. He started building it in 1811. His study was the hub of the house. His desk was illuminated by gaslight (Scott was a director and major shareholder of the Edinburgh Oil Gas Company, and was one of the first private householders in Scotland to install equipment for domestic lighting). In the right-hand corner is a glimpse of the 'Wallace Chair', made from timber believed to have come from the barn in Robroyston in which William Wallace was captured.

The royal visit to Scotland by George IV in 1822 was one of the high points of Sir Walter Scott's public career. He stage-managed the whole event, and persuaded the king and his entourage – and the whole of Edinburgh – to indulge in a frenzy of tartan Highlandism. The levée at the Palace of Holyroodhouse, attended by 456 society ladies with a kilted Sir William Curtis, Lord Mayor of London, in attendance, provided a field-day for English cartoonists like Thomas Rowlandson.

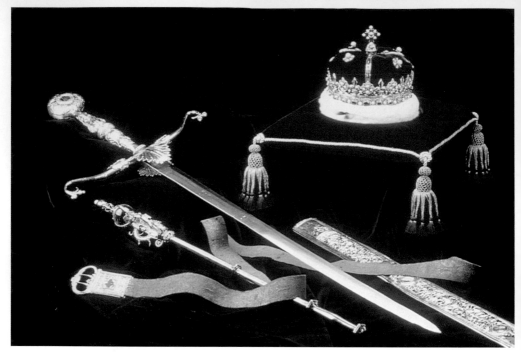

In February 1818 Sir Walter Scott masterminded the recovery of the Scottish Regalia from a bricked-up chamber in Edinburgh Castle. They had been locked away after the Union of the Parliaments in 1707, and no one was quite sure whether they were still in Scotland.

The Queen's progress up Edinburgh's Royal Mile in an open carriage for the official opening of the new Scottish Parliament on 1 July 1999.

a defiant manifesto at the Mercat Cross in Lanark on 12 January 1682. They banded themselves into a 'Union of Correspondence Societies' – in effect, an underground resistance network. To combat it, Claverhouse was given new powers of stop-and-search in the south-west. He has been blamed for every atrocity which took place thereafter (hence the nickname 'Bluidy Clavers'), but it seems that he exercised studied moderation in his own activities ('lest severity alienate the hearts of the whole people').

In September a new Cameronian leader appeared from Holland: James Renwick. As soon as he appeared, the government redoubled its counter-measures. Survivors of old battles were hauled out of their beds, arraigned, and hanged on the spot or taken to Edinburgh for execution. One of them was an eighty-year-old veteran of many battles (including Bothwell Brig), Captain John Paton of Meadowhead.

In June 1684 John Graham of Claverhouse left his own wedding party in Paisley to go in pursuit of a large party of Conventiclers who had been surprised at Blackloch, in Slamannan. He chased them the length of Ayrshire, but lost track of them. Meanwhile, on 29 July, a party of thirty dragoons escorting some Covenanter prisoners from Dumfries to Edinburgh was ambushed at Enterkin Pass near Sanquhar. One of the soldiers was killed, and several of the prisoners escaped. Claverhouse switched his pursuit and caught six of the rescuers near Dumfries on 9 August; they were taken to Edinburgh and hanged. The 'Killing Time' had begun in earnest.

In response, James Renwick issued, on 8 November 1684, an 'Apologetical Declaration and Admonitory Vindication of the True Presbyterians of the Church of Scotland', threatening death to spies and collaborators. A month later, two soldiers were assassinated as they left a tavern in Swyne Abbey, near Bathgate in West Lothian. With hindsight, the parallel with the twentieth-century Troubles in Ireland is uncomfortably close.

The Privy Council was enraged, and escalated the 'anti-terrorist' measures in response. An Abjuration Oath was formulated which required all the people of Scotland to make a formal renunciation of Renwick's 'Apologetical Declaration'. Any person refusing to swear, on demand, could legally be put to death in front of two witnesses.

The war was now open. The Cameronian 'Societies Men', still a tiny Presbyterian minority, embarked on a series of guerrilla raids and murders. The government increased the scope and intensity of its actions. The whole of south-west Scotland was put on a war footing. Even 'Indulged' ministers who had been allowed to return to the fold became the victims of government persecution. Ordinary men and women carrying Bibles were shot on the spot. People working in the fields were summarily executed on the slightest suspicion, even for stammering as they took the Abjuration Oath. This was government terror responding to civil terror, and it was the ordinary people who suffered the most. And yet the spirit of the resistance was never broken.

The end of the 'Killing Time'

King Charles II died of a stroke on 12 February 1685; he had been (as Macaulay put it in his uncompleted *History of England from the Accession of James II*) 'an unconscionable time dying', and it seems as if the political concerns over the succession exacerbated the crisis of the 'Killing Time'. There had been growing tension about the imminent succession to the throne of his brother James. The Duke of Monmouth had been implicated in 1683 in a bizarre scheme to murder the king and eliminate James – the so-called 'Rye House Plot' – and had fled to Holland. The government knew that Monmouth was continuing to make trouble there; he had made alliance with a fellow-exile, the impetuous Earl of Argyll, and they were scheming a simultaneous insurrection in both England and Scotland. For as long as the south-west of Scotland might provide support for an invasion, unrest in the area had to be suppressed with all possible rigour. And then, when the threat of a successful invasion by Argyll had receded, the Terror ended.

The end, or least the culmination, of the 'Killing Time' is usually dated to 13 May 1685. On that day a man named James Kirk was shot on the sands of the Solway Firth for refusing to swear the Abjuration Oath. He had taken part in the Pentland Rising in 1666 but had escaped from Rullion Green, and for nineteen years had wandered round Scotland as an outlaw before he was betrayed by an informer and captured. A cairn and saltire on the roadway on the White Sands at Dumfries marks the spot where he was killed. He was one of the last of the victims of the Terror.

But for the preceding fortnight the field executions had reached their peak. On 1 May, fifty-eight-year-old John Brown, nicknamed the 'Christian Carrier' because he was a runner for the 'correspondence union' of the Cameronian 'Praying Societies', was shot in his home near Priesthill when he refused to swear the Abjuration Oath. His nephew, John Browning, was so unnerved that he revealed the existence of a large subterranean vault stocked with swords and pistols, which Brown had been using as a hiding-place for six years. For his pains, Browning was hanged at Mauchline, along with four others. Five men found hiding in a cave at Ingliston, near Glencairn, were shot on 28 April. Three men were shot in Polmadie on 11 May, and buried in Old Cathcart churchyard. On the same day came perhaps the most horrifically needless execution of all, when two women in Wigtownshire were drowned at the stake. One of them, Margaret Maclauchlan was sixty-three; the other, Margaret Wilson, was eighteen. Both were Radical Conventiclers; arrested when they ventured back from the fields to their homes, they refused to swear the Abjuration Oath and were sentenced to death. They were bound to stakes on the Solway sands below high-water mark at the Bladnoch, outside Wigtown, and were drowned by the incoming tide.

And then suddenly, it seemed, the worst of the Terror was over. There were one or two executions in July. There was a shoot-out between Covenanter fugitives and government troops near Old Cumnock. Finally, the government's Public Enemy Number One, the militant twenty-six-year-old Cameronian preacher James Renwick, was betrayed and captured during a secret visit to Edinburgh. On 17 February 1688 he was hanged, drawn and quartered in the Grassmarket in Edinburgh – the last of the great Covenanting martyrs to die.

Memorials to the martyrs

Halt, Passenger, take heed what you do see –
This Tomb doth show for what some men did die:
Here lies interred the dust of those who stood
'Gainst perjury, resisting unto blood . . .

In the north-east corner of Greyfriars kirkyard in Edinburgh stands the main Martyrs' Memorial in Scotland. It is an unpretentious shrine, erected in 1706 and restored in 1776, built to commemorate the (estimated) eighteen thousand people, from the Marquis of Argyll in May 1661 to James Renwick in February 1688, 'one way or other, murdered and destroyed for the same cause'. About a hundred of them lie underneath the memorial.

Below Greyfriars Kirk, down Candlemaker Row, the Grassmarket has another reminder of these troubled times. At the Bowfoot, in the central reservation, is an enclosure known as the 'Martyrs' Memorial Garden', which was opened in 1954; the centrepiece is a stone roundel which marks the site of the common gibbet: 'On this spot many martyrs and

Covenanters died for the Protestant faith.' A nearby pub, garishly painted in red, is named, with macabre humour, 'The Last Drop'.

But there are martyrs, and there are martyrs. Douglas M. Murray, Principal of Trinity College and Senior Lecturer in Ecclesiastical History at Glasgow University, says:

> *Opinion about the Scottish Covenanters has been divided since the seventeenth century and later generations have viewed them in quite different ways, either as saintly martyrs or as fanatical extremists, or at best as martyrs by mistake . . .*
>
> *There are no simple black-and-white answers. The Covenanters opposed the claims of royal supremacy by the Stewarts (as did the English parliamentarians), but the more extreme Covenanters did not support religious freedom for those who differed from them. They were not fighting for the freedom to worship God in their own way; they opposed what they considered to be an erastian (state-imposed) Church settlement, and sought to establish a Presbyterian theocracy, where all would have had to recognise the Covenants. In that respect, the extremist Covenanters can be seen as political rather than as religious martyrs.*

So what had they all died for, these Covenanters, in the long run? Had it just been an aberrant period of blind blood-letting of religious fanatics by other religious fanatics? Modern historians are in no doubt about the crucial and enduring significance of the Covenanting period. Michael Lynch says:

> *The Covenanting period left different legacies for Scotland. The Covenanters were not simply the militant radicals like Richard Cameron. It represented a mainstream dissent which was totally alienated from the new, restored Episcopalian Church; but it was also alienated from the extremists. What emerged was a very serious fissure in the culture of Scottish Protestantism, which would continue splitting, re-uniting, and splitting again right through the next three centuries. The history of the Covenanters would be used, re-interred, re-used and re-invented for the next three centuries. In the middle of the nineteenth century it would be at the root of the Disruption, the war between the Free Kirk and the Established Church of Scotland; its inspiration would be drawn from this period of Scotland's second Reformation, which had begun with the signing of the National Covenant.*

The Covenanting convulsions formed the setting for one of Sir Walter Scott's most sombre historical novels – *The Tale of Old Mortality* (1816). The original 'Old Mortality' was a kenspeckle character in Scotland at the end of the eighteenth century. His real name was Robert Paterson, a native of the parish of Closeburn in Dumfriesshire, and probably a mason by profession. Scott once met 'Old Mortality' in the churchyard of Dunnottar, in Kincardineshire, cleaning the epitaphs of the Cameronian martyrs.

Scott called his novel a tale in which two sets of 'cruel and bloody bigots' without 'the least idea either of toleration or humanity' opposed one another in ruthless conflict. He contrasted the frenzied courage of the Covenanter with the cruel culture of the cavalier; but through his portrayal of Henry Morton, who seeks to act as an intermediary between the opposing sides, he reflected his own preference for compromise and tolerance, and both parties in the conflict were condemned for their extremism and fanaticism: he condoned neither the government's legalised brutality nor the Covenanters' resort to lawless violence. Above all, Scott explored the true tragedy of the Covenanting period: it was not a conflict between right and wrong, but between right and right.

Chapter 24

JAMES VII & II: THE LAST
STEWART KING (r.1685–88)

*When the Duke of York ascended the throne on the death of his
brother Charles, he assumed the title of James II of England, and
James VII of Scotland.*

TALES OF A GRANDFATHER, CHAPTER LIII

J ames VII & II succeeded to the throne when his brother, Charles
II, died in February 1685. It had been clear for a long time that
the late king's wife, Catherine of Braganza, was unable to bear
children, and that James would succeed. There had been much dispute
about his succession because of the 'Catholic problem': the spectre of
a return to the savage repression of English Protestants by Mary Tudor,
'Bloody Mary', more than a century earlier, was in many people's
minds. Charles II, who had for long been suspected of being a secret
Catholic, had been received into the Catholic Church on his deathbed.
James had been a convert for several years, and his wife, Mary of
Modena, was also Catholic. Parliament, however, trusted him and was
prepared to support him; it passed an Act that the crown must follow
'its natural and legal course of descent', regardless of the heir's religion.
The new king accepted the trust graciously, and pledged himself to
preserve the established order of Church and state:

> *I shall make it my endeavour to preserve this government both
> in Church and state as it is by law established. I know the*

principles of the Church of England are for monarchy and the members of it have shown themselves good and loyal subjects; therefore I shall always take care to defend and support it.

Yet within four years the 'natural and legal course of descent' would be broken, and James VII & II would prove to be the last Stewart king of Britain.

James was fifty-one years old when he ascended the throne. He is usually portrayed as worthy, lugubrious, unimaginative and obstinately obtuse, a 'black-and-white' man who lacked both the intelligence and the subtle skills required to govern his realms at a particularly difficult time. But he had been unswervingly loyal to his brother the king, and had always served him to the best of his ability. He had sown his wild oats in his youth, serving in the Spanish army and later contracting a secret marriage (with Anne Hyde) which had appalled the king at first. His conversion to Catholicism had been an embarrassment, but the deep affection between the brothers had not been soured. James had governed Scotland as Charles's viceroy (1680–82) diligently and not unsuccessfully.

No sooner was he on the throne than he faced armed insurrection, almost simultaneously, in England and in Scotland, led by the exiled Monmouth and the Earl of Argyll. In May 1685 Argyll left Holland with three ships, laden with arms and three hundred men, heading for Scotland. A month later, Monmouth left Holland with a motley crew of eighty followers. Neither rebellion succeeded.

In Scotland, Argyll's attempted rising was a fiasco. He landed briefly in Orkney before raising his standard in Campbeltown on 20 May against 'the hellish mystery of antichristian iniquity and arbitrary tyranny of . . . James, Duke of York, a notorious apostate and bigot Papist'. Argyll had sent the young Covenanter William Cleland, the mastermind of the victory at Drumclog in 1679, to Scotland to link up with the outlawed Cameronians, but the government had moved all extremist prisoners to the dungeons of Dunnottar Castle, in the north-east. Argyll found it difficult to raise any support, even among his own Clan Campbell, but pressed on towards Glasgow nonetheless. Early in June he crossed the Clyde at Kilpatrick, making for Ayrshire, but was captured on 18 June by two militiamen while he was crossing the stripling River Cart near Inchinnan, by Erskine, in peasant clothing. He tried, and failed, to shoot himself, and was put to death on 'the Maiden' – a belated execution of the sentence passed on him in 1681. By government edict, all rebels were to be killed or disabled, their houses burned down and their women and children transported.

In England, Monmouth's rebellion was crushed with equal ease. Monmouth landed at Lyme Regis, in the south-west, and collected an army of seven thousand hastily-armed peasants; his 'cavalry' consisted of farmhands on carthorses. He headed for Taunton in Somerset, where he denounced James VII as a usurper who had poisoned his brother, Charles II. King James sent his favourite commander, John, Lord Churchill (the future Lord Marlborough), to shadow the rebel army. News reached Monmouth that Argyll's rebellion had failed miserably, and he now decided on a desperate gamble. On 5 July he launched a night attack on the royal forces camped at Sedgemoor, and was routed. Two days later he was captured hiding under a hedge, disguised as a shepherd, and was beheaded. His hapless followers were prosecuted with brutal, drunken severity by the notorious Judge George Jeffreys in the 'Bloody Assizes' which ensued: some two hundred people were condemned to death, and another eight hundred were transported to slavery in Barbados.[1]

Scotland had been James's main power-base in the early 1680s, when he was viceroy of the country, and for a time the Scots served him well. He never set foot in Scotland when he was king, but his accession was welcomed at first by the establishment. He claimed to promote religious tolerance, yet more and more people saw this as a stratagem for reversing the Reformation. In 1686 he offered the Scottish parliament free trade with England in return for relieving Roman Catholics of the penal laws against them – legalising Catholicism, in effect. Parliament rebuffed the offer, and was dissolved. King James used his royal prerogative instead. In August 1686 he granted freedom of worship to Catholics in private homes. Six months later he extended this tolerance to moderate Presbyterians and Quakers, provided they did not hold worship in the fields, make processions in the high streets of royal burghs or invade Protestant churches. In June 1687 an even more comprehensive Indulgence granted unlimited toleration to *all* religious denominations: all the king's subjects were allowed 'to meet and serve God after their own way, be it in private houses, chapels,

---

1 One of Monmouth's cavalry commanders was an expatriate Scot named Andrew Fletcher of Saltoun (1653–1716). Fletcher only escaped death as a rebel because he had been sent back to Holland two days after the landing at Lyme Regis: in a quarrel over a horse, he had murdered the expedition's most important local supporter, Thomas Dare. Fletcher would later come to prominence during the protracted debates over the Union of the Parliaments in 1707 (see Chapter 26).

or places purposely hired or built for that use'. Conventicles, however, were still banned.

This Indulgence, so admirable in terms of modern ecumenical attitudes, only irritated and dismayed many in seventeenth-century Scotland – especially the Episcopalians, who saw it as the thin end of the Popery wedge. However, it breathed new life into the Presbyterian Church. Preachers and activists began to come back from exile in Holland; many ministers, freed from compulsion, deserted the 'official' Church and created their own meeting-houses, especially in the southwest. An active Presbyterian party began to develop, with its own regional organisation: Presbyterianism had a future again. In July 1687 a group of Presbyterian ministers, meeting in Edinburgh, even sent a letter of thanks to the king!

James also gave a boost to his nobility. In May 1687 he revived Scotland's premier Order of Chivalry, the Most Ancient and Most Noble Order of the Thistle. He had the nave of Holyrood Abbey refurbished, by Grinling Gibbons, to accommodate the Order, with a throne for himself and twelve stalls for the Knights.[1] James also installed a Jesuit school at Holyrood which offered free education, and had its own printing press.

The king packed his government in Scotland with Catholic placemen. There were, in fact, very few Catholics in Scotland at the time – only about two thousand, according to a contemporary estimate. But it was clear that conversion to Catholicism could help a man's career. Ambitious politicians like the Earl of Perth (the chancellor) and his brother the Earl of Melfort (who became a secretary of state) had earlier ensured their own advancement by returning to the Catholic Church. The Earl of Moray, another secretary of state, followed suit. The command of Edinburgh Castle was given to the Catholic Duke of Gordon. But there was no large-scale conversion in Scotland; the country remained stubbornly Presbyterian and anti-Episcopalian.

Scotland in the 1680s

Although the religious divide and the dissidence of extremist Covenanters dominate the political history of Scotland during the last decade of the Stewart kings, this can give a misleading impression. It was also

---

1   The number of Knights was increased from twelve to sixteen in 1821. A new and richly-decorated Thistle Chapel for the Order, designed by Sir Robert Lorimer, was opened at the east end of St Giles' Cathedral in 1911.

a time of renewed prosperity and intellectual activity, patronised by the king and conducted by men who seemed to have no difficulty in leading double lives.

Take, for example, Robert Sibbald (1641–1722), physician, naturalist and antiquary, Geographer Royal and king's physician. He was one of the founder members of the Royal College of Physicians of Edinburgh, of which James became the patron in 1681 (Sibbald was appointed the first Professor of Medicine at Edinburgh University in 1685). James also supported the Physic Garden in Edinburgh in the grounds of Trinity College Hospital (where Waverley Station is now), which Sibbald had founded in 1667 with Andrew Balfour. Its purpose was practical – to discover which medicinal herbs could be grown in Scotland. It was to be the forerunner of the Royal Botanic Garden in Inverleith. Sibbald is an intriguing illustration of the changing nature of Scottish society. He was originally intended for the Church, but declared:

> *I saw none could enter to the ministrie without ingadging in factions, I preferred a quiet life, wherein I might not be ingadged in factions of Church or State. I fixed upon the studie of medicine, wherein I thought I might be of no faction and might be useful to my generation.*

Despite his concern about 'factions of Church or State', Sibbald converted briefly to Catholicism in 1685 at the persuasion of his patron, the Earl of Perth. It nearly cost him his life: an angry mob broke into his house, and he escaped by the skin of his teeth through a back window. He is remembered first and foremost as a physician, but he also published a geographical and historical description of Scotland, *Scotia Illustrata* (1684), four books on Roman antiquities in Scotland and a *Description of Orkney and Shetland*.

King James also encouraged a major project for the recording of Scotland's architectural heritage by a Dutch draughtsman, Captain John Slezer. The work was not published until 1693, under the title *Theatrum Scotiae* – a magnificent collection of sketches which has provided posterity with a priceless glimpse of the historic monuments of seventeenth-century Scotland.

Another typically versatile virtuoso was Sir George Mackenzie of Rosehaugh (1636–91), who was appointed lord advocate in 1677. He prosecuted the Covenanters with such zeal that he boasted he had never lost a case for the king, and earned the nickname of 'the Bluidy Mackenzie'; but he made other and much more significant contributions. In 1682, as Dean of the Faculty of Advocates, he founded the Advocates' Library, which he called 'this Parnassus and bosom of the Muses'; in 1925 it would form the basis of the National Library of Scotland. In 1684 Mackenzie published his *Institutions of the Law of Scotland*, which tried to give a coherent philosophical structure to the criminal law of Scotland. His literary output was wide and varied, including a prose romance, *Aretina or the Serious Romance* (1661), which is claimed to be the first Scottish novel. He wrote in vigorous but elegant Scots – a tongue ('natural, bold, fiery') which he proclaimed to be superior to English ('weak, courtly and invented') and French.

Men like Robert Sibbald and George Mackenzie laid the foundations for a century of intellectual advance and scholarship in Scotland, and can be said to have been the forerunners of the 'Scottish Enlightenment' in the second half of the next century. But despite the prosperity and the cultural revival of the 1680s, it was religion, after all, which contributed most to the fall of the last Stewart king.

Decline and fall

In England, King James was overtly engaged in a programme of Catholic promotion. The English parliament, like the Scottish parliament, had refused to repeal any anti-Catholic legislation, and was dissolved. James then planted Catholics in high positions in the government, in the universities, in the armed forces, in the Church; and law officers who refused to support these appointments were dismissed. He set up a royal Catholic Council, and established diplomatic links with the papacy.

In April 1687 James issued a Declaration of Indulgence (as he had done in Scotland) which suspended the operation of all laws against Catholics and Protestant Dissenters. This alienated even his High Anglican supporters, and aroused suspicions that his real intention was to bring back popery to Britain. He reissued the Declaration the following April, commanded all the bishops of the Church of England to distribute it and ordered that it be read from every pulpit on two consecutive Sundays. Only two hundred of all the clergymen in England obeyed. Seven bishops, led by the Archbishop of Canterbury, William Sancroft, denounced it and were thrown into the Tower for sedition (they were eventually found not guilty and released).

The last straw came when the queen, Mary of Modena, who had lost five children and suffered several miscarriages and was now forty years old, gave birth to a son and heir – Prince James Francis Edward

– in St James's Palace on 10 June 1688.[1] The king was overjoyed; the country was dismayed: the birth of a son promised a continuing Catholic line, and people simply did not want to believe it. Accordingly, a story was spread that the real prince had been stillborn, and that the infant in question was an impostor who had been smuggled beneath the lying-in sheets in a warming pan. (When the child grew up, however, his resemblance to his parents was unmistakable.)

For the first few weeks of the baby's life there was real doubt as to whether he would live. By August, however, it was clear that he would, and the vehicle of revolution began to move. In the Netherlands, William of Orange, whose wife Mary (James VII & II's daughter) had been heir-apparent until the birth of the baby prince, had been growing increasingly concerned about the prospect of a Catholic England which would doubtless ally itself with the France of Louis XIV and overwhelm little Protestant Holland. He let it be known, discreetly, that if men of goodwill and honest standing wanted him to come over and help to rescue England's religion and nationhood, he would be happy to oblige. Now, with the prospect of a permanent Catholic dynasty looming, seven leading English dignitaries, representatives of the peers and the Churches, sent word to William of Orange, inviting him to intervene.

The Orange invasion (1688)

Immediately on his landing, the Prince published a manifesto, setting forth, in plain and strong terms, the various encroachments made by the reigning monarch upon the British constitution, and upon the rights as well of the church as of private persons and corporate bodies. He came, he said, with an armed force, to protect his person from the King's evil counsellors, but declared that his only purpose was to have a full and free Parliament assembled, in order to procure a general settlement of religion, liberty, and property.

TALES OF A GRANDFATHER, CHAPTER LIV

On 19 October 1688, William set sail from Holland with an armada of sixty warships and five hundred smaller vessels, and a 'personal bodyguard' of fourteen thousand men. A storm drove the fleet back

---

1 Prince James would become better known as the Old Pretender ('James VIII of Scotland'), father of the Young Pretender, Prince Charles ('Bonnie Prince Charlie').

into harbour for a time, but after a delay for repairs it sailed again on 1 November; William landed in the West Country, at Torbay, on 5 November. With him came many Scottish exiles who had been living in Holland. One of the brigades in his army was composed of Scottish soldiers under the experienced command of Captain Hugh Mackay of Scourie. Young William Cleland was there. And so was William of Orange's chaplain, a Scottish prelate of long-standing loyalty to William who would have a huge effect on the future ecclesiastical polity in Scotland – William Carstares. At Torbay the invading army sang Psalm 118 ('O give thanks to the Lord, for he is good'). Then William marched cautiously into Exeter.

In the face of this formidable threat, King James seemed incapable of making a firm, coherent response. He had already, in October, retracted all the measures which had aroused so much opposition, but it was too late – no one trusted his last-minute change of mind. He had a large army of twenty-five thousand men, but was unsure of their loyalty; so he had one of the regiments paraded before him, and told the soldiers that they must either voice their approval of his policies or lay down their arms. All but two of the officers and a few Catholics promptly put down their weapons.

There was always Scotland, however. James ordered a muster of troops there to come to his aid. Graham of Claverhouse, now ennobled as Viscount Dundee, was put in command and crossed the border with six thousand men, leaving only a small garrison in Edinburgh Castle. But by the time they reached London it was already too late: when the king called on his English forces to assemble at Salisbury to confront the Dutch invaders, several of his highest-ranking officers deserted to William – including his favourite protégé, Lord Churchill. The Scottish army was left stranded in Watford, outside London, not knowing what to do or whom to obey.

The cruellest blow, however, was the defection of James's younger daughter, Princess Anne (the future Queen Anne), who was married to Prince George of Denmark. Her closest friend and confidante was Lord Churchill's wife, Sarah. With Churchill's help, they slipped out of London by night and made for Nottingham, where Princess Anne declared for a free Protestant parliament.

King James was distraught. All the fight drained out of him, and he disbanded his English army. The Scottish force was left to fend for itself. James might well have sought safety in Scotland, where he still enjoyed a measure of support. Instead, he chose flight.

The Revolution had started in England, but Scotland was not far behind. When news of William of Orange's relentless advance across England reached Edinburgh, the hatred and fear of Catholicism erupted and a mob went on the rampage on 9 December. It was joined by an enthusiastic crowd of university students and some Covenanters who had moved into the capital from the south-west. In the absence of the army, the Duke of Gordon, Governor of Edinburgh Castle, could only lock the castle gates and take cover. The Chancellor of Scotland, the Earl of Perth, hurriedly left town. The Lord Provost of Edinburgh closed the city gates and posted guards at Holyrood. But nothing could withstand the fury of the mob. As the crowds came down the Royal Mile, the guards in the forecourt of the palace, a hundred strong, opened fire. Twelve students were killed, and many more wounded. The demonstrators regrouped, and attacked again. This time the soldiers were overwhelmed, or joined the rioters. The mob broke into the abbey and vandalised the new splendours of the Chapel Royal. Then they rifled the palace, destroyed the Jesuit school and its printing press, and burned an effigy of the Pope. Finally they broke into the burial vault öf the Stewarts and desecrated the royal tombs.

Meanwhile, in the south-west of Scotland, now stripped of soldiers, the outlawed Cameronians lifted their heads again. Scores of the hated 'king's curates' were forcibly (and frequently brutally) ejected from their manses – they were 'rabbled', as the phrase went. The more extreme Cameronians had no more faith in William than in James, but it was an opportunity to pay off old and long-nursed grievances.

It was James himself who brought the Revolution to a successful conclusion. On 9 December, the day of the Edinburgh riot, he sent his queen and their baby son to France. Two days later he tried to make a run for it himself, but was caught by three Kentish fishermen who were on the lookout for fugitive Catholic priests. He was detained, none too gently, in Faversham for three days, in terror for his life. On 15 December he was brought back to London (where, to his surprise, he was greeted with cheers by the crowds) and placed under house arrest in his palace.

The Viscount of Dundee (Graham of Claverhouse) had left for Scotland with a small loyal troop of only about thirty horsemen. The remainder of the Scottish forces had been put under the command of Captain Mackay and incorporated into William's army.

For William of Orange, who was now in full control in London, the king's presence in London was an embarrassment rather than a threat. The king was his father-in-law, after all, and any use of violence on the king's person – by a foreigner, at that – might well provoke a backlash of sympathy and loyalty for James. William wanted to coerce James, but without the use of force. The king was ordered out of London and commanded to stay at Rochester, from where, as everyone knew, there would be ample opportunity to make his escape abroad. King James took the hint (or the lure) and arranged passage for himself on a frigate bound for France. It was the easiest 'escape' ever engineered.

As King James sailed away he is said to have thrown the Great Seal of England into the Thames. On Christmas Day 1688 he landed at Ambletouse in northern France. He was still the lawful King of Great Britain, but his reign was over. It had lasted for 1,418 days.

Chapter 25

WILLIAM AND MARY: THE 'GLORIOUS REVOLUTION'?

In the meantime, the Revolution had been effected in Scotland, though not with the same unanimity as in England...
TALES OF A GRANDFATHER, CHAPTER LV

In the Pass of Killiecrankie, between Pitlochry and Blair Atholl in Perthshire, the living history of Scotland's roads lies exposed in layers, like the strata of an archaeological excavation.

For hundreds of years the narrow, wooded gorge of the Pass of Killiecrankie was the most difficult and dangerous pass on the main route through the Highlands. Originally, travellers on foot or horse-back would use a winding path beside the tumbling waters of the River Garry. In the 1720s General George Wade built a military road higher up through the Pass to facilitate the movement of government troops to pacify the clans during the Jacobite unrest in the Highlands (see Chapter 27); this became the line of the main through-road to the north – the old A9 – and provided the first route by which wheeled vehicles could travel through the Highlands from Perth to Inverness. In Victorian times a railway was built, with a fine viaduct leading to a busy station at Killiecrankie. Finally, in the 1980s, the dual-carriageway A9 was built high above Killiecrankie to ease traffic congestion down in the gorge.

The Visitor Centre at Killiecrankie, owned by the National Trust for Scotland, sits in the gorge beside the old A9 (now the B8079). The

Centre is designed to celebrate and promote the rich natural heritage of the gorge – the glorious trees and plants, and the abundance of birdlife; but at the southern end of the carpark a small section of General Wade's roughly-paved military road, uncovered by excavation, has been left exposed.

The path at the bottom of the gorge is still there. It was used by Robert Bruce as he retreated north after defeat at the Battle of Methven in 1306; and it was used, in July 1689, by government troops intent on crushing the first Jacobite Rising in Scotland under John Graham of Claverhouse, 'Bonnie Dundee'. Things did not work out quite that way, however, and thereby hangs much more than just a tale: the destiny of Scotland was shaped here, because in 1689 the Battle of Killiecrankie could have altered Scotland's history decisively in the feverish aftermath of the 'Glorious Revolution' of William and Mary.

It was only in England that the turmoil after the departure of James VII & II was hailed as a 'Glorious Revolution', because it had been achieved without bloodshed. But in Scotland there was nothing 'glorious' about it, and there was a great deal of bloodshed.

Since the Union of the Crowns in 1603, the Scots had been under kings who had forced on them a choice they did not want – between their religious allegiance to Presbyterianism and their political allegiance to the Stewart dynasty. This had led to a century of struggle and conflict. Now, suddenly, there was an eerie power-vacuum. Who was in charge? Who was king?

In England the transition was achieved with astonishing blandness. The king had fled the country, had he not? He had absconded, had he not? And therefore, the argument ran, he had effectively abdicated. The fact that this was a legal fiction – he had patently *not* abdicated – was neither here nor there. The throne was vacant. Never mind the fact that the *lawful* male heir was the Catholic infant Prince James; the most *appropriate* heir, in English eyes, was the baby's Protestant half-sister, King James's elder daughter Mary, who was married to William of Orange. Mary was unwilling to ascend the throne without her husband by her side; and William was unwilling to be at her side as a mere consort – his wife's 'gentleman usher', as he put it. For him, it had to be the joint crown, or nothing. So that was how it had to be. What could be clearer, or neater, as far as England was concerned?

Accordingly, on 22 January 1689, a Convention in London declared that James II had 'broken the original contract between King and people', and that he had *de facto* abdicated, if not *de jure*. The Convention then issued a Declaration of Rights as the basis for England's acceptance of William and Mary as king and queen. It stressed the primacy of parliament in government: no laws could be suspended, no moneys levied, no standing army maintained without the consent of parliament. It also stipulated that no Roman Catholic, or spouse of a Roman Catholic, could hold the crown. William and Mary accepted; and on 13 February 1689 they were duly proclaimed King William III and Queen Mary, joint sovereigns of England and Ireland.

William II and Mary II of Scotland

But what of Scotland? In Scotland there was extreme confusion. Thirty peers and eighty 'gentlemen of Scotland' went down to London in January and formally invited the joint sovereigns to take temporary charge of Scottish affairs until a Convention could take place in Edinburgh in March. But it was not a unified delegation. The unrepentant Covenanters of the south-west, who were now practically the only armed force left in southern Scotland, were still undecided about their attitude to the Revolution and to William and Mary. They held an assembly at Lesmahagow on 3 March. The extremists still wanted to have nothing to do with the new monarchs.

A few days later, on 14 March 1689, the Scottish Convention of Estates met to discuss the situation. A division was soon apparent between the 'Williamites' (or 'Whigs') and the 'Jacobites' (Royalist supporters of King James, their name derived from the Latin form of 'James', *Jacobus*). William Douglas-Hamilton, the third Duke of Hamilton,[1] a committed Williamite, who had been appointed William's commissioner to the Convention, arrived with a large body of Cameronians, many of them with arms secreted under their clothing. Hamilton was narrowly elected president of the Convention – a sign of the way in which opinion was forming.

There were two letters to consider – one from William III, and one from James VII & II. William's letter was courteous and conciliatory; he spoke of 'securing the Protestant Religion, the ancient Laws and Liberties of the Kingdom', and expressed a hope for 'a union of both Kingdoms'.[2] James's letter, on the other hand, hastily written on board

---

1 Douglas-Hamilton (1635–94) had come into the dukedom through marriage to Anne, Duchess of Hamilton in her own right.

2 The possibility of a 'union of both kingdoms' was adopted by the Scottish Convention but rejected out of hand by the English parliament. Union did not become a live issue in England

ship on his way to Ireland (see below), was arrogant, rambling and full of woolly promises and vague threats. He hoped

> *that you will neither suffer your selves to be cajoled nor frightened into action misbecoming true hearted Scotsmen, and that to support the honour of your Nation you will contemn the base example of disloyal men and eternise your names by a loyalty suitable to the many professions you have made to us. In doing whereof you will choose the safest part, since thereby you will avoid the danger you must needs undergo. The infamy and disgrace you must bring upon your selves in this world, and the Condemnation due to the Rebellious in the next. And you will likeways have the opportunity to secure to your selves and your posterity the gracious promises we have so often made of securing your Religion, Laws, Property, liberties and rights which we are still resolved to perform.*

Sympathy for the absent king evaporated. On 4 April the Convention decided, almost unanimously, that James VII had 'forefaulted [forfeited] his right to the crown', and that the throne was therefore vacant: James had simply been a bad king who had broken his contract – 'abdication' did not enter into it:

> *They openly declared that James had assumed the throne without taking the oaths appointed by law; that he had proceeded to innovate upon the constitution of the kingdom, with the purpose of converting a limited monarchy into one of despotic authority; they added, that he had employed the power thus illegally assumed, for violating the laws and liberties, and altering the religion of Scotland; and in doing so, had FORFEITED his right to the Crown, and the throne had thereby become vacant.*
>
> TALES OF A GRANDFATHER, CHAPTER LV

The Convention decided to offer the crown of Scotland to 'the Prince and Princess of Orange, now King and Queen of England'; and on 11

---

until the death in 1700 of the eleven-year-old William, Duke of Gloucester, the only surviving child of Queen Mary's sister, Anne, the heir-apparent to the throne (see below). One of the supporters of a full Incorporating Union at this time was Andrew Fletcher of Saltoun, the expatriate Scottish political thinker and radical republican, who wrote to a friend: 'For my own part I think we can never come to any true settlement but by uniting with England in Parliament and Trade.' Fletcher of Saltoun would later argue fiercely against the 1707 Act of Union (see Chapter 26).

April 'William II and Mary II of Scotland' were proclaimed as joint sovereigns at the Mercat Cross in Edinburgh; failing heirs of their bodies, the crown would go to Mary's sister, Princess Anne, and her heirs.

The Convention went on to draw up two documents, the 'Claim of Right' and the 'Articles of Grievances', which set out the main constitutional principles whereby the king and queen should rule. They declared that no Catholic could be king, queen or any officer of state in Scotland; that the royal prerogative could not override the laws of the land; that parliament should meet frequently and debate freely; that no taxes could be raised without the consent of parliament; that any religion other than Presbyterianism was 'contrary to the inclination of the generality of the people'; and that prelacy ('a great and insupportable grievance and trouble to this Nation') should be abolished.

Three commissioners were sent south to offer the Scottish crown to William and Mary on the basis of the Claim of Right and the Articles of Grievances.[1] It is not certain that William and Mary formally agreed to the conditions, but on 11 May 1689 they accepted the crown, and the Scottish commissioners administered the coronation oath to the new sovereigns (there was no coronation). This confusion over whether William and Mary had or had not accepted the constitutional terms laid down by the Convention was to bedevil relations with the monarchy throughout their reign.

The Duke of Hamilton had arranged for William to send to Scotland four of his Scottish regiments under the command of General Hugh Mackay of Scourie; they arrived in Edinburgh late in March 1689. The scattered bands of armed Cameronians were organised into a proper regiment, raised in Douglas by the Marquis of Angus.

But there was another force to be reckoned with in Scotland: the Jacobites. Viscount Dundee (John Graham of Claverhouse) had returned to Scotland after the flight of James VII & II with a troop of fifty horsemen from his old regiment; and Edinburgh Castle was still held by the Royalist Duke of Gordon, although it was now being blockaded by the bands of Cameronians. Viscount Dundee ('Bonnie Dundee', as he would soon be nicknamed, instead of 'Bluidy Clavers') had realised by now that Edinburgh was becoming too dangerous for

---

1   The three commissioners were Archibald Campbell, tenth Earl of Argyll (and later first Duke of Argyll, 1701); Sir James Montgomery of Skelmorlie, an enthusiastic Williamite; and Sir John Dalrymple of Stair, the 'Master of Stair' (1648–1707). Dalrymple was the eldest son of one of the greatest lawyers in Scotland – Sir James Dalrymple, first Viscount Stair (1619–95), author of *Institutions of the Law of Scotland* (1681), popularly known as Stair's Institutes.

him. He scaled the Castle Rock for a conference with the governor (possibly promising him armed support), then galloped north with his fifty troopers to raise the Jacobite standard in the Highlands, where, he knew, there was much residual support for the Royalist cause.

This was not the forlorn, romantic gesture of a Marquis of Montrose. Dundee was aware that the self-exiled James VII & II had sailed from France to Ireland, where he had set up court in Dublin and was planning to create a springboard for an invasion of Scotland and England to recover his lost kingdoms. As James sent an army to deal with the Protestants in the north of Ireland, particularly in Londonderry, Dundee was confident that he would receive reinforcements from Irish Catholic Royalists.

The Battle of Killiecrankie (27 July 1689)

To the Lords of Convention 'twas Claverhouse spoke:
'Ere the King's crown go down there are crowns to be broke,
So each cavalier who loves honour and me,
Let him follow the bonnets o' Bonnie Dundee.
Come fill up my cup, come fill up my can,
Come, saddle my horses, and call out my men;
Unhook the West Port, and let us gae free,
For it's up with the bonnets o' Bonnie Dundee.'
SIR WALTER SCOTT

'Bonnie Dundee' raised the royal standard on Dundee Law and embarked on a muster of clan support in the Highlands. Now an outlaw with a bounty of £20,000 on his head, his name and romantic charisma helped him to raise an army of 2,500 Highlanders from those of the western clans whose chiefs could be persuaded to support the Jacobite cause. However, the expected reinforcements from Ireland turned out to be disappointingly few – only three hundred raw recruits, under the command of Colonel Alexander Cannon – and they brought no money with them. Dundee set up his headquarters in Blair Castle, the imposing seat of the Earls of Atholl in Blair Atholl.

General Mackay was sent to deal with this alarming new threat in the Highlands. In late July he moved to the old cathedral town of Dunkeld, on the north bank of the River Tay, with six regiments of foot, four troops of horse and four of dragoons, and a baggage train of 1,200 packhorses – some four thousand troops in all, many of them new recruits from the Lowlands. At dawn on Saturday, 27 July, Mackay set off northward with the intention of seizing Blair Castle. He reached the Pass of Killiecrankie around noon. His scouts told him that the north end of the Pass was clear, so he started threading his way cautiously along the narrow path through the gorge. At the north end of the Pass he regrouped his forces just above Urrard House.

When 'Bonnie Dundee' heard of Mackay's approach he led his force of 2,500 men and a few horse by a back route to the heights of Craig Eillaich above the north end of the Pass. Mackay saw them on the skyline, and realised that he was in serious trouble. He formed his troops facing uphill on the shelf of land now bisected by the A9, placing his infantry on the wings in long ranks, three or six men deep. What artillery he had was in the centre, with the cavalry behind. In response, Dundee had his Highlanders bunched in three dense divisions, with his cavalry in the centre, opposite Mackay's guns.

Just after 8 p.m., when the glare of the westering sun was fading, Dundee gave the order to charge. The Highlanders fired their muskets before drawing their broadswords and rushing down the hillside in a fearsome barefoot charge. Mackay's infantry unloosed a devastating volley of musket-fire which caused massive casualties, but had no time to fix their bayonets before the clansmen were upon them, overwhelming everyone and everything in their path: men, muskets, bayonets, cannons.

It was all over in a few minutes. Mackay's ranks broke and ran, rushing pell-mell down to the River Garry where one young soldier, Donald MacBean, made an extraordinary life-or-death leap of nearly six metres between two rocks to make his escape.[1] Hundreds of others were not so lucky, and drowned. Only four hundred of Mackay's men managed to ford the river and start heading back towards Perth. But Dundee's troops had suffered grievously as well: almost a third – nearly a thousand – of the clansmen had died in that wild charge. Worst of all, Dundee himself had taken a stray musket-ball under his arm as he waved his horsemen into battle, and died the next day. He was buried in the now ruined church at Old Blair. Officers of both sides were buried in a mass grave on private ground near Urrard House, where a service of commemoration is held each year on the evening of 17 July.

The loss of their leader was a crushing blow for the Jacobites.

---

1 The 'Soldier's Leap' at Killiecrankie is marked, but there is considerable doubt about the precise spot where it happened.

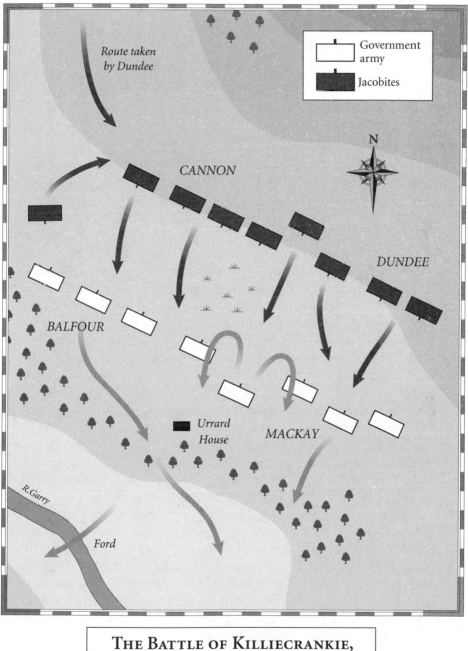

THE BATTLE OF KILLIECRANKIE,
27 JULY 1689

Dundee, and only Dundee, could weld the untamed clansmen into an army; it was his personality and dash which had held it together. His death destroyed any hope of Jacobite success.

The Battle of Dunkeld (21 August 1689)

Dunkeld is one of the most charming little towns in Scotland, nestling beside the majestic River Tay in a bowl of hills. The neatly-grouped whitewashed houses in the centre have been beautifully restored by the National Trust for Scotland. The town holds a significant place in the history of Scotland: it was established as a Celtic fort (*Dun Chaillean*) in about AD 700. The relics of St Columba were brought there for safety at the height of the viking incursions in the Western Isles and Argyll in the ninth century. A fine cathedral was started in 1318, and the 'Wolf of Badenoch' was buried there in 1408. The cathedral was systematically wrecked during the Reformation, in 1560, although the choir was reroofed in 1600 to become the Presbyterian parish church. But the greatest destruction ever visited upon the town was in the summer of 1689, in the aftermath of the Battle of Killiecrankie.

After Killiecrankie, the much-depleted government army under General Mackay regrouped and retreated to Perth, while the Highlanders happily plundered their baggage train. But now the victorious Jacobite army began to disintegrate. Command passed to Colonel Alexander Cannon, leader of the Irish contingent, much to the wrath of the sixty-year-old Sir Ewen Cameron of Lochiel, most formidable of the Highland chiefs, who had come out in person with his clan.[1] Lochiel stalked off in a rage, and many of the clansmen, having tasted the first fierce joys of victory, now began to drift back to their glens and villages.

Colonel Cannon lacked the cavalry to attempt a foray into the Lowlands, so he stayed in Perthshire gathering more recruits to the Jacobite cause. But the government leaders in Edinburgh were unaware of this. They had heard that their army had been annihilated at Killiecrankie (and even that General Mackay had been killed), but not that Dundee was dead. To the best of their knowledge, the Highlanders had broken out of their mountain fastnesses and might even now be poised for a sweep into the south. The Privy Council made hasty plans

---

1 Lochiel is reputed once to have killed an English officer by biting out his throat – 'The sweetest bite I ever took,' he claimed.

to retreat to England if the Highlanders should reach Stirling, the key to the Lowlands.

The belated news of Dundee's death changed all that. While the Highland army was still recouping its losses in Perthshire, the government ordered the Cameronian Regiment to head for Dunkeld, and to hold it at all costs. In command was Colonel William Cleland, only twenty-eight years old but already a veteran soldier; ten years earlier, in charge of a raggle-taggle host of Covenanters, he had worsted Bonnie Dundee – 'Bluidy Clavers' – at the Battle of Drumclog.

The Cameronians, eight hundred strong, reached Dunkeld on Saturday, 17 August after a hurried march from Doune in Stirlingshire, and hastily set to work building defences in the broad Main Street, around the roofless cathedral and behind the walls of a large walled mansion, Dunkeld House, which belonged to the Marquis of Atholl.

On 21 August the Jacobite army appeared in the surrounding hills. It had now increased to a strength of four thousand men, outnumbering the Cameronians by four to one. At 7 a.m. the Jacobites stormed into the attack from all sides; but there was no room in the narrow, winding streets for the fearsome Highland charge. For sixteen furious hours the battle raged. House by hard-fought house the Highlanders advanced; some of them found themselves trapped in houses where they had positioned themselves as snipers, and were burned alive when the Cameronians counter-attacked, locked the doors and set the buildings alight. Little by little, however, the Cameronians were forced back, retreating to the cathedral and to the last redoubt of Dunkeld House as the piles of dead mounted. Dunkeld was ablaze from end to end.

As the Cameronians held off repeated Highland rushes on Dunkeld House, William Cleland took a bullet in the liver and another in the head, and dragged himself away so that his men would not see him fall. All now seemed lost for the defenders. But at 11 p.m., just as the Cameronians were on the point of defeat, the Highlanders – by now exhausted and running low on ammunition – decided to call it a day and withdrew, leaving three hundred of their men lying dead or dying in the blackened shell of the town. The battle was over – a Pyrrhic victory indeed, if either side could claim a victory. In Dunkeld only the cathedral and three houses had not suffered further damage. William Cleland, once again the hero of the Covenanters, was buried at the west end of the medieval nave of Dunkeld Cathedral, three weeks after his old adversary, 'Bluidy Clavers', had been laid to rest as 'Bonnie Dundee'.

In the aftermath of the battle, General Mackay was able to move north through the Pass of Killiecrankie and occupy Blair Castle. The Jacobite dissidents kept up sporadic guerrilla activity, but the threat to the security of the kingdom had diminished. In Ireland, King James had been thwarted by the Protestant citizens of Londonderry, who had withstood a siege of 105 days from April to August 1689; and on 11 July 1690, James was soundly defeated by King William at the Battle of the Boyne, forty kilometres north of Dublin. James fled the field and returned to France, his attempt to reclaim his crown abandoned.[1]

In Scotland, two months earlier, on 1 May 1690, the last Jacobite rebels (about eight hundred Highlanders under the command of Major-General Thomas Buchan) were caught in a night assault near Cromdale, east of Grantown-on-Spey, and routed, some three hundred of the clansmen being killed. It was the end of the 1689 Jacobite Rising, and a decisive outcome for William and the government forces.

How much did it matter, as far as King William was concerned? Alex Murdoch, lecturer in Scottish History at Edinburgh University, says:

> William was a complex man, but above all he was a Dutchman engaged in a long and exhausting struggle with Louis XIV of France; he needed all the financial and military power he could muster in the British Isles, and Scotland was a minor footnote to that struggle. Anything which diverted William from his war with France was an irritant, in the sense that it furthered the French cause; and whenever Scotland required William's attention it was always as this kind of distraction. So, to William, insofar as he cared about Scotland at all, Scotland was always an irritating, even a malevolent, obstacle to his ambitions.

The most pressing problem facing the new government was still the question of religion. King William, an austere, hard-headed man, was by temperament an Erastian; that is to say, he believed that the state should have authority over the Church in all ecclesiastical matters.[2]

---

1 By the terms of the Treaty of Limerick (1692), which ended the war in Ireland, twelve thousand Jacobite soldiers left for France, including hundreds of prominent Roman Catholics. They became known as the 'Wild Geese', and they and their descendants would provide support to Prince Charles Edward Stuart during the Jacobite Rising in 1745.
2 'Erastianism' is named after the Swiss theologian Thomas Erastus (1524–83), to whom this view was attributed.

He had a strong Calvinist background but was tolerant of different forms of Church government, and may well have preferred to see Episcopal Church government in Scotland; but his Scottish chaplain and close confidant William Carstares persuaded him that his real friends were not the Episcopalians, who were all loyal to King James, but the Presbyterians, who had opposed James so bitterly.

The king left the religious question to the Scottish parliament, which in June 1690 passed an Act restoring Presbyterian government and discipline in the Church. In the following month, lay patronage in the Church was abolished and the Act of Supremacy repealed. The Kirk was also given the right to purge all 'insufficient, negligent, scandalous and erroneous ministers'; this was carried out with ruthless militancy against those who refused to take an oath of allegiance: 182 ministers were deprived of their livings for refusing to say public prayers for William and Mary. Over the following twenty-five years about two-thirds of the ministry in Scotland would fall victim in this way.

The problem of the Highlands was equally pressing in the early years of William and Mary's reign. The battles of Killiecrankie and Dunkeld were the beginning but not the end of Jacobite resistance. Certainly, they extinguished Jacobite hopes for the time being; but they sparked off a severe military response to the Highland problem which culminated in the Massacre of Glencoe in 1692.

The Massacre of Glencoe (13 February 1692)

At the northern end of Glencoe ('the narrow glen' in Gaelic) a tall, slender monument commemorates one of the most infamous events in Highland history. Glencoe is the most renowned of all Scotland's magnificent glens: stark, steep and beautiful, and forbidding even in the sunniest weather. Most of the glen is now owned by the National Trust for Scotland which operates a Visitor Centre at Clachaig, in the pastoral lower reaches three kilometres south of the village of Glencoe.[1] The glen provides excellent rock-climbing and skiing facilities, but its celebrity rests chiefly on the tragic event which earned it the by-name of 'the glen of weeping'.

The Jacobite Rising of 1689 had left the Highlands in turmoil. The government hurriedly built a new garrison fortress at Fort William,

---

1   The Visitor Centre at Clachaig attracts more than a hundred thousand visitors a year. A new centre is planned for the present campsite, 'The Clachan', closer to Glencoe Village.

at the head of Loch Linnhe, and troops were deployed at several other strategic points. These were men King William urgently needed in Flanders, where he was embroiled in a war with France. How was the problem to be settled?

In June 1691 John Campbell of Glenorchy, first Earl of Breadalbane,[1] convened a meeting of clan chiefs at Achallader Castle, near Bridge of Orchy in Perthshire. He had brought them together to discuss a proposal for bringing peace to the Highlands: an amnesty for all clan chiefs who had fought against William or fought with one another. In return, the chiefs were to swear personal oaths of allegiance to the king, before a proper magistrate, by 1 January 1692. As a sweetener, William had authorised the payment to the clan chiefs of massive bribes, totalling £12,000, with which to purchase free title to their lands.

The king's secretary of state in Scotland was now the lord advocate, Sir John Dalrymple, the Master of Stair. Dalrymple was an able and dedicated civil servant, totally committed to achieving the security and stability of the new regime. He saw the Highlands as a constant threat, and was convinced that the only way to establish law and order in Scotland was to make an example of one or other of the recalcitrant clans. He was also sure that few of the clan chiefs would submit to William voluntarily, and started drawing up grandiose plans for an exemplary punitive expedition.

But Dalrymple was wrong. By the end of the year it was clear that nearly all the clan chiefs were prepared to swear the required oath of allegiance. By a tragic accident, however, one of the names missing from the official lists of those who had submitted was that of Alasdair MacIain (Macdonald), twelfth Chief of Glencoe, a venerable figure in his sixties, exceptionally tall (well over six feet), with long white hair

---

1 John Campbell of Glenorchy, first Earl of Breadalbane and Holland (1635–1717), was one of the two most powerful clan chiefs in Scotland of his time (the other was the Earl of Argyll). He had taken part in the Royalist rising against Cromwell in 1654, became a Privy Councillor under James VII & II in 1685, and lay low during the 'Glorious Revolution'. He did not play a direct part in the political machinations which led to the Glencoe Massacre – indeed, he seems to have tried to hold back those who were intent on military reprisals in the Highlands; but in 1695, after the publication of the Commission of Inquiry into the Massacre, he was imprisoned for his earlier dealings with the Jacobite chiefs at Achallader, but was released when the king intimated that he had acted with royal approval. After the Union of the Parliaments in 1707 he would sit as a representative peer in the British parliament from 1713 to 1715, but he continued to have dealings with the Jacobites at the time of the 1715 Rising.

and a spiked moustache. The Macdonalds of Glencoe were not a prominent clan; some of them had fought in the Jacobite army at Killiecrankie, but they were noted cattle-thieves and had made themselves highly unpopular with neighbouring clans – especially the Campbells.

By an extraordinary series of mishaps, Alasdair MacIain Macdonald of Glencoe had missed the deadline for taking the oath of binding loyalty to King William. He was one of the many chieftains who had waited for formal permission from 'the king across the water' to take the oath, which permission did not arrive in the Highlands until 28 December. With time running out fast, Macdonald set off at once and presented himself at the newly-built government fortress at Fort William on 31 December. But there he was told that the military commander could not accept the oath – only the sheriff at Inveraray could do that. Macdonald now had to make the freezing, ninety-five-kilometre journey south to Inveraray, carrying a helpful explanatory letter from the commander at Fort William. On the way he was stopped by a party of grenadiers who refused to accept the validity of the letter and held him for twenty-four hours. By the time he reached Inveraray on 3 January 1692 the deadline had passed, and the sheriff, Sir Colin Campbell of Ardkinglass, was absent. As a result, it was not until 6 January that Macdonald was able to make his submission. His oath was forwarded to Edinburgh, but the government lawyers refused to accept responsibility for it, as it had been delivered five days late. Accordingly, Macdonald's name was left off the official list.

So who should be singled out for exemplary punishment for not taking the oath of loyalty to the new government? Some chiefs had made no attempt to submit – men like Macdonald of Glengarry, for instance; but he lived in a well-fortified house at Invergarry in the Great Glen and would be difficult to attack. The Macdonalds of Glencoe, on the other hand, were a much softer target, living in scattered huts at the foot of a glen which could easily be blocked at both ends. According to Dalrymple, they were also 'the only popish clan in the kingdom, and it will be popular to take severe course with them'; in fact, they were probably Episcopalian, if anything. But they were ideal victims for a terrible and symbolic act of punishment to frighten everyone else into submission.

The fate of the Macdonalds of Glencoe was now sealed. King William duly signed the requisite orders given to the commander-in-chief in Scotland, Sir Thomas Livingstone. They included an ominous sentence about Glencoe:

If M'Kean [MacIain Macdonald] of Glencoe and that tribe can be well separated from the rest, it will be a proper vindication of the publick justice to extirpate that sept of thieves.

The soldier chosen to execute this 'proper vindication of the publick justice' was a Campbell – Captain Robert Campbell of Glenlyon, a kinsman of the Earl of Breadalbane; he was sixty years old, an inveterate gambler, and in a notoriously hard-drinking age he drank harder than most. His orders from Dalrymple were that he was to be 'secret and sudden'.

Two companies of Argyll's regiment, with about seventy men in each, set out from Ballachulish on 1 February, led by Glenlyon and a fellow-captain, Thomas Drummond, and marched into Glencoe.[1] They had a warrant for quartering their men in the homes of the five or six hundred Macdonalds living at the foot of the glen; this was a common expedient when collecting arrears of taxation. While the men awaited further orders they spent nearly a fortnight enjoying the hospitality of the Macdonalds, joining enthusiastically in their evening *ceilidhs* (parties).

The orders arrived from Ballachulish on 12 February, signed by Major Robert Duncanson. Glenlyon was playing cards that evening with the chief's sons, John and Alasdair (who was married to Glenlyon's niece). The orders were brutally explicit – Glenlyon's forces were to fall upon their hosts and massacre them:

> *You are hereby ordered to fall upon the Rebells, the MacDonalds of Glenco, and putt all to the sword under seventy. You are to have a special care that the old fox [Alasdair MacIain Macdonald] and his sones doe upon no account escape your hands. You are to secure all the avenues thatt no man escape. This you are to putt in execution at fyve of the clock precisely.*

As it happened, the operation was badly botched. It was snowing hard, and additional contingents from Fort William and Ballachulish who were intended to block off all the escape routes did not arrive on time.

At five in the morning, two of Glenlyon's officers burst into the house of 'the old fox' at Carnoch and shot him as he was getting out of bed. The sound of gunfire there, and in another house at Achtriachtan,

---

1   It should be stressed that this was a government operation, not the outcome of a clan feud; only about a dozen of the soldiers were Campbells.

alerted the rest of the Macdonalds, who ran, half-naked, for the icy sanctuary of the hills. Both of Alasdair MacIain Macdonald's sons, and his baby grandson, escaped.[1] Nevertheless, at least thirty-eight of the clan – men, women and children – were systematically slaughtered; many others died in the raging snowstorm.[2]

From Dalrymple's point of view, the Massacre was only regrettable because it had been a failure – it did not 'extirpate that sept of thieves'. Nor did it succeed in killing off opposition to the change of dynasty. In the long term it did precisely the opposite: it gave a sharp boost to Jacobite sympathies in the western Highlands – and blackened the name of Campbell for ever in Highland memory – because the massacre had been committed in such brutal breach of all the sacrosanct ethics of hospitality.[3]

Such was the public outcry that the Scottish parliament was forced to react when it met in March 1693. A committee was appointed to look into the Massacre, but its report was not published and nothing was done. Two years later, as public revulsion showed no signs of abating, a royal commission was appointed to examine the chain of events leading up to the events in Glencoe. It published its report a month later, in June 1695. This time there was no cover-up: the Massacre had been an act of murder, and the government was condemned for having 'barbarously killed men under trust'. There had to be a scapegoat; the blame was laid squarely at the door of Dalrymple, who resigned his office as secretary of state, unrepentant but totally discredited.[4] Practically everyone else concerned was exonerated – particularly King William himself, who, although he had signed the orders, had perhaps done so without being fully aware of their intended outcome.

---

1   The elder son, John, who became the thirteenth Chief, received a royal pardon and rebuilt the family home at Carnoch. His brother Alasdair fought for the Jacobite cause in 1715 alongside Glenlyon's son, John Campbell. The baby grandson, another Alasdair, became fourteenth Chief of the Macdonalds of Glencoe in his turn; he and his clan joined the 1745 Rising and fought – and lost – at Culloden.

2   The exact number of dead has never been established. The clan never gave its own count.

3   Many commentators have pointed out that Glencoe was by no means the first or the worst atrocity committed by the government in the Highlands in the seventeenth century. There had been a much more savage attack on the Clan Ranald on the island of Eigg in May 1690 by a naval force under the command of an Ulster commodore, Edward Pottinger, when the fighting men of the clan were away. Women were raped and butchered, children were murdered. But this never attracted the horrified fascination which Glencoe has inspired for more than three centuries.

4   Dalrymple was later rehabilitated, and was created Earl of Stair in 1703. He died in 1707.

The Darien Scheme

In his own personal affairs the Scotsman is remarked as cautious, frugal, and prudent, in an extreme degree, not generally aiming at enjoyment or relaxation till he has realized the means of indulgence, and studiously avoiding those temptations of pleasure to which men of other countries most readily give way. But when a number of the natives of Scotland associate for any speculative project, it would seem that their natural caution becomes thawed and dissolved by the union of their joint hopes, and that their imaginations are liable in a peculiar degree to be heated and influenced by any splendid prospect held out to them ... Thus the Scots are often found to attempt splendid designs, which, shipwrecked for want of the necessary expenditure, give foreigners occasion to smile at the great error and equally great misfortune of the nation, – I mean their pride and their poverty. There is no greater instance of this tendency to daring speculation, which rests at the bottom of the coldness and caution of the Scottish character, than the disastrous history of the Darien colony.

TALES OF A GRANDFATHER, CHAPTER LIX

The 'disastrous history of the Darien colony' brought the seventeenth century to a ruinous end for Scotland – and for the 'Glorious Revolution' of William and Mary. It was an ambitious scheme to set up a Scottish merchant colony at Darien, halfway across the isthmus of Panama in central America.[1] From this mercantile entrepôt, Scots entrepreneurs would garner the wealth of both hemispheres and transport the riches of Asia across the narrow neck of land at Panama from the Pacific Ocean to the Caribbean Sea, thus avoiding the long and hazardous sea-journey around either the Cape of Good Hope or Cape Horn. The scheme ended in expensive failure and fiasco – but, like so many disasters, it had seemed an excellent idea at the time.

How did it all come about?

Scotland in the mid-1690s was still smarting from the scandal of

---

1 Darien had been named during the Spanish Conquest. The name would be immortalised by Keats in his sonnet 'On First Looking Into Chapman's Homer':

> *... Or like stout Cortez when with eagle eyes*
> *He star'd at the Pacific – and all his men*
> *Look'd at each other with a wild surmise –*
> *Silent, upon a peak in Darien.*

the Glencoe Massacre, and King William was still embroiled in his war with France. He was also a man in deep grief: in December 1694 his beloved queen, Mary, had died of smallpox at the age of thirty-two. It had been Mary's claim, as the elder daughter of King James VII & II, which had brought William and Mary to the thrones of Scotland and England. William was now king alone; and his interest in Scotland was even more marginal than before. Scotland was very much on its own, and was languishing in the economic doldrums.

To tackle the economic problem, Scotland tried to join the big league in the business of empire-building. In 1693 parliament had passed an Act for 'Encouraging of Foreign Trade', which extended to trading companies the privileges already enjoyed by manufacturing companies. Two years later, in 1695, another Act established a trading corporation entitled the 'Company of Scotland Trading to Africa and the Indies', with extensive powers to found colonies in any unclaimed territories and to make exclusive trade treaties, with the backing of the crown. Mercantilism was all the rage now; and so was the burgeoning science of political economy. One of the pioneers of the new science was a Scots-born financier named William Paterson.[1]

When the Company of Scotland was floated in London it attracted strong support from English merchants who wanted to compete with the East India Company and its monopoly on Oriental trade; of the £600,000 required from its proprietors, £300,000 was subscribed in London. But the East India Company was determined to put a stop to the enterprise, and King William had no enthusiasm for it:

> *I have been ill-served in Scotland, but I hope some remedy may yet be found to meet the inconvenience that may arise from this Act.*

---

1 Paterson (1658–1719) was born in the village of Tynwald, near Lochmaben in Dumfriesshire. He spent much of his childhood in England, where he became a merchant trading with the West Indies (he could only do this from England, because the Navigation Laws prohibited all but English residents from engaging in trade with the English colonies). He came back from his travels in 1681 and settled in London, where he made a small fortune and started proclaiming the advantages of central banking. In 1691 he proposed the establishment of the Bank of England, which was founded in 1694; the subscribers of a total of £1,200,000 to the government (at 8 per cent) were to form the Company of the bank. Paterson was appointed one of the first directors, but resigned after a few months and returned to Scotland, where the Bank of Scotland (which he also helped to found) was established in 1695.

The 'remedy' was a parliamentary decision that any of the Company's proprietors resident in England could be prosecuted; whereupon the £300,000 of investment from London vanished. The Company of Scotland was now on its own. In a new patriotic advertising campaign it promoted itself as a national panacea which would reinvigorate the Scottish economy:

> *This Company . . . is calculat for the general interest of Our Nation . . . Our Nobility and Gentry who are Landed Men will get their rents better paid and raised; our Tenants and Labouring people better employed . . . The Poor will hereby find Work and Food.*

The campaign was extraordinarily successful. Investors in Scotland, large and small, fell over themselves to put their money in. And now William Paterson, the crusader of political economy, came to the fore. He had An Idea – an idea which he had been nursing for several years.

Paterson gave the Company of Scotland a target. He urged it to concentrate on one spectacular target: the Isthmus of Darien, which, he claimed, he had visited in his travels. It was, he said, a land of green jungle, white sand, blue water, great forests and exotic birds and beasts. It was the narrowest point of the Americas, and he called it 'the door of the seas and the key of the universe'. Establishing a colony there would be a sure-fire bonanza:

> *Trade will increase, and money will beget money, and the trading world shall need no more to want work for their hands, but will rather want hands for their work. Thus, the door of the seas and the key of the universe, with anything of a sort of reasonable judgement, will of course enable the proprietors to give laws to both oceans and to become arbitrators of the commercial world without being liable to the fatigues, expenses and dangers, or contracting the guilt and blood of Alexander and Caesar.*

Ah, the temptations of the easy profit, the quick buck. Something like a quarter – a quarter! – of Scotland's liquid assets were invested in the Company of Scotland: £220,000 in total. In 1696 the Company decided to go ahead with the Darien venture. It would not be a colony of conquest, as in South America, or a colony of plantations, as in the West Indies. It would be a free emporium where all the world could exchange goods, without the exploitation of slavery. There was nothing Utopian or pie-in-the-sky about the scheme. Alex Murdoch says:

> *Darien represented a great vision of Scotland as an important player in the history of European expansion overseas. It saw Scotland as integral to this process of tapping into the wealth of the extra-European world as other nations had been doing. It was the Scots, two centuries ahead of the rest of Europe, who saw the strategic importance of Panama as a channel between east and west and who tried to do something which was not successfully completed until the construction of the Panama Canal early in the twentieth century.*

By the summer of 1698, 1,200 eager would-be colonists had enrolled, expecting to make an easy fortune. Many of them were the younger sons of landed gentry; others were officers and men from the Scottish regiments who had fought in the war against the French – among these was Captain Thomas Drummond, who had commanded one of the contingents which had taken part in the Glencoe Massacre. Another colonist was the begetter of the Darien scheme, William Paterson, who took his wife as well.

In July 1698 the expedition set sail from Leith in five ships, full of optimism but short of experience and resources. The ships had been specially built in Amsterdam and Hamburg for the expedition: the *Caledonia*, of 350 tons and carrying fifty guns; the *St Andrew* and the *Unicorn*; and two auxiliary sloops. They carried supplies of beer, brandy, casks of beef (which was already rotten) and biscuits (which were already mouldy), Bibles, axes and needles; they also carried an unlikely cargo of wigs, woollen hose and tartan plaid as trading articles. There were huge crowds on Edinburgh's Calton Hill and along the Fife coast to wave them goodbye.

The voyage took sixteen weeks, via Madeira and the West Indies, and it was a grim journey; there were daily burials at sea of victims of fever or flux. Eventually, in November 1698, the ocean-weary colonists made land in Limon Bay, on the north coast of Panama, and sailed further inland to a sheltered inlet at Darien. They named their settlement 'Caledonia', and set to and built a township of huts which was named 'New Edinburgh'. Meanwhile Captain Thomas Drummond built a makeshift defensive citadel which was robustly named 'Fort St Andrews'. The fact that the land on which they had settled had been claimed by Spain did not deter them for a moment.

Welcoming as it seemed, the isthmus was not the tropical paradise they had expected. The surrounding jungle was dense and impenetrable. When the rainy season came, the downpour was heavy and unceasing. The colonists were soon in dire straits. Their clothes and shoes rotted away. Their supplies were infested with maggots. The beer and brandy were soon finished. One of the sloops made contact with the English colonists on Jamaica, and unsurprisingly found no takers for wigs, woollen hose or tartan plaid. Fever raged. The leaders of the colonists bickered and quarrelled, their ministers preached damnation and hellfire. William Paterson's wife died, and he himself was prostrated by a virulent tropical disease.

And yet the letters which the colonists sent home to Scotland were full of sunny optimism, praising the natural resources of the region and the friendliness of the natives. No doubt they were whistling in the dark; but they also desperately needed reinforcements of supplies, trading stocks and people, and did not want to say anything which might discourage further support from home. The apparently promising news from the settlement electrified Scotland, and 'Darien fever' ran riot. There were wild stories that gold was to be found there for the taking, and a second expedition was planned, with a new flagship, the *Rising Sun*, being fitted out in the Clyde.

But no word of all this activity reached the beleaguered colonists. Instead, blow followed blow. In the middle of May 1699 a Jamaican sloop brought news that the previous month King William had issued instructions to the governors of all of England's colonies on the American seaboard from Boston to Barbados, forbidding English subjects to trade with the Scots or to sell them arms, ammunition or provisions. William had effectively pulled the plug on the Darien colony. But why?

King William was working to his own secret agenda – he was intent on maintaining good relations with Spain. Darien was on Spanish territory, and royal support for the new colony would be taken as a grave breach of treaty obligations. The settlers were now vulnerable to attack by Spanish troops whenever they wished.

This news was enough. In June 1699 it was decided to evacuate Darien. The *Caledonia* and her sister ships sailed northwards to New York, as they were now in no state to hazard the dangers of the Atlantic. At Jamaica the *St Andrew* was abandoned after all her officers and 140 colonists had died at sea. Eventually, only the *Caledonia* was able to make her way back to Scotland; of the original 1,200 colonists, fewer than three hundred had survived.

By the time the *Caledonia* was limping homewards, however, the second Darien expedition had already put to sea. At the end of September 1699 the *Rising Sun*, accompanied by the *Duke of Hamilton* and the *Hope of Bo'ness*, sailed from the Clyde – twelve days before the directors of the Company of Scotland learned from New York that the colony had been abandoned. The Company was horrified by the news, and promptly despatched another expedition of two hundred soldiers under the command of a determined young lieuten-ant-colonel named Alexander Campbell of Fonab, in Breadalbane, with orders 'to repossess yourself, by force of arms, of our shameful deserted colony'.

The second expedition arrived at Darien by the middle of November, after another death-ridden voyage. The new colonists found the much-vaunted settlement deserted and overgrown. Once again fever and hunger took their toll: soon there were six hundred people lying sick in the hovels of New Edinburgh. But at least they now had military support. Colonel Campbell of Fonab took the initiative and marched against a fort which the Spaniards were building nearby at Tubuganti, and won a heartening victory on 17 February 1700. The euphoria did not last long. The Spaniards came back, and on 1 April 1700 the colony was obliged to capitulate.

The surviving colonists were allowed to pack their possessions and sail away in their three ships. By the time they reached Jamaica, another two hundred of them had died. The *Rising Sun* and her sister ships headed for New York. The *Hope of Bo'ness* was wrecked on the rocks off Cuba. The other two ships were overwhelmed by a hurricane off South Carolina, and were lost with all hands.

It was the end of Scotland's attempt to become a major colonial nation. Hundreds of enterprising Scots had died. A quarter of the nation's circulating capital had been lost. And all this had happened while Scotland was suffering five years of dreadful weather which had caused a succession of failed harvests and led to the death, through starvation, of at least a fifth of the population.[1]

Chris Whatley, Professor of Scottish History at Dundee University, says:

The failure of the Darien scheme was a hugely important event, in that it demonstrated how exposed the Scots were in a world

---

1 William Paterson survived, however, and would take an active part, as a pro-Unionist financial adviser, during the long debates on the Act of Union of 1707.

of increasingly rampant mercantilism. It was very difficult to grow economically without naval protection on the high seas. The Scots had a tiny mercantile marine (only two frigates!) compared to that of England, and particularly compared to that of Holland.

Darien would have changed everything for Scotland; but the failure of Darien made it clear to the Scots that some other way would need to be found if they were going to eliminate under-employment and poverty, and deal with the critical situation into which the Scottish economy was falling at the end of the seventeenth century.

How do people react to disaster on such a scale? Scotland was shattered by the news of the Darien venture's collapse – but soon the grief turned to furious anger: anger against the Company of Scotland but, above all, anger against the king who had sabotaged the enterprise so callously. Seditious political pamphlets began to appear, such as *The People of Scotland's Groans and Lamentable Complaints*, which listed the injuries Scotland had suffered as a consequence of the Union of the Crowns in 1603: 'Our Sovereignty and Freedom is violated, and Laws trampled upon, our Trade interrupted.'

In an attempt to diminish the bitterness, King William and the House of Lords proposed a closer union between the two countries. But the House of Commons dismissed it out of hand. Nothing could have been further from people's minds in 1700 than closer union.

The end of the 'Glorious Revolution' (1702)

The two kings of Britain were now approaching their ends.

In France, the exiled James VII & II was living out his last sad years. After his defeat at the Battle of the Boyne in 1690 he had abandoned all hope of recovering his throne; he now lived in permanent exile with his wife, Mary of Modena, at the château of Saint-Germain-en-Laye, twenty kilometres west of Paris, where his great-grandmother, Mary Queen of Scots, had spent her childhood. He was supported by a generous monthly allowance of six hundred thousand *livres* from Louis XIV; it was in Louis's interest to maintain an exiled Jacobite court as a constant threat to King William's regime.

James's only consolation in his last years lay in his family. His wife had borne him a daughter in May 1692 – Louisa Maria Theresa – whom he adored and called 'La Consolatrice'; and his son, Prince

James Francis Edward Stuart,[1] was growing into a handsome young man. In March 1701, James VII & II suffered a debilitating stroke. He never recovered, and died on 5 September; he was sixty-seven years old – the greatest age attained by any Stewart monarch. He was buried in the parish church at Saint-Germain-en-Laye.

Louis XIV immediately recognised the thirteen-year-old Prince James Francis Edward Stuart as 'King James VIII and III of Great Britain', thereby encouraging the Jacobite movement in Scotland. It was seen as tantamount to a declaration of war; and William was forced to start making preparations for another conflict with France.

Meanwhile, the question of the legitimate succession to the throne had reared up again. On 30 July 1700, William Henry Stewart, Duke of Gloucester, son and heir of Queen Mary's sister Anne, died of a fever. He was eleven years old, and had been severely disabled (probably with encephalitis), barely able to walk without support. His death precipitated a huge crisis in the sister kingdoms of the British Isles.

The Duke of Gloucester had been Princess Anne's only surviving child out of the eighteen infants she had borne. She was now thirty-six years old, and it was thought unlikely that she and her husband, Prince George of Denmark, would have another child. William and Mary had never had any children, and William had shown no inclination to remarry after Mary's death in 1694. Anne would become queen after William's death – but who would succeed her? There was no direct and obvious Protestant heir to the throne of Britain.

The choice was both simple, and extremely difficult: either to revert to the main line of Stewart descent (in the person of Prince James Francis Stuart, the Catholic son of James VII & II), or to seek a successor in another, collateral branch of the House of Stewart among the royal houses of Europe. To the English, any return of the Catholic Stewarts was unthinkable. In Europe, one branch seemed the most promising – the House of Hanover. It was descended from King James VI & I through his daughter Elizabeth, the 'Winter Queen' of Bohemia. The present head of the House was Elizabeth's youngest and sole surviving child, Sophia, the sprightly seventy-year-old Electress of Hanover. She had two great advantages: she was staunchly Protestant (albeit Lutheran); and she had a forty-year-old son, who was also Lutheran

---

1 'Stuart' was the French spelling of 'Stewart', and had been used by Mary Queen of Scots. Although the royal line is always called 'Stewart', I use the 'Stuart' spelling for the last Jacobite pretenders to the throne.

– Prince George of Hanover (whom Princess Anne had once rejected as a potential husband!).

So, in the summer of 1701, the English parliament (without consulting or even informing the Scottish parliament) passed the Act of Settlement ('An Act for the further limitation of the Crown and better securing the Rights and Liberties of the Subject'); this Act conferred the thrones of England and Ireland, after the death of William and of Anne, and any heirs of their bodies, on this distant kinswoman, Sophia of Hanover, and her heirs.

On 21 February 1702 King William was out riding near Hampton Court when his horse stumbled on a molehill and threw him. The fall broke William's collarbone. Bronchitis set in, and the king died on 8 March. As far as Scotland was concerned, it was a suitably inglorious end to the 'Glorious Revolution' which had brought little but bloodshed and grief. The Jacobites were jubilant, and from then on they would drink exultant toasts to 'the wee gentleman in velvet' – the mole which had caused the king's fall.

King William had never set foot in his kingdom of Scotland. The 'wee gentleman in velvet' brought to the throne William's sister-in-law, Queen Anne – and led, indirectly, to the ultimate loss of Scotland's 'independence' as a nation with the Union of the Parliaments in 1707.

Chapter 26

QUEEN ANNE (r.1702–14) AND THE
ACT OF UNION (1707)

On the 22nd April, the Parliament of Scotland adjourned for
ever. Seafield, the Chancellor, on an occasion which every Scots-
man ought to have considered as a melancholy one, behaved
himself with a brutal levity, which in more patriotic times would
have cost him his life on the spot, and said that 'there was an
end of an auld sang.'

TALES OF A GRANDFATHER, CHAPTER LX

A former summerhouse, situated in the Holyrood Road vehicle
service access of Moray House College of Education in Edinburgh, was one of the settings for a hugely significant event in the
history of Scotland – the signing of the 1707 Act of Union between
Scotland and England. It was not the only place in which signings of
the Act took place, but the circumstances there were much the most
dramatic; nevertheless this unassuming little stone building, with a
weathered stone greyhound squatting forlornly on its red pantile roof,
has fallen into sad disrepair.

Moray House, once the home of the Earl of Seafield, Lord High
Chancellor of Scotland, was built in 1625.[1] The little building in the

---

1 The house, with its elegant conical gate piers and corbelled balcony, is the finest aristocratic
   mansion to survive in the Canongate. It was inherited in 1643 by the Countess of Moray;
   it was from its balcony that the Argyll wedding party jeered at the captive Marquis of

access lane was part of a garden pavilion – the 'summerhouse' – whose outside door led into a conservatory. When the Act of Union was passed, Seafield and some of his fellow-parliamentarians (who had still to sign the Act) went to their usual haunt, a tavern named the Union Cellar in the High Street, where they became the target of an angry mob protesting against the Union. They fled down the Royal Mile to Moray House, pursued by the baying crowd. The heavy gates were hastily closed and barred, and Seafield and the others retired to the pavilion in the garden to complete the signing of the Act of Union.[1]

The whole area – including the grounds of Moray House – has changed greatly in recent years as a result of large-scale redevelopment; and it is still changing. As Moray House College expanded, the summerhouse, stripped of its conservatory, was moved to its present position at the rear of the grounds; it is set against the adjoining wall of the old Courage brewery (now a brewing research centre belonging to Scottish & Newcastle), and is used as an outhouse for casual storage. The arched doorway and the windows are boarded up. Inside, the decaying ornamental ceiling looks down on a clutter of broken furniture, and the second of the pair of stone greyhounds which used to sit on the roof.

In the entrance hall of Paterson's Land (the main college building) is an intriguing panel in vitreous mosaic representing a highly stylised map of Edinburgh.[2] A circular Latin inscription states:

> In the garden of Moray House on the 1st of May 1707 the ambassadors of Scotland subscribed the Act of Union between England and Scotland.

The design features Moray House, and highlights the summerhouse with its red pantile roof in which the Treaty was signed. Coincidentally, the historic little building (which is A-listed) is only a few yards from the site which has been earmarked for the new Scottish parliament.

Montrose on his way to his trial and execution in 1650. It now serves as the office building of Moray House College of Education, whose buildings cover the extensive original gardens of Moray House.

1 James Grant, in his *History of Old and New Edinburgh*, described the occasion and the pavilion in the garden of Moray House: '. . . the old summer-house, surmounted by two greyhounds – the Moray supporters – wherein, after a flight from "the Union cellar", many of the signatures were affixed to the Act of Union, while the cries of the exasperated mob rang in the streets without the barred gates'.

2 The mosaic, designed by William J. Macaulay, was presented to Moray House in 1938.

How odd, then, that it has been so neglected. What the Earl of Seafield called 'the end of an auld sang' deserves a more dignified memorial.[1]

The long road to union

'Union', in one form or another, had been a large factor in relations between Scotland and England for all of a century. The accession of James VI of Scotland as James I of England had created the Union of the Crowns in 1603. James VI & I had wanted even closer union, and in 1604 commissioners from Scotland and England had discussed a Union of the Parliaments and common citizenship, but nothing came of the idea. Fifty years later, Oliver Cromwell imposed Union by force of arms after annexing Scotland, but this gunshot marriage had been dissolved at the Restoration of Charles II in 1660. Nevertheless, Scotland was far from being an 'independent' state. Tom Devine says:

> Scottish foreign policy had moved with James to London in 1603 and there was a great grievance that, thereafter, foreign policy for both kingdoms was exclusively designed to suit English needs. Thus the three Dutch Wars of the later seventeenth century were fought against a nation that was England's deadliest commercial rival but one of Scotland's main trading partners. Similarly, the fact that the Scots and English shared the same monarch did not prevent the London parliament levying punitive customs dues on such key Scottish exports as linen, cattle, salt and coal, at a time when England was becoming the single most important Scottish market. Increasingly, Scottish interests argued that the Regal Union had to be amended and reformed because of the untold damage it was doing to Scotland.[2]

The furious resentment of the Scots against England's imperious foreign policy was aggravated by the political machinations which had helped to scupper the Darien venture. There were also King William's wars against France, which had a serious effect on Scotland's commercial activities. Even so, the idea of a full Union was far beyond the range of possibility, never mind probability. King William himself had

---

1 Moray House is now part of Edinburgh University, which has plans to restore the summerhouse to its former state and give it its proper place in the historical context of the Royal Mile.

2 T.M. Devine, *The Scottish Nation 1700–2000* (Allen Lane, 1999, p.xxii)

canvassed the idea in 1702, but no one else wanted it, apart from the king's appointees in Scotland. Certainly, the English parliament showed no enthusiasm for it, because it would have allowed the Scots to have a share in the lucrative trade with the English colonies in America.

What eventually brought the debate on Anglo–Scottish union to the forefront of politics on both sides of the border was (not for the first time in Scotland's history) a succession crisis: the long-term implications of the death, on 30 July 1700, of the eleven-year-old William Henry Stewart, Duke of Gloucester, son and heir of King William's sister-in-law, Anne. The Duke of Gloucester, a Protestant like his mother, was the last of the direct royal Stewart line, and his death focused attention with stark clarity on the future of the joint sovereignty of Britain.

The English parliament responded to the crisis by passing, unilaterally, the Act of Settlement of 1701, whereby the eventual succession to the throne was bestowed on the House of Hanover after the death of Queen Anne.

Queen Anne (r.1702–14)

Queen Anne ascended the throne in 1702 after the death of her brother-in-law, King William. She was the last, but by no means the least, Stewart sovereign of Britain. Ironically, she is partly remembered by the rather bizarre popular phrase, 'Queen Anne's dead.'[1]

Anne did not have a happy life. She was the younger sister of Queen Mary II, daughter of James VII & II by his first wife, the Protestant Anne Hyde. At the age of eighteen she married Prince George of Denmark, who was tall and handsome and very little else (Charles II said of him, 'I have tried him drunk, and tried him sober, and there's nothing in him'). She suffered a series of difficult pregnancies – eighteen babies in all, of whom only one (William, Duke of Gloucester) survived infancy.

Anne was always a rather large woman, but as she reached middle age she became enormously fat – so gross that she could scarcely walk. Her face was scarred with smallpox and blotched with erysipelas, her eyesight was failing and she suffered severely from gout and

---

1 The phrase was used as a slighting retort to someone who was retelling stale news. It came about because the government was so concerned about a possible Jacobite rising that the news of her death in 1714 was kept from the public for several weeks.

arthritis. In his *Memoirs*, Sir John Clerk of Penicuik, a baron of the exchequer and a staunch Unionist, described her with anguished sympathy:

> *One day I had occasion to observe the calamities which attend human nature even in the greatest dignities of life. Her Majesty was labouring under a fit of gout, and in extreme pain and agony, and on this occasion every thing about her was much in the same disorder as about the meanest of her subjects. Her face, which was red and spotted, was rendered something frightful by her negligent dress, and the foot affected was tied up with a poultice and some nasty bandages. I was much affected at this sight, and the more when she had occasion to mention her people of Scotland, which she did frequently to the Duke [Queensberry]. What are you, poor mean-like mortal, I thought, who talks in the style of a sovereign?*[1]

When Anne succeeded King William on the throne, there was no question of her kindly but negligible husband (of whom she was extremely fond) becoming king-consort – the possibility was never even considered. Queen Anne was very much her own woman. She worked hard on state papers, despite her failing eyesight. She was stubborn, and quite capable of browbeating her ministers.

Although she was a 'real' Stewart, Anne did not feel herself to be particularly Scottish – in her coronation speech to her first parliament she said, 'I know my heart to be entirely English.' She knew little about Scotland and never went there as queen; but she had spent a few months there as a girl of sixteen when her father, as Duke of York, held court in Scotland in 1681. She called it 'one of the most profound formative experiences' of her life, and was in no doubt about 'Scotland's immense importance to English security'.

Yet after the 1707 Union, and despite the fact that she had concurred in the 1701 Act of Settlement which designated the Hanoverian succession to the throne, Anne would flirt (or pretend to flirt) with the idea of restoring the Stewarts to the throne in the person of her half-brother, Prince James Francis Edward Stuart ('the Pretender' – claimant – as she called him). Like Queen Elizabeth of England, Anne enjoyed creating uncertainty, and even allowed her ministers to visit 'the Pretender' in France. She harboured an intense dislike for her

---

1 J.M. Gray (ed.), *Memoirs of the Life of Sir John Clerk of Penicuik* (Edinburgh, 1892).

designated successors – Sophia, the Electress of Hanover, and her son, the future George I – and would not permit them to visit Britain during her lifetime.[1]

The major preoccupations of Queen Anne's reign were national unity (through the 1707 Act of Union) and the War of the Spanish Succession against France (1702–7). Her captain-general, the Duke of Marlborough (the former Lord John Churchill, who had helped her at the time of the 'Glorious Revolution'), gave her victory after stunning victory – at Blenheim (1704), Ramillies (1706), Oudenarde (1708) and Malplaquet (1709); and Marlborough's wife Sarah enjoyed the queen's intimate favour and confidences. The Whig government was replaced, however, by a Tory administration in 1711, and Queen Anne fell out with the Marlboroughs and transferred her ardent affections to Sarah's cousin, Mrs Abigail Masham.

Above all, Queen Anne was concerned with the stability of her realms. In 1706 she wrote:

> All I desire is my liberty in encouraging and employing all these that concur faithfully in my service, whether they be called Whigs or Tories, not to be tied to one or the other. For if I should be so unfortunate as to fall into the hands of either, I shall not imagine myself, though I have the name of Queen, to be in reality but their slave, which, as it will be my personal ruin, so it will be the destroying of all government; for instead of putting an end to faction it will lay a lasting foundation of it.

For Anne, and for her ministers in England and Scotland, a union of the parliaments was essential for the security of her two fractious realms. But would Scotland be willing to take part in such a union?

Prologue to the 'Great Debate'

After Anne's accession to the throne in 1702, a new Scottish parliament had to be called. The election brought large-scale Jacobite gains. One of the new members of this parliament (the last Scottish parliament, as it turned out) was the radical intellectual Andrew Fletcher of Saltoun, a small estate in East Lothian. Fletcher was an expatriate Scot who loved travelling and preferred to live abroad, but who returned to take up

---

1 When Anne died in 1714, at the age of forty-nine, she had the small satisfaction of having outlived Sophia by a few weeks.

the political cudgels on behalf of Scotland at this critical time in the nation's destiny.[1]

Andrew Fletcher was a political philosopher who believed in pragmatism. For him, necessity was the mother not so much of invention as of opportunity. He saw that England was in difficulties – over the British succession not less than over the War of the Spanish Succession – and needed Scotland's support; this, he claimed, presented the Scots with the opportunity to exact a high price for their acquiescence to union. The growth of mercantilism, he argued, and the impact of commerce on national development, had changed the whole structure of politics and overturned previous ideas of the traditional significance of kingship. In a series of rhetorically-charged speeches he urged his fellow-Scots to seize the opportunity of liberating Scotland from domination by the English administration and of securing Scotland's independence under any future shared king.[2]

The Scottish parliament responded to Fletcher's urgent oratory by passing a flurry of provocative Acts which they knew the English would find insupportable. There was an 'Act anent [concerning] Peace and War', which insisted that no sovereign of the two countries (Anne and her successors) could declare war or make alliances without the Scottish parliament's consent. There was a 'Wine Act', which formally permitted French wines to be imported, in contravention of the English trade embargo on France. There was a 'Wool Act', which encouraged the export of Scottish wool and banned the import of wool from England.

But much the most provocative of all the measures prompted by Fletcher of Saltoun was the 'Act of Security', first put forward in 1703, which declared that when (or if) Queen Anne died without an heir, the Scottish crown was not to go to 'the successor to the crown of England unless there be such conditions of government settled and enacted as may secure the honour and independence of the crown of this kingdom':

Upon the said death of her Majesty, without heirs of her body, or a successor lawfully designed and appointed, the foresaid

---

1   Fletcher (1653–1716) spent most of his life in London or in Continental cities like Amsterdam and Paris, living off the revenues of the Saltoun estate. He was briefly involved in the Duke of Monmouth's rebellion in 1685, but made his name in Europe as a radical political thinker. He was to be elevated into the role of Great Patriot Hero in the pantheon of Jacobite, and now Scottish Nationalist, mythology; but modern historical research (particularly by John Robertson of St Hugh's College, Oxford) suggests that he was rather more of a 'discriminating' patriot than a Patriot Hero.

2   He published his *Speeches by a Member of Parliament* immediately, in 1703.

Estates of Parliament convened or meeting are hereby authorised and empowered to nominate and declare the successor of the Imperial Crown of this Realm, and to settle the succession thereof upon the said successor and the heirs of the successor's body, being always of the Royal Line of Scotland and of the true Protestant religion.

The Act demanded major concessions: Scotland would not be bound to have the same sovereign as England in future unless the English parliament granted to the Scots 'free communication of trade . . . and the liberty of the plantations'. What is more, it demanded that 'there should be such conditions of government settled and enacted as may secure . . . the freedom, frequency, and the power of parliament, and the religion, liberty and trade of the nation from English or any foreign influence'.

This formidable act, which in fact hurled the gauntlet of defiance at the far stronger kingdom of England, was debated in the Scottish Parliament, clause by clause, and article by article, with the utmost fierceness and tumult. 'We were often,' says an eyewitness, 'in the form of a Polish Diet, with our swords in our hands, or at least our hands on our swords.'

The Act of Security was carried in parliament by a decided majority, but the Queen's commissioner refused the royal assent to so violent a statute. The Parliament, on their part, would grant no supplies, and when such were requested by the member of administration, the hall rung with the shouts of 'Liberty before subsidy!' The Parliament was adjourned amidst the mutual discontent of both Ministers and Opposition.

TALES OF A GRANDFATHER, CHAPTER LX

The Act raised, directly and bluntly, the prospect of having, once again, two monarchs in a divided island. In the following year (1704) the Act came up again, and this time the Scots refused to pay the taxes ('supply') to finance the Scottish administration, and threatened to disband the army, unless the Act were accepted by Queen Anne's administration – which, with the greatest reluctance, it was.

The gauntlet had been thrown down, and the English were galvanised into action. The Protestant succession to the throne was at risk. Louis XIV of France had openly supported Scotland's Jacobites by endorsing the young 'James VIII & III' as the true heir to the thrones of Scotland and England, and had even hinted at the possibility of an invasion to help the Jacobite cause in Scotland.

Scotland, in English eyes, was now endangering England's national security in the War of the Spanish Succession against France. Also, the English captain-general, the Duke of Marlborough, needed a constant supply of regiments of Scottish troops in order to maintain his military superiority over the French. The Scottish parliament, which throughout its history had never been much more than a tame poodle, was showing its teeth and running amok.

The only answer, as far as English ministers were concerned, was an 'Incorporating Union' which would dissolve the Scottish parliament and create a new United Kingdom legislature. But the Scots would have to be frightened first. So, in February 1705, the English parliament passed the 'Alien Act':

> An Act for the effectual securing of the kingdom of England from the apparent dangers that may arise from several Acts lately passed by the Parliament of Scotland.

There was no pretence of a velvet glove concealing the iron fist of blackmail. Unless the Scottish parliament appointed commissioners to negotiate, within nine months (by Christmas 1705), for an Incorporating Union between England and Scotland, severe penalties would be imposed: all non-naturalised Scots living in England would be treated as aliens; all Scottish estates in England would be seized; and all the major Scottish exports to England – black cattle, linen and wool – would be barred. The Scots were outraged by this economic bludgeon, of course; they must have expected a response of this sort, but it signalled a dramatic new development: England had now abandoned its traditional opposition to closer union – indeed, was insisting upon it.

The reaction of the Scots was predictably violent. In retaliation for the Darien disaster, agents of the Company of Scotland had arrested an English East India trader, the *Worcester*, on a specious charge of 'piracy' against one of the Company's ships. Now, in a frenzy of anglophobia, the captain of the *Worcester* was put on trial with two of his crew and all three were hanged on 11 April 1705.

The Scottish parliament had little alternative, however, to yielding to England's political pressure. In accordance with the demands of the Alien Act, the Scots agreed to the establishment of a joint parliamentary commission, with thirty-one members each from Scotland and England; in a return gesture, the English parliament repealed the offensive Act.

The man chosen by the government to mastermind the Scottish end of the Union negotiations was John Campbell, second Duke of Argyll, who had recently inherited the title from his father. He was twenty-seven years old, ambitious and arrogant, and was serving as a colonel under Marlborough on the Continent. When Queen Anne's chief minister, the Lord Treasurer of England (the Earl of Godolphin), requested Argyll to go to Scotland to further the Union, he refused until he was given promises of lavish rewards (including an English peerage).

There was no guarantee that the joint commission would be able to agree terms; but when the composition of the Scottish delegation was being discussed in Scotland's parliament, an extraordinary twist took place which made such an outcome much more probable – all because of the premier Scottish peer, the Duke of Hamilton.[1] Hamilton was acclaimed as the patriotic leader of the anti-Union opposition movement (the 'Country Party') in parliament. Late in the evening of 1 September, however, when most of the parliamentarians had left the chamber, Hamilton proposed that the Scottish delegation on the joint commission should be nominated (like the English delegation) by Queen Anne and her English ministers:

> The Parliament is too much in heats and feuds, and can never agree on proper persons; but the Queen, who is free from partiality, may doubtless make a good choice. But if she shall make a bad choice, we will be safe, for all must return to us again, and we may send the Act back to the place whence it came.

The government could hardly believe its luck. A division was rushed through and the proposal was passed, albeit by only four votes. It ensured that the Scottish negotiators would be predominantly pro-Union.

The joint parliamentary commission met in Whitehall in April 1706 to negotiate the Articles of Union. The two sides sat in separate rooms and communicated with one another only in writing. Within ten days

---

1 James Hamilton, the fourth Duke of Hamilton (1658–1712), was the son of Anne, Duchess of Hamilton in her own right, and her husband the third Duke. The family had for long nursed a rather wistful hope that a Hamilton might one day succeed to the throne of Scotland, and throughout the Union debate of 1706–7 the Duke of Hamilton was to play a bafflingly ambiguous part.

they had agreed on the outline shape of the Treaty; within a further ten weeks a set of twenty-five Articles had been agreed. These Articles were then to be debated separately by the two parliaments.

The cardinal principle of the Treaty was full incorporation. The two parliaments were to unite. The Hanoverian succession was to be accepted for both countries. The Scots were to keep their separate civil laws and Church settlements. There was to be complete freedom of trade within Britain and with the colonies. The Scots won some important concessions over trading privileges – but the central issue of a peaceful 'entire union' could be expected to provoke considerable anger and opposition in Scotland. And it did.

Throughout the summer of 1706, as the composition of the Treaty became known, angry opposition to the proposed Union spread throughout Scotland. The Presbyterian Church was deeply concerned about the possibility of Anglican episcopacy being imposed on Scotland, and the General Assembly and the presbyteries fervently opposed the proposed Union; every Sunday the pulpits rang with impassioned denunciations, creating alarm about a general breakdown in law and order. When the Great Debate began, the opposition had not subsided. In his *History of the Union*, Sir John Clerk of Penicuik was later to write of 'a great backwardness in the Parliament of Scotland for a union with England of any kind whatever', and estimated that not even 1 per cent of the population approved of what was being proposed.

'The end of an auld sang'

THAT the Two Kingdoms of England and Scotland shall ... forever after be United into One Kingdom by the name of GREAT BRITAIN.

TREATY OF UNION 1707, ARTICLE I

The stage for the final fateful debate, from 3 October 1706 to 16 January 1707, was Parliament House in Edinburgh. Here the Scottish parliament met to consider the most controversial, the most divisive and the most dramatic Act ever to come before it: an Act which would effectively bring down the curtain on its own existence. Each of the twenty-five Articles agreed by the joint commission was to be debated separately. The failure of any one to be accepted meant that the Treaty, as it stood, could not be ratified; but amendments were permissible with the approval of the commissioners.

The Scottish parliament was a single-chamber assembly with a total of 147 members, representing the nobility, the county members, and the burgesses. The main groupings were clearly defined: the powerful, pro-Unionist, government-controlled 'Court Party' – the largest single party; the 'Jacobites' (or 'Cavaliers', as they called themselves); the patriotic 'Country Party'; and a group of twenty-five members – the 'New Party' – who had broken away from the Country Party and were exotically called the *Squadrone volante* (the 'Flying Squad'!).

Some Scots (mainly the Court Party) wanted an 'Incorporating Union' which would transfer legislative authority for 'Great Britain' to Westminster. Others (the Jacobites) were demanding complete independence for Scotland with a separate monarchy. A few wanted a federal, rather than an incorporating, Union. But all wanted a new and fairer settlement with England and the crown.

The *dramatis personae* were as devious and unpredictable a group of protagonists as Shakespeare himself could have conjured up:

John Campbell, second Duke of Argyll (1678–1743), head of the most powerful clan in Scotland and the political 'manager' of the government Court Party.

John Hamilton, second Lord Belhaven (1656–1708), a committed Jacobite and a strenuous opponent of Union.

Sir John Clerk of Penicuik (1676–1755), a cultured and erudite 'neutral', whose head supported Union but whose heart did not. He was a Scottish delegate to the joint parliamentary commission of 1706. As well as his *Memoirs*, he wrote a Latin *History of the Union of Scotland and England*.

Daniel Defoe (1661–1731), English journalist and novelist, and reporter of the Union debates for the leaders of the English parliament.

Andrew Fletcher of Saltoun, a vehement republican and member of the Country Party; he advocated a federal union instead of an incorporating union.

James Hamilton, fourth Duke of Hamilton, erratic and half-hearted in his convictions, the premier Scottish peer and nominal leader of the Country Party.

George Lockhart of Carnwath (1673–1731), a leading Jacobite lawyer and politician, author of the damning *Memoirs Concerning the Affairs of Scotland* (1714).

John Erskine, sixth Earl of Mar (1675–1732), Secretary of State for Scotland and a leading government minister; later he would become a Jacobite and lead the 1715 Rising.

William Douglas, second Duke of Queensberry (1662–1711), the queen's commissioner to the Scottish parliament.

John Ker, fifth Earl of Roxburgh (later first Duke), a leading member of the *Squadrone volante.*

James Ogilvy, first Earl of Seafield, Lord Chancellor of Scotland, and a leader of the government Court Party.

No one knew how the Great Debate in the Scottish parliament would end: for Union, or against Union. Opinion in the country was generally against, but the opposition in parliament was divided and fragmented. Sir John Clerk of Penicuik played the role of a sort of Greek chorus to the impending drama:

> *Here you may find several persons exalting a union of confederacy [such as Andrew Fletcher of Saltoun], and at the same time exclaiming against that article of the treaty concerning equal duties, customs and excises, as if there could be a union of confederacy . . . without equal burdens.*
>
> *Others quarrel with the charges the nation will be put to in sending sixteen Peers and forty-five Commons to the parliament of Great Britain, and at the same time, both in words and writing, they cry out against that number as a small, dishonourable representation.*
>
> *Some are regretting the extreme poverty of the nation and scarcity of money; yet, notwithstanding, they exclaim against the Union as a thing that will ruin us; not considering how any condition of life we can fall into, can render us more miserable and poor than we are.*
>
> *In a corner of the street you may see a Presbyterian minister, a Popish priest, and an Episcopal prelate, all agreeing in their discourse against the Union, but upon quite different views and contradictory reasons.*

In the wings hovered the threats of an economic blockade and even, as a last resort, military conquest by England.

The Great Debate opened on 3 October 1706, with the Duke of Queensberry presiding as queen's commissioner, supported by the Earl of Mar as secretary of state. When the curtain rose, the noises-off were loud and intimidating as the Edinburgh mob made itself heard. George Lockhart of Carnwath wrote:

> *During this Time, the Nation's Aversion to the Union increas'd; the Parliament-Close, and the Outer-Parliament House, were crowded every Day when the Parliament was met, with an*

infinite Number of People, all exclaiming against the Union, and speaking very free Language concerning the Promoters of it. The Commissioner [the Duke of Queensberry], as he pass'd along the Street, was cursed and reviled to his Face, and the D— of H— [Duke of Hamilton] huzza'd and Convey'd every Night, with a great Number of Apprentices and younger Sort of People, from the Parliament House to the Abbey, exhorting him to stand by the Country and assuring him of his being supported.

The antics of the mob grew ever more threatening. The Duke of Queensberry was pelted with stones and filth and needed a military escort to Parliament House every day. The home of the lord provost (the staunchly pro-Union Sir Patrick Johnston) was broken into and plundered. From that point on, anti-Union demonstrations were almost a daily occurrence in the capital as the mob found the debate an agreeable stimulant to its activities. In November, rioting erupted in the south-west (the stronghold of the ultra-Presbyterian Cameronian Covenanters), and the proposed Articles of Union were ritually burned in Dumfries before a gathering of several thousand Cameronians. In Glasgow, too, the mob rose against Unionist sympathisers, in disturbances which lasted intermittently for more than a month. It was rumoured that plans were being made for an armed uprising, led by the hard-line Covenanters of the south-west. The English government was sufficiently concerned to despatch a powerful force to the border, ready to deal with any insurrection, while the small Scottish standing army of 1,500 troops was stationed on the outskirts of Edinburgh.

Andrew Fletcher of Saltoun had been expected to be the most effective of all the opposition speakers; but he was now a spent force politically. He had for long argued for confederation – a federal union – rather than incorporation; he also demanded a degree of equality with England which, everyone now knew, the English would never tolerate. Scotland, with a population of about a million, was only a fifth the size of England; in terms of relative national wealth it was barely one-fortieth as rich as England. For England, it was incorporation or nothing. Fletcher's speeches in parliament grew more and more intemperate, less and less effective, and his irascible antics antagonised even his previous supporters (he challenged the Earl of Roxburgh to a duel, which was only narrowly averted). Fletcher, alas, failed to capitalise on the historic opportunity which necessity had mothered.[1]

The Duke of Hamilton paraded his patriotic conscience as leader of the Country Party:

> *What! Shall we in half an hour yield what our forefathers maintained with their lives and fortunes for many years? Are none of the descendants here of these worthy patriots who defended the liberty of their country against all invaders, who assisted the great King Robert Bruce to restore the constitution and avenge the falsehood of England and usurpation of Baliol? Where are the Douglasses and the Campbells? Where are the peers, where are the barons, once the bulwark of the nation? Shall we yield up the sovereignty and independence of the nation, when we are commanded by those we represent to preserve the name, and assured of their assistance to support us?*

Lord Belhaven made a memorable, maudlin and flowery speech on behalf of the Jacobites:[2]

> *I see the laborious ploughman, with his corn piling on his hands for want of sale, cursing the day of his birth, dreading the expense of his burial, and uncertain whether to marry or do worse. I see the landed men, fettered under the golden chair of equivalents, their pretty daughters petitioning for want of husbands, and their sons for want of employment. But above all, my lord, I see our ancient mother Caledonia, like Caesar, sitting in the midst of our Senate, ruefully looking around her, covering herself with her royal garment, awaiting the fatal blow, and breathing out her last with an exclamation – 'et tu quoque me fili?' ['and you, my son?'] . . .*
>
> *Our all is at stake. Hannibal, my lord, is at our gates! Hannibal is come within our gates! Hannibal is come to the length of this table! He is at the foot of the throne! He will demolish this throne! If we take not notice, he'll seize upon these regalia, he'll*

---

1 After the Act of Union was passed, Fletcher ceased to have an active political role. He was briefly imprisoned in 1708 on suspicion of involvement in a Jacobite plot, but was released without charge. He left Scotland and spent the rest of his life in London or abroad.

2 There is no original *Hansard* record of Lord Belhaven's speech; but various anglicised versions survive. These extracts are taken from Neil McCallum, *A Small Country*, quoting from John Struthers, *History of Scotland*.

take them as our spolia opima *[choicest spoils] and whip us out
of this house, never to return again.*

The proud Belhaven was on his knees, in tears. The house was deeply
moved. Then the Earl of Marchmont rose to reply:

*We have heard a very long speech, but it requires only a very
short answer. Behold he dreamed, but lo! when he awoke, he
found it was a dream.*

The house was convulsed with merriment, and the debate was
adjourned in great good humour. On Monday, 4 November the first
of the Articles (on the principle of an incorporating union) was carried.
The voting was 115 to eighty-three, a majority of thirty-two (forty-
seven lords, thirty-seven barons and thirty-one burgesses against
twenty-one lords, thirty-three barons and twenty-nine burgesses).
Although the final outcome was by no means a foregone conclusion
yet, the voting on Article I set the pattern for the other twenty-four;
in fact, it was the closest vote the opposition was to achieve.

But for the government managers the majority was uncomfortably,
and unexpectedly, small. On the day of the vote the ministry laid
before parliament a bill designed to allay the fears of the Kirk, the
'Act for the Security of the Church of Scotland'. The Kirk had provided
a powerful anti-Union voice throughout the summer of 1706; with
this inspired political masterstroke, its vociferous opposition was
stifled. The Kirk was effectively sidelined from the debate, and 'the
trumpets of sedition began to fall silent'.

The Duke of Argyll, having completed his assignment to bring the
Bill before parliament, had returned to Flanders. He was sent for again,
and only agreed to go back to Scotland in return for promotion to
major-general and a peerage for his younger brother, Archibald, as
Lord Islay. Argyll was soon busy 'managing' the Court Party supporters
again, offering all manner of inducements in order to ensure their
compliance. A sum of £20,000 was delivered from the English Treasury
and privately distributed as 'payments of arrears of salaries' to selected
recipients.

Petitions protesting against the Union poured in from many parts
of the country; the Duke of Argyll dismissed them with an airy shrug,
saying that they were only fit to be made into paper kites. The opposition parties tried every possible delaying tactic, but one by one each
successive Article was approved. Article II, regarding the Protestant

succession, was passed with only fifty-seven votes against. Article IV, which allowed for 'Freedom and Intercourse of Trade and Navigation', provoked what may, with hindsight, be seen as the most crucial of all the debates. It was passed by the largest majority of all, with a mere nineteen votes against. By the terms of this Article, the Scots were granted access to English markets both at home and in its growing overseas empire – something the English had previously refused to concede. It meant that Scotland would be joining an Anglo-Scottish Common Market which was the largest customs-free area in Europe.

Article VIII, which dealt with the Salt Tax, was described by Daniel Defoe as the 'Grand Affair'. The Earl of Mar called it 'the artickle I was most afraid of'. Salt was a crucial commodity, and an equalising tax on salt would hit every household in Scotland. But the Article was amended to ensure that no tax would be levied on home-produced salt or malt. Other key export commodities, such as coal, grain and black cattle, were granted concessionary status, and major amendments on other economic issues were wrested from the Court Party.

Article XV dealt with the payment to Scotland of a large sum of money known as 'the Equivalent': a total of £398,085.10s (almost £26 million in today's values). This was partly to offset Scotland's future liability towards England's national debt and partly to liquidate Scotland's national debt, but mainly to provide compensation (£232,884.5s) for those investors who had lost heavily on the Darien disaster, including the Duke of Hamilton. The fiscal calculation had been made by none other than the Scotsman William Paterson, begetter of the Darien venture and founder of the Bank of England; ironically, it was the Bank which paid the money.[1]

Article XIX guaranteed the continuance of Scots law and all Scottish courts as a distinct legal system, but subject to alterations 'for the better administration of justice as shall be made by the parliament of Great Britain'.

Article XXII covered the level of representation which Scotland could expect in the new Great Britain parliament: only sixteen peers (in a House of Lords of 206) and forty-five commoners (in a House of Commons of 568). The calculation was based not on population but on national wealth, as measured in terms of the yield from the land tax and from customs and excise revenue. Despite the meagreness of the representation, the Court Party of nobles loyally approved this

---

1 The money was to be distributed by a Commission of the Equivalent, but many shareholders of the Company of Scotland had to wait years for settlement.

Article, like the others. In exchange, the nobility was allowed to keep its local courts and heritable jurisdictions.

The New Year came and went. Article after Article was debated and then accepted by a majority vote. For the opposition in parliament the situation was becoming desperate. Early in January 1707 they decided on a last-ditch ploy: a parliamentary boycott which might prevent the Act being ratified. They planned to present a formal National Protestation and, when this was dismissed, to walk out in a body. It would be an explicit and forceful gesture, and there was a slight chance that it might even succeed. The formal argument was 'that a body of legislators are not the owners or masters of a people. They are not entitled to bargain away the nation they represent, or make it cease to exist.' The opposition intended to claim that the debate on the Union was *ultra vires* (beyond the jurisdiction of parliament). The Duke of Hamilton agreed to lead this move. He exhorted the different factions of the opposition to a last united effort on behalf of their dying country: success could only come if they buried their quarrels and united their strength. The Protestation was duly drawn up, presenting all the arguments against union.

The day of protest arrived. But then the Duke of Hamilton, leader of his country's patriotic conscience, threw his second spanner into the works. He said that he had toothache, and refused to leave his lodgings. Parliament peremptorily demanded him to appear. When he did, he calmly stated that, while he would certainly support the protest, he had no intention of tabling it. It was an extraordinary *volte-face*, which has never been satisfactorily explained. Had he been 'nobbled' by the Duke of Argyll? He was heavily in debt, and may have changed sides in exchange for a secret bribe. Or was he simply so indecisive that he could not bring himself to take action? Whatever the reason, his sudden change of face and heart demoralised the opponents of the Union and dealt the opposition a death-blow.

On 16 January 1707 the Treaty of Union was ratified, by 110 votes to sixty-seven – a majority of forty-three; the Scottish parliament had voted itself out of existence.[1] The Treaty received its ratification in the English parliament in a single sitting on 19 March. The last session of the Scottish parliament was adjourned on 25 March, and formally dissolved by proclamation of the Scottish Privy Council on 28 April. The Earl of Seafield, the lord chancellor, touched the Treaty with the

---

1 It was probably on this occasion that the Edinburgh mob forced Seafield and some of his fellow-signatories to seek refuge in the summerhouse in the grounds of Moray House.

sceptre and handed the papers to the clerk; then he is said to have pronounced the obituary which has echoed down the years: 'Now there's the end of an auld sang.'[1] *Realpolitik* had won.

The Treaty and Act of Union came into force on 1 May 1707. The bells of St Giles' Cathedral saluted the day by pealing out the tune 'Why should I be sad on my wedding day?'

On 5 June Queen Anne issued a historic proclamation:

> *Whereas in pursuance of the two and twentieth article of the Treaty of Union, as the same hath been ratified and confirmed by two Acts of Parliament, the one passed by the Parliament of England and the other in the Parliament of Scotland, we . . . do hereby appoint, that our first Parliament of Great Britain shall meet and be holden at our City of Westminster on Thursday the twenty-third day of October next . . .*

And so, on 23 October 1707, the first ever parliament of Great Britain met at Westminster. Sixteen elected Scottish peers and forty-five nominated Scottish commoners went south to sit in the new parliament. In London, according to the *Memoirs* of Sir John Clerk of Penicuik, they were received with disdain and lodged at prices they could not afford. And all for what?

> *To find themselves obscure and unhonoured in the crowd of English society and the unfamiliar intrigues of English politics, where they were despised for their poverty, ridiculed for their speech, sneered at for their manners, and ignored in spite of their votes by the ministers and government.*

But those who had managed the Treaty were richly rewarded. The Duke of Queensberry was created Duke of Dover in the English peerage, and given a seat in the House of Lords and a pension of £3,000 a year from the revenues of the Post Office. The Duke of Hamilton received the Order of the Garter and was appointed British ambassador to Paris, but was killed in a duel before he could take up the post.

---

1   In a special Addendum to the 25 Articles, it was decided that the Honours of Scotland (the regalia) should never be removed from Scotland. However, they were to be removed from the public view, and secured in a strong chamber, 'lest the sight of these symbols of national sovereignty should irritate the jealous feelings of the Scottish people' (*Tales of a Grandfather*, Chapter XL). See pages 647–8.

The Duke of Argyll was granted an English peerage as Earl (later Duke) of Greenwich.

Causes and effects

For nearly three centuries, commentators and partisans have argued passionately about the 1707 Union of Parliaments. Was it the ultimate betrayal of the Scottish nation? An altruistic act of far-sighted statesmanship? Or simply a pragmatic response to the inevitable?

The anti-Union tone was set by George Lockhart of Carnwath with his *Memoirs Concerning the Affairs of Scotland* (1714), which gave an uncompromisingly Jacobite view of the Union. His tract was a virulent attack on the morals of many of the leading Scottish parliamentarians who, according to Lockhart, had sold Scotland's independence for English gold. Was it downright bribery and corruption, the unacceptable face of eighteenth-century politics? Or were monetary rewards, overt or covert, and lavish patronage just a normal, if unprincipled, aspect of the parliamentary management methods of those days?

The manner of the passing of the Act gave rise to a celebrated jibe by Andrew Fletcher of Saltoun, that Scotland had been sold 'by a parcel of rogues'. In 1792 Robert Burns composed a poem about the end of the Scottish parliament entitled 'Fareweel to a' our Scottish fame':

> . . . *O would, ere I had seen the day*
> *That treason thus could sell us,*
> *My auld grey head had lien [lain] in clay,*
> *Wi' BRUCE and loyal WALLACE!*
> *But pith and power, till my last hour,*
> *I'll mak' this declaration,*
> *We're bought and sold for English gold:*
> *Such a parcel of rogues in a nation!*

Sir John Clerk of Penicuik, who had been a Scottish delegate on the joint parliamentary commission and was a reluctant supporter of the Union, wrote his *History of the Union* partly as a response to Lockhart's *Memoirs*. Clerk had serious qualms about Union. He was profoundly aware of the importance of the loss of an independent Scottish parliament, but was ultimately persuaded that, on balance, considerations of Scottish trade and security had to take precedence over Scotland's ancient and historic freedoms.

Daniel Defoe, the English government's reporter at the Great Debate who has been hailed as 'the father of modern journalism', wrote in his newsletter, *The Review*:

> *I have been a witness to the great transaction of the Union; I know the warmth with which England pursued it; I know the difficulty with which Scotland complied with it.*

The Earl of Roxburgh, one of the leaders of the *Squadrone volante*, had prophesied in November 1705 what he thought would motivate the debate:

> *The motives will be, Trade with most, Hanover with some, ease and security with others, together with a generall aversion to civill discords, intollerable poverty, and the constant oppression of a bad ministry, from generation to generation, without the least regard to the good of the country.*

Chris Whatley, Professor of Scottish History at Dundee University, says:

> *There was undoubtedly a very strong economic dimension to the Union – much stronger than some nationalist writers have allowed. Of the twenty-five Articles which comprised the Act of Union, no fewer than fifteen were concerned with economic matters. These were the most keenly contested, and saw some of the closest votes. Many of them, however, after amendment, were extremely favourable to the Scots: not only did the Scots obtain free trade with England, which was something they had wanted for decades, but several important Scottish economic interests were granted major concessions.*

Those who expected that Union would produce an instant economic miracle for Scotland were disappointed. Free trade could be a mixed blessing for an economy as fragile as Scotland's, and there were fears that Scottish producers would be hit hard by English competition. The short-term effects of the Union were complex, and produced some gains and some losses. Generally speaking, however, economic recovery for Scotland does not seem to have got under way until the 1730s.

Had trade been the clinching factor in the debate? The evidence is confusing, because some burghs were in favour of free trade, whereas others (like Glasgow, for instance) were solidly against it. Perhaps there was another, more deeply-rooted factor in play behind the scenes:

the real possibility of a return to the ancient royal line of Scottish monarchy through the 'Old Pretender', and the equally real fear of what that might involve. A Jacobite restoration in Scotland could provoke another English invasion, only half a century after Cromwell had forced Scotland into union. Michael Lynch says:

> *What was unique about the situation from 1700 onwards was that it was at bottom a crisis of the Stewart succession. In that sense, the complicated web of issues for and against union, often too complex or tangled to result in clear-cut interests, could be refined into a more straightforward choice. Political management, bribery and sweeteners all oil the process of decision-making, but the need to make a decision at all depended on the threat of English invasion and English intransigence, which in 1706 rejected all forms of association other than incorporating union.*[1]

Scotland's immediate reaction to the passing of the Act of Union was one of general discontent. Whatever material benefits might come in the wake of Union, something intangible had been lost – a common identity as a nation, perhaps, a sense of having a real say in the nation's affairs. Sir Walter Scott, whose attitude as a historian was thoroughly pro-Union and pro-British, expressed a much more Scottish nationalist view in his novels. The early chapters of *The Heart of Midlothian*, for instance, are concerned with the story of John Porteous, the notorious captain of the City Guard in 1736, who was sentenced to death for murder after firing indiscriminately at a threatening mob. When a last-minute reprieve arrived, Scott describes the reaction of two members of the disappointed crowd at the gibbet – Peter Plumdamas and old Mrs Howden:

> *'I am judging,' said Mr Plumdamas, 'that this reprieve wadna stand gude in the auld Scots law, when the kingdom was a kingdom.'*
>
> *'I dinna ken muckle about the law,' answered Mrs Howden; 'but I ken, when we had a king, and a chancellor, and parliament-men o' our ain, we could aye peeble them wi' stanes when they werena gude bairns – But naebody's nails can reach the length o' Lunnon.'*

---

1 *Scotland: A New History* (Pimlico, 1992, p.315).

Scottish discontent soon turned to deep resentment as the English administration embarked on a process of 'compleating the Union'. The Scottish Privy Council was abolished in 1708. The House of Lords became a court of appeal in civil cases from the Court of Session in Edinburgh. A series of anti-Presbyterian Acts infuriated the Kirk: in 1712 the Toleration Act granted freedom of worship to Scottish Episcopalians, and the Patronage Act re-established the primary right of local landowners (including the crown) to appoint ministers to vacant parishes and Church offices. In 1713 the House of Commons, contrary to the terms of the Act of Union, imposed a tax on malt in Scotland.

The Scottish members of both houses of parliament were so incensed that they came together and agreed that the only solution was the repeal of the Act of Union. The Earl of Seafield, supported by the Duke of Argyll and the Earl of Mar – three of the leading peers who had managed the Union debate in 1706–7 on behalf of the government – put forward a Resolution to this effect in the House of Lords in June 1713; it was defeated by only a tiny majority of four votes – and proxy votes, at that.

Alex Murdoch says:

> Most Scots had not wanted union with England in 1707. The opinion of those who worked the land, and the smaller group who made their crust in the towns, had been overwhelmingly against any form of political union with an alien race. Even among the political class there had been be a reluctance to accept everything which political union might represent. Hence the famous Resolution in the House of Lords in 1713, to dissolve the Union, on the basis that it was being treated as a takeover rather than as a negotiated political union – which was the way in which the Scottish politicians had always insisted on viewing it.

The narrow vote in the House of Lords reflected a profound disillusionment with union not only among the Scottish nobility, but in England, too. It was also a reflection of the growing strength of the Jacobite movement which would dominate British politics for the next thirty years, in the major Jacobite Risings of 1715 and 1745.

Chapter 27

RISINGS AND RIOTS (1708–36)

The personal adherence of many individuals to the Stewart family might have preserved Jacobite sentiments for a generation, but would scarce have had intensity sufficient to kindle a general flame in the country, had not the sense of the unjust and illiberal manner in which the Union was concluded, come in aid of the zeal of the Jacobites, to create a general or formidable attack on the existing Government.

TALES OF A GRANDFATHER, CHAPTER LXII

The 'end of an auld sang' in 1707 only brought discord, not harmony. It was estimated that two-thirds of Scotland were Stewart in sympathy, and anti-Union sentiment focused on the prospect of a Stewart restoration. Even the anti-Royalists, like the ultra-Presbyterian Cameronians, compared 'the lesser evil of being ruled by a Stewart king with the great evil of being suppressed by an English-Hanoverian dynasty and parliament'. But translating sentiment into action was a different matter entirely.

The first Jacobite Rising: 1708

The first Jacobite Rising fell flat before it had even begun.

When James VII & II had fled back to France after the failure of his expedition to Ireland (1689–91), Louis XIV had granted him a huge annual pension of six hundred thousand *livres* (£50,000) and the use of the royal château at Saint-Germain-en-Laye, near Paris. Here the erstwhile King of Scotland, England and Ireland had set up a Jacobite court in exile, and the town itself became the centre of a large and growing expatriate Jacobite community.

When James VII & II died in 1701, the mantle of Jacobite leadership in exile fell upon 'the Prince of Wales', his thirteen-year-old son, James Francis Edward Stuart (the 'Pretender'), whom Louis XIV recognised formally as 'King James VIII and III of Great Britain'. Louis and his ministers, reeling from Marlborough's resounding victories on the Continent at Blenheim (1704) and Ramillies (1706), kept a close watch on the passage of the 1707 Act of Union and noted the seething Scottish discontent it was causing. From the French perspective, a Jacobite rising in Scotland in favour of Queen Anne's Catholic half-brother James Stuart could create a diversion, at least, for England, and ease the pressure on the French army in Belgium.

Scotland was swarming with spies and agents working for France. One of them was a colourful character named Nathaniel Hooke, an Irish Protestant who had been chaplain to the Duke of Monmouth in the 1685 rebellion; he was now a 'career Jacobite' who had changed his religion and was a colonel in the French army. Hooke had been in Scotland in 1705 to sound out Jacobite support, and again in 1707 in the wake of the Act of Union, meeting the Duke of Hamilton and other notables. He brought back news of several influential noblemen and clan chieftains who, he claimed, were ready to rebel against the Union and the prospect of a Hanoverian succession at the death of the childless Queen Anne.

Encouraged by the promise of an army of twenty-five thousand troops and five thousand horse eager to spring into action in Scotland, the French decided to provide the Pretender with a modicum of military support and land him in Scotland. An expeditionary force of five thousand men was to be sent aboard a French fleet consisting of five men o' war and fifteen transports under the command of Admiral Claude de Forbin. The admiral tried to convince King Louis that the enterprise was crazy, but Louis refused to listen. The expedition gathered at Dunkirk, but not exactly in secret. Before long, a British squadron of men o' war under Admiral Byng was anchored off Gravelines, two leagues (ten kilometres) from Dunkirk.

On 6 March 1708 the twenty-year-old Prince James arrived in Dunkirk. He had caught measles from his little sister at Saint-Germain-en-Laye, and was very ill. The weather was vile, with spring gales raging in the Channel. Nevertheless the French fleet set sail that evening.

They were forced to seek shelter off Ostend, but eventually got away, and on 13 March anchored off the Isle of May, near the south coast of Fife.

A Jacobite welcoming-party was waiting at Burntisland, and the intention was to advance on Stirling. However, the Royal Navy squadron under Byng had shadowed the French ships closely all the way, and now moved into the attack before any troops could be landed. The French escaped northward to the Moray Firth in strong winds and heavy seas with the loss of only one vessel. Prince James begged to be put ashore in a boat (alone, if need be), despite the fact that there was a bounty of £5,000 on his head; but Admiral de Forbin decided to abandon the enterprise and sailed straight back to Dunkirk. After a stormy voyage, Prince James landed back at Dunkirk on 7 April 1708, on the eve of Easter. He had not set foot on his native land. The Rising was over before it had even begun.

Murray Pittock, Professor of Literature at Strathclyde University, says:

> A very large Jacobite army could undoubtedly have been raised in 1708 had there been proper leadership, had there been enough money, and had the French made a landing. Instead, in the aftermath of the failed landing, the House of Commons resolved that the English law of treason, with its barbaric punishment of hanging, drawing and quartering, should be made uniform throughout the kingdom, to ensure that any further Jacobite activities in Scotland would not go unpunished. But the 1708 failure was a clear signal that there was a reservoir of resentment about the way in which the Union treaty was being eroded in the centralised British interest.

The 1715 Rising

It takes a great deal of finding, deep in the heart of gumboot country – the small, lichen-covered 'Gathering Stone', or 'Battle Stone', on the high moorlands of Sheriffmuir, just to the north-east of Dunblane in Perthshire. Under a protective grating of iron hoops, and almost inaccessible to even the most determined pilgrim, the Gathering Stone marks the site of the battle which decided the outcome of the 1715 Jacobite Rising (see page 564). It is not the general area of the extended battlefield which is hard to find, but the unmarked track to the Gathering Stone itself.

The Sheriffmuir Inn, on the route of the old drove road across Sheriffmuir between Dunblane and Greenloaning, is as good a starting-point as any. It was built early in 1715, only six months before the battle; today it is the last survivor of the many inns which used to serve thirsty cattle-drovers. It stands, white-painted like a beacon, isolated but ever-welcoming in the bleak moorlands, and is the gathering-place for an annual commemoration of the battle on the Saturday closest to 13 November.

By the side of the unnumbered road from the Sheriffmuir Inn to Dunblane stands a large stone cairn, the Macrae Monument, which was erected in 1915 to commemorate the bicentenary of the battle and the fighting men of the Clan Macrae who died in it, almost to a man. The track to the Gathering Stone starts here. It goes uphill along a low boundary wall, then forks obliquely left across the moor towards a sheltering copse of conifers. Here, superintended by two tall Scots pines and almost drowning in heather, surrounded by hummocks and hollows which suggest the presence of ancient mass graves, is the Gathering Stone at last. It was here that the Royal Standard of the Jacobite army was planted on the morning of 13 November 1715.

This is how it came about.

The latter years of Queen Anne's reign, after the fiasco of the 1708 Rising, had seen increasing disenchantment in Scotland with the way in which the Union was being 'compleated' by English ministers, and a corresponding increase in Jacobite support – not just in Scotland, but in England too. The High Church Anglicans (the Tories) were dismayed by the Whig administration's measures for greater religious tolerance, and soon Toryism in England became almost synonymous with Jacobitism. When a Tory administration took over in England in 1711, under the Earl of Oxford and the Earl of Bolingbroke, unofficial offers of the throne were made to the Pretender, Prince James, in France, on condition that he converted to Protestantism. But James refused even to consider the suggestion on those terms.

Queen Anne died on 1 August 1714. Seven weeks later her successor George, Elector of Hanover (great-grandson of James VI & I), landed at Greenwich to a less than enthusiastic reception. He was not the most charismatic of men. He could barely speak English, and addressed his ministers in dog-Latin. He also had a skeleton in the cupboard, as it were: in 1682 he had married his cousin Sophia, Duchess of Zell, but had divorced her in 1694 for adultery and thrown her into prison. She was still locked up in the castle of Ahlden, and would stay there until her death in 1726.

There were widespread demonstrations against George in England, including an abortive Jacobite mini-rising in the West Country. In Scotland there was outrage and open ridicule. A popular song was on everyone's lips:

> *What the de'il ha'e we got for a King,*
> *But a wee, wee German lairdie?*

Fuelled by resentment at the Hanoverian succession, Jacobite support was now greater in range and depth than ever before. All that was required was the presence of the star of the show: James Francis Edward Stuart. But where was he? By now James was no longer living in Saint-Germain-en-Laye. France had been forced to make terms with England in the Treaty of Utrecht in 1713, and one of the conditions was that James and his Jacobite court should be expelled from France (although his mother, Mary of Modena, was allowed to remain at Saint-Germain until her death in 1718). James moved to the town of Bar-le-Duc in the still-independent Duchy of Lorraine; he was now living in a house at 22, rue Neve under the title of the Chevalier de Saint George. As soon as possible after Queen Anne's death he hurried to Paris, hoping for a change of policy from Louis XIV; but he was still *persona non grata*, and was sent back empty-handed to Bar-le-Duc.

On 15 October 1714 James published a declaration in which he promised

> *to relieve our Subjects of Scotland from the hardships they groan*
> *under on account of the late unhappy Union, and to restore the*
> *Kingdom to its ancient free and independent state.*

But James lacked both the authority and the force of personality to seize control of the Jacobite movement and bend it to his will.

The Earl of Mar, who had been one of the leading protagonists of the Union in the Great Debate of 1706–7, and who had then presented a Resolution to have the Act of Union repealed in 1713, was the 'third secretary for Great Britain'. The accession of the Hanoverian King George I spelled danger to his political career, and Mar sent the king a grovelling letter of loyalty, signed by many Highland chiefs. When George, who wanted rid of him, snubbed him publicly, Mar decided it was time to throw in his lot with the Jacobites. In August 1715 he left London in disguise on board a collier and sailed to Scotland to launch a new Jacobite Rising.

The prospect of success was very bright – much brighter than in 1708. But everything went disastrously wrong. There was no co-ordination between the planned rising in Scotland and those planned by Jacobites in England. A 'rebellion' in the West Country in September fizzled out and most of its leaders were arrested. In the north of England a small force of English Jacobites wandered about from skirmish to skirmish from October to November, eventually surrendering on 13 November after a desperate stand in the town of Preston. They were all sentenced to execution, forfeiture, or transportation.

But what of Scotland? Could that possibly go wrong? The plan had been for a two-pronged rising, one in the north-east and one in the west. The Earl of Mar raised the standard of 'King James' at Braemar ('Braes of Mar') in the Grampian Highlands on 6 September 1715, which quickly attracted all the great magnates in the north-east. Thousands of fighting men flocked to the standard. Inverness and Aberdeen declared for James, as did all the burghs north of the Firth of Tay. On 14 September Perth fell to a lightning cavalry raid.

The clan rising in the western Highlands was much less successful: the clan chiefs were slow to commit their support. Only three thousand clansmen joined in the first instance, and the strategy of seizing Fort William and other government strongpoints failed dismally. When they joined Mar's forces at Perth on 23 October, the west was still not won.

Nevertheless, Mar had amassed a large following of more than ten thousand men. It was the most impressive military strength Scotland had mustered for many generations. And although it was a Jacobite army, it was by no means an exclusively Highland army: nearly half of its strength consisted of units from the lowlands of the north-east. It was in an important sense a national army, intent on fighting for liberty, breaking the Union with England and restoring the Stewart dynasty to the throne of Scotland. What was even more astonishing was that all these thousands of fighting men had flocked to the standard many weeks before the 'king' had even set foot in his kingdom. The Earl of Mar had raised the standard of rebellion without James's knowledge![1] Even so, the Jacobite cause looked invincible in the autumn of 1715. Most of Scotland north of the Tay was under Mar's control,

---

1 The ineptitude of the timing of the '15 Rising was compounded by the death of Louis XIV on 21 August 1715, leaving the throne to his five-year-old great-grandson, Louis XV. The regent, Philippe, Duc d'Orléans, was much less of an enthusiast for the Jacobite cause, and was not prepared to provide any support, whether of arms, money or men.

and the way was open for a massive drive into southern Scotland to take Edinburgh and Glasgow, and then, perhaps, London itself.

The government had been taken unawares by the scale and size of the Rising. It had no proper army in Scotland to speak of – fewer than four thousand men, at most. John Campbell, second Duke of Argyll ('Red John of the Battles'), was commander-in-chief in Scotland; he had made his reputation fighting in Marlborough's armies, and was considered one of the most able commanders in Europe. He told the government that if he fought, his army would be lost, but that if he retired, the country would be lost. At least, though, he knew the Earl of Mar and his failings. He took up position at Stirling, the gateway to the south, and waited.

The Battle of Sheriffmuir (13 November 1715)

Unaccountably, the Earl of Mar sat on in Perth and waited, too: waited for French help which would not be sent, waited for further recruits from the west to make his position even more unassailable, waited for 'the king over the water' to arrive. Eventually, on 10 November, he lumbered into action; leaving a large garrison in Perth he started to march south towards Dunblane.[1] Mar had worked out an intricate and grandiose plan to bypass Stirling and cross the Forth at four different places, link up with the Jacobites in England, then circle back to trap Argyll's small force. Argyll decided to pre-empt this plan and advanced swiftly to Dunblane, camping his army on the high ground of Sheriffmuir beyond the town; he was familiar with the lie of the land because the local militia used Sheriffmuir as a training ground.

Mar had no alternative now but to give battle on ground not of his own choosing. The Jacobite army which approached Dunblane numbered ten thousand foot and horse. Argyll was outnumbered by more than two to one, but he was superior in heavy cavalry.

Early in the morning of 13 November (the very day on which the beleaguered Jacobites in England surrendered at Preston) the Earl of Mar drew up his forces at the eastern end of Sheriffmuir, in two rows of ten battalions of foot, with the clan battalions in the van and his horse squadrons on his flanks. Argyll, from his vantage-point at the Gathering Stone, could see wave after wave of the Jacobite army approaching across the undulating, frozen ground, and made his dis-

---

1 His guide on the march was that quintessential Highland character, Rob Roy MacGregor (see below).

positions accordingly. He drew up his forces in a single line, to avoid being outflanked, with a small reserve at the back, and positioned himself with the best of his dragoons on the right flank.

The battle which ensued on that icy day was a strange one. Neither side made use of the artillery available. Both armies attacked on one flank only. Argyll attacked with the best of his cavalry down the right wing; after three hours of relentless fighting, during which the Macraes were killed almost to a man, the Jacobite left wing was thrown back and overcome. Meanwhile the Jacobite right wing launched a ferocious Highland charge against Argyll's left wing, which broke under the onslaught and fled back in panic towards Dunblane.

Argyll quickly regrouped his victorious right and joined up with his three battalions in the centre, which had not yet been involved in the fighting. He had barely a thousand men left on the field. The Earl of Mar also regrouped, planting his standard on the Gathering Stone. He now had the advantage of the higher ground, and Argyll's surviving troops were at his mercy. But the short winter's day was passing, and as dusk fell both sides withdrew the way they had come.

Next morning, Argyll's patrols found the field deserted. There was no sign of the Jacobite host. The battle had been a draw, with some three hundred dead on each side; but Argyll could claim a moral victory, for he had stopped in its tracks a mighty host which had desperately needed to win. The Jacobites had thrown away the initiative, and the Rising had lost its way. What was required was inspired leadership, and that was precisely what it lacked. As a politician, the Earl of Mar had always shown astuteness and patience; but as a general, in Tom Devine's words, 'he possessed a fatal combination of caution, timidity and ambiguity'. And the 'king over the water' was *still* just that – a king over the water. James Francis Edward Stuart had missed the boat, you might say.

It was not entirely his fault. The French, under the regent the Duc d'Orléans, had done everything to prevent James from joining the Rising in person. The English ambassador, it is said, had tried to procure James's assassination. James eventually succeeded in reaching Dunkirk, heavily disguised, where he took ship for Scotland on 16 December 1715. On 22 December he reached Peterhead. He had brought neither money nor troops, neither charisma nor spirit; but by then the party, if such it could be called, was practically over.

After the Battle of Sheriffmuir, the Earl of Mar had withdrawn to Perth. The Duke of Argyll had withdrawn to Stirling, there to await government reinforcements. When James landed at Peterhead, Mar escorted him to Aberdeen, where he was enthusiastically received by the Episcopalian clergy, who presented him with a loyal address of welcome to 'his antient kingdom'. James moved south to Dundee, where he made a ceremonial entry, and then to Perth, which he reached on 9 January 1716. There he set up court for three lugubrious weeks. Shy and taciturn at the best of times, he had caught a bad ague, and spent his time huddled in a chair, shivering. A coronation was planned for Scone, and Jacobite ladies offered their jewels so that he might have a makeshift crown. But not even a token coronation ceremony seems to have taken place: the Duke of Argyll was on the move again, reinforced by six thousand Dutch troops.

The Jacobite army was also on the move – homewards. As the Earl of Mar dithered and King James shivered, their impatient forces were dissolving. At last, on 31 January, the Jacobites left Perth, burning Auchterarder, Crieff and Blackford behind them – in order, according to Mar, to slow the advance of the Duke of Argyll. Through Dundee they went, and along the coast to the port of Montrose, where the Pretender was persuaded (without much difficulty) to embark on a ship bound for Flanders. He left Scotland on 4 February 1716; he was not yet twenty-eight years old, and would live for another fifty years, but he would never return. The 1715 Rising was over.[1]

When James returned to Bar-le-Duc in the Duchy of Lorraine he was politely asked to move house again. The Jacobite court went to Avignon, which was still a papal domain, but did not stay for long: in 1717 the pressure of English diplomacy obliged the Pope to persuade James to take up residence in the magnificent ducal palace in another papal city, Urbino, in central Italy. Soon James became bored with the isolation of Urbino, despite its dazzlingly beautiful surroundings in the Apennines, and asked the new Pope, Clement XII, for another home where he could be more involved with social and political life.

The occasion for a move came with James's marriage in 1719 to a seventeen-year-old Polish princess named Clementina Sobieska, a god-daughter of the Pope.[2] She was described as 'sweet, amiable, of an even temper, and gay only in season'. The courtship had been an adventurous one. In response to English pressure, Clementina was

---

1 The Earl of Mar fled the country soon afterwards; he died abroad in 1732. The remainder of the Jacobite army continued its retreat in good order; once the Highland regiments reached the glens and mountains of their homelands, they simply melted away.

2 She was a granddaughter of the heroic John III Sobieski of Poland (1624–96), who defeated the Turks before the walls of Vienna in 1683 with a spectacular cavalry charge.

arrested on her way from Poland to her wedding and imprisoned in the Schloss Ambras in Innsbruck. She was rescued by a daring Irishman, Charles Wogan, one of James's friends, with a group of helpers – his 'Three Musketeers', as they were called. They smuggled a maidservant into the princess's quarters, and removed her dressed as the maid; from there they spirited her safely over the Brenner Pass and into the Papal States.

Clementina brought with her a dowry of twenty-five million francs and the fabled Sobieski rubies, an heirloom of scarcely calculable value. As a wedding present the Pope gave the couple the Palazzo Muti in Rome – a relatively small palace situated at one end of the Piazza dei Santi Apostoli between the Corso and the Quirinale.[1] It was here that their two sons were born: Charles Edward Louis John Casimir Sylvester Xavier Maria Stuart (who would become known to history as 'Bonnie Prince Charlie') on 31 December 1720, and his younger brother Henry Benedict Stuart, a future cardinal, in March 1725. But the marriage was not a success. Clementina was impetuous and wayward, and soon developed a hearty dislike for her husband. She became depressed and turned to religion; after the birth of her second son she retreated for eighteen months to a convent, and on her return she fasted so stringently that she became anorexic. She died in 1735 at the age of thirty-three.[2]

After the death of his wife and the failure of the '45 (see Chapter 28), James's enthusiasm for the Stewart cause waned. The Jacobite court ceased to exist, to all intents and purposes. The 'Old Pretender', as he had become by then, sank into a long and doleful old age, keeping in touch with his supporters abroad, administering his affairs and conferring meaningless peerages on his 'subjects'. He died in 1766.

James's 'antient kingdom' had weathered the storm after the collapse of the 1715 Rising he had so signally failed to lead. The reprisals were much less severe than they would be after the 1745 Rising. A few peers were attainted; two were executed; thirty other Jacobites who had taken leading parts were either shot as deserters or hanged, drawn and quartered; and several hundred were sentenced to transportation. But comparative leniency seems to have been the order of the day. Many Jacobites escaped from prison with suspicious ease (some were freed from the Tolbooth by the mob in Edinburgh). One of the rebels who

---

1 A plaque inside the entrance hall of the Palazzo Muti commemorates the last residence of the Stuart Pretenders.

2 Her heart is preserved in an urn in the church at the other side of the Piazza dei Santa Apostoli opposite the Palazzo Muti.

was attainted for high treason was the man who had acted as guide to the Jacobite army on the way to the Battle of Sheriffmuir: a man who has become a Highland legend – Rob Roy MacGregor.

Rob Roy MacGregor (1671–1734)

My foot is on my native heath,
and my name is Rob Roy MacGregor

This defiant assertion adorns the bronze statue of Rob Roy by Benno Schotz (then the Queen's Sculptor in Ordinary for Scotland) which was unveiled in Stirling, close to the castle, in November 1975. It sums up perfectly the perverse pride and stubborn stance of the man who has become one of Scotland's favourite heroes.[1] Rob Roy MacGregor has become the quintessential Highlander – a curious blend of patriot (like William Wallace), freebooter (like Francis Drake), outlaw (like Robin Hood) and frontiersman (like Buffalo Bill Cody); a man of honour who was also a bandit, a cattle-rustler and the chief of a protection racket known in his time as blackmail (literally, 'black rent'). Daniel Defoe published a 'biography' of him (*Highland Rogue*, 1723); Sir Walter Scott wrote one of his Waverley novels about him (*Rob Roy*, 1818). He was the subject of a swashbuckling film in 1954 (*Rob Roy, the Highland Rogue*), starring Richard Todd; a 1995 film based on his life (*Rob Roy*), shot in Scotland and starring Liam Neeson, had something of the glamour and success of *Braveheart*. The Rob Roy & Trossachs Visitor Centre (a converted church) in the main square of the town of Callander draws a quarter of a million visitors a year to enjoy the multi-media presentations about Rob Roy's life and times in the rugged Trossachs landscapes of his homeland.

Rob Roy MacGregor *was* a frontiersman of his times, in that he and his clansmen lived in the frontier lands between Highlands and Lowlands – the Trossachs at Loch Lomond. He was born in February 1671 at the head of Loch Katrine in the Trossachs, the third son of the fifth chief of his clan, Donald Glas MacGregor of Glengyle; his mother, Mary, was a Campbell.

Rob (the 'Roy' is an anglicisation of the Gaelic *ruadh*, meaning

---

1 Sir Walter Scott was an avid collector of Rob Roy memorabilia. The armoury in Abbotsford displays Rob Roy's flintlock gun, his basket-hilted broadsword, his *sgian dubh* (black-hilted dirk) and his sporran. The showcase in the library contains his dark, cracked leather purse.

'red-haired') grew up to be immensely strong, with exceptionally long arms, and became renowned for his skill with the broadsword. He was an accomplished cattle-drover and tracker of stolen beasts – a trail-boss, he would have been called in the Wild West. Like so many Highlanders he was a Jacobite, and at the age of eighteen he took part in the ferocious Highland charge at Killiecrankie which won the battle for 'Bonnie Dundee' in 1689.

The Clan MacGregor had been officially outlawed in 1603 by James VI & I, and after the failure of the Jacobite rising led by 'Bonnie Dundee', the clan name was proscribed again. To avoid difficulties, Rob Roy adopted the surname of Campbell, which he used in all his correspondence. He set himself up as a dealer in the lucrative trade in black cattle, helping to drive them from the Highlands down to the markets in the Lowlands and England. He prospered, for he had earned a reputation for trustworthiness in his business dealings, and bought land – he acquired the lands of Craigroyston and later became the laird of Inversnaid, on Loch Lomondside.[1]

In 1712, however, everything started to go wrong for Rob Roy MacGregor. In the autumn of the previous year he had raised the huge sum of £1,000 from the Duke of Montrose and other clients to buy cattle for fattening in the Lowlands before the next summer's marts. In the spring of 1712 he sent his chief drover (a MacDonald) to bring in the stock, and gave him the bills of exchange. And then came the thunderbolt: the drover had bought the cattle but sold them on, and promptly absconded. Overnight, Rob Roy was bankrupt. He set off in pursuit of the drover, but failed to find him; by the time he returned, after a month, he found himself accused of having stolen the money himself. The Duke of Montrose took out a warrant for his arrest, and when Rob Roy failed to turn up in court he was outlawed. Montrose immediately attached all Rob Roy's landed property, and sent his factor, Graham of Killearn, to evict Rob's wife Mary and their four young sons from the family home at Craigroyston.

From then on, Rob Roy conducted a private war with the Duke of Montrose, whose base was Mugdock Castle, north of Glasgow. He kidnapped Montrose's factor while he was in the act of collecting the duke's rents, seized £3,227.2s.8d (Scots) of rent-money, and issued fresh receipts for the tenants in the Duke's name. Then he imprisoned the factor on an islet in Loch Katrine and demanded ransom money

---

1   This Loch Lomond beauty spot inspired Gerard Manley Hopkins in 1881 to write the poem 'Inversnaid', which has become an anthem for environmentalists.

for him. When it became clear that the duke had no intention of paying the ransom, Rob Roy characteristically released the man unharmed.

Rob Roy now took to a life of banditry as a cattle-rustler and robber, raiding Montrose's lands whenever possible. He classed all those who had supported the Union as legitimate targets, unless they were prepared to buy him off. Soon he was running a lucrative protection racket, guaranteeing to lay off the herds of his 'clients' in exchange for payment. For his own security, he also put himself under the protection of the Duke of Argyll, implacable enemy of the Duke of Montrose. Argyll was happy to use him as a 'hit-man' to settle old scores or apply pressure on recalcitrant tenants.

During the 1715 Rising, Rob Roy MacGregor joined the Earl of Mar and the Jacobite army. He was despatched to Aberdeenshire to recruit among the MacGregors settled there, and then, because of his intimate knowledge of the terrain, was used as a local 'scout' to guide the Jacobite army on its march from Perth to Dunblane.

As the Jacobites squared up to the Duke of Argyll at Sheriffmuir, Rob Roy was in a dilemma. Argyll was his protector, after all. There are suspicions that Rob Roy was in fact acting as a secret agent for Argyll. Whatever the truth of that, he played no heroic role in the battle, according to a wry Scottish ballad:

> *Rob Roy he stood watch*
> *On a hill for to catch*
> *The booty, for aught that I saw, man;*
> *For he ne'er advanc'd*
> *From the place where he stanc'd*
> *Till nae mair was to do there at a', man.*

His inactivity did not save him after the collapse of the Rising. He was attainted for high treason, and became a fugitive with a price on his head. This did not stop him joining the Jacobite cause again during the abortive 1719 Rising (see below). Apart from that he was constantly on the run, although the Duke of Argyll allowed him to build a refuge on Campbell land in Glen Shira, near Inveraray. To some he was nothing but a highwayman and a gangster; to others he was a latter-day Robin Hood, robbing the rich to give to the poor, ambushing government troops and freeing their prisoners. He was captured on several occasions, but always he managed to escape. His exploits became legendary for their audacity.

Gradually the heat went out of the hunt for him, and he was able to enjoy undisturbed periods with his family. Daniel Defoe's fictitious account of his life in *Highland Rogue* made Rob Roy a 'paper' celebrity. King George himself was enraptured by the tale, and the work became the talk of the court and the coffee-shops. Three years after its publication, in 1726, Rob Roy was granted a royal pardon.

Rob Roy died on 28 December 1734 in his home at Inverlochlarig Beag, at the head of the Glen of Balquhidder, and was buried in Balquhidder. He had become a 'real' national hero by then, all his past racketeering sins forgiven. In a treacherous age he had never betrayed a trust nor broken his word. He had always been his own man. His funeral, on New Year's Day 1735, was attended by a host of mourners of all ranks and most clans from the south, central and west Highlands.

In the churchyard of the roofless Old Kirk in Balquhidder three recumbent old stones mark the graves of Rob Roy, his wife and one of his sons. A new headstone is emblazoned with the MacGregor arms and the defiant motto 'MacGregor Despite Them'. An ornamental bronze rail enclosing the graves gives his age as 'about 70'; in fact he was only sixty-three. But that is the way of legend.[1]

The 1719 Rising: the Battle of Glenshiel (10 June)

The affair of Glenshiel might be called the last faint sparkle of the great Rebellion of 1715, which was fortunately extinguished for want of fuel.

TALES OF A GRANDFATHER, CHAPTER LXXIII

Rob Roy MacGregor had fought in the 1719 Rising – the third time he had taken part in a Jacobite campaign; but to call 1719 a 'rising' at all is a bit of a misnomer – 'fiasco' would again be a better term.

The inspiration for another rising came this time from Spain, which had been paying James Francis Edward Stuart a clandestine pension of £5,000 a year. The main Spanish fleet had been destroyed by Admiral Byng in an engagement off Cape Passero in August 1718, and Spain's

---

1 Walter Scott put the end of Rob Roy's story into the mouth of Francis Osbaldistone: 'I have often visited Scotland, but never again saw the bold Highlander who had such an influence on the early events of my life. I learned, however, from time to time that he continued to maintain his ground among the mountains of Loch Lomond, in despite of his powerful enemies . . . It seemed impossible that his life should have concluded without a violent end. Nevertheless, he died in old age and by a peaceful death, some time about the year 1733, and is still remembered in his country as the Robin Hood of Scotland.'

powerful chief minister, Cardinal Alberoni, was thirsting for revenge. He planned to use the Jacobite movement to make trouble for the British government. The retaliation involved a two-pronged assault: a landing in strength in south-west England, and a diversionary Jacobite bridgehead in the north-west of Scotland.

Early in March 1719 a Spanish armada of twenty-nine ships, crammed with five thousand troops and arms for thirty thousand more, set sail from Cadiz for England, planning to pick up the Pretender at Corunna *en route*. At the same time a couple of frigates, carrying a battalion of 327 hand-picked Spanish infantrymen and enough weapons to arm two thousand, set off from San Sebastian for Scotland.

The intended invasion of England ended long before it had begun. The Spanish armada, like the great fleet which had tried to invade England in 1588, ran into foul weather and was shattered by violent storms off Cape Finisterre; the surviving ships limped into Corunna in tatters.

Meanwhile the little Scottish expedition went on its way, unaware of the disaster which had overtaken the main fleet. In command of the two ships with their token Spanish force was George Keith, the tenth Earl Marischal of Scotland. They made land at Stornoway, on the island of Lewis in the Outer Hebrides, on 2 April. Here they were joined by a small group of Jacobite exiles, including the Earl of Seaforth (the chief of Clan Mackenzie), who had sailed from Le Havre in France. They were led by William, Marquis of Tullibardine, the dispossessed heir of the Duke of Atholl; Tullibardine was carrying a commission from the Chevalier de Saint George, James Francis Edward Stuart, the 'Pretender', drawn up two years earlier, making him commander of all Jacobite forces in Scotland.

That was where the trouble started. Both the Earl Marischal and the Marquis of Tullibardine were high-tempered men, and each refused to defer to the other. The two commanders had rival strategies: Tullibardine wanted to stay on Lewis and await news of the planned Jacobite landing in south-west England; the Earl Marischal wanted to head for the mainland, then make a dash to Inverness to link up with the Earl of Seaforth's clansmen there. Valuable time was wasted in daily councils of war and endless bickering.

The Earl Marischal, who was in command of the two Spanish frigates, had his way. The expedition crossed the Minch in stormy weather and made the shelter of Loch Alsh, where the Jacobites and Spaniards set up their headquarters in the old Mackenzie castle of

Eilean Donan, one of the most picturesque castles in Scotland, on the north side of Loch Duich where it meets Loch Alsh.[1] Here they deposited their arsenal of weapons and ammunition before moving to the head of Loch Duich. More councils of war and more quarrelling ensued. The plan to march to Inverness failed to take shape. Instead, news came of the disaster which had overtaken the armada from Cadiz: suddenly, the sideshow in north-west Scotland had become the main event. Tullibardine urged instant embarkation and withdrawal: it was time to cut their losses and run, he said. The Earl Marischal disagreed, and ordered the two Spanish frigates to sail for home, empty, to forestall any attempt to evacuate.

The expeditionary force was now beleaguered by both sea and land. A Royal Navy squadron of three frigates sailed into Loch Alsh on 10 May and pounded Eilean Donan to destruction, while a government force commanded by Major-General Wightman set out from Inverness with two regiments of infantry, two squadrons of dragoons and 146 grenadiers equipped with six light bronze mortars.

Tullibardine was at Shiel Bridge, near the tiny Loch Shiel.[2] He had been trying to raise the clans, but the news of the failure of the main expedition to make a landing in the south was deeply discouraging. Fewer than a thousand clansmen rallied to the cause – mainly four hundred Seaforth Mackenzies and 150 Camerons; one of the volunteers was Rob Roy with forty MacGregors. On 10 June, as the government army came marching down Glen Shiel, Tullibardine moved eight kilometres up the glen to meet it, taking up a strong defensive position where the glen narrows, just to the east of the old bridge across the river. The Hanoverian army drew up on the flat ground farther to the east, near the ruined croft of Lun an Eorna. The Jacobite forces were deployed on both sides of the glen: Lord George Murray, younger brother of the Marquis of Tullibardine, was to the south of the stream, Tullibardine himself and the Spaniards to the north. The Spanish

---

1 Castle Eilean Donan, so beloved of film-makers and painters, is a familiar sight to travellers on the splendidly scenic A87 from Invergarry to Kyle of Lochalsh. After the 1719 Rising, which reduced it to ruins, it was completely rebuilt; the restoration started in 1912 and was finished in 1932.

2 The Loch Shiel at Shiel Bridge is not to be confused with the sea-loch some forty kilometres to the south, where the standard of the '45 would be raised half a century later at Glenfinnan (Chapter 28). Shiel Bridge lies on the A87 in the lee of the celebrated Five Sisters of Kintail, the mountain range on the north side of Glen Shiel. The glen narrows south of here into a deep ravine with rearing mountains on either side.

regulars, about two hundred in number, took up positions in earthen breastworks on the slope.

The battle began at midday with desultory exchanges of musket-fire, but at 5 p.m. the government grenadiers opened fire with their mortars. The heather was tinder-dry and caught fire, shrouding the battlefield with smoke. Lord George Murray was hit in the leg by shrapnel, and the Earl of Seaforth was wounded by musket-fire. The clansmen were unable to mount one of their typical Highland charges; they repulsed two determined assaults but eventually were forced to withdraw farther up the steep hillside, carrying their wounded with them. As the clans fell back on either side of the stream the Spaniards held their ground, but when they saw that the situation was hopeless they retreated up the steep slope and over the ridge of the Five Sisters to the north. The low point in the ridge where they crossed out of Glen Shiel is known as *Bealach nan Spainnteach* – the 'Pass of the Spaniards'.

The casualties had been relatively light – the Hanoverians apparently lost twenty-one killed and 131 wounded, but legend has it that only one Jacobite was killed. That night the clansmen melted away into the mountains. The white-coated Spanish troops had fought with exemplary courage under their leader, Don Alonzo de Satnarem, but next day, without food and with no idea of where they were, they had no alternative but to surrender. They were well-treated by the authorities, and in October were all sent back home to Spain.[1] Their part in the battle was remembered by the men of Kintail, who named the 'hidden sixth' of the Five Sisters of Kintail in their honour – *Sgurr nan Spainnteach*, the 'Peak of the Spaniards'. There is an interpretive panel at the roadside, just to the east of the old bridge, which explains the course of the battle.

The 1719 Rising had ended in humiliation. But all the Jacobite leaders had escaped – in particular the Marquis of Tullibardine and his brother Lord George Murray. Lord George would be back a quarter of a century later to command the Jacobite forces in the '45. Long before that, some of the wilds of the Highlands would be tamed by an Irish-born Hanoverian soldier with a genius for road-making: General George Wade.

---

1 There was much confusion over who should pay for their return. In the end, the Spaniards signed IOUs for their costs, and it is reported that their commander was held hostage until the debts were settled.

RISINGS AND RIOTS (1708–36)

General Wade: the great road-maker

Had you seen these roads before they were made,
You would hold up your hands and bless General Wade.
ATTRIBUTED TO MAJOR WILLIAM CAULFIELD,
WADE'S INSPECTOR OF ROADS

General George Wade (1673–1748) was a career officer in the army, the son of Anglo-Irish gentry. In 1725 he arrived in Scotland charged with establishing law and order and, in particular, demilitarising the Highland clans. He had seen action in Flanders, Portugal and Spain, and promotion had been rapid: ensign in 1690 at the age of seventeen, lieutenant by 1693, captain-lieutenant by 1695, lieutenant-colonel by 1703, colonel by 1707, brigadier-general by 1708, and major-general by the time he was forty. Wade was not a soldier's soldier, however – not an inspired field commander. He was easy-going and affable, fond of good living and good company. But his *forte* was military intelligence. He was skilful at sniffing out political intrigue and incipient unrest. When the Whig government under Robert Walpole needed someone to cope with a perceived crisis of anti-Hanoverian lawlessness in the Highlands, General George Wade was clearly the man.

The fears of a crisis had been sparked by a disturbing Memoir 'concerning the State of the Highlands', written by Simon Fraser, eleventh Lord Lovat, in 1724.[1] Lovat noted that the Disarming Act of 1716, which had offered compensation for surrendered weapons, had not only proved completely ineffective but had been a windfall for the Jacobite clans, who had imported shiploads of scrap weapons from the Continent and handed them over in return for the bounty. The real weapons were still there, waiting to be used in another Rising. The Highlands, he claimed, were now utterly lawless, with despotic clan chiefs oppressing their clansmen and (like Rob Roy) openly running bandit gangs and protection rackets.

---

1 Lord Lovat (1667–1747) earned an unenviable reputation as a cynical, devious and unscrupulous double-dealer. To get his hands on the title he tried to abduct the daughter and heiress of the late Lord Lovat, then forcibly married his widow. For this he was outlawed in 1698. He was a Jacobite for a time, and proclaimed the Pretender 'King James VIII' at Inverness in 1702 when King William died. He was pardoned for this indiscretion, and supported the government in the 1715 Rising; but he never shook off suspicions of Jacobitism. He would play a characteristically double role in the 1745 Rising, trying to hedge his bets, only to be tried for treason and beheaded at the age of eighty.

Despite Lord Lovat's reputation as a self-serving manipulator, the government could not ignore the warning. On 3 July 1724, at the age of fifty-one, Wade was despatched to Scotland. His instructions were:

> narrowly to inspect the present situation of the Highlanders, their manners, customs, and the state of the country in regard to the depredations said to be committed in that part of his Majesty's dominions; to make strict enquiry into the allegations that the effect of the last Disarming Act had been to leave the loyal party in the Highlands naked and defenceless at the mercy of the disloyal; to report how far Lovat's memorandum was founded on fact, and whether his proposed remedies might properly be applied; and to suggest to the King such other remedies as may conduce to the quiet of his Majesty's faithful subjects and the good settlement of that part of the Kingdom.

After six months, Wade delivered his full report. It made worrying reading for the government. Of twenty-two thousand men in the Highlands capable of bearing arms, he wrote,

> 10,000 are well affected to the Government, the remainder have been engaged in Rebellion against your Majesty, and are ready, whenever encouraged by their Superiors or Chiefs of Clans, to create new Troubles and rise in Arms in favour of the Pretender.

He ended:

> Before I conclude this Report, I presume to observe to your Majesty, the great Disadvantages Regular Troops are under when they engage with those who Inhabit Mountainous Situations . . . The Highlands of Scotland are still more impractible, from the want of Roads and Bridges, and from excessive Rains that almost continually fall in those parts, which by Nature and constant use become habitual to the Natives, but very difficultly supported by Regular Troops.

On Christmas Day 1724 Wade was appointed commander-in-chief of all His Majesty's forces, castles, forts and barracks in North Britain. He asked for £10,000, to be spent over two years. The money was to finance the various proposals he had made in his report: a new fort for Inverness, and major repairs to Edinburgh Castle and Fort William;

six companies of Highlanders, to be raised by their clan chiefs, to provide a militarised police force, or Watch;[1] a new well-armed thirty-ton galley on Loch Ness with a carrying capacity of eighty troops and eight guns; and – crucially – 'Mending the Roads between the garrisons and barracks, for the better Communication of his Majesty's Troops'.

Wade arrived in Scotland in the middle of June 1725, with the authority of a new Disarming Act to help in the pacification of the clans. In the course of the next fifteen years he would organise the building of two great garrison forts: Fort George on the site of Inverness Castle, and Fort Augustus at the southern end of Loch Ness, halfway along the Great Glen, which became the headquarters of the Hanoverian army in Scotland. He transformed Edinburgh Castle and Dumbarton Castle, both of which were now badly run-down.

But it was the roads which were to bring Wade enduring fame. He supervised the building of some four hundred kilometres of metalled military roads, five metres wide, on a base of large boulders covered by smaller broken stones and topped with gravel. He also built forty stone bridges, many of which have endured to this day, like the hump-backed 'Wade' bridge over the River Fechlin on the east side of Loch Ness, and the handsome five-arched bridge over the Tay at Aberfeldy (designed by Scotland's leading architect, William Adam), which is still in use.

Wade created four major routes through the central Highlands: Fort William to Inverness, to link the three fortresses of the Great Glen; Dunkeld to Inverness, creating the line of the modern A9;[2] Crieff to Dalnacardoch (on the Dunkeld–Inverness road); and Dalwhinnie to Fort Augustus over the spectacularly daunting Corrieyairack Pass. He used five teams of what he called his 'Highwaymen' – a hundred regular soldiers in each – with the help of local labour when necessary. This new road network certainly made the policing of the central Highlands much easier. Ironically, it was to be highly beneficial to the Jacobites at the start of the 1745 Rising; the lightning pace of Prince Charles Edward Stuart's advance on Edinburgh owed much to Wade's roads.

Wade's efforts to implement the Disarming Act of 1725 were less

---

1 This was the origin of the Black Watch (*Am Freiceadan Dubh*), so-called from its dark-green government tartan. In 1739 the Watch was increased by four companies and reorganised as a regular 43rd (later 42nd) Regiment of Foot.

2 A short stretch of the Wade road through the Pass of Killiecrankie, uncovered by excavation, is on view at the Visitor Centre there.

successful, on the face of it; no more than 2,685 weapons were surrendered, although Wade estimated that the Jacobite clans could muster as many as twelve thousand fighting men. But more importantly, perhaps, he built up a web of informers who had been suborned by special indemnities; for some years they helped to give the government a much clearer idea of what was going on in the impenetrable hills and glens of the central Highlands.

Wade left Scotland in 1740, his tour of duty done. His military career was by no means over, however. In 1743 he was made a field-marshal, and in 1745 he was appointed commander-in-chief in England. He would lead one of the forces which was closing on the Jacobite army at Derby when the fateful decision was taken to turn back for Scotland.

Apart from his activities in the Highlands, General Wade is also remembered in Scotland for his role in dealing with city rioting during his time as Commander-in-Chief of His Majesty's Forces in North Britain.[1]

The riotous years

While Marshall Wade was employed in pacifying the Highlands, and rendering them accessible to military forces, a subject of discontent broke out in the Lowlands which threatened serious consequences.

TALES OF A GRANDFATHER, CHAPTER LXXIV

The Union had been unpopular in Scotland before it was debated, while it was being debated, and after it had been debated. The 'compleating of the Union' by the new British government had exacerbated Scottish resentment. The government kept chipping away at what the Scots thought they had achieved through the Union; the concessions granted to specific economic interests in Scotland – the coal trade and the salt industry, for example – did not last long. The new taxes, and the appearance of large numbers of efficient new customs and excise officers, sparked countless disorders and riots all over Scotland. Paradoxically, the concessions which had *not* been revoked caused unrest as well: exports of Scottish grain had risen so sharply that there were

---

1   Wade died in London in 1748, at the age of seventy-five. He left a fortune of £100,000 and was buried in Westminster Abbey.

severe shortages in the home market, and in 1720 a series of 'food riots' erupted in Dundee and other east-coast towns.

All this was grist to the mill of popular Jacobitism, not just in the Highlands (where it was endemic) but in the Lowlands as well. Jacobite propaganda blamed all Scotland's ills on the 1707 Union; the only possible remedy was a return to the glorious pre-Revolution Stewart years of the seventeenth century.

In the 1720s the government of Britain – and of Scotland – changed radically. Horace Walpole, 'the first Prime Minister of Great Britain', took power in 1721. In his wake, to govern Scotland, came Archibald Campbell, Lord Islay.[1] For nearly forty years Islay was to be the colossus of Scottish politics, the uncrowned king of Scotland, operating from a base in London; in 1746, George II was to call him, sarcastically, the 'Vice-Roy in Scotland'.

Islay's chief executive in Scotland was Andrew Fletcher, Lord Milton (1692–1766), the nephew of Andrew Fletcher of Saltoun, the anti-Union propagandist; he was an advocate who had found employment in the Board of Excise but suddenly rose to prominence under the patronage of Islay – a Lord of Session at the age of thirty-two, and lord justice clerk by 1734.

Lord Islay, in his capacity as lord chief justice, was despatched to Scotland in 1725 to deal with an emergency. The unpopular malt taxes imposed on Scotland in 1713 had been largely ignored; in 1725 Walpole revived them. This provoked widespread protest in a number of Scottish towns and a brewers' strike in Edinburgh. Even in Glasgow, which had been doing very well out of the tobacco trade with the colonies as a result of the Union, there was a serious riot. On 23 June 1725 – just a few days after General Wade's arrival in Scotland – the elegant new mansion of Daniel Campbell of Shawfield, MP for Glasgow Burghs, a staunch Unionist and one of the earliest of the Glasgow tobacco lords, was looted and burned to the ground. The rioting spread; the city militia was overwhelmed and retreated to the safety of Dumbarton Castle, pursued by a jeering crowd for much of the way. General Wade sent in a large contingent of troops which quelled the insurrection without difficulty, and Lord Islay was sent to Scotland to bring the Glasgow magistrates to trial for dereliction of duty. It was

---

1 Lord Islay (1681–1761) was the younger brother of the second Duke of Argyll; he succeeded his brother as third Duke of Argyll in 1743. He had been created Earl of Islay in 1706 as part of the deal made by his brother to return to Scotland. In 1710 he was made lord justice general for life.

an uneasy situation. Lord Islay was expected to keep Scottish MPs and peers in line, and Wade was expected to keep the Highlands quiet. But Scotland refused to be kept quiet.

The Porteous Riot (7 September 1736)[1]

The coast of Fife, full of little boroughs and petty seaports, was, of course, much frequented by smugglers, men constantly engaged in disputes with the excise officers, which were sometimes attended with violence.

TALES OF A GRANDFATHER, CHAPTER LXXIV

In the spring of 1736 two notorious smugglers in Fife who had been subjected to constant harassment by the commissioner of customs in Kirkcaldy decided to get their own back. They were Andrew Wilson, a former baker who had gone to sea before settling in Fife as a dealer in contraband, and a much younger man named George Robertson. Together with a third, unnamed man they attacked the commissioner of customs while he was on a tour of duty in Pittenweem, forced him to flee from his lodgings and robbed him of £200. All would have been well for the two smugglers if their unnamed accomplice had not lost his nerve and turned informer. Wilson and Robertson were apprehended, tried in Edinburgh and sentenced to be hanged.

It was the custom in those days for condemned criminals to be taken under guard to St Giles' to attend a last service on the Sunday before their execution. On Sunday, 11 April 1736, Wilson and Robertson were paraded into the church. Suddenly Wilson, who was a very large and powerful man, seized hold of his two guards, grabbed the collar of a third with his teeth, and yelled at Robertson to run for it. The worshippers joined in, shouting encouragement. As Robertson broke free from the remaining guard and ran for the door, the congre-

---

1 The story of the Porteous Riot takes up much of the first part of one of Sir Walter Scott's early Waverley novels, *The Heart of Midlothian* (1818). The 'Heart of Midlothian' was the popular name for the old Tolbooth prison in Edinburgh, which at the time Scott was writing his novel was being pulled down. It was a high, turreted building which stood on what is now the open space before the main door of St Giles'. The position of the entrance to the old prison is marked by the design of a heart set into the cobblestones. After the Tolbooth was demolished, Scott acquired the first-floor door through which condemned prisoners were taken out on to the scaffold; he built it, rather incongruously, into an upper wall of Abbotsford House, to the left of the porch. The original iron keys of the Tolbooth hang on the north wall of Abbotsford's entrance hall.

gation made way for him and then closed ranks to hinder the pursuit. Young George Robertson got away from the church and vanished into the tenement closes of the High Street. He was never heard of again.

Wilson was left to face his hanging alone. The authorities were uneasy, and expected trouble: 'the mob' had shown its sympathy for Wilson, not only for helping his young accomplice to escape but also for being a smuggler, which was considered an honourable (and even patriotic) occupation. It was feared that there might be trouble at his hanging, so troops were brought in on stand-by, and the magistrates ordered a strong contingent of the City Guard to attend the execution, under the command of Captain John Porteous, supported by 150 soldiers.

Captain Porteous was a well-known and thoroughly unpopular figure in Edinburgh. A tailor's son, he had joined the army but returned to Edinburgh to marry one of the lord provost's maids in 1715, a connection which was apparently sufficient to land him the job of captain of the City Guard – chief of police, in effect. Since then he had carried out his duties with unflagging relish and severity.

On the morning of Wednesday, 14 April Wilson was brought out of the Tolbooth on to the scaffold. He was roughly handled by Captain Porteous (who, by contemporary accounts, was very drunk); the crowd which had gathered to witness the hanging was displeased, but made no attempt to halt the execution. When Wilson was dead, however, the crowd's temper became ugly. Several people scrambled up on to the scaffold to cut him down. Porteous, either in panic or bravado, seized a musket and fired at them point-blank. The crowd started pelting the City Guards with stones and dung, whereupon Porteous ordered his men to fire. Some aimed over the heads of the crowd, hitting spectators watching from their windows. Nine people were killed, and nearly twenty wounded. Even by the unexacting standards of the time, Porteous had exceeded his authority. He was arrested and charged with murder, tried two months later, and found guilty.

On the morning of 7 September, crowds gathered in the Grassmarket to witness his execution. But nothing happened. Instead, word came that Porteous had been granted a stay of execution the previous day by order of the queen, preliminary to a full pardon.[1] The

---

1   The queen was Caroline of Ansbach, wife of George II, who had succeeded his father, George I, on the throne in 1727. The king was on the Continent at the time, and Queen Caroline was acting as regent in his absence. The government in London felt that the conviction of Porteous had been a flagrant act of defiance against authority.

news of the reprieve infuriated the mob, but it dispersed without trouble, and the City Guard dismantled the scaffold and took it away to its usual place of storage in the basement of Parliament House. Meanwhile, in his cell in the Tolbooth, Porteous was holding a celebration party for his friends.

His celebrations were premature. During the afternoon, ringleaders of the crowd laid plans for a daring *coup*. That same evening, just before the sunset curfew, the gates of the city were seized by well-organised and well-disciplined groups of agitators. When the city had been effectively sealed from outside interference, 'the mob' assembled in the High Street, thousands strong. At 10 p.m. precisely, they surrounded the Tolbooth. Unable to break down the door, they set fire to it and then burst in.

Porteous's locked cell was apparently empty. Porteous, terrified by the tumult outside, had climbed up the chimney in his nightgown, only to find his way blocked by a metal grating. He was dragged down by the legs and frog-marched to the Grassmarket in a grim and disciplined torchlit procession. The silence was perhaps the most chilling aspect of the whole scene. On the way some men broke into a rope-maker's shop and removed a coil of rope, leaving a guinea on the counter for payment. The scaffold in the Grassmarket had been dismantled. Instead, a dyester's pole jutting high above a shop was used for the hanging. As Porteous struggled at the end of the rope, some of the crowd hacked at his bare, kicking legs. When all signs of life had ceased, the mutilated corpse was left hanging from the dyester's pole until morning.

It was lynch law, pure and simple, and could not be ignored by the authorities. The London government was furious, of course. The City Council of Edinburgh was suspended, rewards for information were offered; but no one came forward. After six weeks of investigation the solicitor-general (Charles Erskine) could put names to only half a dozen of the ringleaders, and they were nowhere to be found. A year later one alleged miscreant was put on trial – William McClauchlan, footman to the Countess of Wemyss. He persuaded the jury that he had been so drunk that he had had no idea of what was happening. He was acquitted; but the lord provost was deposed and disqualified for life, and the town of Edinburgh was fined £2,000.

Chapter 28

'BONNIE PRINCE CHARLIE'
AND THE '45

*The unfortunate insurrection of 1745–6 entirely destroyed the
hopes of the Scottish Jacobites, and occasioned the abolition of
the hereditary jurisdictions and military tenures, which had been
at once dangerous to the Government, and a great source of
oppression to the subject. This, though attended with much individual suffering, was the final means of at once removing the
badges of feudal tyranny, extinguishing civil war, and assimilat-
ing Scotland to the sister-country. After this period, the advantages of the Union were gradually perceived and fully experienced.*
TALES OF A GRANDFATHER, CHAPTER LX

The Glenfinnan Monument, at the head of the narrow waters of
Loch Shiel, is one of the most romantic and enduring icons of
Scottish history. It stands twenty metres high, a tall, hollow pillar
surmounted by the statue of a Highland chieftain. Erected in 1815, it
commemorates the place where Prince Charles Edward Stuart – Bonnie
Prince Charlie, the 'Young Pretender' – raised his standard on 19
August 1745 to launch his bid to regain for the Stewart dynasty the
throne of Great Britain and Ireland.

Glenfinnan lies on the A830 between Fort William and Mallaig, the
last lap of the 'Road to the Isles'. At the roadside sits a modest Visitor
Centre, owned and managed by the National Trust for Scotland. It
offers a range of multi-media presentations to illuminate the 1745

583

Rising – a diorama representing the Raising of the Standard, a painting by Chris Collingwood commissioned in 1995 to mark the 250th anniversary of the '45 Rising, multi-language commentaries and (on telephone handsets) examples of *piobaireachd* (pibroch) pipe-playing.

The monument stands about a hundred metres from the Visitor Centre, towards the shores of the loch. Around it is an octagonal stone stockade on which are plaques in Gaelic, English and Latin commemorating those who 'fought and bled in that arduous and unfortunate enterprise'. Access to the top of the monument is through a Tudor Gothic doorway leading to a thirty-two-step spiral staircase, ending in a crawl through a hatch on to the crenellated platform at the top. It is an interesting, if somewhat claustrophobic climb, and well worth the effort. The panoramic view must be one of the finest in Scotland. Glenfinnan lies in a magnificent amphitheatre of hills: great mountains rearing steeply from the narrow waters of the loch. The untamed grandeur of the surrounding landscape adds an epic dimension to the memory of the forlorn enterprise which would end, barely nine months after it began, in the slaughter on Culloden Moor. Yet nothing would have seemed more unlikely, five years earlier, than a major armed rebellion against the Hanoverian throne of Britain.

By the end of the 1730s it appeared that the Jacobite threat was over. With the accession of George II in 1727 the Hanoverian succession began to be more widely accepted as something settled and inevitable. Scotland, too, was beginning to prosper as the long-term effects of the 1707 Union bore fruit at last. The exiled and demoralised Jacobite court in Rome was sunk into a mire of endless intriguing and bickering.

But at least there was now a new figurehead for the Jacobite cause – a younger, better-looking and more charismatic Pretender: Prince Charles Edward Stuart, elder son of 'James VIII & III', who was now eighteen years old. If there was to be any possibility of a Restoration, it would be through him and not through his disappointed and disappointing father.

And then, dramatically, the political scene changed. Sir Robert Walpole had reluctantly gone to war with Spain in 1739 over the mutilation of a British sea-captain named Robert Jenkins in the Caribbean, who claimed that his ear had been cut off. This, the 'War of Jenkins' Ear', was quickly subsumed into a much larger conflict – the War of the Austrian Succession (1740–48): Frederick the Great, the twenty-eight-year-old King of Prussia, invaded the neighbouring territories of Austria and Hungary, newly inherited by the twenty-three-year-old

Empress Maria Theresa. France and Spain sided with Prussia, and Britain sided with Austria.[1]

The war was unpopular in England. In the general election of 1741 Walpole lost much of his parliamentary support, and in February 1742 he was forced to resign. But it was extremely popular with the Jacobites, for it brought England into conflict with the two traditional sources of military support for Jacobitism: France and Spain.

By 1743, France was determined on an invasion of England. Secret plans were drawn up for an army of ten thousand men, under the Comte de Saxe, to sail up the Thames to Maldon, in Essex, then make an immediate advance on London, picking up English Jacobite supporters on the way. Meanwhile there was, apparently, to be a diversionary landing in the north of Scotland involving three thousand troops under the command of the exiled George Keith, the hereditary Earl Marischal of Scotland. There was no intention of involving Prince Charles – but Prince Charles had other ideas: this was one party he was not going to miss.

On 23 December 1743 James Francis Edward Stuart, the Chevalier de Saint George, became the 'Old Pretender': he was persuaded to issue a Declaration which formally appointed his son Charles as prince regent. Charles left Rome before dawn on 30 December, announcing that he was going away 'for a few days' shooting'. Once outside the city he slipped away from his entourage and set off, in disguise, for France. After an adventurous and exhausting eleven-day journey he reached Paris; but he had been unable to keep his travels secret, and soon all of Europe knew that something serious was afoot.

The French army assembled at Dunkirk, and Charles insisted on joining it. By now, however, news of the impending invasion had reached England, and when the French fleet sailed early in February it ran into a score of British ships of the line. Before an engagement could take place a savage storm dispersed the French warships and drove many of the troopships ashore. Several vessels were lost with all hands, but Prince Charles's survived. With the element of surprise gone, the 1744 invasion of England was cancelled, and the Scottish expedition, still waiting in Brest, was disbanded.

Charles was not to be put off, however. He went to Paris to plead with King Louis XV to renew his invasion plans, but France would not contemplate another cross-Channel project. Undeterred, Charles

---

[1] In June 1743 George II personally commanded a joint Anglo-Hanoverian force which defeated the French at Dettingen; he was the last British monarch to command an army in the field.

decided to raise a rebellion on his own initiative. He sent word to selected clan chiefs in Scotland that he would be coming soon with French troops, arms and money. Then he set about raising funds himself. He pawned the 'Sobieski rubies' to raise loans from the Pope and from the Paris banking house of Waters. He made contact with the sons of the 'Wild Geese' who had left Ireland after the Battle of the Boyne in 1690. One of them was a wealthy Franco-Irish slave-trader and ship-owner in Nantes named Antoine Walsh, whose father had brought James VII & II back from the Battle of the Boyne; Walsh offered Charles the use of his eighteen-gun brig, the *Du Teillay*. Another Irish ship-owner who had made a fortune in the slave-trade, Walter Ruttledge, promised him a much larger ship to act as a consort – the *Elisabeth*, of sixty-eight guns and a crew of seven hundred, which could carry weapons and a small band of mercenaries to Scotland.

Throughout the early months of 1745 the young prince, with indefatigable energy and optimism, made his preparations. Most of his closest advisers in France urged him not to make a solo attempt; the Jacobite clan chiefs in Scotland were dismayed at the prospect of a Rising without the backing of foreign troops – 'this rash and desperate undertaking', Cameron of Lochiel called it. But Charles took no heed. He had assembled 3,500 guns, 2,400 swords, twenty artillery pieces and £4,000 in *louis d'or*, most of which were loaded on board the *Elisabeth* along with sixty mercenary marines. He himself embarked on the *Du Teillay*.

The two ships set sail for Scotland on 5 July 1745. As luck would have it they ran into a British man o' war, HMS *Lion*, west of the Lizard. In the ensuing engagement both the *Lion* and the *Elisabeth* were severely damaged. The *Elisabeth*, having suffered two hundred casualties, was forced to return to Brest with all the mercenary troops and most of the weaponry and military stores. The little *Du Teillay* was now on her own. Some of Charles's companions urged him to turn back, too; but he refused.

On 23 July Prince Charles landed on the cockle shore ('Princes Strand') on the west coast of the little Hebridean island of Eriskay,[1] between Barra and South Uist. Tradition has it that the large pink convolvulus which grows on Eriskay and nowhere else in the Western

---

1 The island was to earn itself further fame in 1941, when the merchant ship SS *Politician* foundered in the Sound of Eriskay and broke in two. Part of her cargo consisted of twenty thousand cases of whisky, which were unofficially salvaged by the islanders. The story became the basis of Compton Mackenzie's 1947 novel *Whisky Galore!*, which was filmed (on Barra) as a classic Ealing comedy in 1948.

Isles originates from some seeds which Charles had brought in his pocket from France. From Eriskay he sailed for the mainland, a hundred kilometres away, and dropped anchor by the northern shore of Loch nan Uamh, at the mouth of the Borrodale Burn in Arisaig. He stayed for a week in the old Borrodale House, which was destroyed by Hanoverian troops after the failure of the '45; close by, today, stands the quietly luxurious Arisaig House Hotel at Beasdale on the A830 from Fort William to Mallaig.[1]

The prince's initial welcome was discouraging. He had brought no money to speak of, and none of the promised French support. The lesson of the failure of the 1715 Rising and the fiasco of the 1719 Rising had been that any rebellion in Scotland was doomed unless it was heavily backed with foreign troops. The powerful Skye chieftains, Norman MacLeod of MacLeod and Alexander MacDonald of Sleat, flatly refused to join Charles, and he was strongly advised to go home. His reply has become part of Jacobite legend:

> *I am come home, Sir, and I will entertain no notion at all of returning to the place from whence I came; for I am persuaded my faithful Highlanders will stand by me.*

With that he sent the *Du Teillay* back to France. There was to be no turning back. Charles announced that he would raise his standard at Glenfinnan on 19 August. He headed south across Loch nan Uamh to Glenuig Bay on Moidart for a trek to Kinlochmoidart House, at the head of Loch Moidart, where he made his final preparations. He would find out soon enough how well his 'faithful Highlanders' would stand by him.

'The Seven Men of Moidart'

> *The adventurous Prince, as is well known, proved to be one of those personages who distinguish themselves during some single and extraordinarily brilliant period of their lives, like the course of a shooting star, at which men wonder, as well on account of the briefness as the brilliancy of its splendour.*
>
> SIR WALTER SCOTT, *REDGAUNTLET*, INTRODUCTION

---

1 Arisaig House, built in 1864, was requisitioned during World War II as the training headquarters of the SOE (Special Operations Executive). On the coast just below it are 'Prince Charlie's Cave' and 'Prince's Beach'.

'I landed with seven men,' Prince Charles would say, to underline and romanticise his early success; they would become known as 'The Seven Men of Moidart'. There is a potent, mythical magic about the number seven: think of the Seven Against Thebes, the Seven Bishops, the Seven Samurai, the Seven Deadly Sins, the Seven Sisters (the Pleiades), the Seven Sleepers, the Seven Wonders of the World. Similarly, the phrase 'Seven Men of Moidart' has the aura of larger-than-life heroes marching out of an impossibly brave world of myth to challenge the disconcerting realities of the Britain of 1745.

That is not quite the way it was, alas. For one thing, there were eight of them. For another, Prince Charles's first band of companions was a curiously motley collection of exiles, adventurers and ageing romantics, not all of whom everyone today would call 'heroes'.

Chief in rank among them was William Murray, Marquis of Tullibardine, who had taken part in both the 1715 and the 1719 Risings. His father, the Duke of Atholl, had died in 1724, but a special Act of Parliament had given the title and estate to the marquis's younger brother James, a staunch Hanoverian. Tullibardine's other brother, Lord George Murray, who had taken part in the Battle of Glenshiel in 1719, would be Charles's volatile and resentful general in the campaign.

Aeneas MacDonald, from Kinlochmoidart, was a thirty-five-year-old banker based in Paris. He had important links with the clans in Scotland, and five brothers who would all join the Rising.

Colonel Francis Strickland, from a Westmoreland Jacobite family, was the only Englishman in the group. His father had followed James VII & II to France.

The remaining five were Irish:

Sir Thomas Sheridan, seventy years old, was Charles's former tutor (and said to be his first cousin). His father was from an Irish family which had refused to accept the sovereignty of William and Mary.

The Reverend George Kelly had been imprisoned for ten years in the Tower after declaring his Jacobitism from the pulpit. He was a natural gambler, supporting himself by financial speculation.

Sir John MacDonald (or MacDonnell) was the nominal 'Instructor in Cavalry'. He was also renowned for his prodigious capacity for alcohol.

Antoine Walsh, the French-born and Irish-descended owner of the *Du Teillay*, was knighted by Prince Charles after the successful voyage to Scotland, given a gold-hilted sword and presented with £2,000.

John William O'Sullivan, a large and corpulent soldier of fortune with some military experience, was a former cleric from Kerry. His outstanding characteristic was his blind devotion to, and hero-worship of, Prince Charles. It would bring him into bitter conflict with Lord George Murray in the latter stages of the campaign.

On Moidart, Charles spent a week with Aeneas MacDonald at Kinlochmoidart House, assembling his supplies and planning his next moves.[1] Here he was joined by his friend John Murray of Broughton, whom he appointed his secretary. On Sunday, 11 August, escorted by fifty Clanranald men, he set off from Kinlochmoidart, up Loch Shiel by boat to Glenfinnan.

Monday, 12 August 1745 was a long, long day for Prince Charles Edward Stuart. When he arrived at Glenfinnan in the middle of the morning there was no one there apart from two shepherds who wished him God-speed in Gaelic. He retired to a nearby hut to await events. How many clansmen would respond to his call to arms?

Early in the afternoon a contingent of 150 MacDonalds, under MacDonald of Morar, arrived. So too did James Mor MacGregor, son of the celebrated Rob Roy MacGregor, who brought the welcome news that the MacGregors were on the way.[2] The clan which really mattered, however, was that of Cameron of Lochiel – Young Lochiel, son of the chief who had taken part in the 1715 Rising and was now living in exile in France. Prince Charles had been in contact with Young Lochiel, who had been dismayed by the enterprise but had reluctantly given his bond. At four o'clock in the afternoon the sound of the pipes heralded the coming of the Cameron men – eight hundred of Lochiel's Camerons, followed by Alexander MacDonnell of Keppoch with another three hundred MacDonalds.

For hours it had been touch-and-go. But now, with more than 1,200 clansmen – Camerons and MacDonalds – crowding the level ground at the head of Loch Shiel, the moment had arrived. The Royal Standard of white, blue and red silk was unfurled by the aged Duke William of Atholl (Tullibardine's father). He read out James Francis Edward Stuart's announcement appointing his son as his regent. Charles made a short speech. The assembled clansmen would not have understood a word of the proceedings, but they understood full well

---

1　A line of seven beech trees was planted in the grounds of Kinlochmoidart House by Cameron of Lochiel to commemorate the 'Seven Men'. Five of them are still there

2　James Mor MacGregor was working at the time as a spy for the lord advocate, who had sent him to report on what was going on in the western Highlands.

the significance of the occasion: they cheered themselves hoarse, and hurled their bonnets joyfully into the air in the setting sun.

The Jacobite surge

There was no time to lose. The Jacobites had learned a crucial lesson from previous campaigns – they had to take Edinburgh as quickly as possible and then, if there was to be any lasting success, march on London. There was no future in hanging around in the Highlands. The rebels waited only long enough for reinforcements to join them as word of the successful Raising of the Standard spread through the glens. Then they were up and away. They had the advantage of mobility, particularly as a result of the military roads which General Wade had constructed twenty-five years earlier to open up the central Highlands to Lochaber and Inverness; these could also be used for opening up the way to the Lowlands.

The government quickly got wind of the insurrection and ordered the army to smother it at source. The commander-in-chief of the British army in Scotland was Lieutenant-General Sir John Cope, a competent if not brilliant commander, who was based in Edinburgh. He had at his disposal some 1,400 troops scattered in garrisons and barracks all over Scotland. No one was quite sure of the strength of the Jacobite forces, nor what their plans were, but it was decided that they had to be contained within the Highlands before they could break out into the Lowlands. General Cope mustered all his available troops at Stirling, and made plans to march straight up the Wade roads to the north.

The logistics of the operation defeated him, however. He had to gather supplies for his men, and wait for money to arrive from the south. It was not until 20 August that he was able to set off north, heading for Fort Augustus in the Great Glen *via* the Wade road over the tortuous Corrieyairack Pass from Dalwhinnie. He made slow progress, and by the time he reached the road junction at Dalwhinnie he heard that some two thousand rebels had already bypassed Fort William and were swarming over the hills surrounding the Pass. It was not the terrain which any British commander would choose for an encounter with a Highland clan army, and General Cope bowed to the inevitable. His main task had to be to defend Edinburgh. He sent his supplies back to Stirling, while he himself hastened up the Wade road to the safety of Inverness, where he gathered some desperately-needed reinforcements. From there he swung across to Aberdeen, where he embarked his troops on 15 September for transport by sea to the south. He landed at Dunbar on 17 September.

With General Cope out of the way, the Jacobite army surged southwards, gathering clan reinforcements all the way. It marched triumphantly through Perth on 4 September with pipes playing and colours flying. At Perth the Highlanders were joined by Lord George Murray, younger brother of the Hanoverian Duke of Atholl; he drilled the new recruits on the North Inch, and issued them with knapsacks for carrying meal and cheese as iron rations on the march. The Jacobite army swept on, bypassing Stirling Castle and brushing aside a company of dragoons which tried to halt their progress at Linlithgow. On 16 September, the day before General Cope landed his troops at Dunbar, the Jacobites were at the gates of Edinburgh. The rebels had won the race for Scotland's capital.

At first the city council was determined to resist the prince and his Highland army (even though the lord provost, Sir Archibald Stewart, was suspected of Jacobite sympathies); but when a company of dragoons posted at Corstorphine retreated in disorder to Leith at the Jacobites' approach, their enthusiasm diminished. A force of four hundred middle-class volunteers started drilling on Bruntsfield Links, but melted away quickly as the news of the Jacobites' approach spread.

Edinburgh Castle was still held by the government, but the administration thought it wiser to decamp, and left the capital for the greater safety of Berwick-upon-Tweed. Besides, the castle was in no state to defend the city. Its cannons were obsolete and could probably not even be fired. The garrison was an elderly 'dad's army' of retired or invalided veterans, under an eighty-six-year-old governor.

The main body of the Jacobite army made camp in the King's Park, near Holyrood. The city council sent anxious delegations to parley with them, but to no avail. In the early hours of 17 September, Cameron of Lochiel with nine hundred men followed the carriages of the last delegation back to the city and seized the Netherbow Gate behind them, then marched confidently up the High Street and formed up in front of Parliament House. By the time the citizens of Edinburgh woke up, their city had fallen without bloodshed.[1]

At midday, Prince Charles left his encampment with his staff officers

---

1 The lord provost and lord lieutenant, Archibald Stewart, was suspected of collusion, and would later be tried on that charge. His acquittal, in July 1747, was considered 'an insolent verdict' by the lord justice clerk, Lord Milton.

and rode along the bridle-path to St Anthony's Well. He was in Highland dress, with a blue sash, red velvet breeches, a green velvet bonnet and a white cockade, and wore a silver-hilted broadsword. A huge crowd had gathered to catch a glimpse of him. He gazed down over the Palace of Holyroodhouse where so many of his ancestors had held court, then rode down to the palace. There was loud cheering as he dismounted at the gate and was escorted inside to the royal apartments. That afternoon at the Mercat Cross a crowd of up to twenty thousand excited people heard the prince's father proclaimed as 'James VIII & III, King of Scotland, England, France and Ireland', and Prince Charles as his regent. The 'pretended Union of the Kingdoms' was annulled. The crowd cheered again, and Lochiel's Camerons fired their muskets in the air. Edinburgh now belonged to Prince Charles and the Jacobites.

The Battle of Prestonpans (21 September 1745)

Hey, Johnnie Cope, are ye waukin' [wakened] yet?
Or are your drums a-beating yet?
If ye were waukin', I wad [would] wait,
Tae gang tae the coals in the morning.

On top of a former slagheap, just off the A1 near Prestonpans, a viewpoint offers a clear panorama of the site of one of the shortest battles in Scotland's history – the Battle of Prestonpans, on 21 September 1745.[1] It lasted barely ten minutes, but left a derisive legacy of rhyming ridicule which has haunted the reputation of the unfortunate English commander, General Sir John Cope, ever since.

At Dunbar, Cope had heard the news of the staggering ease with which the capital had fallen to the Highland army. There and then, despite his lack of trained fighting troops, he decided to march on Edinburgh, determined to bring the insurgents to battle as soon as possible. On the morning of 19 September, after resting his weary soldiers, he set off for Haddington. That evening the government forces bivouacked in fields just west of the town.

---

1   The battle-site is easy to reach by car from Edinburgh off the A1. Take the B1361 slip-road for Prestonpans. At the Meadowhill roundabout the B1361 turns left for Prestonpans. An elegant stone cairn on the left of the road in the shape of a recess, inscribed simply '1745', commemorates the battle; a road to the left of the cairn leads to the start of the path to the viewpoint at the top of the slagheap.

The news that Cope was on the march reached Edinburgh the same day. The Highlanders had by now moved their encampment to the area around the attractive little village of Duddingston on the south-eastern outskirts of Edinburgh, overlooking Duddingston Loch and nestling in the lee of Arthur's Seat. That evening Prince Charles held a council of war. The house at 8 The Causeway carries an inscribed panel above the front door:

> *In this house on 19th September 1745*
> *Prince Charles Edward Stuart*
> *held his Council of War before the Battle*
> *of Prestonpans.*

The council of war resolved to march east to intercept General Cope and engage him in battle. Next morning the Jacobite army moved out of its camp and headed towards Musselburgh.

At the same time Cope pushed on towards Haddington. When his scouts brought news that the Jacobites had crossed the River Esk and were now at Musselburgh, he halted and drew up his army on the flat stubble-fields near the hamlet of Prestonpans, less than a mile from the sea, facing west towards Musselburgh with the marshy ground known as the 'Tranent Meadows' protecting his left flank. It was, to his eyes, an impregnable position. He had six squadrons of dragoons, three companies of foot and some Scottish volunteers – about two thousand men in all – and a small artillery battery of six one-and-a-half pounders and four mortars.

The rebels took up position on the high ground around Falside Hill, to the south of the government position. It afforded them an excellent view of Cope's camp, but what they saw caused them some unease. They had no artillery and not many muskets, only the customary Highlanders' armoury of broadswords and dirks. General Cope had wheeled his line to the left, to face the Jacobites on Falside Hill, with the bogs of the Tranent Meadows to his front and the sea at his back. Without artillery support, there seemed no way of attacking the government army except by a frontal assault across the open, reedy marshlands, and that would surely cost heavy casualties.

That evening, however, a local volunteer, Robert Anderson of Whitburgh, came into the Jacobite camp. He knew the marshes well, because he used to go snipe-shooting in them as a boy, and he was aware of a path through them to the east, which would outflank the government position. Under cover of darkness and a dense east-coast haar (sea-mist) the rebel forces, in slender columns three men abreast, started threading their way through the marshes. By dawn they had crept right round Cope's left flank.

'Hey, Johnnie Cope, are ye waukin' yet?' jeers the song. Cope was certainly awake. He had been up all night, expecting some such manoeuvre. Just before first light a dragoon sentry alerted the camp to the movement. Cope quickly swung his whole line round to face east towards the enemy.

As soon as the last Highlanders were in position, just after sunrise, Lochiel's Camerons on the Jacobite left flank charged towards the government artillery, with the MacDonalds racing forward on the right. The speed and ferocity of the Highland charge unnerved the defenders. The Hanoverian artillerymen, with the rising sun full in their faces, broke and fled, followed by the dragoons. Cope's carefully chosen enclosed position was now a death-trap. He tried to rally his men, but could only lead a party of two hundred stragglers up a side lane ('Johnnie Cope's Road') to regroup in an adjacent field, where they refused to return to the battle. Cope and his aide-de-camp could do nothing but gallop off southwards to Lauder and Coldstream and on to the safety of Berwick-upon-Tweed next day. Here, it is alleged (incorrectly), he had the humiliation of being the first general ever to bring to his superiors the news of his own defeat.

As a battle, Prestonpans had lasted less than ten minutes. Some 150 government infantry and dragoons were killed, a hundred were wounded and 1,500 were taken prisoner (many of whom later joined the prince's army). The Highlanders lost thirty killed, and seventy were wounded. They captured all Cope's artillery and ammunition, together with his pay chest and the £2,500 it contained.

In due course, Sir John Cope was 'examined' by a board of general officers (including old General Wade) – an informal court martial. After the evidence was heard, he was cleared of all charges. The Board found that:

> he did his Duty as an Officer, both before, at, and after the
> Action: and that his personal Behaviour was without Reproach.

Balladry has given a different verdict: literally or metaphorically, John-nie Cope was 'caught napping':

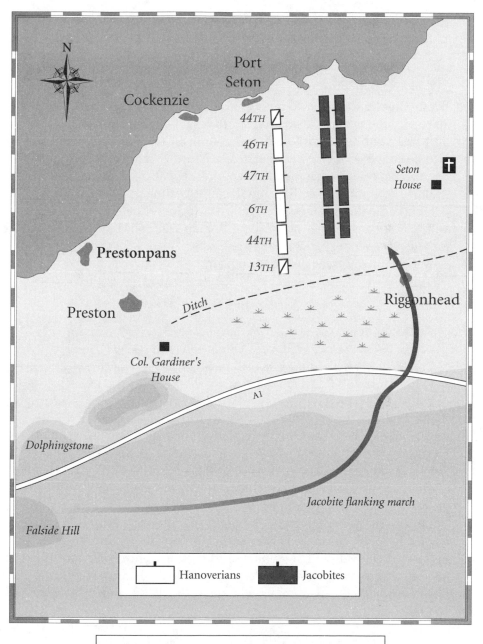

THE BATTLE OF PRESTONPANS,
21 SEPTEMBER 1745

In faith, quo [said] Johnnie, I got sic flegs [such blows]
Wi' their claymores an' philabegs [kilts],
Gin [if] I face them again, de'il brak [break] my legs,
So I wish you a' good morning.[1]

Prince Charles was eager to push on to Berwick-upon-Tweed immediately after the battle as a preliminary to invading England, but he was prevailed upon to return to Edinburgh to instil some military training into his enthusiastic clansmen and to await further clan reinforcements. So, on Sunday, 22 September, the victorious Highland army re-entered the capital with pipes skirling and drums a-beating. At the rear of the column came the prisoners and the spoils of war – the enemy colours and the captured guns – as in some Roman triumph. But the prince forbade any overt expressions of triumphalism: there were to be no bonfires, no rejoicing at the deaths of so many of his father's subjects.

The Prince and the palace

The Court at Holyrood was in those halcyon days of Jacobitism
so much frequented by persons of distinction, that it might almost
have been supposed the restoration had already taken place.
TALES OF A GRANDFATHER, CHAPTER LXXIX

Holyroodhouse was a royal palace which had been longing for royalty for decades. It had been completed during the reign of Charles II, but had never been the home of a reigning monarch. James VII & II had lived there as the Duke of York in 1680–82, and established a glittering court whose brilliance was remembered with nostalgic affection for a generation. Now Holyroodhouse was about to come into its own again.

On his very first evening in Edinburgh, 18 September, Prince Charles had held a hastily-arranged ball for fashionable Edinburgh society. Now, on his return, balls and receptions in the great picture gallery of the palace became regular events. The young Neil Gow, greatest of Scots traditional fiddlers, was summoned to play for Charles and his guests.[2]

---

1 The song was written immediately after the battle by Adam Skirving, a farmer from near Haddington. The pipe march 'Johnnie Cope' is still played at Reveille by most of the Scottish regiments.
2 Gow (1727–1807) was the first of a remarkable family of fiddlers and composers who revived and refreshed the traditional music of reels and strathspeys for Scottish country dancing in the eighteenth century.

The prince, so young, so tall and so handsome, conquered all hearts in a wave of emotional enthusiasm – especially the fluttering hearts of the ladies of Edinburgh, who flocked to his side at every opportunity. But he favoured none of them with a dance, saying, 'I have now another air to dance, and until that be finished I'll dance to none other' – a noble sentiment which caused even more swooning in the ranks.

A formal council was established which met every morning in the prince's drawing-room at the palace. The more optimistic members exulted in the thought that Scotland was now in Jacobite hands. True, the castles in Edinburgh, Stirling and Dumbarton, and the government garrison forts in the Highlands, were still in government hands; but the government had fled to Berwick-upon-Tweed, and James VIII & III had been proclaimed king in all the major towns of Scotland. But the optimism was misplaced.

In the north of Scotland, Duncan Forbes of Culloden (1685–1747), Lord President of the Court of Session, Scotland's premier judge and a leading member of the Whig government, was working hard behind the scenes to rally those chieftains who were still wavering. He had authority to raise twenty independent companies of Highlanders for the government – and raising a company was a lucrative proposition for a clan chieftain. Such was Forbes's personal standing and influence that the far north was holding steady for the government after the Jacobite army had swept southward.

Nor had the people of Edinburgh committed themselves to any real extent, despite the enthusiasm with which the prince had been welcomed. A roster of declared supporters listed only 137 names, consisting of a few merchants, inn-keepers, watchmakers and gold-smiths. The Royal Bank of Scotland had prudently taken its reserves to the castle for safety, but hedged its bets by providing the prince with money to pay his troops.

The south-west of Scotland – particularly Glasgow and Ayrshire – was positively hostile to Charles.

Even more worrying to the prince's advisers was the constant haem-orrhaging of the strength of the Jacobite army. Replete with spoils from Prestonpans, scores of Highlanders were drifting back home for the winter; within a few days of the battle, the numbers in the camp at Duddingston had fallen from two thousand to 1,400.[1] Such a tiny

---

1 The story is told that immediately after the battle, the ageing Robertson of Struan had set off for home in General Cope's personal travelling carriage, wearing his chain and his fur-lined nightgown.

army would never be able to hold Scotland, let alone invade England.

The first priority, then, was to raise reinforcements. Emissaries were despatched all over the Highlands to try to persuade those clans which had not yet made up their minds. Gradually some of the waverers joined the prince's cause. Lord Ogilvie came with six hundred men; Gordon of Glenlivet with four hundred from Strathbogie and Enzie; the scholarly old Alexander Forbes, Lord Pitsligo, with 132 horse and 248 foot from Aberdeen and Banff. Some families were split in their loyalties: Lord Fortrose (son of the attainted Lord Seaforth) joined the government forces, while his wife brought out a number of Mackenzie clansmen for the prince. The incorrigible Simon Fraser, Lord Lovat, played it both ways, as usual – he sent his son, the Master of Lovat, to join the Jacobites, while he himself wrote to Duncan Forbes of Culloden pledging his undying loyalty to the House of Hanover.

By the end of October, the prince's army had grown to some five thousand infantrymen and, more importantly, five hundred cavalry. Support also began to trickle in from France in the wake of the Prestonpans victory. Three French ships evaded the naval blockade and reached Stonehaven and Montrose with arms, equipment and six four-pounder field guns, ten French artillerymen and a personal gift of four thousand guineas from King Louis XV. Late in November, after the Jacobite army had left Edinburgh, Lord John Drummond (the Duke of Perth's brother) would land from France with eight hundred men and an artillery battery of two sixteen-pounders, two twelve-pounders and two eight-pounder guns, and establish his head-quarters at Perth.

News was also filtering through of positive activity in France. On 24 October a treaty was signed at Fontainebleau, committing France to a full-scale invasion of England. The Duc de Richelieu started to organise eighteen battalions of twelve thousand soldiers, together with ships, arms, horses and provisions. Prince Charles's younger brother, Henry Benedict Stuart, made his way to Dunkirk, where the fleet was to assemble. The provisional date of the invasion was set for 15 December.

In England, the government was taking the Rising very seriously indeed after the humiliating defeat at Prestonpans. The king's chief minister, the Duke of Newcastle, wrote gloomily, 'I look upon Scotland as gone.' The king himself, who had been in Hanover, returned in haste to London; as a precaution he had the royal yacht brought up the Thames to the Tower and loaded with his personal belongings, in case he had to make a quick getaway. Thousands of battle-hardened troops were recalled from Flanders – three battalions of Guards, eighteen line regiments, nine squadrons of cavalry and four companies of artillery; and six thousand Dutch troops were sent in support, under the terms of a mutual defence treaty with Holland. Marshal Wade, the road-maker, who was now in his seventies, was appointed commander-in chief of His Majesty's forces in North Britain. The troops in England were formed into three army groups. One group of fourteen thousand men, under Marshal Wade, was despatched to Newcastle; the second, some ten thousand strong, under General Sir John Ligonier, headed for Staffordshire; and the third was deployed along the south-east coast to deal with the threatened French landing. In addition, the Duke of Cumberland, the corpulent younger son of George II, was recalled from Flanders.[1] In Scotland, the third Duke of Argyll (Archibald Campbell, formerly Lord Islay), who had succeeded his brother in 1743, threw his formidable weight behind the government and committed the powerful Clan Campbell to government service, supported by northern clans like the Mackays and the Munros.

England was now mobilised on a full war footing, and ready to meet the looming threat from Scotland. George Wade was even accorded the accolade of having an exhortatory verse in his honour inserted into the National Anthem:

> God grant that Marshal Wade
> May by Thy mighty aid
> Victory bring.
> May he sedition hush,
> And, like a torrent, rush
> Rebellious Scots to crush.
> God save the King.

To Derby – and back

On the 31st of October, 1745, Charles Edward marched out of Edinburgh at the head of his guards, and of Lord Pitsligo's horse; they rendezvoused at Dalkeith, where they were joined by other

---

1 William Augustus, Duke of Cumberland (1721–65), had been educated for the navy, but turned to an army career instead. He fought at Dettingen under his father in 1743, and was then appointed commander-in-chief of the allied army at the age of twenty-three. He was decisively defeated by the French at the Battle of Fontenoy in May 1745, but his troops greatly admired him for his courage in the field.

*corps of their army from the camp at Duddingston, and different
quarters.*

TALES OF A GRANDFATHER, CHAPTER LXXIX

As the October weeks passed, a major difference of opinion was emerging within the council between Charles and his Irish and French advisers (led by O'Sullivan) and the Highland chiefs and Scots officers (led by Lord George Murray). For the Scots on the council, the mission of the Rising had been accomplished: the government had been defeated, the Union had been repealed, and the 'king across the water' had been restored to the throne of Scotland. It was enough now to hold 'fortress Scotland' until such time as the French arrived to help protect it.

For Charles and his Franco-Irish 'Men of Moidart', however, the mission had only just begun. The prince had promised his father three thrones, not one. He insisted that there was a huge Jacobite following in England waiting to rise, and that the French were now totally committed to an invasion of England in support. A determined descent on London, he urged, would carry the day and ensure a Jacobite restoration to the throne of all Britain.

The proposal to enter England was carried, albeit by only one vote, and the Highland chiefs and Scottish officers reluctantly agreed to abide by the decision, in order to encourage and protect an English rising. The prince was all for a frontal attack on Newcastle upon Tyne, a do-or-die confrontation with Marshal Wade which would open the way to London; but Lord George Murray argued cogently for taking the west-coast route through England. The outcome was a compromise between the two strategies: a feint against Newcastle upon Tyne, while the major drive was to be directed against Carlisle.

On 31 October the prince left Edinburgh. On 3 November the army, now numbering five thousand men, left Dalkeith. One column under Tullibardine and the Duke of Perth, bringing the main artillery train, left Edinburgh for Carlisle, marching by Peebles, Moffat and Lockerbie. The other column, led by Prince Charles with Lord George Murray as second-in-command, set off for Lauder and Kelso, as if making for Newcastle, but then turned south-west at Jedburgh to rejoin the other column in the west. The stratagem worked: Marshal Wade stayed in Newcastle, waiting for an assault which never came, and the full Jacobite army regrouped for an unopposed entry into England across the River Esk on 8 November.

Compared with the combined forces which England had mustered

– some thirty thousand troops – the Jacobite army was pitifully small. Nonetheless, the Jacobites proceeded to lay siege to Carlisle. In Newcastle, the elderly Marshal Wade was goaded into action, and moved out to come to the relief of Carlisle. But he was not cut out to 'like a torrent rush, rebellious Scots to crush'. After struggling through deep snow for two days he reached Hexham. By then a thousand of his troops were suffering from exposure, and he turned back for Newcastle.

Prince Charles had welcomed the prospect of fighting Wade in hilly country, and had marched most of his army to Brampton, fourteen kilometres east of Carlisle. When Wade failed to show up, Charles marched back to attend to the siege of Carlisle. The Jacobite artillery was so lightweight that the gunners dared not discharge a single shot – that would have betrayed the smallness of their calibre. Instead, by a mixture of bluff and threat, the citizens of Carlisle were cowed into submission, and the 'Old Pretender' was proclaimed 'King James VIII & III' at the Mercat Cross on 15 November.

The victorious Jacobites in Carlisle were cock-a-hoop. But serious splits in the high command were already developing. The Scottish officers wanted to stay in Carlisle and consolidate their gains, or return to Scotland and defend what they had already won. Lord George Murray, piqued at not having been consulted on some significant decisions, resigned his commission as lieutenant-general of the expedition; only a threatening petition from the army persuaded Prince Charles to overcome his growing dislike of Murray and appoint him as the sole commander of the army. Charles, naturally, wanted to continue the march into England.

After lengthy arguments, the decision was taken to press ahead. On 20 November the first division of the Jacobite army started marching south on what everyone recognised was a distinctly precarious enterprise. They would be hopelessly outnumbered: there were three English armies in the field with a total strength of thirty thousand men, outnumbering the Jacobites by six to one. Marshal Wade was now lumbering slowly towards Lancashire with a force of nine thousand men. The Duke of Cumberland was assembling an army of ten thousand men in Staffordshire. And another force, numbering more than ten thousand, was mustering at Finchley to defend London. But still the Jacobites marched.

They marched via Penrith, Shap, Kendall and Lancaster to Preston, which they reached on 27 November. They were lightly equipped and mobile, travelling fast, and met with little or no opposition. But the promised aid from the English Jacobites, especially in Lancashire, where they had hoped for numerous recruits, was not forthcoming. From Preston they moved quickly on past Wigan until they reached Manchester, where they had high hopes of recruiting supporters in considerable strength.

One of the recruiting sergeants, a young Scotsman named Dickson who had been taken prisoner at Prestonpans and had then joined the Jacobite army, was refused permission by his captain to go ahead to Manchester on his own to drum up recruits in advance of the army's arrival.[1] He went nonetheless, with only his mistress and a drummer for company. The citizens of Manchester tolerated his activities for as long as they thought the Jacobites were close at hand; when no Jacobite army appeared, however, the crowd turned on him, and Dickson had to hold them at bay with a blunderbuss for what seemed like hours before he was rescued by a rival mob of sympathisers. For the rest of the day he strutted through the town with his escort of rescuers, gathering volunteers to join 'the yellow-haired laddie', Prince Charles. By the time his captain arrived with the main body of the army, Sergeant Dickson had enlisted 180 recruits. They were promptly enrolled as a grandly-titled Manchester Regiment, under the command of a Major Macdonald.

When the prince entered Manchester he was greeted with loud cheering and the ringing of bells. But there was disappointment over the level of recruitment – the commanders had expected at least 1,500, but the reality was only 250.

In the Jacobite ranks there was now much talk of turning back, but Prince Charles would not hear of it; he had received a letter from France from his brother, Prince Henry, dated 25 November, assuring him that the planned French invasion would now be launched on 20 December. Elated, the prince marched at the head of his troops, wearing a light plaid belted with a blue sash, a grey wig and a blue bonnet with a white cockade. They forded the Mersey above Stockport, wading through water waist-deep. At Macclesfield they heard that Cumberland was advancing to intercept them and was only twenty-seven kilometres away, at Newcastle-under-Lyme. Lord George Murray went off ahead of the Jacobite column to draw Cumberland out of position with a feint towards the south-west, as if the whole army were planning to join up with Jacobite supporters in Wales. The ruse worked. Cumberland rose to the bait and swung his army farther to the west, while

---

1   The captain was James Johnstone, known as the Chevalier de Johnstone, whose *Memoir of the 'Forty-Five* was first published in 1820.

the main Jacobite army headed purposefully down the unguarded route towards London, through Leek and Ashbourne. On the morning of 4 December 1745 the first Highland troops reached Derby.

The morale of the army was now at its highest. It had outmanoeuvred and bypassed the two large armies with which the government had tried to stop it. London was in a state of panic, stunned by the twin threat of the Jacobite advance and the rumoured French invasion. Many fled into the countryside. Shops closed and windows were shuttered. The City came to a standstill. There was a sharp run on the Bank of England, which only escaped bankruptcy by a neat stratagem to gain time; first-comers were first-served, and the Bank used its own agents to present piles of promissory notes, which were laboriously paid out in sixpences. The agents went out at one door and back by another, so that the *bona fide* holders of notes could not get near enough to present them.

The speed of the Highland advance had taken everyone by surprise. The Jacobites were now only two hundred kilometres from London, and the way was wide open. Surely nothing could stop them now, they felt. But Derby was to be the end of their road.

The retreat from Derby (6 December 1745)

Thus terminated the celebrated march to Derby, and with it every chance, however remote, of the Chevalier's success in his romantic expedition. Whether he ought ever to have entered England, at least without collecting all the forces which he could command, is a very disputable point; but it was clear, that whatever influence he might for a time possess, arose from the boldness of his advance. The charm, however, was broken the moment he showed, by a movement in retreat, that he had undertaken an enterprise too difficult for him to achieve.

TALES OF A GRANDFATHER, CHAPTER LXXIX

They called it 'Black Friday': Friday, 6 December 1745, the day the Jacobites began their retreat from Derby. Why did they stop? Why did they turn back?

On Wednesday, 4 December the Jacobites held a council of war in the handsome mansion of Exeter House in Derby, where the prince had taken residence. It seems that Charles's constant assurances of French and English support were beginning to wear thin. There had been no spontaneous upwelling of support in Cumbria or Lancashire, as he had confidently predicted; and the news from France suggested dithering rather than decisiveness. Lord George Murray feared that if the tiny Jacobite army advanced, it would be crushed between the two massive armies, led by Wade and Cumberland, converging on them. In the unlikely event of them reaching London, they would be slaughtered in the outskirts of the city. Even if the French invaded, their presence would only stiffen the resolve of the English to resist the Jacobite incursion. Murray argued passionately for a retreat to Scotland, where the real Jacobite strength lay.

The meeting lasted from eight o'clock in the morning until nightfall. Only the Irishman John William O'Sullivan and one or two of the 'Men of Moidart' supported the prince. Charles accused Murray and the others of wanting to betray him, and adjourned the meeting in a fury. Next day the council met again. Nothing had changed. It was clear that the prince was not going to have his way. He accepted the decision with angry resignation, and declared that in future he would summon no more councils, but would act as commander-in-chief on his own.

Lord George Murray had won the day; but had he lost the future? For two and a half centuries there has been endless speculation. Derby is one of the great, unanswerable 'ifs' of Scottish history. What the council of war did not know was that the Welsh Jacobites were already on the way to join them, and that the Oxfordshire Jacobites were getting ready to rise. But would that have made any difference? And even if the Jacobites had reached London, would the government have been paralysed into inaction? Would the Londoners have welcomed them (as Prince Charles was convinced) or wiped them out (as Lord George Murray feared)? Above all, perhaps, would it have made any real difference in the long term if the Jacobites had won and the Stewarts had been restored to the throne?

On the morning of 6 December the drums beat 'To Arms' and the Jacobite army, sullen and dejected like its leader, marched out of Derby, heading north. It was a withdrawal rather than a retreat, controlled and sensibly-paced. The weather was appalling – driving rain and sleet all the way. And the mood of the countryside through which they passed had changed markedly. Where there had been friendly curiosity, if not enthusiasm, there was now overt hostility. The retreating columns were pelted with stones and abuse. Stragglers were set upon and never heard of again. In the words of Horace Walpole, the novelist son of the former prime minister Sir Robert Walpole, 'No one is afraid of a rebellion that runs away.'

The Duke of Cumberland was now in hot pursuit with all his cavalry and a thousand mounted infantry, but Prince Charles refused to hurry lest the withdrawal become a headlong flight. The rear of the column, under the command of Lord George Murray, was hampered by the baggage train and ground to a halt on 18 December; when the English cavalry appeared, Murray fought them off in a moonlit rearguard action late in the evening and continued on his way.

The Jacobite army reached Carlisle early in the morning of 19 December, and here the commanders fell out again. The prince was grimly determined to leave a foothold in England; he would not acknowledge that his retreat was anything but temporary, and insisted on leaving behind a garrison of four hundred men and all of his artillery. Despite Lord George Murray's anguished pleas, Charles refused to hold a council to discuss the matter. The four hundred selected officers and men, mostly from the new Manchester Regiment, knew well that Carlisle could not hold out against the English armies, and feared that they were doomed to the hangman's rope or transportation to the colonies. They were right.

On 20 December the Highland army marched the fifteen kilometres to Longtown, where they crossed the River Esk into Scotland again. The normally shallow river was running fast in spate after the incessant rain. Prince Charles and the cavalry formed up in the river, to break the force of the current. The infantry then formed into ranks of ten abreast, locked arms and marched steadily across, with only their heads showing above the icy water. It was an impressive display of discipline and nerve. The Chevalier de Johnstone wrote:

> Fires were kindled to dry our people as soon as they quitted the water, and the bagpipers having commenced playing, the Highlanders began all to dance, expressing the utmost joy on seeing their country again – forgetting the chagrin which had incessantly devoured them, and which they had continually nourished ever since their departure from Derby.

It was a strange ending to the last campaign mounted on English soil, both melancholy and exhilarating at the same time.

1746: the final throes

The state of Scotland had materially changed during the absence of the Prince and his army upon the expedition to Derby; and the nation was now in the situation of one, who, having received a stunning blow, recovers at last from his stupor, and aims, though feebly and with uncertainty, at retaliating the injury which he has sustained.

TALES OF A GRANDFATHER, CHAPTER LXXXI

Once in Scotland, the army divided into two columns. One, led by Lord George Murray, marched by Ecclefechan and Lockerbie to Moffat, where it made a feint along the road to Edinburgh then swerved to march through Hamilton to Glasgow. The other column, led by Prince Charles, followed a more leisurely route. They paused overnight at Dumfries, where the retreating Highlanders stripped the town (and the townspeople) of shoes and exacted £2,000 in ransom for the provost and other merchants. They paused again at Thornhill, where they invaded Drumlanrig Castle, the home of the Duke of Queensberry (whose predecessor had been a chief agent in the passing of the Act of Union in 1707), ransacking it from top to bottom (not forgetting the well-stocked cellar) and, as a parting gesture, slashing to ribbons the duke's portrait of King William. The prince spent Christmas night at Hamilton Palace, and on the following day he entered Glasgow.

Glasgow had previously shown little readiness to support the Jacobite cause, and refused to accept Prince Charles and his council as the legitimate government of the country; in September, when the prince had demanded a contribution of £15,000, the city had paid a grudging £5,000 – and only after being threatened with military action. The citizens of Glasgow felt no more enthusiasm for the Jacobites now, especially when they were presented with a demand for several thousand pairs of shoes and hose, shirts, coats, waistcoats and bonnets. The clansmen were eager to loot the sullen city, and were restrained only by the personal intervention of Cameron of Lochiel.[1]

'The state of Scotland' *had* changed very considerably during Charles's foray into England. The government had been busy shoring up its strength wherever possible. Edinburgh had been retaken soon after the Jacobite army had left. The garrison at Inverness had been

---

1   There is a tradition to this day that the bells of Glasgow are rung to welcome the chief of the Clan Cameron.

greatly strengthened with companies of northern clansmen raised by the lord president, Duncan Forbes of Culloden. And although the traditionally loyalist town of Aberdeen was in Jacobite hands, the castle and town of Stirling were held by the government and its garrison had been reinforced.

The Duke of Cumberland, after reducing the defences of Carlisle and exacting cruel revenge on the garrison which Prince Charles had left there, had called off the pursuit of the retreating Jacobite army when it crossed the Esk to reach Scottish soil. He was recalled to London to face the continuing threat of a French invasion. Lieutenant-General Henry Hawley, a soldier better known for his harshness towards his own men than for his military ability, superseded the ineffective Marshal Wade at Newcastle upon Tyne and started moving his troops northward towards Edinburgh. England was making preparation for a full-scale civil war in Scotland.

However, the Jacobites had mustered a very considerable force in Perth, under Lord John Drummond, during the prince's absence. Drummond's original eight hundred men had been reinforced by thousands of clansmen encouraged by the news of the prince's unopposed march into England, and the Jacobite army in Perth now numbered four thousand men.

That was the position in Scotland when Charles reviewed his refreshed and re-equipped expeditionary army on Glasgow Green on 2 January 1746. Next day the Jacobites moved off in the direction of Stirling, to link up with Lord John Drummond and mount an assault on Stirling Castle.

The Battle of Falkirk Muir (17 January 1746)

The advantage, upon the whole, was undeniably with Charles Edward; but from the want of discipline among the troops he commanded, and the extreme severity of the tempest, it became difficult even to learn the extent of the victory, and to follow it up.
TALES OF A GRANDFATHER, CHAPTER LXXXI·

The Battle of Falkirk Muir on 17 January 1746, which was fought in a blinding storm, can with hindsight be seen to have been the pivotal battle of the Jacobite challenge against the Hanoverian succession. Here a large Jacobite army of six thousand men – the largest assembled throughout the Rising – confronted and defeated the best regular force the Hanoverian government was able to put up. There were more than twelve thousand combatants on the field. The battle itself was a confused, scrambling affair, fought in a storm of wind and driving rain – so confused, indeed, that neither side was sure who had won; but what was of greater importance was the failure of the Jacobite command to take advantage of the encounter. The Jacobites spent most of the month of January in or around Falkirk, and in doing so they threw away whatever initiative they might have gained. They were never to regain it.

When the Jacobite army had eventually left Glasgow on 3 January it divided into two columns, as usual. One column of six Highland battalions, led by Lord George Murray, marched purposefully in the direction of Falkirk, *via* Cumbernauld, as if they were heading for Edinburgh; if they *had* marched on Edinburgh they would have found the capital only half-defended, because General Hawley had not completed his troop movements from Newcastle. Instead Murray swung north before he reached Falkirk and moved to Bannockburn, just outside Stirling – a hallowed place in the military history of Scotland. He posted Lord Elcho to Linlithgow with a detachment of cavalry to patrol the road to Edinburgh, thirty kilometres away.

Prince Charles brought the other column more directly *via* Kilsyth to Bannockburn, where he set up his headquarters. He stayed at Bannockburn House as the guest of Sir Hugh Paterson, a Jacobite supporter; there he met Sir Hugh's handsome twenty-two-year-old niece, Clementina Walkinshaw, with whom he would have an affair (and, much later, an illegitimate daughter).

Lord John Drummond came south from Perth with his four thousand men, ferrying his heavy artillery with the greatest difficulty across the River Forth to Alloa in the face of harassment from British naval frigates. Prince Charles now had at his disposal a force of some eight thousand men or more – double the size of the army with which he had invaded England.

On the evening of 5 January a drummer was sent to Stirling to demand the surrender of the town, which was now almost completely surrounded by Jacobite forces. The garrison of five hundred raw militiamen responded with a fusillade of musket-fire, whereupon the drummer dropped his drum and ran for his life. Three days later the town council thought better of its defiance, and agreed to surrender.

Stirling Castle, however, stood firm. It was held by a small garrison of seasoned regulars and militia, under the command of General William Blakeney. Blakeney, a lively septuagenarian, politely declined to surrender, saying that His Royal Highness would assuredly have a very bad opinion of him were he capable of surrendering the castle in such a cowardly manner.

Prince Charles accordingly ordered the castle to be besieged. He entrusted the task to a French artillery 'expert' of Scottish descent, Monsieur Mirabel de Gordon, known as the Marquis de Mirabelle, who had come from France with Lord John Drummond. The marquis was an exotic figure who claimed to be among the finest engineers in France; but he did nothing to prove it. The Chevalier de Johnstone wrote:

> *It was supposed that a French engineer, of a certain age and decorated with an order, must necessarily be a person of experience, talents and capacity; but it was unfortunately discovered, when too late, that his knowledge as an engineer was extremely limited, and that he was totally destitute of judgement, discernment, and common sense. His figure being as whimsical as his mind, the Highlanders, instead of Monsieur Mirabelle, called him always Mr Admirable.*

Monsieur Mirabelle, who never seemed to be sober, set to work with a will, and ordered the digging of trenches for the Jacobite cannons. Unfortunately he chose a hillside site with only fifteen inches of soil on top of solid rock; what's more, the site was lower than the level of the castle's own guns, and well within their range.

Meanwhile, the simmering dissension among the Jacobite commanders came to the surface again. The Highland chiefs resented the prince's decision not to hold councils, and what they considered his undue reliance on the advice of his Irish 'Men of Moidart' – in particular William O'Sullivan. Lord George Murray handed Charles a petition on the chiefs' behalf, castigating him for lack of coherent command and the decision to sacrifice the Manchester Regiment in a futile attempt to hold Carlisle against the Duke of Cumberland. The prince dashed off a furious reply: 'When I came to Scotland I knew well enough what I was to expect from my Enemies, but I little foresaw what I [would] meet with from my Friends . . .'

Behind the resentment there may well have been another concern – the prince's drinking. Since the decision to turn back at Derby, he had been drinking very heavily late into the night and getting up very late in the morning when the army was already on the move. He seemed to have lost all his gaiety and insouciant charm, and his decisions were becoming wilful, ill-considered and erratic. Modern commentators are unanimous in believing that Prince Charles was already an alcoholic, and a serious liability to the cause for which he was fighting.

While the Jacobite army was frittering its time away around Stirling, the English General Hawley had brought his army of thirteen thousand men from Newcastle to Edinburgh. On 13 January he sent an advance contingent to Linlithgow. The Jacobite commander Lord Elcho fell back to Falkirk, where Lord George Murray had taken up residence. Hawley followed with his main army of six thousand men on 15 January, intent on relieving Stirling Castle, and Murray prudently withdrew to Bannockburn.

The Jacobites drew up in order of battle on the morning of 15 January on Plean Muir, south-east of Bannockburn, expecting an immediate attack from Hawley's forces. No attack came. On the following morning the Jacobites went to battle stations again, but still there was no attack – Hawley had stopped at Falkirk and was encamped there, showing no signs of moving. So, on the morning of 17 January, the Jacobites decided to take the offensive. The army moved cautiously towards Falkirk, skirting the main road to avoid detection and heading for the Hill of Falkirk, a stretch of moorland whose rim overlooked the government encampment below.

The tactic took the government army completely by surprise. General Hawley had been up on the ridge that morning and decided that no action was likely. He had established himself in Callendar House on the other side of Falkirk, the home of Lord Kilmarnock, who was commanding a troop of Jacobite cavalry. After his sketchy reconnaissance, Hawley returned to Callendar House to enjoy a bibulous lunch in the beguiling company of the ardently Jacobite Countess of Kilmarnock. His repast was interrupted at one o'clock by an officer bearing the news that the Jacobites were approaching fast. Hawley refused to believe it; he contented himself with sending instructions for his troops to put on their equipment, as a precaution, and went on with his meal. By two o'clock, however, the Jacobite intent was all too obvious, and a second messenger was sent to Callendar House. Hawley now set off at a furious gallop and arrived, wigless and dishevelled, to take command.

He was too late. The Jacobite regiments were almost at the top of the Hill of Falkirk. Hawley's artillery was bogged down in mire at the foot of the hill, his infantry were not yet ready, so he ordered three regiments of dragoons up the hill. The weather had been worsening all day and was now blowing a gale into the face of the dragoons as they scrambled up the steep slope. Lord George Murray ordered his men to hold their fire until they were all in place. The dragoons reached the top and advanced on the Jacobite ranks at a full trot. Then, and only then, when the dragoons were barely ten paces away, did Murray give the order to fire. The effect of the first volley at point-blank range was devastating: eighty troopers fell dead. Most of the rest turned tail and fled down the hill, trampling some of their own infantrymen who were starting to toil up the slope. Those cavalrymen who continued to advance were now subjected to a highly unusual tactic: the Highlanders dropped their muskets and threw themselves to the ground, disembowelling the horses with their dirks as they passed over them or dragging the riders down by the clothes and stabbing them as they fell.

With the wind at their backs, some of the clansmen plunged down the hillside in pursuit of the fleeing dragoons, but they were caught by enfilading fire and thrown into confusion. Lord George Murray regrouped his remaining regiments and advanced steadily down the hill to demolish the government infantry still on the field. At that moment a squadron of Hanoverian dragoons, having rallied, rode back up the hill to outflank the Highlanders and, if possible, capture Prince Charles. The thrust was foiled in the nick of time by a group of Irish skirmishers who had been held in reserve. The dragoons retreated, and formed a rearguard behind which the government troops still on the battlefield retreated towards Falkirk.

It was now growing very dark, and the storm was raging even more fiercely. Everywhere there was confusion. Lord George Murray called a halt at the bottom of the hill; he had no idea where the enemy was, or even where most of his men were, and further pursuit would be futile and possibly hazardous. Murray gathered his troops as best he could and pushed into Falkirk to seek shelter for the night. News came that the Hanoverian survivors were in full retreat along the road to Linlithgow: the Jacobites had won a spectacular victory, but no one realised it yet.[1]

Next day the storm still raged. It emerged that the Hanoverians had lost some three hundred men, whose naked bodies lay white all

---

1   The only Hanoverian to take pleasure in the result of the Battle of Falkirk was General Johnnie Cope, who had retired to London by this time. He had taken bets amounting to ten thousand guineas in the coffee-houses of London that the first general sent to command an army in Scotland would be defeated, as he himself had been at Prestonpans. In 1927 a battle monument in the shape of a capped obelisk was erected in Falkirk at Maggie Wood's Loan.

over the field in the pouring rain; the Jacobites had lost fifty dead, and eighty others had been wounded. The Jacobites were able to seize the enemy's tents, ammunition and wagons, and three of their cannons.

General Hawley was distraught. On the night after the battle he wrote to the Duke of Cumberland:

> *Sir, my heart is broke. I can't say We are quite beat today, but our Left is beat and their Left is beat. We had enough to beat them for we had Two Thousand Men more than They. But such scandalous Cowardice I never saw before. The whole second line ran away without firing a shot . . .*

Prince Charles was strongly urged to set off immediately in pursuit of Hawley's demoralised army and capture Edinburgh before its defences could be reorganised. But he seemed incapable of taking a rational decision. After a day of dithering in Falkirk he left Lord George Murray and the clan regiments there and moved back to Bannockburn with the rest of the army. He took up residence again in Bannockburn House, where he developed a feverish cold which required constant ministrations from the complaisant Clementina Walkinshaw.

The siege of Stirling Castle was resumed. Monsieur Mirabelle, with unflagging confidence and enthusiasm, continued his futile trench-digging. At last, on 29 January, he had three of the huge cannon dragged into their emplacements. No sooner did they fire than the castle guns opened up in return, and within minutes all three of the Jacobite big guns had been demolished. The siege was over.

It had been a bad ten days for the Jacobites. The Chevalier de Johnstone was to write:

> *We ought to have pursued the English with the rapidity of a torrent, in order to prevent them from recovering from their fright, and we should have kept continuously at their heels, and never relaxed, till they were no longer in a condition to rally . . .*

Instead, Hawley was given the opportunity of reorganising and strengthening his army in Edinburgh. In Stirling, the clansmen were drifting away to their homes. All discipline broke down. Morale in the Jacobite encampment plummeted. The ludicrous failure of the siege of Stirling Castle was the final blow. On the next day, 30 January, the Duke of Cumberland arrived in Edinburgh to take over from

Hawley as commander of the government forces in Scotland. His soldiers loved Cumberland, and Hanoverian morale soared at his arrival. After a day in Edinburgh he set off for Linlithgow.

The last journey north

The chiefs of clans, and men of quality in the army, observing the diminution of their numbers, and disgusted at not being consulted upon the motions of the army, held a council, by their own authority, in the town of Falkirk, and drew up a paper addressed to the Prince, which was signed by them all, advising a retreat to the north.

TALES OF A GRANDFATHER, LXXXII

Once again the submerged antagonisms among the Jacobite leaders broke surface in another outburst of acrimony. The Scottish commanders in Falkirk sent a petition to the prince at Bannockburn House, arguing strongly for an immediate withdrawal to the Highlands, where they could seize the Hanoverian forts and build up an army of at least ten thousand Highlanders for a major offensive in the spring. When Prince Charles received the petition, according to the man who delivered it, 'he struck his head against the wall till he staggered and exclaimed most violently against Lord George Murray'.

Charles had decided on an immediate encounter with Cumberland which would 'decide the fate of Scotland', and was already planning to stage it on the historic field of Bannockburn. But his commanders were adamant for the Highlands, and eventually the prince was forced to give way:

I can't see nothing but ruin and destruction to us all in case we should think of a retreat . . . Why should we be so much afraid now of an Enemy that we attacked and beat a fortnight ago when they were so much more numerous I cannot conceive. Has the loss of so many officers and men killed and wounded and the Shame of their flight made them more formidable? . . . If you are all resolved upon it, I must yield; but I take God to witness that it is with the greatest reluctance, and that I wash my hands of the fatal consequences which I foresee but cannot help.

'I wash my hands of the fatal consequences . . .' These are the words of despair, not confidence, and they were to colour the increasingly arbitrary decisions taken by the prince over the three arduous months to come.

The Jacobite command planned to start an orderly withdrawal on the morning of 1 February. But news came on the previous evening that Cumberland had reached Linlithgow, and before daybreak the army was streaming away from Bannockburn in wild confusion, abandoning artillery and equipment in its headlong flight. Cumberland set off in pursuit, and reached Stirling on 4 February; he reached Crieff next day, and Perth on 6 February. But the Jacobites had vanished. Cumberland thereupon called off the pursuit and returned to Edinburgh to lay plans for a *coup de grâce* in the spring.

The Jacobite leaders had succeeded in imposing a measure of control over their fleeing men by the time they reached Perth. It was decided to divide the army into two again: the prince would lead the clan regiments through the Highlands along the Wade road to Inverness, while Lord George Murray would march the other column to Inverness by the east-coast route *via* Dundee, Montrose, Aberdeen and Peterhead. Accordingly, the Jacobites set off in heavy snow on their last road north on 4 February.

There were to be adventures a-plenty before the two columns were to link up again. Prince Charles, having reduced and set fire to Ruthven Barracks near Kingussie on the way, reached Moy Hall, twelve kilometres south of Inverness off the A9, on the evening of 16 February. Its owner, Lord Mackintosh, chief of Clan Mackintosh, was serving with the Hanoverian forces, but his beautiful and spirited young wife Anne was Jacobite to the core, and despite her husband's leanings she had raised many recruits for the prince's cause. She always wore Mackintosh tartan, trimmed with lace, with a blue bonnet, and rode with a pair of pistols at her saddle-bow. For this she was admiringly known locally as 'Colonel Anne'. When Prince Charles arrived on her doorstep that evening with a retinue of seventy-five staff officers, Colonel Anne whipped up 'a plentiful and genteel supper' for them all and offered the prince and a few of his companions the hospitality of the house.

As soon as Lord Loudoun, who was in charge of the Hanoverian garrison at Inverness, heard that the prince was at Moy Hall, he saw a golden opportunity of capturing him and claiming the bounty of £30,000 which the government had put on Charles's head. That night he assembled a force of 1,200 men, threw a cordon round the town to prevent Jacobite spies leaving, and set out for Moy to kidnap the prince. However, the Dowager Lady Mackintosh, who was living in

Inverness, heard of these preparations and despatched a fleet-footed fifteen-year-old clansman named Lauchlan Mackintosh to slip past the military cordon and run as fast as he could to Moy to raise the alarm. The boy reached Moy Hall in the middle of the night and roused the household. The prince threw on a cape over his nightgown, jammed a bonnet over his nightcap and bolted from the house with his men down to the shelter of the lochside. Colonel Anne called on the blacksmith at Moy, Donald Fraser, to try to delay Loudoun's raiders. When Loudoun's advance-guard under Norman MacLeod of MacLeod arrived, Fraser and a handful of friends opened fire in the darkness, shouting the war-cries of several different clans. Lord Loudoun was so unnerved by this reception that he called off the attack and scurried back to Inverness. His abortive raid became known as 'the Rout of Moy'.

Next morning the prince summoned his forces and advanced on Inverness. Lord Loudoun did not wait for them: he fled with his men north *via* the Kessock Ferry to the Black Isle, and Prince Charles captured Inverness without a shot being fired. The fort in the town (Fort George) promptly surrendered, and was later demolished. From Inverness a contingent of the Jacobite army set out to reduce the other two forts in the Great Glen – Fort Augustus and Fort William. Fort Augustus, which had been built in 1730 and named after William Augustus, Duke of Cumberland, capitulated after a two-day siege; but the Jacobites failed to take Fort William, despite a relentless bombardment which lasted for nearly three weeks.

Meanwhile, Lord George Murray had brought the second column of the Jacobite army safely to Inverness on 21 February after a difficult march up the east coast through heavy snow.

Cumberland was on the move by now with his main army of nine thousand men. He set off from Perth on 20 February, following the same route as Lord George Murray, and reached Aberdeen by the end of the month, closely supported by a flotilla of Royal Navy ships. Here he stayed for a month, training his men in musketry and a new bayonet drill designed to counter the Highlanders' renowned charges.

Murray and the other Scots officers had intended to retire into the hills and conduct a guerrilla campaign against the Hanoverian troops who were gathering in the north. The Jacobites were on their own ground and among friends, so they had every reason to suppose that they could hold the north and wear the Hanoverians down. But Prince Charles could not bear the thought of being seen to retreat in the face of Cumberland's forces. This time he was absolutely determined to make a stand, and nothing could change his mind. Meanwhile, contingents of Jacobites and Hanoverians engaged in a series of skirmishes all over the north of Scotland, with the honours regularly going to the Hanoverians.

The French government had not entirely given up on the rebels, although the plans for a major invasion of England had been abandoned after Derby. Occasional French ships were still trying to outrun the Royal Navy blockade to bring troops and arms to the Jacobites – one ship had reached Aberdeen on 22 February with 130 officers and men and some arms. But an ambitious attempt to bring £12,000 in gold came to grief: the ship (a captured government sloop renamed *Le Prince Charles*) was chased northward into the Pentland Firth, where she grounded at the Kyle of Tongue, and the gold was lost.

The outlook for the Jacobites was growing bleaker, and they were now beginning to feel the effects of dwindling resources and lack of supplies. Cumberland was meanwhile bearing down on Charles's headquarters. Moving along the Moray coast, he reached the last major obstacle between his army and Inverness – the River Spey, greatly swollen from the incessant rain and snow of recent weeks. On Sunday, 13 April a Jacobite force of 2,500 men under the Duke of Perth and his brother John Drummond awaited them on the other side of the river at Fochabers, where there was no bridge. For some unaccountable reason the Jacobites withdrew, leaving Cumberland and his army to make the difficult river-crossing unopposed. On Monday, 14 April Cumberland was at Nairn, twenty kilometres to the east of Inverness, with his infantry camped in the fields of Balblair, on the south-western outskirts of the town, and the cavalry bivouacked at Auldearn, three kilometres to the east.

The Jacobites were faced with a crucial choice: either to stand and fight, or to disperse into the hills and try to maintain a guerrilla campaign. Dispersal would mean abandoning all the ammunition, stores and transport assembled at Inverness, and the precious reserves of oatmeal and salt beef which the Jacobite commissariat had been hoarding there. Without these reserves, the army would starve. Prince Charles, supported as always by O'Sullivan, was adamant: they would stand and fight.

Urgent messages were sent to recall all the units which were away on forays. On 14 April, Charles rode out of Inverness at the head of his troops in a mood of high optimism and set up his headquarters at Culloden House, just to the east of Inverness, which had been hastily vacated by its owner, the lord president, Duncan Forbes of Culloden.

At six o'clock next morning, Tuesday, 15 April, the Jacobite army formed up on the moor at Culloden in full battle order. Prince Charles believed that his fervent wish to meet the Duke of Cumberland in a do-or-die pitched battle was about to be realised. But Cumberland did not appear; he had ordained a rest-day for his troops, and was celebrating his twenty-fifth birthday.

The Battle of Culloden (16 April 1746)

The final act of this great domestic tragedy was now about to begin, yet there remain some other incidents to notice ere we approach that catastrophe.

TALES OF A GRANDFATHER, CHAPTER LXXXIII

They used to call it Drumossie Moor – a bleak stretch of boggy, heather-clad upland moor above Culloden House, south-east of Inverness, overlooking the broad waters of the Moray Firth. This was where the last pitched battle on British soil was fought, on 16 April 1746.

Culloden is now one of the flagship possessions of the National Trust for Scotland. The moor had become unrecognisable as a battle-site. In 1835 a road had been driven right through the graveyards of the fallen clansmen. Much of the land was shrouded under a blanket plantation of sitka spruce, making it impossible to visualise the true setting of the battle. In 1980 the NTS purchased from the Forestry Commission 180 acres of land which had been planted with conifers. The mature trees were felled and the road realigned. At last it was possible to see again the moor as it had been when the encounter took place. The field has been marked with the positions of the kilted Highland clans and the red-coated Hanoverian regiments which took part in the battle. Experienced and well-informed local guides from the Visitor Centre, suitably garbed in Highland dress, conduct visitors over the site, explaining the ebb and flow of battle clearly and objectively. At the side of the field stands the six-metre-high Memorial Cairn, erected in 1881, which proclaims (with more feeling than historical accuracy) that

> THE BATTLE
> OF CULLODEN
> *was fought on this moor*
> *16th April 1746*
> *The Graves of the*

Gallant Highlanders
who fought for
SCOTLAND & PRINCE CHARLIE
are marked by the names
of their clans

The Graves of the Clans lie on either side of the road which was driven across the site in 1835; the traces of its passage through the battlefield graveyard can still be seen. The simple headstones are inscribed with the names of the clans. The trench of the Mackintosh dead measures fifty metres. Something like a thousand clansmen lie here, killed during the fighting or despatched as they lay wounded on the ground. More than a million visitors come every year to try to recapture a sense of that momentous battle. Many leave posies of heather at the gravestones. Culloden today is a place of quiet and dignified remembrance, a fitting open-air monument to massive tragedy.

When the Hanoverian army did not appear on 15 April, Lord George Murray urged that the Jacobites should turn the tables by taking the offensive, and suggested a surprise night attack on Cumberland's sleeping camp. Prince Charles was delighted with this spur-of-the-moment idea, but in reality it was profoundly flawed. The Jacobite army had not been fed for two days, and the men, who had been standing-to all day in the rain, were tired and cold. A night attack with even a small group requires careful preparation and good discipline; to try to lead an army of five thousand men for sixteen kilometres through pitch darkness, over difficult and unfamiliar terrain, was a folly born of despair. To compound the difficulty, a failure of staff work meant that the troops had been issued with only one small biscuit per man.[1] The mission was doomed even before it started.

It was nine o'clock in the evening before the first of the three columns set off, leaving the campfires burning at Culloden to try to disguise their absence. To avoid raising the alarm the Jacobites were to keep off the main road and march cross-country. By two o'clock in the morning the leading column of weary clansmen had covered only six kilometres, with the other two columns stumbling along in

---

1 One of the memorabilia of the '45 which Sir Walter Scott collected, alongside a wisp of Prince Charles's blond hair and a marble-sized musket-ball from Culloden, was a small, round piece of oatcake which had been in the pocket of a Highlander who died on the battlefield – surely the most poignant relic in the whole collection.

disorder and confusion far behind. No one (with the exception of Lord George Murray, perhaps) seemed to know where to go; the officers posted along the route were as confused as everyone else. As first light glimmered in the eastern sky, the attackers were still six kilometres away from the government encampment. Any chance of surprising the enemy had long gone, and the order to retreat was given. When Prince Charles was told that the attack had been called off, he merely shrugged and said, 'It is no matter, then; we shall meet them, and behave like brave fellows.'

When the clansmen got back to Culloden they collapsed from exhaustion where they stood, famished and freezing. All too soon, in the cold dawn of Wednesday, 16 April, the pipes and drums sounded to rouse them to take up their positions again on the moor. Cumberland's cavalry had been sighted only six kilometres away, and approaching fast.

The Jacobite camp was thrown into utter confusion. Only a thousand men answered the call to arms. Officers went galloping in all directions, trying to round up stragglers. By ten o'clock in the morning some five thousand exhausted and disoriented Highlanders were massing on the ground which had been selected for the battle. They still had not been fed. A raw wind was gusting over the moor from the north-east, bringing sharp showers of rain and sleet.

That morning the duke and his Hanoverian troops breakfasted early at Balblair on bread and cheese and a tot of brandy, then set out for Culloden in good order, with bayonets fixed. Cumberland had fifteen infantry regiments of the line, eight hundred mounted dragoons and an artillery train of ten three-pounder guns and six mortars. He was in no hurry. His men halted frequently on the way to rest and keep their ranks in order.

At 11 a.m. the two armies came within sight of one another. The Hanoverians formed up in two lines, facing west with the three-pounders in front and dragoons on the flanks. The edge of the left wing was where the Visitor Centre stands today; the right wing stretched across where the new B9006 now lies. The Jacobite army was outnumbered by two or three thousand. It too was drawn up in two long lines, with the clansman massed in the centre for a traditional Highland charge and the cavalry (such as it was) at the rear towards the flanks, and a few pieces of artillery at the front.

Between the armies lay five hundred metres of level, open moorland which was boggy in places. There has been much argument about the choice of the battleground – Lord George Murray claimed that it was a death-trap for his troops. Others maintain that it was good ground for the Highland clansman to charge over; but it was also ideal terrain for the Hanoverian cavalry.

The engagement began around noon, with a ragged bout of firing from the Jacobite guns. The Hanoverian batteries opened up in reply at once, firing with practised precision for about ten minutes at the massed ranks of the Highlanders, creating much confusion but not very many casualties. The clansmen stood their ground under the bombardment waiting for the word of command to charge – 'Claymore!'; but the line of communications had broken down and the order was delayed for what must have seemed an eternity.

At last the order came. The eight clan regiments, 1,500 men in all, surged forward in a wave of unleashed kilted fury. As they neared the government line, the artillerymen changed from round-shot to grapeshot – canisters of nails, lead balls and iron nails. The effect was devastating as the Jacobite front ranks were mown down by the hail of flying metal. The government infantrymen were now in action with their muskets in well-drilled routine, one rank firing while the others reloaded. It did not stop the Highlanders, but the irresistible impetus of their onslaught had been lost, and now the redcoats put into practice the bayonet drill they had rehearsed in Aberdeen to parry the Highlanders' broadswords: instead of engaging the clansman coming directly at him (thereby catching his bayonet on the enemy's leather shield), each soldier went for the unprotected right-hand side of the man on the attacker's left. The tactic took steady nerves, and complete faith in your comrades – and it proved very effective. Even so, some of the Highlanders managed to break through the left of the Hanoverian line, but only briefly.

The battlefield was now a mass of dead and wounded Jacobites. After the ferocious punishment of the guns, Charles's army was no longer capable of coherent defence. Grimly and defiantly the surviving clansmen fell back, still under heavy fire. There were individual acts of memorable heroism by clan leaders and clansmen alike; but then the dragoons came crashing into them, and the battle was over. It had lasted for less than an hour. The Highlanders, with all the odds stacked against them, had never stood a chance. They had lost at least 1,500 dead; the Hanoverian losses were only fifty dead and 259 wounded.

Cameron of Lochiel, whose ankles had been shattered by a cannon-ball, was carried from the field on the shoulders of a faithful clansman. Lord George Murray, who had fought with exemplary courage and skill, managed to rally some of the right wing and withdraw in good

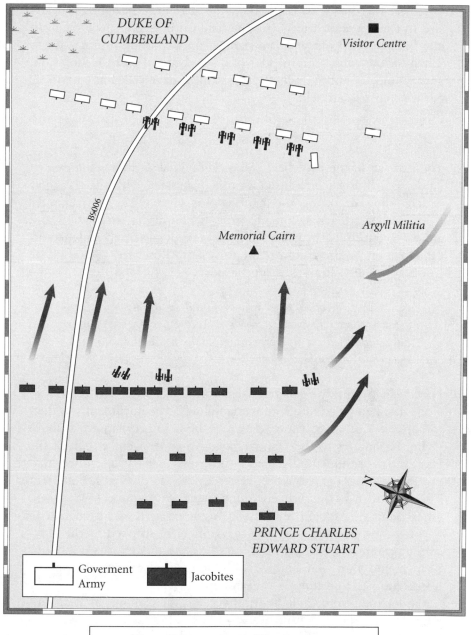

DUKE OF
CUMBERLAND

Visitor Centre

B9006

Memorial Cairn

Argyll Militia

N

PRINCE CHARLES
EDWARD STUART

Goverment
Army

Jacobites

THE BATTLE OF CULLODEN,
16 APRIL 1746

order. He was one of the last to leave the field. Prince Charles, shocked and in tears, was escorted from the field on horseback by O'Sullivan and his Irish staff officers. The sight of the departing prince was too much for the young commander of his bodyguard, Lord Elcho: 'Run, you damned cowardly Italian!' he is said to have yelled at Charles as he fled the stricken field.

Aftermath of defeat

The carnage of the battlefield was sickening, as is always the case in battle. But it paled into insignificance compared with the slaughter which followed. Before the fighting was even over, Cumberland's troops had started a systematic process of murder, mutilation and almost inconceivable brutality which has remained an ugly and ineradicable blot on the annals of British arms. Lord Rosebery, Liberal Prime Minister in 1894, summed it up bleakly:

> *No blacker, bloodier page will be found in the history of any country than that which records the atrocities against a brave but vanquished enemy perpetrated at the command and under the eyes of a British monarch's son.*

Lord George Murray's general orders to the Jacobites, issued the previous day, had fallen into Hanoverian hands. The document was doctored, and a sentence (now known to be a forgery) inserted about giving no quarter to the Hanoverians. An order went out from the Hanoverian command: 'Officers and men will take notice that the Public orders of the rebels yesterday was to give us no quarter.' The hint, with its implicit encouragement of vengeance, was taken. On Drumossie Moor a few of the wounded were despatched with bayonets, pistols and clubs. The survivors were stripped by the Hanoverian camp-followers and left naked on the moor for two days, or thrown into huts and bothies without medical attention, awaiting transfer to jails and dungeons elsewhere.

On the road from Culloden to Inverness, the Hanoverian dragoons slaughtered fugitive clansmen and innocent bystanders alike – men, women and children. Everyone in Highland clothing was assumed to be a rebel; and every rebel deserved to die. The folklore of Culloden weeps with horrifying tales of the merciless price of defeat. In a barn adjoining Old Leanach Cottage (which miraculously survived the battle and now stands next to the Visitor Centre) more than thirty wounded

James Graham, first Marquis of Montrose – 'the Great Marquis' – is one of the most romantic and gallant figures in Scotland's story. He led a spectacular Royalist campaign in Scotland in the mid-1640s in support of King Charles before going into exile; after the king's execution in 1649 he returned to Scotland in 1650 in a vain attempt to bolster the Royalist cause. He was betrayed and captured, and executed in Edinburgh in May 1650. The painting is copied from a portrait by the Dutch artist Willem von Honthorst, completed in 1649 while Montrose was in exile.

The attempt by Charles II to reintroduce episcopacy and sweep away Presbyterianism in Scotland led to armed uprisings by the Covenanters, who held fiercely to the tenets of the National Covenant. Outlawed preachers and their congregations held prayer-meetings in the fields, known as 'conventicles', which were guarded by armed sentries. *The Covenanters' Preaching* by George Harvey is a nineteenth-century depiction of a field conventicle.

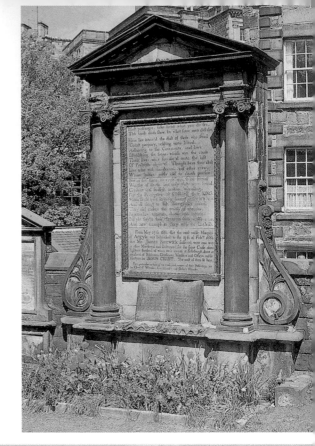

The Martyrs' Memorial in Greyfriars Kirkyard in Edinburgh was erected in 1707 to commemorate the estimated eighteen thousand men and women who died in the Covenanter struggles of the 1680s. There are scores of martyrs' monuments and headstones dotted all over Scotland.

UNVEILING CARGILL MONUMENT, THANKERTON 8TH JULY 1911.

The Reverend Donald Cargill (executed in 1681) was one of the first of the field preachers to advocate sedition against the crown as well as fervent godliness. The monument erected in his memory in 1911 at Thankerton in Maybole, Ayrshire, was constructed of stone from the large rock which Cargill used as his pulpit there two months before his arrest.

John Graham of Claverhouse has come down in history with two contradictory nicknames. He was 'Bluidy Clavers' to the Covenanters whom he hunted down on behalf of the government in the 1680s, and 'Bonnie Dundee' to the Jacobites he led to victory over the forces of William and Mary at the Battle of Killiecrankie in 1689. Portrait by David Paton.

On the night of 13 February 1692 the Macdonalds of Glencoe were assaulted by detachments of government troops (mainly Campbells) who had been enjoying their hospitality for several days. The resulting massacre has come down as one of the blackest deeds of infamy in Scotland's story. This nineteenth-century painting by James Hamilton depicts some of the shivering survivors of the assault.

A dilapidated former summerhouse in the grounds of the Moray House College of Education in Edinburgh was one of the venues for the signing of the 1707 Act of Union between Scotland and England. It was part of a garden pavilion whose outside door led into a conservatory. The Earl of Seafield, Lord Chancellor of Scotland, was the owner of Moray House in 1707; when the Act of Union was passed he and his fellow commissioners were pursued by an angry mob, and sought refuge in Moray House to complete the signing of the Act.

Queen Anne (r.1702–14) was the last Stewart monarch of Britain. She succeeded William III, and superintended the Act of Union of 1707 and the succession of the House of Hanover after her death. Contemporary portrait by Edmund Lilly.

The Articles of Union were drawn up on 27 July 1706. The names of the Scottish commissioners are on the left, headed by the Duke of Queensberry, the Queen's Commissioner in Scotland. The English commissioners are on the right.

Prince James Francis Edward Stuart was the son of the deposed James VII & II. He was involved in the abortive 1715 Rising, and became known as the 'Old Pretender' when his son Bonnie Prince Charlie took up the Jacobite torch. Portrait by M. Horthemals after Alexis Simon Belle.

In 1725 General George Wade, a career officer in the government army, was sent to Scotland to build forts and a new military road system for the Highlands. He built some four hundred kilometres of metalled roads which, ironically, would help the Jacobites to swoop down on Edinburgh at the start of the 1745 Rising. Portrait attributed to J. van Diest.

The Scott Monument in Princes Street, Edinburgh, was completed in 1846, fourteen years after the great writer's death. Under the canopy of the monument, a massive statue sculpted by Sir John Steels depicts a seated Walter Scott accompanied by his favourite deerhound, Maida. In the niches are figurines of many of the characters from the Waverley novels.

Sir Walter Scott was buried in the family plot in the haunting ruins of Dryburgh Abbey in 1832, not far from his beloved home at Abbotsford House. Watercolour by J.E. Alexander.

In January 1919 a major demonstration of 'Red Clydesiders' in Glasgow's George Square panicked the government into violent counter-measures. The raising of the Red Flag was thought to presage a Bolshevik rising.

On 11 April 1951 the young Scottish Nationalists who had abducted the Stone of Destiny from Westminster Abbey deposited it, wrapped in a saltire flag, on the high altar in the ruins of Arbroath Abbey. The Stone was whisked away by the police and promptly returned to London.

officers and men were found hiding; the barn was put to the torch, and they were all burned to death.

The atrocities and the indiscriminate killing went on for several days. Detachments of Hanoverian troops were sent far and wide to scour the Highlands for rebels on the run. The glens were laid waste. Men found bearing weapons were hanged on the spot, and their womenfolk were raped. Whole families were evicted from their blazing hovels and left to starve. Twenty thousand head of livestock – cattle, sheep and goats – were driven off to be sold at market in Fort Augustus, the money to be distributed among the victorious army.

No one in authority in London or Edinburgh complained; on the contrary, the repression of the Rising, however brutal, was welcomed. Aberdeen University appointed the Duke of Cumberland as its chancellor. In Edinburgh, which had welcomed the prince and his Highlanders only six months earlier, there was not a shred of sympathy: in May the General Assembly of the Church of Scotland sent Cumberland a letter, acknowledging that it had been enabled to meet

> in a state of peace and security exceeding our greatest hopes ...
> owing to His Majesty's wisdom and goodness in sending your
> Royal Highness, and to your generous resolution in coming to be
> the deliverer of this Church and Nation.

When Cumberland returned to London it was to a triumphant welcome on a virtually Roman scale. Handel composed an anthem, 'See the conqu'ring hero comes', to greet him. The flowering plant *Dianthus barbatus* was named 'Sweet William' after him; in Scotland, however, where the conquering hero had earned the name of 'Butcher Cumberland', the foul-smelling ragwort *Senecto jacobaea* was nicknamed 'Stinking Willie'.

All the lurking Lowland fear and hatred of the culture of Gaeldom, which had been growing for centuries, was now coming to the surface. The Gaels, with their distinct and 'alien' language and dress and social customs, were subhuman, they were vermin – they deserved no better than extermination. Nowadays it would be called genocide. Cumberland himself advocated his own 'final solution' to the Highland problem: the transportation of whole 'clans such as the Camerons and almost all the tribes of the MacDonalds (excepting some of those in the Isles) and several other lesser clans' – also excepting, of course, the Campbells, most of whom had fought on the Hanoverian side.

The gaols and prison hulks all over Britain were overflowing with

Jacobite captives. In London the Privy Council decreed that the prisoners of the '45 Rising should be tried not in Scotland but in England. Some had played prominent parts in the rebellion; others were accused of nothing more serious than that they had been overheard 'wishing the rebels well' or 'drinking the prince's health'. Serious or trivial, however, all charges could mean transportation or death.

Of the total of 3,471 Jacobite prisoners, 120 were executed: most by hanging, drawing and quartering, four by beheading because they were peers of the realm – the privilege of rank. Of the remainder, more than six hundred died in prison; 936 were transported to the West Indies to be sold as slaves; 121 were banished 'outside our Dominions'; and 1,287 were released or exchanged. Of the fate of the others, no information has survived.

New legislation was brought in to reinforce the military action. The Disarming Acts demanded that all weapons in Scotland be surrendered – including bagpipes, which were considered 'weapons of war'. Also prohibited was the wearing of tartan, the great plaid, the kilt 'or any part whatever of what peculiarly belongs to the Highland garb'. Even the speaking of Gaelic, the language of the hearth, was proscribed.

The escape from Scotland

It was believed that Prince Charles, after leaving the battlefield, was making his way to Fort Augustus, and some of the Jacobite survivors also headed there, believing it to be the rallying-point. The rest – some 1,500 men all told – made their way as best they could southwards to Badenoch, thinking that the rallying-point was to be Ruthven Barracks near Kingussie. There was still a chance of taking to the hills and continuing a guerrilla war of attrition against the Hanoverian victors. But Prince Charles had no intention of staying in Scotland, and told his followers that it was now every man for himself. His only thought was to escape to France. For him, the Rising was over.

Charles and his Irish entourage rode to a Fraser safe-house twenty-five kilometres south-west of Culloden, where he met some of his Scottish officers. There were bitter recriminations. From there the prince set off with his Irish confidants, heading for the west coast in search of a ship. By 20 April, only four days after the battle, they reached Arisaig, and went to Borrodale House, where they had stayed when they first landed on the Scottish mainland nine months before. The prince and O'Sullivan spent a week there before news of redcoats in the vicinity alarmed them into commandeering a small boat to take them to the Outer Isles. As the oarsmen rowed through the night, a furious storm blew up which drove them on to the coast of the island of Benbecula, between North and South Uist.

Had they stayed on Arisaig for another four days, everything would have been very different. The French were still doing what they could to help the prince, either by supporting the Rising or rescuing him if it failed: no fewer than six commando-style rescue attempts would be mounted from France over the next five months. On 30 April, four days after Charles had fled from Arisaig, the first of these materialised when two large, well-armed French frigates, the *Mars* and the *Bellona*, dropped anchor in Loch nan Uamh. They had set sail from Nantes two weeks before the Battle of Culloden, with orders to bring the prince out if he were in trouble, or to land munitions and money (£35,000 in *louis d'or*) if the cause were still alive. After beating off attacks by three smaller British men-o'-war patrolling in Hebridean waters, they reached their destination and landed the money and a large quantity of brandy. But the prince had gone, and the French ships set sail for France, crowded with Jacobite fugitives.

Flora Macdonald

Prince Charles would spend five months on the run in the Highlands and Islands while government troops scoured the country for him and government ships patrolled the sea. There was a price of £30,000 on his head. The hardships and hazards of his life as a hunted fugitive, the narrow escapes and the unswerving courage of his faithful supporters, have become the stuff of legend. But one brief, eleven-day episode has caught the imagination more than any other – the story of Flora Macdonald.

Dr Samuel Johnson, on his tour of the Hebrides with James Boswell in 1773, met Flora, who had become a celebrated national heroine. Later he wrote:

> *Her name will be mentioned in history and, if courage and fidelity are virtues, mentioned with honour.*

In 1746 Flora Macdonald was twenty-four years old, the stepdaughter of minor gentry in Armadale on the Isle of Skye. She had gone to North Uist to help her brother with the cattle and sheep on his summer shieling. The government net was closing on the island, and a desperate scheme was hatched for Charles to accompany Flora back to Skye disguised as her Irish maid, 'Betty Burke'. The prince was fitted out in clothing hastily run up by Flora and Lady Clanranald – a white, blue-sprigged calico gown with a quilted petticoat, a sturdy waterproof overcoat and a woman's head-dress. It was an incongruous disguise, for the prince was a tall man, and kept forgetting to shorten his stride to match that of the slight Flora Macdonald. Not many of the islanders were taken in.

Flora and 'Betty Burke' left North Uist at night on a boat rowed by Jacobite loyalists, and reached Skye before dawn.[1] They were fired on by militia as they approached the coast, but succeeded in landing without further alarms. For a few days they trekked from safe house to safe house, until they parted after a final meal in a tavern called MacNab's Inn (now the Royal Hotel) in Portree.[2] Prince Charles went on his way, first to the island of Raasay (which had already been searched and devastated by government troops) and then on to the mainland. A few days later, Flora Macdonald was arrested and taken to London, where she was held in custody for six months. She was already hailed as a heroine, and the government wisely decided not to make a martyr of her. After her release she returned to Skye, where in December 1750 she married Alan Macdonald of Kingsburgh, by Loch Snizort. They emigrated to America, but lost everything in the American War of Independence, and Flora returned to Skye, where she died in 1790 and was buried at Kilmaur.[3] The prince continued his stravaiging through the western Highlands from Loch Broom in Wester Ross down to Morar, handed on from one group of sympath-

---

1 That night-voyage has been immortalised in one of Scotland's best-loved Jacobite songs – 'The Skye Boat Song'. The words were written by Sir Harold Boulton in 1884:

> *Speed, bonnie boat, like a bird on the wing,*
> *Onward the sailors cry;*
> *Carry the lad that's born to be king*
> *Over the sea to Skye*

2 A romanticised depiction of their parting has adorned countless tins of Walker's shortbread over the years. It was executed in 1891 by George William Joy (1844–1925), an Irish painter of dramatised historical subjects, genre paintings and portraits. The painting shows Prince Charles taking a sentimental farewell of Flora Macdonald, both of them in full Highland costume. George William Joy is now best-known for his *The Bayswater Omnibus* (1895), a delightful picture which shows different social types of passenger aboard a London bus.

3 Such was the appeal of her gallantry that every fragment of the marble slab on her grave was carried off by pilgrims (a new memorial was erected in 1955). Flora Macdonald memorabilia were much sought after. Sir Walter Scott was given a pocket-book embellished by her with a covering of embroidered canvas; it is on display in Abbotsford House, as is the contract for Flora's marriage to Alan Macdonald.

isers to the next, somehow managing to keep a step ahead of his pursuers. Despite the huge bounty on his head, not a single Highlander betrayed his whereabouts. Occasionally word came that yet another French ship was cruising in Hebridean waters, waiting to pick him up, but Charles and his fellow-fugitives were unable to arrange a safe rendezvous.

In the late summer the pressure eased. The Hanoverian commanders either believed that Charles must be dead, or despaired of ever catching him in the trackless wilds of the Highlands. Most of the government regiments were ordered south from Fort Augustus to Stirling, and the naval presence in the Minch was scaled down. Word of this was sent to France, and in early September the sixth and final rescue mission, consisting of two large frigates, *L'Heureux* and *Le Prince de Conti*, set sail. From South Uist they were piloted across to Loch nan Uamh, on Arisaig. There they waited for two nervous weeks while the news was taken to Charles, who was holed up on the slopes of Ben Alder, a hundred kilometres away.

Finally, on 19 September 1746, Prince Charles set sail for France on *L'Heureux* from Arisaig, the place on the mainland where he had landed in Scotland almost fourteen months earlier. To the companions who saw him off on the shore, he said:

> *My lads, be in good spirits. It shall not be long before I shall be with you and shall endeavour to make up for all the loss you have suffered.*

But he never did come back. The Jacobite enterprise was over, although 'Jacobitism' would return.[1] Murray Pittock, Professor of Literature at Strathclyde University, sums up:

> *The '45 is too often portrayed – and romanticised – as a peculiarly Scottish event; but in fact it was an international rising, a play*

---

1 Jacobite sentiment and nostalgia lived on in poetry and song. The immensely popular 'Will ye no come back again?', by Carolina Oliphant, Lady Nairne (1766–1845), was written long after Prince Charles was dead and the Stewart line was extinct; but it still expresses sentimental yearning for the prince's return.

> *Will ye no come back again?*
> *Will ye no come back again?*
> *Better lo'ed [loved] ye canna be –*
> *Will ye no come back again?*

in international power-politics. It was not the 'Last Battle of the Highlanders against the Strangers'.

Some people view it as a lost cause, in the sense that those who were involved knew that they would die but nonetheless, in some kind of sacrificial sense, were prepared to offer themselves on the altar of the Highland way of life, or of Scottish nationhood, or of Roman Catholicism, or of the Stewart dynasty, or what have you.

The countervailing evidence comes from the international dimension: it would not have been a lost cause if the planned French invasion had taken place, if the Continental power-play had been carried through. There are all kinds of near-misses right to the end of the Rising. It very nearly succeeded.

What happened to the Stuarts?

On the whole, if Prince Charles had concluded his life soon after his miraculous escape, his character in history must have stood very high. As it was, his station is amongst those, a certain brilliant portion of whose life forms a remarkable contrast to all which precedes, and all which follows it.

SIR WALTER SCOTT, *WAVERLEY*, CHAPTER 58, NOTE

After the failure of the '45, Charles Edward Stuart was to live for another forty-two years. He was accorded a hero's welcome when he arrived in France, but was soon involved in scandal over a clandestine affair with his first cousin, the twenty-two-year-old Louise de Montbazon, while her husband (a close friend of Charles's) was away on military service. When Louise became pregnant, however, Charles jilted her and started an affair with another married woman, the Princess of Talmont, who was in her forties.

Charles's heavy drinking was now causing acute embarrassment. At the end of 1748, after the Treaty of Aix-la-Chapelle between Britain and France, he was ordered to leave the country. He refused, and remained conspicuous and defiant, ignoring all warnings. Eventually he was seized by French troops one evening when he was on the way to the opera, and bundled over the border to Avignon, which was still a papal enclave. He lived there for a time, until further scandal forced the Pope to ask him to leave.

Charles returned to France in disguise and took up with the Princess of Talmont again. In 1750 he visited London *incognito*. Here he renounced his Roman Catholic faith and became a Protestant. Back in Paris he sent an invitation to Clementina Walkinshaw, who had 'nursed' him in Bannockburn House in Scotland during the Rising, to come and join him. Their relationship lasted for nine tempestuous years, during which she bore him a daughter, Charlotte, whom Charles adored. He became insanely possessive over Clementina, and would beat her in his drunken rages. In 1760 she left him, taking Charlotte with her.

In 1766 Prince Charles's father James Francis Edward Stuart, the 'Old Pretender', died in Rome. Father and son had become estranged after the failure of the '45, and never met again. Charles became, theoretically, the *de jure* 'King Charles III' of Scotland, England and Ireland; but Pope Clement XIII, anxious not to upset the British government, refused to acknowledge him formally as king, and even had the royal coat of arms removed from the entrance to the Palazzo Muti.

In 1772, at the age of fifty-one, Charles married. His wife was an impecunious nineteen-year-old German princess, Louise of Stolberg. Charles curbed his drinking and fondly called Louise his 'Queen of Hearts', but the marriage was childless and soon became loveless; Charles, who had renewed his heavy drinking, once again became tormented by jealousy, and would beat his wife viciously. Within a year she had found a lover, the playwright Count Alfieri, and the marriage collapsed.

In 1774 Charles moved to Florence, where he lived in a palace provided by the Prince Corsini until he acquired the Palazzo Guadigni (later named San Clemente) in the Via San Sebastiano. He now sent for Charlotte, his daughter by Clementina Walkinshaw; she was married by this time, with three small children, but left them to be brought up by their father and went to Florence in 1784, where Charles had her legitimised and created her 'Duchess of Albany'. Father and daughter, both in ailing health, soon left Florence and returned to Rome. There Prince Charles Edward Stuart died on 30 January 1788, in the Palazzo Muti, where he had been born sixty-seven years earlier. Charlotte died shortly afterwards.

With Charles's death the 'succession' passed to his younger brother Henry Benedict, the Duke of York, styled by his followers 'Henry IX of Great Britain'. On the reverse of the medal he struck on his titular accession he inscribed the words 'Not By the Will Of Men But By The Will Of God'.

Henry had taken a cardinal's hat in Rome in 1747, and was known as Cardinal York. He was always conscious of his royal blood, but never made any serious attempt to recover the throne. He held high office at the Vatican, kept court in lavish style at his hilltop palace at Frascati, on the outskirts of Rome, amassed a fine collection of books and paintings and antiques, and gave generously to the poor. In his old age he had to flee for his life after the early campaigns of Napoleon, but was able to return to Rome in modest triumph in 1800. Now that the threat of a Jacobite revival was long since over, the British parliament could afford to be generous, and George III granted Henry an annual pension of £4,000. He lived to become one of the 'sights' of Rome, and died there in July 1807, at the age of eighty-two.

His ashes were deposited with those of his brother and their father James in the crypt of St Peter's in Rome. In 1819 the sculptor Antonio Canova was commissioned by the prince regent (the future George IV) to carve a tomb in the Chapel of the Virgin – among the most spectacular in St Peter's. It was a dignified end to the high drama whose last protagonists had long outlived their roles.

Postscript: Fort George

Fort George, on the jutting spit of land at Ardesier on the Moray Firth, seventeen kilometres from Inverness, is one of the mightiest artillery fortifications in Europe. It is also the most striking and most lasting tribute to the Jacobite Rising of 1745–46. The great fort was built in the worried aftermath of the '45 as a replacement for the old Fort George on its cramped eminence on the castle hill of Inverness, overlooking the river. Fort George (Inverness) had been wrecked by the Jacobites in the prelude to the Battle of Culloden, and the rebellion had exposed alarming weaknesses in the small forts which General Wade had built in the Highlands in the 1730s. The massive new Fort George at Ardesier was planned as an impregnable base from which the Hanoverian army could hinder any further armed threats to law and order. It was designed to the highest standards of artillery fortification; inside was a comprehensive range of buildings on a monumental scale to accommodate the governor and other officers of the fortress, the artillery detachment, and a garrison of 1,600 infantry, all enclosed in an area of forty acres within nearly a mile of fortifications. The buildings included a powder magazine, ordnance and provision stores, a bakehouse, a brewhouse and a chapel. The total cost was £92,673.19s.1d.

When the building work was completed, in 1769, the Highlands were relatively peaceful. Fort George never functioned as a garrison fortress; instead, it assumed a quite different role – that of a recruiting base where young and raw Highland recruits were trained before setting off to fight overseas for king and country – a British, not a Jacobite, king.

Fort George can be said to have been so powerful that it has no history, if 'history' is equated with the alarums and excursions of war, with triumph and disaster, glory and ruination. It never had to fight for its life, never knew the agony of siege or the humiliation of being slighted, never had so much as a single cartridge fired from its ramparts in anger or defiance. As a result, Fort George *is* history. It has a presence as well as a past, and is the most superbly preserved military monument of its time in all Europe. Not only does the entire and intricate defensive system survive, with its many-faceted ramparts and bastions, ravelins and lunettes, casemates and counterscarps; all the garrison buildings stand to this day, too – the officers' blocks and barracks, workshops and ordnance stores, guardhouses and magazine, even the original chapel.

When Johnson and Boswell visited the brand-new fort in 1773 they were lavishly entertained in the governor's house. Boswell enthused:

> *I could not help being struck with some admiration, in finding upon this barren sandy point such buildings – such a dinner – such company; it was like enchantment.*

In the years since then, Fort George has been a regimental depot, a fitting-out place, a station for mustering armies. In 1964, when the fort seemed to have no further military function, it was declared an Ancient Monument. In 1967 it was once more occupied by regular soldiers, the Royal Highland Fusiliers, who found that the stately Georgian fortress was still able to satisfy their needs as a barracks. In June 1986, while I was chairman of the Ancient Monuments Board for Scotland, Michael Ancram (the minister for local government and the environment) formally opened a series of visitor facilities to bring the fort's past to life for the thousands who flock there every year – unaware, perhaps, that Fort George is an even more striking tribute to the 1745 Rising than are the monuments at Culloden or Glenfinnan.

Chapter 29

SIR WALTER SCOTT: 'THE WIZARD OF THE NORTH'

Neither has any thing occurred in Scotland at large to furnish matter for the continuation of these narratives. She has, since 1746, regularly felt her share in the elevation or abasement of the rest of the empire. The civil war, a cruelly severe, yet a most effectual remedy, had destroyed the seeds of disunion which existed in the bosom of Scotland; her commerce gradually increased, and, though checked for a time by the American war, revived after the peace of 1780, with a brilliancy of success hitherto unexampled. The useful arts, agriculture, navigation, and all the aids which natural philosophy affords to industry, came in the train of commerce. The shocks which the country has sustained since the peace of 1815, have arisen out of causes general to the imperial kingdoms, and not peculiar to Scotland. It may be added also, that she has not borne more than her own share of the burden, and may look forward with confidence to be relieved from it as early as any of the sister kingdoms.

TALES OF A GRANDFATHER, CHAPTER LXXXVII

These are the concluding lines of Sir Walter Scott's *Tales of a Grandfather*. In Scott's eyes, the 1707 Act of Union and the end of militant Jacobitism in Scotland were the proper conclusion to the story of Scotland, as the nation's identity became subsumed into the larger, unified identity of Britain. Indeed, in the eyes of a recent

Historiographer Royal in Scotland (Professor Gordon Donaldson), 1707 was the end of the history of Scotland proper – and he refused to write anything about Scotland post-1707!

Yet the decades which followed the end of the '45 brought enormous changes for Scotland. The whole structure, the very fabric, of Scottish society and Scottish thinking, of the Scottish economy and Scottish enterprise, of Scottish towns and the Scottish countryside, was changing – and changing very fast. Tom Devine says:

> There was a kind of Scottish economic miracle in the second half of the eighteenth century. The speed of growth in Scotland at that time was probably the fastest in western Europe. From the 1760s onwards Scotland moved into a period of widespread structural transformation. The world of Scotland in 1830 was completely different from the world of Scotland in 1760.
>
> There was an extraordinary growth in towns and cities, particularly Glasgow. Rural society in both the Highlands and Lowlands was totally reconstructed. In the Highlands there was the break-up of the old clan land-systems and the development of individual crofting tenancies, and of course the beginning of the great Highland Clearances of land for sheep.
>
> In the Lowlands the changes were, if anything, even more revolutionary. In the latter half of the eighteenth century the smallholding (or cotter) class disappeared as agricultural 'Improvements' were introduced and new and larger tenancies were created. Land productivity rose fast, which allowed the growing towns to be fed.
>
> 'Modernity' was born in Scotland in the late eighteenth century as a consequence of all these changes.

Scott used the 1745 Rising as the setting for the first of his Waverley novels, the remarkable sequence of twenty-seven historical novels which he published (mostly anonymously) between 1814 and 1831. *Waverley* was the first. It became an instant best-seller: within two days of its publication on 7 July 1814 the small first edition of a thousand copies had been sold out. By the end of the year it had gone through four impressions. In his memoirs, the judge, writer and reformer Henry Cockburn recalled *Waverley*'s 'instant and universal' impact:

> *The unexpected newness of the thing, the profusion of original characters, the Scotch language, Scotch scenery, Scotch men and*

women, the simplicity of the writing, and the graphic force of the descriptions, all struck us with an electric shock of delight.[1]

The heady success of *Waverley* to a large extent engendered all the rest of Scott's novels, and made him the most prestigious author in Europe and the greatest Scotsman alive.

Waverley *(1814)*

Scott gave *Waverley* a subtitle: *'Tis Sixty Years Since*. That was because he started writing the novel in 1805, sixty years after the 1745 Rising, when – from his perspective – all the old divisions had been healed: Highlander and Lowlander, Jacobite and Hanoverian, Presbyterian and Anglican, Scotsman and Englishman had all been assimilated into a single, peaceful and civilised united kingdom. Scott had been mulling over the theme since boyhood, when he had met men and women with personal memories of the 1745 Rising. *Waverley* was built on the contrast of two worlds: Lowland modernism and Highland medievalism. But it was not the story *of* the 1745 Rising, nor was it a story *about* the '45: it was essentially an exploration of the past in terms of the present.

The eponymous hero of the novel, the young Edward Waverley, is an immature, naive and ineffectual Englishman, son of a Hanoverian and nephew of a wealthy landowner of Jacobite leanings. Waverley is a subaltern in the Hanoverian army, sent north in 1745 to help check the Jacobite Rising. He falls in with various Jacobites, like the eccentric Baron Bradwardine on the edge of the Highlands and his gentle daughter Rose, the desperate young zealot Fergus Mac-Ivor, chief of his clan, and his beautiful sister Flora, headstrong and ardent, with whom Waverley falls in love; eventually he even meets 'the Young Chevalier' Bonnie Prince Charlie himself. Because of his connections with the Jacobites, Waverley is cashiered (unjustly, he feeels). He joins the Jacobite army and shares in the hopeless heroics of the rebellion. In the end he accepts the ineluctable fact of the Hanoverian dynasty and is pardoned. He is rejected as a lover by the spirited Flora Mac-Ivor, who enters a convent after her brother Fergus is executed for treason; instead, Edward Waverley marries the gentle, faithful, non-political Rose Bradwardine.

Waverley is a historical novel – the first of its kind, perhaps. But it

---

1 Henry Cockburn, *Memorials of his Time* (1856).

is not a *romantic* historical novel in the accepted sense of the term; it is above all a heroic adventure story. Scott made no effort to romanticise the Jacobite cause, even though Waverley is dazzled by it. The Jacobite army is described as brave, loyal and astonishingly hardy; but individual Highlanders are mostly portrayed as self-interested and unprincipled. What caught the popular imagination were the marvellous descriptions of wild Highland scenery, the Homeric qualities of the conflict and the extraordinary gallery of ordinary people, comic or tragic but essentially 'real', however exotic; the public also enjoyed, subconsciously perhaps, the essential *safety* of the subject-matter – the sentimental appeal of an atavistic attachment to Jacobitism combined with the realistic and comfortable acceptance of how things were in the readers' own time.

For Scott, the down-to-earth 1707 Act of Union and the fugitive glamour of the 1745 Rising spelled the end of Scotland's Heroic Age; and it was the end of that age which would generate another, much more powerful and profound, 'Jacobite' novel at the culmination of his career as a writer of historical novels: *Redgauntlet*.

Redgauntlet *(1824)*

For many literary critics, *Redgauntlet* is Scott's greatest novel. By the time it was written he was at the peak of his powers. He had written several novels with a Jacobite theme, from *Waverley* to *The Black Dwarf* and *Old Mortality* and *Rob Roy*, using real historical situations as the settings for his own characters. In *Redgauntlet*, however, he freed himself from history and imagined a *third* Jacobite Rising – the 1765. Ian Campbell, Professor of Scottish and Victorian Literature at Edinburgh University, says:

> In Redgauntlet, *Scott turned to fantasy, a 'what-if' story, toying with the idea of a Jacobite rebellion in the 1760s which never happened, trying to force the current of change violently into new channels, to move the slow absorption of past into present into reverse and re-establish the Stewart line on the British throne. What if Bonnie Prince Charlie had come back, although proscribed and in exile, and had landed on the shores of Cumbria in disguise? What if a disaffected Jacobite rebel, like Redgauntlet, had tried to get all the surviving Jacobites together in the 1760s and kick-start another Jacobite rebellion?*

Sir Edward Redgauntlet (Herries of Birrenswork), a fanatical Jacobite, gathers a band of fellow-Jacobites together on the English side of the Solway and proposes another Rising. They all say it's a good idea, but that it has no chance unless Bonnie Prince Charlie returns to lead it: if he were there, they say, of course they would fight. Then Redgauntlet, with a theatrical flourish, produces the prince himself, the Young Pretender in person. The Jacobites realise that they are trapped in a snare of their own making, and have no alternative but to take up arms. Scott imagines a group of Jacobite rebels confronted with their own past and their own ancient loyalties, whose sense of honour allows them no alternative: faced with these imperatives, they would fight (just as Cameron of Lochiel had chosen, however reluctantly, to bring out his clan in the '45).

The dénouement comes with startling suddenness. As the would-be rebels are gathered around their prince discussing what to do, in walks the Hanoverian General Colin Campbell, unarmed and unattended. Campbell, clearly a descendant of that consummate politician the Marquis of Argyll, is the representative of King George III in London. He looks at the Young Pretender and bows to him: 'I do not know this gentleman,' he says, 'and I do not wish to know him; it is a knowledge which would suit neither of us.' He tells the stunned company of partisans that they had been betrayed weeks ago, and that he has been sent to sort things out. 'My commands are to make no arrests, nay, to make no farther inquiries of any kind, if this good assembly will consider their own interest so far as to give up their immediate purpose, and return quietly home to their own houses. And I promise you that this will be remembered against no one.'

With that, the rebellion collapses before it has begun. 'Then, gentlemen,' says Redgauntlet, clasping his hands together as the words burst from him, 'the cause is lost forever.' He goes into exile with the Young Chevalier and becomes a prior, leaving a desolating sense of loss and historical inevitability.

The London government had won the battle through superior espionage; it barely had to lift a finger. That is how conflicts are settled nowadays, Scott was saying: not by bravado, not by courage, not by blind adherence to a cause, but by better information. And how do you defeat someone? Not with a sword or a pistol, but with humiliation: 'Just be good boys and go home, and we won't hold this against you.' Scott the historian knew that what had hurt most after the Jacobite rebellions was that those who had lost their lands, their money, their possessions and their families had been ruined. In the novel,

Campbell promises immunity from that: 'this will be remembered against no one'. The government knows exactly which buttons to press, and it presses them. There is an army waiting just down the road, and a couple of men o' war moored in the Solway Firth; but there is no need to use military muscle any more.

For Ian Campbell, this is the moment when the romance of the past and the reality of the present collide dramatically:

> Scott the historian had moved from Ivanhoe and the old days
> of medieval swashbuckling and had ended up with Redgauntlet,
> only one lifetime away from his own readers' time. And he was
> saying – they're all over, those great, romantic, Jacobite, Scottish
> days, they're past, they're finished. Like it or not, London will
> run things from now on. There was no more need for rebellions
> – London would squash them before they started, anyway. Let
> us co-operate, let us live in the present. It was said with enormous
> regret: 'Then, gentlemen, the cause is lost forever.' Jacobitism had
> become an elegy.
>
> In my view, Scott the historical novelist was making a great
> contribution to understanding the past: you don't live in it, you
> enjoy it; you de-create it, and then you use it the better to
> understand the present.

In a sense, *Redgauntlet* is the most autobiographical of Scott's novels. Its two young heroes, Alan Fairford and Darsie Latimer (Redgauntlet's nephew), between them reflect the duality of Scott's own character. Fairford, an Edinburgh advocate, is the son of a strict, ultra-conservative Edinburgh lawyer; Latimer (who, according to Alan's father, 'has little solidity, Alan, little solidity' – 'solidity' being the ultimate Edinburgh virtue) is the young adventurer seeking to discover the secret of his parentage in the wilds of Dumfriesshire. Alan Fairford is Scott's Edinburgh self; Darsie Latimer his Borders self. Between them, after a series of lively adventures, they discover an ultimate commitment to the Hanoverian peace. It was the story of Walter Scott's own life.

Walter Scott: boy and man

Walter Scott was born in Edinburgh in 1771 in a house (long since demolished) in College Wynd; but he was a Borderer by blood and inheritance. His father, a lawyer, had moved to the capital to advance his legal career. The house in which Walter was born was a high tenement in a narrow, smelly alley. It was a fetid, unhealthy neighbour-hood, and six of Scott's twelve bothers and sisters died in infancy; he himself, at the age of eighteen months, contracted polio in the right leg, which left him with a limp for the rest of his life.

Edinburgh was only one part of his upbringing, however. To recuperate from his illness he was sent first to his grandfather's farm at Sandyknowe in Tweeddale, in the lee of the gaunt old tower-house of Smailholm,[1] and later to his uncle's house in Kelso. The spectacular exploits of the Borderers, and the ballads associated with them, were to set the boy's romantic imagination alight, and Smailholm would feature graphically in *Marmion*:

> *Methought that still with tramp and clang*
> *The gateway's broken arches rang;*
> *Methought grim features, seamed with scars,*
> *Glared through the window's rusty bars,*
> *And ever, by the winter's hearth,*
> *Old tales I heard of woe or mirth,*
> *Of lovers' sleights, of ladies' charms,*
> *Of witches' spells, of warriors' arms:*
> *Of patriot battles won of old*
> *By Wallace wight and Bruce the bold . . .*

Meanwhile, Scott's father's law business prospered and he became a W.S. – a Writer to the Signet, the top accolade for solicitors in the Scottish legal system; in 1774 he could build for his family a compact little house in the more salubrious environment of George Square (now largely redeveloped by the University of Edinburgh). Here young Walter, at the age of eight, rejoined his parents.

In Edinburgh at that time, as Scott was to recall in *Redgauntlet*, there were still many people who had been,

> *as the established phrase gently worded it, 'out in the Forty-Five'*
> *. . . Jacobites were looked on in society as men who had proved*
> *their sincerity by sacrificing their interests to their principles; and*
> *in well-regulated companies, it was held a piece of ill-breeding*
> *to injure their feelings or ridicule the compromises by which they*
> *endeavoured to keep themselves abreast of the current of the day.*

---

1 The rugged border keep of Smailholm Tower, an ancient stronghold overlooking the valley of the Tweed, is now in the care of Historic Scotland.

In the house in George Square, for instance, the young Walter Scott met an old Jacobite, Alexander Stewart of Invernahyle, who had taken part in the 1715 and 1745 Risings, and had crossed swords with the legendary Rob Roy himself.

Scott attended the Royal High School in Edinburgh, which he 'thoroughly detested'.[1] His lameness denied him the chance of becoming a career soldier, which he always longed to be. Instead he was apprenticed to his father and slaved in his office copying legal documents – 'drudgery', he called it. From there he went to the university to study law and was called to the bar in 1792, at the age of twenty-one.

Scott now had his first love-affair. The object of his affections was a young Edinburgh woman named Williamina Belsches-Stuart, daughter of a baronet and granddaughter of an earl. She was well above Scott in rank, however, and in January 1797 she married a wealthy banker, William Forbes. Scott was heartbroken; but that summer, during a riding tour in the Lake District, he met an attractive young French refugee named Charlotte Charpentier of Lyons, who was working as a companion and confidante of the granddaughter of the Bishop of Carlisle. They married in Carlisle Cathedral on Christmas Eve 1797, and remained in contented union until Charlotte's death in 1826. But Scott never forgot Williamina. The marriage, he wrote in a letter to Anne, Marchioness of Abercorn, in 1808,

> *proceeded from the most sincere affection on both sides, which has increased rather than diminished . . . But it was something short of love in all its fervour, which I suspect people only feel once in their lives – folks who have been nearly drowned in bathing rarely venturing a second time out of their depth.*

At first the couple lived partly in Edinburgh and partly at a cottage in Lasswade, Midlothian. In 1799 Scott was appointed sheriff-depute of Selkirkshire. This meant residing for four months of the year in the sheriffdom. The Scotts moved from Lasswade to the rented house of Ashiestel, on the Tweed, ten kilometres above the site where Scott would later build his house, Abbotsford. In 1802 Scott bought a house at 39 Castle Street, in the New Town of Edinburgh. This was to be

---

1 In reaction to his unhappy schooldays, Scott helped to found, in 1824, the Edinburgh Academy, which was designed to provide 'an ampler education' than was available at the High School.

their Edinburgh residence for nearly twenty-five years, until Scott was forced to sell it in the financial crash which overwhelmed his fortunes in 1826 (see below).

Edinburgh was very much a lawyer's city. Scotland's supreme courts, sitting in Parliament House, symbolised the nation's survival through her separate legal system. Scott was appointed a principal clerk to the Court of Session in 1806 (in addition to his sheriff-depute post in Selkirkshire), which kept him busy for six months of the year; it also afforded him an excellent opportunity of seeing the law in all its arcane and, occasionally, ludicrous practice. He enjoyed Edinburgh, and performed his duties with diligence, but it was a place for labour rather than pleasure; his heart was not really in the law – his true life was in his imagination and in his beloved Borders.[1]

Scott's marriage provided him with affection and stability, and soon with children. The first child, a boy, died, but two daughters survived into adulthood: Sophia (1799–1837) and Anne (1803–33). He adored them both, and they in return adored him.[2] He also had another two sons: Walter (born in 1801), who had a military career in the Hussars and inherited his father's baronetcy (he died, childless, in 1847); and Charles (born in 1805), who joined the diplomatic service and died, unmarried, in 1841.

Scott was now starting on his literary career. In 1802 he published a collection of his beloved Border ballads, *The Minstrelsy of the Scottish Border*, which rescued from imminent oblivion the traditional balladry which had so enlivened his boyhood. His own career as a poet began with his first long poem, *The Lay of the Last Minstrel* (1805), a metrical romance set in the Borders of the sixteenth century and told by an old minstrel, the last of his race. It sold forty-four thousand copies and made Scott's reputation as a poet.

---

1 Scott wryly described his relationship with the law in the Introduction to the 1830 edition of *The Lay of the Last Minstrel*: 'My profession and I came to stand nearly upon the same footing which honest Slender consoled himself on having established with Mrs Anne Page [in *The Merry Wives of Windsor*]: "There was no great love between us at the beginning, and it pleased heaven to decrease it on further acquaintance." '

2 Sophia, the elder daughter, was Scott's favourite. In 1820 she married John Gibson Lockhart (1794–1854), an Edinburgh lawyer and writer who became Scott's biographer (*The Life of Sir Walter Scott*, 7 vols, 1837–38); he was also editor of the *Quarterly Review* in London from 1825 to 1853. Their son Johnnie, who died at the age of ten, was the grandson to whom Scott dedicated *Tales of a Grandfather*. Anne Scott, spirited and sharp-tongued, never married; she nursed her father through his declining years after the death of Lady Scott in 1827.

The Lay of the Last Minstrel led to a succession of poetic romances which made Scott the most popular poet of the age, until he was superseded by his more passionate friend Lord Byron. *The Lay* was followed in 1808 by *Marmion*, a historical romance culminating in the Battle of Flodden (1513); this sold thirty thousand copies. In 1810 came *The Lady of the Lake*, which was the most popular of them all. The subject was not the lady of Arthurian legend but Ellen of Loch Katrine; it sold twenty thousand copies in twelve months and helped to make its setting, the Trossachs, a popular tourist resort.[1]

The Lady of the Lake was the last of Scott's successful verse romances. His later efforts all failed commercially: *Rokeby* (set in England in the Civil War) and *The Bridal of Triermain* (an Arthurian romance) in 1813; *The Lord of the Isles* (based on the story of Robert the Bruce) in 1815; and *Harold the Dauntless* (a viking yarn) in 1817. Scott (and his publishers) realised that there was no longer a market for his verse. He had done very well out of his earlier romances; their success had made him wealthy enough to build Abbotsford, his mansion in the Borders, in 1811. The time had come for a change in his literary career, and he turned to prose instead. While he was looking for some fishing tackle in a drawer in his writing-desk at Abbotsford he chanced upon the start of a work he had discarded long ago – the first five chapters of *Waverley*. He completed it in a burst of feverish energy. It was the beginning of a new career, as a novelist.

The Scottish Enlightenment (1730–90)

Walter Scott was, metaphorically, a child of the Scottish Enlightenment, 'that extraordinary outburst of intellectual activity which took place in Scotland in the eighteenth century'.[2] It was a time when an English visitor could observe:

---

1 Soon after the publication of *The Lady of the Lake* a friend wrote to tell Scott that at Loch Katrine his carriage 'was the 279th in the course of this year, and there never had been above 100 before in any one season'. But Scott was not the first, nor the only, promoter of tourism in the Trossachs. The Napoleonic Wars had closed the Continent for the fashionable Grand Tour, and discriminating travellers had been coming to Scotland as a substitute long before the publication of *The Lady of the Lake* – William Wordsworth had made the first of his visits there with his sister Dorothy in 1803.

2 David Daiches, *The Scottish Enlightenment 1730–1790: A Hotbed of Genius* (Edinburgh, 1986).

Here I stand at what is called the Cross of Edinburgh, *and can, in a few minutes, take fifty men of genius and learning by the hand.*[1]

The names of many of these 'men of genius and learning' of the Scottish Enlightenment form a resonant roll-call of honour: Robert Adam, the architect; Joseph Black, the chemist; Adam Ferguson, the sociologist; Henry Home (Lord Kames), the judge and agrarian improver; David Hume, the philosopher; James Hutton, the geologist; Henry Raeburn, the painter; Allan Ramsay, the portraitist and essayist (son of the poet Allan Ramsay); William Robertson, the historiographer; Sir John Sinclair, editor of the *First Statistical Account of Scotland*, which began to appear in 1791; William Smellie, founder of the *Encyclopaedia Britannica*; Adam Smith, the economist. They were all Unionists and Progressives, and together they created a cultural Golden Age of intellectual, literary, scientific and artistic achievement fired by what David Hume called 'the science of man'.

These men set out to discover the secret causes of progress, and then, having discovered them, to apply their knowledge and achieve all the advancement which, in more fortunate countries, had been spread over 250 years. The historian Hugh Trevor-Roper, giving the annual Address at the Sir Walter Scott Club in 1971, said:

> *So serious a task demanded serious application. It could not be carried out lightly, in a detached or fanciful spirit. It entailed hard work: the study and application of economics, statistics, and the laws of social progress. So it was to these subjects, not to decorative learning or elegant literature, that the pioneers of that generation applied themselves. And by so applying themselves, they succeeded. When they had finished, Scotland had made the great leap forward. The archaisms of its society had been repudiated. New agriculture, new industry was prospering. The new sciences of political economy, practical philosophy, sociology, were being taught to the whole world from Edinburgh and Glasgow; and Thomas Jefferson, the greatest scholar-statesman of the New World, could declare that the universities of Edinburgh and Glasgow were the two eyes of the Old.*

---

1 The remark, by 'Mr Amyat, King's Chemist', was recorded by the printer and antiquary William Smellie in *Literary and Characteristic Lives of Gregory, Kames, Hume and Smith* (Edinburgh, 1800).

Such was the generation – the generation of the '45 – whose work provided the cradle-gift at Walter Scott's birth in 1771. Here was reason and rationality, here was sociological study, here was serious historical enquiry, here was a new, British world of practical modernity. To these Scott would add the counterbalance of historical imagination, Scottishness and patriotic fervour.

Four years after Scott was born, another phenomenon erupted which had a huge impact on society and social thinking. The American Revolution (or War of Independence) broke out in 1775, triggered by resentment against the taxes imposed by the British government on the colonists in North America. It was followed, in July 1789, by the start of a social upheaval much nearer home – the overthrow of the French monarchy in the French Revolution. This marked one of the great turning-points of European history, heralding a new order based on sovereignty of the people. The revolutionaries in France declared that all people – irrespective of race, religion, wealth or social origin – had identical civil and political rights, and that the legitimate source of political power was not the will of God but the will of the nation. It was thus that 'democracy' entered the stage of modern European history, and the dramatic impact of its appearance was heightened by the dreadful toll in blood and terror. For ten years, from the fall of the Bastille in July 1789 until Napoleon's seizure of power in 1799, the turbulent course of the French Revolution both fascinated and horrified the rest of Europe.

Elaine MacFarland, senior lecturer in History at Glasgow Caledonian University, says:

> *France was an inspiring example – it was an example that the people could rewrite the constitution. You did not have to accept aristocratic rule as inevitable, as being divinely ordained: people could make history on their own account. For the lower orders, as they were called, it was inspiring, too: the French Revolution was not just a middle-class revolution, it was a popular revolution. The Revolution not only suggested that change could happen – it showed how to make it happen.*

'Democracy', to the authorities in Britain, was synonymous with violence, and the possibility of armed revolution haunted the government's thinking. There were riots in several Scottish cities. Radical political clubs sprang up, inspired by the publication of Thomas Paine's *Rights of Man* in 1792 (in 1796, for example, a secret society called the United

Scotsmen was formed, dedicated to the overthrow of the state and the establishment of a democratic republic – it faded away after the failure of an Irish rising of 1798). The government responded with repressive measures. In Scotland the militia were called out, with orders to suppress any signs of insurrection. During a Napoleonic invasion scare in 1797 Walter Scott, afire with the enthusiasm of his moss-trooper forebears, helped to form the Royal Edinburgh Volunteer Light Dragoons, of which he was appointed quartermaster and organising secretary.[1]

The end of the Napoleonic Wars in 1815 created an acute and widespread economic depression in Scotland. Alex Murdoch, lecturer in Scottish History at Edinburgh University, says:

> The post-war depression led many of those who had been proud to be members of the British war effort, and had served in Scottish regiments against the French before 1815, to question why they had done that, when they and their families were now starving. This led to the rise of a political radicalism which really did flirt with the idea of rejecting completely a constitution which enshrined the privilege of landowners and merchants at the expense of working people.

In England there was the Peterloo Massacre in 1819, the Cato Street Conspiracy in 1820. In Scotland a 'Radical War' raged in 1819–20, culminating in a general strike of sixty thousand workers and an insurrection at Bonnymuir in April 1820; three men were killed in the fight, three radicals were tried and executed and twenty-three were transported. The Whigs saw parliamentary reform as the only means of averting the danger of revolution; the electorate numbered only four thousand people in Scotland at this time, and the Whigs wanted to reform parliamentary elections and extend the franchise. To Walter Scott and others of the propertied classes like him, however, the fundamental stability of society – indeed, the very identity of Scotland as a nation – was under dire threat. He told the reformers:

> Little by little, whatever your wishes may be, you will destroy and undermine till nothing of what makes Scotland shall remain.

---

1 Scott's volunteer service was the closest he came to the military career he had longed to follow. On horseback his lameness no longer mattered, and he derived intense pleasure from the colourful uniforms and arduous drilling of his cavalry unit. His martial passion earned him the nickname of 'Earl Scott'.

Scott became more and more right-wing and reactionary in his politics as anarchy and the threat of widespread violence loomed. Douglas Gifford, Professor of Scottish Literature at Glasgow University, explains:

> *For Scott there was an abyss at hand, and the abyss was the abyss of the world losing structure and order. He had seen Scotland struggle out of the darkness, out of the lawlessness of the Jacobite rebellions. He dreaded the breakdown of order in society. From then on, the key words in Scott's vocabulary were 'prudence', 'temperance' and 'union', because he saw these as stabilising influences. But, echoing the profound dualism at his core, his heart and his head were pulling in different directions. His heart looked back and yearned for the colourful, heroic times of the Jacobite rebellions, but the revolutions in America and France compelled his reason to hold down his imagination.*

Yet, although he was a would-be aristocrat, and held rank and title in considerable regard, if not downright reverence, Scott tried to balance this with a 'natural democracy'. To the end of his life his best friends were commoners – his gamekeeper and shepherd, a former poacher named Tom Purdie, and his farm manager Will Laidlaw, who helped him to run his estate at Abbotsford.

Abbotsford

In 1811, as his literary earnings soared from the sale of his verse romances, Walter Scott decided it was time to put down roots of his own. His seven-year lease of Ashiestel was due to run out, and he wanted to be his own man, not another man's tenant. He bought, for the exorbitant price of four thousand guineas, a farm on 110 acres of land on the River Tweed just to the west of Melrose with the unprepossessing name of Clarty Hale ('Dirty Puddle').[1] He bought it, he wrote in a letter, 'with the intention of "bigging [building] myself a bower" after my own fashion'. Here he created his dream home, a bourgeois-baronial mansion to which he gave the invented name of 'Abbotsford' and into which he built Scotland's history – quite literally: the main entrance was based on the porch of Linlithgow Palace, the

---

1 'Clarty Hale' is perhaps a corruption of the more respectable-sounding 'Cartleyhole' – or *vice versa*.

library ceiling was a copy of that at Roslin Chapel, and the fabric of the house was buttressed by stones salvaged from historical sites all over the Borders. The ceiling of the hall was emblazoned with the heraldic devices of every house or clan to which Scott could claim familial connections. Here he would play the laird in a Scotland which had ceased to exist.

In the words of Jane Millgate, Professor of English Literature at the University of Toronto, Scott 'authored' Abbotsford, just as surely as he did his poems or novels, as a kind of combined status symbol and literary artefact, and it became almost as well-known as those literary works – a magnet for literary excursionists.[1] Scott himself called it his 'conundrum castle', and crammed it with medieval bric-a-brac and armour and historical relics (his 'gabions', as he called them). It was a throwback to earlier times, an extraordinary anachronism, the physical embodiment of a changing Scotland.[2]

Over the next twelve years Scott extended the policies from 110 to 1,400 acres. He planted thousands of trees. He filled his bookshelves with twenty thousand books – not for display, but for reading and for use. He spent a fortune on Abbotsford – and he never grudged a penny of it. Douglas Gifford says:

Abbotsford House is a key to understanding Scott's character. He wanted to be an aristocrat, yes – but a very singular kind of aristocrat. He wanted to be a traditional Border laird. These Border lairds, down-to-earth men, were benign patriarchs. Scott wasn't a snob; he simply wanted to be an anachronism.

It was this profound sense of being a part of living history which inspired Scott in perhaps the most spectacular antiquarian enterprise of his life: the recovery of the Scottish Regalia.

---

1 'Scott and the Victorians', by Jane Millgate (*The Edinburgh Sir Walter Scott Club Bulletin*, 1993–94)

2 Abbotsford was not entirely an anachronism, however. The house was lit by gas (despite the fact that Scott had no sense of smell, which could have been hazardous). Scott was a director and major shareholder of the Edinburgh Oil Gas Company, and was one of the first private householders in Scotland to install gas equipment for domestic lighting.

The Honours of Scotland[1]

The Scottish Regalia lie cocooned in a glass case in a room deep in the heart of Edinburgh Castle. They are a magnet for the thousands of visitors who flock to the castle every year; but the fact that they are on view at all is due entirely to the persistent lobbying and antiquarian fervour of Walter Scott.

In 1815, when Scott was visiting London, he met the prince regent ('Prinny' – the future King George IV). He raised the question of the Honours of Scotland, which had not been seen since 1707, when the lord chancellor, the Earl of Seafield, had touched the Act of Union with the sceptre and handed it to the clerk with the immortal words, 'Now there's the end of an auld sang.' One of the twenty-five Articles of Union stipulated that the Regalia should remain in Scotland 'in all times coming, notwithstanding the Union'. They were locked away in the stone-vaulted Crown Room of Edinburgh Castle, and the openings to the vault were walled up. In time, however, people began to question whether the Regalia had ever been placed in the castle, and rumours circulated that they had been secretly spirited away to London.

Scott was planning to write a novel based on the story of the Regalia, and was anxious to discover whether the Honours were still in Edinburgh Castle: would the prince regent establish a Royal Commission to make an official search for them? In response to Scott's request a royal warrant was issued, empowering the Scottish officers of state to open the sealed Crown Room in search of the Crown, Sceptre and Sword of State, known collectively as the Honours of Scotland.

On 4 February 1818 the members of the Royal Commission gathered on the stair outside the bricked-up entrance to the Crown Room: the lord president of the Court of Session, the lord justice clerk, the lord chief commissioner of the Jury Court, the lord provost of the City of Edinburgh, the commander-in-chief of the army – and Walter Scott. The group watched in silence as the masking masonry was removed from in front of the sealed oak door, and the iron grille inside it was opened. In the dim light beyond it they saw a great, iron-bound, padlocked oak chest, shrouded in a thick layer of dust. They all went inside the chamber. Walter Scott wrote:

---

1 See pages 468–70 for the story of how the Regalia were saved from Cromwell's clutches in 1651 at Dunnottar Castle, then returned to Edinburgh Castle at the Restoration.

The chest seemed to return a hollow and empty sound to the strokes of the hammer, and even those whose expectations had been most sanguine felt at the moment the probability of dis-appointment . . . The joy was therefore extreme when, the ponder-ous lid being forced open, at the expense of time and labour, the Regalia were discovered lying at the bottom covered with linen cloths, exactly as they had been left in the year 1707 . . . The reliques were passed from hand to hand, and greeted with the affectionate reverence which emblems so venerable, restored to public view after the slumber of more than a hundred years, were so peculiarly calculated to excite.

The discovery was instantly communicated to the public by the display of the Royal Standard, and was greeted by shouts of the soldiers in the garrison, and a vast multitude assembled on the Castle Hill; indeed the rejoicing was so general and so sincere as plainly to show that, however altered in other respects, the people of Scotland had lost nothing of that national enthusiasm which formerly had displayed itself in grief for the loss of these emblematic Honours, and now was expressed in joy for their recovery.

The Honours of Scotland, so providentially restored from obscurity and doubt, were put on display to the public in the Crown Room on 26 May 1819; the entry charge was one shilling (nearly £10 at current values). Three years later they were to have a central role in the theatrical pageantry which Scott stage-managed for the royal visit of King George IV. Before then, the grateful monarch conferred on Walter Scott a baronetcy – the first of the new reign.

The royal visit (15–29 August 1822)

On the wall of the tenement apartments at 28 The Shore, in Leith, a plaque commemorates the first royal visit to Scotland since Charles II landed in Garmouth in 1650:

> *KING'S LANDING*
> *Opposite this spot King George IV landed*
> *on 15th August 1822, an historic visit*
> *arranged mainly by Sir Walter Scott,*
> *for the bicentenary of whose birth*
> *this plaque was erected.*

SIR WALTER SCOTT: 'THE WIZARD OF THE NORTH'

The royal visit of 1822 was a miracle of last-minute organisation. The king had made a visit to Dublin in 1821, soon after his accession, and was expected to visit Scotland in 1823; Sir Walter Scott, who was the obvious choice as 'adviser-general' for the pageantry, had already laid some plans for the occasion. On 18 July 1822, however, the Lord Provost of Edinburgh received a letter announcing that the king was resolved to visit Scotland that very summer, and might be expected to reach Edinburgh within a month – on or about 10 August.

Instantly, the city swung into the kind of action associated to this day with VIP visits. A contemporary named Robert Mudie wrote:[1]

> *Various buildings offensive to taste were removed in an instant;*
> *– others were made to change their appearance; – roads were*
> *constructed and repaired; – arches and platforms erected; –*
> *crowds of strangers poured in upon the city . . .*

In his guise as 'A Modern Greek', Mudie took a more sardonic view of the frantic behind-the-scenes activities all over Scotland:

> *The Provost of Aberdeen had been attitudinizing before a great*
> *mirror for a week, and getting his pronunciation translated into*
> *English by Mr Megget, of the Academy, for at least a fortnight*
> *. . . it was sagely inferred that the Provost 'wad get a gryte mickle*
> *purse o' siller, for the gueed o' the ceety, forby a triffle to himsel'*
> *. . . all to wonder at and to admire that mightiest marvel of*
> *human nature – a king.*

As it happened, the date of the king's arrival was mercifully delayed for a few precious days, which provided time for further elocution lessons and other, more public, preparations.

On the afternoon of Wednesday, 14 August 1822 the royal yacht *Royal George* was towed by the steam tug *James Watt* into the Roads of the port of Leith. An official delegation went on board to welcome the king to the country he had never seen. Among the delegation was Sir Walter Scott. 'Walter Scott!' said the king. 'The man in Scotland I most want to see! Let him come up!'

They all drank a toast in cherry brandy to the success of the visit.

---

1 Mudie, an Edinburgh writer and bookseller, published *A Historical Account of His Majesty's Visit to Scotland* (Edinburgh, 1822), as well as a much less reverential anonymous account in *The Modern Athens, by a Modern Greek* (London, 1825).

Sir Walter, ever mindful of his growing collection of 'gabions' at Abbotsford House, humbly begged to be allowed to keep the royal glass as a memento, and tucked it carefully into a hip pocket of his frock-coat. When he got back to his Edinburgh house in Castle Street later that evening – disaster! Heedless of the precious cargo he had stowed in his pocket he sat down heavily, and the glass was smashed. It was the only thing that went awry throughout the whole of the royal visit.

At noon next day the king came ashore and mounted a high platform, crimson-carpeted and strewn with blossoms. A single gun boomed from the royal yacht. The king, very large and portly, was dressed in admiral's uniform with a thistle and a sprig of heather in his hat. A long and colourful procession escorted him up Leith Walk to St Andrews Square and Princes Street, then left into Waterloo Place and up round Calton Hill, and down by way of Abbeyhill to the Palace of Holyroodhouse. There were huge crowds all along the route. Calton Hill was a solid mass of people, and the streets (and even the rooftops) were packed with spectators. Something like three hundred thousand people were crammed into Edinburgh that day – three times the city's normal population.

In Holyrood the king was conducted to a hastily-renovated Presence Chamber. A throne had been brought from Buckingham Palace, and the king seated himself upon it to receive the Honours of Scotland – the regalia which Scott had helped to recover from obscurity in Edinburgh Castle. King George did not stay in the palace, which had become shabby and run-down since those heady days in the autumn of 1745 when Charles Edward Stuart had held court there. Instead, he was lodged in the much greater comfort of Dalkeith Palace as the guest of the young Duke of Buccleuch.

Two days later the king held his first levee at Holyrood, where 1,200 people were shovelled past him in seventy-five minutes – a rate of less than four seconds for each presentation. This was one of the most remarkable occasions of the visit; Scott had decided to make Highland culture the keynote of the pageantry, and the king and his large retinue appeared in full, resplendent Highland dress, the king's bonnet feathered as Chief of Chiefs. Under his kilt he wore flesh-coloured tights or pantaloons to cover his podgy knees, with tartan stockings up to the calves.[1] The king's appearance in Highland dress gave English

---

1   The king's outlay on his Highland rig was huge. It was provided by George Hunter of Edinburgh, who presented an exorbitant bill for £1,254.18s, and included a gold ornament

cartoonists like Thomas Rowlandson a field day – as did the absurd spectacle of the even more ample Lord Mayor of London, Sir William Curtis (a manufacturer of sea-biscuits from Wapping), in what was portrayed as a mini-kilt. Half of Edinburgh cheered; the other half sneered.

On Thursday, 22 August there was another spectacular occasion: a Grand Procession from Holyrood to Edinburgh Castle, in pouring rain. In terms of display and pageantry this was the high-point of the visit. A 'Gathering of the Clans' mustered in the forecourt of the Palace of Holyroodhouse to lead the procession. Heralds and trumpeters preceded the Honours of Scotland, borne by officers of state on magnificently caparisoned horses, and the royal carriage.

The streets were lined with covered stands containing every conceivable group – schoolchildren, university students, academic societies, the Church, the councils and the trade incorporations of the cities and towns of Scotland. These last made a great show – the Caledonian Gardeners' Society had prepared a magnificent floral set-piece of Prince of Wales Feathers made up of variously-hued hollyhocks, and the Deacon of Glassblowers wore a glass hat and carried a glass sword and targe.

Despite the rain, the procession was a sumptuous affair, a riot of coloured silks and satins of white, red, blue, green and gold. At the drawbridge to Edinburgh Castle the king was presented with the keys of the castle; then he processed up the steep, winding passages to the summit. As a finale to the event he emerged on to the Half-Moon bastion overlooking the esplanade and climbed on to a high platform. A royal salute thundered from the ramparts and the bands played 'God Save the King'. The king was entranced. He took off his hat and waved it enthusiastically for a quarter of an hour. A courtier worried that His Majesty would get wet. 'Rain? I feel no rain,' said the king. 'I must cheer the people.' He gazed down through the mist at the crowds thronging the Castle Hill and exclaimed:

---

for the bonnet, gold shoe rosettes 'studded all over with Variegated Gems', a 'Powder horn with variegated Scotch Gems and a Massive Gold Chain', three belts and a brooch, a 'fine White Goatskin Highland Purse with massive Gold spring top', 'Nine rich gold bullion Tassels and Cords', 'a Highland dirk with knife and fork, a fine Basket Hilt Highland sword of Polished steel, Hilt and Mounting inlaid with gold, a pair of fine Highland Pistols inlaid all over', and 109 and a half yards of Royal Stewart tartan (which sounds a bit steep – it only takes ten yards of tartan cloth to make an outsize kilt!). I am indebted for this information to Dr Eric Anderson, Provost of Eton and editor of *The Journal of Sir Walter Scott* (Oxford University Press, 1972).

Good God! What a fine sight! I had no conception there was
such a scene in the world – and to find it in my own dominions!
And the people are as beautiful and extraordinary as the scene.

As darkness fell, illuminations lit up the sky, including a large representation of an imperial crown on top of one of the flues of the Edinburgh gasworks.

There were to be many other events: a Drawing Room (a levee for women only) at Holyrood, where the king kissed 456 pairs of rouged lips in just over an hour; a Peers' Ball in the Assembly Rooms in George Street, and later a Caledonian Ball in the same venue, which was too crowded to allow much dancing; a civic banquet in Parliament Hall, where three hundred guests were treated to thirty-nine toasts and an inordinately lavish menu of grouse soup, lobster, pigeon pâté, sole, veal, venison, roast grouse, hot and cold roasted chicken, haggis and sheep's heads;[1] there was the laying of the foundation stone of the National Monument of Calton Hill;[2] a grand review of three thousand picturesquely-costumed horse and foot on Portobello sands; and a visit to St Giles' for Sunday service.

On his last evening in Edinburgh, at his request, the king attended a Command Performance at the Theatre Royal of a dramatised version of Sir Walter Scott's *Rob Roy* – a handsome compliment to the man who had masterminded the visit so brilliantly. One of the parts was played by the celebrated actress Sarah Siddons. The theatre was jam-packed with crowds who had jostled for entry for hours in the pouring rain. At the end of the performance the National Anthem was played and an additional stanza was sung, specially composed for the occasion:

Bright beams are soon o'ercast,
Soon our brief hour is past,
Losing our King.

---

1 At the dinner the king was presented with a basin and napkin by William Houison Crauford – the service traditionally due for his lands at Braehead. This custom dated back to the reign of James V, the 'Guidman of Ballengeich'. He was also presented with a snuff-box fashioned from the roots of 'Wallace's Oak'.

2 The National Monument, designed to be a replica of the Parthenon in Athens, was never completed. It was intended to celebrate Britain's victory over Napoleon and to commemorate the Scots who died in the Napoleonic Wars; but the money raised by public subscription was not sufficient, and only the western peristyle was erected. The twelve gigantic pillars are formed of blocks of Craigleith stone, each weighing up to fifteen tons. Building work was abandoned in 1830.

SIR WALTER SCOTT: 'THE WIZARD OF THE NORTH'

Honour'd, beloved and dear,
Still shall his parting ear
Our latest accents hear,
God save the King.

It was a far cry from the 'Marshal Wade' verse which had been added to the National Anthem seventy-five years earlier.

The tartan craze

It was the royal visit of 1822 which finally established tartan as the symbol of Scotland rather than just the icon of the Highlands. No one is too sure about the origins of tartan, or how old it is.[1] What seems clear is that, in Scott's day, tartan as a popular fashion was a relatively recent phenomenon: there were no tartans as distinguishing emblems of clan loyalty at Culloden, for instance. However, the Act of Proscription of 1746 had banned the wearing of 'Highland garb' until its repeal in 1782. The only exception was the British Army, whose strength came to rely upon the regiments recruited from dispossessed Highlanders. Army tartans began to proliferate from the green, blue and black of the original government Black Watch as other kilted regiments were formed. When the ban on Highland garb was lifted in 1782, the formal dress and stylised patterns of the military were soon adapted to civilian use.

The early regimental tartans created a huge potential market which was quickly exploited by an enterprising new industry prepared to improvise and invent where necessary. Wilson's of Bannockburn (of course!) brought out a Key Pattern Book full of tartans 'certified' by the Highland Society of London.

Early in the nineteenth century two handsome young men arrived in Edinburgh. They called themselves 'John Sobieski Stolberg Stuart' and 'Charles Edward Stuart', and claimed to be the sons of a legitimate (but previously unknown) son of Bonnie Prince Charlie by his brief marriage to Princess Louise of Stolberg. With their romantic good looks and air of star-crossed mystery they took fashionable Edinburgh by storm; some people even seemed convinced by the validity of their claim to be Jacobite royalty. What created the greatest interest, however, was an old manuscript they had brought with them, called the

---

1 King James V, the father of Mary Queen of Scots, was said to have worn hose of 'Heland tartane' in 1538.

Vestiarium Scoticum and dating back to the sixteenth century, which purported to describe the authentic ancient clan tartans of Scotland. However bogus their claims, the brothers started a craze in the salons of Edinburgh for *haute couture* tartan.

So tartan was already popular when, in 1820, Walter Scott founded the Celtic Society of Edinburgh, whose members, 'kilted and bonneted in the old fashion', held regular convivial dinners in their new attire. It was the Celtic Society members who set the sartorial tone for the tartan frenzy of the 1822 royal visit; they were prominent at all the royal engagements, 'all plaided and plumed in their tartan array'. Many Scots were scornful of what Lockhart called 'Sir Walter's Celtified Pageantry', but the world decided otherwise, and from that time onwards, tartan and Scotland have been synonymous.[1]

But was it all due to Walter Scott? Douglas Gifford thinks not:

> *One has to remember that the whole business of tourism and Scottishness was already going very strongly before the royal visit; there was already an interest in the concept of the 'noble savage', and the garments of the noble savage. The Enlightenment had propounded the idea that we were all emerging from noble savagery and were now rising, through civilisation, to higher plateaux. It helped to rehabilitate the Highlanders, and therefore the Jacobites, after their fall from grace at the 1745 Rising. Scott may have been part of the process, but he was by no means the cause of it.*

The tragic paradox is that fashionable 'Highlandism' and the tartan craze, whether they can be laid at Walter Scott's door or not, coincided with the irreversible decline of indigenous Highland culture, which was being subjected to the barbarous severities of the Highland Clearances (1750–1850), when thousands of impoverished clansmen were ejected from their homes to make way for large-scale sheep-farming.

---

1 In the USA, 6 April, the date of the Declaration of Arbroath, is now known as 'Tartan Day'. According to Senate Resolution 155 (March 1998), 'the American Declaration of Independence was modelled on that inspirational document'. Tartan Day is not by any means a Scottish equivalent of St Patrick's Day, but its existence is a measure of the way in which 'tartanry' has made its mark on the world.

The crash (January 1826)

Walter Scott was one of the wealthiest men of letters who ever lived. By the end of 1825, at the age of fifty-four, he was at the cusp of his life. He was earning between £5,000 and £10,000 a year; he was not only successful but famous, highly respected everywhere in society. He had been created a baronet. He enjoyed, without a hint of vainglory, a towering international reputation (although his authorship of the anonymously published Waverley novels had never been officially acknowledged, everyone assumed by now that they were his[1]). Goethe had hailed him as 'a great genius who does not have an equal'; Lord Byron had called him 'certainly the most wonderful writer of the day'. He had built the home of his dreams – Abbotsford – in which he was contentedly living the life of one of his own fictional Border lairds. And then, with terrible suddenness, everything fell apart. In his journal for Sunday, 18 January 1826 he noted starkly: 'My extremity is come.'

What a dreadful fall it was. Overnight, it seemed, his whole life had collapsed. In a blaze of publicity such as he could never have wished, the material fabric of his achievement was ripped to shreds.

How had it happened? Scott was making more money by his pen than any writer before him, and he had doubled or trebled these earnings by investing heavily – and secretly – in shares in his publishing firm, Constable, and their printers, James Ballantyne & Co., which had been built up by two of his close friends in Kelso, the Ballantyne brothers. This meant that, on top of the royalties from his books, he was also earning dividends from their sales. Both companies had borrowed against future expectations, and Scott himself had also borrowed money in order to purchase more and more land to enlarge the estate at Abbotsford ('Abbotsford has been my Delilah,' he said, 'and so I have often termed it').

Late in December 1825 the Stock Exchange in London crashed. Hundreds of businesses went to the wall, and thousands of investors lost everything they had. One of the companies to fall was Constable's parent company, Hurst Robinson & Co. The effect was catastrophic. Constable fell, and so did their printers, Ballantyne, whose business was found to be in financial chaos. The domino effect overwhelmed Ballantyne's co-owner, Sir Walter Scott. Scott discovered that he was

---

1 Scott publicly acknowledged his authorship of the Waverley novels for the first time at a Theatrical Fund dinner in Edinburgh on 23 February 1827.

in debt to the tune of £130,00, with only Abbotsford and his Edinburgh house (39 Castle Street) as collateral.

On that bleak Sunday, 18 January 1826, he looked back on his life with wry detachment:

> What a life mine has been! – half-educated, almost wholly neg-
> lected or left to myself, stuffing my head with most nonsensical
> trash, and undervalued in society for a time by most of my
> companions, getting forward and held a bold and clever fellow,
> contrary to the opinion of all who thought me a mere dreamer,
> broken-hearted for two years, my heart handsomely pieced again,
> but the crack will remain to my dying day. Rich and poor four
> or five times, once on the verge of ruin, yet opened new sources
> of wealth almost overflowing. Now taken in my pitch of pride,
> and nearly winged (unless the good news hold), because London
> chooses to be in an uproar, and in the tumult of bulls and bears,
> a poor inoffensive lion like myself is pushed to the wall. And
> what is to be the end of it? God knows. And so ends this catechism.

Scott was faced with three alternatives, none of them good. He could opt for sequestration, and get away with an absolute discharge at perhaps seven shillings in the pound; but that would have meant the public shame of declaring himself bankrupt like some ordinary tradesman. He could opt for a *cessio bonorum* ('surrender of goods'), by which an insolvent debtor could put all his goods at the disposal of his creditors: he would remain liable for the full amount of his debts, but could not be imprisoned for a failure to pay. Both of these options would have involved the loss of his library, his furniture and his life-rent of his beloved Abbotsford.[1] The third choice was to set up a Trust Deed for his creditors, which would give him the opportunity to pay his debts in the fullness of time by pledging his future literary earnings. That was the course he adopted – to work his way out of his troubles by the labours of his pen:

> I the said Walter Scott have resolved to employ my time and
> talents on the production of such literary works as shall seem to

---

1 Scott had settled the Abbotsford estate on his son Walter on the occasion of Walter's marriage the previous year, which effectively removed the house from the reach of his creditors; but he feared that malicious tongues would suggest that he had foreseen the crash and had taken to his mind dishonourable, albeit legal, steps to protect Abbotsford.

me most likely to promote the ends I have in view, the sums arising from such works I am also desirous to devote to the payments of the debts owing by me as a Partner of the said Company and as an individual.[1]

The Edinburgh house was sold, and the trustees granted Scott rent-free occupation of Abbotsford and an annual salary of £1,600 in addition to £1,000 a year's income from his pen. It was a generous settlement. And with that, Sir Walter set to work.

It was a heroic undertaking. 'This right hand shall work it off,' he wrote in his journal – and work it off he did. He would make more than £50,000 for his creditors – an extraordinary achievement for a man already overworked, his creative imagination almost exhausted. But it would help to bring him to an early death within six years. In that time he lost his wife of nearly thirty years (in May 1826); and he worked, worked, worked. Abbotsford – dear-bought Abbotsford – became his refuge and his sanctuary. Douglas Gifford says:

> *The motto of Abbotsford is* clausus tutus ero *('I am safe when I am enclosed'). The symbol printed on all the books is a portcullis; these two concepts are clear in the layout of Abbotsford, engirthed by the Tweed and the hills, with its semi-fortalices round about, with its Armoury within that fortalice, with the Library within that armoury, with the Study next to that; and then, most telling of all, the 'Priest's Hole' next door, where he would say his private prayers. Here he was completely on his own. I get a very strong sense in Abbotsford of the winnowing away of Scott down to an essential self; and the image of him coming down at half past four in the morning to pray in the Priest's Hole before going into the study and the library is, for me, profoundly evocative.*

In the little study at Abbotsford he completed a massive nine-volume *Life of Napoleon Buonaparte*, which was published in 1827. He fought a government proposal to abolish banknotes in Scotland in three coruscating newspaper polemics, published under the pseudonym 'Malachi Malagrowther' – and won. He wrote more novels: *Woodstock* (1826), *The Fair Maid of Perth* (1828), *Anne of Geierstein* (1829), *Count Robert of Paris* (1831). He worked tirelessly on an annotated edition of

---

1   The Sederunt Book [Minutes] of the Trust, i.41.

all the Waverley novels (the 'Magnum Opus', he called it) in forty-eight uniform volumes, which began monthly publication in June 1829; sales soared to thirty thousand per volume, and all the profits went to the trustees. And in the midst of all this, he wrote *Tales of a Grandfather*.

Tales of a Grandfather (1827–29)

On 24 May 1827 Walter Scott wrote in his journal:

> *A good thought came in my head to write stories for little Johnnie Lockhart from the History of Scotland like those taken from the History of England [by J.W. Croker, 1817]. I am persuaded both children and the lower class of readers hate books which are written down to their capacity and love those that are more composed for their elders and betters. I will make if possible a book that a child will understand yet a man will feel some temptation to peruse should he chance to take it up. It will require however a simplicity of stile not quite my own. The Grand and interesting consists in ideas not in words. A clever thing of this kind will have a run.*

Scott was right: the 'clever thing of this kind' certainly *did* 'have a run'. *Tales of a Grandfather*, dedicated to his grandson John Hugh Lockhart (who was then six years old), was written in a fury of inspiration and published in three volumes. The first came out at the end of 1827, the third in 1829. The trustees, unwilling to offend the goose which was laying golden eggs so regularly, allowed Scott to keep the proceeds (£3,000) for his personal use. He was then asked to expand the *Tales* (for £1,500) into a 'proper' *History of Scotland* for Dr Lardner's *Cabinet Cyclopaedia*; this was completed by May 1831.

From the time of its first publication, *Tales of a Grandfather* inspired and informed generations of children and adults with a particular view of Scotland's history. What (apart from the pressing need for money) inspired Scott to write it? Alex Murdoch says:

> *Scott had lived through the French Revolution and through the Depression which followed the end of the Napoleonic Wars. He had had to confront what was, to him, the horror of political revolutionary radicalism in Scotland which wanted to do away with the Scottish aristocracy and the landowning class which, for*

Scott, represented the essential continuity of Scottish history. But he also had to try to relate this to the history which his Enlighten-ment mentors, like David Hume and William Robertson, had taught him. Scott wanted the Tales *to be read by the weavers of Glasgow and the mechanics of Falkirk; he wanted to reach out to working people and to communicate to them his own utter conviction that the romance of Scottish history was a gift to every Scot and an inheritance which every Scot should be given to cherish, in these difficult modern times.*

The 'romance of Scottish history' was a gift, certainly. The eminent English historian G.M. Trevelyan wrote of Scott that 'he did more than any professional historian to make mankind advance towards a true conception of history'. But the *Tales* gave a highly personal and selective view of that history. There were whole sections of Scotland's past which were deliberately excluded in order to conform to Scott's vision of a united, British, essentially *Protestant* heritage. Ted Cowan says:

Scott was too close to the French Revolution. Remember, he was just in his teens when the Revolution broke out in 1789. The 'Radical Wars' of 1819–20, which had been provoked by the Depression after the Napoleonic Wars, was seen as something very real, and very threatening, to the well-being of the United Kingdom of Great Britain. So were the activities of the Irish patriots in the 1790s.

It was perfectly legitimate to talk about William Wallace and his revolutionary activities, because Wallace and Bruce between them had safeguarded the independence of Scotland. They had preserved the integrity of the Scottish kingdom so that Scotland could become an equal partner in the Union of 1707: if it had not been for Wallace and Bruce, Edward I would have conquered Scotland, Scotland would have become part of England, and there would have been no need for the Union at all.

But it was not legitimate to talk about the revolutionary anti-monarchist concepts enshrined in the Declaration of Arbroath. It was not legitimate to talk about the huge Irish/ Celtic (i.e. Catholic) part in the original creation of the Scottish nation, through Dalriada. Scott simply didn't want to know – and he didn't want his readers to know.

Walter Scott, in effect, tried to manipulate history to suit the Enlightenment view: the 1707 Act of Union had brought Scotland into the comity of civilised nations, and all was now well. But the democratic forces unleashed by the revolutions of France and America were to shadow his own last days.

The end (21 September 1832)

On 15 February 1829, Walter Scott suffered a minor stroke. He continued to work as energetically as before, however, and when he retired as a clerk of court the following year on a generous pension he had even more time to devote to his writing. But his strength was now becoming dangerously overtaxed, and he suffered another stroke in November 1830.

Scott was also becoming increasingly alarmed by what he considered to be revolutionary political developments. In 1830 the Duke of Wellington's Tory administration fell after the party had been in power for twenty years, to be replaced by a Whig government led by the liberal Earl Grey. Reform was in the air. So was the whiff of popular violence. Scott's family and friends tried to conspire to stop him writing, but he insisted on continuing to work on his last novel, *Count Robert of Paris*, although he never completed it (after Scott's death an ending was cobbled on to it by his son-in-law, John G. Lockhart).

In his enfeebled state of health, Scott's agitation over the movement for franchise reform increased to the point of paranoia. In March 1831 he insisted on proposing a Tory anti-Reform resolution at a meeting in Jedburgh. It was a disaster. His speech was hesitant and largely unintelligible. What *was* intelligible provoked the hostile (and largely unenfranchised) audience to fury:

> *My friends, I am old and failing, and you think me very full of silly prejudices, but I have seen a good deal of public men, and thought a good deal of public affairs in my day, and I can't help suspecting that the manufacturers of this new constitution are like a parcel of schoolboys taking to pieces a watch ... in the conceit that they can put it together again far better than the old watchmaker.*

He was loudly hissed as he left the platform. 'His' Borderers had turned against him. On 22 March 1831 the first Reform Bill (the 'Revolution

Bill', as Scott called it) passed its second reading by only a single vote, and the government called a general election.

There was more mortification to come for Scott. Wednesday, 18 May 1831 was polling day in the general election, and Scott insisted on making the sixteen-kilometre journey in his carriage to register his vote. He found the marketplace in Jedburgh crowded with a vociferous and hostile mob. At the courthouse he cast his vote for his Tory kinsman Sir William Elliot of Stobs, who won comfortably – 'for the last time, I suppose', as Scott noted in his journal. As his carriage left Jedburgh it was stoned, and abuse was hurled at Scott himself. The old man was deeply wounded: in his patriarchal way he had always loved these people, and he had thought that they loved him. Now he saw the future, and it horrified him: 'These unwash'd artificers are from henceforth to select our legislators.'[1]

Scott's friend and fellow-poet James Hogg, 'the Ettrick Shepherd', wrote:

> *I am certain of it, that the democratic ascendancy, and the grievous and shameful insults that he received from the populace of his own country, broke the heart of and killed the greatest man that country ever contained.*

Next year the Reform Act was passed. It was the end of an era, the end of Scotland's *ancien regime*, in which a few hundred landed gentry had controlled the destinies of a whole nation. Scotland was on the brink of revolution in many senses of the word: industrial revolution, agrarian revolution, economic revolution, democratic revolution.

Walter Scott died at Abbotsford on 21 September 1832, at the age of sixty-one, after a long tour abroad which had been intended to improve his health. He had been desperate to get home to his beloved Abbotsford so that he could die there.

On the B6356, on a crest of the road looking west over the meander of the Tweed towards the Eildon Hills and Melrose – and beyond them, Abbotsford – is a layby marked 'Scott's View'. This was where, it is said, Scott would always stop to admire the glorious panorama, and horses travelling the road would rest and graze. On the day of Scott's funeral the horses drawing his coffin paused, from habit, at 'Scott's View'. Then they moved on, drawing the mortal remains of

---

1   A Shakespearean allusion, from *King John*: 'Another lean unwash'd artificer/Cuts off his tale and talks of Arthur's death.'

the great man to his burial plot beside his wife, in the haunting ruins of Dryburgh Abbey.

In 1846 a soaring Gothic steeple dedicated to Sir Walter Scott's memory was completed in Edinburgh's Princes Street. The Scott Monument is probably the largest memorial to a writer anywhere in the world. It was designed by a joiner and carpenter named George Meikle Kemp, who had taught himself draughtsmanship; he had won the design competition for the monument against stiff professional opposition.

The statue enshrined in the open vault of the steeple was carved by Sir John Steell from a huge thirty-ton block of Carrara marble. It shows Sir Walter Scott seated, brooding under his baldachino,[1] dressed in a Border plaid and accompanied by his favourite deerhound, Maida. In the niches are statuettes of many of the characters from the Waverley novels. They, like their creator, live on. As Horace put it in his Odes: *Exegi monumentum aere perennius* – 'I have raised a monument more durable than bronze.'

---

1   Baldachino (or baldequin): 'a canopy of fabric or stone over an altar, shrine or throne in a Christian church'. I am indebted for this enchanting use of the word to Robert Speight, who used it in his presidential address to the Edinburgh Sir Walter Scott Club in 1972.

'There Shall be a Scottish Parliament'

Our journey is now finished, gentle reader; and if your patience has accompanied me through these sheets, the contract is, on your part, strictly fulfilled. Yet, like the driver who has received his full hire, I still linger near you, and make, with becoming diffidence, a trifling additional claim upon your bounty and good nature.

SIR WALTER SCOTT, *WAVERLEY*,
CHAPTER SEVENTY-SECOND

On 1 July 1999, almost three centuries after 'the end of an auld sang' in 1707, Her Majesty the Queen opened the new devolved Scottish parliament in its temporary Edinburgh home, the Assembly Hall of the Church of Scotland. She presented to the parliament a silver mace, symbol of authority for the new politics of Scotland;[1] on its head are inscribed the opening words of the parliament's founding statute (the Scotland Act 1998, Clause 1.1):

'There shall be a Scottish Parliament.'

Donald Dewar, former Secretary of State for Scotland, and now the First Minister of Scotland, made a memorable speech:

Through long years, many long years in the case of many of us, these words were first a hope, then a belief, then a promise. Now they are a reality. This is indeed a moment anchored in history. Today, we can reach back through the long haul to win this parliament, through the struggles of those who brought democracy

---

1 The specially-commissioned mace was fashioned by the silversmith Michael Lloyd.

663

*to Scotland, to that other parliament dissolved in controversy
three hundred years ago.*

*This is about more than our politics and laws. This is about
who we are, how we carry ourselves. In the quiet moments of
the day (if there are any), we might hear some echoes from the
past: the shout of the welder in the din of the great Clyde ship-
yards; the speak of the Mearns, rooted in the land; the discourse
of the Enlightenment, when Edinburgh and Glasgow were indeed
a light held to the intellectual life of Europe; the wild cry of the
great pipes; and back to the distant noise of battles in the days
of Bruce and Wallace.*

Entwined among the symbolic thistles engraved on the mace are the
words 'Wisdom, Justice, Compassion, Integrity'. These concepts were
vividly expressed in the song sung, unaccompanied, on this historic
occasion by the acclaimed Scottish folk-singer Sheena Wellington; it
is the most internationally renowned of all Robert Burns's songs, the
epitome of egalitarianism, written at the height of the French Revolution, in 1795: 'A Man's a Man for a' That', with its rousing finale:

> *For a' that and a' that,*
> *It's coming yet for a' that,*
> *That man to man the world o'er*
> *Shall brothers be for a' that.*

It was a bright and breezy summer's morning, and the centre of
Edinburgh was amiably and decorously *en fête*. The city looked stunning. A team of army paratroopers, the 'Golden Lions', landed with
immaculate precision on Calton Hill, with saltires tied to their ankles.
Saltires and Lions Rampant fluttered bravely, bands played, Gaelic
choirs sang. The loudest cheers went up for the arrival of a special
guest, Sean Connery, Scotland's very own Scottish nationalist film
star, resplendent in Highland dress and looking every inch a king.
A procession of 129 newly-elected MSPs (Members of the Scottish
Parliament), rubbing shoulders with youngsters and with civic and
Westminster dignitaries, ambled with studied informality from Parliament House – the scene of the ending of the last parliament in 1707
– to the Assembly Hall.

The Duke of Hamilton, Scotland's premier peer, signed the crown
of Scotland out of its strongroom in Edinburgh Castle and brought it
to the General Assembly Hall in a glass-topped Rolls-Royce, there to

be laid on a table in the well of the parliament chamber before the sovereign. The queen wore a specially-designed outfit in the light green and purple colours of the thistle; she was driven in a horse-drawn open landau from the Palace of Holyroodhouse (opposite the empty site of the future parliament building) up the Royal Mile along the Canongate, past the High Kirk of St Giles' and Parliament House to the Mound.

There was a flare of fanfares, specially written by the Scottish composer James Macmillan. A twenty-one-gun salute thundered from the battlements of Edinburgh Castle. The 'big bird', Concorde, swooped a thousand feet overhead, mobbed by a pack of Red Arrows trailing a smudged, smoky suggestion of a saltire in the skies – reminiscent of the vision said to have been seen by Unust on the eve of the Battle of Athelstaneford (see pages 30–1). Sixteen hundred youngsters, selected from schools all over Scotland and wearing grey sweatshirts emblazoned with the saltire, paraded down the Mound in quiet pride, carrying banners modelled on long Himalayan prayer-flags.

Everything went well. Very little went wrong. As a royal occasion, it was nothing like as exuberant as the royal visit of 1822, stage-managed by Sir Walter Scott, when King George IV came to Edinburgh. As a parliamentary occasion, it was nothing like as tumultuous as the ending of the parliament in 1707, when the Edinburgh mobs howled for the blood of the commissioners they felt had betrayed them.

This was a new start: understated, forward-looking, a careful blend of traditional pomp and modern pageantry, symptomatic of a pragmatic balance between continuity and change. The Presiding Officer, Sir David Steel, described the event as 'the most significant political achievement in Scotland for nearly three hundred years'. It was the day on which the new parliament assumed its full powers, the day on which Scotland recovered an essential part of its identity as a nation. As Donald Dewar said in his peroration:

> It is a rare privilege in an old nation to open a new parliament. Today is, and must be, a celebration of the principles, the traditions, the democratic imperatives which have brought us to this point and which will sustain us into the future.

It had been a long time a-coming; but when it came, it came quickly, decisively and with conviction.

Scottish nationalism

Sir Walter Scott was both a Tory (that is to say, a Unionist) and a patriot (that is to say, a nationalist), both a Hanoverian and a Jacobite. He revelled in the economic benefits which Scotland had gained by the 1707 Union of the Parliaments; but he also luxuriated in the romantic heritage of Scottish independence which history had bequeathed to the nineteenth century. There was nothing inherently contradictory about such a stance: the Enlightenment theory of Scottish history, which informed Scott's attitudes, was that the Wars of Independence which Wallace and Bruce waged had ensured that Scotland had never been conquered, and this independence had allowed it to enter into union with England in 1707 as a free and equal nation.

Graeme Morton, lecturer in Economic and Social History at Edinburgh University, says:

> *'Nationalism' was, in one sense, very different from how we understand nationalism today. Nationalism today is very much one-against-the-other, in the sense of being 'against' the English or, if not against the English in a racial sense, being against the Union. Scottish nationalists see the Union and the end of the Scottish parliament as demoting the nation to the status of a province; in reality, of course, both Scotland and England lost their individual parliaments and merged them into a new one called the parliament of Great Britain. The loss of Scotland's parliament was no longer a political issue.*
>
> *Nationalism in the nineteenth century was very much about equality between Scotland and England; it supported the union with England, so long as that union was based on equal rights. The nineteenth-century nationalists used the memory of Wallace and Bruce to celebrate the coming together of the nations in 1707, and they wanted to be treated as full partners in that union.*

A National Association for the Vindication of Scottish Rights was formed in 1853 to voice concerns about certain aspects of the union relationship, in particular the number of Scottish MPs – fifty-three in a 658-seat House of Commons at Westminster (this was increased to seventy-two, the present number, in 1884); but the Association lacked political bite and was wound up in 1856. A Home Rule movement began to emerge in the 1880s, designed to achieve administrative reforms which would make the union with England work more effectively. In 1885 the ancient office of secretary for Scotland was revived and a Scottish Office was established in London.

Other and more pressing political issues occupied people's minds. 'Agitation' was becoming the weapon of the disenfranchised. Chartism, the radical philosophy expounded in the People's Charter of 1838, swept the country as the first nationwide political movement of the working class. It combined the liberalism of the middle class with the radicalism of the early trade union movement to empower a class of industrial workers to start thinking about power, and rights, and representation. Catriona Macdonald, lecturer in History at Glasgow Caledonian University, says:

> We see these two classes coming together in terms of the rhetoric they used. It was not the rhetoric of class, but of the common weal of the nation coming together as one people – words like liberty, and justice, and representation. But did they mean Scotland or did they mean Britain?

The other major new factor in Scotland's way of life and way of thinking was Empire. Tom Devine says:

> The essence of nineteenth-century Scottish history was the fact that the nation was yoked to the Union connection with England and was also emphatically a part of the British Empire. The material rewards of the English connection were obvious – but how were 'Scottishness' and 'Scottish identity' to be retained?

Catriona Macdonald says:

> Victorian Scotland was more British than Britain. Scotland prided itself on its role in the Empire, where it was outdoing the rest of the nation: if the English were going to be imperial, the Scots were going to be more imperial. We see that not just in terms of the number of vice-consuls and governor-generals throughout the Empire, but also in Scotland's politics. At no stage was there a successful movement to push for an independent Scotland, separate from Britain, separate from the Empire.

Home Rule only became a serious political issue in the years leading up to World War I. The fledgling Labour Party in Scotland believed passionately in land reform, alcohol prohibition and Home Rule for

Scotland; the Liberals had become converts to the idea of devolving power to all the nations of Britain in the wake of the Irish Home Rule crisis in the 1880s. In 1888 the Scottish Liberal Association voted for Home Rule for Scotland; and in 1900 the radical wing of the Liberal Party set up a Young Scots Society whose membership soon equalled that of the Labour Party (2,500). 'Home Rule' became their joint war-cry. The Young Scots Society argued in 1911:

> A real incorporation of the four nations [of Great Britain] is as impractical as it is undesirable. Each of the four nations requires separate legislation and administration in dealing with the business of four distinct peoples.

A steady stream of private members' Bills was presented to parliament. Home Rule for Scotland seemed merely a question of time. In May 1914 the Liberal prime minister Herbert Asquith introduced a Home Rule Bill on the grounds that the Westminster parliament did not have the time to deal with Scottish business properly. It passed its second reading in the House of Commons, and only the outbreak of war in Europe in August killed its chances of reaching the statute book. It was a close-run thing – but no one had put much thought into what the Scots would do with a parliament of their own once they got one.

The inter-war years

> Though Scotland has not been a nation for some time, it has possessed a distinctly marked style of life; and that is now falling to pieces, for there is no visible and effective power to hold it together ... What stands in the way of Home Rule for Scotland is simply apathy, the apathy of England but chiefly the apathy of Scotland. Consequently the Scottish nationalist movement at its present stage is mainly a movement to rouse Scotland from its indifference.
>
> EDWIN MUIR,[1] SCOTTISH JOURNEY (1935)

World War I convulsed the social and industrial fabric of Scotland. During the war, in 1915, there had been a massive Rent Strike in

---

1 Edwin Muir (1887–1959) was born on Orkney and became one of the outstanding poets and essayists of the 'Scottish literary renaissance' of the inter-war years.

Glasgow as profiteering landlords forced up rents. The city's slum housing became a byword for filth and childhood diseases. The politics of the Scottish Home Rule Association (re-established in 1918) became inextricably entwined with the firebrand revolutionary rhetoric of the 'Red Clydesiders' of the Independent Labour Party (ILP) – Willie Gallacher, John Maclean, Harry McShane, Jimmie Maxton, Emanuel Shinwell, John Wheatley and the rest.[1] In January 1919 the Red Clydesiders called a strike of eighty thousand workers in support of a shorter working week. On 31 January a huge demonstration occupied Glasgow's George Square. The authorities panicked and ordered a police baton charge. The demonstrators, stiffened by angry ex-servicemen,

---

1   *Willie Gallacher* (1881–1966) was a brass-foundryman and a co-founder of the Communist Party of Great Britain; he became the longest-serving Communist MP in British history, as MP for Fife West from 1935 to 1951. *John Maclean* (1879–1923), a schoolteacher in Glasgow Govan who had been sacked for his political activities, was the most militant of the socialist revolutionaries; he became a full-time Marxist organiser and educator. During the war he had been arrested and convicted for sedition thrice and given harsh sentences of penal servitude. After the Russian Revolution of 1917 he was elected an honorary president of the first All-Russian Congress of Soviets, along with Lenin and Trotsky, and was appointed by Lenin 'Bolshevik consul' in Glasgow. He refused to join the British Communist Party when it was formed, and campaigned instead for a Scottish Workers' Republic until his early death. More than ten thousand mourners attended his funeral in Glasgow. *Harry McShane* (1892–1988) lived to the age of ninety-six to become the last survivor of the Red Clydesiders. A working Clydeside engineer, he was also a passionately dedicated trade unionist. A warm, gentle man, he had little schooling, but turned into an intellectual, a philosopher and a scholar. He had a lifelong vision of an ideal society in which people cared for one another, each in his or her own way. *James Maxton* (1885–1946) was a schoolteacher in the East End of Glasgow who was imprisoned for pacifism during the war. In 1922 he was elected MP for Glasgow Bridgeton (a seat which he held until his death), and he campaigned tirelessly against slum housing and poverty wages. In 1923 he was expelled from the House of Commons for calling a minister a murderer; he became famous as 'the conscience of the left', and his gaunt figure, staring eyes and denunciatory forefinger made him every caricaturist's dream of the perennial agitator. *'Manny' Shinwell* (1884–1986) was a Londoner who started work as an errand-boy in Glasgow at the age of twelve. In 1912 he was elected to Glasgow Trades Council and became one of the 'wild men of Clydeside'. He was elected MP for Linlithgow in 1922 and went on to hold several cabinet appointments after World War II. He became the elder statesman of the Labour backbenches and was created a life peer in 1970; he attended the House of Lords on his hundredth birthday. *John Wheatley* (1869–1930), a Catholic, was born in Ireland but moved to Scotland as an infant. He started work as a coalminer at the age of twelve, but later ran a successful publishing and printing business. He joined the ILP in 1906 and fell out with the local Roman Catholic hierarchy for preaching socialism. He became MP for Glasgow Shettleston in 1922, and was appointed housing minister in the first Labour government in 1924. He was successful in introducing generous state subsidies for council house-building.

rioted, tore up tramlines, raised the Red Flag and battled with the police.

Was this the start of a Bolshevik rising? The government thought so. The leaders of the Workers' Committee which had called the strike were arrested and jailed. English troops were sent north to quell any insurrection; the Scottish troops in Glasgow's Maryhill Barracks were locked inside in case they were tempted to join the revolution. Machine-gun nests were set up in Glasgow's main hotels. Six tanks rumbled into the city, and a howitzer was put in place in front of the City Chambers.

Most of those radical leaders of the ILP were elected to parliament in the landslide Labour victory in the general election of 1922. The ten new Red Clydeside MPs were given a rousing send-off as they departed for London from Glasgow's St Enoch's station (now no more) by a huge crowd singing 'The Red Flag'. They were nationalist to the core, and one of their avowed objectives was a parliament in Scotland. Jimmie Maxton, at a rally in Glasgow in 1924, declared passionately:

> Give us our parliament in Scotland. Set it up next year. We will start with no traditions. We will start with ideals. We will start with the aim and object that there will be 134 men and women, pledged to 134 Scottish constituencies, to spend their whole energy, their whole brain power, their whole courage and their whole soul, in making Scotland into a country into which we can take people from all nations of the earth and say: This is our land, this is our Scotland, these are our people, these are our men, our works, our women and children: can you beat it?

The Home Rule Bill of 1924, introduced by George Buchanan, MP for Glasgow Gorbals, was debated at great length, and the Home Rulers seemed to be winning the argument. At the end of the debate, however, the Speaker reneged on an earlier promise to hold a vote, and allowed the Bill to run out of time. There was uproar, and the speaker eventually suspended the sitting because 'grave disorder has arisen in the House'. It was, to all intents and purposes, the end of Labour's interest in Home Rule for several decades: housing and jobs had to come first, and that would require the full resources of the British state – there was no room for separatism.

Nationalism was not dead in Scotland, however. In 1928 the National Party of Scotland was founded by a small group of patriots, including many of the writers of the 'Scottish Renaissance' like the poet Hugh MacDiarmid and the novelists Neil Gunn, Eric Linklater and Compton Mackenzie.[1] The most charismatic of its leaders was the colourful writer and adventurer R.B. Cunninghame Graham, who was elected its first president.[2] It attracted powerful press support from the new *Scottish Daily Express*, which Lord Beaverbrook launched in November 1928. In 1934 the National Party of Scotland amalgamated with the right-wing Scottish Party (founded in 1932) to become the Scottish National Party (SNP), with Cunninghame Graham as its president and more than ten thousand members. In the 1935 general election the SNP contested eight seats, polling an average of 16 per cent. It was to prove a false dawn: by 1939 its membership had dropped to below two thousand.

But administrative devolution, at least, was on the way. On the day

---

1   Hugh MacDiarmid (Christopher Grieve, 1892–1978) was the pioneer and giant of the twentieth-century Scottish literary renaissance. He used a mixture of modern English, older Scots words and Gaelic for expressing Scotland's 'real' identity and culture. His extravagant polemicising and Marxist philosophising sorely tried his fellow-nationalists: he was expelled from the National Party of Scotland in 1934 for his communism, and from the Communist Party in 1938 for his 'nationalist deviation'. He was caricatured in Eric Linklater's novel *Magnus Merriman* (1935) as the poet 'Hugh Skene' fighting a by-election (as Linklater himself did in 1934). MacDiarmid's masterpiece was a verse epic which surveyed the state of Scotland's soul, *A Drunk Man Looks at the Thistle* (1926). He also composed a wonderfully memorable little stanza to express his feelings about Scotland:

> *The rose of all the world is not for me.*
> *I want for my part*
> *Only the little white rose of Scotland*
> *That smells so sweet – and breaks the heart.*

Compton Mackenzie (1883–1972) was the son of an English-born comedy actor and an American actress. He is best-known today for his satirical novel *Whisky Galore* (1947), but he had made a name for himself before World War I as the author of *The Passionate Elopement* (1911) and his story of theatre life, *Carnival* (1912). He became a Roman Catholic convert and a romantic nationalist who devoted his talents unstintingly to promoting the nationalist cause. In 1934 he won the first nationalist electoral victory of any kind when he was elected rector of Glasgow University by its students.

2   Robert Bontine Cunninghame Graham (1852–1936) was a charismatic romantic, the last of the old-style Home Rulers. He was an impoverished minor aristocrat, a flamboyant political rebel and a man of letters who claimed descent from early Scottish kings. He spent much of his youth ranching in Argentina, where he lived as a gaucho and horse-dealer and was known as 'Don Roberto'. He was a radical Liberal and MP for North-West Lanarkshire (1886–92); in 1888 he was a co-founder, with Keir Hardie, of the Scottish Labour Party and became its first president. He was arrested and jailed for six weeks in 1887 for 'illegal assembly' in Trafalgar Square at a mass demonstration during a dockers' strike. He published many books of essays and short stories.

after war was declared on 3 September 1939, St Andrew's House, on the southern slopes of Edinburgh's Calton Hill on the site of the old Calton Jail, was opened to house an army of civil servants. It was to be the headquarters of the Scottish Office – 'Scotland's Whitehall', it was called. St Andrew's House is considered the finest 1930s building in Scotland: solid, formal and authoritative with massive bronze doors and art-deco interiors, while the exterior is embellished with thistled portals and figures representing Agriculture, Architecture, Fisheries, Education, Health and Statecraft. During World War II the Secretary of State for Scotland, Tom Johnston – one of the most effective political operators ever to occupy the post – showed how the existing system could be manipulated to secure concessions from central government without the need for constitutional change.

The post-war years

During the war the SNP – radical and pacifist throughout – had no scruples about breaching the gentlemen's agreement among the major parties about not contesting parliamentary by-elections. In 1944 an SNP candidate took 42 per cent of the vote in a by-election in Kirkcaldy; and in April 1945 the SNP gained its first parliamentary seat when the party's leader Dr Robert McIntyre, a physician at Stirling Royal Infirmary, won the Motherwell and Wishaw by-election.[1] His victory made little impact on the political scene: in the House of Commons he refused to be introduced by any sponsors; when the speaker told him he could not take the oath without sponsors he went away and thought things over, and returned the next day and agreed to be sponsored. At the general election six weeks later, shorn of the monopoly of the anti-government vote, he lost the seat – and never won another, despite many attempts. The SNP trudged off into the political wilderness as a hard-line independence-or-nothing party with a tiny membership. Instead, nationalist sentiment was channelled into an extra-parliamentary movement called the Scottish Convention, which had been founded in 1942 by 'King' John MacCormick.

---

1 McIntyre (1913–98) is considered the 'Father of the Party'. He was chairman (1948–56) and president (1958–80) of the SNP, and provost of Stirling from 1967 to 1975.

EPILOGUE

The National Covenant (1949)

John MacDonald MacCormick (1901–61) was much the most power-ful and influential voice for Home Rule in Scotland; a brilliant orator, not for nothing was he nicknamed 'King'. At Glasgow University he took part in Labour student politics, but then started a university Scottish Nationalist Association in 1927. He helped to found the new National Party of Scotland in 1928, of which he became secretary. In 1942 the SNP, which had merged with the National Party of Scotland in 1932, suffered a disastrous split over policy: MacCormick resigned, taking with him many of the members who favoured a consensual rather than a confrontational approach, and founded his broadly-based Scottish Convention. He joined the Liberal Party in 1945 (because the Liberals, too, supported Home Rule), and in 1948 he stood as a Liberal-sponsored 'National candidate' at a by-election at Paisley; the Tories did not put up a candidate, in order to allow MacCormick a straight fight against Labour. The gambit failed: MacCormick lost the by-election by six thousand votes. The Labour government never for-gave him for having opposed their candidate in what they considered a treacherous piece of politicking.

MacCormick was not finished, however. Through his Scottish Con-vention he planned to appeal to the people with a new 'National Covenant', deliberately reminiscent of the National Covenant of 1638. In April 1949, at a meeting in Aberfoyle, he and his committee sol-emnly drafted the Covenant:

> *We, the people of Scotland who subscribe this engagement, declare our belief that reform in the constitution of our country is neces-sary to secure good government in accordance with our Scottish traditions and to promote the spiritual and economic welfare of our nation.*
>
> *We affirm that the desire for such reform is both deep and widespread through the whole community, transcending all pol-itical differences and sectional interests, and we undertake to continue united in purpose for its achievement.*
>
> *With that end in view we solemnly enter into this Covenant whereby we pledge ourselves, in all loyalty to the Crown and within the framework of the United Kingdom, to do everything in our power to secure for Scotland a Parliament with adequate legislative authority in Scotland's affairs.*

The 'National Covenant for Home Rule' was launched in October 1949 at a 'National Assembly' in the Assembly Hall of the Church of Scotland on the Mound in Edinburgh. It was an impressive gathering of civic, Church and business leaders. MacCormick described it in fulsome terms:

> *Unknown district councillors rubbed shoulders and joined in pledges with the men [e.g. the Duke of Montrose] whose titles had sounded through all the history of Scotland. Working men from the docks of Glasgow or the pits of Fife spoke with the same voice as portly businessmen in pin-striped trousers. It was such a demonstration of national unity as the Scots might never have hoped to see, and when, finally, the scroll upon which the Covenant was inscribed was unrolled for signature, every person in the hall joined patiently in the queue to sign it.*

Copies of the National Covenant were sent off the length and breadth of the country; people hastened to sign it in cities, in towns, in villages, in shops, in churches, in factories, in offices, in railway stations. It generated huge enthusiasm and attracted mass support; within three months it had gathered four hundred thousand signatures, and eventually would claim to have garnered some two million. There were undoubtedly some mischievous forgeries and duplications among them, but it was nonetheless a sensational expression of Scottish middle-ground sentiment in favour of Home Rule (rather than independence). It was bravura gesture politics; but it cut no ice with the politicians (especially the politicians in England) who would have to vote a Home Rule Bill through parliament. The Labour government, still bitterly hostile to MacCormick, simply ignored it; so did the Tory opposition in Scotland.

But four young Scottish nationalists – three men and a woman – did not ignore it. On Christmas Day 1950 they broke into Westminster Abbey and 'liberated' the Stone of Destiny which Edward I had removed from Scotland in 1286.

The Stone of Destiny

You will all have heard by this time of the act of sacrilege that was perpetrated in Westminster Abbey in the early hours of Christmas Day. The Stone of Scone has been stolen. This senseless crime had clearly been carefully planned, and was carried out with great cunning. This precious relic, encased in the Coronation Chair made for it by King Edward I, is treasured by millions throughout the British Commonwealth and Empire, and not least by those who, like myself, see in it the symbol of the Scottish descent of our beloved king.

THE DEAN OF WESTMINSTER, BBC, 25 DECEMBER 1950

The ringleader in this 'senseless crime', this 'act of sacrilege', was Ian Hamilton, a twenty-five-year-old tailor's son from Paisley who was studying law at Glasgow University (he is now a QC). He had been dreaming of recovering the Stone ever since he had heard, in childhood, the story of its theft from Scotland by Edward I, the 'Hammer of the Scots'. The woman in the team was Kay Matheson, from Inverasdale in Wester Ross, who would be known to the media as 'the Stone of Destiny girl' thereafter. She was a twenty-two-year-old teacher at East Park School in Glasgow's Maryhill district, teaching home economics, physical education and Gaelic. The other two members of the team were twenty-four-year-old Gavin Vernon, a powerfully-built young engineering student from Glasgow, and twenty-year-old Alan Stuart, the son of the director of a large engineering company, who had volunteered the use of his car.

Ian Hamilton was an acolyte of 'King' John MacCormick; in the autumn of 1950 he organised the student campaign to have MacCormick elected as rector of Glasgow University. He was also well-versed in nationalist lore. He knew that this was not the first time the idea of recovering the Stone of Destiny had been mooted; it had been suggested many years earlier by R.E. Muirhead, from Bridge of Weir, the organiser and financier of the National Party of Scotland.[1] Hamilton decided it was time for the great dream to be realised, as a symbolic gesture to rouse Scotland from its apathy over Home Rule.

He made a reconnaissance trip to London, where he studied the layout of Westminster Abbey and its practically non-existent security arrangements, and laid his plans, reckoning that it would be a relatively simple job. In the event, it only succeeded after a series of errors, narrow squeaks and almost unbelievable coincidences worthy of an Ealing comedy.

---

1 Roland Eugene Muirhead (d.1964) owned a tannery in Bridge of Weir and was moderately well-off. He paid for the Socialist Home Rule newspaper *Forward*, which Tom Johnston, the future Secretary of State for Scotland, edited; he also financed the party's newspaper, *Scots Independent*, and a host of nationalist pamphlets and booklets.

On the evening of Friday, 22 December the team set off for the south in two small cars – Alan Stuart's, and an old Ford Anglia which Ian Hamilton had hired. They had a long and hazardous journey through ice and snow, and reached London in the afternoon of 23 December. They planned to make the heist that very night; but after Ian had allowed himself to be locked inside the Abbey when it closed to the public he was found by a night-watchman and politely shown out through the West Door.

The quartet spent the night in their cars, to save money. Sunday was Christmas Eve. Well after midnight the raiders left Alan Stuart's car in a carpark off Millbank and drove the Anglia into Old Palace Yard, a lane which led past the Abbey at Poets' Door. The area had been boarded off by builders; leaving Kay Matheson at the wheel, the three men went through the builders' yard and forced Poets' Door open with a jemmy. It made a terrific noise as it crashed open, but no alarm was raised.

The Coronation Chair which housed the Stone of Destiny stood against the wall of the Chapel of Edward the Confessor behind the High Altar. There was no sign of the night-watchman, and the three raiders moved quickly into the chapel. The Stone had an iron ring stapled into it at each end. It lay in a compartment beneath the seat of the Chair, with a wooden bar across the front of it. The wood splintered without difficulty. Then, with immense effort, the Stone was pulled from the base of the chair; it was heavier than they had expected (152 kilograms), and as it was lowered to the ground it broke into two pieces. Hamilton took the smaller piece, carried it out to the car in which Kay was waiting, and dumped it on the back seat. Then he went back inside to help the others with the larger piece. They dragged it to Poets' Door on Ian's raincoat, but when he looked outside he saw their car moving away down the lane towards the main road. He dashed out to tell Kay to bring it back. 'A policeman has spotted me,' she said quietly. 'He's coming across the road.'

With remarkable *sang-froid* Ian slid into the passenger seat, put his arms round Kay and started canoodling. The policeman came over to them with the familiar ''Allo, 'allo, 'allo.' He accepted their story that they were a pair of young lovers who had arrived in London too late to find a bed and were passing the night in dalliance in the car. He took off his helmet, placed it on the roof of the car and lit a cigarette, chatting to them cheerfully. There was a loud thump from inside the Abbey. The policeman grinned and said, 'The old watchman seems to have fallen down the stairs.' Then he asked them to move on, which they did with alacrity.

Because the car had been spotted, and its number might have been taken, Ian told Kay to get out of London with her portion of the Stone at once, heading, as previously planned, for Birmingham, where she would hole up with friends and leave the Anglia. He himself would take the larger fragment in Alan Stuart's car. They moved the Stone into the Anglia's boot, and Kay drove off. While she was still in London the boot sprang open and the section of the Stone fell out on to the road. It weighed forty-five kilograms; Kay, who was accustomed to lifting sacks of peat on her parents' croft in Wester Ross, heaved it back into the car and proceeded to Birmingham, where she left the Anglia with its load in a garage, to be collected later, and made her way back to her home at Inverasdale.

Ian hurried back to the Abbey. He found the second piece of the Stone lying just behind Poets' Door, but there was no sign of Gavin Vernon and Alan Stuart — nor of Ian's raincoat, which had the keys of the second car in the pocket. He decided that the other two must have gone to the car at Millbank; if they had found the keys in the pocket of his raincoat, they would either be in the car, or would be driving it back to the Abbey. He sped back to Millbank, but the car was still there, unattended.

Perhaps the keys had fallen out of the coat pocket while the Stone was being dragged through the Abbey? He rushed back to the Abbey once again, and went inside. It was pitch-dark, and he had no torch. On his hands and knees he crawled back along the route they had taken with the Stone, sweeping the floor with his hands and sparingly using some matches. At last he came across the keys, but this time he dropped his watch. He fetched the car and backed it into Old Palace Yard, then dragged the Stone out of the Abbey and somehow man-handled it into the back seat. He drove off, heading south across Westminster Bridge and into the Old Kent Road. He had no idea where to go, but assumed that the police would soon be setting up road-blocks on every road going north.

He got lost in a maze of side-streets. As he drove aimlessly along he suddenly saw, walking equally aimlessly along the pavement ahead of him, Gavin and Alan. It seemed nothing short of a miracle. The car, with the Stone filling the back seat, could now take only one passenger, so they split up: Gavin was to make his own way back to Glasgow while Ian and Alan drove out into the country and dumped the Stone in a field, covering it with foliage.

There was still one pressing problem: the raincoat, which Alan and Gavin had left lying in the carpark at Millbank when they had wandered off. It had a name-tab marked with Ian's name and that of the tailor who had made it – Ian's father. Ian and Alan decided to drive back into London, knowing that the alarm must have been raised by now. They reached the carpark before nine o'clock. It was Christmas morning, and few people were about. The coat was still there.

They retrieved the Stone from its temporary hiding place, then drove a further twenty miles into Kent where they concealed it in a field near Rochester. Then they turned around and headed for Scotland. It must have been the most ludicrously amateurish burglary ever committed: 'carefully planned and carried out with great cunning' it was not. But they had got away with it.

The news of the heist created a tremendous stir in Scotland, and the newspapers kept the story on their front pages with insatiable relish. 'Police Close Scots Border', blared the *Scottish Daily Mail*: 'All-force hunt for Stone of Destiny'; 'Watch, Jemmy Clues to Abbey Theft'. The more solemn broadsheets, like the *Glasgow Herald*, deplored the exploit as a mischievous prank; but most Scots were highly diverted and privately rather pleased. The Dean of Westminster made an emotional appeal for information:

> It is unbelievable that anyone would destroy it. It must be hidden somewhere. Therefore keep your eyes and your ears open, and if you have any idea where it may be, let the police know; or else let me know, and I will go to the ends of the earth to fetch it back.

There was no need for him to carry out his extravagant promise. When the initial hullabaloo had subsided, Ian slipped over the border with a couple of companions and drove down to Kent, where they retrieved the Stone of Destiny from its field and brought it back to Scotland. Then they collected the Ford Anglia from Birmingham with the smaller portion of the Stone, and took the two pieces for repair to the yard of a sympathetic Glasgow stonemason, Councillor Robert Gray, vice-president of the Scottish Convention. Afterwards they stowed it near Stirling in a small engineering workshop owned by another Covenanting sympathiser. But what to do with the Stone now?

The police soon knew who the perpetrators were: Detective Inspector Willie Kerr, head of the Special Branch in Scotland, had astutely checked the names of people who had borrowed books about the

Stone from the Mitchell Library in Glasgow before the break-in at Westminster Abbey, and Ian Hamilton's name had emerged. Rumour and gossip had done the rest, and all four burglars had been interviewed at length. 'King' John MacCormick made himself permanently available to police and press for comment and interviews, and blandly laid a trail of smokescreens.

Meanwhile, it became clear that the king (George VI) was as distraught as the Dean of Westminster kept claiming he was: he really seemed to believe the old legend that the loss of the Stone presaged the end of his royal line. Ian Hamilton happened to be an ardent monarchist, and was greatly concerned by the news. Moreover, public opinion in Scotland was becoming impatient for a resolution of the situation. The time had come to surrender the Stone. There were endless behind-the-scenes discussions and unofficial negotiations with the authorities.

And so, in the early morning of 11 April 1951, nearly four months after the Christmas Day escapade, the Stone of Destiny, enveloped in the saltire flag of St Andrew, was deposited on the remains of the High Altar in the ruins of Arbroath Abbey, scene of the signing of the Declaration of Independence in 1320. Journalists converged on Arbroath at breakneck speed from all over the country. The police arrived and bore the Stone away on a pallet to Glasgow, where they put it on show at a brief press conference. Then they locked it in a cell in Glasgow's Turnbull Street police station and, at dead of night, whisked it off in the boot of a police car to Westminster Abbey.

No arrests were made. The Home Secretary, Sir David Maxwell Fife (later Lord Kilmuir), told the House of Commons that the 'thieves and vulgar vandals' were known, but that it would not be in the public interest to prosecute them. The Secretary of State for Scotland, Hector McNeil, presented a memorandum to his fellow-cabinet members recommending that the Stone should be returned to Scotland between coronations; he failed to carry his colleagues, however. The Labour government was ousted in October 1951, and in February 1952 the new Prime Minister, Winston Churchill, announced that the Stone was to stay in Westminster Abbey. It was slipped back, without ceremony, under the Coronation Chair in good time to legitimise the coronation of Queen Elizabeth in 1953.

So the story of the Stone of Destiny ended – for a time, at least. The episode gave rise to a new set of myths and fables: the Stone in Westminster Abbey was a substitute, and the real one was still hidden in the basement of a tenement somewhere in Edinburgh; or even that the Stone which Edward I had removed from Scotland had been a substitute. No one really cared now: the abduction had been a splendidly romantic and symbolic gesture, the very stuff of story and contemporary ballad. But no more than that. Neither the theft of the Stone, nor the huge numbers of those who signed the National Covenant, had any effect on the political fortunes of the Scottish National Party. It failed to win a single parliamentary seat at the 1951 general election.

Queen Elizabeth – I or II?

There were more gestures when the government decided that the new queen should be titled Elizabeth II. Why 'II'? There had been an Elizabeth Queen of England, but never an Elizabeth Queen of Scotland – so how could this Elizabeth be other than Elizabeth I of the United Kingdom? James VI of Scotland had not become James VI of England, had he?

Many Scots were outraged when a shiny new red pillar-box was solemnly unveiled in Horse Guards Parade in Whitehall, with the royal cypher EIIR on it. In Edinburgh, the first such pillar-box was unveiled with less ceremony in the New Inch housing estate. Within thirty-six hours it had been smeared with tar. Other pillar-boxes were blown up with crude home-made bombs. No one was injured, and the director of the Post Office in Edinburgh said, 'The whole matter is so trivial that we are letting it take its normal course.' The Secretary of State for Scotland was less complacent, however, and asked the Postmaster-General to think again about the advisability of erecting pillar-boxes with the offending royal cypher on them in Scotland. The Postmaster-General was not impressed, and the pillar-boxes have remained to this day.

It is not that the Scots were anti-royalist: they simply wanted the English to get their history, and their figures, right. Indeed, the new queen was received as affectionately north of the border as elsewhere in her realm when she made her first visit to Scotland in 1954, the year after her coronation. In the courtyard of the Palace of Holyroodhouse thousands of people gathered to serenade their queen, as they had serenaded Mary Queen of Scots in 1561.

For many years after the Stone of Destiny escapade and the EIIR brouhaha the Scottish nationalists seemed an irrelevance. Devolution was no longer on the political agenda, and Labour formally dropped its commitment to Home Rule. Scotland's economy boomed during thirteen years of Tory rule from 1951 to 1964. Prodigious sums of money were poured into prestigious Scottish industrial projects: an integrated iron and steel works at Ravenscraig, near Motherwell; a Rootes car plant in Linwood to make the Hillman Imp; a British Motor Corporation truck plant at Bathgate. But no amount of lavish investment could gloss over the fundamental structural weakness of the Scottish economy – the failure to adapt to changing world markets and to keep up with the new science-based 'sunrise' electronic industries.

There was another, more profound change occurring in Scotland's sense of itself: the concept of 'Britishness'. The spread of the British Empire in the nineteenth century had given rise to a concept of Britain in which Scots had found a lucrative role; Glasgow, with its magnificent, world-beating shipbuilding industry on the Clyde, had proudly called itself 'the Second City of the Empire'. Now, however, as the Empire disintegrated, some Scots became disillusioned with the British side of their dual nationality, their dual identity. Being British was no longer a source of pride; being Scottish was. The one political party which gained from this changing perception was the Scottish National Party.

The rise of the 'Nats'

In November 1967 a thirty-eight-year-old Glasgow lawyer named Winnie Ewing created the most sensational political upset for years by winning a parliamentary by-election at Hamilton for the Scottish National Party. She won 46 per cent of the vote in the safest Labour seat in its heartlands in the west of Scotland. It was a bombshell.[1]

Winnie Ewing's victory was a response to the first tell-tale signs of the underlying weakness of Scotland's economic position, with rising unemployment and falling standards of living in Scotland compared with the rest of the UK. The electors of Hamilton were not necessarily nationalist; they had used the SNP as a stick with which to punish the Labour government. Winnie's victory, coming hard on the heels of a Welsh nationalist (Plaid Cymru) by-election success, terrified Labour. Oliver Brown, a veteran Scottish nationalist, cruelly remarked

---

[1] I remember the occasion all too well, because I was the presenter of the by-election programme on BBC Scotland that night. The Controller of BBC Scotland at the time, Andrew Stewart, took exception to the enthusiasm with which I greeted the news, and I was solemnly banned from further political broadcasting on the BBC for a year.

that 'a shiver ran along the Labour backbenches looking for a spine to run up'.

Winnie Ewing set off for Westminster on a wave of enthusiasm reminiscent of the departure of the Red Clydeside MPs in 1922. Central Station in Glasgow was thronged with well-wishers as she boarded the 'Tartan Express' for London. She was given a hard time by Labour members in the Commons, and would lose her Hamilton seat in 1970; but her victory in 1967 was not to be another false nationalist dawn.

Ted Heath, the Conservative leader, stunned his party by springing his 'Declaration of Perth' on the Scottish Conservative Party conference in 1968; in it he committed the Conservatives to a devolved Scottish assembly. Labour tried to buy time by setting up a Royal Commission on the Constitution, under the Scottish judge Lord Kilbrandon; in the autumn of 1973 it issued its report, which recommended subordinate parliaments for Scotland and Wales. In November of that year the SNP's Margo MacDonald seized yet another rock-solid Labour seat in a by-election, this time at Govan, overturning a Labour majority of sixteen thousand.

The SNP had been learning some hard politics. In the wake of Winnie Ewing's victory at Hamilton a host of SNP local authority members had been elected, but most of them were inexperienced and failed to make a mark; the 1970 general election had seen the SNP vote plummet, with only one parliamentary seat (in the Western Isles). The SNP had not ignored the message. Its party organisation became much more effective, and at by-elections it could swamp a constituency with fervent, disciplined and indefatigable volunteers. When, in the wake of the 1973 Arab–Israeli War, the Organisation of Petroleum Exporting Countries (OPEC) quadrupled the world price of oil, the SNP seized on the economic potential of North Sea oil as a uniquely Scottish asset which England was keeping to itself.

At the general election of February 1974, when the miners' strike forced Ted Heath to go to the country, the SNP made its big breakthrough as a parliamentary force in Scotland. It won seven seats and 22 per cent of the poll as Labour emerged with the most seats at Westminster but without an overall majority. Anxious to secure a majority, Harold Wilson bowed to the inevitable and accepted the principle of devolution, which became part of Labour's manifesto for the second general election of that year, which was held in October. It was not enough to stop the SNP bandwagon: this time the SNP won almost a third of the vote in Scotland and sent eleven MPs to Westminster. The SNP was now the second largest party in Scotland, after Labour; in addition to its eleven MPs, it had come second in a further forty-two constituencies.

In 1975, in accordance with its manifesto commitment, the Labour government issued a devolution White Paper entitled *Our Changing Democracy*. It proposed a Scottish Assembly of 142 members funded by a block grant and exercising control of most of the functions of the Scottish Office, but with no revenue-raising powers of its own. This was an awkward compromise which pleased hardly anyone. The SNP was split: one wing wanted devolution, another denounced it as a fatal dilution of the commitment to independence. Labour was equally split, and the Labour MP for South Ayrshire, Jim Sillars, formed a breakaway Scottish Labour Party in protest. By the time the Scotland Act was agreed by the Commons in February 1978 the government had been forced to concede a referendum in the face of a backbench revolt of 140 Labour MPs. The Act also contained a crucial amendment which had been pushed through by George Cunningham, the Scots-born MP for London Islington. This clause stipulated that at least 40 per cent of the whole Scottish electorate would have to vote yes in the referendum before the Act could be put into effect. Ironically, this amendment was passed on Burns Night, 25 January 1978. After the Act was passed, the empty Royal High School building on Calton Hill, facing St Andrew's House, was refurbished as the future home of the new Assembly.

Referendum day was set for 1 March 1979. The previous winter has become known as the 'Winter of Discontent', when trade union militancy brought James Callaghan's Labour government almost to its knees. The Tories in Scotland ran a confident, well-focused and well-financed 'Scotland Says No' campaign, and made effective use of the hostility of big business to the idea of devolution; the Clydesdale Bank, for instance, sent letters to all its customers explaining why devolution would be bad for them. Some left-wing Labour MPs (such as Robin Cook, later to become Foreign Secretary in the Tony Blair administration) ran an equally effective 'Labour Vote No' campaign – it won a court ruling which halted party political broadcasts (of which three to one were in favour of devolution) on the grounds that the parties neither reflected public opinion nor were as relevant in a referendum campaign as in an election. Tam Dalyell, Labour MP for West Lothian and an inveterate enemy of Home Rule, argued long and persuasively against the proposal on the ground that it would inevitably lead to separation. By contrast, the official 'Yes for Scotland' campaign was woolly, abstract and unfocused.

On the eve of the vote the Scottish former Tory Prime Minister Sir

Alec Douglas-Home (later Lord Home) urged the Scots to vote no, in order to ensure that a better measure could be enacted, with tax-raising powers, proportional representation and fewer assembly members; and the new Conservative leader, Margaret Thatcher, promised that a no vote would not mean an end to devolution.

The turn-out for the vote on 1 March 1979 was disappointingly low – only 63.8 per cent of the electorate. Of those who did cast a vote, 51.6 per cent voted yes while 48.4 per cent voted no; but in terms of the whole electorate, the yes vote was only 39.2 per cent – below the 40 per cent threshold required by the Scotland Act 1978.

Devolution had not been 'defeated', as such; but the vote was not exactly a ringing endorsement of it, either. Barely more than a third of the Scottish people had voted for what would have been the most significant constitutional change in Scotland's history since 1707; and detailed analysis of the result showed that Scotland was deeply divided on the issue – not on party political lines, not on 'class' lines, but geographically: much of the rural north and south voted no, while the huge, more urbanised Strathclyde region voted yes.

The SNP, unwisely as it turned out, tabled a motion of no confidence in the Callaghan administration. It succeeded by a single vote, and the Labour government fell. In the ensuing general election in May 1979 the Conservatives, under Margaret Thatcher, swept to power; the SNP lost nine of its eleven seats. Margaret Thatcher was not going to have any truck with devolution. Almost overnight, the nationalist movement which had dictated Scotland's political agenda throughout the 1970s collapsed.

But the devolution issue had not gone away, and important lessons had been learned; these lessons would ensure victory for the devolutionists at another and much more decisive referendum eighteen years later, in 1997.

The 1980s: devolution in disarray[1]

Margaret Thatcher changed the face of Scottish politics more profoundly than any Scottish politician had ever done. In the recession of the early 1980s the remnants of Scotland's old industrial structure were swept away – including the most potently emotive of Scotland's former heavy industries, shipbuilding. The government switched off

---

1   I am indebted to Tom Devine's *The Scottish Nation 1700-2000* for his spirited and incisive outline of political events in Scotland in the final decades of the twentieth century.

the life-support of state financing. Scotland was left to find its own feet – and did not like it. The burgeoning North Sea oil industry gave Scots business leaders an opportunity, but they were slow to take advantage of it; not until the end of the decade did the performance of the Scottish economy begin to match that of England.

The SNP, demoralised and disillusioned by the outcome of the 1979 referendum, fragmented. The left wing hived off into the '79 Group, led by the former Labour MP Jim Sillars, Margo MacDonald and Alex Salmond, which called for more radical socialist policies in order to mount a more effective challenge to Labour. As a publicity stunt, in October 1981 Sillars and a few companions broke into the Royal High School building and held a debate in the empty chamber (Sillars was arrested and fined £100 for vandalism). The right wing of the SNP formed a group known as *Siol Nan Gaidheal* ('the Seed of the Gael'), posturing as a kind of nationalist militia in Highland dress and indulging in ritual burnings of the Union Jack.

The SNP was in danger of total extinction until the leader, Gordon Wilson, bravely grasped the thistle; at the party's annual conference at Ayr in 1982 all groups were disbanded and six members of the '79 Group (including the future SNP leader, Alex Salmond) were expelled, although they were soon taken back into the fold. The wounds took many years to heal. The SNP's parliamentary representation remained at only two seats. The corner was not turned until the party refined its stated political objective – 'Independence in Europe' was now the slogan, to counter the charge of separatism – and Jim Sillars won a sensational by-election victory over Labour in 1988 at Govan, scene of the 1973 triumph by Margo MacDonald, who was now his wife.

Meanwhile Labour, too, was convulsed by internal troubles. The party lurched far to the left, advocating withdrawal from the EEC and embracing unilateral nuclear disarmament, while its branches were infiltrated by the hard-left Militant Tendency. The 'Gang of Four' (Roy Jenkins, David Owen, Bill Rodgers and Shirley Williams) parted from Labour and founded the more moderate Social Democratic Party (SDP). The Labour disarray led to humiliating defeat at the 1983 general election which gave the Conservatives their greatest victory for half a century. In Scotland, however, Labour more than held its own, returning forty-one MPs – nearly twice as many as the Tories. This was the time when a clutch of talented younger Scots Labour MPs who were to make their mark in the 1990s started to come to the fore: Gordon Brown, Robin Cook, Donald Dewar, George Robertson,

John Smith. Two of them in particular remained passionately committed to devolution – Donald Dewar and John Smith.[1]

The Thatcher government consolidated its position in England with resounding victories in the general elections of 1983 and 1987; but in Scotland, Tory support continued to ebb, and the 1987 election lowered its Scottish Westminster representation to only ten seats – the lowest since 1910. By the end of the 1980s the government's unpopularity in Scotland had reduced the ruling party north of the border to a rump struggling to maintain its credibility, and Margaret Thatcher became the target of virulent personal hostility. All Scotland's ills were laid at her door. She made no secret of the fact that she thought the Scots were 'subsidy junkies' who had to be weaned off their addiction, however painfully. During a visit to Edinburgh in 1988 she delivered a forceful speech to the General Assembly of the Church of Scotland in its Assembly Hall on the Mound; she told the outraged ministers and elders of the Kirk that her Conservative values of hard work, thrift, enterprise and self-reliance were the basic values of Christianity. Her address came to be known, sardonically, as the Sermon on the Mound. Her ill-advised attendance at the Scottish Cup Final at Hampden was loudly booed, and thousands of fans brandished red cards which had been thoughtfully issued to them at the turnstiles before the game.

The last straw was the introduction of a flat-rate Community Charge – the so-called 'Poll Tax' – as a substitute for the traditional rating system on 1 April 1988. The Poll Tax was levied only in Scotland to begin with, giving rise to the suspicion that the Scots were being used as guinea-pigs. There were violent protests and a widespread non-payment campaign – seven hundred thousand summary warrants for non-payment were issued in the first year. When the hated tax was introduced in England the following year it led to riots, and eighteen months later it was withdrawn after Margaret Thatcher herself had been deposed as leader of the Conservative Party and Prime Minister in November 1990.

---

1   John Smith, QC (1938–94) is fondly remembered in Scotland as Labour's 'lost leader'. He succeeded Neil Kinnock as Labour leader after the disastrous general election of 1992 and had started the process of making Labour 'electable' again when he was struck down by a heart attack in 1994. He never lost his unswerving adherence to the cause of devolution – 'the settled will of the Scottish people', he called it; for him, devolution for Scotland was 'unfinished business'. He was buried on the island of Iona, ancient burial place of Scotland's early kings.

EPILOGUE

The Scottish Constitutional Convention

Throughout the 1980s the Home Rule flame had been kept flickering by a cross-party movement called the Campaign for a Scottish Assembly (CSA). It strove to bring together politicians, Church leaders, trade unionists, university notables and business people to plan a way forward for devolution. It culminated in the publication, in July 1988, of *A Claim of Right for Scotland*; the steering committee was chaired by the eminent planner Sir Robert Grieve, and the document was drafted by a retired civil servant named Jim Ross who had long experience in framing the devolution legislation of the 1970s. He produced a powerful, radical, cogently-argued and near-revolutionary document, drawing on historical analysis founded on the thinking of Scotland's foremost contemporary historians. It asserted that 'the Union has always been, and remains, a threat to the survival of a distinctive culture in Scotland,' and accused Margaret Thatcher of wielding more arbitrary power than virtually any Scottish monarch of the past:

> *Scotland faces a crisis of identity and survival. It is now being governed without consent and subject to the declared intention of having imposed upon it a radical change of outlook and behaviour patterns which it shows no sign of wanting. All questions as to whether consent should be a part of government are brushed aside. The comments of Adam Smith are put to uses which would have astonished him, Scottish history is selectively distorted and the Scots are told that their votes are lying: that they secretly vote what they constantly vote against . . .*

A Claim of Right for Scotland proposed the establishment of a 210-strong Constitutional Convention, consisting of MPs, local-authority representatives, trade unionists and Church representatives to discuss how Home Rule should be achieved. It concluded:

> *We are under no illusions about the seriousness of what we recommend. Contesting the authority of established government is not a light matter. We could not recommend it if we did not feel that British government has so decayed that there is little hope of its being reformed within the framework of its traditional procedures. Setting up a Scottish Constitutional Convention and subsequently establishing a Scottish Assembly cannot by themselves achieve the essential reforms of British government, but they*

are essential if any remnant of distinctive Scottish government is
to be saved, and they would create the groundswell necessary to
set the British reform process on its way.

The Campaign for a Scottish Assembly was no longer a lone voice, and the Scottish Constitutional Convention held its inaugural meeting in March 1989. The Conservatives, naturally, refused to take part; so, eventually, did the SNP, fearing that any agreement on devolution might dilute the drive for full independence. But Labour and the Liberal Democrats, the trade unions and Churches and most of Scotland's local authorities all joined, with considerable enthusiasm.

The Convention adopted *A Claim of Right for Scotland* in ringing terms:

> *We, gathered as the Scottish Constitutional Convention, do*
> *hereby acknowledge the sovereign right of the Scottish people to*
> *determine the form of Government best suited to their needs,*
> *and do hereby declare and pledge that in all our actions and*
> *deliberations their interests shall be paramount.*

The first fruits of the Convention, published on 30 November 1990 (St Andrew's Day), were less tasty than had been hoped. The blueprint for a Scottish parliament was somewhat vague and inconclusive. It proposed a legislature elected under proportional representation, financed through 'assigned revenues' from taxes raised in Scotland; it avoided the vexed question of future Scottish representation at Westminster which Tam Dalyell had highlighted so doggedly over many years.

The publication of the document containing the Convention's recommendations made little impact on public opinion at first; press comment wrote it off as a damp squib. Nonetheless it was a significant landmark: Labour (the dominant political party in Scotland) was now firmly ensconced at the heart of the Home Rule movement, even though the Conservatives were still in power in Westminster.[1] The Tory administration in Scotland derided the document, and there was clearly no chance that Scotland would be allowed any kind of parliament or assembly while the Conservatives were in power. But Margaret

---

1   The final report of the Scottish Constitutional Convention, containing detailed proposals for the implementation of its scheme for a Scottish parliament, was published in 1995, entitled *Scotland's Parliament, Scotland's Right.*

Thatcher was forced from the leadership of the Tory party that same month. With the Conservatives in profound trouble internally, it looked as if the party's iron grip on Scotland could well be ended at the next general election; this would surely leave the way open for a Scottish parliament. As the 1992 general election approached, the revitalised SNP coined a new slogan: 'Free by '93'. Political pundits predicted a Tory-free Scotland after polling day. Rupert Murdoch's *Sun* newspaper switched its allegiance from the Conservatives to the SNP with a saltire-draped masthead: *Arise and be a Nation again!*

The celebrations were premature. In April 1992 Margaret Thatcher's successor as Conservative leader and Prime Minister John Major, against all the odds, held on to power, albeit with a reduced majority; and, to most people's surprise, there was a marginal *increase* in the Tory vote in Scotland and an additional parliamentary seat. Once again, the Home Rule issue seemed to be a dead duck. Various *ad hoc* groups were formed to resuscitate it. A relay of dedicated members of 'Democracy for Scotland' kept constant vigil outside the proposed parliament building on Calton Hill opposite St Andrew's House – a marvellously self-sacrificing marathon of loyalty by ordeal. But the death in 1994 of the Labour leader John Smith, so passionate about devolution for Scotland, seemed to bode ill for Labour's future commitment to the cause.

Despite its unexpected general election victory, the Tory administration in Scotland was still in deep, deep trouble. Although the Scottish economy was doing relatively well, the Tories were given no credit for it. In 1995 John Major appointed to the office of Secretary of State for Scotland an unlikely choice: Michael Forsyth, who had made a reputation in the 1980s as Margaret Thatcher's hatchet-man north of the border. Did this herald an intensification of Thatcherism in Scotland?

Not a bit of it. The combative Forsyth, although an unshakeable opponent of constitutional change, metamorphosed himself into a dyed-in-the-wool Scottish patriot. When the film *Braveheart* was premiered in Stirling in 1995, the Secretary of State was there in full Highland dress. He introduced a new Tory slogan: 'Fighting for Scotland'. And then the beleaguered Forsyth made the ultimate gesture of gesture politics: he brought the Stone of Destiny back to Scotland.

The return of the Stone

On 3 July 1996 the Prime Minister rose in the House of Commons to announce that the Queen had agreed that the Stone of Destiny was to be returned to Scotland. Scotland was not impressed – the decision was widely derided as little more than a desperate attempt by the Conservatives to shore up their crumbling support north of the border.

But what was to be the Stone's destination? A cathedral? A castle? A museum? A consultation process was launched by the Scottish Office on 16 July. After a lively public debate, it emerged that the locality favoured by the majority of those who had responded to the consultation was Edinburgh Castle: the Stone should be housed in the Crown Room, alongside the Honours of Scotland. It was to be installed there on St Andrew's Day (30 November).

Removing the Stone from its compartment under the Coronation Chair in Westminster Abbey was a less haphazard operation than its previous removal on Christmas Day 1950. An exact replica was carved, for rehearsal purposes, and a special hand-barrow was constructed. Scaffolding was erected over the Chair to house a block and tackle for lifting the Stone with woven nylon straps. The lifting operation began on the night of 13 November; it took five hours.

The Stone left Westminster Abbey next morning and was brought north under police escort. On the morning of 15 November 1996 it arrived on the English side of Coldstream Bridge over the River Tweed. At the middle of the bridge (the border point) it was received by the kilted Secretary of State for Scotland and conveyed to Edinburgh.

On the morning of 30 November 1996 the Stone was driven up the Royal Mile from the Palace of Holyroodhouse to a service in St Giles' Cathedral. It travelled in state under a perspex bubble on the back of a specially adapted army Land Rover. From St Giles' it was taken on the last stage of its journey up the Lawnmarket and Castle Hill to Edinburgh Castle, escorted by the Royal Company of Archers.

There was considerably more pomp and pageantry than for the royal opening of the new parliament three years later, but despite all the earnest efforts to make the event an occasion of pageantry and national rejoicing, it all fell rather flat. The Stone itself, a grubby-looking lump of sandstone, looks extraordinarily incongruous beside the gleaming elegance of the Honours of Scotland. Curiously enough, once the 'symbol of nationhood' had been officially returned to Scotland, it lost all its potency as a symbol and became just another ordinary and undistinguished chunk of rock.[1]

The mystique of the Stone did nothing to revive the political fortunes of the Tories in Scotland, who had consistently opposed devolution: they lost every single one of their eleven Scottish parliamentary seats at the general election of 1 May 1997. Gesture politics had not been enough.

A parliament for Scotland: the last lap

Despite the overwhelming Labour victory in the 1997 general election, there was no certainty that Home Rule would automatically follow. In June 1996 the Labour shadow cabinet had decided that an election victory would not in itself be sufficient to justify such a momentous constitutional reform: there would have to be a referendum first. In the event, there was no need for devolutionists to be concerned. The Constitutional Convention's final report formed the basis of the devolution policy presented in the Labour Party's manifesto.

Only two months after the election the new Labour administration, with Donald Dewar as Secretary of State for Scotland, issued a White Paper on devolution, entitled *Scotland's Parliament*. It set out the arrangements for the promised referendum; unlike the one in 1979, it would be held *before* the relevant Devolution Bill was introduced to parliament, not after it had been enacted.

The referendum was held on 11 September 1997. It asked two questions: the first on the basic principle of a Scottish parliament, the second on whether such a parliament should have tax-raising powers – the ability to vary the basic rate of income tax by up to 3p in the pound (potentially raising £450 million per annum) – what Michael Forsyth and the Conservatives had repeatedly attacked as a 'tartan tax'.

The outcome of the referendum was incontrovertible: 74.3 per cent of those who voted supported the re-establishment of a Scottish parliament; 63.5 per cent agreed that it should have tax-varying powers. The referendum had triumphantly endorsed what the late John Smith had called 'the settled will of the Scottish people'.

Events now moved with remarkable rapidity. By the end of 1997 the government published its Scotland Parliament Bill, which went

---

1 My personal view is that the Stone should be installed as a centrepiece in the new National Museum of Scotland, where it could be displayed in an imaginative and telling historical setting.

through the Commons without mishap and received the Royal Assent in November 1998. The new parliament would be funded through the existing system of allocation (which provides a budget of around £15 billion). It would have the power to legislate over all the areas of policy not reserved to Westminster: these would include agriculture (plus forestry and fisheries), economic development, education, environment, health, home affairs, housing, law, local government, research and statistics, social work, sport and the arts, training and transport. The Westminster parliament would retain legislative power in respect of the constitution of the UK, defence, foreign policy (including relations with Europe), macro-economic policy and social security and employment. However, the Scottish parliament would be able to debate and form a view on all these reserved matters. A cross-party Consultative Steering Group was established to prepare draft standing orders and procedures. This group concentrated on four key principles: power-sharing, accountability, access and participation, and equal opportunities. It submitted its report in December 1998.

The elections for the Scottish parliament were held on 6 May 1999, with a mixture of first-past-the post and proportional representation. Of the 129 seats, Labour won fifty-six, the SNP thirty-five, the Conservatives eighteen, the Liberal Democrats seventeen, the Scottish Green Party one, the Socialist Party of Scotland one, and there was one independent. Forty-eight of the new MSPs were women – 37 per cent of the total. The new MSPs took their seats on 12 May 1999. Only two years had elapsed since the Westminster general election, an astonishingly short time for such a momentous constitutional change. Suddenly, it had happened. As no single party had obtained an overall majority, a coalition government between the Scottish Labour Party and the Scottish Liberal Democrats was agreed under a 'Partnership for Scotland' on 14 May.

So the Scottish parliament rose from the ashes of the past like a phoenix. Like any infant, its first steps were to attract anxious attention. There were to be arguments about all sorts of things – particularly about the site, and escalating costs, of the new parliament building which had been designed by the Spanish architect the late Enric Miralles. But all the early stutterings, all the uncertainties and concerns, pale into insignificance compared with the magnitude of this new chapter of a nation's story, which the people of Scotland are now beginning to write.

Chronology

10,000 BC End of the last Ice Age
7000 BC Mesolithic Age; hunter-gatherers on the island of Rum
3500 BC Neolithic Age
3100–2600 BC Neolithic village of Skara Brae (Orkney)
3000 BC Chambered tomb of Maes Howe (Orkney)
3000–2000 BC Megalithic standing stones at Calanais (Isle of Lewis)
2500 BC Great Pyramid built in Egypt
2000 BC Bronze Age starts; building of Stonehenge in Wiltshire
600 BC Iron Age starts
500 BC 'Oakbank Crannog' built in Loch Tay
200 BC–AD 200 Broch-building
55–54 BC Julius Caesar invades Britain
AD 80 Agricola invades Lowlands of Scotland
84 Battle of Mons Graupius
122 Hadrian starts building Hadrian's Wall
140–80 Antonine Wall in Scotland
214 The Romans abandon Scotland
297 First reference to 'Picti'
367 The 'Barbarian Conspiracy'; Hadrian's Wall overrun
410 The Romans abandon Britain
500 'Scoti' colonise Dalriada (Argyll); Dunadd
c.550 St Ninian comes to Whithorn (Galloway)

563 St Columba comes to Scotland and the island of Iona
580 Pictish king Bridei mac Máelchú at Craig Phadrig (?)
590 Urien of Rheged assassinated on Lindisfarne
c.600 The Gododdin defeated at Catterick
603 Áedán, king of Dalriada, defeated by the Anglians
638 Angles from Northumbria capture Edinburgh
685 Battle of Dunnichen: the Picts defeat the Northumbrians
750 Battle of Athelstaneford (St Andrew)
793 Start of the viking age: raid on the Holy Isle of Lindisfarne
795 First viking raid on the island of Iona
c.840 Kenneth mac Alpin unites Pictland and Dalriada as *Alba*
849 Iona abandoned; treasures moved to Dunkeld
858 Death of Kenneth I (mac Alpin)
860 Norse earldom established in Orkney and Shetland
870 Vikings storm Dumbarton Castle
874 Norwegian settlers colonise Iceland
890 Vikings storm Dunnottar Castle
900–43 Constantin II rules 'Scotland'

937 Constantin II and his allies
defeated at Brunanburh

1005–34 Reign of Malcolm II

1018 Malcolm II defeats the
Northumbrians at Carham; death
of Owain the Bald, last native
king of Strathclyde

1034 Death of Malcolm II;
accession of Duncan I

1040 Macbeth defeats and kills
Duncan I

1050 Macbeth goes on pilgrimage
to Rome

1057 Macbeth killed by Malcolm
Canmore at Lumphanan

1058 Macbeth's stepson, Lulach,
killed by Malcolm Canmore;
Malcolm Canmore (Malcolm III)
becomes King of Alba

1061 Malcolm III invades
Northumbria

c.1070 Malcolm III marries
Margaret of England
(St Margaret)

1072 William I invades Scotland;
Malcolm III submits

1093 Malcolm III killed at Alnwick;
death of St Margaret; Donald III
(Malcolm's younger brother)
becomes king; Duncan II seizes
the throne, but is soon murdered

1097 Edgar, Malcolm's eldest
surviving son, becomes king

1107 Alexander I (Edgar's brother)
succeeds to the throne

1124 David I, Alexander's brother,
succeeds to the throne

1138 David I defeated at Battle of
the Standard

1153 Death of David I; Malcolm
IV, his grandson, succeeds

1165 Death of Malcolm IV; William
('the Lion'), his brother,
succeeds

1174 William captured by the
English at Alnwick; Treaty of
Falaise: William pays homage for
Scotland

1178 William founds Arbroath
Abbey

1189 The 'Quitclaim of Canterbury'
abrogates Falaise Treaty

1214 Death of William the Lion; his
son Alexander II succeeds

1221 Alexander II marries Joan,
sister of Henry III of England

1230 Norwegian expedition to the
Western Isles

1237 Treaty of York: Alexander
renounces claims in England

1239 Alexander II marries Marie de
Coucy, of France

1244 Alexander II's infant son
Alexander betrothed to Margaret
of England

1249 Alexander II mounts an
expedition to the Hebrides, dies;
Alexander III succeeds, aged seven

1251 Alexander III marries
Margaret, sister of Henry III

1263 'Battle of Largs'

1266 Norway cedes the Western
Isles to Scotland

1272 Edward I comes to the throne
of England

1281 Alexander III's daughter
Margaret marries Erik of Norway

1283 Birth of Margaret, the 'Maid
of Norway'

1284 Death of Alexander III's son
and heir, Alexander; the Maid of
Norway declared heir-
presumptive

1285 Alexander III marries Yolande,
Comtesse de Montford

1286 Death of Alexander III;
Margaret, the Maid of Norway,
declared Queen of Scots

1290 Margaret betrothed to Edward I's son, Edward; death of Margaret

1292 Edward I nominates John Balliol as King of Scotland

1295 Treaty of Paris – the 'Auld Alliance' with France

1296 Edward I invades Scotland, deposes Balliol

1297 William Wallace rebels against the English occupation; Battle of Stirling Bridge: Wallace defeats an English army

1298 Wallace defeated at Battle of Falkirk; John Comyn and Robert Bruce appointed guardians

1302 Robert Bruce defects to Edward I

1304 Scotland submits to Edward I

1305 Wallace captured, and executed in London

1306 Robert Bruce murders John Comyn; Bruce crowned King of Scots; Bruce defeated at Battle of Methven

1307 Bruce emerges from hiding, starts a comeback; death of Edward I

1314 Bruce defeats Edward II at Bannockburn

1320 The Declaration of Arbroath

1327 Edward II deposed

1328 Edward III recognises Scotland's independence; Bruce's son David marries Joan, sister of Edward III

1329 Death of Robert Bruce

1331 David II crowned King of Scots

1332 Edward Balliol invades Scotland, usurps the throne

1333 Edward III defeats the Scots at Halidon Hill; David II and Joan sent to France for safety

1338 'Black Agnes' defends Dunbar Castle

1341 David II returns to Scotland and starts his personal rule

1346 David II captured at Battle of Neville's Cross

1357 David II released and returns to Scotland

1371 David II dies, childless; Robert Stewart, his nephew, succeeds as Robert II

1384 Robert II demits power to his brother John

1388 Battle of Otterburn

1390 The 'Wolf of Badenoch' burns Elgin Cathedral; death of Robert II; John succeeds as Robert III

1396 Battle on the Inch

1401 Duke of Albany kidnaps David, Duke of Rothesay

1402 Rothesay dies during his imprisonment

1406 Robert III's son James flees to France, is captured by the English; death of Robert III; James I succeeds, while a prisoner in England

1411 Battle of Harlaw

1424 James I marries Joan Beaufort, is released and crowned

1425 James I destroys the Albany family

1437 James I assassinated; James II succeeds at the age of six

1440 The 'Black Dinner' in Edinburgh; Douglas beheaded

1449 James II marries Marie de Gueldres

1452 James murders William Douglas

1455 Wars of the Roses break out in England

1460 James II killed by an

exploding cannon; James III succeeds at the age of nine

1463 Death of James III's mother, Marie de Gueldres

1469 James marries Margrethe of Denmark

1482 The Lauder Lynchings; James III arrested

1488 James III dies after Battle of Sauchieburn; James IV succeeds

1503 James IV marries Margaret Tudor

1511 Launch of the *Great Michael*

1513 James IV killed at Battle of Flodden; James V succeeds at the age of seventeen months

1515 Duke of Albany appointed regent

1517 Martin Luther launches the Reformation

1526 James V 'captured' by the Earl of Angus

1528 James 'escapes'

1537 Execution of Lady Glamis; James V marries Madeleine of France

1538 James V marries Marie de Guise

1542 Birth of Mary Queen of Scots; Scots defeated at Battle of Solway Moss; death of James V; Mary succeeds at the age of one week

1543 Mary crowned Queen of Scots; betrothal of Mary to Prince Edward of England fails

1544 Start of the 'Rough Wooing'

1546 George Wishart burned for heresy

1547 John Knox captured and sentenced to the galleys; defeat of the Scots at Battle of Pinkie

1548 Mary betrothed to the Dauphin and sails to France

1557 'Lords of the Congregation' support the Reformation

1558 Mary marries the Dauphin; Elizabeth becomes Queen of England

1559 Mary becomes Queen of France as the wife of François II; John Knox inflames the mob with a sermon in Perth

1560 Mary is widowed; death of Mary's mother, Marie de Guise; parliament accepts the Reformation in Scotland

1561 Mary returns to Scotland, and is berated by John Knox

1565 Mary marries Henry, Lord Darnley

1566 Murder of David Rizzio

1567 Murder of Darnley; Mary marries the Earl of Bothwell; Mary surrenders at Carberry Hill; Mary deposed; James VI crowned king

1568 Mary escapes from Lochleven; Mary defeated at Langside, flees to England; 'trial' of Mary in England

1570–73 Civil war in Scotland

1572 Death of John Knox

1582 The 'Ruthven Raid': the kidnap of James VI

1583 James escapes

1586 The Babington Plot

1587 Execution of Mary Queen of Scots

1589 James VI marries Anne of Denmark

1592 Death of the 'Bonnie Earl of Moray'

1600 The 'Gowrie Conspiracy'

1603 Union of the Crowns: James VI becomes James I

1604 James VI & I proposes a full union of the United Kingdom

CHRONOLOGY

1605 The 'Powder Treason Plot'

1611 The 'King James Bible'

1617 James VI & I pays his only visit to Scotland as king

1625 Death of James VI & I; Charles I succeeds; Charles I marries Henrietta Maria of France

1633 Charles I crowned in Edinburgh

1637 The 'Jenny Geddes' riot against the Prayer Book

1638 The National Covenant launched and signed

1639–40 The 'Bishops' Wars'

1641 Charles I visits Edinburgh

1642 Charles I declares war on Parliament

1643 The Solemn League and Covenant

1644 Scottish troops at Battle of Marston Moor; Montrose starts his great campaign

1645 Montrose defeats the Campbells at Inverlochy; Montrose defeated at Philiphaugh

1646 Charles I surrenders to the Scots at Newark

1648 'The Engagement' forces defeated by Cromwell; the 'Whiggamores Raid'

1649 Execution of Charles I

1650 Montrose invades the north of Scotland, is captured and executed; Charles II lands in Scotland; Cromwell defeats the Scots at Battle of Dunbar

1651 Charles II crowned by the Scots at Scone; Charles II defeated at Worcester, and escapes to France; the rescue of the Scottish Regalia at Dunnottar Castle

1652 Cromwell 'incorporates' Scotland

1658 Death of Cromwell

1660 Restoration of Charles II

1661 Execution of the Marquis of Argyll

1666 The 'Pentland Rising'

1677 William of Orange marries James VII's daughter Mary

1679 Archbishop Sharp murdered by Covenanters; Battle of Drumclog; Battle of Bothwell Brig

1680 James, Duke of York, comes to Scotland

1682–85 The 'Killing Time'

1685 Death of Charles II; James VII & II succeeds

1688 Birth of James Stuart, the 'Old Pretender'; William of Orange lands in England: the 'Glorious Revolution'; James VII & II flees to France

1689 William and Mary crowned in England; William and Mary accept the crown of Scotland; 'Bonnie Dundee' wins Battle of Killiecrankie but is killed; Battle of Dunkeld

1690 James VII & II defeated at Battle of the Boyne

1692 Massacre of Glencoe

1694 Death of Queen Mary

1698–1700 The Darien expedition

1701 Death of James VII & II in exile

1702 Death of King William; accession of Queen Anne

1704 Scotland's parliament passes the Act of Security

1705 England's parliament passes the Alien Act

1706 Joint Parliamentary Commission on Union

1707 Act of Union passed

1708 First Jacobite Rising fails

1714 Death of Queen Anne; George I succeeds

1715 The 1715 Rising; Battle of Sheriffmuir

1716 The 'Old Pretender' returns to France

1717 The 'Old Pretender' marries Clementina Sobieska

1719 The 1719 Rising; Battle of Glenshiel

1720 Birth of Charles Edward Stuart, 'Bonnie Prince Charlie'

1725 General Wade comes to Scotland to build military roads

1736 The Porteous Riot

1745 Prince Charles lands in Scotland; the '45 Rising; Battle of Prestonpans; the march to Derby, and the retreat

1746 Battle of Falkirk Muir; Battle of Culloden; Prince Charles escapes to France

1746–82 Act of Prescription bans Highland dress and language

1771 Birth of Walter Scott

1789 French Revolution

1802 *The Minstrelsy of the Scottish Border*

1805 *The Lay of the Last Minstrel*

1808 *Marmion*

1810 *The Lady of the Lake*

1811 Scott starts to build Abbotsford

1814 *Waverley*

1815 End of Napoleonic Wars

1818 Scott rediscovers the Scottish Crown Jewels

1819–20 'Radical Wars' in Scotland

1820 Cato Street Conspiracy

1822 Royal visit of George IV to Edinburgh

1824 *Redgauntlet*

1826 Scott's financial crash

1827–29 *Tales of a Grandfather*

1831 *History of Scotland*

1831 Scott booed at Jedburgh

1831 First Reform Bill passed

1832 Death of Walter Scott

1838 'People's Charter' – the rise of Chartism

1846 Scott Monument in Edinburgh completed

1853 National Association for the Vindication of Scottish Rights

1885 Scottish Office established in London

1900 Liberal Party's Young Scots Society founded

1914 Home Rule Bill lapses at the start of World War I

1919 'Red Clydeside' riot in Glasgow

1922 'Red Clydesiders' elected to Parliament

1924 Home Rule Bill 'talked out'

1928 National Party of Scotland founded

1932 Scottish Party founded

1934 Scottish National Party (SNP) founded

1939 St Andrew's House opens in Edinburgh

1942 SNP splits; McCormick founds 'Scottish Convention'

1945 SNP wins the Motherwell and Wishaw by-election

1949 National Covenant launched

1950 Young nationalists abduct the Stone of Destiny from Westminster Abbey

1967 Winnie Ewing wins Hamilton by-election for the SNP

1968 Ted Heath makes 'Declaration of Perth'

1974 SNP wins eleven parliamentary seats

1978 Scotland Act 1978 passed

1979 (1 March) Scotland
referendum; (May) general
election: SNP loses nine
parliamentary seats

1988 Margo MacDonald wins
Govan by-election for SNP; *A
Claim of Right for Scotland*
published

1989 Scottish Constitutional
Convention begins

1994 Death of John Smith

1996 Stone of Destiny returns to
Scotland

1997 Referendum on a parliament
for Scotland

1998 Scotland Act 1998 passed

1999 (May) Elections for Scotland's
parliament; (1 July) Royal
opening of Scotland's new
parliament

Kings and Queens of Scotland

Kenneth I (mac Alpin)	c.840–58	Malcolm IV ('the Maiden')	1153–65
Donald I	858–62	William ('the Lion')	1165–1214
Constantin I	862–77	Alexander II	1214–49
Aed	877–78	Alexander III	1249–86
Eochaid	878–89	Margaret ('the Maid of Norway')	1286–90
Donald II	889–900		
Constantin II	900–43	John Balliol ('Toom Tabard')	1292–96
Malcolm I	943–54		
Indulph	954–62	Robert I (Robert Bruce)	1306–29
Malcolm II	1005–34		
Duncan I	1034–40	David II	1329–71
Macbeth	1040–57	Robert II	1371–90
Lulach	1057–58	Robert III	1390–1406
Malcolm III ('Canmore')	1058–93	James I	1406–37
		James II	1437–60
Donald III	1094	James III	1460–88
Duncan II	1094	James IV	1488–1513
Donald III (restored)	1094–97	James V	1513–42
Edgar ('the Peaceable')	1097–1107	Mary ('Queen of Scots')	1542–67
Alexander I ('the Fierce')	1107–24	James VI (James I of Britain	1567–1625 1603–25)
David I	1124–53		

Acknowledgements

Alexander, Wendy (Killiecrankie Visitor Centre); Anderson, Eric (Provost of Eton); Andrian, Barrie (Crannog Centre, Kenmore); Arnold, Kath (Monument Manager, Melrose Abbey); Ashmore, Patrick (Historic Scotland); Atkinson, Norman (Cultural Services, Angus Council); Bain, Carolynn (Archivist, National Trust for Scotland); Barrow, Geoffrey W.A. (Emeritus Professor of History, Edinburgh University); Bennett, Susan (Curator, Elgin Museum); Boardman, Stephen (lecturer in Scottish History, Edinburgh University); Bowgen, Alan (Public Record Office); Bowler, David (Scottish Urban Archaeological Trust); Breeze, David J. (Chief Inspector of Ancient Monuments, Historic Scotland); Brown, Andrew (English Heritage); Brown, Dr Dauvit (lecturer in Scottish History, Glasgow University); Caldwell, Dr David (Curator, Scottish Medieval Collections, Museum of Scotland); Campbell, Ian (Professor of Scottish and Victorian Literature, Edinburgh University); Campbell, Sheila (Reference Library, Kirkcaldy Central Library); Cheape, Hugh (National Museum of Scotland); Courtney, Rena and Graeme (Kings House Hotel, Balquhidder); Cowan, Edward J. (Professor of Scottish History, Glasgow University); Crook, Peter (Chief Marshal, Westminster Abbey); Cruickshank, Graeme (Edinburgh Historical Enterprises); Devine, Tom (University Research Professor, and Director of the Research Institute of Irish and Scottish Studies, Aberdeen University); Dromgoole, Patrick and June (Penkill Castle); Easingwood, Gordon (Dunbar and District History Society); Elgin, Fraser (The Edinburgh Sir Walter Scott Club); Evans, Ros (Otterburn Tourist Information Centre); Fawcett, Richard (Inspector of Ancient Monuments, Historic Scotland); Fojut, Noel (Historic Scotland); Fraser, Lady Antonia (biographer); Gifford, Douglas (Professor of Scottish Literature, Glasgow University); Girvan, Catriona and Wilson (Macbeth Experience, Bankfoot); Glen, Joyce (Isle of Kerrera); Goldie, Sarah (Largs and District Historical Society); Gough, Mary (Boscobel House); Greene, Phil (Langside); Holms, Cathy (Norham Castle); Hunter, Charles (joint editor, *Historic Argyll*, Lorn Archaeological and Historical Society); Jack, Ronnie (Professor of Scottish and Medieval Literature, Edinburgh University); Jardine, Mark (historian and researcher); King, Elspeth (Director, Stirling Smith Art Gallery and Museum); Laing, Julie (Largs Tourist Information Centre); Lambie, Brian (Biggar Museum Trust); Leslie, Graeme and Eileen (1774 Bistro, Perth); Lynch, Declan (radio producer); Lynch, Michael (Professor of Scottish History, Edinburgh University); McCance, Rod (TV weaponry expert, Cambusbarron); Macdonald, Catriona (lecturer in History, Glasgow Caledonian University); McDonald, Joyce (Supervisor, National Wallace Monument); MacFarland, Elaine (senior lecturer in History, Glasgow Caledonian University); McGilp, David Adams (Kilmartin House Museum); MacGowan, Iain (Scottish Natural Heritage); McGregor, Duncan (The Edinburgh Sir Walter Scott Club); MacIvor, Iain (former Chief Inspector of Ancient Monuments, Historic Scotland); McLean, Fiona (Aberdeen and Grampian Tourist Board); Macmillan, Ewen (former manager, Arisaig Estate); Marshall, Rev. Dr James (St Andrews); Mason, Roger (lecturer in Scottish History, St Andrews University); Matheson, Ann (Greenhill Covenanters' House, Biggar Museum Trust); Mathieson, Ailsa (Perth Tourist Information Centre); Michael, Janet (Rob Roy and Trossachs Centre, Callander); Moorcroft, Christine (writer and researcher); Moore, Wilma (Langside Library); Morrison, Fiona (Morrison Graham Media, Edinburgh); Morton, Graeme (lecturer in Economic and Social History, Edinburgh University); Munro, Graeme (Director and Chief Executive, Historic Scotland); Murdoch, Alex (lecturer in Scottish History, Edinburgh University); Murray, Douglas M. (Principal of Trinity College and Senior Lecturer in Ecclesiastical History, Glasgow University); Norris, Morag (Archivist, Scone Palace); Nurick, Commander Rowland (Administrator, Scone Palace); Payne, Susan (Perth Museum and Art Gallery); Perfect, Hugh (Associate Head, Moray House Institute of Education); Pittock, Murray (Professor of Literature, Strathclyde University); Ponting, Gerald and Margaret (Calanais); Ritchie, Anna (archaeologist and writer); Robertson, John (St Hugh's College, Oxford); Robinson, Vicky (indexer); Rodger, Robin (Perth Museum and Art Gallery); Rogers, Gordon (Dick Institute Museum and Art Gallery, Kilmarnock); Rosie, Alison (Curator, National Archives of Scotland); Roy, David (Scottish Covenanter Memorials Association); Scott, Ian (Director, Saltire Society); Scott, Morris S. (The King William the Lion Society, Arbroath); Simpson, John (Honorary Fellow, Edinburgh University); Sinclair, Kelvin (President, Scottish Association of Teachers of History); Smeed, Pauline (Secretary, Dunbar and District History Society); Smith, Christopher (leaseholder, Tutbury Castle); Smither, Ruth (Arisaig House Hotel); Smout, Christopher (Historiographer Royal in Scotland); Storrar, William (Professor of Christian Ethics and Practical Theology, Edinburgh University); Stott, Peter (Assistant Museums Manager, Falkirk Council); Taylor, Ian (Post Office, Garmouth); Thompson, Des (Scottish Natural Heritage); Tindall, Aine (Mill Trail Visitor Centre, Alva); Trewin, Mark (lecturer in Ethnomusicology, School of Scottish Studies); Vallens, Barry (Custodian, Tutbury Castle); Watson, Dr Fiona (senior lecturer in History, Stirling University); Whatley, Christopher (Professor of Scottish History, Dundee University); Whitelaw, Marion (Scottish Natural Heritage); Whitley, Elizabeth (writer); Wickham-Jones, Caroline (archaeologist); Woolf, Dr Alex (lecturer in Scottish History, Edinburgh University); Yeoman, Louise (National Library of Scotland); Young, Alison (Supervisor, Tourist Information Centre, Inverness)

Sources

Anderson, James, *Sir Walter Scott and History* (Edina Press, 1981)

Anderson, W.E.K. (ed.), *The Journal of Sir Walter Scott* (Oxford University Press, 1972; Canongate Classics paperback, 1998)

Armit, Ian, *Celtic Scotland* (Batsford/Historic Scotland, 1997)

Armit, Ian, *Scotland's Hidden History* (Tempus, 1998)

Ash, Marinell, *The Strange Death of Scottish History* (Ramsay Head Press, 1980)

Ashmore, Patrick, *Calanais: The Standing Stones* (Urras nan Tursachan, 1995)

Ashmore, Patrick, *Maes Howe* (Historic Scotland, 1995)

Bailey, Geoff B., *Falkirk or Paradise! The Battle of Falkirk Muir, 17 January 1746* (John Donald, 1996)

Ballingall, J.W. (ed.), *Historical Collections (with notes) Regarding the Royal Burgh and the Parish of Kinghorn* (James W. Duncan, Kirkcaldy, 1905)

Barnes, Michael P., *The Runic Inscriptions of Maeshowe, Orkney* (Uppsala University, 1994)

Barr, W.T., *For a Web Begun: The Story of Dunfermline* (Oliver & Boyd, 1947)

Barrow, Geoffrey W.S., *Robert Bruce and the Community of the Realm of Scotland* (Eyre & Spottiswoode, 1965)

Barrow, Geoffrey W.S., *Kingship and Unity: Scotland 1000–1306* (Edinburgh University Press, 1989)

Bede (trans. Leo Shirley-Price), *A History of the English Church and People* (Penguin Classics, 1968)

Bell, William Scott, *Autobiographical Notes of the Life of William Scott Bell* (2 vols, London, 1892)

Bingham, Caroline, *James VI of Scotland* (Weidenfeld & Nicolson, 1979)

Bingham, Caroline, *James I of England* (Weidenfeld & Nicolson, 1981)

Bingham, Caroline, *Robert the Bruce* (Constable, 1998)

Boardman, Stephen, *The Early Stewart Kings: Robert II and Robert III, 1371–1406* (Tuckwell Press, 1996)

Bold, Alan, *The Palace of Holyroodhouse* (Pitkin Pictorials, 1980)

Bower, Walter (ed. D.E.R. Watt), *Scotichronicon* (Aberdeen University Press, 1987)

Bower, Walter (ed. D.E.R. Watt), *A History Book for Scots: Selections from Scotichronicon* (Mercat Press, 1998)

Bowler, David (ed.), 'Four Excavations in Perth' (*PSAS*, Vol. 125, 1995)

Breeze, David J., *A Queen's Progress* (HMSO, 1987)

Breeze, David J., *Roman Scotland* (Batsford/Historic Scotland, 1996)

Breeze, David J. and Munro, Graeme, *The Stone of Destiny: Symbol of Nationhood* (Historic Scotland, 1997)

Brown, Michael, *James I* (Canongate, 1994)

Burnett, Charles J. and Tabraham, Christopher J., *The Honours of Scotland* (Historic Scotland, 1993)

Butter, Rachel, *Kilmartin: Scotland's Richest Prehistoric Landscape* (Kilmartin House Trust, 1999)

Caldwell, David, *Scotland's Wars and Warriors: Winning Against the Odds* (Stationery Office, 1998)

Cameron, Jamie, *James V: The Personal Rule, 1528–1542* (Tuckwell Press, 1998)

Campbell, Ewan, *Saints and Sea-Kings: The First Kingdom of the Scots* (Canongate, 1999)

Campbell, Ian and Garside, Peter (eds), *Talking About Scott* (Edinburgh Sir Walter Scott Club, 1994)

Campbell, Jack, *A Word for Scotland* (Luath Press, 1998)

Campbell, Marion, *Alexander III, King of Scots* (House of Lochar, 1999)

Campbell, Thorbjörn, *Standing Witnesses: An Illustrated Guide to the Scottish Covenanters* (Saltire Society, 1996)

Carpenter, Sarah, 'Early Scottish Drama' (in *The History of Scottish Literature*, Vol. 1, ed. R.D.S. Jack, Aberdeen University Press, 1988)

Cheape, Hugh, 'The Monymusk Reliquary' (in *The Highlander*, Vol. 36, No. 4, July/August 1998)

Cheetham, J. Keith, *On the Trail of Mary Queen of Scots* (Luath Press, 1999)

Chronicle of Melrose (trans. Joseph Stevenson), (Llanerch Press facsimile, 1991)

Chronicle of Richard of Hexham (in *Chronicles and Memorials of the Reigns of Stephen, Henry II and Richard I*, ed. R. Howlett [Rolls Series, 1886])

Clark, David, *Battlefield Walks: North* (Grange Books, 1995)

Clarke, David and Maguire, Patrick, *Skara Brae* (Historic Scotland, 1996)

Close-Brooks, Joanna, *The Highlands* (HMSO, 1995)

The County of Roxburgh, Vol. II (RCAMS, HMSO, 1956)

Cowan, Edward J., *Montrose: For Covenant and King* (Weidenfeld & Nicolson, 1977)

Cowan, Edward J., 'The Historical MacBeth' (in *Moray: Province and People*, ed. David Sellar, Scottish Society for Northern Studies, 1993)

Crawford, Thomas, *Society and the Lyric: A Study of the Song Culture of Eighteenth Century Scotland* (Scottish Academic Press, 1979)

Cruickshank, Graeme, *Nechtansmere 1300: A Commemoration* (Forfar and District Historical Society, 1985)

Cruickshank, Graeme, *The Battle of Dunnichen* (Pinkfoot Press, 1999)

Cruickshank, Graeme, *The Aberlemno Battle-Scene: A Representation of the Picts' Greatest Victory?* (Pinkfoot Press, 2000)

Cummins, W.A., *The Age of the Picts* (Sutton Publishing, 1995)

SOURCES

Daiches, David, 'Character and History in Scott's Novels' (*The Edinburgh Sir Walter Scott Club Bulletin*, 1993/4)

Daiches, David, Jones, Peter and Jones, Jean (eds), *The Scottish Enlightenment 1730–1790: A Hotbed of Genius* (Edinburgh University Press, 1986)

The Declaration of Arbroath (trans. Sir James Fergusson) (Edinburgh 1970)

Derry, T.K., *A History of Scandinavia* (University of Minnesota Press, 1979)

Devine, T.M., *The Scottish Nation 1700–2000* (Allen Lane, 1999)

Donaldson, Gordon, *The Scottish Reformation* (Cambridge, 1960)

Donaldson, Gordon, *Scotland: James V–James VII* (*The Edinburgh History of Scotland*, Vol. 3, Oliver & Boyd, 1965)

Duncan, A.A.M., *Scotland: The Making of the Kingdom* (Oliver & Boyd, 1975)

Duncan, A.A.M. (ed.), *John Barbour: The Bruce* (Canongate, 1999)

Dunnett, Dorothy, *King Hereafter* (Michael Joseph, 1982)

Durant, David N., *Bess of Hardwick* (Peter Owen, revised edition 1999)

Egil's Saga (trans. Magnus Magnusson), (in *The Icelandic Sagas*, Folio Society, 1999)

Farrer, Alison, *The Pencil, Largs* (North Ayrshire Council, 1999)

Fawcett, Richard, *Arbroath Abbey* (Historic Scotland, 1989)

Ferguson, William, *Scotland: 1689 to the Present* (The Edinburgh History of Scotland, Vol. 4, Oliver & Boyd, 1968)

Field, John, *Kingdom, Power and Glory: A Historical Guide to Westminster Abbey* (James & James, 1996)

Fifeshire Advertiser, Friday, 22 July 1887

Fisher, Andrew, *William Wallace* (John Donald, 1986)

Flodden 1513 (English Heritage: Battlefields Register, 1995)

Forbes, George, *William Wallace: Freedom Fighter* (Lang Syne, 1996)

Foster, Sally M., *Picts, Gaels and Scots* (Batsford/Historic Scotland, 1996)

Fraser, Andrew G., *The Building of Old College* (Edinburgh University Press, 1989)

Fraser, Antonia, *Mary Queen of Scots* (Weidenfeld & Nicolson, 1969)

Fraser, Antonia, *King James VI of Scotland, I of England* (Weidenfeld & Nicolson, 1974)

Fraser, Antonia, *King Charles II* (Weidenfeld & Nicolson, 1979)

Fraser, Antonia, *The Gunpowder Plot: Terror and Faith in 1605* (Weidenfeld & Nicolson, 1996)

Frazer, Allan (ed.), *Sir Walter Scott: An Edinburgh Keepsake* (Edinburgh University Press, 1971)

Freedom is a Noble Thing: Scottish Independence 1286–1329 (Scottish Record Office, 1996)

Froissart, Jean (trans. Geoffrey Brereton), *Chronicles* (Penguin Classics, 1968)

Fry, Plantagenet and Fry, Fiona Somerset, *The History of Scotland* (Routledge, 1982)

Gerhold, Dorian, *Westminster Hall: Nine Hundred Years of History* (James & James, 1999)

Gifford, J., McWilliam, C. and Walker, D., *Edinburgh* (Penguin Books, 1984)

The Gododdin (trans. Joseph P. Clancy), (in *The School Bag*, ed. Seamus Heaney and Ted Hughes, Faber & Faber, 1997)

Goodare, Julian and Lynch, Michael (eds), *The Reign of James VI* (Tuckwell Press, 2000)

Graham-Campbell, James and Batey, Colleen E., *Vikings in Scotland: An Archaeological Survey* (Edinburgh University Press, 1998)

Grainger, John D., *Cromwell Against the Scots: The Last Anglo–Scottish War, 1650–1652* (Tuckwell Press, 1997)

Grant, Alexander, *Independence and Nationhood: Scotland 1306–1469* (London, 1984)

Grant, Alexander, 'The Wolf of Badenoch' (in *Moray: Province and People*, ed. David Sellar, Scottish Society for Northern Studies, 1993)

Gray, D.J., *William Wallace, The King's Enemy* (Robert Hale, 1991)

Halidon Hill 1333 (English Heritage: Battlefields Register, 1995)

Hamilton, Duke of, *Maria R, Queen of Scots: The Crucial Years* (Mainstream, 1991)

Hamilton, Ian, *A Touch of Treason* (Lochar & Neil Wilson Publishing, 1990)

Harvie, Christopher, *Scotland and Nationalism* (Allen & Unwin, 1977; 3rd edition, Routledge, 1998)

Henderson, Ian, *Power Without Glory* (London, 1967)

Johnstone, Chevalier de (ed. Brian Rawson), *A Memoir of the 'Forty-Five* (Folio Society, 1958)

Keay, John and Keay, Julia, *Collins Encyclopaedia of Scotland* (HarperCollins, 1994)

Kennedy, Ludovic, *In Bed with an Elephant: A Journey through Scotland's Past and Present* (Bantam Press, 1995)

Kenyon, John and Ohlmeyer, Jane (eds), *The Civil Wars: A Military History of England, Scotland and Ireland 1638–1660* (OUP, 1998)

King, Elspeth (ed.), *Blind Harry's Wallace: William Hamilton of Gilbertfield* (Luath Press, 1998)

King, Elspeth, *Introducing William Wallace: The Life and Legacy of Scotland's Liberator* (Firtree Publishing, 1997)

Kinross, John, *Discovering Battlefields of England and Scotland* (Shire Publications, 1998)

Laing, Lloyd and Laing, Jenny, *The Picts and the Scots* (Sutton Publishing, 1993)

Lawrie, Archibald Campbell, *Annals of the Reigns of Malcolm and William, Kings of Scotland* (1910)

Lee, Christopher, *This Sceptred Isle* (BBC Books, 1997)

Legge, M.D., 'The Inauguration of Alexander III' (in *Proceedings of the Society of Antiquaries of Scotland*, Vol. LXXX, 1945–46)

Lenman, Bruce P. and Gibson, John S., *The Jacobite Threat: A Source Book* (Scottish Academic Press, 1991)

SOURCES

Linklater, Magnus and Hesketh, Christian, *Bonnie Dundee* (Canongate, 1992)

Linklater, Magnus, *Massacre: The Story of Glencoe* (William Collins, 1982)

Linklater, Magnus and Denniston, Robin, *Anatomy of Scotland* (Chambers, 1992)

Lowe, Chris, *Angels, Fools and Tyrants: Britons and Anglo-Saxons in Southern Scotland* (Canongate, 1999)

Lyle, Emily (ed.), *Scottish Ballads* (Canongate Classics, 1994)

Lynch, Michael, *Scotland: A New History* (Pimlico, 1992)

McCallum, Neil, *A Small Country: Scotland 1700–1839* (James Thin/The Mercat Press, 1983)

McDiarmid, Matthew P. (ed.), *Hary's Wallace* (Scottish Text Society, 1968/69)

MacDougall, H. of MacDougall, *Island of Kerrera: Mirror of History* (published by the author, 1979)

Macdougall, Norman, *James III: A Political Study* (John Donald, 1982)

Macdougall, Norman, *James IV* (Tuckwell Press, 1997)

McGladdery, Christine, *James II* (John Donald, 1990)

MacIvor, Iain, *Edinburgh Castle* (Batsford/Historic Scotland, 1993)

MacIvor, Iain, *Fort George* (Historic Scotland, 1996)

MacIvor, Iain, *A Fortified Frontier* (forthcoming)

Mackay, James, *William Wallace: Brave Heart* (Mainstream, 1995)

Mackay, James, *In My End is My Beginning: A Life of Mary Queen of Scots* (Mainstream, 1999)

Maclean, Fitzroy, *Bonnie Prince Charlie* (Weidenfeld & Nicolson, 1988)

Macleod, John, *Dynasty: The Stuarts 1560–1807* (Hodder & Stoughton, 1999)

McLynn, Frank, *The Jacobite Army in England 1745* (John Donald, 1998)

Magnusson, Magnus, *Vikings!* (Bodley Head, 1980)

Magnusson, Magnus, *Treasures of Scotland* (National Trust for Scotland/ Weidenfeld & Nicolson, 1981)

Magnusson, Magnus (ed.), *Echoes in Stone: 100 Years of Ancient Monuments in Scotland* (Scottish Development Department, 1982)

Magnusson, Magnus, *Hakon the Old – Hakon Who?* (Largs and District Historical Society, 1982)

Magnusson, Magnus, *Lindisfarne, the Cradle Island* (Oriel Press, 1984)

Magnusson, Magnus, 'The Border Abbeys' (in *Journal of the Society of Friends of Dunblane Cathedral*, Vol. XV, Part I, 1986)

Magnusson, Magnus, *Scotland up the Fifties* (BBC radio series, 1994)

Magnusson, Magnus, *Rum: Nature's Island* (Luath Press, 1997)

Magnusson, Magnus and White, Graham (eds), *The Nature of Scotland* (Canongate, 1991)

Marr, Andrew, *The Battle for Scotland* (Penguin, 1992)

Marren, Peter, *Grampian Battlefields* (Aberdeen University Press, 1990)

Marshall, James Scott, *Freuchie Through the Years* (Freuchie Community Council, 1998)

Marshall, Rosalind K., *Queen of Scots* (HMSO, 1986)

Massie, Allan, *101 Great Scots* (W&R Chambers, 1987)

Massie, Allan, *Edinburgh* (Sinclair-Stevenson, 1994)

Massie, Allan, *The Ragged Lion* (Hutchinson, 1994)

Mitchell, Rosalind, *A History of Scotland* (Methuen, 1970)

Moffat, Alastair, *Arthur and the Lost Kingdoms* (Weidenfeld & Nicolson, 1999)

Mudie, Robert, *A Historical Account of His Majesty's Visit to Scotland* (Oliver & Boyd, 1822)

Murray, Douglas M., 'Martyrs or Madmen? The Covenanters, Sir Walter Scott and Dr Thomas McCrie' (*Innes Review*, Vol. XLIII, No. 2, Autumn 1992, pp.166–75)

Murray, W.H., *Rob Roy MacGregor: His Life and Times* (Richard Drew Publishing, 1982)

Neville's Cross 1346 (English Heritage: Battlefields Register, 1995)

Nicholson, Ranald, *Scotland: The Later Middle Ages* (Oliver & Boyd, 1974)

Northallerton (North Yorks) 1138 (English Heritage: Battlefields Register, 1995)

Ollard, Richard, *The Escape of Charles II* (Constable, 1986)

Oram, Richard, *Scotland's Kings and Queens* (Stationery Office, 1997)

Orkneyinga Saga (trans. Hermann Pálsson and Paul Edwards) (Hogarth Press, 1978)

Otterburn 1388 (English Heritage: Battlefields Register, 1995)

Owen, D.D.R., *William the Lion 1143–1214: Kingship and Culture* (Tuckwell, 1997)

The Palace of Holyroodhouse (Official Guide, HMSO, 1988)

Paterson, Raymond Campbell, *A Land Afflicted: Scotland and the Covenanter Wars 1638–1690* (John Donald Publishers, 1998)

Paterson, Wilma (ed.), *Songs of Scotland* (Mainstream, 1996)

Pittock, Murray G.H., *Jacobitism* (Macmillan Press, 1998)

Reese, Peter, *Wallace: A Biography* (Canongate, 1996)

Reese, Peter, *The Scottish Commander* (Canongate, 1999)

Reid, Stuart, *1745: A Military History of the Last Jacobite Rising* (Spellmount, 1996)

Ritchie, Anna, *Picts* (Historic Scotland, 1989)

Ritchie, Anna, *Meigle Museum: Pictish Carved Stones* (Historic Scotland, 1997)

Ritchie, Anna and Breeze, David J., *Invaders of Scotland* (Historic Scotland, 1991)

Ritchie, Graham and Ritchie, Anna, *Scotland: Archaeology and Early History* (Thames & Hudson, 1981)

Robertson, John (ed.), *Andrew Fletcher: Political Works* (Cambridge University Press, 1997)

Ross, David R., *On the Trail of William Wallace* (Luath Press, 1999)

Ross, Stewart, *The Stewart Dynasty* (Thomas & Lochar, 1993)

Ross, Stewart, *Ancient Scotland* (House of Lochar, 1998)

Roy, David, *The Covenanters: The Fifty Years Struggle 1638–1688* (In the Pew Publications, Airdrie, 1997)

SOURCES

Sadler, John, *Scottish Battles from Mons Graupius to Culloden* (Canongate, 1996)

Scott, Sir Walter, *History of Scotland* (in Lardner's *Cabinet Cyclopædia*, Vol. I, 1829)

Sellar, David, 'Sueno's Stone and its Interpreters' (in *Moray: Province and People*, ed. David Sellar, Scottish Society for Northern Studies, 1993)

Sked, Phil, *Culloden* (National Trust for Scotland, 1997)

Sharp, James J., *The Flower of Scotland* (Melven Press, 1981)

Smout, T.C., *A History of the Scottish People 1560–1830* (William Collins, 1969)

Solway Moss 1542 (English Heritage: Battlefields Register, 1995)

Stavert, Marion L., *Perth: A Short History* (Perth and Kinross District Libraries, 1991)

Storrar, William, *Scottish Identity: A Christian Vision* (Handsel Press, 1990)

Sutherland, John, *The Life of Walter Scott* (Blackwell, 1995)

Tabraham, Christopher J., *Smailholm Tower* (Historic Scotland, 1993)

Tabraham, Christopher J., *Lochleven Castle* (Historic Scotland, 1994)

Tabraham, Christopher J., *Edinburgh Castle* (Historic Scotland, 1997)

Tabraham, Christopher J. and Grove, Doreen, *Fortress Scotland and the Jacobites* (Batsford/Historic Scotland, 1995)

Tasioualis, J.A. (ed.), *The Makars: The Poems of Henryson, Dunbar and Douglas* (Canongate Classics, 1999)

Taylor, Cameron, *Bannockburn* (National Trust for Scotland, 1997)

Thomson, Oliver and MacInnes, Hamish, *Glencoe* (National Trust for Scotland, 1994)

Tranter, Nigel, *The Story of Scotland* (Routledge & Kegan Paul, 1987)

Traquair, Peter, *Freedom's Sword* (HarperCollins, 1998)

Wallace, Randall, *Braveheart* (Penguin, 1997)

Watson, Fiona, *Under the Hammer* (Tuckwell Press, 1998)

Weaver, O.J., *Boscobel House and White Ladies Priory* (English Heritage, 1996)

Westminster Abbey: Official Guide (Dean and Chapter of Westminster, 1997)

Whatley, C.A., *Bought and Sold for English Gold? Explaining the Union of 1707* (Economic and Social History Society of Scotland, 1994)

Whitley, Elizabeth, *Plain Mr Knox* (Skeffington, 1960)

Whitley, Elizabeth, *The Two Kingdoms* (Scottish Reformation Society, 1977)

Wickham-Jones, Caroline, *Scotland's First Settlers* (Batsford/Historic Scotland, 1994)

Wilson, A.N., *The Laird of Abbotsford: A View of Sir Walter Scott* (Oxford University Press, 1980)

Yeoman, Louise, *Reportage Scotland: History as it Happens* (Luath Press, 2000)

Young, Alan and Stead, Michael J., *In the Footsteps of Robert Bruce* (Sutton, 1999)

Index

INDEX

INDEX

197–8, 199, 200, 201, 202
Murray, Douglas M. 498
Murray, Lord George: at
Battle of Glenshiel 573,
574; and Jacobite Rising
(1745) 588, 589, 591, 600,
601, 602; retreat from
Derby 604, 605, 606; at
Battle of Falkirk Muir
608, 609, 610, 611;
withdrawal to Highlands
613, 614, 615; at Battle of
Culloden 618, 619–20,
622
Murray, Sir James 422n
Murray, John, of Broughton
589
Myllar, Andrew 285
Mylne, Alexander, Abbot of
Cambuskenneth 304n
Mylne, Walter 336
Mynyddawg Mwynfawr,
King of the Gododdin 26

Nairne, Carolina Oliphant,
Lady: 'Will ye no come
back again?' 627n
Napoleon Bonaparte 630,
643, 644
Naseby, Battle of (1645)
431–2, 441
National Association for the
Vindication of Scottish
Rights 666
'National Covenant' (1638)
423–6, 429, 446, 453,
471–2, 477, 498, see also
Covenanters
National Covenant for
Home Rule (1949) 673–4
National Party of Scotland
(founded 1928) 670–1,
673
National Trust for Scotland
172n, 181, 404n, 510, 617
nationalism/national
consciousness 103–4, 140,
666–8, 681; see Scottish
National Party
Navigation Laws 527n
Navy, Royal 427, 573
Navy, Scottish 286–7

Nechtansmere, battle of see
Dunnichen
'Negative Confession' 386,
424
Neolithic period 5–12;
burial cairns 33n
Neville, Sir Ralph 203, 204
Neville's Cross, Battle of
(1346) 202–4
Newbury, Battle of (1643)
431
Newcastle, Duke of 598
Newcastle upon Tyne 66, 76
Newhaven dockyard 286,
287
Newstead: Roman fort 16
Niddry Castle, nr
Winchburch 366
Ninian, St 37, 63
Nithsdale, Earl of 429
Norfolk, Thomas Howard,
1st Duke of (formerly Earl
of Surrey) 289–90, 292
Norfolk, Thomas Howard,
3rd Duke of 311, 312
Norfolk, Thomas Howard,
4th Duke of 370, 375
Norham: Castle 114–15,
191, 279, 289, 341;
St Cuthbert's Church 117;
Treaty (1209) 85
Normans 63, 65, 66, 69–70,
74, 78, 79, 87
Norsemen 8, 9, 38–40, 44,
45, 49, 93–4
North Sea oil industry 685
Northallerton: 'Battle of the
Standard' (1138) 75–8
Northumberland: Scottish
raids (1296) 120, (1297)
139, (1346) 202–3; see
also Berwick; borders;
Northumbria, kingdom
of; Otterburn, Battle of
Northumberland, Henry,
Earl of 75, 82
Northumberland, Henry
Percy, 2nd Earl of
('Hotspur') 216, 217, 219,
220
Northumberland, Henry
Percy, 9th Earl of 410
Northumbria, kingdom of

27, 33, 40, 44, 45–6, 62,
65–6, 67, 80, 83, 84,
91–2; Battle of Dunnichen
27–30; Battle of
Athelstaneford 30–1; see
Northumberland
Northumbria, Robert de
Mowbray, Earl of
Northumbria 67
Norway 260–1
Nova Scotia 404n
Novantae, the 15, 16

Oates, Titus 482–3
ogam alphabet 34
Ogilvie, Captain George, of
Barras 469
Ogilvie, Lord 598
Ogilvy, Marion 326
Oliphant, Sir William 151
OPEC 682
Order of the Thistle 503
Organisation of Petroleum
Exporting Countries
(OPEC) 682
origin myths, Scottish 41–4
Orkneyinga Saga 10–11, 39,
54, 60, 62, 93
Orkneys 54, 103, 260–2,
442; Broch of Mousa
10–11; earldoms 39, 262;
Kirkwall 101–2; Maes
Howe 7, 8–9; Ring of
Grogar 6, 8; Skara Brae
5–6; Standing Stones of
Stenness 6, 8
Orléans, Philippe, Duc d'
563n, 565
Ormesby, William 135
Ormond, Hugh Douglas,
Earl of 253, 254, 256
Ormonde, James, Marquis of
and Duke of Ross 271
orpiment 36
O'sullivan, John William
588–9, 600, 604, 609, 616,
624
Otterburn, Battle of (1388)
215–17, 218, 219–20
Our Changing Democracy
(White Paper) 683
Overbury, Sir Thomas 415n

727

INDEX

INDEX